Half the
Human Experience

Half the Human Experience

THE PSYCHOLOGY OF WOMEN

FIFTH EDITION

Janet Shibley Hyde
University of Wisconsin—Madison

D. C. Heath and Company
Lexington, Massachusetts   Toronto

Address editorial correspondence to:

D. C. Heath and Company
125 Spring Street
Lexington, MA 02173

Acquisitions Editor: James Miller
Editorial Associate: Tina M. Crowley
Production Editor: Anne Rebecca Starr
Designer: Jan Shapiro
Photo Researcher: Constance S. Gardner
Production Coordinator: Charles Dutton
Permissions Editor: Margaret Roll
Permissions Assistant: Craig Mertens

56789-DOC-00 99

*To Margaret and Luke,
the two best kids a
professor / author / mom
could ever have*

Preface

My basic goal in preparing a fifth edition of *Half the Human Experience* is to provide a text on the psychology of women for undergraduates who have little or no background in psychology—perhaps only an introductory course. Although the book is designed as a core text for psychology of women courses, it may also serve appropriately as one of several texts in a women's studies course or as a supplementary text in a variety of psychology courses.

Three characteristics of this book—its readability, comprehensiveness, and scholarship—were well received in previous editions, and I have worked to retain and improve them. I have come to believe that the readability of texts is a feminist principle. Feminists, as one of their goals, have attempted to demystify science, and as part of that effort we must demystify psychology, including the psychology of women. My goal therefore has been to provide a text with solid and up-to-date scholarship, clearly explained so that students can readily understand it.

What's new in this edition?

Women of Color

The highest priority I had in revising was to integrate the new scholarship on women of color into the book. Beginning with the first edition (1976), I have had a chapter on Black women. By 1990 and the fourth edition, the scholarship on women of many ethnic groups had expanded so that I could cover four major ethnic groups: African Americans, American Indians, Asian Americans, and Latinas. In my endeavors I was helped enormously by a project we had at the University of Wisconsin, funded by the Ford Foundation, to integrate the new scholarship on women of color into the undergraduate curriculum, and I wanted to see this work reflected in this textbook.

With material on women of color, the author and instructor must face the question: separation or integration? That is, should there be a separate chapter focusing on and highlighting research on women of color? Or should this material be integrated throughout the book? I chose a "both/and" strategy. Thus there is a chapter on women of color that provides information on the historical and cultural heritages of women in these four ethnic groups, setting the stage for materials in other chapters. I have also integrated research on women of color throughout all other chapters. I placed the chapter on women of color exactly in the middle of the book, not at the end as an afterthought, in order to make it clear that women of color are central, not peripheral.

Learning Aids

In this revision I focused on increasing and improving the learning aids for students. Two features are especially important: boxed inserts titled "Experience the Research," and a margin glossary.

Each chapter now has a boxed insert at the end, Experience the Research, designed to give students active experience with research or theories in the psychology of women. They include exercises such as collecting a small amount of data from friends to replicate a study in the text, or analyzing the gendered content of computer games at a local store. I hope that students will benefit from these experiences and that faculty will find them useful to assign. We pretested many of the exercises and found that students responded enthusiastically to them. Many thanks to Jan Yoder, Nita McKinley, and Jennifer Lamping, the faculty who helped with the pretest, and to all the students who participated.

I noticed that none of the available psychology of women textbooks has a glossary, much less a margin glossary, although these features have become standard in textbooks in other areas of psychology. I therefore added both a glossary in the margin of the text, with terms defined when they are first mentioned, and a comprehensive glossary at the end of the book. These features should help students learn the meaning of important terms in our field.

Other Revisions

The text has been thoroughly revised and updated throughout. According to my count, 385 new citations were added. Chapter 13, the Victimization of Women, and Chapter 14, Women and Mental Health Issues, received especially extensive revisions. In the mental health chapter, for example, there is a new Focus box on gender and the politics of psychiatric diagnosis in DSM-IV, a new section on addressing the mental health needs of ethnic minority women, and additional coverage of cognitive-behavioral therapy and hopelessness theory. In the chapter on victimization, I rewrote the entire section on rape to include new statistics, research, and theories of the causes of rape, and I added a new Focus box on the debate about recovered memory.

To compensate for all the additions of new research, I needed to make some deletions. Chapter 5 from the previous edition, Masculinity, Femininity, and Androgyny, has been deleted, reflecting reduced interest in these topics; the material on androgyny has been condensed considerably and added to Chapter 3, Gender Stereotypes and Gender Differences.

I also reordered some chapters. Colleagues using the book told me that they thought it did not work well to have the chapter on victimization so close to the end of the book, ending the course on a negative note. I have therefore placed the victimization chapter before the one on mental health issues; students can then see how feminist therapy can empower women to triumph over victimization.

In preparing this new edition, I realized I was revising it approximately twenty years after I did the intensive research and writing on the first edition. Psychology of women as an academic field has changed a great deal in those twenty years. As an author, I found that I faced different problems in 1994 from those I faced in 1973. Two decades ago the problem was that the field was too new and the research therefore too thin. Often I would come to a major point that needed to be addressed and find little data, perhaps not even a single study. In 1994, the problem was the opposite: there was almost too much research—not that there can ever be too much research, but rather that there is more than can possibly be included in a single undergraduate text. Our field of psychology of women is filling the pages of three major journals—*Psychology of Women Quarterly, Sex Roles,* and *Feminism and Psychology*—at impressive rates, and other major psychology journals regularly include articles on gender or the psychology of women. This abundance of research is a marvelous state for our field to be in, but it also means that I had to pick and choose and could not include all studies.

Acknowledgments

I feel deep gratitude to many people who contributed to the quality of this book, although errors, of course, remain my responsibility. Many reviewers were helpful with their critical comments: Veanne N. Anderson, Indiana State University; Karen W. Bauer, University of Delaware; Toni M. Blake, University of Nebraska—Lincoln; Annette M. Brodsky, University of California, Los Angeles Harbor Medical Center; Lynne Carroll, Salisbury State University; Joan Chrisler, Connecticut College; Claire Etaugh, Bradley University; Lucia A. Gilbert, University of Texas at Austin; Margaret M. Gittis, Youngstown State University; Lisa A. Goodman, University of Maryland at College Park; Merle Kelley, Western Oregon State College; Mary P. Koss, University of Arizona; Sydney Langdon, Arizona State University; Marlene Lyons, Western Connecticut State University; Jill Morawski, Wesleyan University; Jan Ochman, University of St. Thomas; Marlene Ramsey, Walla Walla Community College; Esther Rothblum, University of Vermont; Nancy Felipe Russo, Arizona State University; Kenrick S. Thompson, Northern Michigan University; Cheryl Travis, University of Tennessee; Naomi Wagner, West Valley College; Barbara A. Winstead, Old Dominion University; and Deborah R. Winters, New Mexico State University.

Many close colleagues in women's studies at the University of Wisconsin have helped me to enrich my understanding of feminist psychology: Gina

Sapiro, Betsy Draine, and Mariamne Whatley (chairs of Women's Studies over the years), the late Ruth Bleier, Caitilyn Allen, Jane Collins, and Joy Rice.

Many good friends in Division 35, Psychology of Women, of the American Psychological Association have stimulated my thinking about the psychology of women. I am not able to list all of them here because there are so many, and also because I fear that I will leave someone important off the list. But you know who you are, and I thank you.

Wendy Theobald, my library researcher, has done more than any other single person to increase the scholarship of the book. She cheerfully and quickly tracked down obscure references and partial citations, and unearthed many new sources of which I was unaware. My special thanks go to her.

The staff at D. C. Heath have been wonderfully supportive of this project as always. Thanks to acquisitions editors Randall Adams, Vince Duggan, and James Miller, and editorial assistants Heather Monahan and Tina Crowley, and especially to Anne Starr, production editor.

I hope that this new edition of *Half the Human Experience* will help students and faculty alike to gain a deeper, richer, more growth-enhancing understanding of the psychology of women.

Janet Shibley Hyde

Contents

Contents

Contents

1

Introduction

The first thing that strikes the careless observer is that women are unlike men. They are "the opposite sex"—(though why "opposite" I do not know; what is the "neighboring sex"?). But the fundamental thing is that women are more like men than anything else in the world.

DOROTHY SAYERS, UNPOPULAR OPINIONS

One day when my daughter Margaret was four and a half (the half was very important to her), she told me about the games she had been playing at her preschool. She played with her boyfriend, Dimitrios. He said he'd marry her when they grew up. They played "Superfriends." She told me that Dimitrios chose a character he wanted to be, such as Superman, and then she played the female counterpart, Supergirl. Or they played "Dukes of Hazzard," and she was Daisy. I had to sit down for a minute while processing the significance of all she was saying. She hadn't even started kindergarten yet, and her femaleness and its requirements were so clear to her. She understood that the male chooses what he wants to be and then she follows, picking up the female counterpart role. She had learned that he is Super*man* while she is Super*girl*. I tried to talk her out of it. I said if he is Superman, she could be Super*woman*. She said there is no Super-woman. I asked her why Dimitrios always got to choose what they played. Why couldn't she pick Wonderwoman and he could be Wonderman? or Wonderboy? She said it couldn't be played that way. I asked why. She said it just couldn't. After a while I gave up (partly for theoretical reasons that will be discussed in Chapter 3). But the point of the story is that gender, and specifically femaleness, is an important quality in our society. Even preschoolers understand the social significance of these attributes. Margaret and her friends had already learned (and believe me, I didn't tell her all this) that males choose and lead and females follow. They already understood heterosexuality and marriage as important parts of their role requirements.

This book is about being female, what it means in our society, what it means biologically, and how all of this is incorporated into the behavior, thoughts, and feelings of girls and women.

Sex, Gender, and Sexism

Before proceeding, some terms need to be defined. First, it is worth noting that in our language the term *sex* is sometimes used ambiguously. That is, sometimes it is used to refer to sexual behaviors such as sexual intercourse, whereas at other times it is used to refer to males and females. Usually, of course, the meaning is clear from the context. For example, if an employment application says "Sex:—," you don't write, "As often as possible." In that context the question clearly is about whether you are a female or a male. On the other hand, what is the topic of a book entitled *Sex and Temperament in Three Primitive Societies?* Is it about female roles and male roles in those societies, or is it about the sexual behavior of primitive people?

To reduce this ambiguity, I am going to use the term *sex* to refer to sexual behaviors and the term **gender** to refer to males and females (Hyde, 1979, 1994). *Gender differences,* then, refers to differences between females and males. Other scholars have adopted other conventions in this regard. For example, some scholars prefer to use the term *sex differences* to refer to innate or biologically produced differences between females and males, and *gender differences* to refer to male-female differences that result from learning and the social roles of females and males (e.g., Unger, 1979). The problem with this terminology is that studies often document a female-male difference without providing any evidence as to what causes it—biology, society, or both. Furthermore, the sharp distinction between biological causes and cultural causes fails to recognize that biology and culture may interact. Therefore, I am simply going to use the term *gender differences* for male-female differences, and leave their causation as a separate question.

Gender: The state of being male or female.

Sexism is another term that will be relevant to some of the discussions in this book. Sexism can be defined as discrimination or bias against people based on their gender. Some people use the term *reverse sexism* for discrimination against males, although it would seem preferable to use the term *sexism* for discrimination against either females or males on the basis of their gender. (Actually, using my terminology, the term should probably be *genderism,* but it will not be used, because *sexism* and *sex bias* are the standard terms.) Here we will be concerned with sexism as discrimination against women. Some people feel uncomfortable using the term *sexism,* because they think of it as a nasty label to hurl at someone or something. Actually, however, it is a good, legitimate term that describes a particular phenomenon, namely, discrimination on the basis of gender, particularly discrimination against women. It will be used in that spirit in this book, not

Sexism: Discrimination or bias against people based on their gender. Sex bias.

DOONESBURY   **by Garry Trudeau**

FIGURE 1.1

(Source: Copyright, 1974 G. B. Trudeau by Universal Press Syndicate.)

as a form of name-calling. It is also important to recognize that not only men, but women as well, can be sexist.

One final term that needs to be defined in this context is **feminist.** A feminist is a person who favors political, economic, and social equality of women and men, and therefore favors the legal and social changes that will be necessary to achieve that equality. Feminists generally consider this term preferable to others, such as *women's libber,* which is often used in a derogatory manner. A wide spectrum of feminist beliefs exists, ranging from those of women in an organization who want to improve it to those of radical feminists. These different varieties are discussed in Chapter 2.

Let us turn now to the topic at hand.

Feminist: A person who favors political, economic, and social equality of women and men, and therefore favors the legal and social changes necessary to achieve that equality.

Is There a Psychology of Women?

Depending on the inflection, the above question has different meanings, and therefore requires different answers. Is there a *psychology* of women? Stated in that manner, the question refers to whether a psychological approach to understanding women, as compared with, say, a political, historical, or economic one, is valuable. I will leave this question unanswered for the present, but I hope to demonstrate in the course of this book that the psychological approach is both interesting and important, and that attempts to remedy women's political status, by themselves, may leave a host of psychological ills still present and in need of attention.

Is there a psychology of women? The second variation of inflection raises the issue of whether the psychology of women actually exists, whether it is a legitimate area of specialization within the field of psychology. Does the area contain sufficient content, research, and theory to be considered a subdiscipline of psychology? Or is it just a fad, another kind of "pop psych" that will produce a flurry of paperbacks and then be forgotten, a field with which no "respectable" psychologist would want to be associated?

In fact, the psychology of women has quite respectable ancestry in a traditional field of psychology known as *differential psychology.* That people differ one from another in their behavior has probably been obvious ever since humans became self-aware. For the past century these individual differences in behavior have been the subject of scientific study. One particular dimension of individual differences is the differences between males and females, and these have received their due—perhaps more than their due—attention, both in research and in theories. Theorists, from Freud to the modern cognitive theorists, have given considerable attention to observed gender differences in behavior. Generally traditional psychological theories have had the problem (to which we will return later) of viewing the male as normative and the female as a deviation from this norm.

In the past 25 years, the psychology of women has emerged as a distinct area, which already has to its credit the discovery of some phenomena—the psychological effects of sexist language, the psychological responses of rape victims, and, through the research of Masters and Johnson and others, a better understanding of female sexuality. There is no doubt, then, that there *is* a psychology of women, with a long history of theory and research and with a current life of new and important discoveries. Acknowledging this, there is a recognized group (Division 35) in the American Psychological Association on the psychology of women.

Finally: Is there a psychology of *women?* This inflection raises the question of whether women have a special psychology different from that of men. Certainly there are abundant stereotypes implying that women differ psychologically from men—they are reputed to be less logical and more emotional, and to have different attitudes toward and motivations for sex. Psychological research indicates that some of these stereotypes have a basis in reality, and that some simply do not. It is this research—showing when men and women differ psychologically and when they don't, and what this tells us about women's psychology—that is one of the topics of this book.

There is a paradox inherent in trying to understand the psychology of women, a paradox that is captured in the quotation at the beginning of this chapter. Women and men are at once different and similar. Although gender differences are important in defining women's psychology, gender similarities are equally important. Both scientific and nonscientific views of women have concentrated on how they differ from men; this leads to a distorted understanding unless there is equal emphasis on similarities. This paradoxical tension between *gender differences* and **gender similarities** will be a continuing theme throughout the book.

Gender similarities:
Ways in which males and females are similar rather than different.

Why Study the Psychology of Women?

Most textbooks include an introductory section on why people should study that particular topic. Such a section does not seem quite so necessary in a book on the psychology of women. The main reason for studying it is obvious: it is interesting. Many women, for example, take such a course because they want to understand themselves better, a goal they may feel was not met by their other psychology courses. Men may take such a course wanting to understand women better; certainly it is of interest and practical value to understand one's spouse, girlfriend, daughter, boss, or co-worker better. Therefore, many good, practical reasons exist for wanting to study the psychology of women.

There are also some good academic reasons for studying the psychology of women. Many traditional psychological theories have literally been theories about men. They have treated women, at best, as a variation from the norm. Perhaps the best example is psychoanalytic theory, to be discussed in Chapter 2. Similarly, sex bias has existed in many aspects of psychological research, a point to be discussed later in this chapter. As a result, traditional psychology has often

FIGURE 1.2
Robin Williams as Mrs. Doubtfire, 1994. The questioning of traditional gender roles in recent years has made us wonder whether men could take on traditional female roles such as being wonderfully nurturant nannies.

been about men, and it has often operated from very traditional assumptions about gender roles. One way of correcting these biases is by recognizing a psychology of women. The psychology of women thus provides information about a group that has often been overlooked in research and theory, and it opens up new perspectives on gender roles and ways they might be changed.

Finally, one other reason for studying the psychology of women is that the female experience differs *qualitatively* from the male experience in some ways. Only women experience menstruation, pregnancy, childbirth, and breastfeeding. In addition to these biologically produced experiences, there are culturally produced uniquenesses to women's experience produced by the gender roles in our culture. For example, in U.S. culture, walking down the street and being whistled at is an experience nearly unique to women. One of the points of the feminist movement, and particularly of consciousness-raising groups, is that women need to communicate more with one another about these female experiences. Therefore having a course that provides information on these topics is worthwhile, and also gives people a chance to express their feelings about their experiences. Such communication should help women cope better with the female experience, or change the aspects of it that need to be changed.

Sources of Sex Bias in Psychological Research

Research in the psychology of women is progressing at a rapid pace. Certainly I will be able to provide you with much important information about the psychology of women in this book, but there are still more questions yet to be answered than have already been answered. With research on the psychology of women expanding so rapidly, many important discoveries will be made in the next 10 or 20 years. Therefore, someone who takes a course on the psychology of women should do more than just learn what is currently known about women. It is probably even more profitable to gain some skills so as to become a "sophisticated consumer" of psychological research. That is, it is very important that you be able to read intelligently and to evaluate future studies of women that you may find in newspapers, magazines, or scholarly journals. To do this, you need to develop at least three skills: (1) know how psychologists go about doing research, (2) be aware of ways in which sex bias may affect research, and (3) be aware of problems that may exist in research on gender roles or the psychology of women. In general, one of the most valuable things you can get from a college education is the development of *critical thinking skills.* The feminist perspective encourages critical thinking about psychological research and theory. The following discussion is designed to help you develop these skills.

How Psychologists Do Research   Figure 1.3 is a diagram of the process that psychologists go through in doing research, shown in rectangles. The diagram also indicates some of the points at which bias may enter, shown in circles.

The process, in brief, is generally this: the scientist starts with some theoretical model, whether a formal model, such as psychoanalytic theory, or merely a set of personal assumptions. Based on the model or assumptions, the scientist then formulates a question. The purpose of the research is to answer that question. Next, she or he designs the research, which involves several substeps: a behavior must be selected; a way to measure the behavior must be devised; a group of appropriate participants must be chosen; and a research design must be developed. One of these substeps—finding a way to *measure* the behavior—is probably the most fundamental aspect of psychological research. Two interesting examples of measuring behavior relevant to the psychology of women are the tests that measure attitudes toward women (on a scale from traditional to egalitarian) and those that assess attitudes toward rape (Chapter 13).

The next step is for the scientist to collect the data. The data are then analyzed statistically and the results are interpreted. Next, the scientist publishes the results, which are read by other scientists and incorporated into the body of scientific knowledge (and also are put into textbooks). Finally, the system comes full circle, because the results are fed into the theoretical models that other scientists will use in formulating new research.

Now let us consider some of the ways in which sex bias—bias that may af-

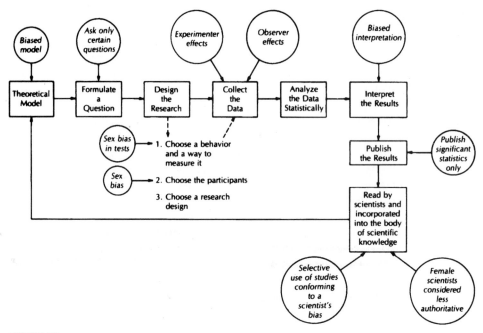

FIGURE 1.3
The process of psychological research (rectangles) and ways in which sex bias may enter (circles).

fect our understanding of the psychology of women or of gender roles—may enter into this process (Caplan and Caplan 1994; Denmark et al., 1988; Grady, 1981; McHugh et al., 1986).

Biased Theoretical Model The theoretical model or set of assumptions the scientist begins with has a profound effect on the outcome of the research. Sex bias may enter if the scientist begins with a biased theoretical model. Perhaps the best example of a biased theoretical model is psychoanalytic theory as formulated by Freud (see Chapter 2). A person with a psychoanalytic orientation might design research to document the presence of penis envy, or masochism, or immature superego in women; someone with a different theoretical orientation wouldn't even think to ask such questions. You need to become sensitive to the theoretical orientation of a scientist reporting a piece of research—and sometimes the theoretical orientation isn't stated, it has to be inferred—because that orientation affects the rest of the research and the conclusions that are drawn.

What Questions Are Asked The questions a scientist asks are shaped not only by a theoretical model but also by gender-role stereotypes. Bias may enter when only certain questions are asked and others ignored, partly as a result of stereotypes. For example, there are many studies of fluctuations in women's moods over monthly cycles. However, until recently no one had thought to ask whether men also might experience monthly mood fluctuations (see, for example, Kimura and Hampson, 1994). Reading the research, one might get the impression that women are moody and men are not; but the research appears to indicate this only because no one has investigated men's mood shifts. Stereotypes about women and men have thus influenced the kinds of questions that have been investigated scientifically.

Feminist scholars advocate an important method for overcoming the problems of biased theoretical models and stereotyped research questions: go to the community of people to be studied and ask them about their lives and what the significant questions are. For example, research on lesbians may be limited if it is conducted by heterosexual women working from theories developed by heterosexual men. It is better scientific practice to begin by asking lesbians for input on the research design. Theories can be built at a later stage, once a firm foundation has been laid beginning from the women's own experience and perspectives.

Sex Bias in Psychological Tests   As shown in Figure 1.3, the next step in psychological research is designing the research, which in turn involves three steps: choosing a behavior or psychological trait and a way to measure it; choosing the participants; and choosing a research design. Let's first consider the step that involves choosing a behavior or trait and a way to measure it.[1]

Psychological measurement: The process of assigning numbers to characteristics of people, such as aggressiveness or intelligence.

Psychological measurement may take many forms. If the researcher wants to measure aggressive behavior in preschool children, the measurement technique may involve having trained observers sit unobtrusively in a preschool classroom and make check marks on a research form every time a child engages in an aggressive act. Here, however, we will concentrate on psychological tests, some of which have been the objects of sharp criticism for problems of sex bias.

Let's take as an example the mathematics portion of the Scholastic Aptitude Test (SAT-Math), which is taken widely by high school seniors who are planning to attend college. The SAT-Math has been criticized a great deal on the grounds that it is biased against women. In 1985, for example, women taking it scored an average of 452, compared with an average of 499 for men (Hyde et al., 1990). How could such a test be biased against women? One major issue is the content and wording of questions. If the content of an item involves situations that men experience more frequently, or requires knowledge to which men have more access, then the item is sex biased. As an example, consider the following item, which appeared on the SAT in 1986:

---

[1]When psychologists measure a trait, they are creating an *operational definition,* which refers to defining some trait by how it is measured, for example, defining intelligence as those abilities that are measured by IQ tests.

A high school basketball team has won 40 percent of its first 15 games. Beginning with the sixteenth game, how many games in a row does the team now have to win in order to have a 55 percent winning record?

(a) 3

(b) 5

(c) 6

(d) 11

(e) 15

Males, who have more experience with team sports and computing win-loss records, have an advantage. There is a direct algebraic solution, which a female could do if she had mastered algebra, but it is time consuming, and the test is timed. A male might say, "I know that 11 out of 20 is a 55 percent record. Will that work? Yes. The answer is 5."

If females score lower than males on a particular psychological test, then, there often are two possible interpretations: (1) females are not as skilled at the ability being measured; or (2) the gender difference simply indicates that the test itself contained biased items.

Sex Bias in Choice of Sample   There is good evidence that bias exists in choosing participants for psychological research. In particular, males are used more frequently as participants than females are. For example, in 1970 in the journal *Psychophysiology,* 38 percent of the articles reported on male-only studies, and in 1990 the percentage was still 35 percent (Gannon et al., 1992). Not only is this true in research with humans, but it is also true in research with animals. In a survey of studies of animal behavior, a colleague and I found that 62 percent of the studies used one gender only, and of those, 75 percent used males only (Hyde and Rosenberg, 1976). Therefore, nearly half of all studies were based on males only.

In research with humans, some entire areas of research have had this problem. A good example is the classic research on achievement motivation, which was based on males only (McClelland et al., 1953). Milgram's (1965, 1974) classic study of obedience to authority—in which people were willing to deliver extraordinarily high levels of shock to another person simply because the experimenter told them to do so—was based on an all-male sample. Such practices can create whole areas of research that have little or no relevance to women's lives. Researchers can make a second error that compounds the use of an all-male sample: the error of **overgeneralization.** That is, having used a single-gender (usually all-male) sample, the researchers then discuss and interpret the results as if they were true of all people, male and female.

The choice of subjects is probably influenced in part by the kind of behavior the psychologist is studying, as well as by gender-role stereotypes. For example, in social psychologists' research on

Overgeneralization: A research error in which the results are said to apply to a broader group than the one sampled; for example, saying that results from an all-male sample are true for all people.

aggression—a "masculine" behavior—nearly 50 percent of the studies were done using males only, as compared with about 10 percent using females only and 40 percent using both genders. This 50 percent is higher than the percentage of male-only research in psychology in general (McKenna and Kessler, 1977). Therefore, it seems that when psychologists study a stereotyped "masculine" behavior—aggression—they are not likely to include females.

The problem with this kind of bias is that it creates not a psychology of human behavior, but rather a psychology of male behavior. Yet the problem is even worse because psychologists have been guilty of an overreliance on college-student samples. Such samples are typically rather homogeneous in several ways, including age (most are between 18 and 22), ethnicity (mostly white), and social class (mostly middle class). Feminist psychologists argue for the importance of recognizing the diversity of human experience. Your family's ethnic group and social class influenced the environment in which you grew up and therefore influenced your behavior. Feminist psychologists urge researchers to use samples that will allow an exploration of ethnic and social class diversity.

Sex Bias in Choice of Research Design Research methods in psychology can be roughly classified into two categories: laboratory experiments and naturalistic observations. In the laboratory experiment, the research participant is brought into the psychologist's laboratory and his or her behavior is manipulated in some way in order to study the phenomenon in question. In contrast, with naturalistic observations, researchers observe people's behavior as it occurs in natural settings and do not attempt to manipulate the behavior. In practice, the distinction between these categories is sometimes muddied; for example, it is possible to conduct an experiment in a naturalistic setting. Nonetheless, the distinction between the two basic categories is useful.

Quasi-experimental design: A research design that uses two or more groups, but participants are not randomly assigned to groups so it is not a true experiment. An example is two-group designs comparing males and females.

Some scholars argue that laboratory experiments are inherently sex biased, although this point is controversial (Peplau and Conrad, 1989). This question will be considered in greater detail later in the chapter.

It is also possible to talk about **quasi-experimental designs** (*quasi* meaning "not quite"). This phrase refers to designs in which there may be two (or possibly more) groups, so that the design looks like an experiment, but the experimenter did not manipulate which group each person was assigned to, so that there is no true experiment. A good example is studies of gender differences: There are two groups, males and females, but certainly the researcher did not randomly assign people to be in one or another group at the beginning of the research session. Studies of gender differences are not true experiments, but rather quasi-experiments.

Experimenter Effects In the step of research in which the data are collected, two important kinds of bias may enter: experimenter effects and observer effects.

Experimenter effects:
When some character-
istics of the experi-
menter affect the way
participants behave
and therefore affect the
research outcome.

Experimenter effects occur when some characteristic of the experimenter affects the way respondents behave, and thus affects the outcome of the experiment. In particular, the gender of the experimenter may affect respondents' behavior. For example, in sex research, respondents report more sexual feelings to an experimenter of the same gender than to one of the opposite gender (Walters et al., 1962). The evidence indicates that children cooperate better with female experimenters, whereas adults cooperate better with male experimenters (Rumenick et al., 1977; see also Harris, 1971).

It is rather disturbing to realize that an experiment might have different outcomes, depending on whether the experimenter was a man or a woman. Moreover, because the majority of psychological research, at least until recently, has been conducted by men, it seems possible that the results might have been quite different had it been conducted by women.

Incidentally, the problem of sex bias from experimenter effects is not unsolvable. The situation can be handled by having several experimenters—half of them female, half of them male—collect the data. This should balance out any effects due to the gender of the experimenter, and demonstrate whether the gender of the experimenter did have an effect on the participants' behavior. Unfortunately, this procedure is seldom used, mostly because it is rather complicated.

Observer Effects   Another important bias that may enter at the stage of data collection is observer effects.

Observer effects: When
the researcher's expec-
tations affect his or her
observations and
recording of the data.

Observer effects occur when the researcher's expectations for the outcome of the research influence his or her observations and recording of the data (Rosenthal, 1966). For example, in one study, observers (really the research participants) were to count the number of turning movements by planaria (flatworms); half the observers had been led to expect a great deal of turning, the other half very little. The observers who expected a great deal of turning reported twice as many turns as the observers who expected little (Cordaro and Ison, 1963). In psychology as in many other areas of life, what you expect is what you get.

Observer effects may be a source of bias in gender-role research and psychology of women research. In particular, scientists are no more immune than laypeople are to having stereotyped expectations for the behavior of females and males. These stereotyped expectations might lead scientists to find stereotyped gender differences in behavior where there are none. As an example, consider research on gender differences in aggression among preschool children. If observers expect more aggression from boys, that may be just what they get, even though the boys and the girls behaved identically. This is analogous to the observers who expected more turns from the planaria and found just that.

The technical procedure that is generally used to guard against observer effects is the "blind" study. It simply means that observers are kept unaware of (blind to) which experimental group participants are in, so that the observers' expectations cannot affect the outcome. Unfortunately, the double-blind method is virtually impossible in gender-differences research, as the gender of a person is almost always obvious from appearance, and therefore the observer cannot be "blind" to it or unaware of it.

One exception is infants and small children, whose gender is notoriously difficult to determine, at least when clothed. This fact was used in a clever study that provides some information on whether observer effects do influence gender-role research. The study is discussed in detail in Chapter 5, but in brief, adults rated the behavior of an infant on a videotape (Condry and Condry, 1976). Half the observers were told the infant was a male, and half were told it was a female. When the infant showed a negative emotional response, those who thought the infant was a male tended to rate the emotion as anger, whereas those observing a "female" rated "her" as showing fear. The observers rated behavior differently depending on whether they thought they were observing a male or a female.

Bias in Interpretations   Once the scientist has collected the data and analyzed them statistically, the results must be interpreted. Often the interpretation a scientist makes is at best a large leap of faith away from the results. Therefore this is also a stage at which bias may enter.

As an example, let us consider a fairly well documented phenomenon of psychological gender differences. A class of students takes its first exam in Introductory Psychology. Immediately after taking the exam, but before getting the results back, the students are asked to estimate how many points (out of a possible 100 points) they got on the exam. On average, males will estimate that they got higher scores than females will estimate they got (see Chapter 3). At this point, the data have been collected and analyzed statistically. It can be stated (neutrally) that there are statistically significant gender differences, with men estimating more points than women. The next question is, How do we interpret that result? The standard interpretation is that it indicates that women lack self-confidence or have low confidence in their abilities. The interpretation that is not made, although it is just as logical, is that men have unrealistically high expectations for their own performance.

The point is that, given a statistically significant gender difference, such a result can often be interpreted in two opposite ways, one of which is favorable to men, one of which is favorable to women.

Female deficit model: A theory or interpretation of research in which women's behavior is seen as deficient.

A persistent tendency has existed in psychology to make interpretations that are favorable to men; these interpretations are essentially based on a **female deficit model.** Sometimes there is no way of verifying which interpretation is right. As it happens in the example above, there is a way, because we can find out how the students actually did on the exam. Those results indicate that women overestimate their scores by about as much as men overestimate theirs (Mednick and Thomas, 1993). Thus the second interpretation is as accurate as the first.

Becoming sensitive to the point at which scientists go beyond their data to interpret them, and becoming aware of when those interpretations may be biased, is extremely important. Other examples of bias in interpretations are the research on gender differences in rod-and-frame test performance (to be discussed in Chapter 6) and gender differences in language (Chapter 4).

Publishing Significant Results Only   Once the data have been analyzed and interpreted, the next step is to publish the results. There is a strong tendency in psychological research to publish "significant" results only. This does not necessarily mean significant in the sense of "important"; it means significant in the sense of being the result of a statistical test that reaches the .05 level of significance.[2]

What are the implications of this tendency for our understanding of gender roles and the psychology of women? It means that there is a tendency to report statistically significant gender differences and to omit mention of nonsignificant gender differences. That is, we tend to hear about it when males and females differ, but we tend not to hear about it when males and females are the same. Thus there would be a bias toward emphasizing gender differences, and ignoring *gender similarities.*

This bias may also enter into psychology of women research such as menstrual-cycle studies (a point to be discussed in detail in Chapter 10).

Other Biases   The final two biases shown in Figure 1.3 are fairly self-explanatory and require little discussion here. If there is a tendency for reports by female scientists to be considered less authoritative than reports by male scientists, this would introduce bias, particularly when combined with bias due to experimenter effects as discussed previously. Research on whether this is really a problem has produced mixed results (Goldberg, 1968; Swim et al., 1989), and so these concerns are somewhat speculative. Also, another kind of bias is introduced if scientists have a tendency to remember and use in their work those studies that conform to their own biases or ideas, and to ignore those that do not.

Conclusion   I have discussed a number of problems with psychological research that may affect our understanding of women—and men. Of course, these problems probably are not present in every study in the area, and certainly I don't mean to suggest that all psychological research is worthless. The point is to learn to think critically about biases that may—or may not—be present when you are reading reports of research. Thinking critically about the theoretical orientation of a writer and about biased interpretations of results is important.

A more general point emerges from this whole discussion of sex bias in research methods in psychology. Traditional psychology has historically viewed itself as an objective and value-free science. Today, many psychologists, feminist psychologists among them, question whether psychological research is objective and value free (Peplau and Conrad, 1989). They point out that psychological re-

---

[2]For those who have not studied statistics, "significant at the .05 level" means roughly that the results that were obtained would have happened by chance only 5 times out of 100.

search might more appropriately be viewed as an interaction between researcher and research participant that occurs in a particular context. To that interaction the researcher brings certain values that may influence its outcome—in short, the results cannot be totally objective.

Psychology, of course, is not the only science that has claimed to be objective and value free when it isn't. Another example is physics and its groundbreaking discoveries of ways to generate nuclear power. These discoveries can be used to manufacture weapons capable of annihilating thousands, or they can be used to generate electricity for cities. Values are closely connected with science.

Feminist Alternatives All the preceding criticisms are important and you should be aware of them, but we need to go beyond those criticisms to offer some constructive alternatives. In doing so, we can think about *gender-fair research* and *feminist research.*

Gender-fair research: Research that is free of gender bias.

Gender-fair research is research that is not guilty of any of the biases discussed in the previous sections (Denmark et al., 1988; Grady, 1981; McHugh et al., 1986). Some characteristics of gender-fair research are as follows: (1) Single-gender research is never, or almost never, done. Even in situations where a single-gender design might seem to be justified—for example, examining women's fluctuations in mood over the menstrual cycle—the demand for gender-fairness and inclusion of the other gender might lead to better understandings—for example, a discovery of fluctuations in men's moods. (2) Theoretical models, underlying assumptions, and the kinds of questions asked should always be examined for gender fairness. For example, the minute someone proposes to do research on the effects of mothers' depression on their children, it should be asked whether fathers' depression also has an effect on children. Otherwise, we assume that only mothers influence children and that fathers have no influence, which is fair to neither mothers nor fathers. (3) Both male and female researchers should collect data in order to avoid experimenter effects. (4) Interpretations of data should always be examined carefully for gender fairness, and possibly several interpretations should be offered. For example, if there is a significant gender difference in the number of points students estimate they will get on an exam, two interpretations should be offered: that women underestimate and lack self-confidence, and that men overestimate and have inflated expectations for their performance. In a sense, then, gender-fair research proposes that we continue to play the research game by the same set of rules it has always had—tight controls, careful interpretations, and so on—but that we improve things so that the rules are observed fairly.

Feminist research: Research growing out of feminist theory, which seeks radical reform of traditional research methods.

Feminist researchers might argue that we need to go even further in reforming psychological research. There really is no single, comprehensive, definitive statement of the principles of **feminist research,** but many scholars have made contributions (e.g., Carlson, 1972; Parlee, 1981; Rabinowitz and Sechzer, 1993; Reinharz, 1992; Wallston, 1981; Wittig, 1985) and I will present some of those ideas here.

Feminist researchers might argue that the classic form of psychological research—the tightly controlled laboratory experiment—needs to be revised. It is manipulative, intended to determine how manipulations of the independent variable cause changes in the dependent variable. It objectifies and dehumanizes the people it studies, calling them "subjects." It emphasizes differentiation, taking people out of their natural environments in order to control all those things the experimenter considers irrelevant. In all these senses—the manipulativeness, the objectification, the differentiation—traditional psychological experimentation might be accused of being masculine or patriarchal.

The feminist alternatives are several: (1) Do not manipulate people, but rather observe them in their natural environment and try to determine how they experience their natural lives and worlds, thus emphasizing relatedness rather than differentiation. (2) Do not call the people who are studied "subjects," but rather "participants." (3) Do not think in simple terms of variable A causing effects on variable B, but rather in terms of complex, interactive relationships in which A and B mutually influence each other. Again, relatedness is emphasized. (4) Devote specific research attention to the special concerns of women. (5) Conduct research that will empower women and eliminate inequities. (6) Do not assume that scientific research and political activism are contradictory activities (Wittig, 1984). Good research—by documenting current conditions—can facilitate social change. And the psychologist who has political activism and social change as goals can still do good research; such researchers are obligated to articulate their values, but that is a good rule for all scientists. All these principles open up new vistas for researchers and you to think about.

Personally, I think we ought to integrate and respect both approaches, gender fair and feminist. The traditional psychological experiment needs reform, but I would hate to throw it out entirely. It functions best when combined with naturalistic research looking at complex mutual influences. Gender-fair research and feminist research might diverge on some issues, though. For example, feminist researchers would value the investigation of battered wives as an issue of special concern to women. Gender-fair researchers would point out that there are some battered husbands and that they should be researched as well. Feminist researchers might reply that there are far more battered wives than battered husbands and that feminist research need not necessarily concern itself with battered husbands. I cannot easily resolve this issue, and so I encourage you to think about it yourself.

Are We Making Progress?   Feminist psychologists began to publish their critiques of traditional research methods over 20 years ago. Has there been any progress? Have psychologists changed their methods to respond to these criticisms?

An analysis of articles published in the most important psychology journals from 1970 to 1990 indicates that there has been some progress, but that some areas still need improvement (Gannon et al., 1992). One issue is the use of all-male samples. In 1970, 42 percent of the articles in the prestigious *Journal of*

Abnormal Psychology were based on all-male samples; by 1990 the use of all-male samples had declined to 20 percent. That represents progress, but still, one article in five was based on males only, even in 1990.

The representation of women as researchers in psychology has seen great progress. For example, in 1970, only 27 percent of the articles in *Developmental Psychology* had a woman as first author; by 1990 that number had risen to 53 percent (Gannon et al., 1992). Similar trends were present for other journals. In 1970 only 6 percent of the articles in *Journal of Personality and Social Psychology* had women as first authors, compared with 30 percent by 1990.

A striking change is the trend toward using nonsexist language (see Chapter 4). In 1970, 29 percent of the articles in *Journal of Personality and Social Psychology* used nonsexist language, compared with 99 percent by 1990 (Gannon et al., 1992). This cannot be attributed entirely to the spontaneous goodwill of psychologists, though. Beginning in 1983, the American Psychological Association's official *Publication Manual* required the use of nonsexist language in all APA journal articles. Institutional norms can definitely have an effect on the behavior of scientists.

In conclusion, then, substantial shifts have been made toward nonsexist methods in psychological research. There are more women researchers and fewer all-male samples, and research is more likely to be reported using nonsexist language. Nonetheless, substantial numbers of studies are still based on all-male samples, and continued monitoring of methods is important.

Looking Ahead

A number of themes will recur in this book. Some of them have appeared repeatedly in history and then crop up in the United States today and are even found in modern psychology. Other themes are derived from current scientific psychological research on women.

Male as normative: A model in which the male is seen as the norm for the species, and the female is seen as a deviation from the norm.

Recurring Themes Rooted in History One historical theme is the **male as normative.** Throughout mythology the male is seen as normative, the female as a variant or deviation. That is, the male is the important one, the major representative of the species, the "normal" one, and the female is a variation on him. As Simone de Beauvoir expressed it, woman is the Other (1952). Or, as another writer put it, woman is little more than a tail wagged by the male ego (Hays, 1964).

In the biblical creation story (Genesis 2), Adam, the man, is created first; Eve, the woman, is later fashioned out of his rib, almost as an afterthought. In this and many other creation myths, man is created first; he is the major, important part of the species. Woman comes second and is only a variant on the male, the normative. There are even myths in which a woman is created by castrating a man.

FIGURE 1.4
The male as normative is a theme throughout history. An example is the Adam and Eve story, in which Adam is created first and Eve is later made from his rib.

Perhaps the best example of the male-as-normative theme is in our language. The word *man* is used to refer not only to a male, but to people in general. When the gender of a person is unknown, the pronoun *he* is used to refer to "him." (Would we dare have said "to refer to her"?) The species as a whole is man; woman is merely a subset. This topic will be discussed in detail in Chapter 4.

To explain the concept of "normativeness," an analogy can be made to handedness. In our society, right-handedness is normative, and left-handedness is considered unusual or deviant. The world is basically set up for right-handed people, and lefties have difficulty adjusting in everything from finding scissors that fit them to finding a satisfactory place at the dinner table. Just as left-handed people live in a world made for the right-handed, so women live in a world made for men, in which the male is normative.

A closely related concept is **androcentrism** (Bem, 1993). It means, literally, male centeredness, or the belief that males are the standard or norm.

Androcentrism: Male centered; the belief that the male is the norm.

Throughout mythology and history, then, a dominant theme is that the male is normative. He is the chief member of the species and woman is a variation or deviation. It seems likely that psychological effects result from this view, particularly as it is expressed in language. This concept of the male as normative crops up in a number of places in modern psychology, including some of the theories discussed in Chapter 2.

A second recurring theme rooted in history is **feminine evil.** One of the clearest images of women in mythology is their portrayal as the source of evil (Hays, 1964). In the Judeo-Christian tradition, Eve disobeyed God's orders and ate from the fruit of the tree of knowledge. As a result, Adam and Eve were forced to leave the Garden of Eden and Eve, the woman, became the source of original sin, responsible for the fall of humanity. In a more ancient myth, the Greek god Zeus ordered Vulcan to create the lovely maiden Pandora to bring misery to earth in revenge for the theft of fire by Prometheus. Pandora was given a box or jar containing all the evils of the world, which she was told not to open. But Pandora opened the box, and thus all the evils it contained spread over the world. In Chinese mythology the two forces yin and yang correspond to feminine and masculine, and yin, the feminine, is seen as the dark, or evil, side of nature.

Feminine evil: The belief that women are the source of evil or immorality in the world, as in the Adam and Eve story.

Historically, perhaps the most frightening manifestation of the belief in feminine evil was the persecution of witches beginning in the Middle Ages and persisting into Puritan America. Guided by the Catholic Church in a papal bull of 1484, the Malleus Maleficarum, the Inquisition tortured or put to death unknown numbers of witches. The objective fact appears to be that the vast majority of those accused and tried were women (Hays, 1964). Thus, it is woman who is seen as being in collaboration with the devil, visiting evil upon humans.

Recurring Themes Rooted in Modern Science Other repeated themes in this book are derived from current scientific research on the psychology of women. One important theme is *gender similarities,* the phenomenon that females and males are psychologically more similar than they are different. Another is the difference between *theory* and *empirical evidence.* Many theories of women's behavior have been proposed. Some have solid data (empirical evidence) backing them, whereas others do not. Not every theory is true, nor is every one a good description or explanation of behavior. Just because Freud said something does not make it true (or false). Readers need to become critical thinkers about the difference between statements based on theory and statements based on empirical evidence.

Trait: An enduring characteristic of a person, such as extraversion.

Another important distinction is **traits** versus *situational determinants* of behavior. A continuing controversy in psychology is whether behavior is determined more by a person's enduring traits (such as a personality trait), or whether behavior is determined more by the particular situation the person is in. Advocates of the latter position point out how inconsistent people's behavior can be from one situation to another—for example, a man may be aggressive toward a business competitor, but passive or nurturant toward his wife. This suggests that his behavior is not determined by an enduring personality trait (aggressiveness), but rather by the particular situation he is in. Later in this book we will also refer to this issue as a distinction between intrapsychic or internal factors (traits) and external (situational) factors. Applied to the psychology of women, the question becomes whether women are more influenced by personality traits that distinguish them from men, or whether their behavior is more determined by the situations they find themselves in. For example, is the lack of professional accomplishments by women due to some trait, such as the motive to avoid success (Chapter 6), or to situational factors, such as job discrimination? This distinction also has practical implications. In trying to improve women's lives, if we decide that the problem is personality traits, then we would try to change the early experiences or child-rearing practices that create those personality traits. If we decide, on the other hand, that situational factors are more important, we would want to change the situations women are in, such as ending job discrimination.

Another recurring theme is the pervasiveness of *female deficit models* in psychology. In the nineteenth century, scientists found women had slightly smaller brains than men and interpreted this as a sure reason why women were not as intelligent as men (Shields, 1975). Today some researchers argue that girls are not as good at math as boys are. No matter the century, researchers always seem to try to find female deficits.

Finally, one other recurring theme is the importance of *values* in a scientific understanding of women. Values affect the scientific theories that are proposed and the way research is done (Rabinowitz and Sechzer, 1993). In particular, they affect the way research is interpreted, a point discussed earlier in the chapter. Readers need to become sensitive to the values expressed by a particular scientific position.

Chapter Previews   In the next chapter we shall look at the contributions to the understanding of female development that have been made by some of the major theoretical systems of psychology—psychoanalytic theory, social learning theory, and cognitive-developmental theory. A controversial theory, sociobiology, is examined, as is gender schema theory and feminist theory.

Following these theoretical views, later chapters will focus on research about what women are actually like psychologically. Chapter 3 reviews evidence on gender stereotypes and gender differences, to see the ways in which women and men differ and the ways in which they are similar. Because feminist scholars have emphasized the importance of language, Chapter 4 is about women and lan-

FOCUS 1.1
PSYCHOLOGY'S FOREMOTHERS

One emphasis of the feminist movement has been recognizing and valuing the accomplishments of women. In part, that involves rediscovering some important contributions women have made. Here is a short self-quiz about some significant achievements made by eminent psychologists. Take the quiz before turning to the answers on the next page.

Q1. Who did the research on Black children that was critical in the U.S. Supreme Court decision to desegregate the nation's schools (*Brown* v. *Board of Education*)?

Q2. Who established that babies can swim?

Q3. Who conducted the famous social psychology study "The Robbers' Cave Experiment"?

Q4. Who authored the famous study "Albert and the White Rat"?

Q5. Who produced the widely used Stanford-Binet IQ Test?

Q6. Who developed the Cattell Infant Intelligence Test Scale?

Q7. What do the following books have in common: *The Growth of Logical Thinking of the Child, The Child's Conception of Space, The Child's Conception of Geometry,* and *The Early Growth of Logic in the Child?*

Q8. Who did the landmark research on the authoritarian personality?

Q9. Who wrote "Learning to Love," the classic report of research on the development of bonds of affection in monkeys?

guage—whether there are gender differences in language use, how the structure of the English language treats women, and how women and men communicate nonverbally. In Chapter 5 we discuss female experiences, adjustment, and roles across the lifespan from birth to old age. We look at women and achievement in Chapter 6, by considering research on gender differences in intellectual abilities, research on achievement in women, and several psychological factors (achievement motivation, the motive to avoid success, and attribution patterns) that may contribute to women's success or lack of it. Chapter 7 is about women and work. And Chapter 8 examines the new scholarship in psychology concerning women of color.

Chapters 9 through 11 are about women in relation to their bodies. Chapter

Here are the answers to the questions on the previous page:

A1. Kenneth Clark and *Mamie Phipps Clark.*

A2. *Myrtle McGraw.*

A3. Muzafer Sherif, O. J. Harvey, W. E. Hood, and *Carolyn Sherif.*

A4. John B. Watson and *Rosalie Raynor.*

A5. Lewis Terman and *Maud Merrill.*

A6. *Psyche Cattell.*

A7. You are partially correct if you said that they were all authored by the famous male psychologist Jean Piaget; but they were all coauthored by his longtime female collaborator, *Bärbel Inhelder.*

A8. *Else Frenkel-Brunswick.*

A9. Harry Harlow and *Margaret Harlow.*

SOURCE: Russo and O'Connell (1980).

9 considers the evidence on whether there are biological influences—such as hormone effects—on gender differences and female behaviors. Chapter 10 discusses psychological research on several women's health issues, including menstruation, menopause, pregnancy and childbirth, abortion, mastectomy, and AIDS. Chapter 11 explores female sexuality, including Masters and Johnson's research on the physiology of female sexual response, research on the psychol-

EXPERIENCE THE RESEARCH

UNDERSTANDING SEX BIAS IN PSYCHOLOGICAL RESEARCH

Design an experiment to determine whether adults are more likely to help a four-year-old child who is crying and apparently lost, depending on whether the adult is alone and there are no other adults close by (no bystander condition) or there are other adults present (bystander condition). Design two versions of the experiment. First, create the experiment as a traditional, pre-feminist psychologist might have done. Then, using Figure 1.3, make a list of all the examples of sex bias in the research. Finally, re-create the experiment to correct all the elements of sex bias, so that it will meet the standards for gender-fair research.

FIGURE 1.5
Dr. Mamie Phipps Clark, who, with her husband, Dr. Kenneth Clark, did the research on Black children that was critical in the 1954 Supreme Court decision to desegregate the nation's schools.

ogy of female sexuality, and sexual dysfunction and therapy for women. Chapter 12 is about lesbians and bisexual women. Chapter 13 centers on the victimization of women as seen in rape, battering, sexual harassment, and incest. Chapter 14 considers various problems that may occur in female adjustment, what happens to women when they seek psychotherapy for their problems, and what new feminist therapies are being developed for women.

In Chapter 15 we examine the "new research," done from a feminist perspective, on the psychology of men and the male role. The final chapter summarizes some of the major themes of the book and suggests important questions for the future.

Suggestions for Further Reading

Caplan, Paula J., & Caplan, Jeremy B. (1994). *Thinking critically about research on sex and gender.* New York: HarperCollins. This brief book includes a feminist critique of several major areas of psychological research on women and provides helpful guides for critical thinking about research.

Denmark, Florence, Russo, Nancy F., Frieze, Irene H., & Sechzer, Jeri A. (1988). Guidelines for avoiding sexism in psychological research. *American Psychologist, 43,* 582–585. This article provides a detailed list of examples of sex bias in psychological research, as well as ways to correct them.

Lewin, Miriam, & Wild, Cheryl L. (1991). The impact of the feminist critique on tests, assessment, and methodology. *Psychology of Women Quarterly, 15,* 581–596. Provides a fascinating look at the way in which feminists have changed psychological testing practices.

Peplau, L. Anne, & Conrad, Eva. (1989). Beyond nonsexist research: The perils of feminist methods in psychology. *Psychology of Women Quarterly, 13,* 381–402. These authors argue that no research method (laboratory experimentation or naturalistic observation) is inherently subject to sex bias and that all research methods can be used in feminist ways in psychology—points that are controversial among feminist scientists.

2

Theoretical Perspectives

> *[Girls] notice the penis of a brother or playmate, strikingly visible and of large proportions, at once recognize it as the superior counterpart of their own small and inconspicuous organ, and from that time forward fall a victim to envy for the penis.*

SIGMUND FREUD, COLLECTED PAPERS

Understanding the nature of the differences between males and females has fascinated people probably since the dawn of the human species. In the past century, science has come to dominate intellectual thought. And so it is not surprising that men (and sometimes also women) have attempted scientific understandings of women. In the present chapter we will examine some major psychological theories, having their roots in science, that have been formulated to explain women and the differences between women and men. The theories are presented in roughly chronological order, beginning with the earliest and most traditional theories and progressing to more modern ones.

In later chapters we shall look at empirical data for a further understanding of women and gender roles. The reader can then contrast these theoretical views with what is known based on scientific data.

Psychoanalytic Theory

Psychoanalytic theory: A psychological theory originated by Freud; its basic assumption is that part of the human psyche is unconscious.

Psychoanalytic theory was formulated by Sigmund Freud. Despite the advent of new models of human psychological development, few can doubt the influence of psychoanalytic theory in psychology, not to mention its penetration into the language and thinking of most laypeople. Psychoanalytic theory not only describes human behavior but also has acted to shape human behavior. For example, Freud's theory of female sexuality (see Chapter 11) held that women could have two kinds of orgasm—vaginal or clitoral—and that the vaginal orgasm was the more "mature," that is, the better, of the two. Some women have spent hours trying to achieve the elusive vaginal orgasm and have sought psychotherapy when they were unable to attain it, all as a result of Freud's theory. Certainly the theory has had an impact on human life, and in particular on women.

Erogenous zones: Areas of the body that are particularly sensitive to sexual stimulation.

Freud viewed humans as being dominated by two basic instincts: *libido* (the sex drive or life force) and *thanatos* (the death force, which causes phenomena such as warfare). The libido is focused on various areas of the body known as the **erogenous zones.** Each zone is a part of the skin or mucous membrane highly endowed with blood supply and nerve endings that are very sensitive to stimulation. The lips and mouth constitute one such region, the anal region another, and the genitals a third. Thus Freud noted that sucking produces pleasure, as do elimination and rubbing the genitals.

Stages of Development   One of Freud's greatest contributions was to promote the view of human personality as being the result of *development*. That is, he saw the personality of an adult as the result of previous experiences, and he believed that early childhood experiences were most critical. He proposed a stage theory of psychosexual development, each stage being characterized by a focus on one of the erogenous zones. According to his view, all humans pass through the stages in a fixed, chronological sequence—first the oral, then the anal, and then the phallic stage—during the first five or six years of life. Thus during the first stage, the oral, the infant derives pleasure from sucking and eating and experiences the world mainly through the mouth. Following this is the anal stage, in which pleasure is focused on defecating.

Phallic stage: The third stage of development in psychoanalytic theory, around 3 to 6 years of age, during which the pleasure zone is the genitals and sexual feelings arise toward the parent of the other gender.

In attempting to explain the development of gender identity and differences between males and females, Freud postulated that boys and girls pass through the first two stages of psychosexual development, the oral and the anal, in a similar manner. For both genders at this time, the mother is the chief object of love. It is during the **phallic stage,** around the ages of three to six, that the development of the genders diverges. As one might suspect from the name for this stage, females will be at somewhat of a disadvantage in passing through it.

Oedipal complex: In psychoanalytic theory, a boy's sexual attraction to and intense love for his mother, and his desire to do away with his father.

During the phallic stage, the boy becomes fascinated with his own penis. It is a rich source of pleasure and interest for him. A critical occurrence during the phallic stage is the formation of the **Oedipal complex,** named for the Greek myth of Oedipus, who unknowingly killed his father and married his mother. In the Oedipal complex, the boy sexually desires his mother. His attachment to her is strong and intense. He also wishes to rid himself of the father, who is a rival for the mother's affection. But the father is too powerful an opponent, and the boy fears that the father will retaliate. He fears that the father will do him bodily harm, particularly to his beloved penis, so that the boy comes to feel *castration anxiety*. The anxiety becomes so great that the boy seeks to resolve the problem. He admits to an inability to possess the mother and do away with the father. He represses his libidinal impulses toward the mother, and makes the critical shift to identifying with the father. In the process of *identification* with the father, the boy introjects (takes into himself as his own) the values, the "thou-shalt-nots," of society as represented by the father and thus comes to have a conscience or **superego.** But more important for our purposes is that in identifying with the father, he comes to acquire his gender identity, taking on the qualities the father supposedly possesses—strength, power, and so on.

Superego: Freud's term for the part of the personality that contains the person's ideals and conscience.

FOCUS 2.1
A CASE HISTORY ILLUSTRATING PENIS ENVY

The following is an example of the sort of case history that a psychoanalyst would see as demonstrating penis envy.

An unsuccessful artist who had always resented being a woman came to treatment very depressed and anxious at having allowed herself to become pregnant. Her husband had recently become extremely successful, and her envy of and competition with him were enormous, especially since she was blocked in her own professional development. She felt that the best way to "show up" her husband was to do the one thing he could not do—bear a child.

She expressed only hatred and contempt for her mother, who had been a dependent, ineffectual housebound woman. This resentment seemed to have started at the birth of her sister, three years younger, at which time the patient hid herself and refused to talk for days. The mother was hospitalized for depression when the patient was twelve. The father was an unsuccessful artist, an exciting, talented person whom the patient adored. She turned away from her mother and spent the next ten years of her life trying to be her father's son. He encouraged her painting and took her to exhibitions. However, he was very inconsistent and bitter, given to terrifying rages; he would alternate between leading her on and slapping her down. Her fantasy of being like a boy was brutally crushed at a time when she was preparing for a bas mitzvah; she thought she would be allowed to have one "as good as a boy's" but was suddenly humiliated publicly at puberty and sent home from the synagogue on the Sabbath because it was decided that she was now a woman and could no longer stay and compete with the men and boys. Menarche intensified her resentment of female functions, but she compensated with fantasies of having a son and traveling around the world with him—self-sufficient, no longer needing her family or her father. While in Europe on a scholarship, she fell in love and,

The sequence of events in the phallic stage is considerably different, more complex, and more difficult for the girl. According to Freud, the first critical event is the girl's stark realization that she has no penis. Because children are so interested in their own and others' genitals during this stage, Freud believed that the girl will inevitably notice the boy's protrusion and her own cavity. Presum-

while petting with the boy, had the only orgasm she has ever experienced. She feared his increasing power over her, experienced a resurgence of dependency needs and fled home. She felt she had spent her life trying to win her father's approval. But when she finally had a solo exhibit of her art, he taunted her, "Why not give it up, go home, and make babies?"

After his death and her professional failure, she became increasingly depressed. At the age of thirty, she decided to get pregnant—after having been married four years. (She had previously been phobic about pregnancy and remained a virgin until her marriage.) She felt that her baby was conceived out of emptiness, not fullness, and then feared that the child would take her life from her. Having a baby trapped her, she felt; she could no longer try to be like a man. It was as though she had had a fantasy penis which she finally had to relinquish.

There was plenty of evidence of typical penis envy in this case. As a girl, the patient even tried to compete with boys in urinary contests, and was furious because she always lost. She first associated her bedwetting with rage at not having a penis, but finally viewed it as a way to punish [her] mother for turning to [the] sister, and as an effort to recover the maternal solicitude she had lost. She envied, and was attracted to, men who had powerful drives for achievement and were free to pursue them. The penis was for her a symbol of such drives; to possess it would also save her from being like her mother. In one sense, she wanted a baby as a substitute for not having a penis; but she also had a burning wish to be a good mother—to prove her own validity as well as to "undo" her past. Her difficulty in achieving this wish forced her to work through her relationship with her mother, which she had contemptuously shelved, finding competition with men more exciting and less anxiety-provoking.

Source: Abridged from Moulton (1970).

ably she recognizes that the penis is superior to her own anatomy. She feels cheated and envious of males, and thus comes to feel *penis envy* (see Focus 2.1). She also feels mutilated, believing that at one time she possessed a penis, but that it had been cut off—indeed Freud believed that the fires of the boy's castration anxiety are fed by the boy's observation of the girl's anatomy, which he sees as living proof of the reality of castration. Her desire for a penis, her penis envy, can never be satisfied directly, and instead becomes transformed into a desire to be impregnated by her father. Holding her mother responsible for her lack of a penis, she renounces her love for her mother and becomes intensely attracted to her father, thus forming her own version of the Oedipal complex, sometimes called the **Electra complex.** Thus the sequence of events is reversed: for the boy, the Oedipal complex leads to castration anxiety, whereas for the girl, the parallel to castration anxiety—penis envy—occurs first and leads to the formation of the Electra complex. The desire to be impregnated by the father is a strong one, and persists in the more general form of maternal urges, according to Freud.

> **Electra complex:** In psychoanalytic theory, a girl's sexual attraction to and intense love for her father.

Passivity, Masochism, and Narcissism Freud believed that there are three key female personality traits: passivity, masochism, and narcissism. Here I shall focus on passivity and masochism.

In the outcomes of the Electra complex Freud saw the origins of the two well-known—at least to Victorians—feminine qualities of *passivity* and **masochism.** In choosing the strategy for obtaining the desired penis by being impregnated by the father, the girl adopts a passive approach—to be impregnated, to be done to, not to do—and this passive strategy persists throughout life. The desire to be impregnated is also masochistic, in that intercourse (in which, in Freudian terminology, the woman is "penetrated") and childbirth are painful. The female, therefore, in desiring to be impregnated seeks to bring pain to herself.

> **Masochism:** The desire to experience pain.

Lest the foregoing strains your credulity, perhaps some quotations from Marie Bonaparte, a follower of Freud, will indicate the strength of these convictions.

> Throughout the whole range of living creatures, animal or vegetable, passivity is characteristic of the female cell, the ovum whose mission is to *await* the male cell, the active mobile spermatozoan to come and *penetrate* it. Such penetration, however, implies infraction of its tissue, but infraction of a living creature's tissue may entail destruction: death as much as life. Thus, the fecundation of the female cell is initiated by a kind of wound; in its way, the female cell is primordially "masochistic." (1953, p. 79)

> All forms of masochism are related, and in essence, more or less female, from the wish to be eaten by the father in the cannibalistic oral phase, through that of being whipped or beaten by him in the sadistic-anal stage, and of being castrated in the phallic stage, to the wish, in the adult feminine stage, to be pierced. (1953, p. 83)

> Vaginal sensitivity in coitus for the adult female, in my opinion, is thus largely based on the existence, and more or less unconscious, acceptance of the child's

immense masochistic beating fantasies. In coitus, the woman, in effect, is subjected to a sort of beating by the man's penis. She receives its blows and often, even, loves their violence. (1953, p. 87)

As we saw, the resolution of the Oedipal complex is critical for the boy's development, being necessary for the formation of his gender identity and superego. Unfortunately, for the girl the resolution of the Electra complex is neither as direct nor as complete. She was led to the Electra complex by her desire for a penis, a desire that can never truly be satisfied. More importantly, the prime motivation in the boy's resolving his Oedipal complex was his overpowering fear of castration. For the girl, castration is an already accomplished fact, and thus her motivation for resolution of the Electra complex is not so strong, being motivated only by the comparatively abstract realization that her desires for her father cannot be gratified.

Immature Superego   For the female, according to the theory, the Electra complex is never as fully resolved as it is for the male. According to Freud, this leads the girl to lifelong feelings of inferiority, to a predisposition to jealousy, and to intense maternal desires. Furthermore, it leads females to be characterized by an *immature superego*. For the boy, one of the positive outcomes of resolving the Oedipal complex is the internalization, or introjection, of society's standards, thereby forming a superego. But the girl's attachment to the parents is never "smashed" as is the boy's, and she continues to be dependent on the parents for her values. She never internalizes her own values as completely as does the boy; continuing to rely on others, she is thus characterized by a less mature sense of morality, or an immature superego. In Freud's own words,

> Their [girls'] superego is never so inexorable, so impersonal, so independent of its emotional origins as we require it to be in men. . . .   That they show less sense of justice than men, that they are less ready to submit to the great necessities of life, that they are more often influenced in their judgments by feelings of affection or hostility—all these would be amply accounted for by the modification in the formation of their superego which we have already inferred. (1948, pp. 196–197)

> . . . Girls remain in it [the Electra conflict] for an indeterminate length of time; they demolish it last, and even so incompletely. In these circumstances the formation of the superego must suffer; it cannot attain the strength and independence which give it its cultural significance. (1933, p. 129)

In summary, Freud postulated a basic model for the acquisition of gender identity in the male, with a parallel model for the female. A primary assumption is the importance and superiority of the male phallus. It is so important to the boy that, in the throes of love for his mother, he fears that his father will harm the penis and he thus gives up his love for his mother and comes to identify with his father, thereby acquiring his own gender identity and introjecting the values of society. For the girl, on the other hand, penis envy—an instant recognition of the superiority of the penis and a sense of envy over not having one—is primary. She turns her love away from her mother and toward her father in an attempt to regain the penis, but is unsuccessful. Her Electra complex is never completely resolved, and as a result her moral development is less adequate.

Criticisms of Psychoanalytic Theory   Numerous general criticisms and feminist criticisms of Freudian theory have been made.

From a scientific point of view, a major problem with psychoanalytic theory is that most of its concepts cannot be evaluated scientifically to see whether they are accurate. Freud believed that many of the most important forces in human behavior are unconscious, and thus they cannot be studied by any of the usual scientific techniques.

Another criticism that is often raised is that Freud derived his ideas almost exclusively from work with patients who sought therapy. Thus his theory may describe not so much human behavior as disturbed human behavior. In particular, his views on women may contain some truth about women who have problems of adjustment, but may have little to do with women who function well psychologically.

Many modern psychologists feel that Freud overemphasized biological determinants of human behavior and did not give sufficient attention to the influence of society and learning in shaping behavior. In particular, his views on the origin of differences between males and females, and on the nature of female personality, are heavily biological, relying mostly on anatomical differences—as the famous phrase has it, "Anatomy is destiny." In relying on anatomy as an explanation, Freud ignored the enormous forces of culture acting to create differences between females and males.

Feminists have raised numerous criticisms of Freudian theory, including those noted above (e.g., Lerman, 1986; Sherman, 1971; Weisstein, 1971). They are particularly critical of Freud's assumption that the clitoris and vagina are inferior to the penis. Freud's views have been termed **phallocentric.** The superiority of the penis may have seemed a reasonable concept in the Victorian era in which Freud wrote, but it is difficult to believe today, and certainly has no scientific documentation backing it.

Phallocentric: Male centered, or, specifically, penis centered.

A related question is whether little girls would, in fact, instantly recognize the superiority of the penis. Although psychoanalysts can provide case histories to document the existence of penis envy among women seeking therapy (see Focus 2.1), it remains to be demonstrated that penis envy is common among women, or that it has a large impact on their development. Indeed, empirical research indicates that in psychiatric studies the penis-envy theme is not nearly so common among women as is castration anxiety among men (Bosselman, 1960). This suggests that Freud, in writing from a male point of view, accurately observed the castration anxiety of the male,[1] but was less accurate when constructing a parallel—penis envy—for the female.

Feminists also note the similarities between psychoanalytic theory and some of the myths about women discussed in Chapter 1. In this context, Freud seems simply to be articulating age-old myths and images about women in "scientific" language. The image of women as sinful and the source of evil is translated into the scientific-sounding "immature superego." Certainly Freud's phallocentrism is a good example of a male-as-normative or *androcentric* model. Basically, for Freud, a female is a castrated male. His model of development describes male development, female development being an inadequate variation on it.

Finally, feminists are critical of Freud's distinction between clitoral and vaginal orgasm and his belief that the vaginal orgasm is the more mature (better) one. This point will be discussed in detail in Chapter 11; briefly, Masters and Johnson, in their carefully conducted laboratory studies, find no evidence for two kinds of orgasm.

Nonetheless, it is important to recognize Freud's contributions in his recognition of the importance of development in shaping human personality, and particularly in shaping gender identity.

Variations on a Freudian Theme

Various attempts have been made within the psychoanalytic school to reform Freud's theory. Here we shall look briefly at some of the proposed variations that are relevant to women.

Karen Horney (1885–1952) Several of the most prominent psychoanalytic theorists were women, and not surprisingly, they made some modifications on Freud's theory. Horney's (pronounced Horn´-eye) theoretical papers show an evolution over time in her own thinking. Originally she accepted Freud's ideas wholeheartedly; in a 1924 paper she eagerly documented the origins of penis envy and of the castration complex in women. However, she soon became critical of these notions, and in a 1926 paper she pointed out that Freudian notions really articulate the childish views boys have of girls (much as I have pointed out that they represent age-old myths), and that Freud's psychological theory of women had been phallocentric.

---

[1]The 1994 case of Lorena Bobbitt and John Wayne Bobbitt speaks volumes on this issue. Lorena Bobbitt cut off her husband's penis with a knife, apparently following years of being beaten by him (surgeons were able to reattach the penis successfully). The story generated enormous publicity and a whole set of "Bobbitt jokes." Why? The case simultaneously touched on and allowed men to express their deep-seated castration anxieties. The publicity was particularly ironic because thousands of women each year have their genitals damaged in sexual assaults and female circumcision rituals. These cases receive little or no publicity.

FIGURE 2.1
Three women who made substantial contributions to psychoanalytic theory: (Left) Helene Deutsch. (Center) Anna Freud. (Right) Karen Horney.

Her chief disagreement with Freud was over his notion that penis envy was the critical factor in female development. Horney used the master's tricks against him and postulated that the critical factor was male envy of the female, particularly of her reproductive potential (**womb envy**), and suggested that male achievement really represents an overcompensation for feelings of anatomical inferiority (a femininity complex). Bettelheim (1962) elaborated on this notion with observations on puberty rites of preliterate tribes, from which he concluded that womb envy is a strong force.

> **Womb envy:** In Horney's analytic theory, the male's envy of woman's uterus and reproductive capacity.

This early work redefining psychoanalytic theory was done while Horney was in her native country, Germany. In 1932 she immigrated to the United States. There she continued her reformulations and articulated a personality theory that—in contrast to Freud's emphasis on biological and intrapsychic forces—emphasized cultural and social influences and human growth (O'Connell, 1990). Indeed, she has the distinction of being the only woman whose theory is included in personality textbooks.

Helene Deutsch (1884–1982) In 1944, Helene Deutsch published a weighty two-volume work entitled *The Psychology of Women,* the major attempt within the psychoanalytic school for a complete understanding of the psychological dynamics of women. In many ways, Deutsch was more of an observer and analyst than she was a theorist; her book contains numerous excerpts from case histories to illustrate major tenets of the psychoanalytic view of women.

Deutsch's major contribution was to extend Freud's analysis of female development, which essentially ended with the phallic stage and Electra complex, to later stages of development. She began in the prepuberty period because she saw the critical processes in woman's psychological development revolving around the transition from being a girl to being a woman. She then continued to describe female development and personality in adolescence and adulthood.

Deutsch largely retained a Freudian orthodoxy in her thinking. For example, she believed that to be a woman one must develop a "feminine core" in the personality, including the traits of narcissism, masochism, and passivity. She also held that instinct and intuition were very important to a feminine personality.

She elaborated on Freud's distinction between the function of the clitoris and the function of the vagina. She saw the switch from clitoral eroticism to a focus on the vagina as being an important task during prepuberty and adolescence. This switch represented a shift from activity to passivity, the clitoris representing the active, masculine component that the woman must give up to be truly feminine (Deutsch, 1924). Deutsch viewed this as the hardest task of libidinal development—a task further complicated by the beginning of menstruation, which revived feelings of castration.

Deutsch coined the term *masculinity complex* to refer to certain instances of women's failure to adjust. Such women are characterized by a predominance of masculine active and aggressive tendencies, which brings them into conflict with both their surrounding environment and their own feminine tendencies.

Deutsch viewed motherhood as the most critical feature in woman's psychological development. Indeed, the whole second volume of *The Psychology of Women* was devoted exclusively to this topic, and she saw prepuberty and adolescence as mainly an anticipation of motherhood.

> Thus woman acquires a tendency to passivity that intensifies the passive nature inherent in her biology and anatomy. She passively awaits fecundation: her life is fully active and rooted in reality only when she becomes a mother. Until then everything that is feminine in the woman, physiology and psychology, is passive, receptive. (1944, Vol. I, p. 140)

Deutsch's view of the psychology of women is at once insightful and laden with the confusion of cultural and biological forces typical of psychoanalytic theory. For example, she believed that female passivity is a result of anatomy and biological functioning and failed to recognize that it is a culturally assigned part of the female role.

Anna Freud (1895–1982)   Although she did not focus specifically on the psychology of women, Anna Freud deserves mention here because she was one of the most—perhaps the most—outstanding contributor to psychoanalytic theory after Sigmund Freud (Fine, 1990). Most importantly, she was the founder of child psychoanalysis.

The youngest of the six children born to Sigmund and Martha Freud, she was the only one to take an interest in her father's work. She was also stimulated by the writings of Maria Montessori, and she originally trained to be an elementary school teacher.

The first major milestone in her career was the publication of her book *Introduction to the Technique of Child Analysis* in 1926. Her important work on ego psychology, *The Ego and the Mechanisms of Defense,* was published in 1936.

By 1938, Nazis had invaded Vienna. After a day of Gestapo interrogation, Anna Freud was convinced that she and her parents must flee to England. There she founded a school for children made homeless by the war. Her observations of these children and their disturbances led to a number of books, including *War and Children* (1943). Many of the major European psychoanalysts were murdered by Nazis, but Anna Freud lived to rebuild the movement following World War II.

Anna Freud's contributions to psychoanalysis were enormous. She founded child psychoanalysis and pioneered such techniques as play therapy for children.

Nancy Chodorow Nancy Chodorow's book *The Reproduction of Mothering* (1978) is a controversial new addition to the psychoanalytic literature. In her book Chodorow fuses psychoanalytic theory, sociological theory, and the feminist perspective (strange alliances, indeed!) in an attempt to answer the question, Why do women mother? That is, why is it that in all cultures it is the women who do almost all of the care of children? Her thesis, in brief, is that childcare done by women produces vastly different experiences for daughters than for sons. Childcare done by mothers produces daughters who want to mother, and thus mothering reproduces itself. Women's mothering also produces sons who dominate and devalue women.

Infants start life in a state of total dependency, and given the current division of labor in the family, those dependency needs are satisfied almost exclusively by the mother. In addition, infants are narcissistic, or self-centered, and have trouble distinguishing between the primary caretaker—the mother—and themselves. Because mothers do such a good job of meeting their every need, infants blissfully assume that mothers have no other interests besides themselves. As babies grow, perhaps as younger siblings are born, unpleasant reality eventually becomes clear as they come to understand that mothers do have other interests.

Chodorow contends that the early, intensely close relationship with the mother affects the sense of self and general attitudes toward women, for both boys and girls. Both males and females continue to expect women to be caring and sacrificing, and that forever shapes their attitudes toward women. The girl's sense of self is profoundly influenced because her intense relationship to her mother is never entirely broken. Therefore, girls never see themselves as separate in the way boys do, and girls and women continue to define themselves more in *relational* terms.

Boys, on the other hand, begin with the same intense attachment to the mother. But in order to develop a masculine identity, they must smash or repress

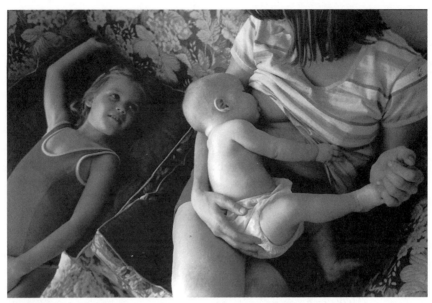

FIGURE 2.2
Chodorow argues that mothering (most childcare being done by women) produces vastly different experiences for boys and girls, resulting in girls who want to mother and boys who dominate and devalue women.

the relationship to the mother. Thus masculinity comes to be defined negatively, as nonfemininity. Masculinity involves denying feminine maternal attachment. And thus all women come to be devalued as part of the male's need to separate himself from his mother (and all women) and define a masculine identity for himself. Fathers are essentially absent, and therefore their masculine qualities become idealized, and the notion of masculine superiority emerges. Simultaneously, men's capacity for parenting is reduced by their denial of relatedness.

In adulthood, men's relational needs are less than women's, and men's needs are satisfied by a relationship with a woman, in which they recapture the warmth of the infant relationship with their mother. Adult women have greater relational needs that cannot entirely be satisfied by a man. So women have babies, their relational needs are satisfied, and the cycle repeats itself.

According to Chodorow's analysis, her question, Why do women mother? is not so small as it might appear. Women's mothering perpetuates the whole division of labor by gender, for once women are committed to be the exclusive child-rearers, men must do the other jobs necessary for society to continue. Furthermore, women's mothering creates the devaluation of women. Thus exclusive childrearing by women is a central issue.

How can Chodorow claim to have integrated feminism into her theory when her ideas so clearly smack of psychoanalytic theory? First, Chodorow makes feminist reconstructions of some of Freud's ideas. For example, she argues that girls' penis envy results not from a girl's recognition of the inherent superiority of the penis (as Freud said), but rather from the fact that the penis symbolizes the power men have in our society. Second, Chodorow does not stop with her analysis of the family dynamics that produce the whole situation. She gives a prescription for social change to eliminate inequities for women. She says that the only way for the cycle to be broken is for men to begin participating equally in childcare. She believes that unless men do so, women will perpetually be devalued. As she concludes,

> Any strategy for change whose goal includes liberation from the constraints of an unequal social organization of gender must take account of the need for a fundamental reorganization of parenting, so that primary parenting is shared between men and women. (Chodorow, 1978, p. 215)

Criticisms of Chodorow's theory have been raised as well (e.g., Lorber et al., 1981). First, the theory has a heterosexist bias. It explains in detail why children grow up heterosexual and seems to assume that all of them would, while making no attempt to understand lesbian development (Rich, 1980). Second, from the viewpoint of feminist theory, Chodorow's theory has been criticized for focusing exclusively on the impact of gender in people's lives, while ignoring the powerful influences of race and social class (Spelman, 1988). Third, most of the evidence Chodorow cites in her book is clinical—that is, it comes from individual histories of people seeking psychotherapy. As such, Chodorow's theory is open to the same criticism that was made of Freud's, namely, that it is based on disturbed personality and experience. On occasion, Chodorow does mention more solid scientific findings, but then proceeds to ignore them. For example, she mentions an important finding that parents tend to treat children quite similarly, regardless of gender, but that finding is not consistent with her theory, and so she dismisses it (Chodorow, 1978, p. 98). Finally, she advocates social change by having fathers participate equally in childcare, but her theory indicates that present-day fathers, who are the products of the last generation of mothering, should be incapable of childrearing. How can change ever be made, then? (Personally, I think that men right now are perfectly capable of being good childrearers, but that idea does not follow logically from her theory.) Nonetheless, many feminists agree that men must participate more equally in childcare.

Sociobiology

Sociobiology: The application of evolutionary theory to explaining the social behavior of animals, including people.

Sociobiology is a controversial theory initially proposed by Harvard biologist E. O. Wilson in his book *Sociobiology: The New Synthesis* (1975), a massive, 700-page work filled with countless examples from insect life. He followed this with a popularized version, *On Human Nature* (1978). David P. Barash has also provided a readable text in his *Sociobiology and Behavior* (1982).

Wilson originally defined sociobiology as "the systematic study of the biological basis of all social behavior" (1975, p. 4). But I think a better definition is provided by Barash (1982): "sociobiology is the application of evolutionary theory to understanding the social behavior of animals, including humans." That is, sociobiologists are specifically concerned with understanding how social behaviors—such as aggression or caring for the young—are the product of evolution. In fact, a better term for this theory would probably be *socioevolution,* but I will stick to *sociobiology* because it is the standard term. *Evolutionary psychology* is another term that is used by some (e.g., Buss, 1991).

To understand what sociobiology has to say about women and gender roles, we must first discuss evolutionary theory. Evolution, as modern biologists understand it, is a product of **natural selection,** a mechanism first proposed by Charles Darwin. His basic observation was that living things overreproduce—that is, they produce far more young than would be needed simply to replace themselves. Yet population sizes remain relatively constant. Therefore, many individuals must not survive. There must be differential survival, with the fittest organisms surviving and others not. In popular conceptions the "fittest" animal is the most aggressive, but evolutionary theory defines fitness differently. **Fitness is defined in this theory as the relative number of genes an animal contributes to the next generation.** The bottom line is producing lots of offspring, specifically healthy, viable offspring. Thus a man who jogs 10 miles a day, lifts weights, and has a 50-inch chest but whose sperm count is zero would be considered to have zero fitness according to sociobiologists. Over generations, there is differential reproduction, the fittest individuals producing the most offspring. Genes that produce fitness characteristics become more frequent, and fitness characteristics ("adaptive" characteristics) become more frequent; genes and associated characteristics that produce poor fitness become less frequent.

Natural selection: According to Darwin, the process by which the fittest animals survive, reproduce, and pass their genes on to the next generation, whereas animals that are less fit do not reproduce and therefore do not pass on their genes.

Fitness: In evolutionary theory, an animal's relative contribution of genes to the next generation.

The basic idea of the sociobiologists is that the evolutionary theory of natural selection can be applied to social behaviors. That is, a particular form of social behavior—let's say, caring for one's young—would be adaptive, in the sense of increasing one's reproductive fitness. Other social behaviors—for example, female infanticide—would be maladaptive, decreasing one's reproductive fitness. Over the many generations of natural selection that have occurred, the maladaptive behaviors should have been weeded out, and we should be left with social behaviors that are adaptive because they are the product of evolutionary selection. From this logic flows the *central theorem of sociobiology:* when a social behavior is genetically influenced, the animal should behave so as to maximize fitness (Barash, 1982).

With this as background, let us now consider some specific arguments of sociobiologists that are of special relevance to women.

Parental Investment   One of the things sociobiologists have attempted to explain is why it is typically the female of the species that does most of the care of offspring. Remember that this phenomenon was also central to Chodorow's theory, but the sociobiologist offers a very different explanation for it. The sociobiologist's explanation rests on the concept of **parental investment,** which refers to behaviors or other investments of the parent with respect to the offspring that increase the offspring's chance of survival, but that also cost the parent something (Trivers, 1972). This all becomes relevant to gender because females generally have a much larger parental investment in their offspring than males do. At the moment of conception, the female has the greater parental investment—she has just contributed one of her precious eggs. The male has contributed merely a sperm. Eggs are precious because they are large cells, and the female produces only one per month (at least in humans, and perhaps only one or several per year in other species of mammals). Sperm are "cheap" because they are small cells and are produced in enormous numbers. For example, there are 300 million sperm in the average human male ejaculate, and a man can produce that number again in 24 to 48 hours. So at the moment of conception the female has invested much with her precious egg, but the male has invested little with a single sperm. In mammals, the female then proceeds to gestate the young (for a period of nine months in humans). Here again she makes an enormous investment of her body's resources, which otherwise could have been invested in doing something else. Then the offspring are born, and the female, at least among mammals, nurses them, once again investing time and energy.

> **Parental investment:** In sociobiology, behaviors or other investments in the offspring by the parent that increase the offspring's chance of survival.

The next step in the logic is this: It is most adaptive for whichever parent has the greater parental investment to continue to care for the offspring. Here we have the female, who has invested her precious egg, her gestation, and her nursing; it would be evolutionary insanity for her to abandon the offspring when they still need more care in order to survive. In contrast, the male has invested relatively little and his best reproductive strategy is to "sleep around" and impregnate as many females as possible, producing more offspring carrying his genes. This works particularly well if he can count on the female to take care of the offspring so that they survive.

In short, the sociobiologist says that women are the ones who do the childcare for two reasons. The first is that the female has a greater parental investment and therefore it is adaptive for her to continue to care for her offspring. The second reason arises from a basic fact: maternity is always certain, whereas paternity is not. The female is sure that the offspring are hers. The sociobiologist would say that she knows that those young carry her genes. The male cannot be sure that they are his offspring, carrying his genes. It is thus adaptive for the female—it increases her fitness—to care for the offspring to make sure that they, and her genes, survive. It does not increase the male's fitness to care for offspring that may not carry his genes. Therefore, females take care of the offspring.

There are exceptions to this pattern, and they are worth considering. One is songbirds, who are notable because the male and female participate quite equally and cooperatively in care of their young (Barash, 1982). But sociobiologists believe that their theory can explain the exception as well as the general rule. Songbirds have a monogamous mating system that makes paternity a near certainty. Thus it is adaptive for the male to care for the young because he can be sure that they carry his genes. In addition, young birds require an enormous amount of food per day. It is doubtful that they could survive on the amount of food brought to them by a single parent. Thus it is highly adaptive for both parents to participate in care of the offspring, and would be highly maladaptive for fathers or mothers to neglect them.

Sociobiologists extend the logic of evolution to explain why female orgasm evolved in humans. The background is that female orgasm is thought to exist in few, if any, other species. Why, then, does it exist in humans?

Sociobiologists say that human female orgasm has evolved because human babies are born particularly helpless, dependent, and in need of parental care (Barash, 1982). Essentially, they need two parents in order to survive. A monogamous mating system, with permanent pairing of mother and father, would be adaptive and favored in evolution. The female orgasm (and the human female's continuous interest in sex at all phases of the menstrual cycle) thus evolved in order to hold together that permanent pair.

Sociobiologists also extend their theorizing to explain the **double standard**—that is, that among humans the male is allowed, even encouraged, to be promiscuous, whereas the female is punished for engaging in promiscuous sex and instead is very careful and selective about whom she has sex with (Barash, 1982). The explanation has to do with that precious egg and those cheap sperm. It is adaptive for her to be careful of what happens to the egg, whereas it is adaptive for him to distribute sperm to as many females as possible. Anticipating her greater parental investment, the female must also be careful about whose genes she mixes with her own. (This line of thinking gives a whole new meaning to the expression "choosy mothers.")

Sexual Selection   Sexual selection is an evolutionary mechanism originally proposed by Darwin as acting in parallel to natural selection and as producing gender differences. Essentially, sexual selection means that different selection pressures act on males and females, and thus males and females become different. **Sexual selection** consists of two processes: (1) members of one gender (usually males) compete among themselves to gain mating privileges with members of the other gender (usually females); and (2) members of the other gender (usually females) have preferences for certain members of the first gender (usually males) and decide

Double standard: Tolerance of male promiscuity and disapproval of female promiscuity.

Sexual selection: According to Darwin, the processes by which members of one gender (usually males) compete with each other for mating privileges with members of the other gender (usually females), and members of the other gender (females) choose to mate only with certain preferred members of the first gender (males).

FIGURE 2.3
Sociobiologists argue that gender differences in aggression in humans and other species are a result of sexual selection in evolution. Here two males fight while the female looks on.

which of them they are willing to mate with. In short, males fight and females choose. Process (1) neatly explains why the males of most species are larger and more aggressive than the females—aggression is adaptive for males in competition, and they are the product of sexual selection. Sexual selection explains, for example, why among many species of birds it is the male that has the gorgeous plumage while the female is rather dowdy. Plumage is a way that males compete among themselves, and females are attracted to the most gorgeous males. Females, on the other hand, in their roles as choosers, need not be gorgeous and have not been selected to be so. Perhaps they have been selected for wisdom (I said that, not a sociobiologist!).

Sexual selection, then, is a mechanism that is used to explain gender differences. It is particularly useful in explaining the greater size, strength, and aggressiveness of males.

Many more examples could be given, but you have seen the main ones dealing with women's issues. The thrust of the argument is clear: The sociobiologist argues that the social behaviors we see in animals and humans today evolved because these behaviors were adaptive, and they continue to be biologically programmed.

Feminist Criticism Feminists are not exactly delighted with sociobiology (for feminist critiques, see Hrdy, 1981; Janson-Smith, 1980; Weisstein, 1982). Three basic criticisms have been raised. First, many feminists are wary of biological explanations of anything. The reason is that biology always seems to end up being a convenient rationalization for perpetuating the status quo. For example, the sociobiologist's belief is that the greater aggression and dominance of males is a result of sexual selection and is controlled by genes. Therefore, men are genetically dominant, and women are genetically subordinate, and the subordinate status of women will have to continue because it is genetic. That kind of logic is a red flag to a feminist. Sociobiologists are not so naive that they ignore environmental influences entirely, and so the argument becomes a question of emphasis, sociobiologists emphasizing biology and feminists emphasizing environment.

Second, feminists object that sociobiologists do a highly selective reading of both data and theories. Sociobiologists tend to view data from an *androcentric* (male-centered) perspective and to talk selectively about those studies that confirm their androcentric theory, ignoring those studies that contradict it. For example, the female chimpanzee—the chimpanzee is our nearest evolutionary relative—is notoriously promiscuous (Janson-Smith, 1980). When she is in estrus ("heat"), she mates indiscriminately with many males. That does not fit into sociobiology, which says that she should be choosy about the male with whom she mates and that the most aggressive, dominant male should be the only one to have the privilege of inseminating her. The sociobiologists tend to ignore chimpanzees.

As another instance of androcentric bias, consider the case of a famous young female macaque (monkey) named Imo, living with her troop on an island off Japan.

> Scientists provisioned the troop there with sweet potatoes. Imo discovered that washing sweet potatoes got the sand off. Her discovery quickly spread among the other juniors in the troop, who then taught their mothers, who in turn, taught their infants. Adult males never learned it. Next, scientists flung grains of wheat in the sand to see what the troop would do. Rather than laboriously picking the wheat out of the sand grain by grain, Imo discovered how to separate the wheat from the sand in one operation. Again this spread from Imo's peers to mothers and infants, and, again, adult males never learned it. The fact that these Japanese macaques had a rudimentary culture has been widely heralded. (Weisstein, 1982, p. 46)

Had the genders been reversed, with Imo being a male and the females being unable to learn, one can imagine the attention these facts would have been given by sociobiologists. They would have made much of the genius of the male and the lack of intelligence of females. As it is, Imo's gender is not discussed, and the learning failure of the males is similarly ignored.[2] Sociobiologists, then, seem to ignore many animal examples that contradict human stereotypes.

---

[2]In case you are not sufficiently impressed with Imo, have you figured out a good way to separate the wheat from the sand? Imo did it by throwing both into the water, where the wheat floated and the sand sunk to the bottom.

From a feminist perspective, even the sociobiologists' attention to theory is selective and androcentric. For example, sexual selection, as noted above, contains two parts. The part that produces competition and aggression in males has received much attention from sociobiologists. But they have ignored the second part, in which females make choices among males. The second part could be used as an explanation for human females' being more intelligent, more perceptive, or more powerful and controlling than human males, but that avenue of thought is never explored by sociobiologists.

Sociobiologists also rely heavily on data from nonindustrial societies, specifically hunter-gatherer societies that are supposed to be like those that existed at the dawn of the human species, millions of years ago. Once again, the emphasis is androcentrically selective. The sociobiologist emphasizes "man the hunter" and how he evolved to be aggressive and have great physical prowess. In discussing this, Wilson (1978, p. 127) makes much of how natural selection for these traits is reflected in men's current superiority in Olympic track events. Later on the same page, he mentions that women are superior in precision archery and small-bore rifle shooting in the Olympics, but does not seem to see this as inconsistent with the evolution of only man as the hunter. "Woman the gatherer" is ignored, although she may have formed the foundation for early human social organization (Janson-Smith, 1980).

Third, sociobiology has been criticized for resting on an outmoded version of evolutionary theory that modern biologists consider naive (Gould, 1987). For example, sociobiology has focused mainly on the individual's struggle for survival, whereas modern biologists focus on more complex issues such as the survival of the group and the species, and the evolution of a successful adaptation between the species and its environment.

The feminist criticisms, then, are that sociobiology can rationalize and perpetuate the subordination of women; that its evidence rests on a selective, androcentric citing of the data, ignoring many contradictions; and that it relies on an outdated and oversimplified view of evolution.

Social Learning Theory

A popular explanation for gender differences in behavior is "conditioning." That is, boys and girls act appropriately for their gender because they have been rewarded for doing some things and punished for doing others. The notion is that principles of operant conditioning explain the acquisition of gender roles. Thus, for girls, some behaviors are rewarded (positively reinforced), whereas others either are not rewarded or are even punished, so that the girl comes to perform the rewarded behaviors more frequently, the unrewarded ones less frequently or not at all. For example, little girls are rewarded for being quiet and obedient, whereas little boys are rewarded for athletics and achievement. Consequently, children acquire gender-typed behaviors because they are rewarded or approved. This is thought to be the essential process creating gender typing.

Reinforcement: In operant conditioning, some-
thing that occurs after a
behavior and makes
the behavior more
likely to occur in the
future.

Imitation: When people
do what they see
others doing.

Observational learning:
When a person
observes someone
doing something, and
then does it at a later
time.

Social learning theory is a major theoretical system in psychology, designed to describe the process involved in human development (see Bandura and Walters, 1963). In particular, it has been
used to explain the development of gender differences (Lott and
Maluso, 1993; Mischel, 1966). In explaining the shaping of children's behavior, social learning theory uses the notion of **reinforcement** described above—that is, the idea that rewards and punishments are given differentially to boys and girls for gender-typed
behaviors, and that children therefore come to perform the rewarded, gender-appropriate behaviors more frequently and the punished, gender-inappropriate behaviors less frequently. But social
learning theory also emphasizes the importance of two additional
processes: **imitation** and **observational learning.** Imitation means
simply that children do what they see others doing. Observational
learning refers to situations in which children learn by observing the
behavior of others, even though they may not actually perform the
behavior at the time, perhaps not using the information until months
or years later. These three mechanisms, then—reinforcement, imitation, and observational learning—are thought to underlie the process
of gender typing, that is, the acquisition of gender-typed behaviors,
according to social learning theory.

Acquiring Gender Roles Given the way roles are divided in our culture, infants of both genders are biologically and psychologically dependent on the
mother. According to the social learning approach, because the mother is the
source of attention and care, the association of the mother's presence with comfort leads the child to value mother-presence and to experience anxiety or discomfort in her absence. Thus, as mother-presence comes to be equated with
pleasure and mother-absence with discomfort, the mother takes on important
meaning to the infant—she becomes an effective reinforcer of the child's behavior. In the course of development, the mother's demands and expectations
for the child's behavior increase and the child learns to perform those acts that
will bring about approval.

Applying the theory to the process of gender-role learning, the mother presumably reacts differently to gender-typed behaviors in her child. For example,
she may react positively when her daughter displays feminine behaviors, such as
nurturance, and negatively when she displays masculine behaviors, such as aggressiveness. In effect, the mother rewards feminine behaviors and may punish
masculine behaviors. Social learning theory asserts that these reinforcements
will be effective in shaping the child's behavior.

Later, stimulus generalization occurs. That is, stimuli that are similar to the
mother—for example, the father and other adults—also become effective reinforcers of behavior. These other adults also presumably react differentially to
gender-typed behavior in the child and apply reinforcements similar to those the
mother has used. Thus male and female children are treated differently, the re-

wards being given in accordance with cultural prescriptions regarding appropriate behavior for males and females.

According to social learning theory, gender typing involves another process, imitation. The child imitates the behavior of other people. The child's imitation is motivated partly by the power of authority figures, so that he or she is particularly likely to imitate parents or other adults. Behaving like a particular person gives the child the sense that she or he possesses that person's power. With regard to gender-role learning, the theory assumes that children tend to imitate the same-gender parent and other same-gender adults more than opposite-gender adults. That is, the little girl imitates her mother and other women more than she does men. This mechanism of imitation helps to explain the acquisition of the complex and subtle aspects of gender roles that probably have not been the object of reinforcements. Furthermore, imitation and reinforcement may interact. For example, the girl may imitate a behavior of her mother's and then be rewarded for it, once again furthering the process of gender typing.

The child does not actually have to perform a behavior in order to learn it. A behavior may become part of the child's repertoire through observational learning. Such information may be stored up for use perhaps 10 or 15 years later, when a situation in adolescence or adulthood calls for a knowledge of gender-appropriate behaviors. For example, a young girl may observe her mother caring

FIGURE 2.4
Children learn gender roles in part by imitation of adults.

for an infant brother or sister. Although the little girl may not perform any infant-care behaviors at the time, much less be rewarded for them, she nonetheless may store up the information about infant care for use when she herself is a mother. Once again, gender typing occurs through mechanisms other than reinforcement.

In more advanced learning, children also learn to anticipate the consequences of their actions. Here also, an action need not be performed for the child to understand the reinforcements or punishments that will result. The little girl knows in advance that her attempts to join Little League will be met with opposition, and perhaps even with punishments. Higher-order conditioning also occurs, so that, for example, verbal cues may serve as strong reinforcements or punishments. The words *sissy* and *mannish* acquire a punishing quality.

According to social learning theory, then, gender typing results from differential rewards and punishments, as well as learning in the absence of reinforcement: by imitation of same-gender models and by observational learning.

Evidence for Social Learning Theory   Social learning theory has stimulated a great deal of research aimed at documenting the existence—or nonexistence—of the mechanisms it proposes. The research makes it possible to begin to assess the adequacy of the social learning model for the development of gender differences.

There have been numerous demonstrations of the effectiveness of imitation and reinforcements in shaping children's behavior, in particular gender-typed behaviors such as aggression. A good example is a study by the psychologist Albert Bandura (1965). In the first phase of this experiment, children were randomly assigned to one of three groups and shown one of three films. In all the films, an adult model was performing aggressive behavior, but in one film the model was rewarded; in another, punished; and in the third, left alone without consequences. The children's aggressive behavior was then observed. As the social learning approach would predict, children who had viewed the model being punished performed the least aggressive behavior. Furthermore, and consistent with the findings of many other investigators (see Chapter 3), boys performed more aggressive behavior than girls. In the second phase of the experiment, the children were offered attractive reinforcements (pretty sticker pictures and juice treats) for performing as many of the model's aggressive responses as they could remember. Gender differences nearly disappeared in this phase, and girls performed nearly as many aggressive behaviors as boys.

This experiment illustrated several important points. The first phase demonstrated that children do imitate, and that they do so differentially depending on the perceived consequences of the behavior. Notice that in this phase the children themselves were not actually reinforced, but simply observed the model being reinforced. The second phase illustrated how gender differences in aggressive behavior can be influenced by reinforcements. When girls were given equal reinforcement for aggression, they were nearly as aggressive as boys. Certainly the experiment is evidence of the power of imitation and reinforcement in shaping children's behavior.

Criticisms of Social Learning Theory   The mechanisms postulated by social learning theory—reinforcement, imitation, and observational learning—intuitively appear to be reasonable explanations for why gender differences develop. Nonetheless, these ideas must be tested scientifically. The study by Bandura discussed above is one kind of test of social learning theory. But we still need to know some other things, namely, (1) do parents and others actually reinforce the behavior of boys and girls differentially, and (2) do children really imitate parents and others of their own gender more than people of the other gender? The available evidence seems to support point (1), but not point (2).

There is evidence that parents treat boys and girls differently, and that they differentially reward some—though certainly not all—behaviors in boys and girls (Block, 1978; Sherman, 1978). Based on a review of 172 studies of parents' socialization practices, the authors concluded that there was a significant tendency for parents to encourage gender-typed activities in their children, especially in areas such as play and household chores (Lytton and Romney, 1991). Interestingly, in some areas where one might expect differential socialization of boys and girls, no differences were found. For example, boys and girls were equally encouraged to achieve.

The evidence does not support, however, the notion that children tend to imitate people of their own gender more than people of the other gender (Maccoby and Jacklin, 1974). When offered an opportunity to imitate either a male or a female model, young children do not tend to behave more like the model whose gender is the same as their own; indeed, their behavior appears to be fairly random with respect to the gender of the model. This raises the distinction between *learning* and *performance*. It is possible that children learn equally from models of both genders, but that they differentially perform what they have learned, depending on the perceived consequences of their behavior and the gender appropriateness of the behavior. This point is illustrated in the study by Bandura mentioned above. Although the girls were less aggressive than the boys in the first phase of the experiment, they were almost equally aggressive in the second phase. The results from the second phase suggest that the girls had learned as much as the boys about the model's aggressive behavior, but that in the first phase they did not perform what they had learned, and did so only in the second phase when encouraged by reinforcements.

In summary, social learning theory postulates that three important mechanisms are involved in the development of gender differences: reinforcement, imitation, and observational learning. The power of reinforcements and imitation in influencing children's behavior has been demonstrated in numerous experiments. It also seems that parents do differentially reinforce some gender-typed behaviors. However, research calls into question whether children do imitate same-gender models more than opposite-gender ones. These latter results suggest that other, more complex processes must be involved, in addition to those postulated by social learning theory, in the development of gender differences. For those who want to see social change in gender roles, this is an optimistic theory. It says that children can and will learn a very different set of gender roles if powerful others—for example, parents and the media—change the behaviors they reinforce and model.

The Cognitive-Developmental Model

In terms of impact, perhaps the closest equivalent in the second half of this century to Freud's work in the first half is the developmental theory founded by Jean Piaget, together with his colleague Bärbel Inhelder. Kohlberg (1966) has extended Piaget and Inhelder's cognitive principles to the realm of gender roles.

Much of Piaget and Inhelder's thinking arose from their observations of the errors children made in answering questions such as those asked on intelligence tests. They concluded that these errors did not indicate that the children were stupid or ignorant, but rather that they had a different worldview, or *cognitive organization,* from that of adults. Piaget and Inhelder discovered that the cognitive organizations of children change systematically over time, and they constructed a stage theory of cognitive (intellectual) development to describe the progression of these changes. Interestingly, concepts of gender and gender identity undergo developmental changes parallel to the development of other concepts.

Gender identity: In cognitive-developmental theory, the individual's concept or knowledge that she or he is a female or male.

Gender Identity   Around the age of 18 months to 2 years, children form a concept of **gender identity;** that is, they know whether they are boys or girls. Soon after this, they learn to identify the gender of their mother and father, and then other people around them generally. However, at this stage they do not realize that gender is a permanent characteristic. That is, a girl may think that when she grows up she can be a boy if she wants to (Kohlberg, 1966).

Gender constancy: According to cognitive-developmental theory, a child's understanding that gender is a permanent, unchanging characteristic of oneself.

Gender Roles and Gender Constancy   If you ask a three-year-old girl whether she is a boy or a girl, she will answer correctly that she is a girl. But if you ask her whether she can grow up to be a daddy, she will incorrectly answer yes. A six- or seven-year-old girl will not make this error. The three-year-old understands the concept of gender, but does not yet have the concept of **gender constancy**—the knowledge that gender is a permanent part of the self or identity. The development of these concepts was amusingly illustrated by Kohlberg (1966, p. 95):

(Jimmy has just turned four, his friend Johnny is four and a half)

JOHNNY: I'm going to be an airplane builder when I grow up.

JIMMY: When I grow up, I'll be a mommy.

JOHNNY: No, you can't be a mommy. You have to be a daddy.

JIMMY: No, I'm going to be a mommy.

JOHNNY: No, you're not a girl, you can't be a mommy.

JIMMY: Yes, I can.

Apparently Johnny has acquired the concept of gender constancy, whereas Jimmy hasn't.

According to Kohlberg, the acquisition of this basic concept of gender constancy (around the ages of four to six) is the crucial basis for the acquisition of gender role. Once the little girl knows she is a girl and will always be a female, this gender identity becomes an important part of personal identity. Gender identity then determines basic valuations (whether a person or behavior is believed to be "good" or "bad"). Motivated to have a positive sense of self, the girl comes to see femaleness as good. She then associates this valuation with cultural stereotypes, so that the female role becomes attractive to her. And finally she identifies with her mother, who is a readily available example of the female role the girl wishes to acquire. Thus children are motivated to adopt gender roles as part of their attempt to understand reality and to develop a stable and positive self-concept.

Cognitive-developmental theory essentially views gender-role learning as one aspect of cognitive development. The child learns a set of rules regarding what males do and what females do, and behaves accordingly. In this theory, gender-role learning is not externally imposed, but rather is largely self-motivated. The child essentially engages in self-socialization and self-selects the behaviors to be learned and performed on the basis of rules regarding the gender appropriateness of the behavior.

Cognitive-developmental theory points up an important potential problem in female development. It asserts, quite reasonably, that normal, healthy children tend to value the self, and therefore their own gender. Therefore little girls start to grow up thinking "female is good." Unfortunately, this does not correspond to cultural valuations of gender roles, in which the male role is valued more highly. Thus the girl is placed in a conflict situation in which her human need is to value the female role, yet culture informs her that it is not a valued role. We shall discuss the implications of this situation further in the next chapters.

Criticisms of Cognitive-Developmental Theory Kohlberg's basic argument is that the acquisition of the concept of gender constancy and, with it, the concept of gender identity is the important first step in gender typing. Once these concepts have been formed, say, at around five to seven years of age, the child essentially "self-socializes." What evidence is there supporting these ideas?

First, a concept of gender constancy clearly develops in children around the ages of five to seven. Evidence comes from children's comments such as those quoted earlier in this chapter and from their responses to direct questioning by psychologists (e.g., Marcus and Overton, 1978). There is also some evidence that kindergartners who have acquired gender constancy prefer to observe same-gender models, as compared with opposite-gender models, whereas children who do not yet have a concept of gender constancy have no such preference

(Slaby, 1974, cited in Maccoby and Jacklin, 1974, p. 365). Preschoolers who have acquired gender constancy are more stereotyped in their views of adult occupations than preschoolers who do not have gender constancy are (O'Keefe and Hyde, 1983).

However, children's gender-typed interests appear when they are far too young to have acquired the concept of gender constancy (Maccoby and Jacklin, 1974; O'Keefe and Hyde, 1983). That is, gender-typed toy and game preferences appear when children are two or three, yet children do not develop gender constancy until they are between the ages of five and seven. This is inconsistent with Kohlberg's theory, which would say that gender-typed interests should not appear until after gender constancy develops.

It seems reasonable to conclude that Kohlberg's notion of gender constancy and "self-socialization" explains some aspects of gender-role development, but that other mechanisms—such as those in social learning theory—are also functioning.

According to the theory, one of the child's main motives for adopting a gender role is the power and value the child sees in that role; yet the female role has less power and value. Is the girl therefore less motivated to adopt her role than the boy is? Kohlberg (1966, pp. 121–122) attempted to avoid this problem by saying that girls are motivated by the competency and "niceness" they perceive the female role to represent. Certainly it would be desirable to have a more complete explication of the process of female gender-role development from the cognitive-developmental point of view.

Kohlberg on Moral Development   Kohlberg's other major contribution to psychology has been his analysis of moral development, that is, children's changing cognitions or understandings about morality (Kohlberg, 1969; Colby et al., 1983). Although the analysis is not directly about women, it has important implications for women. First, you need to know how Kohlberg studied moral development and how he determined that there are stages in the development of moral reasoning.

Kohlberg studied moral thought by presenting children or adults with a moral dilemma, of which the following is an example:

> In Europe, a woman was near death from a special kind of cancer. There was one drug that the doctors thought might save her. It was a form of radium that a druggist in the same town had recently discovered. The drug was expensive to make, but the druggist was charging 10 times what the drug cost him to make. He paid $200 for the radium and charged $2,000 for a small dose of the drug. The sick woman's husband, Heinz, went to everyone he knew to borrow the money, but he could only get together about $1,000, which is half of what it cost. He told the druggist that his wife was dying and asked him to sell it cheaper or let him pay later. But the druggist said, "No, I discovered the drug and I'm going to make money from it." So Heinz gets desperate and considers breaking into the man's store to steal the drug for his wife.

Following presentation of the dilemma, the participant is asked a number of questions, such as whether Heinz should steal the drug and why. The important part is not whether the person says Heinz should or should not steal, but rather the person's answer to the question, Why?—which reflects the stage of development of moral reasoning.

Based on his research, Kohlberg concluded that people go through a series of three levels in their moral reasoning as they mature, and that each level is divided into two stages, for a total of six stages. These stages are defined on the left side of Table 2.1. In Level I, **preconventional morality,** children (usually preschoolers) have little sense of rules and obey simply to avoid punishments or to obtain rewards. For example, Heinz should not steal because he might get caught and put in jail. In Level II, **conventional morality,** children (usually beginning in elementary school) are well aware of society's rules and laws and conform to them rigidly; there is a law-and-order mentality and a desire to look good in front of others. For example, Heinz should not steal because stealing is against the law. Finally, in Level III, **postconventional morality,** a person transcends the rules and laws of society and instead behaves in accordance with an internal, self-defined set of ethical principles. For example, it is acceptable for Heinz to steal because human life is more important than property. In Level III, it might be judged acceptable to violate laws in some instances in which they were unjust. The perfect example of Level III morality is the life of Mahatma Gandhi as shown so clearly in the movie *Gandhi.* For him, equality and freedom were self-accepted, internalized values that allowed him to violate the laws of his country, and he persisted in following his own principles despite the disapproval of authorities, which was sometimes so severe that he was beaten.

According to Kohlberg's research, most adults never reach Level III, and instead persist in Stages 3 and 4 of Level II, stoutly believing in law and order and conforming to rules in order to avoid the disapproval of their neighbors.

Kohlberg also found evidence of gender differences in moral development, and here the interest for the psychology of women begins. Kohlberg found that most males eventually reach Stage 4, whereas most females only reach Stage 3. From this it might be concluded that females have a less well developed sense of morality. Freud's immature superego returns dressed up in a modern, scientific costume.

In evaluating Kohlberg's theory, there is evidence that children pass through the early stages he specified, in the order in which he specified them (e.g., Kuhn, 1976). On the other hand, certain value judgments are involved in setting up the hierarchy of stages in the way he did; in particular, it seems odd to have a Level III that few adults ever reach (someone once joked that the only

Preconventional morality: In Kohlberg's theory, the earliest stage of moral reasoning, in which children do the right thing simply to gain rewards or avoid punishments.

Conventional morality: In Kohlberg's theory, an intermediate level of moral reasoning, in which children and adults understand rules and obey them rigidly.

Postconventional morality: In Kohlberg's theory, the most mature level of moral reasoning, in which the person understands that rules are not absolute, but rather are part of a social contract; the person behaves from internalized ethical principles.

TABLE 2.1
Kohlberg's and Gilligan's Understanding of Moral Development

Kohlberg's Levels and Stages	Kohlberg's Definition	Gilligan's Levels
Level I. Preconventional morality		
Stage 1. Punishment orientation	Obey rules to avoid punishment	Concern for the self and survival
Stage 2. Naive reward orientation	Obey rules to get rewards, share in order to get returns	
Level II. Conventional morality		
Stage 3. Good-boy/ good-girl orientation	Conform to rules that are defined by others' approval/disapproval	Concern for being responsible, caring for others
Stage 4. Authority orientation	Rigid conformity to society's rules, law-and-order mentality, avoid censure for rule breaking	
Level III. Postconventional morality		
Stage 5. Social-contract orientation	More flexible understanding that we obey rules because they are necessary for social order, but the rules could be changed if there were better alternatives.	Concern for self and others as interdependent
Stage 6. Morality of individual principles and conscience	Behavior conforms to internal principles (justice, equality) to avoid self-condemnation, and sometimes may violate society's rules	

people who reached Level III were Kohlberg and his graduate students). One of the most influential critiques of Kohlberg's ideas is the feminist analysis by Gilligan (1982).

Gilligan: A Different Perspective on Moral Development Harvard psychologist Carol Gilligan provided a feminist critique of Kohlberg's work on moral de-

velopment in her book *In a Different Voice* (1982). She also provided a reformulation of moral development from a woman's point of view.

Several of Gilligan's criticisms follow from our earlier discussion of sex
bias in research. The main character of Kohlberg's dilemma is Heinz, a man.
Perhaps females have trouble identifying with him. Some of the other moral
dilemmas Kohlberg used are more gender-neutral, but one is about the captain of
a company of marines. Once again, women may find this a bit hard to relate to.
Gilligan (1982, p. 18) also pointed out that the people who formed the basis for
Kohlberg's theorizing were a group of 84 *males,* whom he followed for 20 years,
beginning in their childhood. When a theory is based on evidence from males, it
is not surprising that it does not apply well to females. Finally, Gilligan pointed
out a bias in Kohlberg's interpretation: The phenomenon that women reach only
Stage 3 is interpreted as a deficiency in female development, whereas it might
just as easily be interpreted as being a deficiency in Kohlberg's theory, which
may not adequately describe female development.

Gilligan did not stop with a critique of Kohlberg. She extended her analysis
to provide a feminist reformulation of moral development. Her reformulation is
based on the belief that women are reasoning differently about the moral dilemmas—that is, they are speaking in a different voice (hence the title of her
book)—and that their voices have not been listened to. To understand her ideas,
listen to the voices of 11-year-old Jake and 11-year-old Amy responding to the
Heinz dilemma. First Jake:

> For one thing, human life is worth more than money, and if the druggist only
> makes $1,000, he is still going to live, but if Heinz doesn't steal the drug, his
> wife is going to die. (*Why is life worth more than money?*) Because the druggist
> can get a thousand dollars later from rich people with cancer, but Heinz can't
> get his wife again. (Gilligan, 1982, p. 26)

Now Amy, asked if Heinz should steal the drug:

> Well, I don't think so. I think there might be other ways besides stealing it, like
> if he could borrow the money or make a loan or something, but he really
> shouldn't steal the drug—but his wife shouldn't die either. (*Why shouldn't he
> steal the drug?*) If he stole the drug, he might save his wife then, but if he did,
> he might have to go to jail, and then his wife might get sicker again, and he
> couldn't get more of the drug, and it might not be good. So, they should really
> just talk it out and find some other way to make the money. (Gilligan, 1982, p. 28)

Jake would be scored as showing a mixture of Stages 3 and 4, but also as reaching some elements of mature Level III morality (Gilligan, 1982, p. 27). Amy, on
the other hand, just doesn't fit very well into the scoring system. Jake, like
Kohlberg, sees the issue as one of rules and balancing the rights of individuals:
the right of the druggist to profit, and the right of Heinz's wife (who remains

nameless) to life. In contrast, Amy sees the issue as one of relationships: the problem that the druggist fails to live up to a relationship to the dying woman, the need to preserve the relationship between Heinz and his wife, and the need to avoid a bad relationship between Heinz and the druggist. Amy's solution similarly does not involve rules, but rather relationships—they should "talk it out" and mend the relationships.

Justice perspective:
According to Gilligan, an approach to moral reasoning that emphasizes fairness and the rights of the individual.

Gilligan contrasts these two approaches to moral reasoning in several ways. The **justice perspective** views people as differentiated and standing alone and focuses on the rights of the individual; the **care perspective** emphasizes relatedness between people and communication. According to Gilligan, males tend to stress justice; females tend to stress caring. Males focus on contracts between people; females focus on attachments between people. In essence, women tend to think differently about moral questions. Kohlberg devised his stages of moral reasoning with the male as norm; thus women's answers appear immature, when in fact they are simply based on different concerns. Interestingly, many of the great European philosophers—such as Locke and Kant—argue from a perspective based on the morality of justice.

Care perspective:
According to Gilligan, an approach to moral reasoning that emphasizes relationships between people and caring for others and the self.

What evidence is there for Gilligan's theorizing? Two studies, one with college students and one with adolescents, demonstrated that women's moral judgments, compared with men's, are more tied to feelings of empathy and compassion (Haan, 1975; Holstein, 1976). Gilligan herself also presented several studies in support of her views. Here I will consider one of these, the abortion decision study. She interviewed 29 women between the ages of 15 and 33, all of whom were in the first trimester of pregnancy and were considering abortion. They were interviewed a second time one year later. Notice how she shifted the moral dilemma from a male stranger named Heinz to an issue that is far more central to women. Just as Kohlberg saw three major levels of moral reasoning, so Gilligan found three levels among these women, but the focus for the levels was different (see the right-hand side of Table 2.1). In Level I, preconventional morality, the woman making the abortion decision is concerned only for herself and her survival. An example is Susan, an 18-year-old, who was asked what she thought when she found out that she was pregnant:

> I really didn't think anything except that I didn't want it. (*Why was that?*) I didn't want it, I wasn't ready for it, and next year will be my last year and I want to go to school. (Gilligan, 1982, p. 75)

Women who have reached Level II have shifted their focus to being responsible and to caring for others, specifically for a potential child. Women in Level II see their previous, less mature Level I responses as selfish. These themes are articulated by Josie, a 17-year-old, in discussing her reaction to being pregnant:

> I started feeling really good about being pregnant instead of feeling really bad, because I wasn't looking at the situation realistically. I was looking at it from my own sort of selfish needs, because I was lonely. Things weren't really going good for me, so I was looking at it that I could have a baby that I could take care of or something that was part of me, and that made me feel good. But I wasn't looking at the realistic side, at the responsibility I would have to take on. I came to this decision that I was going to have an abortion because I realized how much responsibility goes with having a child. Like you have to be there; you can't go out of the house all the time, which is one thing I like to do. And I decided that I have to take on responsibility for myself and I have to work out a lot of things. (Gilligan, 1982, p. 77)

Typical of Level II thinking, Josie sees Level I thinking as selfish, and shifts her concern to being responsible to the child. Notice that deciding to have an abortion or not to have an abortion is not what differentiates Level I from Level II. Either decision can be reached at either level. For example, in Level I the concern for self and survival can lead to having an abortion so that a baby does not interfere with one's life. However, the Level I concern for self and survival can also lead one not to have an abortion in order to have a baby for fun, giving and receiving love, and so on.

Finally, in Level III moral reasoning, the self and others are seen as interdependent, and there is a focus on balancing caring for others (the fetus, the father, parents) with caring for oneself. A woman must have reasonably high self-esteem to reach this level, for without it the "caring for self" aspect looks like a return to the selfishness of earlier levels, rather than a complex balancing of care extended to all, including herself. In this stage, caring is not the crude product of female socialization, but is rather a universal ethical principle that all should follow. A recapitulation of her earlier moral reasoning and her current balancing of caring is articulated by Sarah, who is faced with a second abortion:

> Well, the pros for having the baby are all the admiration that you would get from being a single woman, alone, martyr, struggling, having the adoring love of this beautiful Gerber baby. Just more of a home life than I have had in a long time, and that basically was it, which is pretty fantasyland. It is not very realistic. Cons against having the baby: it was going to hasten what is looking to be the inevitable end of the relationship with the man I am presently with. I was going to have to go on welfare. My parents were going to hate me for the rest of my life. I was going to lose a really good job that I have. I would lose a lot of independence. Solitude. And I would have to be put in a position of asking help from a lot of people a lot of the time. Con against having the abortion is having to face up to the guilt. And pros for having the abortion are I would be able to handle my deteriorating relation with [the father] with a lot more capability and a lot more responsibility for myself. I would not have to go through the realization that for the next twenty-five years of my life I would be punishing myself for being foolish enough to get pregnant again and forcing myself to bring up a

kid just because I did this. Having to face the guilt of a second abortion seemed like not exactly—well, exactly the lesser of two evils, but also the one that would pay off for me personally in the long run because, by looking at why I am pregnant again and subsequently have decided to have a second abortion, I have to face up to some things about myself. (Gilligan, 1982, p. 92)

Gilligan summarized the differences between men's and women's moral reasoning as follows:

> The moral imperative that emerges repeatedly in interviews with women is an injunction to care, a responsibility to discern and alleviate the "real and recognizable trouble" of this world. For men, the moral imperative appears rather as an injunction to respect the rights of others and thus to protect from interference the rights to life and self-fulfillment. . . . Development for both sexes would therefore seem to entail an integration of rights and responsibilities through the discovery of the complementarity of these disparate views. (Gilligan, 1982, p. 100)

How good is Gilligan's theory? First, it is an example of many of the qualities of the "new feminist scholarship." She detected the male centeredness of Kohlberg's analysis of moral reasoning. She then reconstructed the theory after listening to what females said and shaped a developmental model from it. My reservation about it comes from my own firm belief in gender similarities. Much of Gilligan's writing sounds as though men display one kind of moral thinking and women display a totally different kind. I am certain that there are some men who show "female" moral reasoning of the kind quoted earlier and some women who display "male" moral reasoning.

By now, several important studies have tested various aspects of Gilligan's theory. One was a major meta-analysis (for an explanation of meta-analysis, see Chapter 3) of studies that had examined gender differences in responses to Kohlberg's moral dilemmas; the conclusion from this review was that there were no gender differences (Walker, 1984; see also Mednick, 1989). That is, there is no evidence to support Gilligan's basic observation that Kohlberg's scales shortchange women and cause them to score as less morally mature. Females score at the same moral level, on average, as males.

In another study, college students read four moral dilemmas and then rated the importance of various considerations in deciding how the protagonist should respond in each (Friedman et al., 1987). Half the considerations rated by respondents reflected Kohlberg's stages (e.g., the relative weights of life and property), and the other half reflected Gilligan's stages (e.g., does Heinz have a responsibility to care for his wife?). There were no significant gender differences in either Kohlberg-type reasoning or Gilligan-type reasoning, again confirming the notion of gender similarities in moral reasoning.

In conclusion, Gilligan's main contribution was to articulate a different side of moral reasoning, one based on relationship and caring. Probably there are no gender differences in the use of either the justice or the caring perspective; both males and females use both (Friedman et al., 1987; Jadack et al., 1995).

Gender Schema Theory

This brainteaser has been popular for the past few years:

> A father and his son were involved in a car accident in which the father was killed and the son was seriously injured. The father was pronounced dead at the scene of the accident and his body was taken to a local mortuary. The son was taken by ambulance to a hospital and was immediately wheeled into an operating room. A surgeon was called. Upon seeing the patient, the attending surgeon exclaimed, "Oh my God, it's my son!"
>
> Can you explain this? (Keep in mind that the father who was killed in the accident is not a stepfather, nor is the attending physician the boy's stepfather.)

If you have not heard this before, give yourself some time to solve it before reading the next paragraph, which contains the solution.

The solution is that the surgeon is the boy's *mother.* But why is it so difficult for most people to think of this solution? It is exactly this sort of question that is addressed by psychologist Sandra Bem's gender schema theory (1981).

Schema: In cognitive psychology, a general knowledge framework that a person has about a particular topic; the schema then processes and organizes new information on that topic.

First, you need to understand what a schema is. Schema is a concept from cognitive psychology, the branch of psychology that investigates how we think, perceive, process, and remember information (for a good summary of schema theory, not applied to gender, see Alba and Hasher, 1983). A **schema** is a general knowledge framework that a person has about a particular topic. A schema organizes and guides perception. To gain a more specific understanding of what a schema is, read the following description carefully and then, without looking back at it, answer the questions that follow.

> You decide to go to your favorite restaurant for dinner. You enter the restaurant and are seated at a table with a white tablecloth. You study the menu. You tell the waiter that you want prime rib, medium rare, a baked potato with sour cream, and a salad with blue cheese dressing on it. You also order red wine. A few minutes later the waiter returns with your salad. Later he brings the rest of the meal, all of which you enjoy, except the prime rib is a bit overdone.

Now answer the following questions:

1. What kind of salad dressing did you order?

2. Was the tablecloth red-checked?

3. What did you order to drink?

4. Did the waiter give you a menu?

You probably found the questions easy to answer. The important point is, what was your answer for question 4? The correct answer is no, because there is no mention in the story of the waiter handing you a menu. Many people incorrectly answer yes to this question. The reason is that most of us have a restaurant schema in our stored knowledge. This schema contains certain characteristics that are common to most restaurants, as well as events that generally occur in most restaurants. A schema typically helps us process and remember information, and your restaurant schema may have helped you answer questions 1, 2, and 3. But schemas also act to *filter and interpret* information, and they can therefore cause errors in memory. A common part of a restaurant schema is that a waiter hands you a menu. Therefore, your restaurant schema probably filled in this piece of information that really was not described in the story and thereby caused you to make an error. An individual's perception and memory of information, then, is a result of the interaction of the incoming information with the individual's preexisting schema.

Gender schema: A person's general knowledge framework about gender; it processes and organizes information on the basis of gender-linked associations.

Psychologist Sandra Bem (1981) has applied schema theory to understanding the gender-typing process in her gender schema theory (see also Martin and Halverson, 1983). Her proposal is that each one of us has as part of our knowledge structure a **gender schema,** a set of gender-linked associations. Furthermore, the gender schema represents a basic predisposition to process information on the basis of gender. That is, it represents our tendency to see many things as gender-related and to want to dichotomize things on the basis of gender. The gender schema processes new, incoming information, filtering and interpreting it. Thus gender schema theory provides a ready answer for why the brainteaser at the beginning of this section is so difficult. Most of us have a gender schema that contains a link between man and sur-

FIGURE 2.5

Our gender schemas make us assume that the head of the household is male, and we are amused when it's not. *(Source: Reprinted with special permission of King Features Syndicate.)*

geon. Therefore, making an association from surgeon to woman or mother is difficult, if not impossible.

Bem says that the developmental process of gender typing or gender-role acquisition in children is a result of the child's gradual learning of the content of society's gender schema. The gender-linked associations that form the schema are many: girls wear dresses and boys don't; boys are strong and tough, girls are pretty (perhaps learned simply from the adjectives adults apply to children, rarely or never calling boys *pretty,* rarely or never calling girls *tough*); girls grow up to be mommies, boys don't.

There is a further process. The gender schema becomes closely linked to the self-concept. Thus five-year-old Maria knows she is a girl and also has a girl schema that she attaches to her own sense of girlhood. Maria's self-esteem then begins to be dependent on how well she measures up to her girl schema. At that point, she becomes internally motivated to conform to society's female gender role (a point much like Kohlberg's). Society does not have to force her into the role. She gladly does it herself and feels good about herself in the process. Finally, Bem postulates that different individuals have, to some extent, different gender schemas. The content of the schema varies from one person to the next, perhaps as a result of the kinds of gender information to which one is exposed in one's family throughout childhood. And the gender schema is more central to self-concept for some people, those who are highly gender typed (traditionally masculine males and feminine females).

Evidence for Gender Schema Theory   Let us look at three studies that illustrate how the theory can be tested, all of which support the theory.

In one study, Bem (1981) gave a list of 61 words, in random order, to respondents who were college students. Some of the words were proper names, some were animals, some verbs, and some articles of clothing. Half the names were masculine and half were feminine. One-third of the animal words were masculine (*gorilla*), one-third were feminine (*butterfly*), and one-third were neutral (*ant*). Similarly, one-third of the verbs and the articles of clothing were each masculine, feminine, and neutral. The participants' task was to recall as many of the 61 words as they could, in any order. It is known from many previous studies that in memory tasks such as these, people tend to cluster words into categories based on similar meaning; this is indicated by the order in which they recall the words. For example, if the person organized the words according to gender, the recall order might be *gorilla, bull, trousers;* but if the organization was according to animals, the recall order might be *gorilla, butterfly, ant.* If gender-typed people (masculine males and feminine females, as measured by the Bem Sex Role Inventory, a test to be discussed in Chapter 3) do possess a gender schema that they use to organize information, then they should cluster their recalled words into gender groupings. That is exactly what occurred. Gender-typed persons tended to cluster words according to gender, a result that supports gender schema theory.

In another experiment, five- and six-year-old children were shown pictures

FIGURE 2.6
Pictures used in the Martin and Halverson research on gender schemas and children's memory. (Left) A girl engaged in a stereotype-consistent activity. (Right) Girls engaged in a stereotype-inconsistent activity. In a test of recall a week later, children tended to distort the stereotype-inconsistent pictures to make them stereotype-consistent; for example, they remembered that they had seen boys boxing. *(Source: National Institute of Mental Health.)*

of males and females performing stereotype-consistent activities (such as a boy playing with a train) and stereotype-inconsistent activities (such as a girl sawing wood) (Martin and Halverson, 1983). One week later the children were tested for their recall of the pictures. The results indicated that the children distorted information by changing the gender of the people in the stereotype-inconsistent pictures, while not making such changes for the stereotype-consistent pictures. That is, children tended to remember the picture of the girl sawing wood as having been a picture of a boy sawing wood. That result is just what would be predicted by gender schema theory: Incoming information that is inconsistent with the gender schema is *filtered out* and *reinterpreted* to be consistent with the gender schema. This study also indicates that the gender schema is present even in five-year-olds. (For other evidence of gender schemas in children, see Levy, 1994.)

In a third study, Bem (1981) measured the reaction times of college students to gender-linked adjectives, such as *independent, feminine, competitive,* and *loves children.* The words were projected, one at a time, on a screen. The participant's task was to press one of two buttons, "me" or "not me," according to whether or not the adjective was characteristic of him or her. The reaction time is the amount of time from presentation of the word until the person presses either button. If there is a gender schema that processes incoming information, then information that is consistent with one's gender schema, particularly as it relates to the self, should be processed faster than information that is not consistent with the gender self-schema. As an example, if I asked you "Is a robin a bird?" you would probably respond quickly. If I asked you "Is a penguin a bird?" you would probably respond more slowly. Robins fit your bird schema, and so you can process that question quickly. Penguins do not fit your bird schema as well, and so that question is processed more slowly—essentially you have to think about it longer. The results were that gender-typed participants did indeed make schema-consistent judgments faster than they made schema-inconsistent judgments, a result that supports gender schema theory.

Criticisms of Gender Schema Theory   Psychologists Janet Spence (president of the American Psychological Association in 1983) and Robert Helmreich (1981) have provided a critique of Bem's gender schema theory. Although most of their points are meant for a professional audience and are too technical to be included here, one criticism is that Bem's measuring of gender typing includes only a narrow part of the masculinity and the femininity in people's personalities. Thus her measuring of individual differences in the gender schema may lose much of the complexity of people's masculinity and femininity. And Bem's focus on the gender typing of personality as measured on paper-and-pencil checklists says nothing about gender typing in actual behavior or about how actual behaviors are affected by the gender schema.

Feminist Theories

Many people view the feminist movement as a political group with a particular set of goals to work for, a lobbying group trying to serve its own ends, as the National Rifle Association does. What is less recognized is that feminism has an articulated theoretical basis. Thus it is appropriate to include the feminist perspective as one of the theoretical approaches in this chapter. This viewpoint spans many areas besides psychology, but it certainly fits well in any psychological approach to understanding women.

The feminist perspective was created by no single person. Instead, numerous writers have contributed their ideas. This is quite consistent with the desire of feminists to avoid power hierarchies and not to have a single person become the authority. But it also means that the feminist perspective as I have crystallized it here has been drawn from many sources. For that reason, I have titled this section "Feminist Theories," rather than "Feminist Theory." Some of the central concepts and issues of feminist theories follow.

Gender As Status and Power   Feminists view gender as similar to a *class* variable in our society. That is, males and females are unequal just as the lower class, the working class, the middle class, and the upper class are unequal. Men and women are of unequal *status,* women having the lower status.

After reviewing studies of people's interactions in small groups, two sociol-

FIGURE 2.7
A key point of the feminist perspective is that women have less power than men do in many areas: political, interpersonal, economic. (*Source: © 1983 King Features Syndicate, Inc.*)

ogists concluded that the best explanation for the results was the gender-as-a-status-variable hypothesis proposed by feminists (Meeker and Weitzel-O'Neill, 1977). When a small group of people are brought together to work on a task, sharp gender differences sometimes emerge: The men are highly task-oriented, making lots of comments to "get things done," whereas the women are more oriented toward the relationships among the group members. Yet other studies do not find this pattern of gender differences. The authors concluded that these contradictory results can best be explained by the hypothesis that men have higher status than women. Thus in small-group interactions men are expected to be more competent than women, and competitive and dominating behavior is therefore seen as legitimate for men but not for women. However, in certain special circumstances these effects can be reversed, and assertive, competitive behavior becomes legitimate for women; examples of such situations are (1) when a woman has been appointed to be the leader of the group by an authoritative outsider such as the experimenter, and (2) when the content of the task is seen as an area of competence for women rather than for men, such as evaluating the quality of daycare centers. Thus these authors concluded that the evidence—at least from studies of small-group interactions—supports the hypothesis that gender is a basic status variable.

From the observation of the lesser status of women comes another basic feminist argument, that sexism is pervasive. Women are discriminated against in diverse ways, from the failure of the passage of the Equal Rights Amendment (which means that it is still legal to discriminate on the basis of gender) to the male centeredness of psychological theories, from the different pay scales for women and men to the boss pinching his secretary. Thus sexism exists in many spheres: political, academic, economic, and interpersonal.

A closely related concept is the inequality of *power* between men and women, men having more power than women. One of the classic works of the feminist movement is Kate Millett's *Sexual Politics* (1969); she defined "politics" as the study of power, and thus in analyzing sexual politics she focused on power relationships between women and men. Once again, the areas of greater male power are diverse. Most political leaders are men, and thus men have the power to pass laws that affect women's lives. That is an obvious example of male power. But feminist analysis has extended the power concept to many other areas, for example, to seeing rape not as a sexual act but as an expression of men's power over women (e.g., Brownmiller, 1975). The concept of power is key to feminist analysis (Yoder and Kahn, 1992).

One saying of the feminist movement has been "the personal is political" (MacKinnon, 1982). Once again, "political" refers to expressions of power. Feminists have reconceptualized many acts that were traditionally viewed as personal, as simple interactions between individuals, into acts that are seen as political, or expressions of power. As examples, Mr. Executive pats the fanny of Miss Secretary, or John rapes Mary. Traditionally, these have been thought of as personal, individual acts. They were understood to be the product of an obnoxious individual such as Mr. Executive, or of a rare, disturbed individual such as John, or of the inappropriately seductive behavior of Miss Secretary or Mary. The feminist recasts these, not as personal acts, but as political expressions of men's power over women. The greater status of men gives them a sense of entitlement to engage in such acts. At the same time, the acts exert power and control by men over women.

Sexuality   One of the central issues for feminists is sexuality (MacKinnon, 1982). There have been many specific feminist issues: rape, incest, abortion, birth control, sexual harassment on the job, pornography. Although these issues are diverse, note that all have the common link of sexuality. Female sexuality has been repressed and depressed, but rarely expressed. The problem, according to feminist analysis, is that women's sexuality is controlled by men. The issue, again, is power: Men have the power to control and exploit women's sexuality, for example, the power to deny abortion. As law professor Catharine MacKinnon put it, "Sexuality is to feminism what work is to marxism: that which is most one's own, yet most taken away" (1982, p. 1).

Two other central issues in the feminist perspective are *the family* and *work*. Space does not permit a discussion of those issues here, but Chapter 7 is devoted to women and work, and Chapter 5 discusses women in relation to the family (for extended discussions, see Deckard, 1983; Jaggar and Struhl, 1978).

Gender Roles and Socialization   Feminists have highlighted the importance of gender roles and socialization in our culture. American society has well-defined roles for males and for females. From their earliest years, children are socialized to conform to these roles. In this regard, the feminist perspective is in close agreement with social learning theory. The feminist sees these roles as constricting to individuals. Essentially, gender roles tell children that there are certain things they may not do, whether telling a girl that she cannot be a physicist or a boy that he cannot be a nurse. Because gender roles shut off individual potentials and aspirations, feminists believe that we would be better off without such roles, or at least that they need to be radically revised.

Cross-cultural evidence indicates that American society is not unique in its emphasis on gender roles and socialization. Anthropologists such as Margaret Mead (1935, 1949) have discovered that other cultures have gender roles considerably different from our own; for example, in some other cultures men are reputed to be the gossips, and women are thought to be the appropriate ones to carry heavy loads. Despite all the cross-cultural diversity in gender roles, one universal principle seems to hold: Every known society recognizes and elaborates gender differences (Rosaldo, 1974), a point that is consistent with feminists' emphasis on the power and pervasiveness of gender roles.

Beyond this recognition of the universality of gender roles, there is disagreement among feminist anthropologists. Some argue that the male role, whatever it is, is always valued more (Mead, 1935; Rosaldo, 1974). For example, in some parts of New Guinea the women grow sweet potatoes and the men grow yams; but yams are the prestige food, the food used in important ceremonies. Even in this case where the labor of females and males is virtually identical, what the male does is valued more. This finding is consistent with the feminist concept of gender as a class or status variable. On the other hand, other anthropologists argue that there are exceptions to the rule that the male role is always valued more. They point to societies in which there is gender equality or in which the female role is valued more (Sanday, 1988). For example, the Minangkabau of West Sumatra are proud of being described as a matriarchate (a society in which many important activities are matricentered, or female centered, and women are more important than men) (Sanday, 1988). Members of that society say that men are dominant in matters related to traditions and customs, but that women are dominant in matters related to property. Such discussions often end in laughter as everyone agrees that the sexes are equal. I cannot resolve this debate here, except to note that patriarchal societies are by far in the majority, and egalitarian or matriarchal societies, if they exist, constitute a small minority.

External Versus Internal Attributions of Problems Kim was raped; Suzanne is depressed. Traditional psychological analyses focus on the internal nature and causes of these women's problems. Kim might be viewed as having brought on the rape by her seductive behavior. Suzanne might be viewed as having personal problems of adjustment. Feminists are critical of analyses that assume women's problems are caused by internal or personal factors. Feminists instead view the *sources of women's problems as being external.* Kim's problem is recast as having its roots in a society that condones, indeed encourages, male aggression. Suzanne's problem is recast as having its roots in a society that attaches little value and recognition to being a housewife and mother. This theme of external factors will recur in Chapter 14 in the discussion of the theoretical basis of feminist therapy.

Consciousness Raising In the late 1960s and early 1970s, as the modern feminist movement gained momentum, consciousness-raising (C-R) groups were popular. Ideally, such groups begin with a small group of women sharing their personal feelings and experiences; they then move to a feminist theoretical analysis of these feelings and experiences, and from this should flow action, whether it involves an individual woman restructuring her relationship with her partner, or a group of women lobbying for a new law to be passed. Although C-R groups are not as common as they were a decade or two ago, the process of consciousness raising remains central to feminism.

There is a temptation to see C-R groups as merely a fun sort of activity that some feminists engage in. However, consciousness raising occupies a far more fundamental and serious position within feminism. As one theorist put it,

> Consciousness raising is the major technique of analysis, structure of organization, method of practice, and theory of social change of the women's movement. (MacKinnon, 1982, p. 5)

Thus consciousness raising is central to the feminist perspective for a number of reasons. First, it is a means for women to get in touch with their experiences and understand themselves. Previously, the only tools women had for understanding themselves were various psychological theories, such as psychoanalytic theory, that were male centered and defined women from a male point of view. Through the sharing of personal feelings and experiences, women in C-R groups can come to know and understand women from a female point of view. But consciousness raising does not stop with sharing. It proceeds to theoretical analysis. Women come to see that what they had perceived as individual problems are actually common and are rooted in external causes. For example, Linda has been beaten by her husband. In the C-R group, she discovers that three of the other women have also been beaten by husbands or lovers. In so doing, she comes to recognize two central points: that the personal is political (the individual beating by her husband is part of a larger pattern of power in society), and that the sources of her problems are external, rooted in the structure of society, rather than a result of her own internal deficiencies. Finally, the C-R group becomes the power base for political action. Linda and the other three women might decide to found a shelter for battered women.

Varieties of Feminism   One of the difficulties in writing this section on the feminist perspective is that there are actually several different kinds of feminism, differing in everything from their theoretical analysis to their model for social change to their vision of the ideal society. One method of categorization is to conceptualize three major types of feminism: (1) liberal or moderate feminism, (2) Marxist or socialist feminism, and (3) radical feminism (e.g., Deckard, 1983; Jaggar and Struhl, 1978; Jaggar, 1977).

Liberal feminism holds that women should have opportunities and rights equal to those of men. Basically, liberal feminists believe in working within the system for reform. The liberal feminist position is exemplified by organizations such as NOW (National Organization for Women), which is the major group that lobbied for passage of the Equal Rights Amendment. The notion here is that American society is founded on basically good ideals, such as justice and freedom for all, but the justice and freedom need to be extended to women. Some would argue that liberal feminism can be credited with many of the educational and legal reforms that have improved women's lives in the United States over the last several decades (Tong, 1989).

Marxist or *socialist feminism* argues that the liberal feminist analysis of the problem is superficial and does not get to the deeper roots of the problem. Marxist feminism views the oppression of women as just one instance of oppression based on class, oppression that is rooted in capitalism. Marxist feminists, for example, point out the extent to which the capitalist system benefits from oppressing women in ways such as wage discrimination. What would happen to the average American corporation if it had to start paying all of its secretaries as much as plumbers earn (both jobs require a high school education and a certain amount of manual dexterity and specific skills)? The answer is that most corporations would find their economic structure ruined. Women's situation will not improve, according to this point of view, without a drastic reform of American society, including a complete overhaul of the capitalist economic system and the concept of private property.

Radical feminists such as Shulamith Firestone (1970) find the Marxist feminist analysis too superficial. Radical feminists argue that the oppression of women can occur in any economic system. Ironically, radical feminists return the focus to biology. They argue that the oppression of women is rooted in biology, specifically in the biological differences between genders, and particularly in the fact that only women can bear children. These feminists believe that the latter fact explains the prehistoric origins of the lower status of women: Women were physically incapacitated by pregnancy and the care of infants, women became dependent on men, and men thus gained power over women. Radical feminists look hopefully to technology—such as test-tube babies, artificial insemination of surrogate mothers, perhaps even cloning—to free women from the biological functions that oppress them. For radical feminists, women's situation will not improve substantially until all gender distinctions are eliminated, both socially and biologically. Among radical feminists, however, a different subgroup has formed, called *maternists.* They believe that reproductive technologies are not the answer and may even make matters worse because men control the technology (see Tong, 1989, for more detail on maternists).

The point here is that not all feminists and not all feminist viewpoints are alike. There is a wide spectrum of belief. Probably most of the academic feminist psychologists who have contributed to the psychology of women would be classified as liberal feminists, working for reform within institutions. But Marxist feminists or radical feminists might also be found within the field of psychology, and certainly they are common in some other academic disciplines, such as sociology and philosophy.

Gender, Race/Ethnicity, and Class Feminist theories emphasize the critical importance of gender. But feminist theorists argue that gender cannot be understood as a social variable in isolation; it can be understood only in the context of

FIGURE 2.8
A key point of feminist theory is that not
only gender, but also race and class,
shape one's life experiences profoundly.

race and social class as well (e.g., Dugger, 1988). That is, feminist theories place
emphasis on the simultaneous importance of gender, race, and social class, as
these shape everything from social institutions to individual behavior.

We will take up these concepts in more detail in Chapter 8, "Women of
Color." As a brief example here, clearly women's attitudes about gender roles
and feminist issues vary as a function of their race or ethnicity (Dugger, 1988).
Feminists of any race or ethnicity, for example, have readily recognized that
white men oppress white women. Black feminists, on the other hand, have emphasized that the oppression of Black women by Black men can be understood
only in the context of the fact that Black men themselves are oppressed by
whites. Gender and race interact in powerful ways when we discuss feminist issues. As one scholar put it,

> A necessary next step is the development of theoretical and conceptual frame-
> works for analyzing the interaction of race and gender stratification. Separate

models exist for analyzing race, ethnic or gender stratification. Although the "double" (race, gender) and "triple" (race, gender, class) oppression of racial ethnic women are widely acknowledged, no satisfactory theory has been developed to analyze what happens when these systems of oppression intersect. . . . Race, gender and class interact in such a way that the histories of white and racial ethnic women are intertwined. . . . The situation of white women has depended on the situation of women of color. White women have gained advantages from the exploitation of racial ethnic women. (Glenn, 1985, pp. 87, 105)

The Social Construction of Gender   Feminist theorists view gender not as a biologically created reality, but as a socially constructed phenomenon (Beall, 1993; Hare-Mustin and Marecek, 1988). The basic position of *constructivism* is that people—including scientists—do not discover reality; rather, they construct or invent it (Watzlawick, 1984). According to **social constructionism,** we do not experience reality directly. Instead, we actively construct meanings for events in the environment based on our own prior experiences and predispositions. This theoretical view, then, shares much in common with schema theory, discussed earlier in this chapter.

Social constructionism: A theoretical viewpoint that humans do not discover reality directly; rather, they construct meanings for events in the environment based on their own prior experiences and beliefs.

The extent to which we socially construct gender becomes clearer if we view the issues through the lenses of other cultures. In white cultures it is perfectly obvious—a clear reality—that there are two genders, males and females. However, among some American Indians, such as the Sioux, Cheyenne, and Zuni, there is a third category, the **Two-Spirit** (also called *berdache*), people who dress as and completely take on the role of the other gender. Some of these tribes consider the berdache to be a third gender, and it is perfectly clear in their culture that there are three genders (Beall, 1993; Kessler and McKenna, 1985). The Navajo in the United States and the Hijara of India believe that there are males, females, and intersexed individuals who are both male and female (Martin and Voorhies, 1975). Again, the belief is that there are three genders. Therefore, what seems like an obvious reality to whites, that there are only two genders, turns out to be a social construction, which becomes clear when we see that other cultures have constructed the categories differently.

Two-Spirit: Among Native Americans, a third gender category.

Processes closely related to gender are also socially constructed. For example, whites are quite sure of the reality that women typically feel tired after giving birth, because they have gone through a physically exhausting process. Other societies, though, have the **couvade,** which is practiced in Asia, Africa, South America, and some parts of North America (Hall and Dawson, 1989). The couvade consists of elaborate rituals that are based on the assumption that the father, not the mother, is the main contributor of effort in childbirth. After the mother gives birth, the baby is given to the

Couvade: A custom in which the man is assumed to be the major contributor to childbirth, and therefore suffers the symptoms such as fatigue.

father, and he rests for several days to overcome his fatigue, whereas the mother returns to work immediately because she is believed not to need rest. The contribution of the father to childbirth, and his fatigue following it, are clear reality to people in these cultures. Again, our Euro-American notions of women's contributions to childbirth are challenged, and we see the extent to which such events are socially constructed.

Social constructionism, then, argues that these processes occur in at least three areas: (1) the individual engages in social constructions, for example, reacting to another person differently depending on whether that person is male or female; (2) the society or culture provides a set of social constructions of gender, for example, whether there are two genders or more; and (3) scientists socially construct gender by the way they construct their research.

Among other things, this view that notions of gender are socially constructed challenges the belief that social sciences such as psychology are fundamentally objective (Hare-Mustin and Marecek, 1988), a point that was discussed in Chapter 1. Scientific knowledge, like all other knowledge, is shaped by the values and presuppositions of the perceiver, in this case the scientist.

Feminist psychologists have noted that gender is not only a person variable (as traditional psychology has maintained) but also a stimulus variable (e.g., Grady, 1979). By saying that gender is a person variable, I mean that gender is a characteristic of the individual; this point of view leads to the study of gender differences, a pursuit that has occupied some traditional psychologists and some feminist psychologists (see Chapter 3). By saying that gender is also a stimulus variable, I mean that a person's gender has a profound impact on the way others react to that person. Our understanding of an individual—that is, our social construction of that individual—is in part determined by our knowledge of that individual's gender. This point of view leads to an area of research in which participants are led to believe that a particular piece of work was done by a male or a female, or that a particular infant is a male or female; their responses to the work or the infant can then be studied as a function of the gender they believe it to be (see Chapters 5 and 7 for examples). Therefore, gender is both a personal characteristic and a stimulus variable.

Attitudes Toward Feminism   What do most women think about the feminist movement? TIME/CNN commissioned a well-sampled poll of adult women in the United States; 1,000 women were surveyed by telephone in October 1989 (*Time,* December 4, 1989).

Among these women, who presumably are a representative cross section of women in the United States, 33 percent said that they considered themselves to be feminists; 58 percent said they did not, and the remaining were unsure. We can conclude that fully one-third of U.S. women are willing to call themselves feminists.

Support for feminist issues is even more widespread. When asked, "Which issues are very important to women?", 94 percent agreed that equal pay for equal work was important, 90 percent agreed for day care, 88 percent agreed on the issue of rape, 84 percent agreed for maternity leave at work, 82 percent agreed on the issue of job discrimination, and 74 percent agreed for abortion. We can conclude that there is widespread support for feminist issues. Interestingly, four of the top five issues are work/family issues (for more details, see Chapter 7, "Women and Work").

Attitudes toward the women's movement were generally positive. For example, 94 percent agreed that the women's movement has helped women become more independent and 82 percent agreed that the movement is still improving the lives of women.

The feminist movement is not the same as it was in 1970, and the issues have shifted to some extent. But there is no evidence in these statistics that the feminist movement or feminist issues are dead!

Summary   Feminist theories generally highlight a number of points: (a) Gender is a status and power variable, with men having power over women; (b) gender roles and gender-role socialization are powerful forces in any culture; (c) many of women's problems are better conceptualized as being caused by external forces than internal ones; (d) consciousness raising is an essential process for women to get in touch with themselves; (e) gender, race, and class interact in influencing the behavior of individuals as well as social institutions; and (f) knowledge, in particular our understanding of gender, is socially constructed.

Evaluation of Feminist Theories   One criticism of the feminist perspective comes from the New Right and other conservative groups (see, for example, Eisenstein, 1982). They believe that women's roles and status are rooted in biology, perhaps ordained by God, and certainly "natural." They therefore find the feminist viewpoint just plain wrong. These arguments involve basic questions of value and cannot be addressed at a scientific level.

Feminist theories span many disciplines and were not specifically proposed as scientific theories. That means that some of their propositions are difficult to evaluate scientifically. The notion of men as a class having power over women will recur in several studies mentioned later in this book; an example is the sexual harassment of women (see Chapter 13). Also, the data on issues of sexuality for women are the focus in several later chapters (9, 10, 11, and 12). Feminists' concepts about gender roles and socialization are supported by anthropologists' evidence, as discussed earlier. I don't mean to evade the question, but it seems to me that the issues raised by feminist theory are so broad that it is best to wait until you have read the rest of this book before attempting an evaluation.

In Conclusion

In this chapter I have presented six major theoretical perspectives: psychoanalytic theory, sociobiology, social learning theory, cognitive-developmental theory, gender schema theory, and feminist theories. They operate from vastly different underlying assumptions and provide considerably different views of women. Psychoanalytic theory and sociobiology both see the nature of women and gender differences as rooted in biology: evolution, genes, and anatomy. Social learning theory falls at the other end of the nature-nurture continuum, seeing gender differences and gender roles as products of the social environment. Feminist theories, too, emphasize society as the creator of gender roles. Cognitive-developmental theory is an interactionist theory, emphasizing the interaction between the state of the organism (stage of cognitive development) and the information available from the culture. Gender schema theory also emphasizes the cognitive aspects of gender typing and the interaction between the knowledge structures in the individual and the incoming information from the environment.

With regard to scientific evidence for the various theories, certainly there are far more studies supporting social learning theory and cognitive-developmental theory than there are supporting psychoanalytic theory. The evidence concerning the tenets of sociobiology is quite mixed. Gender schema theory has some supporting evidence, but is too new to have been tested enough. The same is true of the feminist perspective.

Because our basic purpose is to understand women and gender-role development, what insights do these theories give us? No one theory by itself is adequate for understanding women—there is no "right" theory. Yet no theory is completely wrong. Each contributes something to our understanding. Freudian theory was important historically in emphasizing the notion of psychosexual development, highlighting the notion that an individual's gender identity and behavior have their roots in previous experiences. To understand an individual's gender identity as an adult, or at any age, for that matter, one must look at the person's life history. A second important contribution from psychoanalytic theory is the concept of *identification*. Though one might dispute the factors Freud postulated as creating identification, the fact remains that children usually do identify strongly with the same-gender parent, and this identification is an important force in gender-role development.

Social learning theory is important in its emphasis on the social and cultural components of gender-role development—the importance of society in shaping gender-typed behaviors. It points out, quite correctly, that boys and girls are treated differently. Social learning investigators have contributed some very impressive laboratory demonstrations of the power of reinforcements in shaping children's behavior, in particular gender-typed behaviors. Social learning theory also highlights the importance of imitation in the acquisition of gender role. Modern mothers who are concerned about freeing their children from gender-role restrictions might do well to keep these forces in mind. It is axiomatic that children do as you do (they imitate). If a mother wants to avoid restrictive gender-role stereotypes for her daughter, it may help to encourage her to be a doctor or a lawyer; but in the end, the mother's own behavior may have a much greater impact than her verbal encouragements. I found myself assembling a child's rocker one Christmas Eve for these very reasons. My daughter Margaret, age four at the time, was watching, and the rocker needed to be put together in order to be her little brother Luke's present the next morning. I started to call my husband to do "his" job. But then I realized the consequences of such an action. I stiffened my upper lip, got the screwdriver, and started following the instructions. A half-hour later, the rocker was in one beautiful piece, I felt triumphant,

EXPERIENCE THE RESEARCH

GENDER SCHEMA THEORY

Ask six friends to participate, individually, in a memory study that you are conducting. Collect the data in a quiet place, free from distractions. Before giving the memory task, write on the back of the paper whether this friend is male or female, and whether, knowing this person, you would categorize the person as feminine, masculine, or androgynous. Then give the following set of instructions to the person:

> I am going to read to you a list of 12 words. As soon as I finish, I would like you to recall the words for me, in any order. I want to see how many words you remember.

Then read them the following words, in exactly this order:

gorilla	(M)	stepping	(N)
Daniel	(M)	butterfly	(F)
blushing	(F)	trousers	(M)
hurling	(M)	bikini	(F)
ant	(N)	bull	(M)
Susie	(F)	dress	(F)

Read the words slowly and clearly, with about 1 second between each. Write the words down as your friend recalls them, in exactly the order they are recalled. If the person responds quickly, you may need to abbreviate the words.

Does the pattern of results for your friends look like those that Sandra Bem obtained for her research on gender schemas? That is, did people cluster the words into groups on the basis of gender associations ("butterfly" and "dress" close together, "trousers" and "bull" close together), or on the basis of other categories ("trousers" and "dress" together, "butterfly" and "bull" together)? Did gender-typed people (masculine or feminine) seem to do more clustering on the basis of gender than androgynous people?

and Margaret was impressed. I don't know what the long-term consequences for her may be, but I do know that I don't want her to imitate helplessness.

The feminist perspective shares with social learning theory an emphasis on external, social, environmental shaping of gender roles. Ironically, it shares with psychoanalytic theory an emphasis on sexuality as a critical issue in the lives of humans. Feminism adds the concepts of power, status, race, and class in male-female relations. It also emphasizes the importance of the social construction of gender.

Finally, cognitive-developmental theory emphasizes that gender-role learning is a part of the rational learning processes of childhood (as contrasted with the libidinal motivations postulated by psychoanalytic theory). Gender schema theory shares the emphasis on cognition, or the intellectual processes underlying gender typing. It points out the extent to which we process information in terms of gender and distort information that is not consistent with our gender-typed expectations. Further, cognitive-developmental theory emphasizes that gender-role learning results not solely from externally imposed forces of society, but at least in part from intrinsic motivation. Children actively seek to acquire gender roles, sometimes to the dismay of parents who want their children to be untouched by gender-role stereotypes. Gender roles seem to be helpful to children in structuring and understanding the reality of the world about them.

Suggestions for Further Reading

Bem, Sandra L. (1983). Gender schema theory and its implications for child development: Raising gender-aschematic children in a gender-schematic society. *Signs, 8,* 598–616. In this provocative article, Bem discusses the implications of her gender schema theory for parents who wish to do feminist childrearing.

Bem, Sandra L. (1993). *The lenses of gender.* New Haven, CT: Yale University Press. This book presents Bem's latest theorizing, in which she argues that three lenses—androcentrism, gender polarization, and biological essentialism—shape how people perceive social reality.

Gilligan, Carol. (1982). *In a different voice.* Cambridge, MA: Harvard University Press. Gilligan's reconstruction of moral development from a female point of view is insightful.

Hare-Mustin, Rachel T., & Marecek, Jeanne. (1988). The meaning of difference: Gender theory, postmodernism, and psychology. *American Psychologist, 43,* 455–464. This article presents some recent developments in feminist theory and the psychology of gender.

Lorber, Judith, & Farrell, Susan A. (Eds.) (1991). *The social construction of gender.* Newbury Park, CA: Sage. This collection of articles, mostly by sociologists, provides many examples of research conducted from a social constructionist perspective.

Gender Stereotypes and Gender Differences

> *Man should be trained for war and woman for the recreation of the warrior.*
>
> NIETZSCHE

All of you have probably heard dialogues such as the following:

MCP*: "Of course she did that, because she's so emotional. Women are just more emotional than men."

AF[†]: "Women *are not* more emotional than men. How can you say that?"

MCP: "Yes they are."

AF: "No they're not."

et cetera, et cetera.

Debates such as these are often unproductive because they essentially end up setting one person's opinion against another's. The more productive approach is to realize that MCP's statement, "Women are just more emotional than men," is scientifically testable. That is, one can collect actual data on men and women to see if it is true. In this chapter we shall consider research that has done just that—looked at gender differences in various personality characteristics and behaviors—to see how different the personalities of women and men are. Research on gender differences in abilities will be discussed in Chapter 6.

Stereotypes, Real Differences, and the Nature-Nurture Issue

Before we look at the various personality characteristics and behaviors that have been investigated, it is important to make a distinction among the following: gender-role stereotypes; psychological gender differences that have been empirically determined to exist ("real" differences); and the causes of gender differences, whether biological or environmental.

Gender-role stereotypes are simply a set of shared cultural beliefs about males' and females' behavior, personality traits, and other attributes. Research shows that even in modern American society, and even among college students, there is a belief that males and females do differ psychologically in many ways (Rosenkrantz et al., 1968; Ruble, 1983). Research also shows that these stereotypes have not changed much at all since 1972 (Bergen and Williams, 1991). A list of these stereotyped traits is given in Table 3.1.

Gender-role stereotypes: A set of shared cultural beliefs about males' and females' behavior, personality traits, and other attributes.

---

*MCP = male chauvinist pig

[†]AF = ardent feminist

TABLE 3.1
Stereotyped Personality Characteristics

Americans generally believe that the following are characteristics of men and women.

Masculine Characteristics Considered Socially Desirable	Feminine Characteristics Considered Socially Desirable
Very aggressive	Very tactful
Very independent	Very gentle
Not at all emotional	Very aware of feelings of others
Not at all easily influenced	Very religious
Very dominant	Very neat in habits
Likes math and science very much	Very strong need for security
Not at all excitable in a minor crisis	Enjoys art and literature very much
Very active	Easily expresses tender feelings
Very competitive	
Very skilled in business	
Knows the ways of the world	
Very adventurous	
Can make decisions easily	
Almost always acts as a leader	
Very self-confident	
Not at all uncomfortable about being aggressive	
Very ambitious	

SOURCE: Ruble (1983).

One of the essential points of feminist theory (see Chapter 2) is that gender and ethnicity interact. For example, stereotypes about women and men may be different for different ethnic groups. In one recent study, data were collected about this very issue (Niemann et al., 1994). College students at the University of Houston—51 percent of whom were Euro-American and the rest of whom were, in order of frequency, Hispanic, African American, Asian American, and Native American—were asked to list ten adjectives that came to mind when they thought of members of the following groups: Anglo-American males, Anglo-American females, African American males, African American females, Asian American males, Asian American females, Mexican American males, and Mexican American females. The most frequently listed adjectives are shown in Table 3.2.

TABLE 3.2

Gender and Ethnicity: Stereotypes of Males and Females from Different Ethnic Groups

Males	Females
Anglo-American	**Anglo-American**
Intelligent	Attractive
Egotistical	Intelligent
Upper class	Egotistical
Pleasant/friendly	Pleasant/friendly
Racist	Blond/light hair
Achievement oriented	Sociable
African American	**African American**
Athletic	Speak loudly
Antagonistic	Dark skin
Dark skin	Antagonistic
Muscular appearance	Athletic
Criminal activities	Pleasant/friendly
Speak loudly	Unmannerly
	Sociable
Asian American	**Asian American**
Intelligent	Intelligent
Short	Speak softly
Achievement oriented	Pleasant/friendly
Speak softly	Short
Hard workers	
Mexican American	**Mexican American**
Lower class	Black/brown/dark hair
Hard workers	Attractive
Antagonistic	Pleasant/friendly
Dark skin	Dark skin
Non-college education	Lower class
Pleasant/friendly	Overweight
Black/brown/dark hair	Baby makers
Ambitionless	Family oriented

SOURCE: Niemann et al. *Personality and Social Psychology Bulletin*, 1994, *20.*
Copyright © 1994, reprinted by permission of Sage Publications, Inc.

Two important patterns can be seen in Table 3.2: (1) Within an ethnic group, males and females have some stereotyped traits in common, but also some that differ. For example, both Mexican American males and Mexican American females are stereotyped as pleasant and friendly; however, Mexican American females are stereotyped as overweight but Mexican American males are not. (2) Within a gender, some stereotyped traits are common across ethnic groups, but others differ. For example, females from all ethnic groups are stereotyped as pleasant and friendly; however, Anglo-American and Asian American females are stereotyped as intelligent, whereas African American and Mexican American females are not.

When data are collected on the actual behavior and personality of females and males, the stereotypes turn out to be true in some cases ("real" differences), but not in others. For example, there is a stereotype that males are more aggressive than females; this turns out to be a real difference, as we will see later in this chapter. On the other hand, there is a stereotype that women are less intelligent than men, although actual research shows this not to be true; there are no gender differences in IQ. In this case, the stereotype is false. A *real difference,* then, is a gender difference that has been found to exist based on data collected on the personality or behavior of males and females.

Finally, if a gender difference (a real difference) is found, it requires one more step of analysis—and a very difficult one—to determine *whether the difference is biologically or environmentally caused.* For example, because there is a well-documented gender difference in aggression, we cannot automatically infer that this gender difference is biologically caused (e.g., by sex hormones), nor can we automatically decide that it is produced by environmental factors (e.g., socialization). Gender differences may be caused by environmental factors, biological factors, or an interaction between the two. Sophisticated research is necessary to uncover the complex interplay of biological and environmental forces at work.

Research by social psychologist Kay Deaux indicates that adults of the 1980s and 1990s view the male stereotype and the female stereotype as two overlapping categories rather than as two separate and distinct categories. For example, people no longer think that men are strong and women are weak. Rather, they believe that men are likelier to be stronger than women. To get at this idea, Deaux has research participants estimate probabilities that a fictitious character will have a certain characteristic. For example, if participants are given only the gender cue (the person is a man, or the person is a woman), they estimate the probability that a man is strong as .66 and that a woman is strong as .44 (Deaux and Lewis, 1983).

Deaux's research also indicates that as we learn more information about a person, gender per se has less influence on our impressions of that person (Deaux and Lewis, 1984). We are not totally ruled by gender stereotypes. They are most important in the very first impression we form of a person. Stereotypes are also influential when we are thinking about strangers or some category of people. But as we learn more about an individual, that is, about his or her actual behavior and personality, this information becomes far more important in our opinion of that person.

FOCUS 3.1
STEREOTYPES AND POWER

Social psychologist Susan Fiske (1993) has proposed an insightful analysis of the ways in which power and stereotypes influence each other. Two processes are involved. First, stereotyping exerts control or power over people, thus justifying and maintaining the status quo. Second, powerful people stereotype the less powerful. Given that gender is an important status or power variable, you can read "men" for "powerful people" and "women" for "less powerful people." The theory, of course, extends to other categories, such as ethnic groups.

First, stereotyping exerts control over people. Some stereotypes are descriptive; that is, they describe how most people in the group supposedly behave. Stereotypes claim that women are emotional, that African Americans are athletic, and that Jews are academically talented. These stereotypes then exert pressure on people in the group to conform to them.

Other stereotypes are prescriptive; that is, they tell how people of a certain group *should* behave. For example, women should be nice, Asian Americans should be good at math, adolescent boys should be athletic. If one fails to meet the demands of the stereotype, penalties can be severe (Eagly, Makhijani, and Klonsky, 1992). Again, stereotypes exert control over people.

Let us now turn to the second process: The powerful group stereotypes the less powerful group. Generally, less powerful people pay more attention to powerful people than the reverse; less powerful people therefore have more information about the powerful and tend to stereotype them less. Less powerful people need to pay attention because powerful people control important aspects of their lives and bear close watching. Servants know far more about their employers than the reverse, for example. In contrast, powerful people pay less attention to the less powerful, for three reasons: (1) the less powerful do not control outcomes of the powerful very much, so the powerful do not need to pay attention; (2) the powerful tend to be overloaded with information, and therefore have less attention to devote to the less powerful; and (3) powerful people who have a high need for dominance (not every powerful person does) may not want to pay attention to the less powerful. Because the powerful pay less attention, they have little information about the less powerful, and therefore the powerful rely on stereotypes of the less powerful.

FIGURE 3.1

According to Fiske's analysis of power and stereotypes, powerful people pay little attention to less powerful people, whereas the less powerful pay great attention to the powerful. Here the men focus on each other, ignoring the woman, while she pays close attention to them.

Fiske (1993) has conducted many clever experiments to test various aspects of her theory. In one, undergraduates were given the power to evaluate the summer job applications of high school students. Some undergraduates were given more power in the final decision, and others were given less power. The students who were given more power actually paid less attention to the applicants, consistent with Fiske's theory.

Fiske's theory and research were influential in an important Supreme Court case, *Price Waterhouse* v. *Hopkins.* Ann Hopkins was denied a partnership in the prestigious accounting firm of Price Waterhouse. Compared with her male colleagues who were being considered for partnership, she worked more billable hours, was well liked by clients, and brought in millions of dollars in accounts. She was denied partnership not because her performance was inadequate (it was in fact superb), but rather because she was not considered feminine in the way she dressed, walked, and talked. Stereotype violation, in short, was seen as legitimate grounds for the denial of a promotion.

Based on Fiske's analysis, we can see how the power of

stereotypes operated at several levels in this case. Men were in power at Price Waterhouse, and women were outnumbered. The powerful men were therefore likely to hold stereotyped expectations about the women. Hopkins, by being a successful woman in a male-dominated profession, management, was a stereotype violator and received punishment for it. The senior partners were probably overloaded with work, evaluating 88 partner candidates that year on top of an otherwise grueling workload, contributing to their lack of attention to Hopkins's qualifications.

The Supreme Court and other courts ruled in favor of Hopkins, and the brief filed by the American Psychological Association, reporting Susan Fiske's research, was highly influential in the decisions. As of this writing Ann Hopkins is a partner at Price Waterhouse.

SOURCE: Fiske (1993).

Gender Stereotypes, Ethnicity, and Social Class

Gender stereotypes vary not only cross-culturally, but also across various ethnic groups and social classes in the United States. We will return to this point in Chapter 8, "Women of Color," but for now, let's consider an experiment that clearly demonstrates different stereotyping of women from different classes and ethnic groups.

Psychologist Hope Landrine (1985) had undergraduates rate four stimulus groups—middle-class Black women, middle-class white women, lower-class Black women, and lower-class white women—on a series of 23 adjectives that are commonly stereotyped qualities. The results indicated that ratings were significantly different as a function of race. White women, compared with Black women, were rated as significantly more dependent, emotional, intelligent, passive, vain, and warm. Black women, compared with white women, were rated as more hostile and superstitious. Social class exerted a larger effect on the ratings than did race. That is, middle-class white women and middle-class Black women received more similar ratings than middle-class white women and lower-class white women.

Lists of stereotypes of women in the United States typically include qualities such as dependent, passive, and vain. Landrine's research shows that these traits are not seen to be as characteristic of Black women. Therefore, much of the research on gender stereotypes probably tells us about gender stereotypes among whites but may tell us little about gender stereotypes among other ethnic groups.

Gender Differences Versus Individual Differences

Suppose we say that a particular study of kindergarten children showed boys to be more aggressive than girls. Just what does that mean?

Such a statement generally means that there were average differences between males and females, and that these differences were statistically significant. It most certainly does not mean, however, that all the males were more aggressive than all the females. With data on gender differences, the distributions, although showing average differences, generally overlap to a great extent (see Figure 3.2). Typically there is a great deal of variability among members of one gender (individual differences). Therefore one should not be surprised to find an aggressive little girl in the kindergarten in our imaginary study. There may be some very aggressive little girls, but on average, the boys are more aggressive. And particularly if the number of people is large, a statistically significant gender difference may be found even though the average scores of males and females are fairly close.

The point is that even when there are average gender differences in a particular trait, almost always there are still large individual differences—differences from one female to the next and from one male to the next. Often these individual differences are more important than the average gender differences. A finding that females are less aggressive than males should certainly not lead one to expect that all females are unaggressive.

Often in this book I will make a statement such as "Males are more ag-

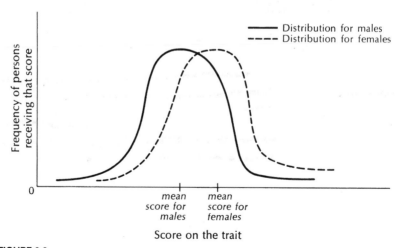

FIGURE 3.2

Examples of distributions of scores for males and females that might lead to statistically significant gender differences in the trait.

gressive than females" as a kind of shorthand for the more precise—but awk-ward—"Males, on average, are more aggressive than females." Individual differences and the great overlap of distributions should always be kept in mind, however.

Meta-Analysis

At this point, there are literally thousands of studies investigating psychological gender differences. These studies have attempted to document the "real differences," using the terminology introduced earlier. This should mean that we have a thorough understanding of which behaviors show gender differences and which do not. Unfortunately, things are a bit more complicated than that. Often the results of different studies contradict one another. For example, some studies of gender differences in infants' activity levels find that boys are more active, whereas others find no differences. In such cases, what should we conclude? Are boys more active than girls?

Another problem is that sometimes a single study that finds a gender difference will be widely cited and included in textbooks, and the five other studies of the same behavior that found no gender difference will be ignored. It seems likely that this occurs particularly when a finding of gender differences confirms the stereotypes held by authors and the general public. As an example, many child psychology texts cite the finding that boys are more active than girls and further argue that this may be a source of later gender differences and of the active assertiveness of the adult male role. However, in the actual studies of infants' activity levels, one of the reports found gender differences that were not statistically significant (Lewis et al., 1963). According to the rules of science, a gender difference should be statistically significant before it is worth talking about. A second study that is cited as evidence in fact used only male infants as subjects (Bell, 1960). It is difficult to see how such a study could be evidence for gender differences.

Meta-analysis: A statistical technique that allows a researcher to combine the results of many separate research studies.

Meta-analysis is a new technique that allows researchers to bring order out of this seeming chaos of sometimes contradictory studies (Hyde and Linn, 1986). Meta-analysis is a statistical technique. It allows the researcher to statistically combine the results from all previous studies of the question of interest to determine what, taken together, the studies say. In conducting a meta-analysis, the researcher goes through three steps:

1. The researcher locates all previous studies on the question being investigated (e.g., gender differences in aggression). This step can often be done today using computerized library searches.

2. For each study, the researcher computes a statistic that measures how big the difference between males and females was, and what the direction of the dif-

ference was (males scoring higher or females scoring higher). This statistic is called *d*. The formula for it is

$$d = \frac{M_M - M_F}{s}$$

where M_M is the mean or average score for males and M_F is the mean or average score for females; s is the average standard deviation of the male scores and the female scores. If you've studied statistics, you know what a standard deviation is. For those of you who haven't, the standard deviation is a measure of how much variability there is in the scores. For example, if the average score for females on test Q is 20 and all the scores fall between 19 and 21, then there is little variability and the standard deviation would be small. If, on the other hand, the average score for females is 20 and scores range from 0 to 40, then there is great variability and the standard deviation will be large. The *d* statistic, then, tells us, for a particular study, how big the difference between the male and female means was, relative to the variability in scores. If *d* is a positive value, then males scored higher; if *d* is negative, females scored higher; and if *d* is zero, there was no difference.

3. The researcher averages all the values of *d* over all the studies that were located. This average *d* value tells, when all studies are combined, what the direction of the gender difference is (whether males score higher or females score higher) and how large the difference is.

Although there is some disagreement among experts, a general guide is that a *d* of .20 is a small difference, a *d* of .50 is a moderate difference, and a *d* of .80 is a large difference (Cohen, 1969).

A substantial number of meta-analyses of gender differences are now available, most of them based on large numbers of studies. Meta-analyses, whenever available, will form the basis for the conclusions presented in this chapter.

We shouldn't leave this discussion without noting a moral that emerges. Often a very interesting gender difference will be found in a study, and the study will be given a great deal of publicity, including being discussed in textbooks and professors' lectures. Students need to develop a critical attitude in such cases. The first question one should ask when hearing such a report is, Has this finding been replicated? **Replicated** means that the study has been repeated independently by other scientists and the same results obtained. A single study that finds a gender difference is not very convincing. Are there other studies of the same behavior that find no difference? Or have many different scientists all found this difference consistently? One study doth not a gender difference make.

Replicate: To repeat a research study and obtain the same basic results.

Now let us proceed to see whether there is evidence for gender differences in a variety of personality characteristics and behaviors. I have put them in roughly the following order: those for which there is good evidence of a gender difference come first, those where the evidence is somewhat mixed come next, and, finally, those in which there appear to be no gender difference are last.

Aggressive Behavior

Gender Differences One of the most consistently documented psychological gender differences is in aggressive behavior, with males being more aggressive than females (Maccoby and Jacklin, 1974). Psychologists generally define **aggression** as behavior intended to harm another person. This gender difference holds up for every one of the many different kinds of aggression that have been studied, including physical aggression and verbal aggression (Hyde, 1984b). Furthermore, this gender difference has been found in all cultures in which the appropriate data have been collected (Maccoby and Jacklin, 1974).

Aggression: Behavior intended to harm another person.

Developmentally, this difference appears about as early as children begin playing with one another, around the age of two or two and a half. The difference continues consistently throughout the school years. Of course, as people get older they become less aggressive, at least in the physical sense. It is rare to see adults rolling around on the floor as they punch each other, compared with the frequency with which that occurs on an elementary school playground. We have less information available on gender differences in adult aggression, but we do know that the vast majority of crimes of violence are committed by men (although female crime is on the increase). According to the results of social psychologists' research on aggression (most of it done in the laboratory with college students), there are some situations in which there are no gender differences; but it is rare for women to be more aggressive than men (Frodi et al., 1977). In particular, women are likely to be as aggressive as men when it appears that it would be justified or even prosocial to be aggressive. It also seems that men and women react differently to provocation: what angers a man (and leads him to be aggressive) tends to make a woman anxious, not angry or aggressive.

Because I was interested in finding out how large gender differences in aggression are, I reviewed a large number of studies (143, to be exact) of gender differences in aggression, using the technique of meta-analysis (Hyde, 1984b; see also Eagly and Steffen, 1986). I found that gender differences in aggression do appear consistently, but the difference is moderate relative to the individual differences—in fact, the size of the difference is approximately as large as that shown in Figure 3.2. The value of *d* computed in the meta-analysis was 0.50, which is a moderate difference. The analysis also showed that gender differences in aggression are largest among preschoolers; gender differences become smaller with age and are quite small among college-age subjects.

What Causes the Gender Difference? The causes of the gender difference in aggressive behavior have been hotly debated, with the nature and nurture teams battling against each other. The nature team attributes gender differences in ag-

FIGURE 3.3
Gender differences in aggressiveness appear early.

gressiveness to the greater size and musculature of males and/or differences in the levels of the sex hormone testosterone. These factors will be discussed in detail in Chapter 9.

On the nurture side, a number of environmental forces might produce the observed gender difference: (1) Aggressiveness is a key part of the male role in our society, and unaggressiveness or passivity a key part of the female role. Following the logic of cognitive-developmental theory, as soon as children become aware of gender roles, girls realize that they are not supposed to be aggressive and boys know that they should be. As I noted in Chapter 2, this logic does not work very well in explaining how gender differences develop so early, but it may be helpful in explaining gender differences among older children. (2) Children imitate same-gender adults more than opposite-gender adults, and they see far more aggression in men than in women, particularly on TV and in movies. Hence boys imitate men, who are aggressive, and girls imitate women, who are unaggressive. (3) Boys receive more rewards for aggression and less punishment for it than girls do. These reinforcements and punishments might be in a physical form, such as spanking, or in a verbal form, such as comments from adults like "Boys will be boys" in response to a boy's aggression, and "Nice young ladies don't do that" to a girl's aggression. Boys may also be rewarded in the form of status or respect from their peers for being aggressive, whereas girls receive no such reward. Actual studies, however, indicate that boys are punished more for aggression than girls are by both parents and teachers (Maccoby and Jacklin, 1974; Serbin et al., 1973). This poses a problem for this explanation. However, psychologists believe that some kinds of punishments for aggression may actually increase a child's aggression rather than decrease it. Therefore the punishments that boys receive may actually make them more aggressive. (4) A somewhat more complex cultural argument takes into account the fact that, simply because of the way our culture organizes childcare, the major disciplinarians of small children are women—mothers and teachers. Research indicates that children's identification with a punishing adult is important in what kind of effects the punishment will have. If the child is highly identified with the adult, punishment will decrease aggression, whereas if the child is not identified with the adult, punishment will increase aggression (Eron et al., 1974). Little girls are more highly identified with their mothers and female teachers than boys are. Hence punishment by mothers and female teachers would decrease the aggression of girls and increase the aggression of boys. There are some empirical data to support this explanation (Hyde and Schuck, 1977). One implication of this line of reasoning is that if we want to reduce the aggressiveness of boys, or increase the aggressiveness of girls, or minimize gender differences, we will need to get fathers more involved in caring for their children and get more men to be preschool and elementary school teachers.

One interesting experiment tested the first hypothesis stated above, that gender roles are a powerful force creating gender differences in aggression (Lightdale and Prentice, 1994). The researchers used the technique of deindividuation to produce a situation that removed the influences of gender roles. **Deindividuation** refers to a state in which the person has lost his or her individual identity; that is, the person has become anonymous. Under such conditions, people feel no obligation to conform to social norms such as gender roles. Deindividuation essentially places the individual in a situation free of gender roles. Half the participants were placed in an individuated condition by having them sit

Deindividuation: A state in which a person has become anonymous and has therefore lost his or her individual identity.

FOCUS 3.2
HOW ACCURATE ARE PEOPLE'S GENDER STEREOTYPES?

We sometimes hear a person say "It's only a stereotype," meaning that stereotypes about gender differences are not real differences, or that stereotypes are not at all accurate. Yet the evidence indicates that sometimes stereotypes correspond to real differences. For example, there is a stereotype that males are more aggressive than females and, as we saw earlier in this chapter, there is a moderate gender difference in aggression.

Psychologist Janet Swim (1994) devised a clever technique to determine the accuracy of people's gender stereotypes. She had research participants estimate how large gender differences were for a list of behaviors for which meta-analyses are available. The participants estimated whether males or females scored higher, and they made their estimates along the scale shown in Figure 3.4. Using that scale, they were told that 0 meant no gender difference, .20 was a small difference, .50 was a moderate difference, .80 was a large difference, and that they could go even higher for a really large difference.

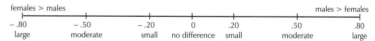

FIGURE 3.4
The rating scale used in Swim's study of the accuracy of people's gender stereotypes. *(Source: Swim, 1994. Copyright © 1994, the American Psychological Association.)*

The results indicated that people are fairly accurate about or, if anything, tend to underestimate the magnitude of gender differences. That is, they don't hold stereotypes that blow the differences way out of proportion. For example, the average estimate of the size of the gender difference in aggression was .51, and the meta-analysis discussed earlier in this chapter found $d = .50$ (Hyde, 1984b). The actual size of the gender difference on the SAT-Math is .39 (Hyde et al., 1990), but participants estimated .12, that is, they underestimated.

The results, then, indicate that people—or at least college students—do not have wildly inflated notions about how large psychological gender differences are.

SOURCE: Swim 1994.

close to the experimenter, identify themselves by name, wear large name tags, and answer personal questions. Deindividuated participants sat far from the experimenter and were simply told to wait quietly. All participants were also told that the experiment required information from only half the participants, whose behavior would be monitored, and that the other half would remain anonymous. Next, the participants played an interactive video game in which they first defended and then attacked by dropping bombs. The number of bombs dropped was the measure of aggressive behavior.

The results indicated that, in the individuated condition, men dropped significantly more bombs (31.1, on average) than women did (26.8, on average). In the deindividuated condition—that is, in the absence of gender roles—there were no significant gender differences. In fact, females dropped somewhat more bombs (41.1, on average) than males did (36.8, on average). In short, the significant gender differences in aggression disappeared when the influences of gender roles were removed.

The question of what causes gender differences in aggressiveness is a complex one that has not been completely resolved by scientific data. Perhaps the best conclusion to make at this point, and the one that seems to agree best with the existing data, is that there are probably rather small biologically based gender differences in aggressiveness and that cultural forces act to magnify these differences considerably.

Self-Confidence

Suppose a group of students take their first exam in Introductory Psychology. Immediately after they complete the exam and before they receive their grades, we ask them to estimate how many points (out of a possible 100 points) they think they got on the exam. Most studies indicate that we will find a gender difference, with females estimating that they will get fewer points than males estimate (Mednick and Thomas, 1993). Psychologists interpret this as indicating that females have lower self-confidence than males do.

This difference between males and females has been found consistently in many studies. Even in a study involving a group of preschoolers, with an average age of four and a half years, girls had lower expectancies for their performance on various tasks than boys did (Crandall, 1978).

The gender difference in self-confidence is an important one. There is evidence that people with low expectations for success avoid engaging in challenging tasks. Thus this gender difference may have important effects on women's careers and accomplishments, a point to be discussed further in Chapter 7.

Although the gender difference in self-confidence is fairly consistent, we need to place some qualifications on the general result (Lenney, 1977, 1981; Mednick and Thomas, 1993). First, whether females give lower estimates of their expectancies depends on the kinds of tasks involved. For example, females do not give lower estimates if they are made to think a task is gender appropriate for them. Second, the gender difference depends on the kind of feedback given to people about their performance. If females are given clear and unambiguous feedback about how well they are doing, or how good their abilities are, then their estimates are not lower than males'. Finally, the gender difference depends on the presence or absence of social comparisons or social evaluations. If other people are present and everyone is being compared with one another, then women give low estimates; but if they work alone or in situations where they do not expect their performance to be compared with others', then their estimates are not lower. Therefore it seems that women have lower self-confidence than men in some situations, but not in others.

Before leaving the topic of self-confidence, I need to note one further complication, namely, interpretation of the results. The objective, statistical result in the studies we have been discussing is that males estimate they will get more points on the exam or some other task. To use the terminology of Chapter 1, the *interpretation* of this result is that males have more self-confidence than females, or that *females are lacking in self-confidence.* This is a *female-deficit* interpretation. Would it be possible to make a different interpretation that would still be consistent with the data? An alternative interpretation is that males' estimates are too high (rather than females' being too low) and that males are unrealistically overconfident. This alternative is just as reasonable an interpretation of the gender difference, but this interpretation implies a problem for males. As it turns out, with tasks such as these it is possible to decide which interpretation is more accurate, because we can find out how students actually did on the exam. In fact, males do tend to overestimate their performance by about as much as females underestimate theirs, although some studies find females' estimates to be accurate and males' to be inflated (Mednick and Thomas, 1993). Therefore, there is some truth in each interpretation—men are probably a bit overconfident and women a bit underconfident.

Also, girls are socialized for *modesty*—that is, not to brag about their accomplishments, but rather to be modest about them. According to this interpretation, women give lower estimates of their expected performance than they may actually think they will get in order to conform to the social norm of modesty. In a study designed to test this hypothesis, first-year college students estimated their first semester grade point averages (GPAs) either in public conditions (the student reported it out loud to the student experimenter) or in private conditions (the student wrote it on an index card out of sight of the experimenter and then sealed it in an envelope) (Heatherington et al., 1993). In the public conditions, in which women presumably would feel the pressure of the modesty norm, a significant gender difference in prediction of grades was found, with women predicting lower grades for themselves than men did. However, there was no significant gender difference in the private condition. It seems when there is no need to be modest, there is no gender difference. In a second experiment by the same researchers, college students were asked to predict their GPAs publicly either to a nonvulnerable person or to a vulnerable person (a person who revealed he or she had earned a low GPA). Women's estimates were lower than men's only in the second condition, that is, when reporting to the vulnerable person. This result suggests that it is more than modesty at work, but also a desire to care for others and maintain relationships.

In summary, then, women give lower estimates of their achievements than men do. However, men may overestimate by as much as women underestimate. And women may simply be conforming to norms that they be modest about their achievements and that they not hurt the feelings of someone who may have achieved less. Given all these findings, one would be mistaken to conclude that women lack self-confidence in achievement situations.

Activity

There has been quite a bit of debate among psychologists as to whether gender differences in activity level exist. Certainly if you ask the average parent or teacher, they will tell you that boys are more active, and most child psychology texts have maintained that this is true.

A major meta-analysis found that d was approximately .50, that is, that there is a moderate gender difference in activity, with males having the higher activity level (Eaton and Enns, 1986). Among infants, d was .29; it was .44 for preschoolers and .64 older children. Thus, the difference is present from infancy and seems to get larger with age, at least among children.

The findings for gender differences in activity level parallel those for many other gender differences in an important way: They depend on the *situation* in which the activity is measured. For example, the gender difference is significantly larger when peers are present (d = .62) than when they are absent (d = .44). That is, the activity level of boys, relative to that of girls, seems to increase when other kids are there.

This meta-analysis was based on samples of children from the general population. In samples of hyperactive children, about 80 percent are boys (Holborow and Berry, 1986).

What causes this gender difference? The arguments are similar to those made about aggressive behavior, and the issue has not been resolved in either case. What we do not know is how much the developmental precocity of girls contributes to this difference. Stated briefly, girls are ahead of boys in development. As children grow older, they learn to control their activity more. It might be, then, that the lower activity level of girls represents simply a greater ability to control activity because of their being somewhat more mature than boys.

Helping Behavior

Social psychologists have studied helping behavior extensively. A meta-analysis of studies of gender differences in helping behavior found that d = .34 (Eagly and Crowley, 1986). The positive value indicates that males, on average, helped more than females and that the gender difference is somewhere in the small-to-moderate range. This finding may be somewhat surprising because helping or nurturing is an important part of the female role, and therefore we might have expected a negative value for *d*. To clarify this finding, the researchers, Alice Eagly and Maureen Crowley, probed into those kinds of situations that produced more helping by males and those that produced more helping by females. They noted that some kinds of helping are part of the male role and some are part of the female role. Helping that is heroic or chivalrous falls within the male role, whereas nurturance and caretaking fall within the female role.

Consistent with these predictions from social roles, Eagly and Crowley found that the tendency for males to help more was especially pronounced when the situation might involve danger (such as stopping to help a motorist with a flat tire). The tendency was also stronger when the helping was observed by others (rather than the person needing help and the research participant being alone). Helping that involves danger and that carries with it a crowd of onlookers has greater potential for heroism, and that kind of helping is part of the male role.

The plot thickens because social psychologists have spent most of their time studying precisely these kinds of helping behaviors—the ones that occur in relatively short-term encounters with strangers. They have devoted little research to the kind of caretaking and helping that is characteristic of the female role—the kind of behavior that more often occurs in the context of a long-term relationship, such as a mother helping her child. Therefore, the gender difference found by Eagly and Crowley, showing that males help more, is probably no more than an artifact of the kinds of helping that psychologists have studied and the kinds of helping that they have overlooked.

Again we see that the pattern of gender differences is highly dependent on the situation in which they are observed.

Anxiety

Most studies show that girls and women are more fearful and anxious than boys and men. A recent meta-analysis found $d = -.30$ for general anxiety (Feingold, 1995). The difference is significant, but not large. Girls also report more fears than boys do (Brody et al., 1990; Gullone and King, 1992). Once again, though, the difference is not simple. Most of the studies that find differences are based on self-reports, but studies based on direct observations often find no gender difference (Maccoby and Jacklin, 1974). To illustrate the difference between self-reports and direct observations, suppose a psychologist is trying to determine whether girls are more fearful of dogs than boys are. If the psychologist is using the self-report method, he or she would interview children and ask them if they are afraid of dogs. Using the method of direct observation, the psychologist would bring a dog into the room and see whether the children behave fearfully.

What we know, then, is that girls and women are more willing to admit that they have anxieties and fears. It is possible that these self-reports reflect that females actually are more fearful and anxious than males. But it is also possible that males and females experience the same levels of fear and anxiety and that females are only more willing to admit them. This might be a result of gender-role stereotypes, which portray women as fearful and timid and men as fearless and brave. This would encourage women to admit their feelings and men to pretend not to have them. At this point, however, studies have not been able to resolve this issue.

Most of the studies just discussed are based on samples of the general population and the kinds of fears and anxieties most of us experience routinely. If, on the other hand, we consider psychiatrically diagnosable phobias, women clearly outnumber men (Robins et al., 1984; Russo, 1990).

Empathy

Empathy means feeling the emotion another person is feeling. It essentially involves putting yourself in another's place emotionally. According to stereotypes, females are more empathic than males, as part of the general stereotype of emotional expressivity in females and emotional inexpressivity in males. Does this stereotype reflect a real difference?

Psychologists Nancy Eisenberg and Randy Lennon (1983) reviewed studies of empathy and found that the results on gender differences were rather mixed. Gender differences in empathy seem to depend on the way in which they are measured. When people respond to self-report questionnaires containing items like "Seeing people cry upsets me," the gender difference is large, with females showing more empathy. When researchers use a different measure, designed to measure "empathy" in newborn infants, girl infants are more likely to cry when they hear a tape recording of another infant crying, but the size of this gender difference is only moderate. Finally, when actual psychological measures of emotional responding are used, or when researchers unobtrusively observe actual behavior (facial expressions, tone of voice), gender differences are small. Perhaps gender differences are largest with the questionnaires because the questions tap gender-stereotyped responses. For example, the item mentioned earlier, "Seeing people cry upsets me," sounds a lot like the stereotypes of women as being emotional and aware of the feelings of others, discussed in the first section of this chapter. The items may measure stereotypes more than reality. Thus, although the evidence does indicate that females are somewhat more empathic than males are, the difference is a small one.

Leadership

Psychologists have collected a substantial amount of data on the leadership behaviors of women and men. A large-scale meta-analysis of studies of leadership found a *d* of .03, indicating that there is no overall gender difference (Eagly and Johnson, 1990). However, in one particular area there was a consistent—though small—difference: in the use of autocratic (authoritarian) versus democratic leadership styles, *d* was −.22. The results indicate that women, compared with men, are more likely to use democratic rather than autocratic leadership styles.

Leadership is important as more women move into corporations and politics. The trend in corporations is away from rigid, hierarchical structures and toward more participatory, democratic ones. It is gratifying to know that women tend to use precisely those styles that represent the new trend in organizations.

Beyond Gender Stereotypes: Androgyny?

With the last 25 years of feminist thought has come a desire for new models of human behavior that overcome gender stereotypes. One prominent alternative that has been suggested is **androgyny,** the combining of masculine and feminine characteristics in an individual. Psychologists quickly moved to develop tests to measure androgyny (e.g., Bem, 1974). But to understand these tests, we must first go back several decades and examine psychologists' traditional understandings of masculinity and femininity (M-F) and how they measured them before androgyny arrived on the scene.

Androgyny: The combination of masculine and feminine psychological characteristics in an individual.

Psychologists' Traditional Views of M-F   Psychologists' traditional view was that masculinity and femininity were at opposite ends of a single scale—that is, that a unidimensional, bipolar continuum described variations in M-F (see Section 1 of Figure 3.5).

One of the traditional tests to measure M-F is the FE (for femininity) scale of the California Psychological Inventory (Gough, 1957). Some items from it are shown in Table 3.3. It is a simple paper-and-pencil test, with a person responding true or false to items, depending on whether the items describe the person or not. Then a score is computed that places the person at some point along the bipolar continuum.

Items were chosen for such tests in a simple way—the criterion being that they must differentiate biological males from biological females. That is, an item was chosen if it showed marked gender differences, meaning that a much different proportion of males as compared with females respond true to it. Therefore, an item such as "I prefer a tub bath to a shower" can appear on such tests, not because it reflects anything profound about the essence of masculinity or femininity, but simply because males tend to prefer showers and females tend to prefer tub baths. The implicit assumption, then, is that "femininity" is the quality of women that differentiates them from men.

Feminist psychologists raised a number of criticisms of M-F tests (Constantinople, 1973). A serious question is whether M-F is so simple that it can be scored on a single scale or dimension or whether, instead, it might require two or several scales to capture its complexity. A second criticism is that the psychologists who constructed M-F tests never really defined precisely what they meant by "femininity" or "masculinity." They typically settled for the definition of gen-

1. The unidimensional, bipolar continuum

2. The two-dimensional scheme

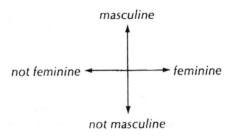

3. The multidimensional scheme

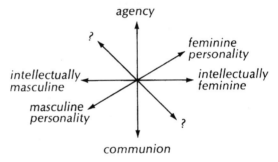

FIGURE 3.5
Progressive conceptualizations of masculinity-femininity.

der differences when they chose items, with an implicit definition that femininity is whatever women are that men aren't. This may be a practical definition, but it does not give us much insight into what femininity or masculinity is.

The Concept of Androgyny The question that needs to be raised is, Why can't a person be both feminine and masculine? In fact, most of us know people who are both. An example would be a woman who has strong achievement drives, is very successful at her career, plays tennis very well, and likes to wear jeans, and who at the same time likes to cook and sew, likes to wear long dresses, and is very sensitive and caring. The problem is that traditional M-F tests can't handle her. The research on androgyny was designed to study such people.

Androgyny means having both masculine and feminine psychological characteristics. It is derived from the Greek roots *andro,* meaning "man" (as in *an-*

TABLE 3.3

Some Sample Items That Differentiate Males from Females and Are Therefore Used to Measure Masculinity-Femininity

Item	Response Indicating Femininity
Sometimes I have the same dream over and over.	True
I am somewhat afraid of the dark.	True
I think I could do better than most of the present politicians if I were in office.	False
I would like to be a soldier.	False
I think I would like the work of a librarian.	True
I want to be an important person in the community.	False

SOURCE: Reproduced by special permission from California Psychological Inventory by Harrison G. Gough, Ph.D. Copyright 1956 by Consulting Psychologists Press, Inc.

drogens—sex hormones that are found in high concentrations in males), and *gyn,* meaning "woman" (as in *gynecologist*). An androgynous person, then, is a person who has both masculine and feminine psychological characteristics.

As shown in Figure 3.5, the concept of androgyny is based on a two-dimensional model of masculinity-femininity. The idea is that instead of masculinity and femininity being opposite ends of a single scale, they are two separate dimensions, one running from not feminine to very feminine, and the other from not masculine to very masculine. This would allow for androgynous people, that is, people who are high in both femininity and masculinity. It would also allow for feminine people and for masculine people. In the second diagram of Figure 3.5, the androgynous people would be the ones falling in the upper-right-hand quadrant. The two-dimensional model—unlike the unidimensional, bipolar model—allows for people who are both highly masculine and highly feminine, that is, androgynous.

Measuring Androgyny   Psychologist Sandra Bem (1974) constructed a test to measure androgyny (see also Spence and Helmreich, 1978) that is shown in Table 3.4. It consists of 60 adjectives or descriptive phrases. Respondents are asked to indicate, for each, how well it describes them on a scale from 1 (never or almost never true) to 7 (always or almost always true). Of the 60 adjectives, 20 are

---

[1]Unlike the constructors of the M-F tests, Bem did not avoid defining M and F by simply relying on gender differences. Instead, femininity was defined as those characteristics that are considered socially desirable for women in our culture, and similarly for masculinity.

TABLE 3.4
Are You Androgynous?

The following items are the Bem Sex Role Inventory. To find out whether you score as androgynous on it, first rate yourself on each item, on a scale from 1 (never or almost never true) to 7 (always or almost always true).

1. self-reliant	22. analytical	41. warm
2. yielding	23. sympathetic	42. solemn
3. helpful	24. jealous	43. willing to take a stand
4. defends own beliefs	25. has leadership abilities	44. tender
5. cheerful	26. sensitive to the needs	45. friendly
6. moody	of others	46. aggressive
7. independent	27. truthful	47. gullible
8. shy	28. willing to take risks	48. inefficient
9. conscientious	29. understanding	49. acts as a leader
10. athletic	30. secretive	50. childlike
11. affectionate	31. makes decisions easily	51. adaptable
12. theatrical	32. compassionate	52. individualistic
13. assertive	33. sincere	53. does not use harsh
14. flatterable	34. self-sufficient	language
15. happy	35. eager to soothe hurt	54. unsystematic
16. strong personality	feelings	55. competitive
17. loyal	36. conceited	56. loves children
18. unpredictable	37. dominant	57. tactful
19. forceful	38. soft-spoken	58. ambitious
20. feminine	39. likable	59. gentle
21. reliable	40. masculine	60. conventional

SCORING:

(a) Add up your ratings for items 1, 4, 7, 10, 13, 16, 19, 22, 25, 28, 31, 34, 37, 40, 43, 46, 49, 52, 55, and 58. Divide the total by 20. That is your masculinity score.

(b) Add up your ratings for items 2, 5, 8, 11, 14, 17, 20, 23, 26, 29, 32, 35, 38, 41, 44, 47, 50, 53, 56, and 59. Divide the total by 20. That is your femininity score.

(c) If your masculinity score is above 4.9 (the approximate median for the masculinity scale) and your femininity score is above 4.9 (the approximate femininity median), then you would be classified as androgynous on Bem's scale.

SOURCE: Bem (1974, 1977), Hyde and Phillis (1979).

stereotypically feminine,[1] 20 are stereotypically masculine, and 20 are neutral, that is, not gender typed. Items 1, 4, 7, and so on in Table 3.4 are masculine; items 2, 5, 8, and so on are feminine; and 3, 6, 9, and so on are neutral. Therefore *self-reliant* is a masculine characteristic, *yielding* is feminine, and *helpful* is neutral.

Once the test has been taken, people are given two scores: a masculinity score and a femininity score. The masculinity score is the average of their self-ratings of the masculinity items, and their femininity score is the average of their self-ratings of the femininity items. This will give each person a score on each of the two scales shown in the two-dimensional diagram in Figure 3.5. The androgynous people should be in the upper-right-hand part, which means they should be high in masculinity and high in femininity. Bem (1977) defines "high" as being above the median (the median is a kind of average). Therefore people are androgynous if they are above the median on masculinity and above the median on femininity (the median on each of these scales is generally about 4.9). A feminine person who scores high (above the median) on femininity but low (below the median) on masculinity would fall in the lower-right-hand quadrant in Figure 3.5. Similarly, a masculine person who scores high on the masculinity scale but low on the femininity scale would fall in the upper-left-hand quadrant. Finally, people who score low on both scales fall in the lower-left-hand quadrant and are called "undifferentiated" because they don't rate themselves very highly on any of the adjectives, masculine or feminine. Therefore, having taken the Bem Sex Role Inventory, an individual can be placed in one of four categories: masculine, feminine, androgynous, or undifferentiated.

In her work with college students, Bem typically finds that about one-third of them are androgynous, according to her scale (see Table 3.5).

Is It Better to Be Androgynous?   As an ideal, androgyny sounds good. It permits freedom from gender-role stereotypes and allows people to express their opposite-gender tendencies. But what are androgynous people like in reality? Do

TABLE 3.5

Percentages of College Students Classified as Androgynous, Masculine, Feminine, or Undifferentiated

	Androgynous	Masculine	Feminine	Undifferentiated
Females	27	14	32	28
Males	32	34	8	25

Based on a sample of 715 students at the University of Texas.

SOURCE: From *Masculinity and Femininity: Their Psychological Dimensions, Correlates, and Antecedents* by Janet T. Spence and Robert L. Helmreich, Copyright © 1978. Reprinted by permission of the author and the University of Texas Press.

they function well psychologically? Does society view them suspiciously because of their gender-role nonconformity? There are a number of studies that give us some answers to these questions.

Pressure-to-Conform Study Bem has done several studies to find out how androgynous people, as compared with masculine or feminine people, actually behave in various demanding situations (Bem, 1975; Bem and Lenney, 1976; Bem et al., 1976). Her general prediction in these studies is that androgynous people should do better in a wider variety of situations, because they are capable of being feminine or masculine when the situation calls for it. Masculine or feminine people, on the other hand, may do well when stereotyped behavior is required, but in situations demanding nonstereotyped behavior, they will do poorly.

The "pressure-to-conform study" was one such experiment (Bem, 1975). College students were brought to the laboratory in groups of four males and four females. They were then placed in individual booths equipped with microphones and earphones. Their task was to judge how funny some cartoons were; they thought they were participating in an experiment on humor. The cartoons had previously been rated by an independent set of judges, and half of them had been judged very funny, half of them not at all funny.

Participants were asked to rate how funny each cartoon was. Before giving their rating, however, they heard what they thought were the others in their group giving their ratings. In fact what they were hearing was a tape recording, with voices saying that a particular cartoon was funny when it wasn't and vice versa.

The idea was that people who stuck to their guns and gave their opinions of the cartoons honestly, refusing to be influenced by the others, would be displaying the "masculine" trait of independence. Those whose opinions were swayed by the others and gave ratings similar to them, rather than really telling how funny the cartoons were, would be showing the "feminine" characteristic of compliance or conformity.

Bem's prediction for the outcome of the study was that those people who had been classified as masculine by the Bem Sex Role Inventory would be independent or nonconforming. Feminine people, on the other hand, would be more likely to conform. Androgynous people should be able to be masculine or feminine. In this situation, Bem believes that independence is the most desirable behavior, and therefore she predicted that androgynous people would be independent. The results turned out exactly as predicted—masculine and androgynous people did not differ significantly from each other, and both groups were significantly more independent than the feminine people.[2]

Good-Listener Study In another study, the participant listened as a lonely transfer student (who was actually a confederate of the experimenter's) poured out a list of troubles in adjusting to college life (Bem, 1975). The interaction was

---

[2]If you are a psychology student, you might want to notice that this and the next study are means by which Bem can establish the *validity* of the Bem Sex Role Inventory. That is, to be valid, the scale should be able to differentiate various groups of people based on theoretical predictions. That is precisely what this study does.

watched from behind a one-way mirror, and participants were scored for their responsiveness and sympathy for the talker, as a measure of their nurturance.

The idea is that the "feminine" quality of nurturance is what is called for in this situation. Bem predicted that feminine people would be more nurturant than masculine people. Androgynous people, able to be either masculine or feminine, should do what is appropriate, namely, be nurturant. The results turned out as predicted: feminine people and androgynous people of both genders did not differ from each other, and both groups were significantly more nurturant than masculine people.

In sum, these two studies, when taken together, indicate that androgynous people probably function better in a wider variety of situations than gender-typed people do. Because they have both masculine and feminine characteristics in their repertoire, they are capable of being masculine when that is appropriate (as in the pressure-to-conform study, where independence is appropriate) and they are capable of being feminine when that is appropriate (as in the good-listener study, where nurturance is most appropriate). In short, androgynous people have an advantage because they are flexible.

Self-Esteem   The traditional assumption in psychology was that gender typing was a good thing in terms of personal adjustment. That is, it was thought that the well-adjusted person would be appropriately gender typed (feminine if a female, masculine if a male) and that people who were not so gender typed would be poorly adjusted.

With a test to measure androgyny available, we are in a position to see how well adjusted androgynous people are, and how their adjustment compares with that of gender-typed people. Research indicates that androgynous people and masculine people tend to be high in self-esteem, in comparison with feminine people and undifferentiated people, who tend to be lower in self-esteem (Bem, 1977; Spence et al., 1975). The ordering of groups, from highest to lowest in self-esteem, has been found consistently to be as follows: androgynous, masculine, feminine, undifferentiated (Spence and Helmreich, 1978). These results, then, indicate that androgynous people have high self-esteem, an important psychological characteristic. The point that masculine people tend to have higher self-esteem than feminine people is certainly worth noting. The implications of this finding will be discussed further in Chapter 14.

Two conclusions emerged in a major review of the dozens of studies of the psychological implications of androgyny (Taylor and Hall, 1982). First, there is no support for psychologists' traditional assumption that masculinity is best for men and femininity is best for women. For example, masculinity is highly correlated with self-esteem for men, but masculinity is also highly correlated with self-esteem for women. Thus the purely gender-typed feminine woman is at a disadvantage in terms of psychological health. Second, although both masculinity and femininity are positively correlated with self-esteem, masculinity shows a consistently higher correlation. In short, whether one is a man or a woman, one's masculine characteristics seem most related to self-esteem and other measures of psychological health.

Problems? Androgyny sounds wonderful, but are there any problems with it? Several criticisms have been raised. (For a summary of feminist criticisms of androgyny, see Lott, 1981.)

First, androgyny is advantageous in freeing people from the restrictions of rigid gender-role stereotypes. In so doing, however, it may be setting up an extraordinarily demanding, perhaps impossible, ideal. For example, in the good old days, a woman could be considered reasonably competent ("successful") if she could cook well. To meet new standards and be androgynous, she not only has to cook well, but also has to repair cars. That is, androgyny demands that people be good at more diverse things, and that may be difficult. Indeed, the characteristics required to be androgynous sometimes seem almost mutually contradictory. For example, on the Bem Sex Role Inventory, in order to be androgynous, one needs to be forceful and dominant ("masculine" items) and also shy and soft-spoken ("feminine" items). It is hard to see how a person could be all of those at once. Of course, the ideal androgyn would be expected to display different characteristics in different situations, depending on what was most appropriate; but knowing what is most appropriate is also rather difficult.

Some feminist scholars have also raised a second criticism of androgyny (Orloff, 1978). They regard it as essentially a "sellout" to men. That is, to become androgynous, women need to add masculine traits to their personalities, or become more like men. The argument has been made that what we should do, rather than to encourage women to become more like men, is to concentrate on valuing those things that women do and are. To these scholars, rediscovering and cherishing womanhood would be preferable to encouraging androgyny. This, of course, is a matter of personal values.

A third criticism is that the very definition of androgyny rests on traditional assumptions about masculinity and femininity. To be classified as androgynous, the person merely scores high on two scales that consist of stereotyped masculine and feminine traits. As such, the concept of androgyny is hardly radical or liberating (Bem, 1981).

Other scholars have pointed out that we need to be careful about generalizing from androgyny in *personality* traits (as measured by the Bem Sex Role Inventory) to expecting androgyny in actual *behavior* or in *attitudes* about gender roles (Spence and Helmreich, 1980). That is, just because a person is rated as androgynous on the Bem Sex Role Inventory does not mean he or she will necessarily behave flexibly in all situations, or that he or she will have liberal attitudes about women's roles.

Stages of Gender-Role Development

A friend of mine recounted the following story. Both she and her husband hold Ph.D.'s and are professors of political science. Both are feminists, and they try to have an egalitarian marriage and run an egalitarian household. Yet one day their son came home from kindergarten, glibly telling them how women could be nurses and not doctors, and men could be doctors and not nurses. To say the least, my friend was quite dismayed by this. She had certainly never told her son such things, and in fact had told him quite the opposite. Probably some of you have had similar experiences, or know of people who have, and can appreciate the frustration parents feel when, after all their efforts to teach their children about gender-role equality and freedom, the children still keep coming up with the same tired old stereotypes that people have traditionally held. However, some research and theory in psychology provide an explanation for this phenomenon, not to mention a ray of hope for parents.

Psychologist Joseph Pleck (1975) has proposed that children go through stages in their understanding of gender roles. Basically, he has applied cognitive-developmental theory to children's understanding of gender roles, much as Kohlberg did (as discussed in Chapter 2). Kohlberg, however, stopped his theoretical descriptions when children were five or six; Pleck has extended the theory to describe older children and adults (for other, similar theorizing, see Block, 1973; Rebecca et al., 1976; Ullian, 1976).

According to Pleck's theory, there are three stages of gender-role development, and these stages parallel the stages of moral development in children. In the first stage of moral development in children, the premoral or preconventional phase, children are dominated by their desire to gratify their own impulses, and seek to be good only to avoid punishment. In the corresponding *first stage of gender-role development,* the child's gender-role concepts are disorganized. The child may not even know her or his own gender yet, and has not yet learned that only men are supposed to do certain things, only women others. (In Kohlberg's terms, such children have not yet acquired the concepts of gender identity or gender constancy.) In the second stage of moral development, conventional role conformity, children understand rules and conform to them mostly to get approval from others, particularly authorities. In the corresponding *second stage of gender-role development,* children know the rules of gender roles and are highly motivated to conform to them themselves and also to make others conform to them. This stage begins in childhood and probably reaches its peak in adolescence when gender-role conformity is strongest. In the third stage of moral development, the postconventional phase, moral judgments are made on the basis of internalized, self-accepted principles rather than on the basis of external forces. In the corresponding *third stage of gender-role development,* people manage to go beyond (transcend) the limitations of gender roles imposed by society; such individuals develop psychological androgyny in response to their own inner needs and values. Pleck, then, views androgyny as a stage of development.

Of course, many adults never make it out of the second stage of moral development to move on to the third stage. An example would be the man who donates a lot of money to a charity because doing so will get him respect and approval from important people, rather than because of an internalized belief that the charity is a good cause and he should support it. So, too, some people never go beyond the second stage of gender-role development and move on to androgyny; they remain for their entire lives restricted by tight limitations of gender roles.

Pleck's theory is informative in answering the question originally posed, namely, Why do children who should have very flexible ideas about gender roles instead have rigid—sometimes absurdly rigid—ideas? This theory suggests that children, as part of their cognitive development and their attempts to understand how the world works, must go through a stage of gender-role restrictiveness. Essentially, they must first learn the common preconception that only men can be doctors and only women can be nurses. Then they can learn that there are exceptions to this rule and that girls can become doctors. Feminist parents probably cannot realistically expect that their children will skip the second stage of gender-role development. What they can hope for, and provide the stimulus for, is their children eventually reaching the third stage and androgyny.

What evidence is there concerning Pleck's theory? Eileen O'Keefe and I did a study to test some of the predictions of Pleck's model (O'Keefe and Hyde, 1983). We studied the occupational gender-role stereotypes (e.g., only men can be doctors, only women can be nurses) of preschoolers, kindergartners, third-graders, and sixth-graders. If Pleck is correct, preschoolers should show relatively less stereotyping, being in the preconventional or first stage. Kindergartners, third-graders, and sixth-graders should all be highly stereotyped because they are in the conventional or second stage. Stereotyping would decline in late adolescence and adulthood, although we did not interview people in those age groups. In agreement with Pleck's predictions, stereotyping did increase somewhat from the preschool group to the kindergarten group. However, in contradiction to Pleck's model, stereotyping of adult occupations declined sharply among the third-graders and sixth-graders. Sixth-graders seemed convinced that all jobs could be done by men or by women. Thus it seems that the decline in stereotyping occurs earlier than Pleck says it should, so that his theory did not receive much support in our study. On the other hand, as Pleck noted, the theory helps to make sense out of some apparently conflicting studies. For example, some studies have shown that daughters of working mothers have quite traditional gender-role concepts when they are young (Hartley, 1959, 1960); but another study showed that maternal employment is associated with daughters' high achievement and androgyny later in life (Siegel et al., 1963). Perhaps the kinds of roles parents model make little difference in childhood, when all children are in a conforming stage, but by late adolescence or adulthood these people are able to benefit from the liberated models their parents provided.

In Conclusion

In this chapter we first discussed the nature of gender stereotypes in the United States and how these stereotypes may vary as a function of race/ethnicity and social class. Then I presented the evidence for gender differences in some important psychological characteristics, basing the conclusions primarily on the results

EXPERIENCE THE RESEARCH

HOW ACCURATE ARE PEOPLE'S BELIEFS ABOUT GENDER DIFFERENCES?

Ask four people you know to provide you, individually, with some data. When you interview a person, tell her or him that you want to determine how accurate people are in estimating the size of some psychological gender differences. Have the person fill out the following form, explaining what they are to do. Be sure that they understand that they can give any number they want; that is, they do not have to answer just .20 or .50, but could give an answer like .34. Also be sure that they understand the importance of the difference between negative numbers and positive numbers. Negative numbers on this scale mean that females have higher scores than males, and positive numbers mean males score higher than females. This is the form to use:

1. Aggressive behavior among preschoolers.

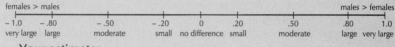

Your estimate: _____

2. Math computations by elementary school children, such as, what is 5×7?

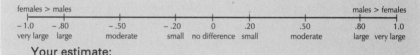

Your estimate: _____

3. Approval of a couple engaging in sexual intercourse when they are only casually acquainted.

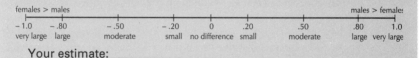

Your estimate: _____

How accurate were your respondents? Meta-analyses show that among preschoolers, males are more aggressive, $d = .58$. For accuracy of math computations by elementary school children, $d = -.20$; girls do somewhat better. For approval of a couple engaging in sexual intercourse when they are only casually acquainted, $d = .81$; males are more approving.

SOURCE: Based on Swim (1994).

of meta-analyses. For some characteristics—particularly for aggressive behavior and activity level—there was good evidence of a difference. For others—self-confidence, anxiety, helping, and empathy—there seemed to be a gender difference, but a smaller one, and the gender difference seemed to depend more on the situation or on the way in which the trait was measured.

The danger in focusing so much on gender differences is that we will start to think that males and females have entirely different personalities. Although there are some differences, as we have seen, what is perhaps more impressive are the similarities. Even for aggressive behavior, the gender difference is not large. And we have not even begun to discuss a long list of characteristics that have probably never shown a gender difference in anyone's research and have, therefore, been omitted from mention—for example, honesty, conscientiousness, sincerity. It is important to remember that *gender similarities* are probably more the rule than gender differences.

It is equally important to remember that gender differences often depend heavily on the *situation* or *context.* For example, as we saw in the section on helping behaviors, males are more likely than females to help in a situation that involves some personal danger, whereas females are more likely to engage in nurturant helping with children. Therefore, it makes no sense to refer to women as "the helping sex" or to men as "the aggressive sex." The gender difference found in one situation may not be found in another.

In the last sections of the chapter, we discussed androgyny as an alternative to traditional standards of masculinity and femininity. Twenty years after the concept of androgyny was introduced into psychology, I think we can say two things about it. First, it challenges our traditional notions of masculinity-femininity and suggests new ways of behaving that may be more adaptive and satisfying. That is good. Second, androgyny is not an instant remedy for all the gender-related injustices in society. Although it is an interesting and important concept, we cannot expect too much of it. Research and theorizing must move on.

Suggestions for Further Reading

Eagly, Alice H. (1987). *Sex differences in social behavior: A social role interpretation.* Hillsdale, NJ: Erlbaum. In this book Eagly articulates her social role theory of gender differences and summarizes many meta-analyses, including those on aggressive behavior, helping behavior, and influenceability.

Fiske, Susan T. (1993). Controlling other people: The impact of power on stereotyping. *American Psychologist, 48,* 621–628. This article describes the Supreme Court case on sex discrimination, *Price Waterhouse* v. *Hopkins,* and how Fiske's research on gender stereotyping was relevant.

4

Gender and Language

Gender Differences in Language Use

Body Language: Nonverbal
  Communication

How Women Are Treated in Language

Some Practical Suggestions

> *Women are the decorative sex. They never have anything to say, but they say it charmingly.*

OSCAR WILDE

Suppose you found the following caption, torn from a cartoon: "That sunset blends such lovely shades of pink and magenta, doesn't it?" If you had to guess the gender of the speaker, what would you say? Most people would guess that the speaker was a woman. Most of us have ideas about what is "appropriate" speech for males and females, and *lovely* and *magenta* just don't sound like things a man would (or should) say. In this chapter we shall explore the evidence on the differences between how women and men speak and communicate non-verbally, and on how women are treated in the English language.

Gender Differences in Language Use

The example given above illustrates certain stereotypes about men's and women's speech—namely, that women use adjectives like *lovely* and *magenta* and men don't. The noted linguist Deborah Tannen, in her widely read books such as *You Just Don't Understand: Women and Men in Conversation,* has popularized the belief that men and women essentially belong to different linguistic communities. That is, in some sense they don't speak the same language, leading to painful communication problems. What evidence exists on the actual speech patterns of women and men? Table 4.1 summarizes some of the differences. Details on research on these differences is provided in the following sections.

Tag Questions   Linguist Robin Lakoff (1973) originally hypothesized that women use more tag questions than men. A tag question is a short phrase at the end of a declarative sentence that turns it into a question. An example would be "This is a great game, isn't it?" The sentence about the sunset at the beginning of this chapter is another example.

Data have been collected to see whether Lakoff's ideas are correct (McMillan et al., 1977; see also Carli, 1990). College students participated in a group problem-solving task in either same-gender or mixed-gender groups of five to seven people. The discussions, which involved solving a mystery and which lasted 30 minutes, were tape-recorded, and later were coded and analyzed by the experimenters. They found that the women used about twice as many tag questions as the men, a difference that was statistically significant.

Using the terminology of Chapter 1, we have a statistical result that women use significantly more tag questions than men do. How should that finding be interpreted? The standard interpretation has been that men's tendency not to use tag questions indicates the self-confidence and forcefulness of their speech. Women's tendency to use tag questions is interpreted as indicating uncertainty or weak patterns of speech. As Lakoff put it,

TABLE 4.1

A Comparison of Women's and Men's Typical Speech Patterns

Women's Speech	Men's Speech
1. Goal: establish and maintain relationships	1. Goal: exert control, preserve independence, enhance status
2. Match experiences, show support ("I've felt that way, too")	2. Exhibit knowledge or skill, avoid disclosing personal information indicating one is vulnerable
3. Conversation maintenance ("How was your day?")	3. Conversational dominance (interrupting, greater talking time)
4. Responsiveness (nodding in response to another's talk)	4. Less responsive ("yeah")
5. Personal, concrete style	5. More abstract style
6. Tentativeness	6. Forceful, absolute, authoritative

SOURCE: Wood (1994).

> These sentence types provide a means whereby a speaker can avoid committing himself [*sic*], and thereby avoid coming into conflict with the addressee. The problem is that, by so doing, a speaker may also give the impression of not being really sure of himself, of looking to the addressee for confirmation, even of having no views of his own. (1975, pp. 16–17)

This interpretation implies that women's speech is somehow deficient, reflecting undesirable traits such as uncertainty. Are other interpretations possible? To interpret this difference in a way that would be more favorable to women, we might say that the tag question is intended to encourage communication, rather than to shut things off with a simple declarative statement. The tag question encourages the other person to express an opinion. Rather than reflecting uncertainty, women's greater use of tag questions may reflect greater interpersonal sensitivity and warmth (McMillan et al., 1977).

The researchers in the experiment discussed above attempted to determine which of these interpretations was more accurate (McMillan et al., 1977). They did this by comparing the use of tag questions in same-gender versus mixed-gender groups. They reasoned that if tag questions reflect uncertainty, then women should use more tag questions when men are present (mixed-gender groups) than when only women are present (all-female groups). This hypothesis was confirmed by the data, thus supporting the "greater female uncertainty" interpretation. However, the men in the study also used more tag questions in the mixed-gender groups than they did in the all-male groups. The researchers had not hypothesized this, as it did not seem that men should be more uncertain when women were present. Thus the interpretation of this gender difference is still unclear, and more sophisticated experiments will be necessary before a definitive statement can be made. The more important point to keep in mind, however, is that often alternative interpretations, one favoring men, the other favoring women, can be made of the same statistical results.

Tentativeness The tendency of women to use more tag questions is sometimes interpreted as indicating tentativeness and a decided lack of forcefulness. Two other gender differences in speech patterns that signal tentativeness have also been documented (Carli, 1990). Disclaimers are phrases such as "I may be wrong, but . . . " Hedges are expressions such as "sort of" or "kind of." Women are more likely than men to use disclaimers and hedges. Again, this may make women's speech seem tentative. On the other hand, it leaves the communication open for others to respond (Wood, 1994).

Intonation Say the phrase "Are you coming?" in a number of different ways. By varying the way you say it, you can convey a variety of feelings, from cheerful politeness to stern irritation. This is done by varying the intonation pattern, that is, the combination of high pitches plus low pitches.

Studies indicate that females and males tend to use somewhat different intonation patterns (Brend, 1971; McConnell-Ginet, 1978). Women are more likely to use intonation patterns of surprise, cheerfulness, and politeness. Further, men have only three contrasting levels of pitch in their intonation, whereas women have four; the additional level that women have is the highest one. The distinctive intonation patterns used by women are probably advantageous in allowing them to express a wider range of emotions. However, those patterns may also contribute to women's speech appearing emotional and high-pitched.

Correctness Some research indicates that women's speech tends to be more "correct" than men's (Haas, 1979; Thorne and Henley, 1975, p. 17). For example, in one study of the pronunciation of words ending in *-ing,* males pronounced it "in' " 62 percent of the time, compared with only 29 percent for females (Shuy, 1969). This gender difference has been found in both white and Black samples; that is, Black women's speech is more correct than Black men's (Haas, 1979). Generally, it seems that females' speech is closer to the normative speech of the culture, whereas males' is more likely to contain errors or subcultural forms (Kramer, 1974b).

Interruptions Researchers have repeatedly found that men interrupt women considerably more often than women interrupt men (McMillan et al., 1977; West and Zimmerman, 1983; Zimmerman and West, 1975). To give an idea of the magnitude of the difference, some data from one study are shown in Table 4.2. Notice that women interrupt women about as often as men interrupt men. However, women very seldom interrupt men, whereas men quite frequently interrupt women.

TABLE 4.2
**Mean Number of Interruptions per Half Hour
in Mixed-Gender Groups**

| | Gender of Interrupter | |
Gender of Interruptee	*Female*	*Male*
Female	2.50	5.24
Male	0.93	2.36

SOURCE: McMillan et al. (1977).

Once again, we have a statistical result that men interrupt women considerably more than women interrupt men. How should this gender difference be interpreted? The typical interpretation made by feminist social scientists involves the assumption that interruptions are an expression of *power* or *dominance*. That is, the interrupter gains control of a conversation, and that is a kind of interpersonal power. The gender difference, then, is interpreted as indicating that men are expressing power and dominance over women. This pattern may reflect the subtle persistence of traditional gender roles; it may also help to perpetuate traditional roles.

This power interpretation will also be discussed in the section on nonverbal communication later in this chapter. Such interpretations are central to feminist research and theory, as noted in Chapter 2.

Research also indicates that the content of interruptions varies as a function of gender. Men interrupt men with supportive comments, whereas they interrupt women with neutral or disagreeing remarks (Smith-Lovin and Brody, 1989).

Total Talking Time The stereotype is that women talk a lot more than men. Women are reputedly always gabbing on the telephone or chatting at the kitchen table with a neighbor.

What about the empirical data? Is this stereotype a real difference? In fact, there does seem to be a real difference, but it is just the opposite of the stereotype: in terms of total talking time, men talk more than women (Argyle et al., 1968; Strodtbeck et al., 1957; Swacker, 1975).

Talking time may also be interpreted as indicating dominance or power. One study examined couples who were living together (Kollock, Blumstein, and Schwartz, 1985). The power of each person relative to the other was assessed by self-report. Couples were then selected on the basis of these responses so that for half of them power was shared equally, whereas for the other half one person had more power. There were five male-female couples, five male-male couples, and five female-female couples. The results indicated that, overall, men talked more than women. However, women who had greater power in the couple talked more than their partner. Again, talking time may both reflect and perpetuate power.

Other Differences Some other gender differences in speech have been documented. For example, males use more hostile verbs than females do (Gilley and Collier, 1970). Women say more supportive words, such as *mm hmm* (Hirschmann, 1974, cited in Thorne and Henley, 1975, p. 231; Fishman, 1978; Haas, 1979). Generally, the differences fall along the lines one would expect from gender-role stereotypes.

The gender differences in language use that we have discussed are found rather consistently. Indeed, male-female differences in language are found in all cultures around the world (Bodine, 1975a). Nonetheless, it is important not to overestimate the extent of the differences. In many ways, females and males use essentially the same vocabulary and grammar. Thus, although certain features of male and female language differ, one would be unwise to say that there are separate female and male languages. Gender similarities are the rule in language just as they are in other behaviors (Kramer et al., 1978).

Body Language: Nonverbal Communication

The popularizers of the "body language" concept have pointed out that we often communicate far more with our body than with the words we speak. For example, suppose you say the sentence "How nice to see you" while standing only six inches from another person or while actually brushing up against him or her. Then imagine, in contrast, that you say the sentence while standing six feet from the person. The sentence conveys a much different meaning in the two instances. In the first, it will probably convey warmth and possibly sexiness. In the second case, the meaning will seem formal and perhaps cold. As another example, a sentence coming from a smiling face conveys a much different meaning from that of the same sentence coming from a stern or frowning face.

Here I shall present what evidence there is on whether there are differences between women and men in nonverbal styles of communication, and what those differences mean (for a good, detailed discussion, see Mayo and Henley, 1981; and for meta-analyses, see Hall, 1984).

Interpersonal Distance Generally it seems that in the United States, men prefer a greater distance between themselves and another person, whereas there tends to be a smaller distance between women and others. For example, women stand closer to other women in public exhibits than men do to men (Baxter, 1970). In another study, subjects seated themselves an average of 4.6 feet from a female stimulus person and an average of 8.5 feet from a male—that is, they sat about twice as far from the male as from the female (Wittig and Skolnick, 1978).

FIGURE 4.1
Men tend to keep a larger interpersonal distance between each other than
women do.

Meta-analyses indicate that these gender differences are moderately large. For women approaching others, $d = -.54$ (to use the statistics introduced in Chapter 3), and for others approaching women, $d = -.86$ (Hall, 1984).

How should these results be interpreted? One possibility is that women essentially have their personal space, or "territory," violated, and that this expresses dominance over them. On the other hand, an alternative interpretation would be that women have a small interpersonal distance as a result of, or in order to express, warmth or friendliness. More sophisticated research will be necessary to sort out these possibilities (see, for example, Wittig and Skolnick, 1978).

Smiling   Women tend to smile more than men. Meta-analysis indicates that the difference is moderately large (d = -.60) (Hall, 1984). Once again, however, it is not clear how this difference should be interpreted (LaFrance, 1981; Ragan, 1982). Smiling has been called the female version of the "Uncle Tom shuffle"— that is, rather than indicating happiness or friendliness, it may serve as an appeasement gesture, communicating, in effect, "Please don't hit me or be nasty."

FIGURE 4.2
Smiling is a part of the female role. Do women's smiles indicate happiness and friendliness, or are they forced because of role expectations?

Smiling seems to be a part of the female role. Most women can remember having their faces feel stiff and sore from smiling at a party or some other public gathering at which they were expected to smile. The smile, of course, reflected not happiness, but rather a belief that smiling was the appropriate thing to do. Women's smiles, then, do not necessarily reflect positive feelings and may even be associated with negative feelings. This pattern of smiling varies as a function of ethnicity; the pattern is more characteristic of white women than African American women (Halberstadt and Saitta, 1987).

One interesting study examined smiling in interactions between parents and children (Bugental et al., 1971). When fathers were smiling they tended to make more positive statements to their children, compared with when they were not smiling. Mothers' statements, on the other hand, were no more positive when they were smiling than when they were not. Parents, and particularly mothers, smiled more when they thought they were being observed than when they thought they were not being observed. This suggests that smiling is indeed part of a role people play. Finally, it seemed that children had learned to sort out the contradictory messages (smile accompanied by a negative statement) they got from their mothers; they ignored the smile and responded to the negative statement.

In another study, participants were given a written description of a person, accompanied by a photograph of a male or female who was smiling or not smiling (Deutsch et al., 1987). The results indicated that the women who were not smiling were given more negative evaluations: they were rated as less happy and less relaxed in comparison with men and in comparison with women who were smiling. The results indicate that people react negatively when women fail to perform this part of the female role.

Eye Contact Eye contact between two people when speaking to each other reflects patterns of power and dominance. In North American cultures, higher-status people tend to look at the other person while they (the dominant people) are speaking. Lower-status people tend to look at the other person while listening. Researchers in this area compute a *visual dominance ratio,* defined as the ratio of the percentage of time looking while speaking relative to the percentage of time looking while listening (Dovidio et al., 1988).

Social psychologist John Dovidio has done a series of studies investigating the connection between visual dominance and social power. His research indicates, for example, that patterns of visual dominance are expressed across different levels of military rank and different levels of educational attainment (e.g., Dovidio et al., 1988).

One of these experiments investigated visual dominance as a function of both gender and power (Dovidio et al., 1988). College students were assigned to mixed-gender dyads. Each pair discussed three topics in sequence. The first discussion was on a neutral topic and there was no manipulation of power. For the second topic, one member of the pair evaluated the other member and had the power to award extra credit points to that person. For the third topic, the roles were reversed, and the person who had been evaluated became the evaluator.

In the control condition, men looked at their partner more while speaking and women looked more while listening, as predicted based on considerations of the relative status or power associated with gender. However, in the second and third discussions, when women were in the powerful role, they looked more than men while speaking, and men looked more while listening. That is, when women were given social power, they became visually dominant. These results again support a power or status interpretation of gender differences in visual dominance. And, as women gain more power in society, patterns of visual dominance may well change.

How Women Are Treated in Language

To this point I have discussed women's communication styles, both verbal and nonverbal. The other aspect that needs to be addressed on the topic of women and language is how women and the concept of gender are treated in our language. Feminists have sensitized the public to the peculiar properties of terms like *man* used to refer to the entire species.[1] Here we shall discuss patterns that emerge in the way the English language treats women and concepts of gender.

Male as Normative   One of the clearest patterns in our language is the normativeness of the male, a concept discussed in Chapter 1 (Hamilton, 1991). The male is regarded as the normative (standard) member of the species, and this is expressed in many ways in language: for example, the use of *man* to refer to all human beings, and the use of *he* for a neutral pronoun (as in the sentence "The infant typically begins to sit up around six months of age; he may begin crawling at about the same time"). The male-as-normative principle in language can lead to some absolutely absurd statements. For example, there is a state law that reads, "No person may require another person to perform, participate in, or undergo an abortion of pregnancy against his will" (Key, 1975).

Sometimes students in their essays mistakenly use the phrase "the male species" (the expression they really mean to use is "the male of the species"). But in a way they are expressing the principle well—the male is the species.

At the very least, the male-as-normative usage introduces ambiguity into our language. When someone uses the word *men,* does *he* mean males, or does he mean people in general? When Dr. Karl Menninger writes a book entitled *Man Against Himself,* is it a book about people generally, or is it a book about the tensions experienced by males?

Some people excuse such usage by saying that terms like *man* are generic.

---

[1]Someone once commented cutely that feminists have a bad case of "pronoun envy" (Key, 1975).

Such an explanation, however, is not adequate. To illustrate how weak the "generic" logic is, consider the objections raised by some men who joined the League of Women Voters. They complained that the name of the organization should be changed, for it no longer adequately describes its members, some of whom are now men. Suppose in response to their objection they were told that by *woman* is meant "generic woman," which of course includes men. Do you think they would feel satisfied?

The male-as-normative principle is also reflected in the **female-as-the-exception phenomenon.** A newspaper reported the results of the Bowling Green State University women's swimming team and men's swimming team in two articles close to each other. The headline reporting the men's results was "BG Swimmers Defeated." The one for the women was "BG Women Swimmers Win." As another example, when the University of Wisconsin picked a new chancellor, the headline read, "UW Picks Woman Chancellor." It is hard to believe that had a man been chosen, the headline would have been "UW Picks Man Chancellor." His maleness would not have been considered newsworthy. The point is that we consider athletes and prestigious professionals to be normatively male. In cases where they are female it seems important to note this fact as an exception.

Female-as-the-exception phenomenon: If a category is considered normatively male and there is a female example of the category, gender is noted because the female is the exception. A byproduct of androcentrism.

Parallel Words   Another interesting phenomenon in our language is how parallel words for males and females often have quite different connotations (Key, 1975; Lakoff, 1973; Schulz, 1975). For example, consider the following list of parallel male and female words:

Male	*Female*
dog	bitch
master	mistress
bachelor	spinster
stud	slut

Note that the female forms of the words generally have negative connotations; a bachelor is viewed as a carefree, happy person, whereas a spinster is the object of pity. Also note that the negative connotation to the female words is often sexual in nature. For example, a man who is a master is good at what he does or is powerful, but a woman who is a mistress is someone who is financially supported in return for her sexual services.

Of course, many of these parallel words originally had equivalent meanings for male and female. An example is *master* and *mistress,* terms originally used to refer to the male and female heads of the household. Over time, however, the female term took on negative connotations, a process known as **pejoration.** Linguist Muriel Schulz (1975) has argued that this process is caused simply by prejudice. That is, terms applied to women take on negative meanings because of prejudice against women (see also Allport, 1954).

Pejoration: The process by which a term takes on negative connotations.

Euphemisms   Generally when there are many euphemisms for a word, it is a reflection of the fact that people find the word and what it stands for to be distasteful or stressful (Schulz, 1975). For example, consider all the various terms we use instead of *bathroom* or *toilet*. And then there is the great variety of terms such as *pass away* that we substitute for *die*.

Feminist linguists have argued that we similarly have a strong tendency to use euphemisms for the word *woman* (Lakoff, 1973; Schulz, 1975). That is, people have a tendency to avoid using the word *woman,* and instead substitute a variety of terms that seem more "polite" or less threatening, the most common euphemisms being *lady* and *girl*. In contrast to the word *man,* which is used quite frequently and comfortably, *woman* is used less frequently and apparently causes some discomfort or we wouldn't use euphemisms for it.

Infantilizing   A 25-year-old man wrote to an advice columnist, depressed because he wanted to get married but had never had a date. Part of the columnist's response was

> Just scan the society pages and look at the people who are getting married every day. Are the men all handsome? Are the girls all beautiful?

This is an illustration of the way in which people, rather than using *woman* as the parallel to *man,* substitute *girl* instead. As noted in the previous section, this in part reflects the use of a euphemism. But it is also true that *boy* refers to young males, *man* to adult males. Somehow *girl,* which in a strict sense should refer only to young females, is used for adult women as well. Women are called by a term that seems to make them less mature than they are; women are thus *infantilized* in language. Just as the term *boy* became very offensive to Black activists, so *girl* has become offensive to feminists.

There are many other illustrations of this **infantilizing** theme. When a ship sinks, it's "Women and children first," putting women and children in the same category. Other examples in language are expressions for women such as *baby, babe,* and *chick*. The problem with these terms is that they carry a meaning of immaturity and perhaps irresponsibility.

Infantilizing: Treating people, for example, women, as if they were children or babies.

How Important Is All This?   Although many of the tenets of the women's movement—such as equal pay for equal work—have gained widespread acceptance, the importance of changing our language to eliminate sexism has not. Many people regard these issues as silly or trivial. Just how important is the issue of sexism in language? (For a review, see Blaubergs, 1978.)

It is true that language reflects thought processes. This being the case, sexism in language may be the symptom, not the disease (Lakoff, 1973). That is, things like the generic use of *man* and *he* may simply reflect the fact that we do think of the male as the norm for the species. The practical conclusion from this is that what needs to be changed is our thought processes, and once they change, language will change with them.

On the other hand, one of the classic theories of psycholinguistics, the **Whorfian hypothesis** (Whorf, 1956), states that the specific language we learn influences our mental processes. If that is true, then things like the generic use of *man* make us think that the male is normative. This process might start with very young children when they are just beginning to learn the language. If such processes do occur, then social reformers need to pay careful attention to eliminate sexism in language because of its effect on our thought processes.

Whorfian hypothesis: The theory that the language we learn influences how we think.

An important study demonstrated that even when *he* and *his* are used in explicitly gender-neutral contexts, people tend to think of males (Moulton et al., 1978). College students were asked to make up stories creating a fictional character who would fit the theme of a stimulus sentence. The students were divided into six groups; for three of the groups, the stimulus sentence was as follows:

> In a large coeducational institution the average student will feel isolated in _____ introductory courses.

One of the groups received *his* in the blank space, another received *their,* and the third received *his or her.* The other three groups received one of those alternative pronouns in this stimulus sentence:

> Most people are concerned with appearance. Each person knows when _____ appearance is unattractive.

Averaging the responses of all groups, when the pronoun was *his,* only 35 percent of the stories were about females; for *their,* 46 percent were about females; and for *his or her,* 56 percent were about females. Females were chosen as characters more often for the second stimulus sentence (concerned about appearance) than for the first. But the important point is that even though a sentence referred to "the average student," when *his* was used most people thought of males. Though a linguist may say that *he* and *his* are gender neutral, they are certainly not gender neutral in a psychological sense.

It seems likely that both processes—thought influencing language and language influencing thought—occur to some extent. Insofar as language does have the potential for influencing our thinking, sexism in language becomes a critical issue (e.g., Martyna, 1980; Moulton et al., 1978).

I became interested in a related question raised earlier—namely, the effect of sexist language on children—and so I began a series of studies to investigate the question (Hyde, 1984a). First, I generated an age-appropriate sentence like the one used by Moulton and her colleagues and asked first-, third-, and fifth-grade children to tell stories in response to it:

> When a kid goes to school, _____ often feels excited on the first day.

As in the study by Moulton and her colleagues, one-third of the children received *he* for the blank, one-third received *they,* and one-third received *he or she.* The results were even more dramatic than those of Moulton and her colleagues with college students. When the pronoun was *he,* only 12 percent of the stories were about females. In fact, when the pronoun was *he,* not a single elementary school boy told a story about a girl. Clearly, then, when children hear *he* in a gender-neutral context, they think of a male. I also asked the children some questions to see if they understood the grammatical rule that *he* in certain contexts refers to everyone, both males and females. Few understood the rule; for example, only 28 percent of the first-graders gave answers showing that they knew the rule.

I also had the children fill in the blanks in some sentences such as the following:

> If a kid likes candy, _____ might eat too much.

The children overwhelmingly supplied *he* for the blank; even 72 percent of the first-graders did so.

This research shows two things. First, the majority of elementary school children have learned to supply *he* in gender-neutral contexts (as evidenced by the fill-in task). Second, the majority of elementary school children do not know the rule that *he* in gender-neutral contexts refers to both males and females and have a strong tendency to think of males in creating stories from neutral *he* cues. For them, then, the chain of concepts is as follows: (1) The typical person is a "he." (2) *He* refers only to males. Logically, then, might they not conclude that (3) the typical person is a male?

In a previous chapter we saw that girls have less self-confidence and lower expectations for success than boys do. I wonder whether part of that is due to language and the sort of thinking by children outlined above. Further research will be needed to test this speculation.

In a final task, I created a fictitious, gender-neutral occupation: wudgemaker.

> Few people have heard of a job in factories, being a wudgemaker. Wudges are made of plastic, oddly shaped, and are an important part of video games. The wudgemaker works from a plan or pattern posted at eye level as _____ puts together the pieces at a table while _____ is sitting down. Eleven plastic pieces must be snapped together. Some of the pieces are tiny, so that _____ must have good coordination in _____ fingers. Once all eleven pieces are put together, _____ must test out the wudge to make sure that all of the moving pieces move properly. The wudgemaker is well paid, and must be a high school graduate, but _____ does not have to have gone to college to get the job.

One-quarter of the children received *he* in all the blanks, one-quarter received *they,* one-quarter received *he or she,* and one-quarter received *she.* I then asked

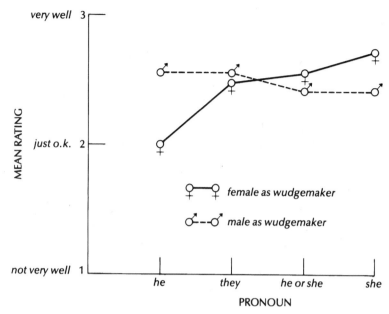

FIGURE 4.3

Children's ratings of the competence of women and men as wudgemakers, as a function of the pronoun they heard repeatedly in the description of the wudgemaker. Women are rated as having only medium competence when the pronoun is *he,* but their ratings rise for *they* and *he or she.* When *she* is used in the description, women are rated near the top of the scale. *(Source: Mean Rating Graph by Janet Hyde.* Developmental Psychology, 20, *697–706. Copyright © 1984 by the American Psychological Association. Reprinted by permission of the author.)*

the children to rate how well a woman could do the job on a 3-point scale: 3 for very well, 2 for just okay, and 1 for not very well. Next, I asked the children how well a man could do the job, giving ratings on the same scale. The results are shown in Figure 4.3. Which pronoun the children were given didn't seem to affect their ratings of men as wudgemakers, but the pronoun had a big effect on how women were rated as wudgemakers. Notice in the graph that when the pronoun *he* was used, women were rated at the middle of the scale, or just okay. The ratings of women rose for the pronouns *they* and *he or she,* and finally were close to the top of the scale when children heard the wudgemaker described as *she.* These results, then, demonstrate that pronoun choice does have an effect on the concepts children form; in particular, children who heard *he* in the job description thought that women were significantly less competent at the job than children who heard other pronouns did.

In another experiment, males remembered material better when it had been written with generic masculine forms, but females remembered it better when it had been written with gender-neutral forms (Crawford and English, 1984).

In answer to the original question of whether this pronoun business is really important, I think it is. We need to be concerned about the effects that sexist pronoun usage has on children; my research demonstrates that it can affect the concepts children form of occupations, and I think there is also reason for concern about its effect on broader issues, such as girls' self-confidence. Sexist language can even affect how much females can remember about a passage they've read.

One final bold experiment deserves discussion. To see what happens when pronoun usage changes away from the traditional sexist use of *he,* a psychologist used *she* as the generic pronoun with two of her child development classes, and compared the student responses with those of students in a class in which she did not follow this practice (Adamsky, 1981). Strikingly, students in the experimental group started using the generic *she* in their written essays. Although many people think that the sexist usage of pronouns in English cannot be changed, this study demonstrates convincingly that it can be. Here are some student responses (all are from female students) to use of the generic *she:*

> Once I started using the "she" I found it hard to stop. I liked using the generic "she"—it gave me a sense of equality—power even.

> I felt surprisingly proud when I used it.

> I could picture a female in roles so often pictured as strictly male. (Adamsky, 1981, pp. 777–778)

You might try using *she* as the generic form for a day and try to analyze the reactions, both in yourself and in others. It's a wonderful consciousness-raising device.

Some Practical Suggestions

Some people believe in theory that it would be a good idea to eliminate sexism from language, but in practice they find themselves having difficulty doing this in their speaking or writing. Here we shall discuss some practical suggestions for avoiding sexist language (for reviews, see Blaubergs, 1978; Miller and Swift, 1991) and for dealing with some other relevant situations.

Toward Nonsexist Language   The use of generic masculine forms is probably the most widespread and difficult problem of sexist language. The following are some ways to eliminate or avoid these usages.

One possibility is to switch from the singular to the plural, because plural pronouns do not signify gender. Therefore, the generic masculine in sentence 1 can be modified as in sentence 2:

1. When a doctor prescribes birth control pills, he should first inquire whether the patient has a history of blood clotting problems.

2. When doctors prescribe birth control pills, they should first inquire whether the patient has a history of blood clotting problems.

Another possibility is to reword the sentence so that there is no necessity for a pronoun, as in this example:

3. A doctor prescribing birth control pills should first inquire whether the patient has a history of blood clotting problems.

One of the simplest solutions is to use *he or she* instead of the generic *he, him or her* instead of *him,* and so on. Therefore, the generic masculine in sentence 1 can be modified as follows:

4. When a doctor prescribes birth control pills, he or she should first inquire whether the patient has a history of blood clotting problems.

Many feminist scholars, however, believe that the order should be varied, so that *he or she* and *she or he* appear with equal frequency. If *he or she* is the only form that is used, women still end up second!

One final possibility is the singular use of *they* and *their.* For years people have been saying sentences like "Will everyone pick up their pencil?" and English teachers have been correcting them, saying that the correct form is "Will everyone pick up his pencil?" Actually, singular *they* was standard usage in English until the late 1700s, when a group of grammarians decided it was wrong (Bodine, 1975b). Because it is so natural to use the plural in this situation, and to do so eliminates the sexism, why not go ahead and do it?

With a little practice, these strategies can be used to eliminate the generic masculine.

Space does not permit a complete discussion of all possible practical problems that may arise in trying to avoid sexist language. Usually a little thought and imagination can solve most problems. For example, the salutation in a letter, "Dear Sir," can easily be changed to "Dear Madam or Sir," "Dear Sir or Madam," "Dear Colleague," or simply "To Whom It May Concern." The tendency to use euphemisms for *woman* can be changed by becoming sensitive to this tendency and by making efforts to use the word *woman.*

One other solution to the problem of generic masculine pronouns should also be mentioned—namely, the creation of some new singular pronouns that are gender neutral. Unfortunately, at least ten alternatives for these new pronouns have been proposed, confusing the situation somewhat (Blaubergs, 1978). One set that has been proposed is *tey* for "he" or "she," *tem* for "him" or "her," and *ter* for "his" or "her." Thus one might say, "The scientist pursues ter work; tey

FOCUS 4.1
THE MS. STEREOTYPE

The concern in the last few decades over sexism in language use has prompted some suggestions for change. One form is the use of the title Ms. as an alternative to Miss or Mrs. The reasoning is that the female titles Miss and Mrs. indicate the woman's marital status, whereas the male title Mr. does not, and that women's marital status should not be highlighted more than men's. Ms. is the alternative that does not indicate a woman's marital status. But does its use indicate other things about the woman? And are those things primarily negative?

Psychologists Kenneth Dion and Albert Cota have conducted a series of studies to assess the stereotypes that people hold about women who use the Ms. title compared with the traditional Miss or Mrs. In one of these studies, they administered questionnaires to 230 adults from Canada and the United States, ranging in age from 17 to 80. In all cases, the participants were presented with a very brief description of a stimulus person, B. Moore, who is "21 years old and presently employed at a full-time job with a large corporation." One-third of the participants received the title Ms. for the stimulus person, one-third received Mrs., and one-third received Miss. Then participants rated their stimulus person on a series of personality dimensions from the Personal Attributes Questionnaire (PAQ). Two of the scales from the PAQ assessed instrumental ("masculine") qualities; one scale measured positive instrumental qualities (for example, independence), and the other scale measured negative instrumental qualities (for example, arrogance, boastfulness). The other two scales from the PAQ assessed expressive ("feminine") qualities; one scale measured positive expressive qualities (for example, being understanding of others), and the other measured negative expressive qualities (for example, spinelessness).

reads avidly and strives to overcome obstacles that beset tem." Entire books have been written with this usage (e.g., Sherman, 1978). Although in an ideal sense these new pronouns have a great deal of merit, they do not seem to be catching on. Probably they would need to be adopted by a number of respected, widely circulated sources in order to find their way into the ordinary person's language. If the *New York Times,* the *Washington Post, Time, Newsweek,* Dan Rather, and the president all started using *ter, tey,* and *tem,* these terms would probably have

The results indicated that when the woman's title was Ms., she was rated higher on both positive and negative aspects of instrumentality. Essentially she was thought to possess more masculine-stereotyped qualities than women with the title Miss or Mrs. But this association of Ms. with masculine qualities extended to both negative and positive qualities—that is, the Ms. stereotype is not entirely negative. The results also indicated that women identified as Ms. were rated lower on feminine, expressive qualities, both the positive and the negative ones.

Dion and Cota also varied whether the brief description indicated that the woman explicitly preferred Ms. (or Miss or Mrs.), or whether there was no mention of preference and the title was simply present. The results indicated that the stereotyped responses to Ms. occurred only in the condition in which participants were told that the woman had an explicit preference for Ms.

The Ms. title, then, evokes stereotyped responses from people, at least when there is an indication that the woman explicitly prefers this title. Women who are deciding what title they will use as, for example, they begin to build their careers, should consider these issues carefully. The use of Ms. may not necessarily evoke stereotypes of "women's libber"; instead, it may make the woman seem to be high on instrumental characteristics, which are precisely the qualities—at least the positive ones—that are crucial to success in the business world. Indeed, a recent survey of American women business executives under age 40 indicated that the majority preferred the title Ms.

SOURCE: Dion and Cota (1991).

a chance. Such widespread adoption does not seem to be a very immediate possibility, however.

This brings us to the topic of institutional change in language use.

Institutional Change   A number of institutions have committed themselves to using and encouraging nonsexist language. For example, several textbook publishers have issued guidelines for nonsexist language and refuse to publish books that include sexism (e.g., McGraw-Hill Book Company in 1974; Scott, Foresman and Company in 1972). The American Psychological Association requires the use of nonsexist language in articles in the journals it publishes (APA, 1994). The new *Webster's Dictionary* now has a policy of avoiding masculine generics and other forms of sexist language ("No sexism please," 1991). These are all good sources for the reader wanting more detail on how to eliminate sexist language.

Many occupational titles, particularly in government agencies, have also changed. For those who worry about the linguistic properties of nonsexist language, it is worth noting that some of the changes introduce definite improvements. For example, *firemen* has been changed to *firefighters*. In addition to being nonsexist, the newer term makes more sense, because what the people do is fight fires, not start them, as one might infer from the older term.

Language, Women, and Careers   The discussion of gender differences in language use in the first part of the chapter raises an important practical question for women aspiring to careers in male-dominated occupations such as business executive. From the data presented in that part of the chapter, it seems reasonable to conclude that the average woman has some language characteristics that suggest she is uncertain of herself or lacking in confidence. These are surely not qualities that help one get ahead in the business world. Should women attempt to modify their language on the job, much as African Americans speak standard English when the situation calls for it? And how should women modify their language?

One possibility is for women to become conscious of their "feminine" speech patterns, to eliminate them, and to substitute "masculine" ones. Women could stop using tag questions and high tones and start interrupting more. Although I have no data on the point, it is my opinion that this approach would probably not work very well, simply because many people feel threatened by "masculine" women. This approach also adopts male values and assumes that the male should be the norm.

As an alternative, I would suggest that women try to achieve androgynous speech—or perhaps a better term is *nonstereotyped speech*—that is, speech that has both the desirable qualities of "feminine" speech and the desirable qualities of "masculine" speech. Such speech would convey confidence and forcefulness together with a concern for the feelings of others. Such a combination of qualities should contribute to success in many careers.

On the other hand, women should not have to bear the burden of making all the changes. Men must become more conscious of the issues involved in sexist language and strive to use nonsexist, inclusive language.

One interesting experiment assessed the impact of women using traditional patterns of tentative speech compared with assertive speech (Carli, 1990). Participants listened to an audiotape of a persuasive speech delivered by either a woman or a man. On one of the tapes, the woman used many tag questions ("Great day, isn't it?"), hedges ("sort of"), and disclaimers ("I'm no expert, but . . . "), indicating tentativeness. On another tape, she used no tag questions,

EXPERIENCE THE RESEARCH

GENDER AND CONVERSATIONAL STYLES

Recruit four students, two men and two women not in this class, to participate. Pair one man and one woman together alone in a room and tell them that you are going to give them a topic to discuss and that you want to tape record their discussion to analyze it for a class. Be sure to obtain their permission to record the conversation, and assure them that you will not reveal to anyone the identity of your participants. Then give the pair a controversial topic to discuss—perhaps a current controversy on your campus or in national politics. Be sure that the topic is not gender stereotyped so that one person will feel superiority over the other. For example, "How good is the new quarterback on the football team?" would not be a good topic. "Would you vote for the new crime bill before Congress and why?" is a good topic. Tell them that you will record their discussion for about 10 minutes. You should remain in the room and note any observations you have of their discussion. Specifically, count the number of times each person nods in response to what the other is saying.

Repeat this procedure with the second male-female pair. You now have two tapes for data. Analyze the tapes in the following ways:

1. Count the number of times the man interrupted the woman and the woman interrupted the man. Did men interrupt women more than the reverse?
2. Count the number of tag questions (see text for explanation). Did women use more tag questions than men did? Having listened to their conversation, how would you interpret the difference you found? Were the women indicating uncertainty, or were they trying to encourage communication and maintain the relationship?
3. Count the number of hedges (e.g., "sort of"). Did women use more hedges than men?
4. Did women nod more in response to what men were saying or the reverse?

hedges, or disclaimers, thus indicating assertiveness. In the third tape, a man used tentative speech, and in a fourth tape, a man used assertive speech. The results indicated that the female speaker who used tentative speech was more influential to men than the assertive female speaker. For women listeners, the effect was just the reverse: They were more influenced by the woman using assertive speech than by the woman with tentative speech. Interestingly, men were equally influential whether their speech was tentative or assertive. Apparently men acquire their status and influence simply by being male; speech style makes little difference. But to return to the implications for women and careers, the results of this study indicate that changing from tentative to forceful speech for women is likely to have different effects, depending on whether the woman is speaking to a man or a woman. Tentative speech seems to work best with men, and assertive speech works best with women.

Suggestions for Further Reading

Miller, Casey, & Swift, Kate. (1991). *Words and women: New language in new times.* 2d ed., New York: HarperCollins. The authors, both professional journalists, have done an excellent job in this readable and thought-provoking review of the feminist critique of sexist language issues. They provide very useful suggestions for nonsexist language as well.

Tannen, Deborah. (1991). *You just don't understand: Women and men in conversation.* New York: Ballantine. Tannen is a noted linguistics expert, and this book on the communications gap has been a best-seller.

Tannen, Deborah. (1994). *Talking from 9 to 5: How women's and men's conversational styles affect who gets heard, who gets credit, and what gets done at work.* New York: Morrow. This is Tannen's latest book on gender and communications.

Wood, Julia T. (1994). *Gendered lives: Communication, gender, and culture.* Belmont, CA: Wadsworth. This is an excellent textbook on gender and communication, including verbal and nonverbal communication and the impact of the media.

5

From Infancy to Old Age: Development Across the Lifespan

*At age twelve I was among the first of my friends to begin
to menstruate and to wear a bra. I felt a mixture of pride
and embarrassment. For all of my life I had been a chubby,
introspective child, but a growth spurt of a few inches,
along with my developing breasts, transformed me one
summer into a surprisingly slim and shapely child-woman.
The funny thing was that on one level I had always known
this would happen. Yet it was as if a fairy godmother had
visited me. I felt turned on, but I was mostly turned on to
myself and the narcissistic pleasure of finding I was
attractive to boys.*

FROM OUR BODIES, OURSELVES

When my daughter was five, she loved to look at the family photograph albums.
She begged to see the pictures of herself as a baby or a two-year-old and to hear
the stories of the funny things she had done or said at that age. She nagged to see
the pictures of me dressed in my cowgirl outfit at age five and to hear how I had
wanted to be Dale Evans (Roy Rogers's other half) when I grew up. Then she tri-
umphantly announced, "But you didn't, you're a professor." She saw the picture
of me as an awkward-looking eight-year-old, dressed in a ballet costume for my
first dance recital, and we laughed together at how I still didn't dance very well.
She was fascinated, as most people are, with the process of psychological development—how different she was at five from the way she had been at two, how
different adults are from what they as children thought they would be, how predictable some things are from childhood to adulthood. In this chapter we shall
consider the development of female personality and roles across the lifespan.

Infancy

Psychologists have spent an extraordinary amount of time studying children, particularly preschoolers and infants. Studies of gender differences have been extensive. Investigations of infant gender differences have had two primary motives.
First, it has been thought that if gender differences were found in newborns—
say, when they are only one day old—those differences must surely be due to biological factors, because gender-role socialization can scarcely have had time to
have an effect. The idea, then, was to try to discover the biological causes of
gender differences by studying newborns. Second, many investigators think it is
important to study the way parents and other adults treat infants, in order to discover the subtle (and perhaps not-so-subtle) differences in the way adults treat
boy babies and girl babies, beginning the process of socialization at a tender age.
I shall review research in these two areas below.

Infant Gender Differences   Establishing what behaviors in infants show gender differences has the same complications as does establishing any gender difference (as discussed in Chapter 3). To this is added the further complication of trying to establish whether these differences really mean anything in terms of later behavior, in childhood or adulthood.

First, most infant behaviors do not show gender differences. That is, *gender similarities* are the rule for most behaviors. For example, in a study of infants at three weeks of age and again at three months, 12 behaviors were measured (Moss, 1967). At three weeks, only 6 of the 12 behaviors showed significant gender differences, and at three months, only 4 of the 6 behaviors still showed gender differences (males fussed more, were more irritable [cried and fussed], and were more often awake and passive, whereas females slept more). Only 4 of 12 variables, then, showed stable gender differences at three weeks and three months. The majority of behaviors showed gender similarities.

There are differences in *activity level,* with boys having the higher activity. In small infants, this may be measured by counting the number of times they swing their arms or kick their legs. In older babies, it might be measured by counting the number of squares the baby crawls across on a playroom floor. A major meta-analysis found that $d = +.29$ for gender differences in infants' activity level (Eaton and Enns, 1986.) That is, male infants are more active, but the difference is small. The difference is larger among preschoolers ($d = .44$) and older children ($d = .64$).

Some evidence does exist, then, for very early gender differences in at least one behavior, activity level. The next question is, What does this mean? The results by themselves are of little interest, except perhaps to a trivia expert. They become important if they predict later behavior, in childhood or adulthood. For example, if high activity level in infancy predicts hyperactivity in elementary school, then the higher activity level of infant boys might predict the greater incidence of hyperactivity and behavior problems that boys have in school (discussed in Chapter 15). To get evidence for this supposition, however, requires *longitudinal developmental research.* This means starting out with a group of infants and following them through their lives until they are adults. The research for a project of this type is very time consuming and costly, and so not much of it has been done. Further research in this area should be extremely informative.

Adults' Treatment of Infants   The other area of interest in infant research concerns whether, even at this early age, parents and other adults treat males and females differently.

Once again, *gender similarities* seem to be the rule; for the most part parents treat male and female babies similarly (Maccoby and Jacklin, 1974). Nonetheless, there do seem to be some differences. Boys are handled more roughly (Maccoby and Jacklin, 1974), and boys generally receive more responses from adults, such as being held by the mother (Lewis, 1972).

Some of these studies are based on direct observations of parent-child interactions, whereas others are based on parents' self-reports of their behavior toward their babies. The problem with this is that not only do parents influence infants, but infants also influence parents. Therefore, if there are differences in the behavior of boys and girls, these may cause the differences in parental treatment rather than the reverse. For example, if boys cry more, that may explain why they are held more.

A well-designed experiment, the *Baby X Study,* controlled these factors (Seavey et al., 1975; for a review of similar studies, see Stern and Karraker, 1989). The adult participants (all nonparents) were told they were taking part in a study on infants' responses to strangers. They were brought into an observation room and a three-month-old infant (actually a female) in a yellow jumpsuit was put on the floor in the room with them. One-third of the adults were told the baby was a boy, one-third were told she was a girl, and the other third were given no gender information. Three toys were near the baby—a small rubber football (a "masculine" toy), a Raggedy Ann doll (a "feminine" toy), and a plastic ring (a "neutral" toy). The interactions between the adult and the baby were observed from behind a one-way mirror for three minutes. The frequency of using each of the toys was recorded, and ratings were made of the behavior of the adults toward the infant. Afterward, the adults also rated their own impressions of the infant.

A number of interesting results emerged. With regard to choice of toy, there was an interaction between the gender of the adult and the gender-label of the baby. The results are shown in Table 5.1. The football was not really very popular in any condition, probably because a football does not seem to be a very appropriate toy for such a small baby. As expected, the doll was used most fre-

TABLE 5.1

Mean Frequency of Toy Choices for Babies by the Adults in the Baby X Study

		Toy		
Gender of Adult	*Baby Labeled*	*Football*	*Doll*	*Teething Ring*
Male	Boy	.33	.72	.61
	Girl	.50	1.61	.94
	No label	.85	.71	1.42
Female	Boy	.57	.71	1.00
	Girl	.50	1.27	1.05
	No label	.40	1.23	.70

SOURCE: From "Baby X: The effects of gender labels on adult responses to infants," by Carol Seavey et al., 1975, *Sex Roles,* 1. Published by Plenum Publishing Corporation. Reprinted by permission.

quently when the baby was introduced as a girl. On the ratings of the interactions, and on the adults' ratings of the babies, however, there were no significant differences depending on the label given to the baby. Some of the most interesting results came from the neutral-label group. Many of these adults inquired what the baby's gender was. Most of them had formed an opinion of what the baby's gender was by the end of the session (57 percent of men and 70 percent of women thought that it was a boy) and had stereotyped rationales for their beliefs. Those who thought the baby was a boy noted the strength of the grasp or lack of hair, whereas those who thought it was a girl remarked on the baby's roundness, softness, and fragility.

What can we conclude from this study? It would seem that gender is important in adults' interactions with children, something that is particularly evident when adults are not told a child's gender. However, the effects are not simple, and they may not be large. None of the ratings of the interactions showed gender-label effects. For example, the adults did not automatically give a football to the "boy." Further, the effects depended not only on the gender-label given the baby, but also on the gender of the adult.

In a related study, a videotape was made of a baby's emotional responses to the opening of a jack-in-the-box (Condry and Condry, 1976). The baby stared and then cried. The videotape was shown to adults, half of whom were told the baby was a boy and half of whom were told it was a girl. When the adults thought the baby was a boy, they labeled the emotions "anger," whereas they called the "girl's" emotions "fear." Our interpretations of emotions are stereotyped: What is anger in a male is fear in a female. Children, of course, are frequently given feedback by adults about the emotions they are feeling when they display reactions such as a frowning face. According to the results of this study, boys are taught that they are feeling anger and girls are taught that they are feeling fearful or anxious. These are powerful messages, and in this manner adults' treatment of infants and children may have a great impact.

Childhood

Gender Differences   Already by the early preschool years, several reliable gender differences have appeared. One is in *toy and game preference.* Preschool children between the ages of three and five have a strong preference for gender-typed toys and same-gender playmates (Martin and Little, 1990). What we don't know is what causes this early gender typing of activities or interests. It may be that it has some biological basis, because it appears so early. But it is also true that there has been a chance for several years of socialization to take place.

Another difference that appears early is in *aggressive behavior.* About as soon as aggressive behavior appears in children, around the age of two, there are gender differences; boys are more aggressive than girls. This difference persists throughout the school years (see Chapter 3).

Socialization: The process by which society conveys to the individual its expectations for his or her behavior, values, and beliefs.

Socialization   The forces of gender-role socialization become more prominent in childhood (Lips, 1989). **Socialization** refers to the ways in which society conveys to the individual its expectations for his or her behavior. The child's own immediate family may begin to have different expectations for her or him. For example, girls may be expected to help with the dinner dishes, boys to take out the garbage. A major meta-analysis of parents' gender-role socialization found that parents for the most part treat boys and girls similarly (Lytton and Romney, 1991). However, there was one major exception: encouragement of sex-typed activities, where the difference was large ($d = .71$ for preschoolers). There is strong evidence, then, that parents socialize their children toward sex-typed activities.

It is also true that there is considerable variation from one family to the next in the way children are socialized to gender roles. Very "liberated" parents may take great pains to give trucks to their daughters and dolls to their sons and to make sure that the mother and father share equally in childcare duties. A more traditional family will probably encourage more traditional roles.

One factor that creates variation both between and within families in socialization forces is the size of the family and the child's ordinal position among siblings (Sutton-Smith and Rosenberg, 1970). For example, girls with sisters, as compared with girls with brothers, are significantly more interested in "feminine" activities.

The *schools,* whether purposely or unwittingly, often transmit the information of gender-role stereotypes (Lips, 1989). I recently heard the story of a second-grade teacher urging on a little girl balking at doing a mathematics problem by saying, "You must learn to do your arithmetic so you'll be able to do the marketing for your husband when you grow up." Research based on classroom observations in preschools and elementary schools indicates that teachers treat boys and girls differently. Teachers, on average, pay more attention to boys (Golombok and Fivush, 1994). When teachers praise students, the compliments go to girls for decorous conduct and to boys for good academic performance (Dweck et al., 1980; Golombok and Fivush, 1994). When children make mistakes, boys are given more precise feedback and are encouraged to keep trying until they get it right; girls are more likely to be told not to worry about the mistake, and teachers spend less time with them suggesting new approaches. Girls are more often not told even whether their answers are right or wrong (Sadker and Sadker, 1985).

As we will see repeatedly throughout this book, both gender and ethnicity are factors, in this case in predicting teachers' interactions with students (e.g., Irvine, 1985, 1986). One study replicated the finding that white girls receive significantly less communication from teachers than white boys do (Irvine, 1985). In contrast, in the early elementary grades (K through 2), Black girls receive as much feedback from the teacher as Black boys do (Irvine, 1986). However, by the later grades (3 through 5), Black girls are receiving less attention than Black boys; they have been molded into the invisibility found among white girls. The researcher suggested that this developmental pattern occurs because Black girls are not socialized by their parents to be passive in the same way that white girls are, so that Black girls are assertive when they enter school in kindergarten. However, by the later grades they have assumed the same passive roles as white girls.

The *media* are powerful socializing agents. Many people assume that things have changed a lot in the past 20 years and that gender stereotypes are a thing of the past. On the contrary, an analysis of the Sunday comics in 1974 and again in 1984 indicated that not much has changed (Brabant and Mooney, 1986). Males were still depicted more often—in 67 percent of the strips in 1974 and 74 percent in 1984, compared with women's 52 percent in 1974 and 59 percent in 1984. That is, men were more visible and women were less visible. Women were shown in the home in 69 percent of the strips in 1974, compared with 32 percent for men; in 1984 the numbers had hardly changed—72 percent for women and 33 percent for men. The domestic role is still most prominent for females.

An analysis of children's picture books published between 1937 and 1989 showed that 26 percent of the pictures showed female characters, compared with 74 percent showing male characters—females were simply less visible (Crabb and Bielawski, 1994; see also Kortenhaus and Demarest, 1993). In addition, female characters were considerably more likely to be shown holding household items (e.g., a broom), although males were increasingly shown with such objects. Males were considerably more likely to hold items such as plows and guns, and the proportion of females with such objects showed no change over time. Stereotyping, then, is very much present in children's picture books.

Analyses of gender in television programs indicated that, in the 1950s, male characters outnumbered female characters two to one; a recent analysis showed that today, male characters still outnumber female characters two to one (Davis, 1990). Some change is so slow that there's no change at all!

Television—both the programs and the commercials—continues to show stereotyped roles (Bretl and Cantor, 1988; Kalisch and Kalisch, 1984). An analysis of television commercials from 1971 to 1985 indicated that in 1971, 89 percent of the commercials were narrated by men; in 1985, 91 percent were (Bretl and Cantor, 1988; see also Lovdal, 1989). The voice of authority is male, with no change over 14 years. In the meager 9 percent of commercials with female narrators, the woman spoke not to the TV viewing audience, but rather to dogs, cats, babies, and female dieters (Lovdal, 1989). On the other hand, there have been some trends away from stereotyping (Bretl and Cantor, 1988). For example, men are increasingly being shown in the role of spouse or parent in commercials.

The stereotyping of television messages has been demonstrated to have an actual effect on children's behavior. In one study, four- to six-year-old children viewed a film similar to "Sesame Street" shows in which Muppet-like characters said that a set of toys belong to a boy; another group of children saw the same film, except that the characters said the toys were a girl's; and a third group of children saw a version of the film in which the characters said the toys could be for either boys or girls (Cobb et al., 1982). After viewing the film, children played more with the toys that had been described as gender appropriate for

FIGURE 5.1
Research indicates that children's books continue to show children in traditional gender-stereotyped activities, such as girls doing household chores (Top left), and boys doing outdoor work (Top right). More illustrations are needed showing children involved in non-traditional activities (Bottom).

them. In the condition in which the toys were described as being appropriate for both boys and girls, the children preferred those toys (compared with toys not shown in the film). This result suggests that children can respond positively to nonstereotypical messages on television.

School It seems that girls make the adjustment to school with greater ease than boys do. Boys are referred to principals, psychologists, or guidance counselors for serious behavioral problems about ten times more frequently than girls are (Golombok and Fivush, 1994). This is due in part to the fact that the incidence of hyperactivity is far higher in boys than in girls; the common estimate is that boys outnumber girls by about four to one (Holborow and Berry, 1986). (Note how this contrasts with adjustment problems in adulthood; see Chapter 14.) Girls' interactions with teachers, in contrast, seem to be more pleasant and less full of conflict.

Tomboys   Despite the results on gender differences and socialization, not every girl conforms. One study found that 63 percent of a group of junior high girls said they were tomboys, and 51 percent of a sample of adult women recalled having been tomboys in childhood (Hyde et al., 1977). Not every girl, then, is staying at home playing with dolls. In fact, probably the majority are engaging in the active games that have traditionally been called "masculine." Perhaps tomboyism is simply childhood's version of androgyny (Hemmer and Kleiber, 1981).

Although many social critics emphasize the restrictiveness of girls' socialization, stereotype-inconsistent behavior is probably far less tolerated for boys than it is for girls. Many parents tolerate their daughters climbing trees and playing baseball, but get upset at a son playing with dolls. It is, after all, far worse to be a sissy than to be a tomboy. As one investigator commented,

> . . . demands that boys conform to social notions of what is manly come much earlier and are enforced with much more vigor than similar attitudes with respect to girls. (Hartley, 1959, p. 458)

It seems, then, that particular areas exist in which there are gender differences in childhood, and that socialization does occur to some extent. However, gender similarities are the rule, and many girls are allowed a great deal of freedom and are encouraged to achieve in school. Severe gender-role pressures probably do not come until adolescence. But in a sense, this may be even more difficult for the girl than consistent gender-role restrictions would be. Throughout most of her childhood she is free to pursue achievements, and only later is she told that continuing these behaviors is not appropriate.

Adolescence

If the behavior and development of males and females are so similar for about the first ten years of life, how do the gender differences in adult personality and roles arise? In the early years, girls do better in school and have fewer adjustment problems than boys. Yet adult women, on the average, have lower-status jobs than men (Chapter 7) and have a higher incidence of certain kinds of adjustment problems (Chapter 14). Although the groundwork for these differences is prepared in childhood, the real precipitating factors most likely occur in adolescence. These will be discussed below.

Femininity-achievement incompatibility: The cultural belief that, beginning in adolescence, achievement is not appropriately feminine for girls.

The Femininity-Achievement Incompatibility   In adolescence, a cultural rule starts to be enforced on the girl: **femininity-achievement incompatibility**—that is, to achieve is gender inappropriate. If the girl continues to achieve she will be unfeminine, and to be feminine is not to achieve. The girl is caught in a situation in which two equally important systems of values are in conflict. One is the desire for a positive sense of self, the sense that one is a worthwhile,

FIGURE 5.2

In early adolescence, the girl learns that her status will be determined by her attractiveness, not her achievements.

productive person. Achieving, getting good grades, and excelling have been encouraged and rewarded so far, providing a major avenue for establishing the self as having worth and value. But the reward system changes abruptly at adolescence. The competing system is the desire to be a good female, to conform to gender-role expectations, and to be feminine, with whatever rewards that carries. The desire to be a competent, worthwhile person is now incompatible with the desire to be good in the female role; but society at large does not value the female role.

The situation is actually a bit more complex because not all achievements are considered gender inappropriate for girls. It is perfectly acceptable to be preparing to be a nurse or teacher, but achievement in male-stereotyped areas—such as being a welder or car mechanic—is inappropriate and subject to sanctions (e.g., Cherry and Deaux, 1978).

The reward system may change in adolescence for either or both of two reasons. One is that heterosexual relationships, popularity, and dating rise to importance; thus the peer group may begin enforcing the rules of the femininity-achievement incompatibility. Parents, too, may change their teachings as they begin to see popularity and marriageability as important for their daughter. The timing of the change in the parents' emphasis, of course, varies greatly from one family to the next. In one, the girl may be urged to stop studying and to start having boyfriends when she is in sixth grade, whereas in another, achieving a college education will be viewed as far more important than dating, and the parents do not begin asking about marriage prospects until the young woman announces that she is going to go to graduate school and get a Ph.D.

Data on the changing social emphases at adolescence and their impact on the girl are rather slim. One study compared preadolescent (fifth-grade) girls and adolescent (tenth-grade) girls on a measure of gender-role stereotyping. The tenth-grade girls had significantly higher stereotyping scores, indicating that the tenth-grade girls rated women significantly lower than men on socially valued traits related to competence (Baruch, 1975).

Perhaps most relevant is a study of the self-concept of students in the third through twelfth grades (Rosenberg and Simmons, 1975). The results indicated that gender differences were small among the younger children and that striking gender differences emerged during adolescence. At that time, girls became more self-conscious than boys; the adolescent girls were increasingly people oriented, whereas the adolescent boys stressed achievement and competence. In another study, high school juniors and seniors were asked whether they would most like to be independent, successful, or well liked (Rosenberg, 1965). Adolescent girls emphasized being well liked (60 percent compared with 35 percent of the boys), whereas boys were much more likely to stress success (46 percent compared with 29 percent).

Certainly the origin of the *double-bind* for females lies in the conflict between achievement and femininity (Horner, 1970a, 1972). The adolescent girl is caught in a classic double-bind situation in which she wants both of two alternatives, but the two alternatives are incompatible. She wants both to be feminine and to achieve, but the two are perceived as being incompatible. Certainly here would appear to be the origins of much of the *ambivalence* and conflict that females face—the adolescent girl finding it difficult to combine, because of imposed cultural contingencies, being a worthwhile individual and being a proper female (Broverman et al., 1972; Earle and Harris, 1985). In this we see one source of the adjustment problems some adult women have.

Dating and Friendship   The rituals of dating are also an important force influencing adolescent female personality development. Competition against other girls for the attention of boys becomes essential to success; other females become the enemy. The competition is in itself somewhat frustrating because the competitor must remain passive in such an important battle; the girl is not supposed to directly choose the boy and call him for a date. On the other hand, the passive aspects of this social interaction for the female should not be overemphasized. The techniques displayed by many teenage girls in their attempts to attract male attention are about as passive as a three-ring circus complete with wild animals and neon lights.

One rule that becomes quickly apparent in the dating game is that females are valued for their appearance, males for their achievements. This phenomenon has been documented in a number of social psychology studies (Jackson, 1992). For example, in one study snapshots were taken of college women and men (Berscheid et al., 1971). A dating history of each person was also obtained. Judges then rated the attractiveness of the women and men in the photographs. For the women there was a fairly strong relationship between attractiveness and popularity; the women judged more attractive had had more dates in the prior year than the less attractive women. There was some relationship between appearance and popularity for men, but it was not so marked as it was for women. In a long-term study, high school girls were rated as to the attractiveness of their appearance (Udry and Eckland, 1984). Fifteen years later, the more attractive the adolescent, the more "successful" she had been in getting a husband. The most beautiful girls had married well-to-do, successful men. For men, interestingly, the relationship was reversed: the males who had been the least attractive in high school now had the most education and the highest occupational status. It seems that a woman's status is determined by her appearance, a man's by his achievements.

Another noticeable phenomenon among adolescent girls is the formation of girl-groups or cliques, tight-knit groups of girls engaging in mutual sharing and often more than a little plotting. It has been suggested that these groups are important in learning social definitions of femininity and in learning about sexual impulses (Douvan and Adelson, 1966). Unfortunately, the latter function, at least, is not as well served for girls, who are less likely than boys to exchange sexual information (Kinsey et al., 1953).

Women's friendship patterns in adulthood have attracted quite a bit of research attention recently, and some of the results will be discussed later in this chapter.

The Search for Identity   According to Erik Erikson (1950), adolescence is the stage in which the primary developmental crisis is a quest for identity. For the male, adult identity will be defined largely in occupational terms (Angrist, 1969)—"I am a doctor." Adolescence and the growing identity then become a preparation for this adult identity—"I must start to take science courses and become a responsible student in order to become a doctor."

For the adolescent girl, however, this process seems to be considerably different. Traditionally, girls did not anticipate that work outside the home would be a major source of identity for them (Douvan, 1970). Even today, college women often say they are preparing themselves to be teachers or social workers, not because they want to educate the minds of youth or do good works for humanity, but rather so that they "will have something to fall back on" (in case of unexpected widowhood or divorce). Job or occupation is simply not seen as a major source of identity. Instead, the main priority is still family (Greenglass and Devins, 1982) and the major source of identity is the husband and later the children—that is, the wife-mother role. The man sees himself as a doctor; the woman sees herself as a doctor's wife.

A 1985 study of senior women at the University of California at Berkeley was entitled "Talking Career, Thinking Job," expressing the notion that young women of today talk about having careers, but the details of their life expectations are still so traditional that the expectations are consistent with having a job, not a career (Machung, 1986). For example, 31 percent of the women in the survey indicated that they planned to interrupt work from 1 to 5 years to stay home with young children, and an additional 17 percent planned to be off between 6 and 17 years—that is, approximately half planned major interruptions, and that is something one can do with a job, but usually not with a career. The expectations for division of labor were traditional: 62 percent of the women (but only 6 percent of the men, who were also surveyed) expected to have primary responsibility for making daycare arrangements for their children, and 54 percent of the women (but only 13 percent of the men) expected to take primary responsibility for missing an important meeting at work when a child was sick. And 54 percent of the women (and 63 percent of the men) expected the husband's job to have top priority. Research indicates that although college women have been expanding their career options into areas that were traditionally male dominated, there has been little reciprocal change in thinking about the primacy of mothering (Baber and Monaghan, 1988). Perhaps there shouldn't have to be such trade-offs. Nonetheless, college women probably do not have very realistic notions about the work/family dilemmas faced by adult women today (see Chapter 7). They unrealistically think they can simultaneously fulfill the traditional role of wife and mother while still having an exciting career, without having to make hard choices along the way.

In the late adolescent period, when the male is actively striving to develop an adult identity, we see the female postponing identity formation in an attempt to maintain a flexible identity that can adapt itself to the as-yet-unknown husband (Angrist, 1969). Forming a distinctive identity might make the girl unmarriageable. For example, a girl may decide to become the best nuclear physicist in the world. But if she later meets the man of her dreams, with the one exception that he has no plans to be married to the world's best nuclear physicist, she may have eliminated a good marriage prospect for herself. Shirley Angrist (1969) uses the term *contingency training* to describe this phenomenon. Flexibility is built into women's personalities in the socialization process by contingency training. A woman lives by adjusting to and preparing for anticipated and unanticipated contingencies: the unknown qualities of the future husband, lack of guarantee of marriage, possible economic necessity of work, possible childlessness, children leaving home, and divorce or widowhood. For the adolescent female, the marriage/unknown-husband contingency is certainly the most salient (Psathas, 1968). Although flexibly moving from one job to another or in and out of the work force may be a detriment to professional achievement (Chapter 7), in other areas flexibility may be very valuable. If contingencies are truly beyond one's control, the ability to adapt is very functional.

Today, then, it seems that three alternative female identity patterns have emerged (Dellas and Gaier, 1975):

1. Traditional role and stereotype—Awaiting marriage

2. Achievement and role success—Achievement in valued areas of our andro-centric society

3. Bimodal identity—Commitment to family and career

Unfortunately, none of these three alternatives escapes the double-bind (Denmark and Goodfield, 1978) that will remain as long as there is an incompatibility between femininity and achievement. The adolescent girl who chooses the traditional role today may find herself and others wondering why she didn't accomplish more in the world of work (Luria, 1974). The girl who chooses the achievement-oriented identity will be questioned for her lack of husband and children. And the girl who chooses the bimodal identity will suffer the pulls between the conflicting areas of her life (Hodgson and Fischer, 1981).

Self-Esteem One of the major changes for girls in adolescence is in self-esteem. In 1991, the American Association of University Women (AAUW) released a report entitled *Shortchanging Girls, Shortchanging America.* Based on interviews with 3,000 school-aged girls and boys, the report revealed declines in self-esteem for both boys and girls during adolescence, but a much sharper drop for girls. On one item, for example, 60 percent of elementary school girls and 69 percent of elementary school boys said they were "happy the way I am." But by high school, girls' agreement with that statement fell to 29 percent, compared with 46 percent for boys.

These effects vary as a function of ethnicity. Among African American girls in elementary school, 65 percent said they were "happy the way I am," and this percentage remained high, at 58 percent, in high school. African American girls, then, do not seem to suffer the adolescent loss of self-esteem that white girls do. However, Hispanic girls seem to go through a crisis that is at least as striking as that of white girls. In elementary school, 68 percent of Hispanic girls say "I am happy the way I am," compared with 30 percent in high school.

The AAUW report concluded that gender inequity in the schools was a major force diminishing girls' self-esteem. Creating gender-fair classrooms is the key in reversing these negative trends (AAUW, 1991).

In sum, although I have suggested that development may be quite similar in females and males during infancy and childhood, adolescence represents a major divergence. The expectations for the girl suddenly change and become conflicting: Achievement is not rewarded as it was formerly, femininity is demanded, and achievement and femininity are seen as being incompatible, creating a double-bind, or ambivalence, for girls. Later in adolescence, identity formation becomes a key process, but the contingencies are such that it may not occur at this stage and may instead be postponed. There is also evidence of serious losses of self-esteem for adolescent girls, at least among whites and Hispanics.

Early Adulthood

Wife, Housewife, Mother   The wife and mother roles are important to the identity of many adult women.

The relationship between marriage and women's adjustment is complex (Voydanoff and Donnelly, 1989). For example, depression is greatest among women with strained marriages, intermediate for unmarried women, and least for women in happy marriages (Aneshensel, 1986).

Sociologist Ann Oakley (1974) did a major study on housewives and their feelings about housework. The basic assumption of her study—that housework could be thought of and analyzed as work—was an unusual one because the general public, as well as social scientists, has tended to think that housework is not really work. The traditional logic goes like this:

1. Women belong in the family, whereas men belong "at work."

2. Therefore men work, and women do not work.

3. Therefore housework is not a form of work. (Oakley, 1974, p. 25)

FIGURE 5.3
Will this marriage last? Statistics indicate that 50 percent of today's marriages will end in divorce. One implication is that women need to have the education and skills necessary to support themselves.

Oakley believes that housework is a form of work just like any other job, except that it is not paid. She found that housewives are sensitive to the categorization of their work as nonwork. As an ex-typist put it:

> I think housewives work just as hard. I can't stand husbands who come home and say, "Oh look you've done nothing all day, only a bit of housework and looked after the child." But I reckon that's tiring myself, well, not tiring, it's just as hard as doing a job—I don't care what any man says. . . . My husband says this—that's why I feel so strongly about it. (Oakley, 1974, p. 45)

In general, Oakley found that housework evokes a mixture of feelings, but dissatisfaction predominates: 70 percent of the London housewives she interviewed were dissatisfied with housework. The common reasons for dissatisfaction were monotony, loneliness, lack of structure, and long hours. The average woman spent 77 hours per week on housework. The smallest number of hours spent on housework by any woman in Oakley's sample was 48 hours per week, and that was reported by one of the women who was employed full-time outside the home. Some women also commented on the unconstructive nature of housework—for example, every morning the housewife makes the beds, which will only be unmade that evening and have to be made again the next morning.

Autonomy—being one's own boss—was the most valued part of the housewife role. An ex–computer programmer put it this way:

> To an extent you're your own master . . . you can decide what you want to do and when you want to do it . . . it's not like being at work when somebody rings you up and you've got to go down and see them or you've got to do this and that within half an hour. (Oakley, 1974, p. 42)

The women's previous experiences with jobs outside the home were related to their satisfactions or dissatisfactions with housework. Specifically, women who had previously had high-status jobs (computer programmer, fashion model) were all dissatisfied with housework.

A recent study of houseworkers (a few of whom were men) compared with paid workers reached generally similar conclusions (Bird and Ross, 1993). Housework was reported to seem very routine and offered little intrinsic gratification. Neither did it yield many extrinsic rewards such as money or recognition. The most positive aspect reported by houseworkers was a sense of autonomy.

The women in Oakley's study differed from one another in the extent of their personal identification with the housewife role. Those who were highly identified with it tended to structure the job by establishing routines (Monday is the day we wash our clothes, Tuesday we iron them . . .) and by setting high standards for the work. A critical factor in shaping high or low identification with housework was the identification with that role modeled by the woman's own mother. Many women have told me of the guilt they experience as they walk out the door, leaving a messy kitchen; the guilt is related to an almost tangible ghost of one's own mother sitting on one's shoulder saying, "Bad, bad, bad." Women need to analyze their own identification with the housewife role and how this was shaped by their mothers. They can then begin to analyze how they can experience more satisfaction—or at least less guilt—in regard to housework. Personally, I am very grateful that my own mother was a feminist long before it was fashionable to be one. She saw housework as something to be gotten done as quickly as possible, through using one's wits, so that one could do more satisfying things, like playing the piano. As a result, I think, I rarely experience the housework "guilt ghost." Right on, Mom!

The mother role is probably the most satisfying part of the traditional complex of female roles. Even here, however, there may be problems. The feeding demands of small infants leave many mothers constantly exhausted, and it is not until infants are several months old that they can respond with one of their heartwarming smiles. Interactions with young children are stimulating in their own way, but many women feel a need for some interactions with other adults during the day. Research shows that although marriage and employment are both generally associated with positive adjustment for women, parenthood is generally associated with greater psychological distress (McLanahan and Adams, 1987).

Motherhood is so basic an assumption of the female role that it is easy to forget that society pressures women to be mothers; indeed, the pressure is so strong that the situation has been called the **motherhood mandate** (Russo, 1979). And, in fact, 90 percent of ever-married American women have had at least one child (Etaugh, 1993). Consistent with the idea of a motherhood mandate, research indicates that people who choose to be childless tend to be viewed as poorly adjusted and misguided (Peterson, 1983; but see Shields and Cooper, 1983, for contradictory evidence). Interestingly, however, married couples without children report greater happiness than married couples with children do (Campbell et al., 1975).

Motherhood mandate: The cultural belief that all women should have children, that is, be mothers.

Whether or not a woman wants children and how many children she wants can be predicted by a number of factors; her memory of her mother's love in early childhood, a feminine gender-role identification, and antifeminist attitudes are all related to a desire to have children (Gerson, 1980). Also, women from large families—women having three or more siblings—express more desire for children than women from smaller families do (Gerson, 1980).

One option that is being recognized increasingly is *voluntary childlessness.* Terminology makes a difference here. Some reject the term *childless,* which may seem to imply some sort of deficit, in favor of *child-free.* Research shows that women arrive at the decision to remain childless through different paths. Some women arrive at the decision fairly early in life, perhaps even before marriage; they are called "early articulators" (Houseknecht, 1979). Others marry and postpone the decision many times, finally deciding for childlessness relatively late; these are called "postponers." Both of these groups of voluntarily childless women tend to be high in autonomy and achievement orientation (Houseknecht, 1979). A high level of autonomy or independence would be expected from these women because they have been able to make a decision that goes against a great deal of societal pressure. The high levels of achievement orientation also make sense: These women tend to want high levels of achievement in their careers, which may seem incompatible with having children. Early articulators differ from postponers in some ways. In particular, early articulators tend to report less warmth in their families when growing up and less compatibility of attitudes with their parents. Perhaps they have no desire to re-create a family situation that was not particularly pleasant for them, and thus they make the decision to remain childless early. Research also shows that a supportive reference group is extremely important to women making the decision to remain childless (Houseknecht, 1979). For example, a young woman in her second year of medical school may begin to think that it would be impossible to maintain a medical practice and rear children. If she has many women friends who are also medical students and are also reaching similar conclusions, and who offer her positive support for her decision, she is more likely to decide to be child-free.

Women and Work   The work role is increasingly important for adult women. For that reason, I have devoted an entire chapter to the topic of women and work (see Chapter 7) and will postpone discussion until then.

Divorce   Between 1970 and 1980, the divorce rate in the United States more than doubled, rising to more than one million divorces each year (Arendell, 1987). But then divorce rates leveled off in the 1980s and show no signs of increasing in the 1990s. Among marriages today, approximately 50 percent will eventually divorce (Cherlin, 1992). On the other hand, remarriage rates are high; 70 to 75 percent of divorced women remarry (Norton and Moorman, 1987). These statistics vary as a function of ethnicity. For example, among women born in the 1950s, 91 percent of white women, compared with 75 percent of Black women, will ever marry (Cherlin, 1992). Divorce rates also differ; 47 percent of married Black women separate or divorce within ten years of marriage, compared with 28 percent of non-Hispanic whites, and 26 percent for Mexican Americans (Cherlin, 1992). For remarriage rates, 32 percent of Black women remarry within ten years of divorce or separation, compared with 72 percent for non-Hispanic whites and 53 percent for Mexican Americans. Black women, then, are less likely to marry, more likely to divorce, and less likely to remarry (Cherlin, 1992).

A study of women and divorce by sociologist Lenore Weitzman (1986) has attracted a great deal of attention. She found that divorced women and their children are becoming the new underclass; whereas divorced men experience a 42 percent increase in their standard of living, divorced women experience a 73 percent decrease. These are the unintended consequences of no-fault divorce, which in the 1970s was thought to be a positive for women. The problem is that divorce settlements often make the liberated assumption that women will go out and become self-sufficient earners, ignoring the great disparity between women's wages and men's wages in the United States. In short, no-fault divorce has been an economic disaster for those women who do not have professional training, job skills, or strong work experience. I don't mean to suggest, of course, that no-fault divorce is all bad for women. For example, it makes it easier for a woman to get out of a marriage in which she is battered. Weitzman's statistics have also been criticized for exaggerating divorced women's economic decline (Faludi, 1991). A decline of 33 percent—not 73 percent—is probably more accurate (Duncan and Hoffman, 1988). But a 33 percent decline in standard of living is not exactly pleasant, either.

In addition to financial stress, divorced women experience stresses in a number of other areas (Etaugh, 1993). Divorced people are generally perceived somewhat negatively and are considered to be less stable, less reliable, and less satisfied than married people. And, indeed, divorced women do typically experience an emotional upheaval in the months leading up to, and the year following, a divorce. They report feeling anxious, depressed, angry, rejected, and incompetent.

They also may experience role strains and role overload. They may have to manage a household by themselves, including doing tasks such as repairs that the husband may have done previously. Divorced women with children may feel that their social life has become extremely limited and that they are socially isolated from other adults.

Support from family and friends is extremely important in helping women adjust following divorce (Etaugh, 1993).

The Single Woman   It is difficult today to comprehend how radical the concept of the "Mary Tyler Moore Show" was when it began in 1970 (Atkin, 1991). This TV show was about an attractive, bright woman in her thirties who was *happily single,* and who never, in the course of the series, got married. The concept of a woman being purposely single and being happy was a new one.

In the 1960s, the number of high school and college women who did not intend to marry was about 5 to 6 percent (Douvan and Adelson, 1966). Even in a 1985 sample, 90 percent of college women reported wanting to marry and have children (Machung, 1986). And, in fact, 90 percent of women eventually marry (Cherlin, 1992).

Nonetheless, being a single woman is increasingly being viewed as a valid alternative lifestyle for women. In 1987, 20.9 percent of white women, 36.4 percent of African American women, and 26.6 percent of Hispanic women were in the "single, never married" category (Rix, 1988, p. 354). These statistics are up from 1960, a result of trends toward not marrying and toward marrying later.

Two advantages are typically mentioned in discussions of being a single woman (Donelson, 1977; Etaugh, 1993). One is freedom. There is no necessity to agree with someone else on what to have for dinner, what TV program to watch, or how to spend money. There is the freedom to move when doing so is advantageous to one's career—or to stay put and not to move to follow a husband's career. The other advantage is a sense of self-sufficiency and competence. The single woman has to deal with the irritation of fixing the leaky faucet herself, but having done so, she gains a sense that she is competent to do such things. As noted earlier, single women have higher reported life satisfaction than married women. Among single women, life satisfaction is correlated with having good health, not being lonely, living with a female housemate, having many casual friends, and being highly involved with work (Loewenstein et al., 1981).

In a society as marriage oriented as ours, it is not surprising that there are disadvantages to being a single woman. Most of the social structures for adults involve couples' activities, and the single person is often excluded. Loneliness is another disadvantage that is mentioned frequently.

In one study, one-quarter of childless single women expressed regret at not having had children—but that means that three-quarters expressed no such regret (Loewenstein et al., 1981).

Sociological studies indicate that higher levels of intelligence, education, and occupation are associated with singleness among women (Spreitzer and Riley, 1974). Single women tend to value achievement and personal growth, whereas married women tend to value personal relationships (Gigy, 1980). One sociologist concluded that high-achieving women may consider marriage too confining and therefore choose not to marry (Havens, 1973). Note that this is a much different matter from saying that such women are not likely to be chosen. The decision is apparently theirs. For most women, however, being single is not a result of an early, explicit decision, but rather is a result of many small choices, many not made deliberately (McGinnis, 1974). These women may essentially drift into singleness and, once there, discover that they like it.

Friendship Lucia and Eva are best friends. They eat lunch together while they tell each other about the joys and sorrows they have experienced since they last saw each other. Sam and David are also best friends. They relax as they shoot baskets together on Saturday morning.

Research has focused on the nature of female friendships and whether or not female friendships differ in nature from male friendships (Caldwell and Peplau, 1982; Davidson and Duberman, 1982; Wright, 1982). Although there are great similarities between male friendships and female friendships, the scenarios described above reflect the sorts of differences that have been found. In general, women tend to emphasize talking and emotional sharing in their friendships, whereas men tend to emphasize activities and doing things together (Caldwell and Peplau, 1982). Topics of conversation between best friends also differ (Davidson and Duberman, 1982). Men are far more likely to talk about topical, external matters, such as current events, whereas women are more likely to spread the conversation out to include feelings and personal matters. For example, one man said:

> We are pretty open with each other, I guess. Mostly we talk about sex, horses, guns, and the Army. (Davidson and Duberman, 1982, p. 815)

Compare that with this report from a woman:

> We discuss everything with each other. From what we're doing, to how each of us might be feeling, or what's happening to us, to discussing what happens between the two of us. No matter how bad it is, I don't want to hide my feelings. (Davidson and Duberman, 1982, p. 814)

Research on friendship patterns in a group of women ranging in age from 14 to 80 indicates that friendship serves three important functions for women (Candy et al., 1981):

1. Intimacy and assistance—This involves disclosing personal feelings to the friend and helping the friend, points that are consistent with the findings on gender differences in friendship discussed above.

2. Status—This involves gaining status by having a particular person as a friend.

3. Power—This involves being able to influence the friend or give advice, or have the friend do the same to you.

Research also shows that women find their best friendships to be therapeutic (Davidson and Packard, 1981). This is true in a number of senses: best friends are reported to provide guidance, an opportunity to express feelings, feedback, the instillation of hope, and understanding.

In sum, it is clear that women's friendships in adulthood meet some important psychological functions. Men's and women's friendships are generally similar, but they also differ in some respects, with women emphasizing self-disclosure and emotional sharing and men emphasizing shared activities.

Middle Age

Middle age for women involves both biological and social changes. Hormone levels decline with menopause (Chapter 10) and children leave home. What are the psychological consequences?

Empty Nest or Prime of Life?   During a woman's middle age her children may leave home—to go to work, to go away to college, to get married. For the middle-aged woman, a major source of identity—motherhood—has been taken away. The term **empty nest syndrome** has been used to describe the cases of depression in women at this time. Sociologist Pauline Bart (1971) has investigated the empty nest syndrome. Interestingly, her research indicates that it is the "supermothers," not those who chose nontraditional careers, who are most susceptible to this depression. The supermothers have invested so much

Empty nest syndrome: Depression that middle-aged people supposedly feel when their children are grown and have left home, leaving an empty nest.

FIGURE 5.4
Although traditional stereotypes held that women lapse into empty nest depression in middle age, research shows this not to be true. The women's movement has helped many women find new opportunities. Here, a woman runs in the Senior Olympics.

of themselves in the mother role that they have the most to lose when it has ended. Confirming these results, a study of graduates of an eastern women's college who had been out of college 35 years and were in their late fifties indicated that women employed full-time had significantly lower symptom scores than women not employed outside the home (Powell, 1977).

Sociologist Lillian B. Rubin (1979) has challenged many ideas about the empty nest syndrome. Her results are based on a study of 160 women, a cross section of white mothers aged 35 to 54, from the working, middle, and professional classes. To be included in the sample, they had to have given up work or careers after a minimum of three years and to have assumed the traditional role of housewife and mother for at least ten years after the birth of their first child. Therefore this group should be the most prone to the empty nest syndrome. Typically these women said, "My career was my child." Contrary to the empty nest, Rubin found that, although some women were momentarily sad, lonely, or frightened, they were not depressed in response to the departure or impending departure of their children. The predominant feeling of every woman except one was a feeling of relief. For mothers who have sacrificed so much for their children, such a reaction is probably not too surprising. Rather than experiencing an immobilizing depression, most of the women found new jobs and reorganized their daily lives. Rubin felt that the women's movement had helped many of the women by raising their sights to other careers and opportunities.

Psychologists Valory Mitchell and Ravenna Helson (1990) go one step further and argue that the early fifties are the *prime of life* for women. In a sample of college graduates between 26 and 80, women in their early fifties were the group most likely to describe their lives as "first rate." There were more empty nests (but they may not be so bad), there was better health, and there was higher income compared with other ages. Women at this age displayed confidence, involvement, security, and depth in their personalities.

What should we conclude, then? Probably some women experience empty nest depression, but they are not the majority, and among those who do experience such depression, it may be brief. What is more important is the ability of the majority of women to adjust to the changes that occur in their lives and roles at this time. A feminist reframing of the issues suggests that the early fifties may actually be the prime of life.

Mothers and Daughters   The topic of the mother-daughter relationship has attracted much attention, with books such as journalist Nancy Friday's *My Mother, My Self* (1977) chalking up big sales. In psychological theory, too, the mother-daughter relationship is thought to be critical, whether the theory is psychoanalytic, as is Nancy Chodorow's (see Chapter 2), or is social learning theory.

A major review of research on the mother-daughter relationship concluded that many popular views of it as conflict ridden are inaccurate (Boyd, 1989). Although there are conflicts in the relationship when the daughter is in adolescence, the relationship undergoes many transitions as the daughter grows older and moves through life stages herself. Early conflicts give way to reports of increased closeness, greater empathy, and greater mutuality. The adult mother-daughter relationship is described as rewarding and close; mothers and daughters help and care for each other. Thus mothers and daughters, rather than being their own worst enemies, may contribute positively to each other's psychological well-being.

Old Age

Double standard of aging: Cultural norms by which men's status increases with age but women's decreases.

There is a **double standard of aging** (Berman et al., 1981; Etaugh, 1993; Sontag, 1979). That is, as a man reaches middle age and beyond, he may appear more distinguished and handsome, but a woman of the same age does not seem to become more beautiful. As we saw in a previous section, a woman's value in her youth is often judged by her appearance, which may decline with age. Here I shall examine some of the research on women in old age.

Physical Health   Despite the fact that women live longer than men, women have more illnesses. Compared with elderly men, elderly women have higher rates of arthritis and rheumatism (both of which can be extremely painful), diabetes, hypertension, osteoporosis (brittle bones), and vision problems (Etaugh, 1993; Kart et al., 1988).

Do women actually have more illnesses than men, or do they just report them more? Again, there is a finding of a gender difference and there are two possible interpretations. The first is that women are neurotic and whiny, complaining over slight aches and pains, whereas men are tough and brave and don't let little things get them down. This is a female-deficit interpretation. The alternative interpretation is that men deny illnesses when they have them, which can be quite dangerous and may even lead to death (and men's higher mortality rate), whereas women are sensitive to danger signs and report them to a physician (Etaugh, 1993).

Grandmotherhood   The stereotype of a grandmother is a white-haired lady baking cookies for the little ones. However, women can become grandmothers at vastly different ages. One woman becomes a grandmother at age 30, and another does at age 65. Nonetheless, because a great many elderly women are grandmothers, we will discuss the topic in this section on elderly women.

In one study of grandparents, most of them women, five aspects of their experience of grandparenthood emerged: (1) centrality, in which grandparenthood is a central part of the woman's life and identity; (2) valued elder, in which the woman passes on family traditions and ethnic or cultural traditions; (3) immortality through the clan, in which the woman has a sense that she lives on through her descendants; (4) reinvolvement with personal past, in which the woman relives her earlier life, when she was the age of her grandchildren, and identifies with her own grandmother; and (5) indulgence, in which the woman is lenient with and "spoils" her grandchildren (Kivnick, 1983).

The grandparenting role is likely to differ for different ethnic groups as a result of different family structures and cultural traditions. Unfortunately, this question has received little research, but I can mention a few relevant studies. In one, African American grandparents were much more likely to assume an authoritative or influential role with grandchildren than were Euro-American grandparents (Cherlin and Furstenberg, 1985). In another study, Mexican American grandparents had more contact with their grandchildren and reported more satisfying relationships with them than did white or Black grandparents (Bengtson, 1985).

In some cases, grandmothers end up rearing their grandchildren. In one sample of Black grandmothers, 10 percent lived in the same home with their grandchildren (Pearson et al., 1990). In some cases, of course, the mother and father were also present. But in other cases they were not, and the grandmother then was responsible for raising the grandchildren. Grandmothers raising children because the parent or parents are drug addicted report that it is rewarding to raise their grandchildren; but research also shows heightened levels of stress in this group as evidenced by signs such as heart attacks and depression (Burton, 1992).

Retirement   Most of the studies of retirement have been based on all-male samples (Etaugh, 1993), no doubt based on the researchers' assumption that women do not hold paying jobs and therefore cannot retire from them. Nothing could be further from the truth, of course (see Chapter 7). Women are committed to their jobs, and retirement has important consequences for them, just as it does for men (George et al., 1984).

Women are more likely than men to retire because of a spouse's retirement—particularly because women tend to be married to men who are somewhat older than they are—and because of a spouse's ill health (Shaw, 1984). Professional women and self-employed women are less likely to retire early than are other women (Shaw, 1984).

Income is a concern for retired women. Women are more likely than men to report that their retirement incomes are not adequate (Etaugh, 1993). One reason is that retired women, on the average, receive considerably smaller Social Security checks than retired men do. This occurs because Social Security payments are based on one's preretirement earnings, and the gender gap in wages ensures that women receive smaller payments.

Widowhood There are far more widows than widowers. In the United States the ratio of widows to widowers is estimated, depending on race, to be about 3:1 to 5:1 (Rix, 1988, p. 334). Among adults over 75, 24 percent of men are widowed, compared with 66 percent of women (U.S. Bureau of the Census, 1990a). This is the result of two trends: the longer life expectancy of women, and the tendency of women to marry men older than they themselves. Opportunities for remarriage are limited because there are so few men compared with women in the "appropriate" age group. Therefore it is fairly common for women to face the last 15 years or so of their lives alone.

A number of factors affect how women respond following the death of a spouse, including the woman's age, whether the death was anticipated or unexpected, and her financial and social resources (Etaugh, 1993). Older widows tend to have an advantage over younger widows (say, widows under 45), because older widows tend to be more financially secure and are not responsible for young children. Older widows also tend to have friends in the same circumstances and tend to be psychologically prepared for a husband's death.

Two problems are especially common among widows: loneliness and financial strain (Etaugh, 1993). Widows may become socially isolated; contact with their children, and especially with friends, is important. Financial strain can be severe. There is loss of the husband's income, and the couple's savings may have been depleted by medical expenses associated with the husband's illness. Elderly women are more likely than elderly men to live in poverty, and older minority women are even more likely to be poor than white women.

The death of a spouse is harder on men than it is on women, as evidenced by low morale, mental disorders, and high death and suicide rates (Bock and Webber, 1972; Spreitzer et al., 1975; for an excellent review, see Stroebe and Stroebe, 1983). Put another way, women seem to cope better with widowhood. One reason for this is that women are more likely to have deep friendships that they have developed over the years and from which they can draw emotional support (Blau, 1973). In one study of people over 65, women had 38 percent more friends than men did (Fischer and Phillips, cited in Peplau et al., 1982). Although widowed men are significantly lonelier than married men, widowed women are no lonelier than married women (Perlman et al., 1978; for a review of loneliness, see Peplau et al., 1982).

Research indicates that in modern American cities, roles and social support systems do not come automatically to widows as they might in a more traditional society (Lopata, 1979). In short, the widow has to be assertive to get the kinds of support and services she needs. Unfortunately, today's widows are from precisely that generation of women who were socialized not to be assertive. Lopata also found that women who are the most family oriented and husband dependent are the most devastated by widowhood.

Gender Roles and Androgyny   Some scholars have suggested that gender roles become more relaxed or even reversed among the elderly. With the children grown, the woman is less restricted to the mother role. In some marriages, because the husband is older than the wife, he may have retired while she continues to hold a job. Thus he may do many of the household chores while she is the breadwinner.

This shifting of gender roles might suggest that the elderly are more androgynous than younger adults. To see whether this is true, people from age 13 to 86 were asked to complete the Bem Sex Role Inventory, discussed in Chapter 3 (Hyde et al., 1991). Based on their scores, they were categorized as androgynous, feminine, masculine, or undifferentiated. The results, shown in Table 5.2, indicate that older men are more androgynous than younger men.[1] In contrast,

TABLE 5.2

Percentages of Males and Females Who Are Classified as Androgynous in Four Age Groups

	Age			
Gender	*13–20*	*21–40*	*41–60*	*61 and over*
Females	36	12	17	23
Males	18	13	15	41

SOURCE: Hyde et al. (1991).

[1]These data were cross-sectional (collected on many different people at different ages) and not longitudinal (collected on the same group of people repeatedly as they grew older). Therefore it is important to be cautious in concluding from them too much about actual developmental changes.

EXPERIENCE THE RESEARCH

ELDERLY WOMEN

For this exercise, interview an older woman, over the age of 65. You might choose a female relative or a woman from a local senior citizens center. Record her age, marital status, and ethnic group. Ask her the following questions, and either tape record or take notes on her answers:

1. What does she feel were the three major events in her life? Why?
2. Did she spend most of her life as a homemaker or having a job or career? Reflecting back on that role, what were the good things about it? What were the negative things?
3. If she is single, is she lonely? Why or why not?

the percentage of feminine women increased in the oldest age categories. Perhaps this means that both men and women become more feminine with age, resulting in more androgynous men and more feminine women.

In Conclusion

I have traced female development across the lifespan. Gender similarities seem to be the rule in infancy and childhood, with many gender differences not emerging until adolescence. The femininity-achievement incompatibility exerts an important force on female development. Declines in girls' self-esteem in adolescence are cause for concern.

Suggestions for Further Reading

Baruch, Grace, Barnett, Rosalind, & Rivers, Caryl. (1983). *Lifeprints: New patterns of love and work for today's women.* New York: McGraw-Hill. Writing for a general audience, developmental psychologists Baruch and Barnett teamed up with journalist Rivers to report their findings on women's adult development.

Jackson, Linda A. (1992). *Physical appearance and gender.* Albany: State University of New York Press. Jackson explores the evidence that physical appearance is more important to women's life outcomes than men's, and why this occurs.

6

Abilities, Achievement, and Motivation

> *When Samuel Johnson was asked which is more intelligent,*
> *man or woman, he replied, "Which man, which woman?"*

Part of the lore of the culture is that women are less intelligent than men. Put bluntly, they are dumb—witness the expressions *dumb broad* and *dumb blonde*. An additional stereotype is that women's thought processes are less rational, more illogical than men's, more influenced by emotion. A familiar scene in movies and comics is the male shaking his head over his inability to understand the mind of his wife or girlfriend.

Is there any scientific evidence to support the notion that women are less intellectually competent than men? In this chapter we shall explore empirical evidence regarding the intellectual and achievement characteristics of women, and whether these characteristics seem to differ from those of men. It is important to remember that the finding of a gender difference does not say anything about what causes it, that is, whether biological or environmental factors are responsible. We shall then examine motivational differences between females and males with the goal of better understanding the relationship between women's abilities and their achievements.

Abilities

General Intelligence   There is no evidence to support the hypothesis that females are less intelligent than males. In fact, research has consistently shown that there are no gender differences in general intelligence (Maccoby and Jacklin, 1974).

These results need to be interpreted with some caution, because of the nature of IQ-test construction. It became clear to the early test constructors that because of both biological and cultural factors, boys would do better on some kinds of items, whereas girls would do better on others. They decided to balance these subtests so that there would be no gender differences in overall measured intelligence. Therefore, saying that there are no gender differences in overall tested intelligence essentially means that the test constructors succeeded in their goal of eliminating gender differences.

Rather than looking at global assessments, it is more revealing to analyze patterns of specific abilities in males and in females, such as mathematical ability or verbal ability.

For years, psychology textbooks have told students that there were gender differences in three basic abilities: verbal ability, spatial ability, and mathematical ability. Often these conclusions were based on an important review by Maccoby and Jacklin (1974). However, we now have modern meta-analyses to give us a more accurate and detailed understanding of whether there are gender differences in these abilities and, if so, how large the differences are.

Verbal Ability Although it was traditionally thought that females showed better verbal ability than males, a meta-analysis found that the gender difference in verbal ability is so small that we can say there is no gender difference (Hyde and Linn, 1988). Overall, $d = -0.11$, indicating a slight female superiority, but one that is so small it can be called zero. The analysis also looked at different types of verbal ability, such as vocabulary, analogies, reading comprehension, and essay writing. The gender difference was small for all types of verbal ability.

Another interesting finding emerged: There was evidence that gender differences had grown smaller over time. For studies published in 1973 or earlier, $d = -0.23$, whereas for studies published after 1973, $d = -0.10$. That is, the gender difference was cut approximately in half. We can't be certain what has caused this narrowing of the gender gap. One possibility is that gender-role socialization practices have become more flexible in the past two decades, and the result is a reduction in the size of gender differences. Another is that those who produce standardized tests have become more sensitive about gender-equity issues, resulting in tests that show no gender differences.

Spatial Ability A major meta-analysis of gender differences in spatial ability discovered that there are actually three different types of spatial ability, each showing a different pattern of gender differences (Linn and Petersen, 1985). The first type, which the researchers called *spatial visualization,* involves finding a figure in a more complex one, like the hidden figures games you may have played as a child. This type of spatial ability shows a gender difference favoring males, but the difference is so small that we can consider it zero, $d = +.13$. The second type of spatial ability, *spatial perception,* requires a person to identify a true vertical or true horizontal line when there is distracting or misleading information around it. This type of spatial ability showed a moderate gender difference favoring males, $d = +.44$. The third type of spatial ability, *mental rotation,* requires the test taker to mentally rotate an object in three dimensions in order to obtain a correct answer. A sample of such an item is shown in Figure 6.1. This is the type of spatial ability that shows a large gender difference favoring males, $d = +.73$.

Although many occupations do not rely heavily on spatial ability of the last kind, there are some in which it is very important, such as those in engineering. It might therefore be tempting to attribute the small number of women in engineering to women's lower spatial ability. However, the gender difference in spatial ability is not nearly large enough to account for the fact that only 1 percent of the engineers in the United States are women (Hyde, 1981).

Scores on spatial ability tests can be improved by training (Baenninger and Newcombe, 1989). The schools generally offer little training in spatial performance in the curriculum; it would be an important addition to a gender-fair curriculum for girls.

Mathematics Ability A major meta-analysis of gender differences surveyed 100 studies, representing the testing of more than 3 million persons (Hyde et al.,

The test below is made up of pictures of blocks turned different ways. The block at the left is the reference block and the five blocks to the right are the answer blocks. One of these five blocks is the same as the reference block except that it has been turned and is seen from a different point of view. The other four blocks could not be obtained by turning the reference block. For example:

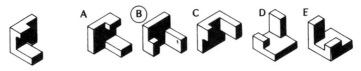

The illustration below shows that "B" is the correct answer.

FIGURE 6.1

Sample item and solution from a test of spatial ability. *(Source: From R. E. Stafford,* Identical Blocks, *form AA, 1962. Used with the permission of R. E. Stafford and Harold Gulliksen).*

1990). The results were surprising, because psychologists have said for so long that boys are better at math than girls. In fact, the average effect size was $d = -.05$ averaged over all samples of the general population (not counting special, selective samples, such as studies of mathematically gifted adolescents). That is, there was a slight female superiority, but basically the gender difference was zero.

The results were a bit more complex, though. Mathematics tests differ in the difficulty of the problems. They may tap simple computation, or real understanding of mathematical concepts, or, at the highest cognitive level, problem solving such as word problems or story problems that ask the student to go beyond memorized math facts. The meta-analysis indicated that girls outperformed boys in computation in elementary school and middle school, and the difference was zero in high school. In understanding of concepts, the gender difference was close to zero at all ages. In problem solving, the difference was zero in the elementary and middle school years, but then became more noticeable in high school ($d = +.29$) and college ($d = +.32$), with the difference favoring males. Therefore, although the results indicated that there were generally no gender differences in math performance, the gender difference in problem solving that emerges in high school is a cause of concern, because problem solving of that type is important for success in courses and careers in the sciences. It is just in the high school years that boys are more likely than girls to choose math courses, and this difference in course taking no doubt accounts for a good part of the gender difference in tested performance. We will return to this issue of choosing to take math courses later in this chapter.

One final result of the meta-analysis is also worth noting. Like the results for verbal ability mentioned earlier, the size of the gender difference in math performance has declined over the years. For studies published in 1973 or earlier, $d = +.31$, whereas for studies published in 1974 or later, $d = +.14$. That is, this gender difference declined to about half its former size. Again, this may be a result of changes in gender-role socialization practices.

Perceptual Speed The ability known as perceptual speed involves being able to perceive details quickly and accurately and to shift attention from one item to the next rapidly. Tests of perceptual speed are generally timed, and involve comparison of two strings of letters or numbers to see whether they are identical (Table 6.1). This seems to be the basic aptitude necessary for most forms of clerical work.

Women perform consistently better than men on these tests. A meta-analysis indicated that $d = -.32$; that is, the difference is in the small to moderate range (Feingold, 1988).

TABLE 6.1
Sample Items from a Test of Perceptual Speed

Instructions: Compare each line of the COPY at the bottom of the page with the corresponding line of the ORIGINAL at the top. Each *word* or *abbreviation* or *digit* in the copy that is not exactly the same as in the original is one error. In each line, mark every word or abbreviation or figure that is wrong. Then count the errors you have marked in the line and enter the total number in the column at the right. The first line has been done correctly to show you just how to mark and where to enter the total number of errors in the line. Work quickly and accurately.

ORIGINAL

Name	Address	Amount
Mr. Kevin Johnson	Auburn, ME	$2783.78
Miss Janine Adams	Austin, TX	4784.12

COPY

Name	Address	Amount	Number of Errors
Mr. Kevin Johnston	Auburn, AL	$2788.78	3
Dr. Janice Adams	Austing, TX	4784.21	5

SOURCE: Sample item from the *General Clerical Test.* Copyright © 1969 by The Psychological Corporation. Reproduced by permission. All rights reserved.

Physical Performance and Athletics Gender differences in physical and athletic characteristics provide a contrast to the findings for cognitive abilities (Linn and Hyde, 1990). For example, $d = +2.60$ for physical height, a difference that is about four times greater than any of the differences in cognitive abilities (Thomas and French, 1985).

Large gender differences in athletic performance tend to emerge in adolescence (Eaton and Enns, 1986). For example, for speed in the 50-yard dash, $d = +.63$ when averaged over all ages, but $d = +2.5$ for adolescence and beyond. For throwing distance, $d = +1.98$. On the other hand, for some other aspects of athletic performance, gender differences are small or zero; for example, on tests of balance, $d = +.09$.

Athletic performance is also strongly responsive to training and diet, as we have seen in the past 20 years with the great advances made in these areas. Figure 6.2 shows record performance in the Olympics over the years for males and females for the 100-meter dash (top part of the illustration) and for swimming the 100-meter freestyle (lower part). As you can see, the women who win today swim faster than the record-breaking men of 1952, and the gender gap is narrowing.

Summary A number of conclusions emerge from this discussion of gender differences in abilities:

1. There are no gender differences in verbal ability.

2. There are no gender differences in mathematical performance except in problem solving beginning in the high school years, and this may be accounted for by girls not taking as many math courses as boys.

3. There are gender differences in only one type of spatial ability, mental rotations, an ability that is important in career fields like engineering. However, spatial ability can be improved by training.

4. Gender differences in some kinds of athletic performance are large beginning in adolescence.

5. There is evidence that gender differences in abilities have become smaller in the past 20 years.

6. Gender differences in cognitive abilities are so small as to be irrelevant in practical situations such as job counseling. It would be a great mistake, for example, to urge a high school girl against pursuing an engineering career just because females on average score lower than males on tests of spatial ability. The gender difference is still far too small, and there is too much variability from one female to the next to predict that an individual woman will not have adequate spatial ability for such a career. A far better indicator would be her own score on a spatial ability test.

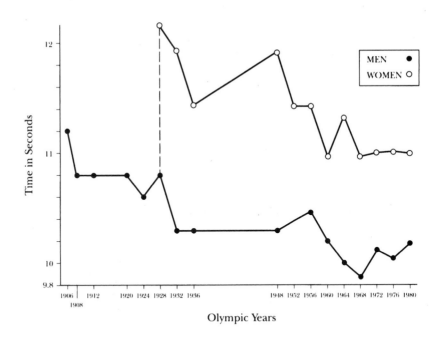

Olympic Years

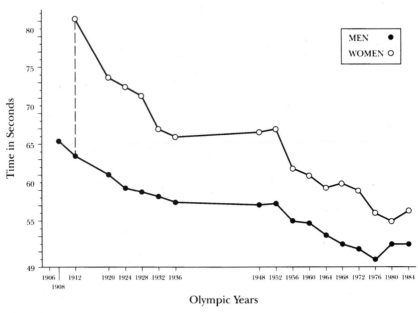

Olympic Years

FIGURE 6.2
Record performance of men and women on the 100-meter dash (top) and
100-meter freestyle (bottom) in the Olympic Games. *(Source: Linn and Hyde, 1990.*
Educational Researcher 1989. Copyright 1989 by the American Educational Research Association.
Reproduced by permission.)

Choosing Courses: How to Avoid Math

I hope that you didn't begin reading this section thinking that I would tell you how to avoid math courses, because that is not my intention at all. What I am going to tell you is that, beginning in high school, girls stop taking math courses—or they avoid math courses—and that the consequences are serious, keeping them out of many attractive careers.

I am convinced that the traditional approach of looking at gender differences in abilities (e.g., math ability) is not productive. Whether or not a significant gender difference is found, where does that approach get us, either in terms of better scientific understanding or in terms of helping women? Not very far. Psychologist Jacquelynne Eccles has broken ground with what I think is a much more productive approach—understanding why students choose or do not choose to take certain courses (e.g., Eccles, 1987; Meece et al., 1982).

Eccles points out that gender differences in math performance do not appear consistently until the tenth grade. That is just about the time when females become less likely than males to enroll in high school math courses. By the time women emerge from college, they have fewer mathematical skills than men, probably because they have not been taking math.

This in turn is significant because mathematical skills are important to success in many attractive occupations. Indeed, mathematics has been called the "critical filter" (Sherman, 1982) keeping women out of careers in engineering, computer science, the physical sciences, business, and finance. The point that should be investigated by researchers, then, is not whether females have less mathematical ability than males, but rather why it is that females stop taking math courses. If we understood the reasons behind this choice, it might be possible to help women to take more math courses and perhaps to help them expand their career options.

Eccles has proposed an elegant model to explain why students choose or avoid certain courses, such as math courses. A diagram of the model is shown in Figure 6.3. The final behavior Eccles is trying to predict is achievement behavior—specifically, choosing a math course—and it is shown in the box on the far right in Figure 6.3. The multiple factors feeding into the choice of a course are shown in the other boxes in the diagram.

In overall terms, Eccles has used an *expectation × value model* of achievement (course choice). That is, any particular achievement behavior is a product of the person's expectations and the person's values. Kim is a high school sophomore contemplating taking an optional course in geometry. The model says that she will sign up for geometry only if she has both positive expectations for success in the course (if she thinks she'll get an F, she won't sign up) and positive values with respect to the course (if she thinks the course will be of value to her both now and in the future; but she may instead think that geometry will be of no value if she expects to spend the rest of her life as a housewife). The values part of the model is shown in the top half of Figure 6.3, and the expectancies part is shown in the bottom half.

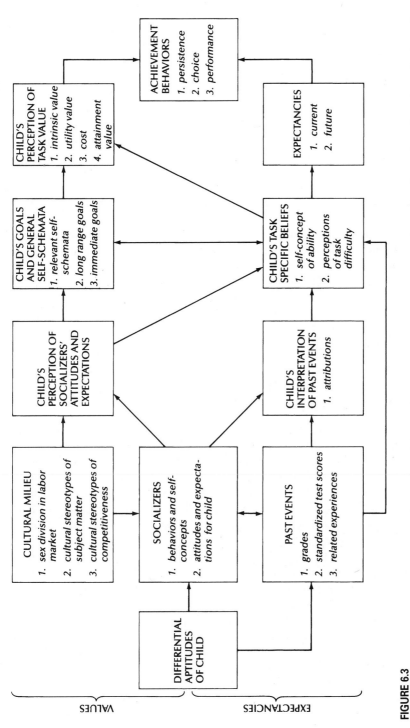

FIGURE 6.3

Eccles's model of academic course choice shows how girls' expectations and values may be shaped so that they do not take math courses in high school. *(Source: From "Sex Differences in Math Achievement," 1982, The Psychological Bulletin, 91. Copyright © 1982 by the American Psychological Association. Reprinted by permission of Judith L. Meece, Jacquelynne Eccles-Parsons et al. Also from J. E. Parsons et al. in Achievement and Achievement Motives edited by Janet T. Spence. Copyright © 1983 by W. H. Freeman and Company. Used by permission.)*

Many factors shape Kim's values regarding math courses and her expectations for success in them. In the area of values are the following:

1. The cultural milieu—Kim probably perceives the division of labor by gender in the United States and notes that women are not found in math-related jobs. Furthermore, math as a subject is stereotyped as a masculine domain. And success in an advanced math course may seem competitive to Kim, and competitiveness is not regarded as feminine.

2. Goals and self-schema—Kim has already formed a self-schema or self-concept and has some tentative occupational goals. If these involve being a housewife or a secretary, math courses will not be valued.

In the area of expectancies for success are the following factors:

1. Aptitudes and grades—Kim has some idea of her aptitude for math from a variety of sources, including her grades in past courses and her scores on standardized achievement tests. It is strange that in elementary school and junior high, girls' grades in math are as good as those of boys, yet in high school, girls stop taking math courses and boys don't. This tendency is explained in part by the next factor.

2. Interpretations or attributions—Kim may have gotten B's in all her math courses, but may fail to attribute the good grades to her own abilities (see the section on attributions later in this chapter). She may think that the courses so far have just been easy. As a result, she has low expectations for success in future math courses.

Eccles and her colleagues have done a number of studies testing various links in the model, and they have reviewed numerous pertinent studies done by others (Meece et al., 1982). Space does not permit me to review all of this research, but the model has generally been upheld. Although many links in it have been supported with data, a few have not. For example, one study showed that parents do not have lower expectations for their daughters' mathematical performance than they have for their sons', which is contrary to what the model would predict. On the other hand, research shows that by junior high, boys have higher perceptions of their math ability than girls do, and self-concept of math ability is related to one's decisions to enroll in optional math courses. These findings support key points in the model. Like most models, this one isn't perfect, but I think it is good.

As an interesting exercise, you might want to trace through the model, thinking of yourself, trying to see how it predicts why you did or did not continue taking math courses.

What are the practical implications of Eccles's model? Suppose that our goal were to get more girls enrolled in math courses so as to expand their career options. How would we do that? We could work on the expectancies side of the model or on the values side or on both. On the expectancies side, we would try to get high school girls to have higher expectancies for success in math courses. This could be done in a number of ways: by stressing that there are no average gender differences in math ability prior to high school, by pointing to an individual girl's pattern of success in math courses, and by encouraging girls to attribute their previous good grades in math to their own abilities. On the values side, we would need to increase the value girls attach to math and math courses. Girls are probably not aware of the wide variety of careers that require math. Individual counseling sessions might examine each girl's anticipated career and the math required for it.

In sum, Eccles has provided a detailed model for why girls choose or avoid math courses. In general, data support the model, although it needs to be tested further by independent researchers. It provides exciting avenues for intervening to get girls into math classes, which should have the beneficial result of expanding their career options.

Cognitive Style

Field independence: Witkin's term for the ability to make perceptual judgments and not be influenced by misleading surroundings.

Field Dependence Psychologist Herman Witkin and his colleagues (1954, 1964) have carried out a series of experiments from which they conclude that women have a field-dependent style, whereas men are **field independent.** This contrast has also been termed analytical versus global functioning—men are analytical, whereas women are global in their perceptions. Typical of the tests used in these studies is the rod-and-frame test (Figure 6.4).

Error in judgment of the true vertical indicates field-dependence.

Accuracy in judgment of the true vertical indicates field-independence.

FIGURE 6.4
The rod-and-frame apparatus is used to measure field dependence and field independence.

FOCUS 6.1

WOMEN AND COMPUTERS: THE NEW FRONTIER OF GENDER DIFFERENCES?

It used to be said that mathematics was the "critical filter" keeping women out of many desirable college majors and careers. Today, it may well be that computers are the critical filter keeping women not only out of lucrative and important careers in the computer field, but also out of dozens of other fields in which computers play a major role.

The statistics on women and computers are cause for concern. Although the great majority of computer operators are women, only 30 percent of computer scientists and 10 percent of Ph.D.-level computer scientists are women. Although 37 percent of college computer science majors are women, they comprise only 10 percent of Ph.D. degrees (McCormick and McCormick, 1991).

Female disenchantment begins early. Elementary school girls, compared with boys, feel less anxious and more excited when computers are first introduced into the classroom (Loyd et al., 1987). However, over time boys become considerably more enthusiastic than girls about computers—almost all children attending computer science camps are boys and boys dominate the use of computers at home and at school. From grades kindergarten through 12, girls have increasingly negative attitudes about computers.

What leads to girls' and women's disenchantment with computers? Gender stereotypes lead the list of explanations. Computer software is male stereotyped, often involving violence such as bombing. Boys and girls have different preferences for computer games. For example, boys like the fantasy of arrows popping balloons, which girls dislike; girls like music in a game, but boys do not (Malone and Lepper, 1986). Furthermore, computers—and technology more broadly—are stereotyped as a male domain.

Computer resources often exist in a masculine environment. Based on observations of high school computer labs, one researcher noted that they tend to be dominated by an unsympathetic male teacher and unappealing boys:

[There are] three or four boys who can control the computers with what seems to be an incomprehensible flair. They know its language and routines and flash their expertise in a way that makes everyone else feel disenfranchised and stupid. The computer teacher, a man

FIGURE 6.5
Boys and girls are interested in different uses for computers. Boys are more interested in violent games, and this kind of software dominates the market. *(Source: Illustration 1994 by Nicole Hollander)*

who teaches mathematics most of the day, has a high regard for these students, introducing them to visitors with something . . . almost like awe. (Collis, 1985, p. 211)

Research shows that computer software designers' gender stereotypes influence their design of software (Huff and Cooper, 1987). In one study, software designers were instructed to create software for either boys, girls, or students. For girls, the resulting programs were learning tools, whereas the resulting programs for boys were games. Most importantly, the software designed for "students" was similar to that designed for boys. The male-as-normative principle strikes again, but this time in computer-land. In short, the male stereotyping of computer software and of the computer lab environment powerfully contributes to girls' negative attitudes toward computers.

What can be done about this situation? First, computer lab aides could be recruited for more than their technical expertise, such as for interpersonal sensitivity and tutoring ability. The result would be lab aides who, rather than exhibitionistically flashing their own skills, would nurture girls' and women's computer skills. Recruiting women lab aides would, of course, be important as well. Faculty who teach computer science should be vigilant about monitoring software for sex bias, looking for software that is equally appealing to males and females. The curriculum is also important. Girls and women show the most interest in applications of computers, such as in doing research, writing, and drawing. The computer science curriculum, at least at the introductory level, should emphasize interesting applications rather than formal, mathematical introductions.

As computers more and more become a way of life in the United States, as well as a prerequisite for many important careers, we must move quickly to reverse sex bias.

SOURCES: Huff and Cooper (1987), Loyd et al. (1987), Malone and Lepper (1986), McCormick and McCormick (1991), Wilder et al. (1985).

The participant is seated in a dark room facing a luminous rod inside a luminous frame. Both the rod and the frame are tilted at an angle, and the person's task is to adjust the rod to the true vertical. The tilt of the frame serves as a distraction in the task, so that people make errors from the true vertical in adjusting the rod. People who are very accurate in judging the true vertical are called field independent because they have been able to make their judgments independent of the misleading frame or field, whereas people who make errors are said to be field dependent. Because women make larger errors on average than men do on this test, Witkin infers that women are field dependent, men field independent, in their cognitive styles. Note that this may hold only in visual tests. In other tasks, performed with their eyes closed, women did as well as men.

The interpretation Witkin places on his research is an interesting instance of the large leap of faith that is often made between results and interpretations, particularly when research confirms stereotyped expectations (Chapter 1). Some psychologists think that what is essentially a gender difference in susceptibility to an illusion has unjustifiably been interpreted to conform to gender-role stereotypes, namely, that women are dependent and men independent. Consider this reinterpretation, which is equally consistent with the data: Women are context sensitive and men are context insensitive.

The rod-and-frame test also may be just another measure of spatial ability. It is basically a measure of what we called spatial perception earlier in the chapter. As such, it isn't a separate gender difference, but rather the same old gender difference in spatial ability.

On the basis of these criticisms, it is difficult to know what these results on cognitive style mean, except that women and men have different styles of perceiving and processing information, in this instance, when the field or context is misleading.

Achievement

School Achievement   At all grade levels, girls consistently get better grades than boys, even in those areas in which boys score higher in ability tests (e.g., Kimball, 1989). The school progress of girls is also superior to that of boys. Girls less frequently have to repeat a grade and are more frequently accelerated and promoted.

Vocational Achievement   Stop for a moment and think of the name of a famous woman scientist. Write it down. Probably at least 90 percent of you wrote "Marie Curie," and the rest of you wrote nothing because you couldn't think of her name. Who else is there? This illustrates how few women have achieved real eminence in science and how little recognition we give to those who have. (Other examples would be Anna Freud, Jane Goodall, Dian Fossey, and Margaret Mead.)

An early statistical study of eminent women, collecting a total of 868 names representing 42 nations and extending from the seventh century B.C. to 1913, showed that the largest number (38 percent) had achieved eminence in literature. However, the highest degree of eminence (as measured by the number of lines allotted in the biographical dictionaries) was obtained by sovereigns, political leaders, and mothers and mistresses of eminent men. Women achieved eminence in a number of other nonintellectual ways, such as tragic fate, beauty, and being immortalized in literature (Castle, 1913).

Even in fields traditionally assigned to women, the top-ranking, most prestigious positions are held by men. Professional interior decorating and clothing design are dominated by men. The chefs who achieve renown and "greatness" are men. Teachers are women, but principals and superintendents of schools are more likely to be men.

In more recent years, there still remains a gap between the accomplishments of women and those of men. We will discuss women and work in far greater detail in Chapter 7. Suffice it to say here that the majority of women are concentrated in a relatively narrow range of female-dominated occupations (occupations in which 80 percent or more of the workers are female); these include librarians, health technicians, secretaries, nurses, bank tellers, telephone operators, childcare workers, and dental workers (Reskin and Hartmann, 1986). In contrast, the majority of men are spread out over 229 occupations that are at least 80 percent male, including natural scientists, physicians, dentists, and lawyers. There is a great deal of difference between the status of the male-dominated occupations and that of the female-dominated occupations.

FOCUS 6.2
THE STORY OF A GIFTED WOMAN: BEATRIX POTTER

Beatrix Potter is best known as the author and illustrator of *The Tale of Peter Rabbit.* But her biography reveals a great deal about the struggles of a gifted woman trying to express her talent in the field of biology.

She was born in 1866, and by the age of eight, was already carefully drawing and labeling caterpillars. She became particularly interested in fungi, and through her teens and twenties she devoted as many hours as possible of every day to a search for new species she had not previously observed. She then painted each one that she saw.

By 1894, her studies of fungi and lichens were sufficiently advanced for her to take an interest in research from abroad suggesting that lichens result from symbiosis, a relationship between two organisms in which each is necessary for the other's survival. To test this hypothesis, she enlisted the help of her uncle, a distinguished chemist. On the basis of her research, Potter discovered the intimate interdependency between the fungus and alga which together formed the lichen.

It was through her uncle that she gained her first audience with the scientific establishment. He took her to the Royal

FIGURE 6.6
Beatrix Potter's genius is shown in her superb scientific drawings; she encountered such obstacles to a career in science, however, that she channeled her talents into writing and illustrating children's books.

Botanic Gardens to present her work. One after another of the scientists greeted her with apathy. The director dismissed her paintings of fungi as being too artistic to meet scientific criteria. Although continually rebuffed by the scientific community, she continued her work on lichens, began work on spores, and started drafts of a paper describing her findings. As such, she was the first Britisher to explain the symbiotic relationship involved in a lichen and to begin to understand the germination of spores.

Her uncle became increasingly furious over her rejections by the scientific establishment and determined that her views would be heard. In 1897 a paper entitled "On the Germination of the Spores of Agaricineae" by Helen B. Potter was read to the Linnaean Society of London. It was read by a friend; Beatrix Potter was not present because only men were allowed to attend the meetings.

But the prospects for her work to be appreciated remained nonexistent. Two years later she gave up her study of spores, finding the response of children to the books she wrote and illustrated to be much more satisfying. Her first book, complete with illustrations, was about a rabbit. Unable to get a publisher, she paid to have it printed. *The Tale of Peter Rabbit* has been on the list of children's best-sellers ever since its publication 90 years ago. Many of the psychological themes of Potter's own life are reflected in the characters, most notably frustration, a sense of being kept from a desired goal. For example, Peter Rabbit can't roam the garden at will because of the upraised rake of the pursuing gardener, MacGregor. Gifted in both science and art, Beatrix Potter finally found a socially acceptable, gender-appropriate way to express her creativity, by writing and illustrating children's books.

At the age of 47 she married, for the first time, a lawyer and spent her last 30 years living happily in the country. One wonders what great contributions she might have made to science had she not been so thwarted in her efforts.

SOURCE: From Gilpatrick (1972).

This situation is compounded by the fact that women who do make exceptional achievements often remain invisible. For example, when you think of the discovery of the structure of the genetic molecule DNA, you probably think of the two male scientists Watson and Crick. Lost from the story told to the public was the essential contribution of their female colleague, Rosalind Franklin (Sayre, 1978). Examples of a number of women who contributed to major advances in psychology were given in Chapter 1. It is important not only to remove barriers to women's achievement, but also to recognize the work of those who already have achieved.

Studying the adult achievements of women labeled as gifted during the school years provides some insight into the "gap at the top" syndrome. The Stanford Gifted Child Study (Terman and Oden, 1947) is perhaps the most extensive research of its kind. More than 600 children with IQ's above 135 (which represents the upper 1 percent of the population) were identified in the California schools. Their progress was then followed into adulthood. The adult occupations of the women, whose childhood IQ's were in the same range as the men's, were on the whole undistinguished. Few became professionals. Although IQ showed a fairly close relationship to accomplishment among men, it showed essentially no relationship among women. In fact, two-thirds of the women with IQ's of 170 or above (certainly at the genius level) were housewives or office workers. One cannot help but be struck by the enormous waste of resources this represents. It would be interesting to repeat this study today, when so many more opportunities for women have opened up.

In summary, in terms of achievement, girls surpass boys in school achievement in all areas, but in terms of career achievement, females lag behind males. This deficit in achievement is particularly surprising in view of girls' school successes and intellectual abilities; it is probably a result of a variety of forces, including discrimination and gender-role socialization. In the next sections of this chapter we shall explore various motivational factors that may also help to account for the lesser professional achievements of women.

Achievement Motivation

A striking paradox has emerged in this chapter. Women start out in life with good abilities, yet they end up in adulthood with lower-status jobs and less recognized achievement than men. Girls also do better in school. Yet in adulthood we find them in unpaid occupations such as housewives, or in lower-status, lower-paying ones such as clerks. Why?

There is currently a high consciousness about discrimination against women, and certainly discrimination is an important source of women's low achievement. (See Chapter 7 for a more complete discussion.)

However, psychologists believe that discrimination on the basis of gender is not the entire explanation for the *ability-achievement gap.* Society has subtler ways of achieving its goals, ways in which some women may internalize low drives to achieve and may perpetuate this pattern in other women. Some of the personality factors that have been proposed to explain this gap are achievement motivation, the motive to avoid success, and expectations about success. We shall examine these processes in women in this and the following sections.

Achievement motivation is the desire to accomplish something of value or importance through one's own efforts, to meet standards of excellence in what one does. There are several methods for measuring it. The most commonly used is a projective technique in which participants' stories in response to an ambiguous cue are scored for achievement imagery (McClelland et al., 1953). Subjects are shown a series of pictures and are asked to write a story about each picture after being told that this is a test of creative imagination. They are told to cover such questions as the following: What is happening? What has led up to this situation? What will happen? What is being thought? One of the pictures shows a young man standing on a sidewalk with a broom in his hand, looking off into the distance. Below are two stories written by different respondents about this picture:

> The boy works in the grocery store. He has just graduated from high school and hasn't enough money to go to college. He is standing there thinking about how long it will take him to save enough to get his education. He doesn't want to remain a store clerk all his life, and wants to make something of himself.

> It seems that this young man has been told by his father to clean up the sidewalk. This has prevented him from going off to the beach for the day with his pals. He is watching them go off in their car and is feeling left out and sore at his father.

The first story would be scored as indicating a high achievement motive, whereas the second indicates a low achievement motive.

Most of the classic literature on gender differences asserts that females have a lower level of achievement motivation than males (Hoffman, 1972; Tyler, 1965). These gender differences are of considerable interest because achievement motivation is related to achievement behaviors such as test performance and occupational choice. Thus, the lower achievement motivation of females might help to explain their lesser occupational achievement and might therefore represent a kind of "internalized barrier to achievement." Theories were constructed to explain the developmental forces, such as socialization, that might lead females to have low achievement motivation (Hoffman, 1972). It was also believed that although females were not motivated for achievement, they were motivated by social concerns, or by a need for affiliation. That is, females were thought to be motivated not by internalized standards of excellence (achievement motivation), but rather by a desire for approval from other people (Hoffman, 1972). Indeed, some authors even suggested that girls' achievement behavior (for example, in school) was not motivated by achievement motivation as it was for boys, but rather by a need for affiliation (the teacher's approval).

Achievement motivation: The desire to accomplish something of value or importance through one's efforts; the desire to meet standards of excellence.

These results need to be reassessed, however. From reviews of available research, there actually appears to be little evidence for lower achievement motivation in females (Maccoby and Jacklin, 1974; Mednick and Thomas, 1993; Stewart and Chester, 1982). The results are complex because achievement motivation may be tested under any of several conditions. In the simplest case (the "neutral" or "relaxed" condition), participants are simply given the test. Under such conditions, females actually show higher achievement motivation than males. The test may also be given under "achievement arousal" conditions. For example, before taking the test of achievement motivation, participants might be given an anagrams test that they are told measures not only intelligence, but also capacity to organize and to evaluate situations quickly and accurately, and to be a leader. Under these conditions, males' achievement motivation increases sharply, whereas females' does not. However, these studies have been criticized for sex bias in their designs (Stewart and Chester, 1982). Therefore, the research on gender and achievement motivation is muddled, and there is not much that we can conclude from it.

Gender differences in achievement motivation probably also depend on age and stage of development. Although females may generally have a high level of achievement motivation, at various periods of a woman's life achievement may become anxiety provoking, so that she temporarily suppresses her achievement motivation (Bardwick, 1971). Research indicates that in college, the influence of male peers and a peer-group culture that stresses romance may lead women to forget career plans (Holland and Eisenhart, 1990). For instance, a girl who, because of a strong desire to go to medical school and become a doctor, has earned straight A's through her junior year in college suddenly meets the man of her dreams. He has no plans for being married to a doctor, but rather wants a competent wife, housewife, and mother for his children. So she abandons all medical school plans. However, after her children are all in school, she may revive her educational goals and become a successful professional.

The belief in women's need for affiliation also should be reassessed (Maccoby and Jacklin, 1974; Stein and Bailey, 1973). This belief was based on the notion that females are more sensitive to interpersonal reinforcement; yet available research does not indicate that this is true. Much of what appears to be affiliative needs in females may actually be achievement needs expressed in a gender-appropriate fashion. Thus the traditional middle-class housewife may be highly motivated to be an outstanding cook and to throw fantastic dinner parties not because of her needs for social approval, but because this is a socially acceptable, gender-appropriate means of expressing her very real achievement strivings. She is displaying achievement that is gender appropriate for women.

In summary, females appear to have high levels of achievement motivation on the average. This motivation, however, is not aroused by traditional achievement-arousal conditions, as is the case with males. Gender differences in achievement motivation appear to depend on the situation in which they are tested, as well as on the stage of development.

Motive to Avoid Success

In 1969 Matina Horner reported on the results of research on an anxiety about success called **motive to avoid success** or *fear of success,* among bright, high-achieving women.

In attempting to understand the basis of gender differences in achievement motivation, Horner first observed that achievement situations, such as test taking, are more anxiety provoking for females than for males. To measure this phenomenon, Horner devised a projective test in which respondents were asked to complete a story that begins: "After first-term finals, Anne (John) finds herself (himself) at the top of her (his) medical-school class." Females wrote about Anne, males about John.

Males' stories generally indicated happiness and feelings of satisfaction over achievement. For example:

> John is a conscientious young man who worked hard. He is pleased with himself. John has always wanted to go into medicine and is very dedicated. . . . John continues working hard and eventually graduates at the top of his class.

Females' responses, on the other hand, were often bizarre:

> Anne starts proclaiming her surprise and joy. Her fellow classmates are so disgusted with her behavior that they jump on her in a body and beat her. She is maimed for life.

The negative imagery expressed by females generally fell into one of three categories—fear of social rejection, worries about maintaining womanhood, and denial of the reality of success. For example:

Social rejection fears:

> Anne is an acne-faced bookworm. She runs to the bulletin board and finds she's at the top. As usual she smarts off. A chorus of groans is the rest of the class's reply. . . .

Worries about womanhood:

> Unfortunately Anne no longer feels so certain that she really wants to be a doctor. She is worried about herself and wonders if perhaps she isn't normal. . . . Anne decides not to continue with her medical work but to take courses that have a deeper personal meaning for her.

Denial of reality:

> Anne is a code name of a nonexistent person created by a group of medical students. They take turns writing exams for Anne.

In her sample of undergraduates at the University of Michigan, Horner found that 65 percent of the females, as compared with less than 10 percent of the males, told stories that fell into one of these three categories.

Presumably the motive to avoid success is related to the perceived conflict between achievement and femininity and the perceived connection between achievement and aggressiveness, which is also gender inappropriate for females. Thus, for women, the rewards of achievement are contaminated by the accompanying anxiety.

Horner collected her original data in 1965 for her doctoral dissertation. The results were published in a 1969 *Psychology Today* article. They attracted quite a bit of attention, to put it mildly. The *New York Times* and other newspapers featured stories about the research. The article was reprinted a number of times and was required reading for many students. The research was—and is—appealing for a number of reasons. It appeared just at the time of rising interest in women and the women's movement. In particular, it seemed to offer a sensible explanation for why more women had not succeeded in high-status occupations—they simply feared success.

In the cold light of day some 30 years later, the research doesn't seem to provide the surefire answers it originally did. Horner's research has been criticized on a number of grounds (Mednick, 1989; Shaver, 1976; Tresemer, 1974; Zuckerman and Wheeler, 1975): (1) Other studies using Horner's techniques often find men having fear-of-success imagery as much as or more than women. Therefore there is no reason to believe that the motive to avoid success is found only in women, or even that it is more frequent in women. If that is the case, then it cannot be used to explain the lesser occupational achievements of women. (2) Anne's success was in a stereotype-inappropriate field, namely, medical school. Therefore the research may not indicate a generalized fear of success, but rather a fear of being successful at something that violates stereotypes. Perhaps if Anne were presented as doing well in nursing school, she would not evoke much anxiety. One study has shown just that (Cherry and Deaux, 1978). (3) Women are responding to another woman, Anne, not themselves, in writing the stories. Perhaps they feel anxious about Anne's success, but would not feel anxious about their own success. (4) In technical language, Horner's technique confounds gender of participants with gender of the stimulus cue. That is, women write about Anne, men about John. From this, we cannot tell whether women are higher in fear of success than men, or whether successful women (cues) arouse more anxiety than successful men. Perhaps if men wrote about Anne, they too would indicate bizarre reactions to her. In fact, one study showed that to be exactly what happens (Monahan et al., 1974). This suggests that Horner's techniques may simply be measuring cultural stereotypes about women rather than murky unconscious conflicts.

Where does this leave us? Is there a motive to avoid success that keeps some women from achieving, or that at least makes them miserable if they do? My belief is that there probably is such a phenomenon, but I must also say that there is not much scientific evidence for it. In Chapter 1, I noted that one of the critical

Projective test: A method of psychological measurement that uses ambiguous stimuli; the person's responses are thought to reflect his or her personality based on the assumption that one's personality is projected onto the ambiguous stimulus.

steps in psychological research is *measurement*. That is, when a researcher has some phenomenon to study, she or he must first devise a way to measure it. In Horner's case, she chose to measure the motive to avoid success by using a **projective test.** The idea is that people are given an ambiguous cue. Their stories about that cue presumably reflect a projection of their own unconscious motives. Many psychologists now consider projective tests to be poor methods of measurement and might prefer some more direct method, perhaps a paper-and-pencil checklist (such as Bem used in measuring androgyny, as discussed in Chapter 3). My belief is that the motive to avoid success probably exists in some people, but no one has been able to measure it adequately as yet (Macdonald and Hyde, 1980), and it may affect both women and men.

Attributions: When a Woman Succeeds, Is It Just Luck?

Suppose a college woman gets an A on a calculus exam. When she thinks about her success, or when others think about it, what will they believe caused it? To what will she or others attribute her success? This is called the **attribution** process, and it has been studied in detail by social psychologists. Typically four kinds of causes have been studied: ability, effort, luck, and task difficulty. Applied to the example given here, people might think that the woman got an A because of her own high mathematical ability, because she studied hard (effort), simply because she was lucky, or because the exam was easy. These four kinds of causes can be further categorized into two groups, those attributing the event to *internal* sources (factors within the individual, that is, ability and effort) and those attributing the event to *external* sources (forces outside the individual, that is, luck and task difficulty).

Attribution: The process by which people make judgments about the causes of behavior.

Early research in this area tended to document gender differences in attribution patterns. Women were found to be more likely than men to attribute their own success to external sources, in particular, luck; men, in contrast, attributed their success to their own abilities (e.g., Simon and Feather, 1973). These results were also found when people explained the performance of another person; they thought that a woman succeeds because of luck and that a man succeeds because of his skill or ability (Deaux and Emswiller, 1974). The early research also showed that, when people are explaining their failures, women are more likely than men to attribute failure to internal sources, namely, to their own lack of abilities (McMahan, 1971, 1972).

Irene Frieze and her colleagues (1982; see also Sohn, 1982; Whitley et al., 1986) then conducted a meta-analysis of all available studies on attribution patterns to see whether gender differences appeared consistently. Their results indicated that the size of the gender differences described above is essentially zero. Once again, gender similarities in behavior are the reality.

Research may yet uncover important gender differences in causal attributions if the study designs become more complex, particularly if attention is given to situational factors, such as the type of task that is used (McHugh et al., 1982). For example, if the task involves spatial ability problems or some kind of athletic performance, women might attribute their successes to luck, whereas if the task involves establishing a friendship with a new person or establishing a nurturant relationship with someone in need, then women might be more likely to attribute their successes to ability. But for now it must be said that we don't know whether there are gender differences in causal attributions.

At this stage of the research and theorizing, causal attributions are not going to be much help in explaining gender differences in achievements. What may be more helpful is a related result discussed in Chapter 3. It has been found that women have lower expectations for success than men do, for a wide variety of tasks and age groups (Mednick and Thomas, 1993). Indeed, this gender difference has been discovered as early as the preschool years. Further, people with high expectations of success tend to do better (Crandall, 1978). For example, when people are randomly assigned to high-expectancy and low-expectancy groups, the high-expectancy group tends to perform better (Tyler, 1958). Therefore, women may achieve less because they expect to achieve less. Expectations may be more important than attributions.

It is important to recognize the situational and social factors influencing these phenomena. As noted above, in competitive situations women have lower expectations for success than men do; however, in noncompetitive situations, women state expectancies similar to men's (House, 1974). Apparently gender-role concerns can become inhibiting to women when the situation involves competition.

In Conclusion

In this chapter I reviewed evidence on gender differences in abilities, noting that there are no gender differences in verbal ability or mathematical performance, except that boys start doing better in problem solving beginning in high school; and there are gender differences favoring males on only one type of spatial ability, mental rotations. Girls do better in school, yet men achieve higher-status positions in the world of work. There is a disparity, then, between the abilities and school achievement of females, on one hand, and the status of their jobs in adulthood, on the other.

Two general classes of factors help to explain this discrepancy: (1) external[1]

---

[1]The use of *external* and *internal* here should not be confused with the language of external and internal used in discussing causal attributions earlier in this chapter.

barriers to achievement and (2) internal (or intrapsychic) barriers to achievement. External barriers are factors such as job discrimination and, as noted in Chapter 7, there is ample evidence that this exists, in both obvious and subtle forms. Internal barriers or intrapsychic factors—such as low expectations for success—and low value placed on some areas such as developing math skills—also seem to exist. Of course, the internal barriers may be caused by external forces; for example, a woman may have low expectations for success on her job because she has experienced job discrimination. Thus, a combination of external and internal factors is important in explaining the work achievements of women. It is also important to recognize both sets of factors when trying to bring about the social change necessary to allow women to achieve more.

EXPERIENCE THE RESEARCH

GIRLS, BOYS, AND COMPUTERS

This exercise has two parts:

1. Visit a local store that sells computer games. Examine ten games that are currently being sold. Based on the information on the package and what you know about the games, classify each game as male oriented, female oriented, or neutral. To do this, you will have to specify your criteria for each of these categories. For example, you might decide that any game that involves violence is male oriented. Specify your criteria clearly and write them down. If there is not enough information on the package to classify a game, ask a salesperson in the store to give you more details about it.

   Overall, what were your findings? What percentage of the games were male oriented? Female oriented? Neutral? What are the implications of your findings?

2. Find out whether the local high school has an after-school computer lab. If it does, visit the lab twice to make observations. On each occasion, count the number of male students and female students who are there. Next, observe the computer activity in which each student is engaging, such as playing a game (what kind of game?) or programming.

   Do the boys' computer activities differ systematically from the girls'? Do there seem to be power dynamics in the lab, with some people dominating over others? What is the pattern of those power dynamics?

Suggestions for Further Reading

Holland, Dorothy C., & Eisenhart, Margaret A. (1990). *Educated in romance: Women, achievement, and college culture.* Chicago: University of Chicago Press. The authors used anthropologists' methods to study a predominantly white, southern university and a southern historically Black college. They found that the faculty and administration had relatively little impact. Rather, it was the peer culture stressing romance that led women to abandon their career plans.

Mednick, Martha T. (1989). On the politics of psychological constructs: Stop the bandwagon, I want to get off. *American Psychologist, 44,* 1118–1123. Discusses the demise of the concept of fear of success and some other popular constructs in the psychology of women, and why these constructs failed to deliver as promised.

7

Women and Work

The token woman is a black Chicana fluent in Chinese
Who has borne 1.2 babies
(not on the premises, no child care provided)
owns a Ph.D., will teach freshmen English
for a decade and bleach your laundry
with tears, silent as a china egg.
Your department orders her from a taxidermist's catalog
and she comes luxuriously stuffed with goose down
able to double as sleeping
or punching bag.

FROM MARGE PIERCY, THE TOKEN WOMAN

The majority of American women hold paying jobs. Among women between the ages of 25 and 54, 75 percent hold jobs (U.S. Department of Labor, 1993). The working woman, then, is not a variation from the norm; she *is* the norm.

Why do women choose to hold or not to hold jobs? A distinction can be made between the process of *career choice* (Betz, 1993) and the *decision to work* (Nieva and Gutek, 1981). Career choice generally involves matching one's interests, abilities, and training with the requirements of a particular job. However, many factors can be barriers to women's career choices, including gender stereotypes about occupations, lack of role models, and gender-biased career counseling.

The decision to work is usually the product of a number of situational factors (Nieva and Gutek, 1981). One of these is economics. If the woman is single, she usually must work to support herself and possibly her children if she is a single parent. For many married women, the decision to work is influenced by how adequate the husband's income is as support for the family. Another factor is children. The more children a woman has, the less likely she is to hold a paying job (Nieva and Gutek, 1981). However, this is a correlational result and causality should not be inferred from it. In fact, there is evidence that the influence works in the opposite direction: participating in the labor force reduces the number of children that women want and have (Nieva and Gutek, 1981).

Stereotypes About Women and Work

There are many stereotypes about women and work. Below I shall consider some of them, and what the actual data say.

Stereotype 1: Women are working only for a little extra money. The idea behind this stereotype is that most women are only providing a second income, that the husband supports the family, and that the wife is working only to provide a few frills. In fact, however, most women work because of stark economic necessity. Nearly two-thirds of all women in the labor force are single, widowed, divorced, or separated or have husbands whose earnings were less than $15,000

FIGURE 7.1
The majority of American women (75 percent) hold jobs outside of the home.

(U.S. Department of Labor, 1988). The majority of women workers are the sole support of their families, or are married to men whose incomes would have put them below the poverty line. The presence of working wives decreases the poverty rate of married couples by 35 percent among whites, 39 percent among Blacks, and 26 percent among Hispanics (Blank, 1988). In 1991, the average income of married-couple families with the wife in the paid labor force was $48,000, compared with $30,000 for those without the wife in the labor force (U.S. Department of Labor, 1993).

Stereotype 2: Women shouldn't be hired for jobs requiring training, because they will just quit when they get married or pregnant. The assumption here is that women are more likely to quit their jobs than men are. Overall, that is true. However, the gap between men's and women's turnover rates has narrowed substantially in the past several decades. In 1961, men's turnover rate was 108.5 and women's was 132.9;[1] by 1981, men's was 105.5 and women's was down to 114.0 (Blau and Ferber, 1985). Thus women have an increasing stability in the work force. Moreover, when occupational level and income are controlled, males and females do not differ significantly in turnover rates (Mead and Kaplan, 1965, p. 52). This simply means that women are found disproportionately in dull, dead-

---

[1]These numbers are calculated in a manner that is too technical and too far off the subject to explain here.

"AS FAR AS I'M CONCERNED, THE REAL EROGENOUS
ZONE IS WALL STREET!"

FIGURE 7.2
(Source: Shiong/Rothco.)

end jobs, and there is a high turnover rate in those jobs, whether men or women are in them. Given the same job and the same pay, females and males have about the same turnover rate. Today, most women are in the labor force for more than just a few years. The average woman can expect to spend 29.3 years of her life in the labor force (U.S. Department of Labor, 1988).

Stereotype 3: A woman who is really ambitious and qualified can get ahead anyway. It is true that some women get ahead, but they are relatively few in number. All other factors aside, what the woman worker must often face is simple job discrimination. For example, the average woman worker is as well educated as the average man worker—both have a median of 12.6 years of schooling—but she makes only 75 cents for every dollar he earns when both work full-time, year-round (U.S. Department of Labor, 1993). Most investigators agree that women are discriminated against in employment. Given the same education, job, experience, and so on, they are given less pay and are promoted more slowly (e.g., Adelman, 1991; Betz, 1993; Morrison et al., 1992).

Sex Discrimination in the Workplace

Sex discrimination in the workplace may take a number of forms, including discrimination in the evaluation of women's work, discrimination in pay, discrimination in hiring and promotion, and people refusing to work for a woman boss.

Discrimination in the Evaluation of Women's Work Psychologists have contributed some interesting experiments that investigate whether there is discrimination in the evaluation of women's work. A classic study demonstrated that even when the work of a female is identical to that of a male, it is judged to be inferior (Goldberg, 1968; replicated by Pheterson et al., 1971). Female college students were given scholarly essays in a number of academic fields to evaluate. All of the students rated the same essays, but half of them rated essays bearing the names of male authors (for example, John T. McKay), whereas the other half rated the same essays with the names of female authors (Joan T. McKay). The essays were identical except for the names of the authors. The results were that the essays were rated higher when the author was male, even when the essay was in a traditionally feminine field such as dietetics. It appears that the work of males is valued more even if it is identical to that of females. It is interesting to note that the raters in this study, those who gave lower value to female work, were themselves females.

In another study of gender and discrimination in the evaluation of work, the opposite effect was found; it was called the "talking platypus effect" (Abramson et al., 1977). Undergraduates read a one-page biography of a stimulus person. Half of them read about a male, and half about a female; further, in half of the biographies the person was a lawyer, and in the other half the person was a paralegal. Interestingly, the female attorney was rated as *more* competent than the male attorney. The authors believe that with public awareness of the obstacles to achievement that women face, people actually overvalue a woman who has demonstrated a high level of achievement: If you hear a platypus talking, it doesn't much matter what it says; it is simply a wonder that it can say anything at all.

How can we resolve these two apparently contradictory studies, one showing discrimination against women and one showing discrimination against men? A meta-analysis reviewed 106 articles reporting studies of this type (Swim et al., 1989). The authors concluded that there was little evidence of bias in the evaluation of women's work; the average effect size d was $-.07$, the negative sign indicating that women's work was given slightly lower ratings than men's work, but the d was so small that we could say it was zero. Notice that—in contrast to other meta-analyses I have reported, in which d reflected the difference between the performance of males and the performance of females—here the effect is for the difference between evaluations of work with a male's name on it and evaluations of work with a female's name on it. The effect size d, in this instance, is a measure of the extent of sex bias or discrimination.

It would be a rather happy conclusion to say that there is no bias in the evaluation of women's work. However, there were complexities in the meta-analysis. First, the effect size depended quite a bit on the kind of material that was rated, and it was larger when that material was an employment application ($d = -.25$) than when it was something else, such as written work ($d = -.14$). Thus discrimination against women was greatest for employment applications, and that is a serious matter.

The other complexity was that the effect size (amount of sex bias) depended on the amount of information given to the rater. When raters were given only a small amount of information—just a male or female name—bias was greatest ($d = -.38$), whereas when raters were given a paragraph or more of information, the effect size was small ($d = -.08$). This is consistent with a general finding in social psychology, that people stereotype others less the more they know about them. This is a rather optimistic finding in that it means we do not always have to be ruled by stereotypes. On the other hand, there are some very important situations, such as job interviews, when an interviewer is making a critical decision based on a first impression and a small amount of information, and that is just when stereotyping and bias are most likely to occur.

A serious limitation to the meta-analysis was that virtually all the studies reviewed were laboratory experiments with college students serving as the raters. In short, the studies do not directly measure what is of most concern: sex discrimination in the actual evaluations of the work of real women, as evaluated by their actual supervisors, by people actually making hiring decisions, or by other powerful persons. The studies in the meta-analysis provide only analogies to the real situation, and for that reason are called *analog studies*. We are left wondering, then, whether there is more or less discrimination in the real world of work.

A real-world study investigated the impact of both gender and race on evaluations of work (Greenhaus and Parasuraman, 1993). A total of 1,628 managers in corporations (814 African Americans and 814 whites) and their supervisors participated. Supervisors gave an attribution rating—that is, to what extent they thought the satisfactory performance of the manager was due to ability. The results indicated that, among the most highly successful managers, the performance of the women was less likely to be attributed to ability than it was for men. The performance of African American managers was less likely to be attributed to ability and effort and was more likely to be attributed to help from others than was the performance of white managers. On the other hand, the effects were generally small; for example, for race differences in attributions to ability, $d = .18$. Furthermore, these attribution effects were strongest when the manager and supervisor had little experience with each other. With longer experience, the race differences in attributions became smaller. This study, then, provides evidence of gender bias and race bias in evaluations of work in a real-world setting; however, the effects are small, and they become smaller when the supervisor and manager have had more experience together.

Pay Equity Sex discrimination in pay is another serious issue. For many women, especially those who are single heads of households, it is literally a bread-and-butter issue. By 1991, women's earnings had climbed to an average of $20,553 for full-time, yearly workers, compared with $29,421 for men (U.S. Department of Labor, 1993). And this occurs despite the fact that, on average, women are as educated as men.

The wage gap is not only a gender issue, but a race issue as well. Table 7.1 shows annual earnings as a function of both gender and ethnicity. These statistics clearly show that both women and minorities have lower wages than white men.

TABLE 7.1
Median Annual Earnings for Full-Time, Year-Round Workers, 1991

	Women	Men	Ratio* (wage gap)
All races	$20,553	$29,421	.70
Whites	$20,794	$30,266	.69
Blacks	$18,720	$22,075	.62
Hispanics	$16,244	$19,771	.54

*This ratio gives women's earnings as a percentage of white males' earnings.
Source: U.S. Department of Labor (1993).

What causes the wage gap? One clear factor is job segregation, to be discussed in the next section. Very few jobs have a 50:50 male:female ratio. Most are held predominantly by one sex or the other, and the higher the percentage of women in an occupation, the lower the pay. In extreme cases, when the gender ratio shifts so that women take over a formerly male-dominated occupation, wages drop. An example in the United States is pharmacy, which was once a predominantly male occupation in which men owned their own stores and were businessmen as well as pharmacists, bringing in high earnings. These stores are now being replaced by chain drugstores, where women pharmacists dispense drugs and earn much smaller incomes (Bernstein, 1988).

It was the recognition of the gender gap in wages, and the fact that it was an outgrowth of gender-segregated occupations, that led, in the late 1970s, to the concept of **comparable worth.** The idea behind comparable worth is that people should be paid equally for work in comparable jobs—that is, jobs with equivalent responsibility, educational requirements, level in the organization, and required experience. As an illustration of the need for principles of comparable worth, in one state both liquor store clerks and librarians are employed by the state government. Liquor store clerks are almost all men, and the job requires only a high school education. Librarians are almost all women, and the job requires a college education. But in this state, liquor store clerks are paid more than librarians. The principle of comparable worth argues against this pattern. It says that librarians should be paid at least as much as, and probably more than, liquor store clerks because librarians must be college graduates.

Comparable worth: The principle that people should be paid equally for work that is comparable in responsibility, educational requirements, and so forth.

Several states—including my own, Wisconsin—have enacted comparable-worth legislation, stating that at least all those who are government employees must be paid on a comparable-worth basis. This necessitates extensive job analyses by industrial/organizational psychologists to determine which jobs—ignoring gender—have equivalent requirements in terms of responsibilities, education,

FOCUS 7.1
GENDER, ENTITLEMENT, AND THE WAGE GAP

Among full-time, year-round workers, women earn only 75 cents for every dollar earned by men (U.S. Department of Labor, 1993). This is a gross injustice. Why are women not rioting in the streets, protesting this massive problem?

Psychologist Brenda Major has developed a theory of entitlement that helps to explain both the wage gap and why women tolerate it. *Entitlement* refers simply to the individual's sense of what she or he is entitled to receive (e.g., pay). Major's model is shown in Figure 7.4.

The process begins with inequalities in the social structure in the United States. These include the gender segregation of most jobs, the chronic underpayment of women and of women's jobs, and the lack of equal opportunities for women. These inequalities in the social structure then lead women and men to have different

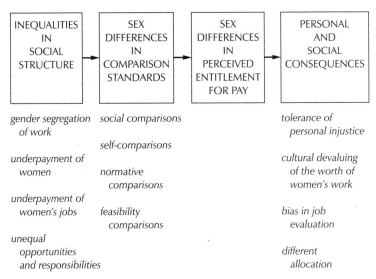

INEQUALITIES IN SOCIAL STRUCTURE	SEX DIFFERENCES IN COMPARISON STANDARDS	SEX DIFFERENCES IN PERCEIVED ENTITLEMENT FOR PAY	PERSONAL AND SOCIAL CONSEQUENCES

gender segregation of work　　*social comparisons*　　　　　　　　　　*tolerance of personal injustice*

　　　　　　　　　　self-comparisons

underpayment of women　　　　　　　　　　　　　　　　　　*cultural devaluing of the worth of women's work*
　　　　　　　　　normative comparisons

underpayment of women's jobs　　*feasibility comparisons*　　　　　　*bias in job evaluation*

unequal opportunities and responsibilities　　　　　　　　　　　　　　*different allocation*

FIGURE 7.3
Major's model of the causes of gender differences in the sense of entitlement and how this gender difference contributes to the wage gap.
(Source: From "Gender differences in comparison and entitlement: Implications for comparable worth" by Brenda Major, Journal of Social Issues 45, 4, p. 101.
Reprinted by permission of the author and the Society for the Psychological Study of Social Issues.)

standards of comparison, that is, standards against which they compare their own pay when deciding whether it is equitable. The result is that women compare their pay with that of other women and with others in their typically female-dominated occupation. Women see other women and those in their own occupation as the appropriate comparison group because of a proximity effect—that is, those are the people who are around them and about whom they have information. The average telephone operator is unlikely to have information on what electricians earn. Self-protective factors may also play a part. An underpaid female librarian who is a college graduate does not want to know what a male high school graduate working in a skilled trade earns. It will just make her feel bad. Her tendency will be to compare her pay with that of other female librarians, and then she won't be doing so badly.

These gender differences in standards of comparison then have a great impact on women's and men's perceptions of their entitlement to pay. Many women do not feel entitled to high pay for their work in the way that men do because (1) their pay is reasonable relative to those with whom they compare themselves; (2) their pay is reasonable compared with their own past pay; and (3) their pay is reasonable according to what is realistically attainable given restricted job opportunities for women.

The result is that women have less of a sense of entitlement to high pay than men do. This in turn leads them to tolerate wage injustice. Another consequence is that others come to believe that women will settle for less in pay, precisely because many women do, leading to further bias in setting wage rates. And so the cycle continues.

What evidence is there to support this theory? Many experiments have been conducted testing various aspects of it, and virtually all of them support it. I will discuss two examples here (Major, 1989). In one, female and male undergraduates worked on a gender-neutral task in a research laboratory for a fixed amount of time. Afterward, they paid themselves privately from a pot containing $4.00. In one of the experimental groups, the participants simply paid themselves what they thought their work was worth, in the absence of any social comparison information. In the other group, participants were given bogus information about how much money previous participants had paid themselves for the same work. In the first condition, with no information about others' pay, women paid themselves an average of $1.95, whereas men paid themselves an average of $3.18. However, when comparison information was given, there were no gender differences; men and women both matched their pay to the comparison standard.

Another study, closer to a real-world situation, found that female and male management students who had equal qualifications had different perceptions of what graduates in their field earned; women thought the pay was lower.

As I noted in Chapter 1, we must be careful of interpretations of these phenomena, so that this theory does not become another female deficit model. One interpretation is that women have a low sense of personal entitlement compared with men, that is, that women have a deficit in their sense of entitlement. The other possible interpretation is that men have too great a sense of entitlement—a sense that they are entitled to more than they are worth. An inflated sense of entitlement characterizes many dominant groups, including men, whites, and those from the upper social classes.

This theory is an excellent example of the ways in which social institutions, such as the gender segregation of occupations (an external factor) interact with psychological processes such as a sense of entitlement (an internal factor) to create gender bias.

Source: Major (1989, 1994).

FIGURE 7.4

(Source: © 1992 Cathy Guisewite. Reprinted by permission of Universal Press Syndicate. All rights reserved.)

and so on. Preliminary results in states that have legislated this principle are promising. Despite dire predictions from the business community, it turns out not to be terribly expensive for employers to pay on a comparable-worth basis.

A second factor that seems to be related to the gender gap in wages is women's family roles (O'Neill, 1985). Marriage and children raise the amount of home-related work for both women and men, but the effect is much greater for women. We will discuss these issues more later in this chapter, in the section on work and family issues. The important point for this discussion of pay equity is that women's greater family responsibilities may lead them to make certain choices (or force them to make certain choices) that will result in lower wages. For example, to be a successful partner in a law firm or to earn tenure as a college professor requires considerably more than 40 hours of work per week—often 60 to 80 hours. Some (though certainly not all) women in this situation may choose not to commit the extra hours, because they want to spend them with their family, or family commitments simply prevent work beyond 40 hours per week. These women then choose or settle for the lower and less well paid levels of their occupations—lawyer but not partner, lecturer but not tenured professor. There is much questioning of why women's family responsibilities should interfere with their job advancement, a point to which we will return later in this chapter.

Discrimination in Hiring and Promotion   As noted earlier in this chapter, there is some evidence of gender bias in the evaluation of employment applications. Here we will focus on discrimination in promotions.

A series of studies by Laurie Larwood and her colleagues (1988) demonstrates the continuing existence of sex discrimination in the selection of people for work assignments. The research shows that men are preferred for more important assignments, for assignments in which the client is a man, and for assignments in which the work is stereotyped as appropriate for men. Women, on the other hand, are preferred when assignments are less important, when the client is a woman, when the client is known to oppose sex discrimination, when the work is stereotyped as appropriate for women, or when the woman herself has been independently recognized as talented. These experiments illuminate the complex factors that can contribute to discrimination against women, preventing them from being given important assignments and the opportunity for promotion.

Most of what has been said here about sex discrimination also characterizes race discrimination. For example, the same series of studies by Larwood and her colleagues showed that a Black woman is preferred for an assignment if the client is a Black woman, but that a white man is preferred if the client is a white man—and in most of the business world, the client is a white man.

On a purely logical basis, discrimination in hiring and promotion doesn't make sense. All companies ought to benefit the most from hiring and promoting the best-qualified individuals, regardless of gender or race. Why, then, does discrimination continue?

According to a complex theory advanced by Larwood and her colleagues (1988), discrimination occurs because managers who are in charge of making assignments or granting promotions behave in a highly self-interested way. Furthermore, these managers generally perceive that the norms of the business world *support* discrimination. Thus managers essentially believe that it is in their best interest to behave the way the bosses of the corporation want them to—assigning women to stereotyped jobs, keeping them out of important assignments, and so on. Of course, managers may misperceive the beliefs of top executives, but the research shows that if they are unsure about those beliefs, they will discriminate.

Are there any solutions to these thorny problems? Larwood's research does offer some helpful suggestions. It demonstrates quite clearly that if a client or the president of the company has spoken out against discrimination, that action affects the behavior of managers, who are then less likely to discriminate in making assignments. Perhaps most important, therefore, is establishing a corporate climate in which it is clear that those at the top are opposed to discrimination. Managers, still operating out of self-interest, will then be more likely to engage in gender-fair practices.

Glass ceiling:
"Invisible" barriers to the promotion of women and ethnic minorities into upper management and executive levels.

The Glass Ceiling The term **glass ceiling** refers to the phenomenon that, in many instances, women seem to be promoted and to advance well in their company up to a certain point, and then there seems to be a barrier or ceiling that prevents them from rising further (Morrison et al., 1992; Task Force on the Glass Ceiling Initiative, 1993; U.S. Department of Labor, 1992). For example, some women make it to the upper levels of management, but can't seem to break into executive positions—they can see the executive suite through the glass, but they can't crack through the barrier.

What evidence is there that a glass ceiling exists? A 1992 U.S. Department of Labor study of Fortune 1000–sized companies found that, although 37 percent of all employees in these companies were women, women comprised only 16.9 percent of managers (including everyone from supervisors of clerical pools to CEOs) (Table 7.2). At the highest level of the company, women were only 6.6 percent of executives. Exactly the same pattern holds for people of color (see Table 7.2). The higher one goes in corporations, the fewer women and people of color there are, and that is exactly what is meant by the glass ceiling.

In a survey of women in management in Wisconsin, we found that 58 percent of the women reported the existence of a glass ceiling at their current or previous companies (Task Force on the Glass Ceiling Initiative, 1993). Among those women who said there was a glass ceiling at their previous company, 80 percent said it was an important reason why they left. Typically either these women moved to a company with a more equitable environment for women, or they started their own business. The study found that women-owned businesses were thriving. This phenomenon is evidence of **women's resistance.** Many talented women do not stay and passively suffer with a glass ceiling; instead, they move to another company or start their own business, and those women-owned businesses often compete successfully with ones they left.

Women's resistance:
Occurs when women do not passively accept discriminatory treatment, but instead take active steps to resist it.

TABLE 7.2

Statistics on the Glass Ceiling: Percentage of Women and Minorities at Different Levels of Fortune 1000 Corporations

	Women	Ethnic Minorities
All employees	37.2	15.5
All managers	16.9	5.0
Executives	6.6	2.6

SOURCE: U.S. Department of Labor (1992).

Leadership Issues   Surveys show that some people do not want to work for a woman boss (Kanter, 1977). Social psychology studies have documented that it is difficult for a woman to assume and be recognized in a leadership role. For example, one study investigated this by using the phenomenon that the person seated at the head of a table is usually recognized as being the leader of a group (Porter et al., 1978). Participants were shown photographs of groups seated around a table and were asked to rate the leadership attributes of each member of the group. A man seated at the head of the table in a mixed-gender group was clearly seen as the group's leader, but a woman occupying that position was ignored. Women at the head of the table were recognized as leaders only when the group was all-female.

When women occupy positions of leadership—for example, as a supervisor on a job—the evidence, then, indicates that they tend to be stereotyped as not having the right characteristics to be successful leaders. In real-world job situations, there are three possible reasons that women leaders might be viewed in this way. One is that they are truly lacking in personality traits, interpersonal skills, and so on that are necessary in the supervisory role. A second reason is that people simply are biased in their evaluations of women who are leaders. A third reason is that women supervisors, as part of the complex network in a corporation, have less power than their male counterparts do (Nieva and Gutek, 1981). Power involves such things as being able to grant pay raises or promotions to subordinates or being able to influence the decisions of those higher up the corporate ladder. If workers perceive women supervisors as having less power, it should be no surprise if they are unenthusiastic about working for them.

One interesting study investigated the first hypothesis above—namely, that when women are placed in supervisory roles they behave differently, perhaps less skillfully, than men do. In a simulation of an organizational setting, a male or female undergraduate was placed in the role of supervisor of either a three-man or a three-woman work group in the adjacent room (Instone et al., 1983). The workers did some rather trivial clerical tasks and were in fact confederates of the experimenters. In some cases the workers were compliant, continuing to produce work

FIGURE 7.5
Women aspiring to nontraditional careers may face various forms of psychological discrimination; for example, some people have difficulty recognizing a woman in a leadership role. This photograph shows a woman attorney and her client. When you saw the picture, did you perceive him as being her boss?

at a high rate. In other cases the workers were noncompliant—their productivity dropped sharply, and they expressed negative attitudes such as "I'm bored, this is a pain." Supervisors were permitted to do a number of things in dealing with the workers: they could do positive things, such as give pay increases or give positive talks; or they could do negative things, such as give pay decreases or fire the workers. (Notice that in this cleverly controlled laboratory study, the third hypothesis discussed above—that females have less access to power in corporations—is ruled out because male and female supervisors were given identical power in the experiment.) The question was, Do females behave differently as supervisors from the way males do? The results did show some gender differences consistent with stereotypes. Compared with males, females made fewer attempts to influence their workers. Females were also less likely to use rewarding strategies, particularly promises of pay increases, and were more likely to use negative, coercive strategies, such as pay deductions. However, these differences were small, supporting the notion that gender similarities are the rule.

An additional finding of the study by Instone and colleagues is important. The female research participants reported strikingly less confidence in their ability to supervise their workers than male participants did. This gender difference in self-confidence has been found in other research (Chapter 3). Previous research has shown that men in leadership positions who have low self-confidence are less likely to exert influence and more likely to use coercive techniques than men who have high self-confidence are. The leadership behaviors of the women in this study, then, may be more a result of their lack of self-confidence than of any kind of innate lack of leadership ability. Their lack of self-confidence is odd given that the female participants actually reported as much prior experience in supervisory roles as the male participants did. On the other hand, the authors noted a positive correlation between amount of supervisory experience and self-confidence in women—the more experience a woman had, the more self-confidence she had. Therefore, the authors concluded on a hopeful note: the more supervisory experience women are given, the more their self-confidence will increase, which in turn will improve their supervisory behaviors, so that they will make more influence attempts and use more positive strategies in dealing with their workers.

The second hypothesis is that people simply are biased in their evaluation of women leaders. A meta-analysis was performed on laboratory studies in which women and men occupying leadership roles were evaluated, with all other factors controlled (Eagly, Makhijani, and Klonsky, 1992). The results indicated that, overall, there was little evidence of gender bias; women and men leaders were given similar evaluations in general ($d = .05$). However, under certain conditions women received notably worse evaluations. If women used an autocratic leadership style (a dictatorial style rather than a more democratic, nurturant one), they received lower evaluations ($d = .30$). It may be, then, that it is not so much a question of bias against women leaders as bias against women leaders who behave in a counterstereotyped, masculine style. People have trouble with autocratic, pushy women, although the same behaviors would probably not seem nearly so pushy coming from a man. Other research shows that, perhaps fortunately, women are more likely to use a democratic style of leadership and men are more likely to use an autocratic one (Eagly and Johnson, 1990). These are important findings for women as they assume leadership roles and consider the management style they adopt.

The third hypothesis above—that women as leaders have less power in organizations—implies that women also need to find ways to increase their power (for an excellent summary and analysis, see Smith and Grenier, 1982). Some of this will involve women's getting specific instruction—for example, assertiveness training or instruction on how to plan careers. But women also need to learn how to use the structural bases of power that exist within organizations. Legitimate power can come from any of three sources (Smith and Grenier, 1982): (1) participating in activities critical to the organization's survival or its current pressing problems; (2) participating in activities that control uncertainty (if the computer breaks down frequently at inopportune moments, then the computer repairperson has power); and (3) participating in activities controlling resources such as money, people, or information. Women can learn to use any or all of these strategies for gaining power. (There are, of course, many illegitimate sources of power, such as sexual harassment and threats; however, I can't recommend that women learn to use these.)

Feminist psychologists have also suggested new models of leadership (Astin and Leland, 1991; Denmark, 1993). Specifically, they suggest a new model of **empowerment.** Replacing the old belief that leaders have the power to control, this new model suggests that leaders have the power to empower. This view "treats power as an expandable resource that is produced and shared through interaction by leader and followers alike" (Astin and Leland, 1991, p. 1). In a study of successful women leaders, their strategies for empowerment included the following: communicating with others on their own level, listening, employing strong people and not feeling threatened by them, offering positive feedback, and working through consensus and collegiality (a democratic style) (Astin and Leland, 1991).

Empowerment:
Helping people to find their own strength.

In summary, then, women face some barriers—some internalized, but most external—when they assume leadership roles. They may lack self-confidence in their abilities to lead. People may be biased in their evaluation of women leaders, particularly women who adopt an autocratic style. And women may lack power in their organization, so that employees are less enthusiastic about working for them. Feminist psychologists have suggested strategies for women to gain power in their organization, and they have proposed a new model of leadership that involves empowerment.

Occupational Segregation

Most occupations are segregated by gender (Reskin, 1988). Some relevant statistics are shown in Table 7.3. Notice that most occupations are highly segregated by gender, with 90 percent or more of the workers coming from one gender. Men dominate as airline pilots, auto mechanics, carpenters, dentists, and welders. Women dominate as childcare workers, data entry keyers, dental assistants, and registered nurses. Only a few occupations come close to a 50 to 50 gender ratio: bus drivers, editors and reporters, social workers, and college and university teachers.

Occupational segregation is a critical issue for two reasons. First, the stereotyping of occupations severely limits people's work options. A man might think himself well suited to being a registered nurse, or a woman might love carpentry, but they are discouraged from following their dreams because certain occupations are not considered gender appropriate for them. Second, occupational segregation is a major contributor to the gender gap in wages. As I noted earlier, women earn only 75 cents for every dollar earned by men. Statistics indicate that about 30 to 45 percent of that wage gap is due to occupational segregation (Reskin, 1988). Occupations that are predominantly female are almost invariably low paying.

TABLE 7.3

Women as a Percentage of All Workers in Selected Occupations, 1975, 1989, and 1992

Occupation	Women as Percentage of Total Employed		
	1975	*1989*	*1992*
Airline pilot	0	3.8	2.3
Auto mechanic	0.5	0.7	0.8
Bus driver	37.7	54.8	41.7
Carpenter	0.6	1.2	1.0
Childcare worker	98.4	97.1	97.1
Data entry keyer	92.8	87.8	84.9
Dentist	1.8	8.6	8.5
Dental assistant	100.0	98.9	98.6
Editor, reporter	44.6	49.2	49.7
Elementary school teacher	85.4	84.7	85.4
College/university teacher	31.1	38.7	40.9
Lawyer, judge	7.1	22.3	21.4
Librarian	81.1	87.3	87.6
Physician	13.0	17.9	20.4
Registered nurse	97.0	94.2	94.3
Social worker	60.8	68.1	68.9
Telephone installer, repairer	4.8	10.8	3.4
Telephone operator	93.3	89.8	89.9
Welder	4.4	6.6	4.2

SOURCE: U.S. Bureau of Labor Statistics (1976, 1990, 1993).

Are We Making Any Progress?   As we have reviewed evidence of continuing sex discrimination and occupational segregation in the 1990s, you might be wondering whether any progress has been made as the women's movement has pressed its case for equality. The answer is yes, in some areas. For example, in certain fields, women have quickly risen to earn substantial numbers of professional degrees. Some statistics from professions in which women have made the greatest advances are shown in Table 7.4. Now that women are earning substantial numbers of the professional degrees in these areas, occupational segregation will surely decrease. It is particularly interesting to note that all of these are high-paying, high-status occupations. I speak with some feeling when I say that education can be one of the most important solutions to the problems women face in the work force.

FIGURE 7.6
Most occupations are gender segregated. (Above) Male autoworkers. (Below) Female nurses.

TABLE 7.4
**Percentages of Professional Degrees Awarded to Women
in Selected Professions in Which There Have Been Substantial
Advances, 1970, 1980, 1990**

Field	1970	1980	1990
Dentistry	0.9%	13.3%	30.9%
Medicine (M.D.)	8.4%	23.4%	34.0%
Law	5.4%	30.2%	42.2%

SOURCES: From *The American Woman 1988–1989,* edited by Sara Rix, 1988, p. 363.
Used by permission of W. W. Norton & Company, Inc.; U.S. Bureau of the Census (1993).

Work and Family Issues

Women have traditionally been responsible for maintaining the family, and particularly for caring for children. As women marched into the paid work force in the 1970s and 1980s, they added the responsibilities of their new jobs, but they didn't give up their family obligations. Therefore, combining work and family— both for women and for men—is one of the most important social issues of the 1990s. Work and family issues rank high on the feminist agenda, and corporate executives realize their importance. Even the U.S. government has recognized this fact; as of this writing the ABC bill (Act for Better Child Care) is making its way through Congress, and legislation on parental leave went into effect in 1993 (see Focus 7.2, "Psychology and Public Policy: The Parental Leave Debate").

Work and Women's Psychological Well-being   The American woman of the 1990s holds a full-time job while managing a household and marriage and raising a preschooler or caring for an elderly parent. Is she on overload, stressed out with all her responsibilities, prone to physical and mental illness? Or is she supermom, able to have it all and be happy? Quite a bit of scientific data is available to answer these questions.

Scarcity hypothesis: In research on women and multiple roles, the hypothesis that adding a role (e.g., worker) creates stress, which has negative consequences for mental health and physical health.

Within the framework of the social sciences, we are asking questions about the effects of multiple roles (e.g., worker, mother, wife) on health. Researchers in this area have taken two major theoretical approaches (Baruch et al., 1987):

1. The **scarcity hypothesis**—This approach assumes that each human has a fixed amount of energy and that any role makes demands on this pool of energy. Therefore, the greater the number of roles, the greater the stress and the more negative the conse-

FOCUS 7.2

PSYCHOLOGY AND PUBLIC POLICY: THE PARENTAL LEAVE DEBATE

In Sweden at the time of the birth of a baby, the parents have a right to 12 months of leave from work at 90 percent of normal pay (up to a certain maximum). The parents can split the leave however they wish. For example, the whole 12 months might be taken by the mother, or the whole 12 months might be taken by the father, or they might split it. They can have an additional 3 months' leave at pay that is further reduced, and they can have an additional 3 months' leave (taking them up to the baby's eighteenth month) at pay that is still further reduced. At 18 months, each baby in Sweden is entitled to a place in a childcare center. Furthermore, Swedish parents are entitled to work at 75 percent time at 75 percent pay, if they so choose, until the child is 8 years old. This sounds to me like a true profamily policy.

Until 1993, the United States was one of only two industrialized nations in the world (the other being South Africa) that did not have a nationally legislated policy on parental leave. The term *parental leave* refers to leave from work for purposes of recovering from childbirth and/or caring for a child at the time of the birth (or possibly adoption) of a child. An even broader term, *family leave,* refers to leave from work to care for a new baby, an ill spouse, or an elderly parent. With the exception of a few states that passed parental leave legislation around 1987, in most states until 1993 a woman could give birth to a baby, return to work quickly—say, a month later—and find that she had lost her job, and it was perfectly legal for her employer to have fired her. There was an urgent need for legislation that ensured mothers and fathers the right to care for their newborn infant and know they had their jobs waiting for them; among other things, they obviously need the income to support the baby.

The federal legislation—the Family and Medical Leave Act—that went into effect in 1993 mandates that employers must allow mothers and fathers a minimum of 12 weeks of job-guaranteed, unpaid leave at the time of a birth or adoption. This legislation has several important features. First, it is gender fair—that is, fathers have equal rights to mothers to take the leave, and some couples might choose to take the leaves back-to-back, so that one parent would be home with the baby for a total of 24 weeks, or nearly 6 months. I think this is unlikely right now for most couples, for reasons I will describe below. A second feature is that the leave is job guaranteed, which means that the employee has a right to return to the same or a comparable job (in terms of pay and responsibilities). A third feature is that the leave is unpaid, at least as a minimum standard. Most couples cannot afford to lose the wife's income for very long, if at all, and even fewer couples can afford to lose the husband's income, which generally is higher. It is for that reason that I think it is not very likely that many couples would take back-to-back leaves totaling 24 weeks. A fourth feature is that the legislation sets a minimum standard. Employers may be more generous. It's like the minimum wage—if it is $4.85 per hour, employers are perfectly free to pay a highly skilled person $20 per hour; they just can't pay anyone less that $4.85. In the same way, employers can be more generous with parental leave. They can allow more than 12 weeks, or they can provide paid leave. Some progressive corporations have realized that it is beneficial to provide paid leaves and are already doing so.

Clearly the legislation could be improved in a number of ways. Providing paid leave is a major necessary improvement. Employers worry about how costly this would be to them, but there are rather simple methods for paying for the leaves. Both Canada and the state of New Jersey have a system using a small payroll tax shared by employer and employee, and functioning much like the Social Security tax. This creates a fund, and employees on leave are paid from the fund. A second improvement needed is to have more employers and employees covered. The legislation applies only to employers with 50 or more employees; that is, small employers don't have to follow the rules. Women work disproportionately for small businesses, and it is important to extend the coverage to all mothers and fathers. A friend of mine recently told me that she had been fired in the first week after returning to work after having a baby. I exclaimed in outrage, "But that's illegal!" She replied that it was perfectly legal because there were only 12 employees at this company and they weren't covered by the legislation.

We have made enormous strides in the last decade with legislation that supports women as they combine work and family. And yet there is always a catch—in this case some women are still legally fired after taking parental leave.

Where does psychology come into the picture? Often as Congress considers legislation, it calls on expert witnesses, such as psychologists, who can provide evidence on the kind of impact the legislation—or lack thereof—might have. Psychologists' research on this topic can have one of two foci: effects on infants and effects on parents. The consensus that has emerged among developmental psychologists is that infants need to spend approximately the first four months of life with a stable caregiver—usually the mother, but equally well the father or some other caring adult, such as a grandparent. This pattern allows infants to form strong and stable attachments to the caregiver and to establish self-regulation of body processes, such as sleeping regularly through the night, feeding at regular times, and learning that they can trust that the food will be there. Therefore, psychologists such as Edward Zigler testified before Congress that legislation should provide four months of parental leave to meet the important developmental needs of an infant. This expert testimony on psychological research was influential in the passage of the bill.

As a specialist in the psychology of women, I immediately noticed that the well-being of mothers was invisible in the debate. Therefore, my colleagues and I are conducting a large-scale research project that adds a second focus to the psychological research: the effects of parental leave, or the lack of it, on mothers and fathers. Our study was begun before the federal legislation, but there was legislation in Wisconsin that provided 6 weeks of parental leave. Under those conditions, men took an average of 5 days of leave and women took an average of 8 weeks. We are studying the impact of taking a short leave (6 weeks or less) compared with a long leave (12 weeks or more) on women's mental health. We have found that a short leave seems to act as a risk factor for problems such as depression when the short leave is combined with some other risk factor such as a stressful marriage or stressful job. For example, women who took short leaves and had many concerns about their marriage had elevated levels of depression, compared with women who took longer leaves or who took short leaves but had happy marriages. We also found that many of the women in our sample wished they could have taken a longer leave than they did. The leading reason why they didn't take a longer leave was that they could not afford to do so.

This research and the research of developmental psychologists on infants' attachment needs illustrate how important psychological research can be in framing legislation that will have an impact on most of us at some time in our lives.

Sources: Hyde and Essex (1991); Hyde, Essex, and Horton (1993); Hyde, Klein, Essex, and Clark (1995); Zigler and Frank (1988).

quences on health. The conclusion from this view, then, is that as women take on increased work responsibilities in addition to their family responsibilities, stress and negative health consequences must result.

Enhancement hypothesis: In research on women and multiple roles, the hypothesis that multiple roles are good for mental health, because they provide more opportunities for stimulation, self-esteem, and so on.

2. The **enhancement hypothesis**—This approach assumes that people's energy resources are not limited, just as a regular program of exercise makes one feel more energetic, not less energetic. According to this approach, the more roles one has, the more the opportunities for enhanced self-esteem, stimulation, social status, and identity. Indeed, one might be cushioned from a traumatic occurrence in one role by the support one was receiving in another role.

If the second theoretical approach is correct, we need not worry about stress from women's combining work and family roles. The combination might actually enhance mental and physical health rather than threaten it. It might also be true that both theoretical approaches have some validity.

Actual research on the effects of paid employment on women's health shows a generally positive, but also complex, picture (see the review by Repetti et al., 1989). Employment does not appear to have a negative effect on women's physical and mental health. In fact, employment seems to improve the health of both unmarried women and married women who hold positive attitudes toward employment. Women generally gain social support from colleagues and supervisors by being employed, and this factor seems to be important to the health-enhancing effects of employment for women. Many women, of course, are not in such rosy situations; the woman whose work situation exposes her to sexual harassment or the frustrations of discrimination in pay and promotion will probably not enjoy positive health benefits from employment.

Childcare is another critical factor when one considers the relation between employment and women's mental health. If the woman cannot find childcare, or if she feels that such resources do not offer high-quality care for her child or are so expensive that she cannot afford them, then combining work and motherhood becomes stressful. If, on the other hand, the childcare is excellent, then work and family roles are more likely to enhance each other. In one study, the investigators found that children increased depression among nonemployed wives. In contrast, for employed mothers, if childcare was accessible and husbands shared in childcare, depression levels were low. However, employed mothers without accessible childcare and with sole responsibility for the children had extremely high levels of depression (Ross and Mirowsky, 1988).

The Second Shift In 1989, sociologist Arlie Hochschild published a book entitled *The Second Shift: Working Parents and the Revolution at Home.* The title reflects her finding that most employed women put in a full day of work on the job and then return home to perform a second shift of house and family work.

Studies in the 1970s found that if work is defined to include work for pay outside the home plus work done in the home, then women work, on average, 15 hours more per week than men do (Hochschild, 1989). Over the course of a year, women work an extra month of 24-hour days. In earlier sections of this chapter, we have discussed the wage gap between women and men. Here what we see is a leisure gap.

The problem of the dual duty for women—job and family work—is more than just a question of hours, though. Hochschild found that women were also more emotionally torn between the demands of work and the demands of family. In addition, the second shift creates a struggle in many marriages. The wife, in

FIGURE 7.7
Work/family issues are among those at the top of the feminist agenda. Does combining work and motherhood serve as a source of stress, or does it enhance women's well-being?

many cases, struggles to convince the husband to share the housework equally; alternatively, she does almost all of it and resents the fact that she does. And even when husbands share slightly or equally in doing the housework, women are still *responsible* for all of it.

Hochschild concluded that we are in a time of transition amidst a social revolution in which gender roles have changed and women have been catapulted into the world of paid work. In this period of transition, we have not yet arrived at stabilized social structures. In a sense, the revolution is stalled. We no longer have the mythical, stable but patriarchal, white, middle-class family, with the wife at home, having no economic power. On the other hand, we have not yet achieved a system in which women have equal relationships with men at work and at home.

Hochschild's arguments have been challenged by some researchers (e.g., Gilbert, 1993; Pleck, 1992). These researchers raise two basic issues: (1) Hochschild may have taken insufficient account of changes over the last 20 years. The evidence shows, for example, that men's contributions to family work have increased from 1970 to the present time, although gradually, and there is still not equity. (2) Hochschild did not sufficiently recognize the diversity of arrangements that couples make in regard to sharing household tasks. For example, research by Lucia Gilbert on dual-career couples shows that they fall into three types: traditional/conventional, modern/participant, and egalitarian/role-sharing (Gilbert, 1985; Gilbert and Dancer, 1992). In the conventional dual-earner family, both partners are involved in careers, but the woman keeps all the responsibility for household work and childcare. Typically both members of the couple agree that work within the home is "women's work," and men should be free of these obligations to pursue their careers, although they may "help out" a bit if time permits. Typically the man earns a much higher salary than the woman. These sound like the people in Hochschild's study. On the other hand, there are other types.

In the modern/participant type of relationship, parenting is shared between husband and wife, but household work is still the woman's responsibility. There is less male dominance and less division of labor by gender. Most of these men are highly motivated to be active fathers and to have close relationships with their children, but they are less interested in other aspects of family work.

The egalitarian/role-sharing couples participate equally in pursuing their careers, in parenting, and in household work. This is the most egalitarian pattern, and the one toward which many couples aspire. However, only approximately one-third of dual-career couples fall into this category, with one-third in the modern/participant and one-third in the traditional/conventional category.

In conclusion, then, the picture may not be quite as bleak as Hochschild painted it. Some men are contributing more toward home and family work, although more toward family than home. And Hochschild's portrait is still quite accurate for a large number of dual-earner couples—just not all of them.

What directions do we need to take for the future? In my view, we need a combination of private change and public change. In the private realm, gender roles must continue to change so that men contribute equally to and feel equal responsibility for household and childcare tasks. In the public realm, we need new social policies planned by the government that provide real support for two-earner families—policies that are truly profamily. If our society wants to continue to have children reared within the nuclear family, it will have to offer some supports to that family. The government urgently needs to promote high-quality, affordable childcare. The U.S. government needs to encourage companies to provide paid parental leave for new mothers and fathers, and opportunities for part-time work, flextime, and job sharing. We must have a uniform policy of pay equity so that women are paid fairly for the work they do. Many women, for example, would gladly work at 75 percent time if their full-time wage was decent, thereby easing some work and family tension. Only through this combination of private change and public change can we arrive at a new kind of social stability.

EXPERIENCE THE RESEARCH

ENTITLEMENT

In this exercise you will investigate Brenda Major's notion of entitlement and how it is related to the gender gap in wages.

Interview four psychology majors, two men and two women, preferably seniors. In each case, read to them the following paragraph:

Imagine that you have just graduated with your degree in psychology. You decide to get some research experience before deciding whether to go to graduate school. You manage to land a job as a full-time research assistant in the laboratory of a professor at the University of Wisconsin. What do you think your pay would be for your first year at that full-time job? How did you come up with that number—that is, what factors did you take into account?

Write down the gender of your respondent, his or her estimate of pay (be sure to get it in terms of an annual salary, not an hourly wage), and his or her reasoning about the pay.

Were your results consistent with Major's theory of entitlement? Did the men estimate higher salaries than the women? What factors did women take into account in deciding on the salary? Were these factors different from men's?

Suggestions for Further Reading

Costello, Cynthia, & Stone, Anne J. (Eds.). (1994). *The American woman* 1994–95. New York: Norton. Updated every two years, this book contains a wealth of statistical information on women and work, as well as many other women's issues.

Crosby, Faye. (1991). *Juggling: The unexpected advantages of balancing career and home for women and their families.* New York: Free Press. Crosby is a psychologist specializing in women and work; this book, written for a general audience, contains a lot of wisdom about balancing—or juggling—work and family.

Gilbert, Lucia A. (1989). *Sharing it all: The rewards and struggles of two-career families.* New York: Plenum. Gilbert, an authority on the psychology of women and dual-earner couples, offers insightful advice on how to make dual-earner marriages work.

8

Women of Color

An odd thing occurs in the minds of Americans when Indian civilization is mentioned: little or nothing. As I write this, I am aware of how far removed my version of the roots of American feminism must seem to those steeped in either mainstream or radical versions of feminism's history. . . . I am intensely conscious of popular notions of Indian women as beasts of burden, squaws, traitors. . . . How odd, then, must my contention seem that the gynocratic tribes of the American continent provided the basis for all the dreams of liberation that characterize the modern world.

PAULA GUNN ALLEN, THE SACRED HOOP: RECOVERING THE FEMININE IN AMERICAN INDIAN TRADITIONS

Introduction

We must confront a serious problem: Much of the scholarship on "the psychology of women" is, in reality, a psychology of white middle-class American women. But are phenomena such as difficulties balancing work and family common among all women? When we consider women of diverse racial and ethnic origins in the United States, it quickly becomes apparent that the different and complex social forces acting on them may result in differences in gender roles and behaviors. Among these forces are higher rates of poverty, discrimination, variations in family structures, identification with ethnic liberation movements, and evaluation of appearance by white, dominant-culture standards of beauty.

In this chapter we will focus on women in four major U.S. ethnic groups: African Americans, Hispanics, Asian Americans, and American Indians. The purpose of the chapter is to provide important background information about the cultures and heritages of these ethnic groups as well as an overview of gender roles in these cultures. This background and overview will provide the context for more specific discussions of research on ethnic minority women that occur in other chapters throughout the book.

Before we proceed, though, we need a brief discussion of terminology. The term **Hispanics** refers to all people of Spanish origin, whether from Puerto Rico, Cuba, Mexico, or elsewhere. **Chicanos** are Americans of Mexican origin. *Chicano* also refers specifically to men and **Chicana**[1] to women, an example of the fa-

Hispanics: People of Spanish descent, whether from Mexico, Puerto Rico, or elsewhere.

Chicanos: Americans of Mexican descent; may also refer specifically to male Mexican Americans.

Chicana: A female of Mexican descent.

---

[1]"Chicana" has some negative connotations to some, so the broader term "Latina" is generally preferable. "Hispanic" is also not favored by some because it was a term imposed by the U.S. Bureau of the Census.

Latinos: Latin
Americans.

Latina: A female Latin
American.

miliar male-as-normative problem in language. Another general term is **Latinos,** which refers to Latin Americans. Again, the term *Latino* refers both to all Latinos and to males, whereas **Latina** refers to females.

For Americans of African origin, there has been a steady evolution in terminology. Prior to the 1960s, *Negro* was the respectful term. With the 1960s, the Black Power movement was ushered in, and its followers urged the use of the term *Black* to connote pride in the very qualities that were the basis of discrimination, and promoted slogans such as "Black Is Beautiful." In the late 1980s, as ties to Africa and pride in one's heritage came to be emphasized, there was a shift to the term *African Americans.*

Asian Americans:
Americans of Asian descent.

Asian Americans (replacing terms such as *Orientals*) and *American Indians* or *Native Americans* are additional terms that are preferred, replacing various slang or older terms that are now considered disrespectful.

Even the terms *white* and *Caucasian* now seem to be problematic. For example, many Hispanics are white in skin color, yet when most people use the term *white* they don't mean to include Hispanics in the category. They really mean "white, not of Hispanic origin," but that phrase is too long to be used conveniently. The alternative that has been proposed for *white* is

Euro-Americans: White
Americans of European
descent. An alternative
to the term *whites.*

Euro-American. It has the advantage of being parallel to other terms, such as Asian American and African American, and places the emphasis on the group's cultural heritage.

Two themes will recur throughout this chapter. One is the theme of similarities and differences. Just as we have approached the issue of gender differences by emphasizing that there are both differences and similarities, so, too, will we approach the topic of ethnicity by recognizing both *differences and similarities.* As we look at African American women, Latinas, Asian American women, American Indian women, and white American women, we will see that there are some similarities, some common experiences such as childbirth and motherhood that women from all these cultures share. On the other hand, we will see that there are some profound differences, some resulting from differences in culture in the land of origin, others resulting from the greater poverty and discrimination experienced by members of some ethnic groups. These twin themes, then—similarities and differences—must always be kept in mind.

A second recurring theme in this chapter is simultaneous *oppression and strength.* Women in all these groups have a heritage of oppression, including slavery for African American women and internment in U.S. prison camps during World War II for Japanese American women. Current oppression, in the form of race discrimination and sex discrimination, persists. In the midst of this oppression, though, it would be a mistake to regard these women as victims. Instead, one sees enormous strength in them and in their lives. Thus strength in the face of oppression is another continuing theme.

An Ethnic/Cultural Critique of Psychological Research

In Chapter 1 we considered a gender-based critique of possible sources of sex bias in psychological research. In this section we will consider a parallel critique, namely, an ethnic/cultural critique that examines psychological research for sources of race bias (Landrine et al., 1992; Yoder and Kahn, 1993).

First, the very concept of **race,** as it has been used in psychology over the last 100 years, is problematic (Betancourt and Lopez, 1993; Jones, 1991). The biological concept of race implies a group of people with a common set of physical features, such as skin color, hair texture and color, and so on, who have mated exclusively with other members of their race and not with members of other races. The minute interbreeding with members of another race occurs, there is no "pure" race. Interbreeding, of course, has been the rule rather than the exception in many countries around the world. For example, an African American woman in the United States, whose skin color is black, may have 50 percent of her ancestors of African heritage and 50 percent of European heritage. The existence of such people renders the concept of race useless. Nonetheless, this woman may have grown up in the culture of an African American community and may identify herself as African American. For this reason, terms such as *culture* and *ethnicity* are generally preferable to *race.* The term **ethnic group** generally refers to a group that shares a common culture and language.

Race: A biological concept referring to a group of people with a common set of physical features who have mated only within their race.

Ethnic group: A group of people who share a common culture and language.

Second, just as males have been the norm in psychological research, so have Euro-Americans been the norm. As one critic put it, "Even the rat was white" (Guthrie, 1976). Basing studies exclusively on samples of white college students or other samples of Euro-Americans has been considered perfectly acceptable methodology. In part this is just bad science. It involves making an unjustified inference from an all-white sample to all people. In addition, the experience of persons of other ethnic groups then becomes invisible. The consequence is that whites represent "people," and everyone else becomes "subcultures" (Landrine et al., 1992).

Third, psychological research has ignored the different meanings that may be attached to different words, gestures, and so on by people from different ethnic groups (Landrine et al., 1992). The culture in which we grow up teaches us the meaning of various words. Therefore, two different ethnic groups (for example, African Americans and Euro-Americans) may have different understandings of the meanings of words even though both groups speak the same language (for example, English). This quickly becomes a radical critique of methods in psychological research, because it means that standardized tests, many of which were normed on exclusively white samples, may contain terms that are defined differently by other ethnic groups. The tests, then, might measure something quite different for African Americans or Hispanic Americans. To demonstrate this problem, Hope Landrine and her colleagues (1992) administered the Bem

Sex Role Inventory (BSRI), which measures androgyny (see Chapter 3), to 71 white women and 67 women of color. The women first rated themselves on each adjective, and then chose, from among several choices, the phrase that best defined that term for them. Overall, there were no differences between the Euro-American women and the women of color in their scores on the BSRI—that is, there were ethnic group similarities. However, there were major differences between the groups in the definitions chosen. For example, for the term *passive,* white women most frequently chose the definition "am laid-back/easy-going," whereas women of color most frequently chose "don't say what I really think." That is, there were large ethnic or cultural differences in the meanings that the women attached to the terms. Such findings imply that we need to go back to the very beginning with many psychological tests to determine how people from various ethnic groups understand the terms used in the tests.

A fourth criticism concerns possible bias in interpretation of results. If Euro-Americans are the norm, then the behavior and experiences of people of color are interpreted as being deficient—much as we have seen examples of female deficiency models. Just as the latter bias is often called androcentrism, so the former bias can be called **ethnocentrism** or, more specifically, **Eurocentrism.** As an example of such bias, viewed through the eyes of white researchers, the African American family has generally looked deficient.

As we look at psychological research on women of color in the United States, then, we must bear in mind that both androcentrism and Eurocentrism have permeated much of the traditional research and that new research is badly needed that is both gender fair and race/ethnic fair.

Ethnocentrism: The tendency to regard one's own ethnic group as superior to others and to believe that its customs and way of life are the standards by which other cultures should be judged.

Eurocentricism: The tendency to view the world from a Euro-American point of view and to evaluate other ethnic groups in reference to Euro-Americans.

Cultural Heritages of Women of Color in the United States

Before we can consider current gender roles and women's issues for women of color, we must first understand the cultural, historical heritage of these women. This heritage includes the cultures in the lands of origin (Africa, Asia, Latin America), the impact on those cultures of the process of migrating to the United States, and the impact of the dominant Euro-American culture of the United States.

The Cultural Heritage of Asian American Women Chinese—almost all of them men—were recruited first in the 1840s to come to America as laborers in the West and later in the 1860s to work on the transcontinental railroad (for an excellent summary of the cultural heritage of Asian Americans, see Tsai and Uemura, 1988; much of what follows comes from their discussion). Racist sentiment against the Chinese grew, however, and there was a shift to recruiting first Japanese and Koreans, and then Filipinos. An immigration control law passed in 1924 virtually ended the immigration of Asian Americans until the act was revoked in 1965. Then in the late 1960s and the 1970s, there was a mass exodus to the United States of refugees from war-torn Southeast Asia.

Today, Asian Americans are composed of 21 percent Chinese, 20 percent Filipinos, 15 percent Japanese, 12 percent Vietnamese, 11 percent Koreans, 10 percent Asian Indians, and many smaller groups.

Examples of racism directed against Asian Americans are many. Perhaps the most blatant was the internment of Japanese Americans during World War II. Japanese Americans had their property confiscated and were forcibly moved to prison camps in the United States.

The cultural values of Asian Americans are in some ways consistent with white middle-class American values, but in other ways contradict them. Asian Americans share with the white middle class an emphasis on achievement and on the importance of education. On the other hand, Asian Americans value family and group interdependence, interpersonal harmony, and stoicism (nonexpression or control of emotions), whereas the dominant American culture places great emphasis on individualism and self-sufficiency.

For Asian Americans, the family is a great source of emotional nurturance; for them, the family includes not only the nuclear family, but ancestors and the family of the future as well. One has an obligation to the family, and the needs of the family must take precedence over the needs of the individual. Maintaining harmonious relations with others, especially one's family, is important. Shame and the threat of loss of face, which can apply both to the individual and to his or her family, are powerful forces shaping good behavior. Often what may appear to be passivity in Asian Americans more accurately represents conscientious efforts to maintain dignity and harmony.

Asian American women have a high interracial marriage rate (Lott, 1990). This pattern began when U.S. servicemen married Asian women in World War II, the Korean War, and the Vietnam War. In second and later generations the interracial marriage rate can be as high as 50 percent.

Subcultural Variations You would not expect all Europeans—say, French, Germans, and Italians—to be alike and have similar cultures. Similarly, although Asians share some similarities in culture, there are also great variations. One Asian American woman is a Chinese American who is a fourth-generation descendant of a man brought to work on the transcontinental railroad, and who is herself a physician, as is her father. Another is a woman who escaped from Vietnam in a leaky boat in 1975, nearly died several times, and is heroically coping with a new language and a new culture. There are great subcultural variations among Asian American women.

Research on these cultures is beginning to appear. One example is a study of Khmer refugee women (Thompson, 1991; for a similar study of Vietnamese refugee women, see Kibria, 1990). The Khmer are an ethnic group from Cambo-

FIGURE 8.1
A Hmong refugee woman in the United States. Large subcultural variations exist among Asian American women. Refugee women, for example, would have very different experiences from Chinese women who are fifth generation in the United States.

dia, in Southeast Asia. Many fled to the United States in the 1970s when Cambodia was invaded during the Vietnam War. The research began with understanding the role of women in Cambodia before the war, the culture in which these women had grown up and been socialized. Peasant women had responsibility for childcare and household work, but they also tended fish traps and were coworkers in the important activities involved in cultivating the rice fields. Buddhism, a dominant religious influence, assigns a superior status to men. Many marriages were arranged, and the women felt that they had been sexually assaulted on their wedding night.

The women had experienced many forms of war-related and refugee-related trauma, including rape, abduction, and torture. The ethics of feminist research posed a dilemma for the researchers in this project, because they wanted to learn more about the traumatic experiences, but questioning the women about them itself seemed to cause pain by reactivating traumatic memories. The researchers tried to achieve a balance between the goal of giving voice to these women's experiences, while at the same time not traumatizing them further.

The researchers were particularly impressed by the fact that these women were survivors who possessed incredible strength. The women had survived—both physically and mentally—severe traumas and were now successfully coping with a vastly different culture.

The Cultural Heritage of Latinas   Hispanic Americans are currently the nation's second largest minority and are expected to be the largest by the year 2000 (Vasquez and Baron, 1988). Of those living on the mainland, their backgrounds are as follows: 61 percent Mexican, 15 percent Puerto Rican, 6 percent Cuban, and 18 percent from other Central and South American countries and Spain (Amaro and Russo, 1987).

When we speak of the cultural heritage of Latinos, we must first understand the concept of acculturation. **Acculturation** is the process of incorporating the beliefs and customs of a new culture (Vasquez and Baron, 1988). The culture of Chicanos is different from both the culture of Mexico and the dominant Euro-American culture of the United States. Chicano culture is based on the Mexican heritage, modified through acculturation to incorporate Euro-American components.

Acculturation: The process by which one takes on the beliefs and customs of a new culture as one's own.

In understanding Latino culture, two factors are especially significant: (1) bilingualism and (2) the importance of the family. **Bilingualism,** or knowing two languages, is important because Hispanic children often grow up learning two languages and thus two cultures. Spanish is more often the language of home and family, and English the language of school and job. Those Latinas who are immigrants often know no English at first, and therefore the language barrier is a problem in finding employment and in other areas of daily life.

Bilingualism: Knowing two languages.

The family is the central focus of Latino life. Traditional Latinos place a high value on family loyalty and on warm, mutually supportive relationships. Family solidarity is highly valued, as are ties to the extended family (Segura and Pierce, 1993). A Hispanic girl is likely to be "mothered" not only by her own mother, but by aunts or grandmothers as well. This emphasis on family is in many ways at odds with the dominant culture's emphasis on individualism. Furthermore, this emphasis on family places especially severe stresses on employed Latinas, who are expected to be the preservers of family and culture and to do so by staying in the home.

The process of *migration* is also critical in understanding the background of Hispanic women. While the majority of Mexican Americans (75 percent) were born in the mainland United States, 55 percent of Puerto Ricans and 75 percent of Cubans were born elsewhere (Amaro and Russo, 1987). The process of migration can be extremely stressful (Espin, 1987a; Salgado de Snyder et al., 1990). For a woman who leaves her homeland and friends, acute feelings of loss and grief are to be expected.

The Cultural Heritage of American Indian Women   To understand the heritage of American Indian women, one needs to understand the cultures of traditional Indian societies. Just as we have recognized subcultural variations for women of other ethnic groups, we must do the same for Indian women, this time recognizing tribal variations, which are in some cases great. Indian societies, however, were invaded by Euro-Americans, so that many current Indian practices resemble Euro-American culture as a result of forced acculturation, Christianization, and economic changes (LaFromboise et al., 1990).

The Spirit World is essential to Indian life, and especially to the life of Indian women. Women are seen as extensions of the Spirit Mother and as keys to the continuation of their people (LaFromboise et al., 1990).

A harmonious relationship with the Earth is an important part of Indian life. Interestingly, the Earth is referred to as Mother Earth, so that women are seen as connected with this important part of existence.

Thus Indian women see themselves as part of a collective, fulfilling harmonious roles in the biological, spiritual, and social realms: biologically, they value being mothers; spiritually, they are in tune with the Spirit Mother; and socially, they preserve and transmit culture and are the caretakers of their children and relatives (LaFromboise et al., 1990).

The Cultural Heritage of African American Women   Two factors are especially significant in the cultural heritage of African American women: the heritage of African culture, and the experience of slavery in America and subsequent racial oppression. Two characteristics of the African woman's role were maintained during slavery: an important economic function, and a strong bond between mother and child (Dobert, 1975; Ladner, 1971). African women have traditionally been economically independent, functioning in the marketplace and as traders. Black women in the United States continue to assume this crucial economic function in the family to the present day. Mother-child bonds also continue to be extremely important in the structure of Black society.

African American culture, like that of the other ethnic groups discussed earlier, but in contrast to Euro-American society, emphasizes the collective or tribe over the individual (Fairchild, 1988). It recognizes the important connections between generations, and it is concerned with the individual's harmonious relationship with others, in contrast to the "me generation" of contemporary white culture and contemporary white psychology.

In the 1800s, when it was popular in the United States to put white women on a pedestal, Black women were viewed as beasts of burden and subjected to performing the same demeaning labor as Black men (Dugger, 1988). Angela Davis has argued that this heritage created an alternative definition of womanhood for Black women, one that includes a tradition of "hard work, perseverance

FIGURE 8.2
Mother-child bonds are very important in African
American culture.

and self-reliance, a legacy of tenacity, resistance, and an insistence on sexual equality" (1981, p. 29).

Gender Roles and Ethnicity

Against this background of the cultural heritages of women of color in the United States, let us consider the gender roles that have evolved in these various ethnic communities. A basic tenet of feminist theory is that gender and ethnicity interact as social norms are formed and as they affect behavior. Thus gender roles are defined in the cultural context of a particular ethnic group, and it is not surprising that there are variations in gender roles from one ethnic group to another.

Gender Roles Among American Indians   It is clear today that the early work of anthropologists misrepresented women's roles in Indian culture (LaFromboise et al., 1990). The tale is an interesting one of how sex bias and race bias can easily pervade research in the social sciences. The researchers were male and non-Indian. As such, they focused on male activities and had greater access to male informants. A stereotyped dichotomy of Indian woman as either princess or squaw emerged, much like the saint/slut dichotomy that was drawn for Victorian white women. Furthermore, because the anthropologists were non-Indians and therefore outsiders, they were able to observe only public behaviors and how Indians interacted with outsiders, thereby missing private interactions. In some tribes, dealing with outsiders was an activity assigned to men. Therefore, researchers overestimated male power within the tribe because they did not observe Indian women's powerful roles within the private sphere. In some tribes, for example, there was a matrilineal system of inheritance, meaning that women could own property and that property passed from mother to daughter. Indian women, doubtless wary after the legacy of white violence against Indians, were unlikely to share their intimate rituals or feelings with these outsiders.

As an example of the problems with this early research, scholars claimed that there was a pattern of isolating menstruating women from the tribe and its activities, keeping them in a secluded menstrual hut, based on the Indian view that women were contaminated at this time (e.g., Stephens, 1961). Firsthand accounts from Indian writers, however, provide a different interpretation (LaFromboise et al., 1990). Menstruating women were not shunned as unclean, but rather were considered extremely powerful, with tremendous capacities for destruction. Women's spiritual forces were thought to be especially strong during menstruation, and women were generally thought to possess powers so great that they could counteract or weaken men's powers. The interpretation makes all the difference—shifting from a view of a shunned, powerless woman to that of a too-powerful woman.

A woman's identity and gender roles in traditional Indian culture were rooted in her spirituality, extended family, and tribe (LaFromboise et al., 1990). The emphasis was on the collective and on harmony with the spiritual world, the world of one's family and tribe, and the natural world.

The evidence shows that some North American Indian tribes had a system of egalitarian gender roles, in which separate but equally valued tasks were assigned to males and females (Blackwood, 1984). It is important to remember tribal variations, for not all tribes had such egalitarian patterns, but certainly some—for example, the Klamath—did.

There is also evidence that some tribes—such as the Canadian Blackfeet—had institutionalized alternative female roles. There was the role of the "manly hearted woman," a role that a woman who was exceptionally independent and aggressive could take on. There was a "warrior woman" role among the Apache, Crow, Cheyenne, Blackfoot, and Pawnee tribes (e.g., Buchanan, 1986). In both cases, women could express "masculine" traits or participate in male-stereotyped activities while continuing to live and dress as a woman.

Gender Roles Among African American Women A methodological point must be recognized, one that is apparent in research on African Americans but is a problem with research on other ethnic groups as well. The problem in much of the research to be cited is the *confounding of ethnicity and social class.* Because Blacks tend to be overrepresented in the lower class and whites in the middle class, it is generally not clear whether differences between Blacks and whites should be attributed to race or to social class. Research techniques generally have not been powerful enough to conquer this ambiguity. As you read this material on gender and ethnicity, you should keep in mind that much of what seem to be ethnic group differences may actually be due to social-class differences.

Multiple gender roles—mother, worker, head of household, wife—have been a reality for African American women for generations, in contrast to the situation for white middle-class American women, for whom these multiple roles are more recent. Reflecting on the absurdity of defining women's role on the pedestal in white middle-class Victorian terms, the Black abolitionist Sojourner Truth commented at a women's rights convention in the 1800s:

> That man over there says that women need to be helped into carriages, and lifted over ditches, and to have the best place everywhere. Nobody ever helps me into carriages, or over mud puddles, or gives me any best places. . . . And ain't I a woman? Look at me! Look at my arm! . . . I have plowed and planted, and gathered into barns, and no man could head me—and ain't I a woman? I could work as much and eat as much as a man (when I could get it), and bear the lash as well—and ain't I a woman? I have borne thirteen children and seen most of them sold off into slavery, and when I cried out with a woman's grief, none but Jesus heard—and ain't I a woman? (*Abolitionist,* 1831)

African American women have had to define their identity in terms of roles other than exclusively housewife-mother. Although motherhood is still a prime gender-role definer, African American women have taken on additional roles, such as worker and head of household. Black women generally expect that they must hold paying jobs as adults (Dickson, 1993), and this expectation has important consequences for their educational and occupational attainments, as we shall see later. Indeed, since 1986 the number of employed Black women in America has exceeded the number of employed Black men (Dickson, 1993).

The role of the African American woman as head of household has received a great deal of publicity under the term *Black matriarchy,* suggesting that the Black woman has greater power than the man does in the Black family and culture. The high frequency with which Black households, as compared with white households, are headed by women is usually given as evidence for this phenomenon. In 1992, 47 percent of Black households were maintained by women, compared with 24 percent for Hispanic families and 14 percent for white families (U.S. Department of Labor, 1993). This pattern has increased over time. For example, in 1990, of Black families with children under 18, 56 percent were headed by women, compared with only 25 percent in 1965 (Dickson, 1993).

A number of factors contribute to the greater rates of female-headed households among African Americans (Dickson, 1993).

1. Lower marriage and higher divorce rates among Blacks.   Among Black women between the ages of 30 and 34 in 1990, only 39 percent were married and living with a husband, compared with 65 percent in 1960. In 1990, the divorce ratio was 28.2 divorces per 100 marriages among Blacks, compared with 13 divorces per 100 marriages among whites. This pattern of lower marriage rates and higher divorce rates in turn is a result of many of the factors listed below.

2. The obstacles African American men have encountered in seeking and maintaining jobs necessary to support their families.   Since World War II, the number of manufacturing jobs in the United States has declined dramatically. These jobs were a major source of employment for working-class Black men. The result has been a decline in the Black working class and an expansion of the Black underclass. Joblessness among Black men contributes to low marriage rates and high divorce rates.

3. The unequal gender ratio among African Americans.   In 1990, among 30- to 34-year-olds, there were only 85 Black men for every 100 Black women, compared with 101 white men per 100 white women and 98 Hispanic men per 100 Hispanic women (U.S. Bureau of the Census, 1990b).

4. Welfare policies.   Current welfare policies discourage marriage for poor Black mothers, because they will lose benefits if they are married.

5. Interracial dating and marriage patterns of Black men.   Black men are far more likely to marry white women than Black women are to marry white men.

In short, there are just not enough men—particularly not enough good men—to go around, and so African American women find themselves as single-parent heads of households.

On the other hand, the stereotype of matriarchal domination of African American families ignores the fact that if 47 percent of Black households are headed by women, then 53 percent must be headed by men and women jointly or by men. Thus, the female-headed household, although more common among Blacks than whites, is not the only pattern—in fact, the majority of Black households are headed jointly by men and women or by men. Furthermore, there is a clear trend toward an increase in the number of female-headed households among whites.

The unequal gender ratio among African Americans deserves further comment, because it is likely to have far-reaching psychological implications. The important theorizing and research of Guttentag and Secord (1983) found that, in cultures in which men are in short supply, men essentially become a scarce and therefore precious resource. Some have argued that this applies among African

Americans and that, as a result, Black men hold the power in an emotional relationship (Dickson, 1993). They do not have to work at a relationship or even commit to one. They can always find another woman. On the other hand, this encourages self-reliance in women, including a drive for more education and a desire to be self-supporting.

At the very least, the term *Black matriarchy* oversimplifies the complex relationships between Black men and women.

Among the elderly, the role of Black women also differs from that of white women. The feelings of uselessness and the lack of roles experienced by white women in their youth-oriented culture are not so common among African Americans. The extended-family structure among Blacks provides a secure position and role for the elderly. The "granny" role—helping to care for young grandchildren, giving advice based on experience—is a meaningful and valued role for the elderly Black woman (Bart, 1971). Elderly Black women seem to have a more purposeful and respected role than elderly white women do. This pattern of seeing elderly women as wise and respected is also found among American Indians.

Gender Roles Among Asian American Women   It is popular in the 1990s to think of Asian Americans as the "model minority." According to the 1980 census, for example, the median earning of Asian Americans was $23,600, higher than the median of $20,800 for whites. Currently, 42 percent of Asian Americans graduate from college—a rate double that of whites. Nonetheless, feminist Asian Americans believe that Asian American women are victims of both racism and sexism. For example, the model minority stereotype hides the plight of recently arrived refugees, as the earlier discussion of Khmer refugee women illustrated. And distorted stereotypes remain in the mass media (Sue and Morishima, 1982), such as the Asian man as the violent Kung Fu warrior.

The expectations from traditional culture—for family interdependence, preservation of group harmony, and stoicism—are expected of Asian American women specifically. Asian American women, as part of a bicultural existence, experience gender-role conflict, the gender roles expected in traditional culture being considerably different from those expected in modern Euro-American culture, which increasingly prizes independence and assertiveness for women. Another conflict involves the Euro-American emphasis on equality in male-female relationships, an emphasis that is at odds with the traditional Asian focus on female subservience (Tsai and Uemera, 1988).

Gender Roles Among Latinos   In traditional Latin American cultures, gender roles are rigidly defined (Comas-Diaz, 1987). Such roles are emphasized early in the socialization process for children. Boys are given greater freedom, are encouraged in sexual exploits, and are not expected to share in household work. Girls are expected to be passive, obedient, and weak, and to stay in the home.

Machismo: The ideal of manliness in Latino cultures.

These rigid roles are epitomized in the concepts of machismo and marianismo (Comas-Diaz, 1987). The term **machismo,** or *macho,* has come to be used rather loosely in American culture today. Literally, *machismo* means "maleness" or "virility." More generally, it refers to the "mystique of manliness" (Ruth, 1990). The cultural code of machismo among Latin Americans mandates that the male must be the provider and the one responsible for the well-being and honor of his family. Males hold a privileged position and are to be treated as authority figures. In extreme forms, machismo has come to include glorification of sexual conquests and the often violent physical domination of women.

Marianismo is the female counterpart of machismo (Comas-Diaz, 1987). The term derives from the Catholic worship of Mother Mary, who is both virgin and madonna. According to the ideal of marianismo, women, like Mary, are spiritually superior and therefore capable of enduring the suffering inflicted by men. Latin American culture attributes high status to motherhood. The woman is expected to be self-sacrificing in relation to her children and the rest of her family, but Latino culture at the same time holds mothers in high esteem. Although superficially these roles may seem to endorse male domination and female submissiveness, the true situation is complex. Women who do exceptionally well in the marianista role come to be revered as they grow older and their children feel strong alliances with them, so that they wield considerable power within the family.

Marianismo: The ideal of womanliness in Latino cultures.

Most Latin American cultures assign the healing role to women. Most *espiritistas* (spiritual healers) are female (Comas-Diaz, 1987). According to research on Hispanic female healers in the United States, the role is associated with power and status (Espin, 1987a).

Thus, although the traditional role for Latinas involves passivity and subservience, this generalization masks the powerful roles that these women play within the family, and that they may gain in certain specialized roles, such as that of *espiritista.* In addition, recent research on Latino families has found that there is a great deal of variability, ranging from patriarchal to egalitarian family forms (Segura and Pierce, 1993).

Education

Immigrants to the United States have long realized that education was the best avenue for improving their job success, their status, and their standard of living. Worldwide, education and literacy are critical issues for women. Therefore, as we examine women's achievements, it is important to look at education.

Table 8.1 shows the educational attainments of Americans as a function of gender and ethnicity. Focusing first on the section of the table that deals with high school graduation, you can see that there is some problem with high school dropouts among whites and Asian Americans, but basically about 80 to 90 percent of each group do graduate from high school. On the other hand, graduation rates are considerably lower for African Americans and Latinos. This pattern is

TABLE 8.1

Educational Attainments of U.S-Born Americans
(Aged 25 and Over in 1991), as a Function of Gender and Ethnicity

Ethnic Group	High School Graduate		1–3 Years of College		4 or More Years of College	
	M	F	M	F	M	F
Whites	80%	80%	19%	19%	26%	19%
African Americans	68	67	17	18	12	12
Hispanics	53	53	13	12	10	10
Asian Americans	90	82	25	19	46	42

SOURCE: Costello and Stone (1994), Tables 2.1 and 2.2.

not particularly gender differentiated, though: the graduation rate for females is about the same as the rate for males.

Examining the section on those who complete some college (one to three years) but do not graduate, you can see that the rates are about the same for all ethnic groups, ranging around 17 to 25 percent, except for Latinos, who have a lower rate of attendance. Many of these prospective Latino students are themselves immigrants and may have come from an impoverished school system and be dealing with the problems of a second language as well. Again, the rates for attending one to three years of college are not gender differentiated.

The section on those who graduate from college (four or more years of college) indicates that a gender differentiation begins for whites, with fewer women than men graduating. For the other groups, though, women have rates as high as men's of graduating from college. Notice, too, that Asian Americans graduate from college at approximately twice the rate for whites.

There has been much discussion of the dynamics behind Black women's educational parity with Black men (e.g., Sanders, 1988). Indeed, recent statistics indicate that African American women are now somewhat ahead of African American men in educational achievements, as well as in professional achievements. For every Black professional man, there are nearly two Black professional women (Sanders, 1988), although it should be remembered that nursing and teaching are counted in the professions and women are often limited to these professions. In explaining these successes, Paula Giddings commented,

> Prejudice against their race and sex forced Black women to work and simultaneously limited the kinds of work they could perform. The only choice Black women had were the professions—where until recently there was less competition from White women—or domestic work. Since education is the key to the

FIGURE 8.3
Asian Americans, like white, middle-class Americans, emphasize the importance of education, including education for women. In fact, a larger percentage of Asian American women graduate from college than do white men.

more attractive occupations, Black women have a history of striving for education beyond what their gender or their color seemed to prescribe. Black men, on the other hand, have not had the same motivation, historically, because they had a greater range of options—including blue-collar work, which often pays better than the traditional women's professions (teaching, social work, nursing, and so on). (Giddings, 1984, p. 7)

American Indian women, on the other hand, are often the most conflicted about pursuing a college education (LaFromboise et al., 1990). It is difficult for them to adapt to the competitive nature of higher education. Furthermore, family and community members often discourage Indian women from going to college. In one survey of Indian women undergraduates, 90 percent said that they felt they were going against their culture by attending college (Kidwell, 1976).

Beyond these statistics are also important issues of campus climate (Moses, 1989). For African American women, of course, the climate is considerably different, depending on whether they attend a historically Black college or a primarily white college. Parallels to the historically Black colleges do not exist for other minority groups.

In terms of classroom dynamics, women of color suffer double prejudice based on both their race and their gender. Leadership and academic competence are associated with white males, and so women of color are doubly distanced from possessing these admirable qualities. Furthermore, women of color are often exposed to stereotypical comments unwittingly made by faculty. As one researcher commented,

> Black students often report that the professors' tone of voice or facial expressions display disbelief or surprise when they respond correctly or otherwise show good performance. . . . Black students report that professors offer little guidance and criticism of Black students' work. . . . Professors will often make stereotypical comments about Blacks without being aware of the hurtful impact that these comments can have on Black students, particularly when they imply that Blacks are less competent than whites. (Katz, 1983, p. 36)

In predominantly white institutions, women of color often experience the paradox of underattention and overattention. On the one hand, their comments may be ignored or they may not receive the help they need in a lab. On the other hand, if the discussion focuses on women of color, they may be called on to represent the views of all women of their ethnic group (if you are a white student, how would you like it if the class asked you to tell them what all white women, or all white men, think about issue X?).

It is also important to look at what happens before the college years, for the schools are important socializers of students' behaviors and aspirations. Research on Black girls in desegregated elementary schools indicates that they undergo a process of socialization toward a Black female role (Grant, 1984). In this research, teachers described Black girls as mature, self-sufficient, and helpful. In each of the classrooms that was observed, one Black girl emerged in the role of go-between, that is, serving as a social integrator, linking children with each other and with the teacher. The social position of Black girls seems to enable them to reach out to children from all the other race/gender groups. For example, in one such interaction, Camille, a Black girl, responded to the appeal of Felix, a Black boy, that he needed a replacement for a broken shoelace, came to his side, and then contacted the teacher. This position earns high status for the girl among her peers. On the other hand, it perhaps encourages her social skills at the expense of her academic skills.

In summary, in this section on education we have examined the interaction of race and gender at two levels: the microlevel (classroom interactions) and the macrolevel (statistics on graduate degrees awarded to people of color in the United States). Two important points emerge from this discussion:

1. Gender and race are powerful factors in classroom dynamics, whether in elementary school or college. Women of color may receive stereotypical responses that encourage neither their academic achievement nor their sense of their own academic competence.

2. With the exception of Asian Americans, women of color in the United States are not graduating from college or pursuing graduate education at a rate comparable to that of whites. This lack of education in turn precludes many occupations and limits earnings. Therefore, the recruitment and retention of women of color in higher education need to be a top priority.

Work Issues

In Chapter 7 we discussed issues of women and work. We noted the interaction of gender and ethnicity in these issues; for example, women of color consistently receive the lowest wage of the race/gender groups. Thus work issues for women of color in many ways parallel those for white women—pay equity, access to childcare and parental leave options, and sexual harassment (see Chapter 13) — but to this is added racial harassment.

Here we will consider work and family issues, the impact of multiple roles (worker, mother, wife), and the implications for the mental health of women of color. As we have already seen, gender roles vary for these different ethnic groups. Therefore, working outside the home may seem far more appropriate in some groups (African Americans) than in others (Latinos).

Recall from the discussion of work and mental health in Chapter 7 that there are two competing theories: the scarcity hypothesis and the enhancement hypothesis. The first argues that multiple roles (worker, mother, wife) are stressful to women, whereas the second argues that multiple roles are actually beneficial to mental health. The picture is complex, though, and more than just multiple roles are involved: the woman's attitude toward work, the supportiveness of the work environment, and whether the woman is married or single. Are these same factors important among women of color?

Results from a large-scale, national survey of Hispanic women indicate that holding a job, by itself, is not related to depression (Saenz et al., 1989). However, employed Hispanic women whose husbands help with housework and who report higher levels of marital satisfaction do show lower levels of depression than other groups exhibit. Furthermore, among employed women, those holding more prestigious jobs report less depression than those holding less prestigious jobs. These patterns are quite similar to those found among Euro-Americans (see Chapter 7).

One study involving middle-aged and older Black women examined the effects of the roles of parent, spouse, and worker on mental and physical health (Coleman et al., 1987). Of these three roles, only employment had a significant impact on well-being. Among both the middle-aged and the older groups, employed women had higher self-esteem and better health. The sheer number of roles did not benefit well-being; rather, it was a particular role (employment) or cluster of roles (employment and marriage) that enhanced mental and physical well-being. Unfortunately, this study did not examine other factors, such as satisfaction with work or marital satisfaction, and so we do not know to what extent they may play a part, too.

Another study examined work, family, and psychological well-being among Hispanic women professionals (Amaro et al., 1987). Support from one's spouse and the ethnicity of the spouse were significantly related to stress in balancing work and family roles. Cuban women (compared with Mexican American women) and women married to non-Hispanic men experienced less stress. Again we see evidence of subcultural variations. Of course, those with more supportive husbands reported less stress. In addition, those reporting less stress were more likely to have more supportive co-workers and not to have experienced discrimination at work. Again, work environment is critical when we analyze the effects of work on women's mental health.

From these studies we can conclude the following:

1. Like the research with predominantly white samples, this research demonstrates that work outside the home is not injurious to women's health, mental or physical. If anything, employment enhances women's well-being, in all the ethnic groups studied.

FIGURE 8.4
In the last two decades, many new role models for women of color have emerged. (Left) Marian Wright Edelman, head of the Children's Defense Fund and author of *The Measure of Our Success: A Letter to My Children and Yours.* (Right) News reporter and anchor Connie Chung.

2. More complex factors are involved than just employment per se. These may include satisfaction with one's marriage, one's attitudes toward work, the quality of the work environment and social supports available in it, and occupational prestige.

When We've Made It, Let's Help Others In many ethnic communities, a feeling exists among those who have "made it" that there is an obligation to help others in the community who have not. One of the hallmarks of the new Black middle-class successful woman is a concern for the Black underclass (Sanders, 1988). Similarly, many Indian women are moving into professional roles—as social workers, psychologists, writers, artists, political leaders, and so on—with the intent of serving their community or tribe (LaFromboise et al., 1990). These women of color can be powerful forces in uplifting their communities.

Mental Health Issues

The history of clinical psychology and its treatment of people of color in the United States is heavily laden with racial stereotypes and downright racism. For example, the census of 1840 reported that Blacks in the Northern states had far higher rates of psychopathology than Blacks in the slave states. Psychiatrists of the day interpreted this finding to indicate that the supervision and control of Blacks that slavery provided were essential to Blacks' well-being; thus, the data and methods of social science were used to defend slavery as good for Blacks (Deutsch, 1944). That part of the census data was later demonstrated to have been fabricated, but the record remained uncorrected.

Psychologists in the early 1900s—among them the greats such as G. Stanley Hall—advanced theories that perpetuated racial stereotyping. For example, it was thought that Blacks were innately happy-go-lucky and therefore immune to depression (Landrine, 1988b; Thomas and Sillen, 1972).

Contemporary clinicians often perpetuate these stereotyped views, although in fancier social science jargon than their predecessors. For example, immunity to depression is attributed no longer to happy-go-luckiness, but rather to a belief that Blacks have nothing to lose—no jobs, property, or self-esteem (Prange and Vitols, 1962). Such views may be caused by and in turn may cause depressed Blacks to be misdiagnosed, often as schizophrenics (Landrine, 1988b; Simon and Fleiss, 1973).

Definitions of the term *normal* given in psychology texts often include such characteristics as emotional control, independence, the capacity for abstract and logical thinking, the ability to delay gratification, happiness, a concern with developing one's own potential to the fullest, and a sense of the self as an autonomous individual who is able to exert control over the environment (e.g., Jourard, 1974). The problem is that this definition is based on white middle-class males' experience of the self and health. It may not reflect the experience of women or of people of color. As we have seen in many chapters, women often have less power and control over their environment. And for the ethnic groups we have discussed, there is often more of a concern for relations with one's family and community than for advancing oneself as an individual. Thus the very definitions that psychology offers for normalcy may not be appropriate for women of color (Landrine, 1988b).

For American Indians, the definition of well-being and the method of treating disturbances are at odds with mainstream psychotherapy in the United States. In most Indian cultures, a person is considered to be in a state of well-being when she or he is peaceful and is exuding strength through self-control and adherence to Indian cultural values (LaFromboise et al., 1990). When a person is troubled, traditional healing systems are used, which involve a community process that helps the troubled individual while also reaffirming the norms of the community; the emphasis of the process is holistic and naturalistic (LaFromboise et al., 1990).

Whether on the reservation or off, Indian women experience intense stressors, but they appear to be reluctant to use mental health services (LaFromboise et al., 1990). In part this reluctance is caused by the fact that they view the existing services as unresponsive to them and their needs (Medicine, 1982). Indians who do use mental health services often express concern that these services shape their behavior in a direction that is incompatible with Indian culture.

Asian American women also experience stresses from racism and sexism, and refugees have been exposed to particularly extreme stresses. Yet statistics indicate that Asian Americans, compared with Euro-Americans, underutilize mental health services (Sue, 1977). The traditional explanation is that Asian Americans simply have a low rate of mental disturbance. Yet it now seems more accurate to say that Asian American culture attaches great stigma and shame to mental disturbance, so that individuals do not seek help until a true crisis has developed and all family and community resources have been tried. Furthermore, when Asian Americans do seek therapy, they often find that it is not sensitive to the values of Asian American culture.

Latinos, too, are underrepresented in the use of mental health facilities, and Hispanic women are less likely to use them than Hispanic men are (Russo et al., 1987). A number of factors have been proposed to explain why Hispanics are less likely to use these services: existing services may be inaccessible to Hispanics; some segments of the Hispanic population may use traditional methods for dealing with problems, rather than mainstream psychotherapy; and Spanish-speaking clinicians may be lacking.

This discussion indicates that an important task for clinical psychology in the future will be to develop culturally sensitive methods of psychotherapy (True, 1990). An additional task is to increase the number of ethnic minority psychologists, who bring important cultural sensitivities with them.

Feminism and Women of Color

Women of color have emerged as powerful forces in the feminist movement, shaping feminism to reflect their experiences and priorities (Comas-Diaz, 1991). Their writings recognize that the oppression of women of color results from intertwined systems of race, gender, and class oppression.

An example is Black feminist thought (Collins, 1989; James and Busia, 1993). Black feminist thought is not a new invention, but has historic origins in activists such as Sojourner Truth, Ida Wells-Barnett, and Fannie Lou Hamer. Indeed, Sojourner Truth attended the famed Seneca Falls convention that shaped the feminist manifesto of the 1800s.

Nor is Black feminist thought purely the product of scholars and activists; instead, its origins lie in the actions of common Black women and their everyday acts of resistance, beginning in the days of slavery (Collins, 1989). Above all, contemporary Black feminist thought "specializes in formulating and rearticulat-

FIGURE 8.5
Women of color have emerged as a powerful force in the feminist movement.

ing the distinctive, self-defined standpoint of African American women" (Collins, 1989, p. 750). As such, it seeks to recognize and validate the lived experience of African American women, in the belief that this experience has been ignored by the traditional academic disciplines, as well as by white women's studies scholars and male African American studies scholars.

Black feminism values an ethic of caring (see the parallels in the work of Gilligan, Chapter 2). Emotions are appropriate and should be validated, not repressed. Empathy should be cultivated. Black feminist thought also holds that viewpoints and opinions are personal rather than objective (recall the feminist critique of the objectivity of science, Chapter 1), and that individuals are also personally accountable for their beliefs. Thus a psychologist whose theorizing perpetuates racial stereotypes or racism is held responsible for those effects and cannot hide behind the mask of scientific objectivity. And finally, and perhaps most importantly, Black feminist thought recognizes that both racism and sexism affect the lives of Black women.

Chicana feminism has also emerged (see, for example, Garcia, 1989). In the 1960s, at much the same time as the Black Power movement was very active, a Chicano liberation movement was also a vital force. Probably the best-known facet of this movement was the unionization of the United Farmworkers. Chicanas were an important part of this movement. Like African American women in the Black liberation movement, they gained experience with activism, but at the same time became disturbed at the male dominance and sexism within the Chicano movement. Chicana feminism grew from these roots. Chicana feminists thus have dual goals of working toward both cultural nationalism (liberation for Hispanics) and feminism (liberation for women).

A particularly inspiring story is found in American Indian feminism. First, it is important to provide some background on one of the new discoveries in American history. There is now good evidence that the foundation for our American democracy as shaped by the "fathers" of our country in the Constitution lay not in the government of Britain—after all, the patriots were not exactly thinking kind thoughts about the British right then—but in the government of the great Iroquois nation (Grinde, 1977). The founding fathers had a good deal of contact with the nearby Iroquois and apparently observed their system of governance with interest. The Iroquois system was composed of local or "state" bodies, plus a federal government consisting of legislative, executive, and judicial branches. There were important differences, however. Iroquois women had the vote, that is, had an equal say in the choice of leaders; and the executive branch consisted of a Council of Matrons, that is, wise women elders (Allen, 1986). The idea of women having power was taken for granted. Therefore, the roots of the structure of American government may well lie in the government and social structure of an American Indian group, the Iroquois.

I should not imply that the picture is completely rosy. The topic of women of color and feminism is a delicate one. Many believe that American feminism has been dominated by white middle-class women who have put their issues at the top of the agenda while ignoring issues that are more important to women of color. At the same time, many women of color feel that feminism divides their loyalties within their own community and that they should put their energies into fighting racism (Comas-Diaz, 1991). They may feel that feminism creates conflicts for them with their men; for example, African American men often feel that African American women should provide support for them when they experience instances of racism. The feeling among some is that African Americans should unite and that feminism only divides them along gender lines.

EXPERIENCE THE RESEARCH

GENDER ROLES AND ETHNICITY ON PRIME TIME

Identify three current (that is, no reruns) television series that focus on an African American family. Then identify three comparison series that focus on a Euro-American family. Ideally, choose comparison series that air at the same time, or perhaps are shown immediately following, as the shows about the African American families but on a different station. Observe each program twice, on two consecutive weeks. As you observe the programs, answer the following questions:

1. How are gender roles portrayed on the program? Does the main female character have a paying job? What kind of job is it? Does the main male character have a paying job? What is it? Who does the cooking? Who does the grocery shopping?
2. How is the family portrayed on the program? Is it a traditional married couple with children, or is it a female-headed household or some other kind of family?
3. How is emotional expressiveness portrayed on the program? What emotions do women express? What emotions do men express?

After you have completed your observations, compare the results for the African American family shows and the Euro-American family shows. What are the differences? What are the similarities? What impact do you think these programs have on African American and Euro-American viewers?

Finally, locate three comparable programs that focus on Asian American families, Hispanic families, and Native American families. Were you able to do it? If so, how are gender roles portrayed on those programs?

The important point is that the feminist movement should be for all women and that all have essential contributions to make, whatever the color of their skin. Only by combining the perspectives and scholarship of women of all ethnic groups can we achieve a women's movement that is effective in promoting the equality of all women with all men.

Suggestions for Further Reading

Allen, Paula Gunn. (1986). *The sacred hoop: Recovering the feminine in American Indian traditions.* Boston: Beacon Press. This collection of essays includes poetry, mythology, and literary analyses, all defining the identities of American Indian women.

Giddings, Paula. (1984). *When and where I enter: The impact of black women on race and sex in America.* New York: Bantam Books (Paperback). This is a sweeping history of Black women in the United States, including portraits of such greats as the antilynching journalist Ida Wells-Barnett and presidential candidate Shirley Chisholm. Important reading for those who wish to understand the social and political context of contemporary African American women.

James, Stanlie, & Busia, Abena. (Eds.). (1993). *Theorizing Black feminisms: The visionary pragmatism of Black women.* New York: Routledge. This collection of essays provides a current view of Black feminism.

Marchetti, Gina. (1993). *Romance and the "yellow peril": Race, sex, and discursive strategies in Hollywood fiction.* Berkeley: University of California Press. This is a fascinating analysis of images of Asian women and men in American film.

Many novels and autobiographies are available that help the reader to grasp more profoundly the experience of women of color. A list of important ones, to name but a few, includes Maxine Hong Kingston's *The Woman Warrior,* Wong's *Fifth Chinese Daughter,* and Amy Tan's *Joy Luck Club* (Asian American women); Toni Morrison's novels such as *Beloved* and *The Bluest Eye* (African American women); and Louise Erdrich's *Bingo Palace* and *Love Medicine* (Native American women).

9

Biological Influences on Women's Behavior

> *. . . an extraordinarily important part of the brain
> necessary for spiritual life, the frontal convolutions
> and the temporal lobes are less well developed in
> women and this difference is inborn. . . . If we wish a
> woman to fulfill her task of motherhood fully, she
> cannot possess a masculine brain. If the feminine
> abilities were developed to the same degree as those
> of the male, her maternal organs would suffer, and
> we should have before us a repulsive and useless
> hybrid.*

MOEBIUS, CONCERNING THE PHYSIOLOGICAL INTELLECTUAL
FEEBLENESS OF WOMEN, 1907

Traditionally it was believed that psychological differences between females and males were created by biological differences. It was also popularly thought that biological influences were particularly potent forces on women's behavior. The turn-of-the-century psychologist quoted above believed that male and female brains differed and that the female brain was defective. Women have also been thought to be the victims of their "raging hormones." In this chapter we shall examine the evidence on whether biological gender differences create psychological gender differences, and on whether women's behavior is controlled by biological forces.

The biological factors that may influence women and gender differences fall into three major categories: genetic factors, sex hormones, and brain differences.

Genes

Normal humans possess a set of 46 chromosomes. Because chromosomes occur in pairs, there are 23 pairs, classified as 22 pairs of autosomes (nonsex chromosomes) and one pair of sex chromosomes. The female has a sex chromosome pair denoted XX, whereas the male sex chromosome pair is XY. Therefore, there are no genetic differences between males and females except for the sex chromosomes.

Sex-linked trait: A trait controlled by a gene on the X chromosome (and occasionally on the Y chromosome).

Traits that are controlled by genes on the sex chromosomes are called **sex-linked traits** (for an excellent explanation of sex-linked genetic effects as related to the psychology of women, see Wittig, 1979). For such traits, the female will have a pair of genes controlling a particular sex-linked trait, but the male will have only one gene for that trait, because he has only one X chromosome. (The Y chromosome is small compared with the X and contains little genetic information except for determining gender.) Sex linkage is a source of gender differences when one form of a gene (*allele*) is dominant or recessive to the other possible allele, as in the example of blue eyes (b) recessive to brown eyes (B). Normally, to manifest a recessive trait, both alleles must be recessive, whereas the dominant trait is manifested if both members of the pair are dominant, or one is dominant and one recessive. However, for genes on the X chromosome, a male will have only one allele and will therefore manifest the recessive if the one allele present is recessive. The female, of course, with two X's, needs two recessives to manifest the recessive trait. Thus if a trait is sex-linked recessive, it will be manifested more frequently by males than by females. A good example is color blindness.

This basic genetic gender difference is thought to be a source of the biologi-

FIGURE 9.1
There is no evidence that genes influence math ability or other abilities, but the media are delighted by images of genetic female inferiority at math. This cartoon accompanied a story about the Benbow and Stanley research (see Chapter 6 for further discussion). *(Source: Kimble Mead.)*

cal resiliency of the female compared with that of the male (for a popularized discussion, see Montagu, 1964). Women are known to be generally less susceptible to sex-linked recessive genetic diseases, such as hemophilia. Most genetic diseases or other harmful genetic effects are recessive, whereas beneficial effects are generally dominant (the biological utility of this system is apparent). As stated above, it is easier for a man to manifest a sex-linked recessive trait, because he needs only one recessive gene, whereas a woman needs two recessives. Therefore, men are more likely than women to be affected by sex-linked recessive defects such as hemophilia and color blindness.

Except for color vision, there are no behaviors or abilities or other psychological characteristics for which there is good evidence of sex-linked genetic influence. There was some early evidence that spatial visualizing ability was influenced by an X-linked gene (Bock and Kolakowski, 1973; Hartlage, 1970; Stafford, 1961; Yen, 1975). However, later studies using larger samples failed to find evidence for this (Bouchard and McGee, 1977; DeFries et al., 1976).

Another important function of the sex chromosomes is to direct the course of prenatal gender differentiation. In doing this, the sex chromosomes interact with hormones. This brings us to a second biological factor that may influence gender differences.

Sex Hormones

Testosterone: A "male" sex hormone; one of the androgens.

Androgens: A group of "male" sex hormones, including testosterone, produced more abundantly in males than females.

Estrogen: A "female" sex hormone produced by the ovaries; also produced in smaller quantities in males.

Progesterone: A "female" sex hormone produced by the ovaries; also produced in smaller quantities in males.

Hormones are powerful chemical substances manufactured by the various endocrine glands of the body. Endocrine glands secrete hormones into the bloodstream so that they can have effects throughout the body, including effects on target organs far from the endocrine gland that secreted them. Among the endocrine glands are the gonads (ovaries and testes), pancreatic islets, pituitary, thyroid, and adrenal glands.

The "male" sex hormone is called **testosterone.** It is one of a group of "male" hormones called **androgens,** which are manufactured by the testes. The "female" sex hormones are **estrogen** and **progesterone,** which are manufactured by the ovaries. If these hormones influence behavior, then they may create gender differences.

Actually, it is a mistake to call testosterone the "male" sex hormone and estrogen and progesterone "female" hormones. Testosterone, for example, is found in females as well as males. The difference is in amount, not presence or absence. In women, testosterone is manufactured by the adrenal gland, and the level in women's blood is about one-sixth that in men's (Salhanick and Margulis, 1968). "Female" hormones are also found in men's blood.

The differences in levels of sex hormones may affect behavior at two major stages of development: prenatally (the time between conception and birth), and during and after puberty (adulthood). Endocrinologists refer to the effects that occur prenatally as *organizing effects,* because they cause a relatively permanent effect in the organization of some structure, whether in the nervous system or the reproductive system. Hormone effects in adulthood are called *activating effects* because they activate or deactivate certain behaviors. To understand the **prenatal** effects, we need to examine the process of prenatal gender differentiation first.

Prenatal: Before birth.

Prenatal Gender Differentiation Gender differences exist at the moment of conception. If the fertilized egg contains two X chromosomes, then the genetic gender of the individual is female; if it contains one X and one Y chromosome, the genetic gender is male. The single cell then divides repeatedly, becoming an embryo, then a fetus. Interestingly, during the first six weeks of human prenatal development, the only differences between females and males are in genetic gender. That is, anatomically and physiologically males and females develop identically during this period. Beginning approximately during the sixth week of pregnancy, and continuing through about the sixth month, the process of prenatal gender differentiation occurs (for an extended discussion, see Money and Ehrhardt, 1972). First, the sex chromosomes direct the differentiation of the gonads (Figure 9.2). An XX chromosome complement directs the differentiation of ovaries; an XY complement produces testes. The gonads then begin secreting

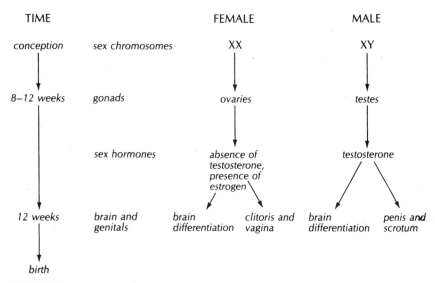

FIGURE 9.2
The sequences of prenatal differentiation of females and males.

sex hormones. Thus the internal environment becomes different for females and males because of hormonal differences.

The sex hormones further affect the course of fetal differentiation. In particular, the male testes produce testosterone. If testosterone is present, the male penis forms. If testosterone is not present, a clitoris and vagina differentiate. New research indicates that the presence of estrogen may also be critical for the development of female sexual organs (Fausto-Sterling, 1992; Wilson et al., 1984). In addition to influencing the process of anatomical gender differentiation, the sex hormones also influence the developing brain. The structure most affected seems to be the hypothalamus. The importance of this differentiation will be discussed later in the chapter.

Prenatal Sex Hormone Effects   Male fetuses and female fetuses, then, live in different hormonal environments. Does this have any effect on their later behaviors?

Most of the evidence in this area is based on experiments done with animals. It may be that the effects on humans would not be the same. But let us consider the animal experiments, and then see what is known about similar processes in humans. (For a review, see Ehrhardt and Meyer-Bahlburg, 1981.)

Prenatal sex hormone exposure seems to affect mainly two behaviors: *sexual behavior* and *aggressive behavior*. The organizing effects of sex hormones on sexual behavior have been well documented. In a classic experiment, testosterone was administered to pregnant female guinea pigs (Phoenix et al., 1959). The female offspring that had been exposed to testosterone prenatally were, in adulthood, incapable of displaying female sexual behavior (in particular, lordosis, which is a sexual posturing involving arching of the back and raising the hindquarters so that the male can insert the penis). It is thought that this occurred because the testosterone "organized" the brain tissue (particularly the hypothalamus) in a male fashion. These female offspring were also born with masculinized genitals, and thus their reproductive systems had also been organized in the male direction. But the important point here is that the prenatal doses of testosterone had masculinized their sexual behavior. Similar results have been obtained in experiments with many other species as well (Hines and Collaer, 1993).

In adulthood, these hormonally masculinized females displayed mounting behavior, a male sexual behavior. When they were given testosterone in adulthood, they showed about as much mounting behavior as males did. Thus the testosterone administered in adulthood *activated* male patterns of sexual behavior.

The analogous experiment on males would be castration at birth followed by administration of female sex hormones in adulthood. When this was done with rats, female sexual behavior resulted. These male rats responded to mating attempts from normal males the way females usually do (Harris and Levine, 1965). Apparently the brain tissue had been organized in a female direction during an early critical period when testosterone was absent, and the female behavior patterns were activated in adulthood by administration of ovarian hormones.

Similar effects have also been demonstrated for aggressive behavior. Early exposure to testosterone increases the fighting behavior of female mice (Edwards, 1969). Female rhesus monkeys given early exposure to testosterone show a higher incidence of rough-and-tumble play (Young et al., 1964). Thus early exposure to testosterone also organizes aggressive behavior in a "masculine" direction.

What relevance do these studies have for humans? (For a review, see Hines, 1982). It would be unethical, of course, to do experiments like the ones discussed above on human participants. Nonetheless, a number of "natural" experiments and "accidental" experiments of this sort occur. The natural experiments are the result of a few genetic conditions that cause abnormal hormone functioning prenatally. The accidental experiments have occurred when pregnant women were given drugs containing hormones. (These drugs are no longer administered during pregnancy.) We will consider one of the genetic syndromes.

Congenital adrenal hyperplasia (CAH): A rare genetic condition that causes the fetus's adrenal glands to produce abnormally large amounts of androgens. In genetic females, the result may be a girl born with masculinized genitals. Also called adrenogenital syndrome.

Congenital adrenal hyperplasia (CAH, also known as adrenogenital syndrome or AGS) is a rare recessive genetic condition that causes the fetus's adrenal glands to produce abnormally large amounts of androgens (testosterone) beginning about three months after conception. CAH is most interesting in genetic females, for whom the testosterone exposure is particularly abnormal. Researchers have studied the behavior of CAH girls (Berenbaum and Hines, 1992; Hines and Kaufman, 1994). CAH girls are significantly more likely, compared with a control group of non-CAH sisters, to choose male-stereotyped toys for play. On the other hand, CAH girls do not differ from their control sisters in the amount of rough play. These results, then, are not consistent with the research showing that prenatal exposure of genetic female animals to testosterone results in higher levels of rough, aggressive behavior.

Some cautions must be sounded about the research with humans. First, CAH girls are born with masculine-appearing genitals and generally must undergo surgery to correct the problem. We have no idea how traumatic that might be, nor whether that trauma would have an effect on behavior. Second, the girl's parents know about the genetic condition. Might, parents of CAH girls treat them differently than they would normal daughters?

Biology and Gender Identity   Gender identity—the knowledge that one is a male or a female, and the integration of this fact into one's personal identity—is a very basic psychological characteristic. Is gender identity biologically determined (by chromosomes, by hormones, or by anatomical sex characteristics), or is it modifiable by environment?

On the basis of a long program of research, psychologist John Money concluded that the acquisition of gender role and of basic gender identity is dependent upon the environment (Money and Ehrhardt, 1972). Many of the data come from individuals with anatomical abnormalities so that there are contradictions among their various sexual characteristics.

To discuss gender identity, we must first distinguish among the six variables of gender: (1) chromosomal gender (that is, XX in the female or XY in the male); (2) gonadal gender (ovaries or testes); (3) hormonal gender (estrogen and progesterone or testosterone); (4) internal accessory organs (uterus and vagina or prostate and seminal vesicles); (5) external genital appearance (clitoris and vaginal opening or penis and scrotum); and (6) assigned gender ("It's a girl!" or "It's a boy!") and gender role. Normally, of course, all these variables are in agreement, apparently indicating that chromosomal gender determines gender identity. That is, normally the female's XX chromosome complement causes differentiation of the ovaries during fetal development (actually, it is not the presence of XX, but the absence of a Y chromosome that causes this), and the ovaries produce the appropriate female hormones, which cause further feminine differentiation of the internal organs and external genitals. The appearance of the external genitalia determines the gender assignment—the announcement "It's a girl!" — which then leads to rearing as a female.

However, a number of "accidents" during the course of development may result in the gender indicated by one or more of these variables disagreeing with the gender indicated by the others. In these cases, the gender of assignment and rearing may or may not correspond to the genetic gender, but the child seems to accept the assigned gender and to develop successfully in it.

Pseudohermaphrodite:
An individual who has a mixture of male and female reproductive structures, so that it is not clear whether the individual is a male or female.

One sort of individual they have studied is the **pseudohermaphrodite,** in whom there is a mixture of male and female reproductive structures, as well as contradictions between external genital appearance and one of the other biological gender variables (genetic gender, gonads, hormones, or internal reproductive structures). In genetic females, this often results from CAH, discussed in the previous section. These females as fetuses develop ovaries normally, but during the course of prenatal development, the adrenal gland begins to function abnormally and excess amounts of androgens are produced. Prenatal sexual differentiation does not follow the normal course. As a result, the external genitals are partly or completely male in appearance—the labia are partly or totally fused, and the clitoris is enlarged to the size of a small penis. Hence, at birth, these genetic females are identified as being males.

Money and Ehrhardt (1972) cited one case of a matched pair of these individuals. Both were diagnosed as males at birth. One was from that time on reared as a male. He developed normally as a male; functioned normally in groups of boys; had outdoor, athletic, and sporting interests; and easily accepted the stereotype of the male role in marriage. The other child, because of further medical problems, returned for treatment and was at that time correctly rediagnosed as a female. Her external genitals were feminized surgically, and the internal reproductive structures were already feminine. She was reared as a female, and managed fairly successfully to adopt the female role, although she did have tendencies toward what Money calls "tomboyism." Despite identical genetic gender and genitals, these individuals could become either males or females, depending on the gender of the assignment and rearing.

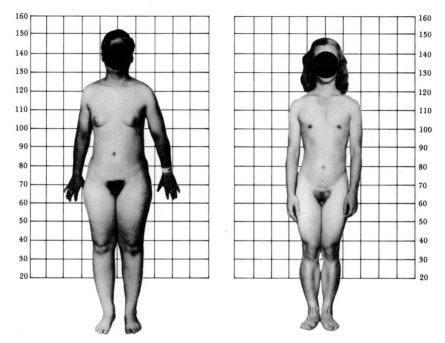

FIGURE 9.3
A matched pair of individuals who are genetic females born with CAH. The one on the right was reared as a female, with hormonal treatments and surgical treatment of her genitals. The one on the left was reared as a male, with hormonal treatments; no genital surgery was necessary. The one on the right has a female gender identity; the one on the left has a male gender identity.

An important related finding is that there appears to be a critical period for gender assignment and for the formation of gender identity. Up until the age of about 18 months, the child's gender may be almost arbitrarily reassigned, as in the case of the pseudohermaphrodite, and the child will accept the new gender and develop normally in it. Reassignment after that age can lead to serious conflicts in the child, and normal development in the new gender is unlikely. Note that this is in agreement with the view of cognitive-developmental theory (Chapter 2), which asserts that the formation of gender identity occurs at about the age of two or three years and that this becomes a permanent lifelong concept.

Money's argument for the importance of the environment in the formation of gender identity has not been accepted without challenge (e.g., Diamond, 1965, 1979; Rogers and Walsh, 1982). First, in almost all the cases given as evidence, sex reassignment was supplemented by appropriate surgical or hormonal therapy. That is, the individual's biological characteristics were modified to correspond to the assigned gender. Hence, it is not reasonable to say that gender could be assigned independent of biological gender characteristics. In fact, the very success of the reassignment often depends on the proper anatomical and hormonal modifications. Furthermore, it is difficult to know how relevant the abnormal cases studied by Money are to understanding the normal process of acquiring a gender identity.

A major study by Julianne Imperato-McGinley and her colleagues (1974) provides evidence that clearly contradicts Money's theory. Imperato-McGinley and her colleagues studied 38 individuals among rural people called the Guevodoces in Santo Domingo; all had a genetically inherited deficiency for an androgen known as dihydrotestosterone. All 38 had ambiguous genitalia, but 18 were raised as females. At puberty, their voices deepened and they grew adult-size penises and scrotums. This phenomenon is common enough in these villages that the individuals are not treated as freaks, and there is even a term used among the villagers, *penis-at-twelve,* to describe them. Of the 18 children raised as girls, 16 seemed successfully to assume a male gender role and gender identity, marrying and fathering children. These observations contradict Money's notion that gender identity is determined by early environmental factors. Instead, they indicate that biology (in this case, testosterone suddenly increasing at puberty) can have an important effect on gender identity, and can do so much later than early childhood (for a critique of this study, see Bem, 1993).

Data such as these have led reproductive biologist Milton Diamond (1965, 1979, 1982) to propose a *biased interaction model* of the development of gender identity. According to his model, gender identity is influenced by environmental forces interacting with the individual's biological makeup, specifically genes and hormones, and that biology biases the interaction. That is, most individuals have a gender identity that is consistent with their biological gender. The Guevodoces, according to Diamond, are a perfect case in point.

Diamond's interaction model is consistent with the general position in modern psychology that biology and environment are best viewed as interacting in their influence on psychological characteristics.

Hormone Effects in Adulthood   The effects of sex hormones in adulthood that are of interest to us fall into two categories. First, sex hormone levels in women fluctuate over the menstrual cycle. This raises the question of whether these hormone fluctuations would cause fluctuations in mood or other psychological characteristics. This topic will be discussed in detail in Chapter 10. Second, levels of sex hormones differ in men and women. For example, as noted earlier, women have only about one-sixth the level of testosterone in the blood that men do. Could it be that these different levels of hormones "activate" different behaviors in men and women?

As noted above, studies done with animals indicate that sex hormones in adulthood have effects on both aggressive behavior and sexual behavior. Once again, however, less information is available for humans and the results are more mixed (Rubin et al., 1981). Testosterone has well-documented effects on libido or sex drive in humans (Carani et al., 1990; Everitt and Bancroft, 1991). For example, men deprived of their main source of testosterone by castration show a dramatic decrease in sexual behavior in some, but not all, cases. Testosterone therefore has an activating effect in maintaining sexual desire in adult men. Recent research shows that testosterone, not estrogen, is related to libido in women, although the effects are not quite as strong (Bancroft, 1987; Sherwin, 1991). For example, if all sources of testosterone in women are removed (the adrenals and the ovaries), women lose sexual desire.

Probably sex hormone levels do have some effects on adult human behaviors, particularly aggressive and sexual behaviors. It is also likely that these effects are not so strong as they are in animals, and that they are more complex and interact more with environmental factors.

The Brain

In this section we will consider various hypotheses that have been proposed about differences between male and female brains and what effects those differences might have on behavior.

Brain Size A century ago, scientists discovered that human males had somewhat larger brains than human females. In the culture of the time, they concluded that this brain difference was the cause of the well-known lesser intelligence of women. The hypothesis was later discredited when other scientists found that males' larger brain size was almost entirely accounted for by their greater body size. Elephants have pretty big brains, too, but you wouldn't want to use that as a basis for putting them in charge of the space program.

Amazingly, this same brain size hypothesis resurfaced in the 1990s. Two different scientists found that men's brains were larger in volume and weighed more than women's, and they argued that this brain difference had an impact on gender differences in intelligence (Ankney, 1992; Rushton, 1992). Interestingly, the same scientists also claimed that Caucasian Americans had larger brains than African Americans and that Asian Americans had larger brains than either group (Rushton, 1992)—so the argument had racial dimensions as well, but here we will focus on the argument about gender.

Feminist biologist Anne Fausto-Sterling provided a detailed critique of this work (Fausto-Sterling, 1993). First, there is disagreement among scientists about how large the difference in brain size is—estimates range between 10 percent and 17 percent. Second, some of the studies have not actually measured brain size directly. Some have measured the inside volume of skulls, but there is more inside the skull than just the brain, so this isn't a good measure of brain size. And Rushton, the leading proponent of the brain size argument, actually just measured the outside of people's heads. Third, Rushton used a complicated and questionable formula that indicated that men had larger brains relative to body size than women did; however, according to Fausto-Sterling's computations, if

FIGURE 9.4
There has been much publicity about differences between male and female brains. However, research evidence is ambiguous and inconsistent.

you simply take the ratio of brain size to body weight, women actually had relatively larger brains. Finally, the question still remains whether brain size has anything to do with intelligence. No one has good evidence—pro or con—on whether it does. Therefore, there doesn't seem to be any reason to stay awake at night worrying about women's somewhat smaller brains.

Hypothalamus: A part of the brain that is important in regulating certain body functions, including sex hormone production.

The Hypothalamus   Gender differences do exist in the **hypothalamus,** a tiny region of the brain on its lower side (Gibbons, 1991; MacLusky and Naftolia, 1981). These differences are the result of differentiation of brain tissue in the course of fetal development, much as is the case for the reproductive organs (see Figure 9.2). Recall that the sequence of normal development consists of the sex chromosomes directing the differentiation of gonadal tissue into ovaries or testes. The gonads then secrete appropriate-gender hormones, which cause further reproductive-system differentiation. The fetal sex hormones also cause gender differentiation of the hypothalamus.

Basically, then, brain differentiation in the fetus is a process much like reproductive-system differentiation. Earlier researchers believed that the embryo began with no differentiation on the basis of gender and therefore humans were inherently gender neutral. It now appears to be more accurate to say that nature's primary impulse is to create a female. That is, if no additional forces intervene, female development occurs. The critical variable is the presence or absence of testosterone. If it is present, male characteristics develop; if absent, female characteristics. Thus it seems that, biologically, the female is normative! The male is a variant created by the addition of testosterone.

One of the most important organizing effects of prenatal sex hormones is the determination of the estrogen sensitivity of certain cells in the hypothalamus (for a review, see Taleisnik et al., 1971). Once again, it is the presence or absence of testosterone that is critical. If testosterone is present during fetal development, certain specialized receptor cells in the hypothalamus become insensitive to estrogen; if no testosterone is present, these cells are highly sensitive to levels of estrogen in the bloodstream. This is important because of the hypothalamic-pituitary-gonadal regulating feedback loop (see Chapter 10). In this process, gonadal hormone output is regulated by the pituitary, which is in turn regulated by the hypothalamus. The hypothalamus responds to the level of gonadal hormones in the bloodstream. Male hypothalamic cells are relatively insensitive to estrogen levels, whereas female hypothalamic cells are highly sensitive to them. We also know that estrogen (and progesterone as well) lowers the threshold of central nervous system (CNS) excitability in adults. Hence, the estrogen-sensitivity effect amounts to a much greater increase in CNS excitability in response to estrogen in the female than it does in the male. The estrogen-sensitivity effect is a result of the organizing effect of hormones. Hormones administered in adulthood activate male and female nervous systems differentially depending on prenatal determination (organizing effects) of estrogen sensitivity.

What are the observable consequences of these gender differences in the hypothalamus? One consequence is the determination of a cyclic or acyclic pattern of pituitary release of hormones (e.g., Barraclough and Gorski, 1961). The hypothalamus directs pituitary hormone secretion. A hypothalamus that has undergone female differentiation will direct the pituitary to release hormones cyclically, creating a menstrual cycle, whereas a male hypothalamus directs a relatively steady production of pituitary hormones.

The gender differences in the hypothalamus may have some consequences for behavior, too, although these have not been well documented in humans (for a review, see Reinisch, 1974). As discussed earlier, the organization of the hypothalamus in a male or a female direction may have some influence on both sexual and aggressive behavior.

Right Hemisphere, Left Hemisphere   The brain is divided into two halves, a right hemisphere and a left hemisphere. It is thought that these two hemispheres carry out somewhat different functions. In particular, in right-handed, normal persons, the left hemisphere seems specialized for verbal tasks, and the right

Lateralization: The extent to which one hemisphere of the brain organizes a particular mental process or behavior.

hemisphere for spatial tasks. The term **lateralization** usually refers to the extent to which a particular function, say, verbal processing, is handled by one hemisphere rather than both. Thus, for example, if verbal processing in one person is handled entirely in the left hemisphere, we would say that that person is highly lateralized or completely lateralized. If another person processes verbal material using both hemispheres, we would say that that person is bilateral for verbal functioning.

Brain lateralization research currently is an active area in psychological research. Based on the old belief that there are gender differences in both verbal ability and spatial ability (see Chapter 6), various theories have been proposed using gender differences in brain lateralization to account for the supposed differences in abilities. We shall review one of these theories and the evidence for it below (for detailed reviews, see Halpern, 1992; Sherman, 1978).

The *cognitive crowding hypothesis* was proposed by psychologist Jere Levy (Levy, 1976; Levy-Agresti and Sperry, 1968). Levy believes that spatial ability is optimized when it is strongly lateralized in one hemisphere. Furthermore, she believes that when verbal processes are lateralized completely in one hemisphere, and spatial processes in the other, the neural connections function the best and performance is best. If lateralization is not strong, then the processes for two different abilities (verbal ability and spatial ability) will occur in the same hemisphere, but essentially there is not enough "neural space" for this to work well, and performance is impaired. Furthermore, Levy argues that, in such cases, verbal processes dominate and spatial ability therefore suffers.

Levy believes that females are less lateralized than males and are therefore more likely to be bilateral for verbal ability. More neural space is devoted to verbal ability, therefore females outperform males on tests of verbal ability. At the same time, spatial performance suffers. So, in one neat package, Levy explains both females' superior verbal performance and their inferior spatial performance.

What evidence is there for the cognitive crowding hypothesis? Psychologists typically use two types of tasks in brain lateralization research. One is the dichotic listening task. The researcher presents different stimuli to each ear through headphones. As it turns out, people have ear—or hearing—dominance on the same side as hand dominance. If you are right-handed, you are also right-eared! That is, your right ear is more ready, willing, and able to process stimuli than your left ear is. This, in turn, connects to the hemispheres of the brain. Researchers in this field believe that the more dominant your right ear is (in accuracy and speed of processing stimuli), the more lateralized you are; the same would be true if you were very left-ear dominant. The other task used in this research is the split visual field, in which different stimuli are presented to different sides of your eyes, much like the different stimuli to different ears.

What does the evidence for the cognitive crowding hypothesis say? Dichotic listening tasks tend to show that males have a greater right-ear dominance for verbal stimuli than females do, indicating that males are more lateralized for verbal processes (for a review, see Halpern, 1992). Males also show greater right visual field superiority for verbal stimuli than females do, again indicating that males are more lateralized than females are for verbal processes. These findings, then, are consistent with the hypothesis. Nonetheless, some studies find inconsistent results. Some of these inconsistencies may be due to technical issues such as problems with the dichotic listening tasks.

In my view, the most serious criticism of the hypothesis is that it is designed to explain gender differences in verbal abilities and spatial abilities, yet the results of meta-analyses indicate that currently there are no gender differences in verbal ability, and there are large gender differences in only one type of spatial ability (see Chapter 6).

Brain lateralization is a very active area of research, and there are often flashy newspaper or magazine articles on a scientist who has discovered *the* cause of gender differences in abilities based on right-hemisphere/left-hemisphere differences. It is worthwhile for you to know the kinds of theories that have been proposed and the fact that there is inconsistent evidence. When the next theory comes along, you should know that it needs to be evaluated carefully, and how one could go about testing it—for example, by using dichotic listening or split visual field tasks. Such theories are also sometimes evaluated using clinical studies of brain-damaged people.

In sum, there do seem to be some gender differences in the use of the hemispheres of the brain. In particular, some evidence shows that males' brains are more strongly lateralized for some cognitive functions (Halpern, 1992). However, the exact differences and the effect these have on gender differences in abilities have yet to be untangled by research.

EXPERIENCE THE RESEARCH

BIOLOGY AND GENDER DIFFERENCES IN THE MEDIA

Search through old issues of *Time, Newsweek, U.S. News & World Reports,* or your local newspaper to find at least two articles that report on gender differences. Do the articles report on a psychological gender difference or a biological one? If it is a psychological gender difference, what explanation does the author of the article offer—does the author imply that it is biologically caused or environmentally caused, or is there a balanced discussion of both possibilities? If the article is about a biological gender difference, what is it? Is the information consistent with what you have learned in this chapter?

In Conclusion

We have considered three major classes of biological influences on gender differences and women's behavior: genes, hormones, and brain factors. Genes are not likely to be sources of gender differences, except when the genes are on the X chromosome, as for traits such as color blindness. Hormones have effects prenatally as well as in adulthood, particularly on sexual and aggressive behaviors, and possibly on behaviors related to the menstrual cycle. Regarding brain factors, males have slightly larger brains than females, but it is unclear whether this means anything. Gender differentiation of the hypothalamus in a female direction controls the cyclic functioning of the menstrual cycle and may be related to both aggressive and sexual behaviors. Finally, there may be some gender differences in the functioning of the hemispheres of the brain, but the exact nature of these differences is not yet well known.

Suggestion for Further Reading

Fausto-Sterling, Anne. (1992). *Myths of gender: Biological theories about women and men* (2d ed.) New York: Basic Books. Fausto-Sterling, who is a developmental biologist at Brown University, has written a brilliant critique of theories of biological gender differences.

10

Psychology and Women's Health Issues

[There is] an imperative need for women everywhere to learn about our bodies in order to have control over them and over our lives. We seek to communicate our excitement about the power of shared information; to assert that in an age of professionals, we are the best experts on ourselves and our feelings; to continue the collective struggle for adequate health care.

FROM OUR BODIES, OURSELVES

One of the most important parts of the feminist movement of the past decades has been the women's health movement. It is based on the belief that women need to know more about their bodies in order to have more control over them. One of the best books to come out of that movement is *Our Bodies, Ourselves,* written by the Boston Women's Health Book Collective (1976, 1984).

In this chapter we shall consider some of the topics that are important in the women's health movement—menstruation, menopause, pregnancy and childbirth, abortion, breast cancer, and AIDS. I will give brief information on the physical and medical aspects of each of these topics and concentrate on the psychological research that has been done on them. But first, I will review the overall statistics on gender and health and how women fare in the health care system.

Gender and Health

At every moment from conception to death, males have a higher death rate than females (Strickland, 1988). Approximately 125 male fetuses are conceived for every 100 female fetuses (it is thought that the Y chromosome–bearing sperm are a bit lighter and swim faster to the egg), yet only 106 live male babies are born for every 100 female babies. At the other end of the lifespan, among those who are 100 or older, there are five women for every man. For a baby born in the United States today, the average life expectancy is 79 years for women and 72 years for men (Collins et al., 1994).

Data on the leading causes of death are shown in Table 10.1. Notice that males have higher death rates from just about everything. Notice also that ethnicity is a factor. African Americans, for example, have a considerably higher death rate from diseases of the heart; African American women have a higher death rate from heart disease than white women, but the rate is still below that of white men.

There is a gender similarity, too. For both males and females, heart disease is a leading cause of death. Yet the stereotype is that men have the heart attacks. Furthermore, much of the medical research on treatments for heart disease has

TABLE 10.1

Leading Causes of Death for Males and Females (number of deaths per 100,000 people in the population)

	Females		Males	
	White	*Black*	*White*	*Black*
Cancers	111	137	160	248
Heart disease	103	168	202	276
Cerebrovascular (stroke)	24	43	28	56
Accidents	18	20	46	62
Lung disease	15	11	27	27
Pneumonia and influenza	11	14	18	29
Diabetes	10	25	11	24
Liver disease and cirrhosis	5	12	12	20
Suicide	5	2	20	12
Blood poisoning	3	8	4	12

SOURCE: Collins et al. (1994).

been done with all-male samples. If women are going to have heart attacks, they need to be part of this research!

It is thought that the higher mortality rates for males—or higher survival rates for females—are due to a combination of biological factors and cultural factors, the latter having to do with gender roles and what some have termed the "lethal" aspects of the male role.

At the same time, women report more short-term illnesses than men do, and 65 percent of surgery patients in the United States are women. Gynecological surgeries lead the list as the more frequent surgeries (Strickland, 1988; Travis, 1993). The majority of those are for tubal ligations (the female sterilization operation); also included in the category are **hysterectomies** (surgical removal of the uterus). The data indicate that 25 percent of hysterectomies are elective, that is, not medically necessary (Travis, 1993). There is a concern, then, that many unnecessary hysterectomies are being performed, which leads to concerns about the health care system.

Hysterectomy: Surgical removal of the uterus.

Women and the Health Care System

Feminists have been critical of the treatment of women in the health care system. These criticisms can be summarized in the following four points (Travis, 1988a; 1993):

1. The physician-patient relationship reflects the subordinate status of women in society, with the physician (usually male) having power and control over the female patient.

2. The medical profession has actively discriminated against women as practitioners (Walsh, 1977). Around the turn of the century, most medical schools refused to admit women. Women were not admitted to the American Medical Association until 1915. Although women now earn 34 percent of M.D. degrees (U.S. Bureau of the Census, 1993), they still generally receive their medical training in an atmosphere that is hostile to women. For example, in a study done on the treatment of women in the medical school at my own university, it was found that women doing their residency in surgery were often referred to by the male surgeons as "skirts." The status of nurses (over 90 percent of whom are women) in relation to physicians also reflects the higher status of male-dominated professions and the lower status of female-dominated professions.

3. Medical care offered to women is often inadequate, uncaring, or irresponsible. There are problems of misdiagnosis and overmedication. For example, women are 1.5 times as likely as men to receive prescriptions for psychotherapeutic drugs such as tranquilizers (Svarstad, 1987), perhaps reflecting the stereotype that women are hysterical or neurotic. Even when women go to doctors and present physical symptoms, they are still twice as likely as men to receive a psychotherapeutic drug (Gomberg, 1986). As noted earlier, as many as 25 percent of hysterectomies are elective, and this may indicate irresponsible care of women.

4. Medical research conducted on women is often irresponsible. For example, far more contraceptives have been developed for females than for males, and thus the health risks associated with them have been borne disproportionately by women. One notorious example is the Dalkon Shield, an IUD (intrauterine device) that was withdrawn from the market after 17 women died of pelvic inflammatory disease directly traceable to the IUD (Travis, 1988a). Ethnicity is also a factor relating to risky research. For example, the initial field trials for the birth control pill, whose risk was unknown at the time, were conducted among poor women in Puerto Rico.

Health Needs of Poor and Minority Women Feminist theory emphasizes the importance not only of gender, but of ethnicity and social class as well. That principle is important as we consider the health care system.

Ethnic minority women have a number of special health concerns (Zambrana, 1988):

1. Ethnic minority women experience higher rates of infant mortality than white women. This in turn is related to higher rates of low-birth-weight babies among ethnic minority women. And this in turn is related to more fre-

quent adolescent childbearing among ethnic minorities. That is, adolescent mothers are more likely to have low-birth-weight babies, who have a higher death rate.

2. Chronic diseases are more prevalent among ethnic minority women than among white women. Examples include diabetes, high blood pressure, heart disease, and cervical cancer.

3. The life expectancy of ethnic minority women is five to seven years less than that of white women. This is a result, at least in part, of less access to medical care that would allow early detection and prevention of many diseases.

Ethnic minority women are overrepresented among the poor. We have, then, a combination of ethnicity and poverty contributing to reduced access to necessary health care. This is turn creates more health problems for these women. There is an urgent need for equal access to health care.

Menstruation

Ovum: An egg.

Follicle: The capsule of cells surrounding an egg in the ovary.

Follicular phase: The first phase of the menstrual cycle, beginning just after menstruation.

Ovulation: Release of an egg from an ovary.

Luteal phase: The third phase of the menstrual cycle, after ovulation.

Menstruation: A bloody discharge of the lining of the uterus; the fourth phase of the menstrual cycle.

Biology of the Menstrual Cycle   The human female is born with approximately 400,000 primary follicles in both ovaries, each follicle containing an egg or **ovum.** (The term **follicle** here refers to a group of cells in the ovary that encapsulates an egg and has nothing to do with the term *hair follicle.*) A single menstrual cycle involves the release of one egg from a follicle, allowing it to move down the fallopian tube for possible fertilization and implantation in the uterus. Hence not more than 400 eggs are ovulated from puberty through menopause. The remaining follicles degenerate. (See Figure 10.1 for a diagram of women's reproductive anatomy.)

A menstrual cycle can be separated into four phases, each describing the state of the follicle and egg within that phase (see Figure 10.2). It would be most convenient to call the period of menstruation the first phase, because it is easily identifiable, but physiologically it represents the last. The first phase, called the **follicular phase,** extends approximately from day 4 to day 14 after menstruation begins. (In counting days of the cycle, day 1 is the first day of menstruation.) During this phase, a follicle matures and swells. The termination of this phase is marked by the rupturing of the follicle and the release of the egg (**ovulation**). During the next phase, the **luteal phase,** a group of reddish yellow cells, called the corpus luteum, forms in the ruptured follicle. The final phase, marked by **menstruation,** represents a sloughing off of the inner lining (endometrium) of the uterus, which had built up in preparation for nourishing a fertilized egg.

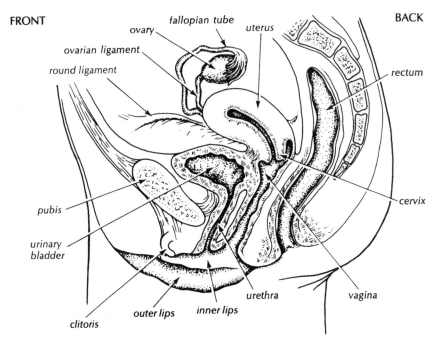

FRONT   BACK

fallopian tube

ovary

uterus

ovarian ligament

round ligament

rectum

pubis

cervix

urinary
bladder

urethra   vagina

outer lips   inner lips

clitoris

FIGURE 10.1
Schematic cross section of the female pelvis, showing sexual and reproductive organs.

Follicle-stimulating hormone (FSH): A hormone secreted by the pituitary; in females it stimulates follicle and egg development.

Luteinizing hormone (LH): A hormone secreted by the pituitary; in females it triggers ovulation.

Gonadotropin-releasing hormone (Gn-RH): A hormone secreted by the hypothalamus that regulates the pituitary's secretion of hormones.

These cyclic phases are regulated by hormones that act in a negative feedback loop with one another (Figure 10.3), so that the production of a hormone increases to a high level, producing a desired physiological change. The level is then automatically reduced through the negative feedback loop. Here we are concerned with two basic groups of hormones—those produced by the ovaries, most importantly estrogen and progesterone, and those produced by the pituitary gland, most importantly **follicle-stimulating hormone (FSH)** and **luteinizing hormone (LH).** We also need to consider control of the activity of the pituitary by the hypothalamus, an important region of the brain on its lower side (Figure 10.3), by Gn-RH (**gonadotropin-releasing hormone**). The overall pattern of the negative feedback loop is that the activity of the ovary, including its production of estrogen and progesterone, is regulated by the pituitary, which in turn is regulated by the hypothalamus, which is sensitive to the levels of estrogen produced by the ovaries.

The regulation of the menstrual cycle involves interactions among the levels of these hormones. The follicular phase of the cycle is initiated by the pitituary gland sending out follicle-stimulat-

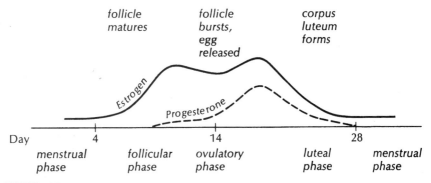

follicle
matures

follicle
bursts,
egg
released

corpus
luteum
forms

Estrogen

Progesterone

Day   4   14   28

menstrual   follicular   ovulatory   luteal   menstrual
phase   phase   phase   phase   phase

FIGURE 10.2
Changes in hormone levels over the phases of the menstrual cycle.

ing hormone (FSH), which signals the ovaries to increase production of estrogen and to bring several follicles to maturity. The resulting high level of estrogen, through the feedback loop, signals the pituitary to decrease production of FSH and to begin production of luteinizing hormone (LH), whose chief function is to trigger ovulation. Temporarily, FSH and LH induce even more estrogen production, which further lowers the amount of FSH. At this point the LH becomes dominant, causing the follicle to rupture and release the egg. The corpus luteum then forms in the ruptured follicle. The corpus luteum is a major source of progesterone. When progesterone levels are sufficiently high, they will, through the negative feedback loop, inhibit production of LH, and simultaneously stimulate the production of FSH, beginning the cycle over again.

Estrogen has a number of functions and effects in the body. It maintains the lining of the vagina and uterus and provides the initial stimulation for breast growth. Its nonreproductive functions include increasing water content and thickness of skin and retarding growth rate. At the beginning and the end of the menstrual cycle, estrogen is at a low level. In between these two times, it reaches two peaks, one immediately prior to and during ovulation, the other in the middle of the luteal phase (Figure 10.2). It appears that mature ovarian follicles are the major producers of estrogen.

Progesterone is especially important in preparing the uterus for implantation of the fertilized ovum, maintaining pregnancy, and regulating the accessory organs during the reproductive cycle. Because the corpus luteum is a major source of progesterone, progesterone level peaks during the luteal phase and is otherwise low.

A Health Function for Menstruation? Biologist Margie Profet (1993) argues that menstruation, rather than being just a pain in the abdomen, has a disease-preventing function. Sperm can carry bacteria; bacteria from either the male or

259

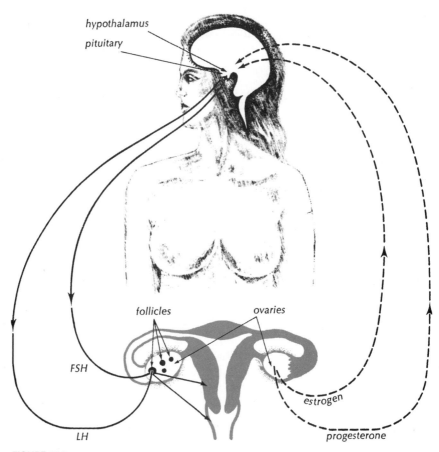

FIGURE 10.3
Schematic diagram illustrating the negative feedback loops controlling hormone levels during the menstrual cycle. FSH and LH are produced by the pituitary gland and influence production of estrogen and progesterone in the ovaries. The hypothalamus is sensitive to levels of these hormones and, in turn, regulates levels of FSH and LH. (See text for further explanation.)

female genitals regularly attach themselves to the tails of sperm. With this free ride, during heterosexual intercourse they are transported not only into the vagina, but also into the uterus and fallopian tubes. Menstruation cleans out the uterus and also delivers large numbers of immune cells into the uterus. Menstruation, then, may have a bacteria-fighting function.

If Profet is right, then there is cause for concern about a number of situations in which women do not menstruate, such as women who exercise strenuously and are very lean, anorexic women, and post-menopausal women. These women, if they engage in heterosexual intercourse, should consider using a barrier method such as a condom or diaphragm to reduce the risk of infections.

Dysmenorrhea: Painful menstruation; cramps.

Menstrual Problems: Cramps   Painful cramps during menstruation are called **dysmenorrhea.** Some women experience them regularly, some women experience them some of the time, and some women don't experience them. There are serious problems of understanding another person's experience here. It is very difficult for a man, or for a woman who does not experience severe dysmenorrhea, to understand precisely how those who do experience it feel, a point that is expressed poignantly in Focus 10.1, "A Woman Describes Her Experiences with Menstrual Pain."

Traditional medical remedies have not been completely successful in treating the problem. Over-the-counter drugs such as Midol help some people some of the time, but they do not help everyone. In fact, until a few years ago, it seemed that the best treatment was plain old aspirin. However, in the past several years there has been a major breakthrough in understanding the biology of cramps and corresponding advances in treating them.

Prostaglandins: Hormone-like biochemicals that stimulate the muscles of the uterus to contract.

Prostaglandins are currently thought to be the culprit responsible for cramps (Budoff, 1981; Golub, 1992). Prostaglandins are hormonelike substances produced by many tissues of the body, including the lining of the uterus. Prostaglandins cause smooth muscle to contract and can affect the size of blood vessels. Women with severe menstrual pain have unusually high levels of prostaglandins. The high levels cause intense uterine contractions, which are painful; these contractions in turn choke off some of the uterus's supply of oxygen-carrying blood, a painful process that resembles somewhat what occurs in a heart attack. Prostaglandins may also cause greater sensitivity in nerve endings. The combination of the uterine contractions, lack of oxygen, and heightened nerve sensitivity produces cramps.

As a result of this analysis of the causes of cramps, a new treatment is the use of *antiprostaglandin drugs.* The drug is mefanamic acid and is sold with brand names such as Ponstel. Other, similar drugs are Motrin, Naprosyn, and Anaprox. Interestingly, its application to menstrual cramps was discovered by a woman physician, Dr. Penny Wise Budoff (1981). In her research, 85 percent of the women tested reported significant relief from menstrual pain and symptoms such as nausea, vomiting, dizziness, and weakness. Not coincidentally, one of the traditional cures for cramps, aspirin, is a weak antiprostaglandin. The work on antiprostaglandin drugs looks promising enough to me that I would recommend that any woman who has suffered severe problems with cramps and has not received satisfactory treatment consult a doctor about possibly receiving an antiprostaglandin drug (these drugs are available by prescription only).

In 1982 the Nobel Prize in medicine was awarded to the three scientists who pioneered prostaglandin research *(Time,* October 25, 1982). The news coverage

FOCUS 10.1

A WOMAN DESCRIBES HER EXPERIENCES
WITH MENSTRUAL PAIN

I started to menstruate when I was 12. The pain did not occur the first few times. The first time it happened I was in the kitchen getting tea for my mother. Suddenly, a terrible pain doubled me over, and I could hardly get my breath. I could not stand straight and when I reached my mother she told me to sit on my bed, and that it would pass. She was quite nice that time and told me that sometimes it had been bad for her, too. Later on, after a half-year had passed, she was fed up with me. She began to hate my crying and twisting in pain. . . . Finally, one day when I was thirteen she told me that if I didn't stop crying that instant, she would walk out on me and leave me alone. I sat there and shuddered, but I didn't make any more noise. My mother made it plain. I learned that I could not cry out or she and other people would withdraw from me.

When I got older, this lesson was reinforced. I could mention my problem once, maybe twice, but then the school nurses and personnel all turned a deaf ear. Teachers would not help me cope; they shook their heads at such absurdity, believing that I had suddenly turned into a goldbrick. . . . Past history also seemed to count for nothing. I always loved basketball and participated enthusiastically in gym. Once a month, however, I would incur the wrath of my gym teacher who decided that I suddenly just didn't want to improve my basketball skills. Her attitude cooled the attitudes of the girls in my class for me, also. Who would want to associate with such an unreliable person? . . .

When I was 18, I had a horseback-riding accident in which I broke my back in the middle. The first doctor who examined me failed to X-ray the middle back and said there was nothing wrong but some bruises. I seemed to have too much pain for bruises. . . . Two weeks later my father, who did not like the way I

focused on the physiology of prostaglandins and discussed applications in the treatment of ulcers, arthritis, and pain associated with heart attacks. Only fleeting mention was made of the application of prostaglandins to the treatment of menstrual pain. Millions of women who are sufferers might say that the menstrual-pain application is just as important.

was moving, sent me to Knickerbocker Hospital for more X-rays. There they found out that my spine had been broken (in addition to my coccyx) and proceeded to put me in a wheelchair and tell me that I must not take another step, which I thought was pretty funny (except for the pain) because for two weeks I had been walking, cleaning, living on my own, and even hiking in that condition. As you know, Knickerbocker is a busy New York City hospital, used to seeing plenty of the rougher side of life. Yet that night, the resident who had examined me and taken the X-rays stopped by my room to speak to me. He said, "I just wanted to see how the bravest girl I've ever met is getting along." His kindness surprised me, but so did the fact that he thought my talking calmly, normally, and not crying or fainting with the enormous pain I was in, was surprising. . . . The rest of the hospital staff also found my behavior very surprising. . . .

There was one thing they did not know, however, about my ability to take pain. It's not that I don't feel it; I have the same number of nerve endings per square foot as anyone else. The difference is that I had been in training for years to endure it. I was used to coping through a haze of nauseating pain, used to having a conversation when every nerve in me was screaming out, used to getting dressed and getting on a bus when I felt as though a red-hot iron was going to knock my stomach out. I got my training every month without fail, when my period came.

I, of course, developed such techniques as I could for enduring this experience, such as mentally talking myself through something, step by step. . . .

These great techniques were not much. Obviously they only helped me to endure what I had to endure anyway to live up to our society's conviction that this condition does not exist and need not be remedied.

SOURCE: Budoff (1981), pp. 35–37.

Psychological Aspects of the Menstrual Cycle   "Why do I get so emotional?" screams the ad for Midol PMS in *Teen* magazine. The notion that women experience changes in personality or mood depending on the phase of the menstrual cycle is well known to the layperson and scientist alike. In this section we shall examine the evidence on the nature and extent of these moods and behavior shifts and their relationship to the hormone cycles occurring during the menstrual cycle.

In 1931, R. T. Frank gave the name *premenstrual tension* to the mood changes that occur during the three or four days immediately preceding menstruation (approximately days 23 to 26 or 28 of the cycle). There is by now an extensive body of research on this phenomenon, and the more general one of fluctuations in mood and behavior corresponding to the menstrual cycle (see Golub, 1992, and Parlee, 1973, for critical reviews).

Four types of studies have been used to document the existence of a premenstrual syndrome. First, attempts have been made to correlate observable behaviors with cycle phase. For example, it has been found that a large proportion of the suicides and criminal acts of violence committed by women occur during the four premenstrual and four menstrual days of the cycle (Dalton, 1964). Forty-five percent of the female industrial workers who call in sick, 46 percent of the women admitted to psychiatric care, and 52 percent of female accident-emergency admissions are in the eight premenstrual or menstrual days. In addition, 54 percent of the children brought to a clinic with minor colds were brought during their mothers' eight premenstrual and menstrual days, perhaps indicating an increase in the mothers' anxiety at this time (Dalton, 1966). The premenstrual syndrome, then, may have rather important and far-reaching consequences. On the other hand, the eight premenstrual and menstrual days do constitute 36 percent of the total days in a cycle. Hence a statistic like "49 percent of criminal acts committed by women occur during this time," which appears impressive considered by itself, may not represent a substantial or meaningful increase over the 36 percent expected randomly. And even with these presumed hormone effects, women commit far fewer crimes than men do.

A second type of study used to document the premenstrual syndrome is based on questionnaires requesting that women report retrospectively their symptoms and moods at various phases of the cycle. Such studies are largely useless because retrospective accounts, particularly of such subjective phenomena as moods in relation to menstrual cycle, are notoriously unreliable and have not been demonstrated to correlate with other indicators of premenstrual symptoms; that is, their validity is not established (Parlee, 1973).

A third type of study uses daily self-reports made by women throughout the cycle. Such studies generally find positive moods around the time of ovulation, and various symptoms, such as anxiety, irritability, depression, fatigue, and headaches, premenstrually (see summary by Parlee, 1973). On the other hand, the fluctuations are not large, on average. In one study, the mean depression score of women was 6.84 around ovulation and 9.30 premenstrually, compared with a mean of 16.03 for depressed psychiatric patients (Golub, 1992). Women are not ready for the psychiatric ward premenstrually!

A fourth approach avoids direct questioning of women about symptoms and instead uses a projective technique, in which participants tell stories at regular intervals throughout the cycle. These stories are then subjected to a standardized scoring for themes manifested in them. An example is a study by Ivey and Bardwick (1968), who recorded the spontaneous stories of 26 college women at ovulation and premenstruation over two menstrual cycles and then scored the stories using Gottschalk and Gleser's Verbal Anxiety Scale. Their findings for these normal women were that anxiety about death, mutilation, and separation were highest premenstrually, whereas self-confidence and self-esteem were higher at ovulation. Ivey and Bardwick provided the following examples:

From one woman at ovulation:

> We took our skis and packed them on top of the car and then we took off for up north. We used to go for long walks in the snow, and it was just really great, really quiet and peaceful.

Mutilation anxiety from the same woman premenstrually:

> . . . came around a curve and did a double flip and landed upside down. I remember this car coming down on my hand and slicing it right open and all this blood was all over the place. Later they thought it was broken because every time I touched the finger, it felt like a nail was going through my hand.

From another woman at ovulation:

> Talk about my trip to Europe. It was just the greatest summer of my life. We met all kinds of terrific people everywhere we went, and just the most terrific things happened.

Hostility from this same woman premenstrually:

> . . . talk about my brother and his wife. I hated her. I just couldn't stand her. . . . I used to do terrible things to separate them.

In summary, the results of the research using all these approaches do seem to indicate that there are fluctuations in mood corresponding to the phases of the menstrual cycle.

It is tempting to speculate that these mood changes are related to, or perhaps even caused by, changes in hormone levels occurring during the cycle (Bardwick, 1971). In particular, it seems that high levels of estrogen (at ovulation) are associated with positive moods, whereas low levels of estrogen premenstrually are associated with negative moods.

However, such a conclusion has been criticized on a number of counts (Parlee, 1973). First, virtually all the data (with some exceptions discussed below) presented to support this contention are correlational in nature; causal inferences are then made from these data, an unwise procedure at best. That is, the data simply demonstrate a correlation between cycle phase or hormone levels and mood. From this it is unwarranted to infer that hormones actually cause or influence mood. From these data an equally tenable conclusion would be that the direction of causality is the reverse—that psychological factors affect hormone levels and menstrual-cycle phase. For example, gynecology texts state that stress may delay menstruation or precipitate its onset; many women in concentration camps during World War II ceased menstruating. Social factors may also have an influence; for example, women living together in a college dormitory came to have menstrual cycles more closely synchronized as the academic year progressed (McClintock, 1971). In sum, the inference that hormone level influences mood is not completely justifiable on the basis of the available data, although further data may yet substantiate this conclusion.

One study that partially answers the objection about correlational data involved scoring the spoken stories of 102 married women four times during a single menstrual cycle: on days 4, 10, 16, and two days before the onset of menstruation (Paige, 1971). Other data were also collected to try to disguise the purpose of the study. The women were classified into three groups: (1) those who were not taking oral contraceptives and never had; (2) those who were taking a combination pill (combination pills provide a steady high dose of both estrogen and progestin, a synthetic progesterone, for 20 or 21 days); and (3) those who were taking sequential-type pills (which provide 15 days of estrogen, followed by 5 days of estrogen-progestin, similar to the natural cycle, but at higher levels). Nonpill women experienced statistically significant variation in their anxiety and hostility levels over the menstrual cycle, as previous studies had shown. Women taking the sequential pill showed the same mood changes that nonpill women did, which agrees with the predicted outcome, because their artificial hormone cycle parallels the natural one. Combination-pill women showed *no* mood shifts corresponding to the menstrual cycle: their hostility and anxiety levels remained constant. Therefore it appears that the steady high level of both hormones leads to a steady level of mood. This study serves as a quasi-experiment with respect to hormone levels, thereby answering, in part, the objections with regard to causal inferences on hormone-behavior relations.

Premenstrual syndrome (PMS): A combination of severe physical and psychological symptoms (such as depression) occurring in some women for a few days before menstruation.

A second criticism of this area of research is that the term **premenstrual syndrome (PMS)** or *premenstrual tension syndrome* is only vaguely defined. For instance, some authors have defined it so broadly as to include "any combination of emotional or physical features which occur cyclically in a female before menstruation" (Sutherland and Stewart, 1965, p. 1182). While it would be worthwhile to know what percentage of the female population is afflicted with premenstrual symptoms, estimates of this percentage vary considerably from one study to another. In one study, premenstrual irritability was found in 69 percent of the sample, depression in 63 percent, and both symptoms together in 45 percent (Sutherland and Stewart, 1965). In another study, the responses of approximately 30 to 50 percent of 839 young married women to a questionnaire indicated mood cycles in irritability, tension, and depression (Moos, 1968). In view of the vagueness of definition, it is not surprising that these estimates are not consistent, and until the "syndrome" is more clearly defined, we can have no really accurate estimate of its incidence. At least from these data it seems fair to conclude that the premenstrual syndrome is far from universal among women. It is possible that 50 percent of women have no premenstrual symptoms.

A third problem with this area of research is the problem of participants' expectations. Research participants may report more negative feelings premenstrually because such feelings are culturally prescribed—brainwashing through menstrual drug ads—or because they feel the experimenter expects those feelings, because the women must certainly be aware of the investigator's interest in their menstrual cycle.

Psychologist Diane Ruble (1977; see also Klebanov and Jemmott, 1992) did a clever experiment to determine whether people's expectations influence their reporting of premenstrual symptoms. College students were tested on the sixth or seventh day before the onset of their next menstrual period. They were told that they would participate in a study on a new technique for predicting the expected date of menstruation using an electroencephalogram (EEG), a method that had already been successfully tested with older women. After the EEG had been run, the woman was informed of when her next period was to occur, depending on which of three experimental groups she had been assigned to: (1) she was told she was "premenstrual" and her period was due in one or two days, (2) she was told she was "intermenstrual" or "midcycle" and her period was not expected for at least a week to ten days, or (3) she was given no information at all about the expected date of menstruation (control group). The women then completed a self-report menstrual-distress questionnaire. The results indicated that those who had been led to believe they were in the premenstrual phase reported significantly more water retention, pain, and changes in eating habits than those who had been led to believe they were around midcycle did. (In fact, women in these groups did not differ significantly in when their periods actually arrived.) There were no significant differences between the groups in ratings of negative moods, however. This study indicates that, probably because of learned beliefs, women overstate the changes in body states that occur over the menstrual cycle. When they think they are in the premenstrual phase, they report more problems than when they think they are at midcycle.

A subtle problem of interpretation exists in menstrual-cycle research. A typical conclusion is that symptoms increase or that mood is negative premenstrually. Perhaps, however, the premenstrual state is the "usual" one, and what occurs is really a decrease in symptoms, or a positive mood shift, at ovulation. This is essentially a problem of establishing a baseline of behavior—and what should that be? Should it be the average for males? Or are males irrelevant to this research? This is a complex question needing further resolution.

Also noteworthy are the tremendous cultural influences on menstrual-cycle mood shifts. In many preliterate societies and religions, a menstruating woman is seen as unclean, and many taboos arise to prevent her uncleanness from spreading to others (Stephens, 1961). For example, she may not be permitted to cook while menstruating, or she may even be isolated from the rest of the community

FOCUS 10.2
THE SOCIAL CONSTRUCTION OF PMS

"Why do I get so emotional?" asks the young woman in the ad for Midol PMS. You can bet the emotion she's talking about is not happiness—more likely anger, irritability, or sadness. As we discussed in Chapter 2, feminist theory emphasizes the social construction of gender phenomena—that is, that the way we interpret our experiences is shaped in large part by social and cultural forces. PMS, it has been argued, is socially constructed.

The expression of emotions is carefully regulated by social norms. You wouldn't, for example, laugh heartily in the middle of a funeral, and if you did, you would certainly receive negative responses from those around you. There are gender norms for emotions. For most emotions—love, sadness—it is far more acceptable for women to express them than for men. Anger is the exception. The expression of anger by men is tolerated; it is not for women. A woman who expresses anger is violating a social norm.

The expression of anger in women is unacceptable in large part because it interferes with the performance of their social roles. Women's family roles call for them to provide nurturance and emotional support to others. An angry person cannot be nurturant and emotionally supportive. The same is true for work roles. Women are found disproportionately in service occupations, and again anger interferes with performance of the job. No one wants to be cared for by an angry nurse.

On the other hand, many women have plenty to be angry about—low-status jobs, unequal pay for equal work, and battering, to name a few.

In sum, then, many women feel angry or irritable, but feeling these emotions—much less expressing them—is a serious deviation from social norms. This leads the woman herself and those around her to seek some socially acceptable explanation for her emotions. Enter PMS.

in a separate hut outside the village. Such superstitions become subtler in modern America, but they still persist. For example, many couples abstain from sexual intercourse during the woman's period. A survey of 960 California families showed that half the men and women had *never* had sex during menstruation (Paige, 1973). There is also considerable evidence of cultural influences on menstrual distress. For example, groups of married women were compared, accord-

From a psychological or social constructionist point of view, PMS can be seen as an attribution (attributions were discussed in Chapter 6). A woman experiences or expresses a particular emotion. To what does she attribute it? If the emotion is a socially unacceptable one, such as anger or irritability, she and others seek a socially acceptable attribution, and society makes PMS a readily available attribution. Magically, she isn't really angry, she is just in that temporary state of insanity, PMS. With a single stroke of attribution, her emotion no longer violates social norms; but at the same time, any real feelings of true anger she may have, perhaps toward her husband or her boss, are also brushed away.

Interestingly, PMS became a popular concept beginning in the 1980s, just as the feminist movement was urging women to discover their anger.

There may be a bit of a paradox here, though, from the viewpoint of feminist theory. The theory argues, on the one hand, that PMS is a social creation. On the other hand, feminist theory argues that we should accept and validate the lived experiences of women. A lot of women truly believe that they experience the emotional symptoms of PMS in a profound way. How can this paradox be resolved? The answer is that these women do experience the emotions they report, but that society has created a particular explanation or attribution for them in the few days before menstruation. When a woman experiences these negative emotions at some other time in the cycle, she may ignore them or seek some other attribution, such as just being in a bad mood that day, or perhaps being truly angry at her boss as a result of something he or she said to her. The PMS attribution, then, becomes a self-fulfilling prophecy.

SOURCES: Pugliesi (1992), Rodin (1992).

ing to their religious preference, on attitudes toward menstruation and variations in anxiety during the cycle (Paige, 1973). Most of the Jews and Catholics said they would never have sex during menstruation, as compared with less than half the Protestants. Protestants did not experience much fluctuation in anxiety level between the ovulation and premenstrual phases, whereas Catholics showed extreme fluctuations. These cultural variations in menstrual attitudes and symptoms may be related to religious teaching regarding menstruation (Paige, 1973). In any case, Protestant, Catholic, and Jewish women all have the same hormone cycles, but the correlated psychological cycles are different, so that the psychological cycles must surely be influenced by culture.

Finally, this area of research has seen too little attention devoted to coping mechanisms (Maccoby, 1972). Most women are simply not dissolved in tears, reduced to a state of incompetency, for three to six days each month. Certainly women must develop mechanisms for coping with these mood shifts, particularly if such shifts are regular and predictable. In fact, it might be reasonable to expect that the women who experience the largest mood shifts would develop the best strategies for coping with them. Unfortunately, we have little empirical evidence on these points. My own interviews with undergraduates suggest that increased activity, "keeping busy," is the most common coping strategy. Another common coping mechanism is sleeping more than usual—a kind of escapism, but also a practical means of dealing with feelings of fatigue. In addition, because the premenstrual syndrome is so well known, it is easy to deal with accompanying symptoms such as depression—most women quickly recognize that the depression is associated with the onset of menstruation and proceed about their business, unconcerned that they are displaying serious psychological symptoms because they know that the symptoms will disappear in a few days.

Feminist approaches to science often point up alternative interpretations of phenomena. But it is also true that the perspectives of different ethnic groups can suggest new interpretations (see Chapter 8). American Indian women believe that menstruation is a time of centering and balancing oneself (Hernandez, 1990). The flow out of the body washes away impurities and the negative things that have occurred during the month. Reflecting the close connection of the Indian people to nature, Indian women refer to the menstrual period as being "on the moon," which is considered a positive time.

Practical Implications   In assessing the practical implications of research on mood shift and menstrual phase, some important considerations should be kept in mind. First, the *magnitude* of the mood shift depends on the individual woman. It is a function of her psychological adjustment, as well as her current experiences. Certainly in practical situations, the magnitude and content of the mood shift are most significant. For instance, it is much more essential to know that a particular woman experiences mood shifts so small as to be unnoticeable in her work and interpersonal relations than it is to know that she experiences slight mood shifts detectable only by sensitive psychological tests. Hence the most important characteristics are individual ones, just as they are for men.

Second, in making practical decisions about hiring people, *performance* is certainly more crucial than mood. Research on performance—such as intellectual or athletic performance—generally shows no fluctuations over the cycle (Golub, 1976, 1992; Sommer, 1973). Research has found no fluctuations in academic performance, problem solving, memory, or creative thinking (Golub,

1992). Therefore, there is no evidence of cycle fluctuations in the kinds of performance that are important on the job.

In addition, it is likely that monthly hormonal cycles exist in men also (Delaney et al., 1976; Hersey, 1931; Parlee, 1978; Ramey, 1972), but until quite recently such cycles have not been the subject of scientific investigation—probably because they produce no obvious physical changes like menstruation. One study in fact found no differences between men and women in day-to-day mood changes—men were no more nor less changeable than women (McFarlane et al., 1988; see also McFarlane and Williams, 1994).

In summary, research suggests that menstrual-cycle changes in hormone levels may be related to corresponding changes in mood. Mood is generally positive at ovulation or midcycle, when estrogen levels are high, whereas it is negative, with feelings of depression, anxiety, and irritability, at the time of low estrogen levels premenstrually. The existing research has many problems: most of it is correlational in nature, and expectations complicate interpretations. Cultural factors may also contribute to mood shifts. Probably a substantial proportion of women either do not experience such mood cycles, or their cyclic fluctuations are so small as to be undetectable. In addition, there is no evidence of fluctuation in performance.

Other Menstrual-Cycle Fluctuations   Research has demonstrated that there are menstrual-cycle fluctuations in the sensitivity of the senses: vision, smell, hearing, taste, and touch (Parlee, 1983). For example, sensitivity to the smell of certain compounds is greatest around the time of ovulation and is reduced during menstruation. In the search for psychological characteristics that are controlled by biological factors fluctuating over the menstrual cycle, these basic sensory processes may be a better place to look than more diffuse attributes such as moods, which are far more influenced by environment, socialization, and cognitions.

Menopause

Physical and Psychological Changes   A number of physical as well as psychological changes occur during the climacteric. *Climacteric* refers to the gradual aging of the ovaries over the years, leading to a decline in their efficiency. Most importantly, estrogen production declines, leading to the most obvious symptom of the climacteric, menopause (the ceasing of menstruation), which occurs on average around the age of 51. Another effect is the loss of elasticity of the vagina and shrinking of the breasts.

A number of symptoms occur at this time: physical symptoms such as "hot flashes"; and psychological symptoms such as depression, irritability, crying spells, and inability to concentrate. About 10 percent of women suffer from serious depression during menopause. Less severe depression during menopause is more common.

Do all women experience these menopausal symptoms? In a survey of 638 women, aged 45 to 55, conducted in London in 1964–1965, about 50 percent of the women experienced hot flashes, and half of the 50 percent said the flashes were acutely uncomfortable (McKinlay and Jeffreys, 1974). Hot flashes are the most common menopausal symptom.

Unfortunately, much of the research on women at menopause has been based on women seeking some form of health care—that is, on a "patient" population. A stereotype of the menopausal woman has emerged in which she is seen to have many and diffuse symptoms. A challenge to this stereotype is presented by a study of a representative sample of 2,500 women, aged 45 to 55 years, from the state of Massachusetts (McKinlay et al., 1987). The women were followed over 27 months. The results indicated clearly that menopause itself does not cause poorer health, whether mental health or physical health. Specifically, there was no relationship between menopause and depression.

There is another subtle problem of interpretation similar to the one mentioned in conjunction with the premenstrual tension syndrome. Women are said to have "more" problems during menopause. More than what? more than men? more than at other times in their own lives? Investigating the latter question, psychologists Bernice Neugarten and Ruth Kraines (1965) studied symptoms among women of different age groups. They found that adolescents and menopausal women reported the largest number of problematic symptoms. Postmenopausal women reported the smallest number of problematic symptoms. Apparently, menopause does not permanently "wreck" a woman. Among the adolescents, psychological symptoms were the most common (for example, tension), whereas among the menopausal women, physical symptoms such as hot flashes were most common. Thus menopause does not seem to be the worst time of a woman's life psychologically; probably it is not as bad as adolescence.

In sum, the evidence indicates that menopause does not bring on an avalanche of problems, whether one looks at well-sampled studies of middle-aged women, or compares middle-aged women with other age groups. A few limited symptoms do appear, particularly hot flashes.

Biology, Culture, or Both? The difficulties associated with menopause are attributed to biology (in particular, to hormones) by some and to culture and its expectations by others. In this discussion, we must distinguish between physical symptoms (e.g., hot flashes) and psychological symptoms (e.g., depression). As we saw in the previous section, there is an increase at menopause in physical symptoms, but not in psychological symptoms. It therefore makes no sense to debate whether increased depression is due to biology or culture if there is no increase in depression.

Estrogen-deficiency theory: The hypothesis that the symptoms of menopause are due to low levels of estrogen.

From the biological perspective, menopausal problems appear to be due to the woman's hormonal state. In particular, the symptoms appear to be related either to low estrogen levels or to hormonal imbalance. The former hypothesis, called the **estrogen-deficiency the-**

ory, has been the subject of the most research. Proponents of this theory argue that the physical symptoms, such as hot flashes, are caused by declining amounts of estrogen in the body.

Estrogen-replacement therapy (ERT): Replacement doses of estrogen given to some women to treat menopausal symptoms.

The best evidence for the estrogen-deficiency theory comes from the success of **estrogen-replacement therapy (ERT).** Physicians may prescribe estrogen either in its natural form, Premarin, or in a synthetic form, such as Stilbestrol, Progynon, or Meprane. Estrogen-replacement therapy is successful in relieving low-estrogen menopausal symptoms like hot flashes, sweating, cold hands and feet, osteoporosis (brittle bones), and vaginal discharges (Golub, 1992). The success of this therapy suggests that low estrogen levels cause menopausal symptoms and that increasing estrogen levels relieves the symptoms.

Any possible benefits of estrogen-replacement therapy should be weighed against the dangers, because there is increasing evidence linking it to cancer of the uterus (Jick et al., 1980; Mack et al., 1976; Marx, 1976; Weiss et al, 1976). On the other hand, estrogen replacement protects women from osteoporosis, or brittle bones, which may cause broken hips, which may in turn cause death. More women die annually from hip fractures than from endometrial cancer. Thus, on balance, not only may estrogen replacement be relatively safe; it may actually be relatively healthy (Budoff, 1981), particularly when taken together with progesterone (Golub, 1992).

On the other hand, advocates of the environmental point of view note the cultural forces that may act to produce psychological stress in women around the time of menopause. The aging process itself may be psychologically stressful in our youth-oriented culture. The menopausal years remind a woman forcefully that she is aging. Menopause also means that the woman can no longer bear children. For women who have a great psychological investment in motherhood, this can be a difficult realization. In Chapter 5 we reviewed research on the empty nest syndrome and found that some investigators question whether this is a time of depression among women. Further, I noted that menopausal symptoms do not occur in women in cultures where women's status rises at this time (Bart, 1971).

We have a strong cultural bias toward expecting menopausal symptoms. Thus any quirk in a middle-aged woman's behavior is attributed to the "change." It simultaneously becomes the cause of, and explanation for, all the problems and complaints of the middle-aged woman. Given such expectations, it is not surprising that the average person perceives widespread evidence of menopausal symptoms. Ironically, idiosyncrasies in women of childbearing age are blamed on menstruation, whereas problems experienced by women who are past that age are blamed on the *lack* of it.

As a way of resolving this biology-culture controversy, it seems reasonable to conclude that the physical symptoms of menopause, such as hot flashes, are probably due to declining estrogen levels, and that the belief that there are psychological symptoms, such as depression, is a product of culture.

Pregnancy and Childbirth

Pregnancy is marked by radical hormone changes, in which both estrogen and progesterone levels are high. Early in pregnancy, the corpus luteum is responsible for this production, and later in pregnancy, the placenta is the major source of the two hormones.

Emotional state is related to stage of pregnancy (Sherman, 1971, p. 177). During the first three months, depression and fatigue may occur. Women's emotions are generally more positive during the second trimester (months 4 to 6). The last trimester may be more stressful and anxious, as the woman begins to worry about how the delivery will go, whether the baby will be healthy, and so on. The incidence of depression increases during the third trimester (O'Hara, 1986).

An intensive study by Myra Leifer (1980) found generally similar results. Nineteen women, all pregnant for the first time, were interviewed once during each trimester of pregnancy, on the third day after giving birth, and at six to eight weeks postpartum; a questionnaire was also mailed to them at seven months postpartum. Leifer's general findings were that, rather than being a time of calm and bliss, pregnancy was, for most of the women in her sample, difficult and turbulent. She also found that emotional changes during pregnancy and after giving birth were strongly related to the emotional support and help the woman received from her husband. The women tended to experience mood shifts and to be anxious. Specifically, in the first trimester, anxieties centered on the possibility of miscarriage. In the first trimester, only the four women for whom the pregnancy was unplanned expressed overall negative emotions. The other women were either positive or ambivalent during the first trimester. The second trimester was the high point psychologically—there was the most happiness and pride in pregnancy. Fears of miscarriage diminished as the women could feel the fetus moving, and there was an intense feeling of relief that the fetus was alive. In the third trimester, anxiety about the delivery and about possible deformity of the baby increased.

In sum, not all pregnant women are blissfully happy. A woman's psychological state depends on a number of factors: whether the baby was wanted, the stage of pregnancy, physical comfort or discomfort, and a variety of social factors such as support from husband or friends.

Pregnancy is probably best regarded as a major developmental transition, with emotional upheavals that can be either positive or negative. Psychologists generally agree that there are three important psychological tasks for the woman during pregnancy: attachment, separation-individuation, and identity formation (Seegmiller, 1993). During the first trimester, the fetus is experienced as part of the self rather than as a separate being, and there is therefore little sense of attachment to it. Things change, though, in the second trimester with the quickening, or first sense of movement of the fetus. The woman then begins to think of the fetus as a separate individual (the process of *separation-individuation*). She also forms a growing emotional *attachment* to it. Although much has been written about the attachments that parents form for their infants after birth, attachment, in fact, begins long before birth. Some women, of course, develop stronger attachments than others. Finally, the woman renegotiates her relationship with her own mother. For some, this is difficult because there are many conflicts in the relationship, whereas for others it is a time for sharing and affection. The important outcome of the process is for the pregnant woman to go beyond feeling dependent on her own mother to forming a sense of *identity* as a mother herself, with an independent, adult sense of competence.

Childbirth represents a major shock to the body. Estrogen and progesterone levels drop sharply, and it may take several months for the levels to return to normal and for menstruation to resume. Within a couple of days after delivery, many women experience depression and periods of crying. These mood swings range from mild to severe (O'Hara et al., 1990). In the mildest type, *baby blues,* the woman experiences sadness and periods of crying, but this mood lasts only a few days. Between 50 and 80 percent of women experience mild baby-blues postpartum (O'Hara et al., 1990). Moderate *postpartum depression* is experienced by approximately 10 percent of women and typically lasts six to eight weeks (Campbell and Cohn, 1991). Postpartum depression is characterized by a depressed mood, insomnia, tearfulness, feelings of inadequacy and inability to cope, irritability, and fatigue. Finally, the most severe disturbance is *postpartum depressive psychosis;* fortunately, it is rare, affecting only 0.01 percent of women following birth (Hopkins et al., 1984).

Psychological and social influences on the symptoms of the pregnancy and postpartum periods should be noted. Our culture is full of lore on the psychological characteristics of pregnant women—the glow of radiant contentment, the desire for dill pickles and ice cream. The proper behavior for pregnancy is learned through the process of gender-role socialization, and the behaviors are displayed when the time comes. Positive moods might be further related to a strong desire for a child. Negative moods might be related to not wanting the child, fear of the dangers of childbirth, or fear of responsibility for the child. Postpartum depression might be related to the sudden change that has occurred in one's life, not wanting the baby, fearing responsibility for it, or even such a simple factor as being in a hospital and being separated from one's husband and family. It has been demonstrated that postpartum emotional reactions are influenced by both past and present stresses (Gordon et al., 1965). Thus depression symptoms could be as easily explained by psychological and social factors as by hormonal ones. Probably, in reality, postpartum depression is a result of a combination of biological factors (shock to the body, radically diminished hormone levels) and social-psychological factors.

Contraception

Detailed information on the various methods of contraception is available elsewhere (e.g., Hyde, 1994). What I want to do here is concentrate on the psychological aspects of contraceptive use—or, more accurately, of nonuse.

In the United States there are 1.5 million legal abortions every year; nearly one-third of all pregnant women terminate the pregnancy with an abortion (Henshaw, 1990). In an era when highly effective contraceptives are readily available, why should so many unwanted pregnancies, leading to abortion, occur? The basic answer is that lots of women have sexual intercourse while using no contraceptive, even though they are single and don't want to get pregnant. For example, among sexually active teenage girls, 21 percent use no method of contraception (Forrest and Singh, 1990). Similar statistics are reported at many universities.

Why? Why is there such widespread nonuse of contraceptives, and so many resulting abortions? There were two traditional theories to explain this phenomenon (for a summary, see Luker, 1975). One is the *contraceptive ignorance theory*. It holds that women fail to use contraceptives and have unwanted pregnancies because they lack knowledge about or access to contraceptives. The theory goes on to say that if women had more information about contraceptives, about their advantages, disadvantages, and so on, they would use them. That is probably true for some women, but not for the majority in the United States. In one study of women who were undergoing abortions, more than half reported having previously used a prescription method of contraception (usually the pill), and the majority displayed some or considerable knowledge about birth control when interviewed (Luker, 1975).

A second theory is the *intrapsychic conflict theory*. It holds that women generally have adequate skills in contraception, but that they fail to use contraceptives because of internal psychological conflicts. According to this view, a woman might use an "accidental" pregnancy to trap a man into marrying her, or to get back at parents whom she feels have not given her enough love. This model portrays women as neurotic and manipulative. Stereotypes strike again!

Sociologist Kristin Luker (1975) has formulated an excellent alternative theory about why unwanted pregnancies occur, in her book *Taking Chances: Abortion and the Decision Not to Contracept*. The cause of unwanted pregnancies, she argues, is *contraceptive risk taking*, which results from conscious decision-making processes about whether to use contraceptives in any given sexual encounter. She believes that the decision not to use contraceptives is analogous to the decision not to fasten one's seat belt when driving.

According to Luker's theory, the woman engages in an informal cost-benefit analysis (although she might not be able to articulate it) in which she weighs the costs and benefits of contraception against the costs and benefits of pregnancy. The woman must assess the risk or uncertainty (probability) of pregnancy (which is actually unknown, even to scientists), and she generally decides that it is very low. Thus if there are many costs associated with contraception, the woman begins to engage in risk taking. Luker's model is based on data she collected at an abortion clinic in northern California, by analyzing the medical records of 500 women treated at the clinic and by doing in-depth interviews with 50 women undergoing abortions at the clinic.

What are the costs of contraception? First, there are a number of social-psychological costs. Using, and planning to use, contraceptives involves acknowledging that one is a sexually active woman, and this is difficult for many

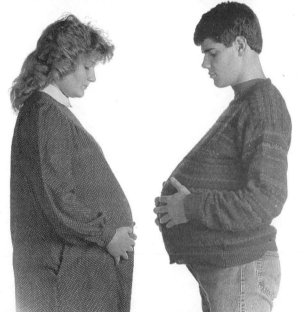

IF YOUR GIRLFRIEND GETS PREGNANT, SO DO YOU!

PLANNED PARENTHOOD
CALL FOR CONFIDENTIAL BIRTH CONTROL COUNSELING
BEFORE IT'S TOO LATE

FIGURE 10.4
Organizations such as Planned Parenthood and the Children's Defense Fund continually wage informational campaigns about contraception. Nonetheless, there are about 1.5 million legal abortions per year in the United States, indicating a great many unwanted pregnancies which, according to Kristin Luker, result from contraceptive risk taking.

women, even today. Using a contraceptive such as the pill signals that one is always sexually available, and this may be seen as decreasing the woman's right to say no. Some methods, particularly foam and the diaphragm, decrease the spontaneity of sex, which for some people is a psychological cost. Second, there are structurally created costs—women must call for an appointment with a physician for some methods, and they may be told that no appointments are available for several weeks. They are expected to have high motivation and to use abstinence or to call repeatedly for appointments. Even the "drugstore" methods (foam or condoms) involve going into the store and openly acknowledging to the world—or at least to the people in the store—that one is sexually active. Third, there may be costs to the relationship—the woman may fear negative reactions from the man if she uses a contraceptive such as foam or a diaphragm, or rejection if she asks him to use a condom. Finally, there are biological-medical costs, particularly fears of side effects from the pill.

Luker also points out that the woman may anticipate benefits from pregnancy. Some people view pregnancy as proof of womanhood, and this may be particularly important in a society with a fluctuating view of gender roles. Pregnancy may enhance one's feeling of self-worth, proving that one is a valuable person who can produce children. Unarguably, pregnancy is a proof of fertility, and some women may feel a need for this proof—fully two-thirds of the women interviewed by Luker said that their gynecologists had told them they would have trouble getting pregnant because of problems in their reproductive systems. Pregnancy can be a way of accomplishing something with a significant other, perhaps forcing a man to define the relationship more clearly or perhaps going from living together to marriage. Finally, the pure excitement of risk taking itself may be fun for some.

Given all this, Luker argues, the woman weighs the costs and benefits and often decides to take the risk. The costs and benefits, of course, vary from one woman to the next and at different times in a woman's life. The costs of pregnancy to a single college student are probably far greater than they are to a married woman with two children who would rather have no more. Risk taking, if successful, may foster more risk taking: "I got away with it once; surely I can again." And so the cycle goes, eventually ending in an unwanted pregnancy. But the costs of this failure are no longer terribly high, as long as abortion is legal and available. Accordingly, many women leave the abortion clinic with no plans to use an effective method in the future, and the risk taking begins again.

On a more hopeful note, Luker argues that as women become more aware of their own decision-making processes, they will become more effective in using contraceptives to achieve the goals they truly desire.

Abortion

A number of methods of abortion are available (see Hyde, 1994, for a more complete discussion). The most commonly used method, accounting for 94 percent of abortions in the United States today (Koonin et al., 1991), is **vacuum**

curettage, also called dilation and evacuation (D and E), vacuum suction, and vacuum aspiration. It is done on an outpatient basis with a local anesthetic. The procedure itself takes only about ten minutes and the woman stays in the doctor's office, clinic, or hospital for a few hours. The woman is prepared as she would be for a pelvic exam, and an instrument is inserted into the vagina (Figure 10.5). The in-

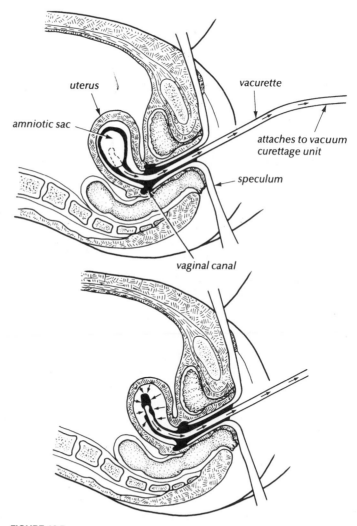

FIGURE 10.5
The procedures involved in vacuum curettage abortion. A tube is inserted through the vagina and the cervix and into the uterus. The uterine contents are then suctioned out.

strument dilates (stretches open) the opening in the cervix. A tube is then inserted through the opening until one end is in the uterus. The other end is attached to a suction-producing machine, and the contents of the uterus, including the fetal tissue, are sucked out. Statistics indicate that D and E is the safest method of abortion, not only during the first trimester, but through the twentieth week of pregnancy (U.S. Public Health Service, 1976).

It is a common belief that making the decision to have an abortion and having one are times of extreme psychological stress and that psychological problems may result. A major review of the methodologically sound studies of the psychological responses of U.S. women having legal abortions concluded that severe problems are rare and that, in fact, the worst stress occurs before the abortion (Adler et al., 1990, 1992). For example, in one study women were interviewed two weeks after first trimester abortions (Lazarus, 1985). The most common feeling was relief, reported by 76 percent of the women; the most common negative feeling was guilt, reported by 17 percent.

In one particularly well done study, 360 adolescents seeking pregnancy tests were interviewed (Zabin et al., 1989). They were then classified into three groups: (1) those whose test was negative, meaning they weren't pregnant; (2) those who were pregnant and carried the baby to term; and (3) those who were pregnant and had an abortion. The women were then interviewed one year later and again two years later. After two years, the women who had had abortions were more likely to have graduated from high school or still to be in school and in the appropriate grade than either those who carried the pregnancy to term or those who were not pregnant. And two years later the abortion group showed, if anything, a more positive psychological profile—in terms of measures such as anxiety and self-esteem—than the other two groups. (See also Burnell and Norfleet, 1987; Shusterman, 1979.)

In January 1989, then–Surgeon General C. Everett Koop released a report reviewing studies on the psychological effects of abortion. He, too, concluded that there was no scientific evidence that abortion had negative effects on mental health (Holden, 1989). In the antiabortion Reagan administration, the report was quickly suppressed (Roberts, 1990).

It is also important to consider the possible consequences of restricting abortion, that is, denying abortions to some women, and the implications for children born to women in this situation. Such research is impossible to conduct in the United States now, because abortion has been legal since 1973 (although the Supreme Court decision of 1989 giving states the right to limit access to abortion may again give us a population of women denied permission for abortion). In some other countries, access to abortion depends on obtaining official approval. In Czechoslovakia, for example, researchers followed the situations of 220 children born to women denied abortion (the "study group") and 220 children born to women who had not requested abortion; the children were studied when they were 9 years old, again when they were 14 to 16 years old, and again in their 20s (David, 1992; David and Matejcek, 1981). By age 14, 43 children from the study group, but only 30 from the control group, had been referred for counseling. Although there were no differences between the groups in tested intelligence, children in the study group did less well in school and were more likely to drop out. At age 16 the boys (but not the girls) in the study group more frequently rated themselves as feeling neglected or rejected by their mothers and felt that their mothers were less satisfied with them. In their early twenties, the study group reported less job satisfaction, more conflicts with co-workers and supervisors, and fewer and less satisfying friendships. Several other studies have found results similar to the Czechoslovakian one (David et al., 1988). These results point to the serious long-term consequences for children whose mothers would have preferred to have an abortion.

In sum, legal, first-trimester abortion does not seem to be dangerous to mental health, on average. The evidence also indicates that there may be long-term negative consequences for children born to women denied access to abortion.

Breast Cancer

Breast cancer is the most common form of cancer in women. It is rare in women under 25, and a woman's chances of developing it increase every year after that age. About one out of every nine American women has breast cancer at some time in her life. Every year, 44,000 women in the United States die of breast cancer (American Cancer Society, 1991).

Because breast cancer is relatively common, every woman should do a breast self-exam monthly, around midcycle (*not* during one's period, when there may be natural lumps). Unfortunately, psychological factors such as fear prevent some women from doing the self-exam or, if they discover a lump, from seeing a doctor immediately. This is unfortunate because the more quickly breast cancer is discovered and treated, the better the chances of recovery. If the cancer has not spread beyond the breast, the survival rate is 91 percent five years after treatment (American Cancer Society, 1991).

In fact, not all breast lumps are cancerous. There are three kinds of breast lumps: cysts (fluid-filled sacs, also called fibrocystic disease or cystic mastitis), fibroadenomas, and malignant tumors. The important thing to realize is that 80 percent of breast lumps are cysts or fibroadenomas and are therefore benign, that is, not dangerous. Techniques for diagnosis of breast cancer are controversial. Most physicians feel that the most definitive method is the excisional biopsy, in which a small slit is made in the breast, the lump is removed, and a pathologist determines whether it is cancerous. Other diagnostic techniques include needle aspiration, thermography, mammography, and xeroradiography.

Radical mastectomy: A surgical treatment for breast cancer in which the entire breast, as well as underlying muscle and lymph nodes, is removed.

If a malignancy is confirmed, what is the best treatment? This is also controversial. The treatment usually is some form of mastectomy, that is, surgical removal of the breast. In **radical mastectomy,** the most serious form of the surgery, the entire breast, as well as the lymph nodes and underlying muscles, is removed. Advocates

■ WHY DO THE BREAST SELF-EXAM?

There are many good reasons for doing a breast self-exam each month. One reason is that it is easy to do and the more you do it, the better you will get at it. When you get to know how your breasts normally feel, you will quickly be able to feel any change, and early detection is the key to successful treatment and cure.

Remember: A breast self-exam could save your breast—and save your life. Most breast lumps are found by women themselves, but, in fact, most lumps in the breast are not cancer. Be safe, be sure.

Finger Pads

■ WHEN TO DO BREAST SELF-EXAM

The best time to do breast self-exam is right after your period, when breasts are not tender or swollen. If you do not have regular periods or sometimes skip a month, do it on the same day every month.

■ NOW, HOW TO DO BREAST SELF-EXAM

1. Lie down and put a pillow under your right shoulder. Place your right arm behind your head.

2. Use the finger pads of your three middle fingers on your left hand to feel for lumps or thickening. Your finger pads are the top third of each finger.

3. Press firmly enough to know how your breast feels. If you're not sure how hard to press, ask your health care provider. Or try to copy the way your health care provider uses the finger pads during a breast exam. Learn what your breast feels like most of the time. A firm ridge in the lower curve of each breast is normal.

4. Move around the breast in a set way. You can choose either the circle (A), the up and down line (B), or the wedge (C). Do it the same way every time. It will help you to make sure that you've gone over the entire breast area, and to remember how your breast feels.

5. Now examine your left breast using right hand finger pads.

6. If you find any changes, see your doctor right away.

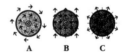

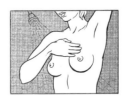

A   B   C

■ FOR ADDED SAFETY:

You should also check your breasts while standing in front of a mirror right after you do your breast self-exam each month. See if there are any changes in the way your breasts look: dimpling of the skin, changes in the nipple, or redness or swelling.

You might also want to do a breast self-exam while you're in the shower. Your soapy hands will glide over the wet skin making it easy to check how your breasts feel.

FIGURE 10.6

of this procedure argue that it is best to be as thorough as possible, and that the muscle and lymph nodes should be removed in case the cancer has spread to them. In *modified radical mastectomy,* the entire breast and lymph nodes, but not the muscles, are removed. In *simple mastectomy,* only the breast, and possibly a few lymph nodes, is removed. In partial mastectomy, or **lumpectomy,** only the lump and some surrounding tissue are removed. Research indicates that in cases of early breast cancer, lumpectomy or quadrantectomy (removal of the quarter of the breast containing the lump) is as effective as old-fashioned radical mastectomy (Henahan, 1984; Veronesi et al., 1981) and obviously much preferable.

Lumpectomy: A surgical treatment for breast cancer in which only the lump and a small bit of surrounding tissue are removed.

What are the psychological consequences? A systematic study of 41 women who had had mastectomies indicated that 60 percent judged their postmastectomy emotional adjustment to be excellent or very good, but 10 percent judged it to be not very good, poor, or very poor (Jamison et al., 1978; see review by Meyerowitz, 1980). About one-fourth of the women reported having suicidal thoughts following the mastectomy. About 15 percent sought professional help for their emotional problems related to the mastectomy. Interestingly, however, it was not the postmastectomy period that was rated as most difficult psychologically; rather, the period immediately following discovery of the lump was reported as being the worst. About three-quarters of the women reported that their sexual satisfaction in marriage had not changed or was better, but one-quarter reported a change for the worse. In sum, this study provides evidence of successful coping by the majority of mastectomy patients, but it also indicates that a substantial minority of women suffer considerable psychological stress. It is extremely important for mastectomy patients and their partners to have counseling available. The American Cancer Society has organized support groups for mastectomy patients in many towns.

Women and HIV

AIDS refers to acquired immunodeficiency syndrome, a disease that destroys the body's natural immunity to infection, so that the person is susceptible to and may die from diseases such as pneumonia and cancer. *HIV* stands for human immunodeficiency virus, the virus that causes AIDS. The disease is spread by exchange of body fluids, which occurs, specifically, through (1) sexual intercourse (either penis-in-vagina intercourse or anal intercourse); (2) contaminated blood (blood transfusion with HIV-contaminated blood); (3) contaminated hypodermic needles (a risk for those who abuse intravenous drugs); and (4) passage from an infected pregnant woman to her baby during pregnancy or childbirth. There is about a 30 percent chance that a baby born to an infected woman will be infected (Gentry, 1993).

Because approximately 90 percent of the cases of AIDS in the United States have been men (most of them gay men or male injection drug users), most

FOCUS 10.3

AIDS: HOW IT CHANGED ONE WOMAN'S LIFE

I met Michael the summer after I graduated from college. I was on vacation and was in good spirits and ready to take hold of anything life handed me. I first encountered Michael when he asked me to dance in a bar. A few dances turned into a few drinks, which led to hours of talking. We fell for each other instantly.

I knew immediately that Michael was the type of man I had always wanted to marry. He was intelligent, funny, handsome, masculine, sensitive, and so romantic. Two days after we met, we made love. Michael was insistent that we use a condom, because I wasn't on any birth control. I was comforted by the fact that he was responsible about sex. Most men I had had sex with didn't want anything to do with condoms.

Two days later he told me he loved me and wanted to marry me. But I felt I couldn't commit myself to him yet. So when I returned home from vacation our long-distance relationship began. There were many expensive phone calls, long letters, and plane rides.

As the months went by, I found myself falling in love with Michael. When I called him and told him this, he asked me to marry him. I said yes. We bought the engagement ring that weekend, and it was gorgeous. Hours before we were to leave for the airport, we realized we had run out of condoms. We decided to risk it that one time and have sex without protection.

When I kissed Michael goodbye at the airport, I thought of what we had talked about after our lovemaking that day. We had talked about how scary AIDS is, and how we had both thought about getting tested. We had talked about how many partners we had both had. Although we didn't talk about actual numbers, we joked that I could count mine on my fingers and he could count his on his fingers and toes. He also told me that he had had an operation four years ago that had required two units of blood. I knew this put him at a higher risk for the AIDS virus, but I didn't really think about it because, after all, he was my fiancé. He *couldn't* be infected. But even so, our talk had disturbed me enough that I decided to get tested for the HIV antibody.

When I told Michael what I had done, he went in for his own test. A few weeks later, I found out that my test was negative. I called Michael and I could hear him crying. He had tested positive for the HIV antibody.

I comforted Michael the best I could, reassuring him that I loved him. I fell to my knees after I hung up the phone and started crying. My heart was pounding as my whole world died.

My first thought was "I love you, Michael, but I can't marry you," and my second one was "Oh my God, I'm going to get AIDS."

Christmas with my family was hell. I wanted to die when I was given a place setting in my silver pattern and the card was for Michael and me. It killed me to watch my nieces and nephews and think that Michael and I would never have children. The questions my family asked about Michael and me, the wedding, our jobs, our plans for children—all these were like scissors cutting up my insides. I felt I couldn't tell my family the truth because I didn't want to hurt or scare them. I was so overwhelmed with it all. I was scared, so scared.

After the holidays, I went back to the clinic and told the nurse the news. She told me to come back 14 weeks after the date Michael and I had last had unprotected sex. I flew to visit Michael and we sat down and made rules about our lovemaking. We wouldn't French kiss, I would not perform fellatio, and Michael would use two rubbers and pull out before he ejaculated. At times I wondered if the rules were too extreme, but it was the only way I could feel even fairly safe.

Physically and mentally, I felt awful. I caught a cold that lasted two weeks, followed by a urinary tract infection. I lost weight. When I finally told Michael I did not think I could marry him, we both cried. Michael was, for the most part, pretty understanding of my feelings. I felt as if I were abandoning him when he needed me most. I felt immense guilt but, most of all, I felt frightened. I didn't know if I was HIV positive or negative yet.

For many days, all I could do was cry, sleep, eat a little, and cry some more. I was angry with God for doing this to Michael and me. I felt immense jealousy when I heard about friends of mine getting married.

After the 14 weeks, I got retested. After the test, I had to wait another 7 days to get the results. During that time, I flew up to see Michael again. As before, we were very careful during sex . . . but then it happened. When Michael pulled out, the rubbers were still inside me. We didn't know if he had ejaculated inside me or if his penis was completely outside. It was then I realized that even though I loved him very, very much, I could not have sex with him again. It was making me crazy.

When I returned home, I found out that my test results had come back negative. I told the nurse what had happened to us with the rubbers the weekend before, and she told me to come back in another 14 weeks. She said that, most likely, my results would be negative again, because Michael and I had been so careful. She also said that if I did not have sex with Michael or anyone else in the next 14 weeks, and if my test came back negative again, then, according to the Centers for Disease Control, I would not have the virus.

Right now I do not know what the result of my next test will be. Michael knows that if it is negative, I will leave him. Considering the circumstances, he has been very loving and supportive of my decision. Sometimes I feel very guilty and selfish, but I know I cannot mentally handle having sex with him and being constantly worried about whether we have been careful enough. I know in my heart that I am doing the right thing for myself.

I will never, ever have unprotected sex again. And if I ever get married, my future husband will have to get tested, because I will never put myself through this again.

Now I must go on with my life and think about my future, not the past. But this doesn't stop me from thinking about all the beautiful, dark-haired, blue-eyed babies we could have had together.

SOURCE: Personal communication to the author.

attention has been focused on them. However, in Africa AIDS infects men and women nearly equally, and so it is clear that women can and do become infected. Moreover, the number of infected women in the United States is rising rapidly; thus there is an increasing need to address the needs of women with AIDS.

Among women with AIDS, the largest group (44 percent) had been infected by injection drug use (Gentry, 1993). However, the second largest group (40 percent), and the fastest-growing group, contracted the disease through sexual intercourse with infected men.

AIDS is an issue for women on several counts. First, it is an issue for women who themselves become infected. In addition, because women are disproportionately in caregiving roles such as nursing, they bear a huge burden in the care of HIV-infected patients. Women also are the mothers, wives, and sisters of infected men and suffer with the suffering of the infected person. Focus 10.3, "AIDS: How It Changed One Woman's Life," provides one woman's story about the impact of AIDS on her.

HIV-infected women are more likely than infected men to be unemployed or to be employed in situations in which they feel vulnerable to being fired (Gentry, 1993). They have serious fears that they will lose their job if their HIV status becomes known. Moreover, HIV-infected women are more likely than infected men to have sole responsibility for their children, and they worry about what will happen to their children if they die. Or they may fear losing custody of their children if they become seriously ill and have difficulty caring for them. They may also worry that their children will be ostracized at school if the mother's infection becomes known.

Race and ethnicity are also important issues in AIDS (Amaro, 1988; Mays and Cochran, 1987; Peterson and Bakeman, 1988). Approximately 40 percent of AIDS cases in the United States are found among nonwhites, which is greatly disproportionate to nonwhites' representation in the general population. For example, African Americans make up about 12 percent of the American population, but they constitute 25 percent of AIDS cases (Mays and Cochran, 1987). African American women account for 53 percent of adult female AIDS cases (Gentry, 1993). Hispanics represent 7 percent of the general population, but 15 percent of those with AIDS (Amaro, 1988). The pattern of transmission of AIDS tends to be different in minority populations from its pattern among whites. Among African Americans, for example, transmission occurs more often by heterosexual contacts, whereas in the white population it occurs more often through homosexual contacts (Mays and Cochran, 1987).

Programs of AIDS intervention and education for women of color need to be culturally sensitive. For example, programs need to be designed for low-income women. Such women may need to be reached for education in special ways, such as working through social welfare agencies. Educational programs need to be sensitive to different attitudes about contraception in different ethnic groups and to the resistance of some to using condoms. Prevention efforts will probably work best if they involve the entire community, including Spanish radio and television programs, bilingual telephone hot lines, tenant groups, church groups, and neighborhood organizations.

In our efforts to address the needs of men with AIDs, we must not forget that women, too, are at risk.

In Conclusion

In this chapter we have discussed the psychological aspects of some topics considered important by the women's health movement. We reviewed statistics on gender and health and examined how women are treated by the health care system. We considered the evidence on whether women experienced menstrual-cycle fluctuations in mood and whether these shifts are caused by fluctuating hormone levels. Although a great deal of research has been done in this area, there are fundamental problems with the research itself that make it difficult to draw firm conclusions. My conclusion is that some, though not all, women expe-

EXPERIENCE THE RESEARCH

WOMEN'S EXPERIENCE OF PMS

Interview four women friends on the topic of PMS. Ask each the following questions and record their answers:

1. Do you experience PMS? (Continue with questions 2 through 6 if the answer is yes; use questions 7 through 9 if the answer is no.)
2. What symptoms of PMS do you experience? Include both physical symptoms and psychological symptoms.
3. About how frequently do you experience PMS? That is, out of ten menstrual periods, for how many of them do you experience PMS?
4. About how long do the symptoms of PMS last for you? How many days before your period do they begin? For how many days do they last?
5. How much does the PMS interfere with your functioning? Do you continue pretty much as you normally would, or do you have to stay in bed for a while?
6. How do you treat the PMS? Do you take any medication for it? If so, what? Is it effective? What symptoms does it relieve? If you do not take any medication, how do you try to relieve the PMS symptoms?

[This ends the questions for those with PMS.]

7. Do you have any ideas about why you don't have PMS?
8. Do you experience any symptoms or changes over your menstrual cycle? Do you experience any symptoms during your menstrual period, such as cramps?
9. How do you feel about women with PMS?

What can you conclude from your interviews? How common is PMS? What are its symptoms? How do women cope with it?

rience menstrual-cycle fluctuations in mood. There is evidence of both hormonal and cultural influences on the fluctuations; it seems likely that cultural forces act to increase the woman's perception of relatively small body changes.

The conclusions about menopause were similar. Some, though not all, women experience psychological symptoms such as depression and irritability, and many experience hot flashes. Once again, the perception of a body change is magnified by cultural factors—expectations that there should be menopausal depression, loss of role and the empty nest, and so on.

Research on the psychological aspects of pregnancy indicates that a woman's psychological state depends on the stage of pregnancy she is in; negative moods are more common in the first and third trimesters, and positive moods are more common in the second. Once again, environmental factors probably influence the woman's perception of her body changes.

Research on the psychological consequences of having an abortion indicate that it is generally not a traumatic experience, but more complex research is needed on this topic.

I emphasized the psychological aspects of breast cancer, something physicians often fail to recognize.

AIDS is not just a gay men's disease. It affects women, too, in growing numbers.

In all these cases, I feel that as women inform themselves more about the functioning of their bodies, they should inform themselves about the *psychological* aspects of these processes.

Suggestions for Further Reading

Golub, Sharon (1992). *Periods: From menarche to menopause.* Newbury Park, CA: Sage. This book tells you everything you always wanted to know about menstruation and menopause, including biological, psychological, and social factors.

Travis, Cheryl B. (1988). *Women and health psychology: Biomedical issues.* Hillsdale, NJ: Erlbaum. This is a readable, up-to-date book on women's health issues, including menstruation and menopause, contraception, pregnancy, hysterectomy, and breast cancer.

White, Evelyn C. (Ed.) (1994). *The Black women's health book.* Seattle: Seal Press. This book provides information on the health concerns of Black women.

11

Female Sexuality

*Clitoral stimulation is more intensive and produces a more
violent reaction. . . . Vaginal stimulation is much more
relaxing and less intense. I like it. I love clitoral
stimulation . . . vaginal stimulation is soothing and
produces a rhythmical rocking and rotating of the pelvis.
. . . It is never as intense as clitoral stimulation, yet feels
extremely good in its own way. The best analogy I can
contrive is the difference between someone lightly and
caressingly stroking your bare back or arm or face and
being violently, exhaustingly tickled. The former resembles
vaginal, the latter clitoral stimulation. Vaginal stimulation
soothes me and produces an involuntary contented hum
deep in my throat. The vaginal stimulation of intercourse
produces a closeness, a coordination, a sense of oneness
unmatched by any other sexual activity.*

A woman respondent quoted in S. FISHER, *UNDERSTANDING THE
FEMALE ORGASM*

It is not coincidental that the women's movement and the sexual revolution grew
together. Historically, sex for women always meant pregnancy, which meant babies, and which, in turn, meant a life devoted to motherhood. For the first time in
the history of our species, because of the development of highly reliable methods
of contraception, we are now able to separate sex from reproduction, both in theory and in practice.

In the 1970s, because of advances in contraception, women came to see
themselves as free to be sexy without making a 20-year commitment to motherhood. The AIDS and herpes epidemics of the 1980s and 1990s have complicated
the picture of sexual freedom. Nonetheless, female sexuality has been let out of
the bag and is unlikely to return to hiding.

Physiology

Only recently has female sexual physiology been the subject of scientific investigation. Most of our contemporary knowledge in this area is due to
the important work of William Masters and Virginia Johnson (1966).

Vasocongestion: An accumulation of blood in
the blood vessels of a
region of the body,
especially the genitals;
a swelling or erection
results.

Masters and Johnson distinguish four phases in sexual response,
although these stages actually flow together. The first phase is *excitement.* In the female, the primary response is **vasocongestion** or
engorgement of the tissues surrounding the vagina. This simply
means that a great deal of blood accumulates in the blood vessels
of the pelvic region. A secondary response is the contraction of vari-

Myotonia: Muscle
contraction.

ous muscle fibers (termed **myotonia**), which results, among other things, in erection of the nipples.

Perhaps the most noticeable response in the excitement phase is the moistening of the vagina with a lubricating fluid. This seems quite different from the most noticeable response in males, erection of the penis. In fact, Masters and Johnson discovered that the underlying physiological mechanisms are the same, namely, vasocongestion (the blood vessels becoming engorged with blood). It is fairly common knowledge that vasocongestion causes erection in the male. Masters and Johnson believe that the droplets of moisture that appear on the walls of the vagina during sexual excitation are fluids that have seeped out of the congested blood vessels in the surrounding region. Hence the physiological underpinnings are the same in males and in females, although the observable response seems different.

Lubrication marks only the beginning of female sexual response, however. In the excitement phase, a number of other changes take place, most notably in the clitoris. The clitoris, located just in front of the vagina (see Figure 11.2), is, like the penis, a shaft with a bulb, or *glans*, at the tip. The glans is densely packed with highly sensitive nerve endings. The clitoris is therefore the most sexually sensitive organ in the female body. In response to further arousal, the clitoral glans swells, and the shaft increases in diameter, probably also due to vasocongestion. The clitoris is interesting because it is the only exclusively sexual organ in the human body; all the others, such as the penis, have both sexual and reproductive functions. The clitoris is purely for sexual pleasure.

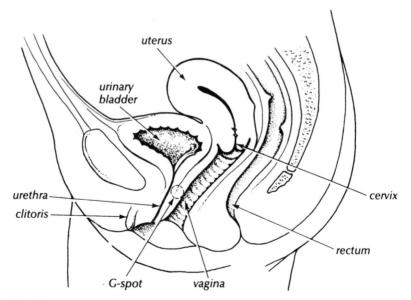

FIGURE 11.1
Female sexual and reproductive anatomy.

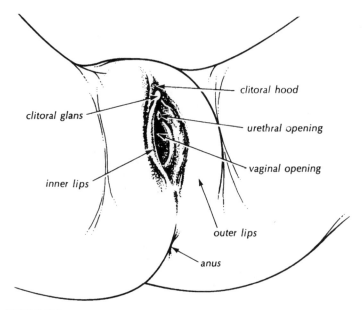

FIGURE 11.2
The vulva, or external genitals, of the human female.

The vagina also responds in the excitement phase. Think of the vagina as an uninflated balloon in the unaroused state, divided into an outer third (or lower third, in a woman standing upright) and an inner two-thirds (or upper two-thirds). During the successive stages of sexual response, the inner and outer portions react in very different ways. In the latter part of the excitement phase, the inner two-thirds of the vagina undergoes a dramatic expansion, or ballooning. This produces a tenting, or pulling apart, of the vaginal walls surrounding the cervix (see Figure 11.3).

In the second phase of the woman's sexual response, the *plateau phase*, the major change is the appearance of the "orgasmic platform" (Masters and Johnson, 1966). This refers to the outer third of the vagina when it swells and is engorged with blood, with its diameter reduced by as much as 50 percent (Figure 11.3). While the upper portion of the vagina expands during excitement, the lower or outer portion narrows during the plateau phase. The orgasmic platform therefore grips the penis (if there happens to be a penis in the vagina at that point), resulting in a noticeable increase in the erotic stimulation experienced by the male.

The other major change occurring during the plateau phase is the elevation of the clitoris. The clitoris retracts and draws into the body, but continues to respond to stimulation. A number of autonomic responses also occur, including an increase in pulse rate and a rise in blood pressure and in rate of breathing.

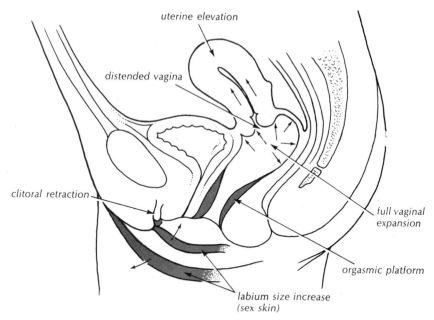

uterine elevation

distended vagina

clitoral retraction

full vaginal expansion

orgasmic platform

labium size increase (sex skin)

FIGURE 11.3
Female sexual and reproductive organs during the plateau phase of sexual response. Notice the ballooning of the upper part of the vagina, the elevation of the uterus, and the formation of the orgasmic platform.

Once again, these complex changes seem to be the result of two basic physiological processes, vasocongestion and increased myotonia or muscular tension, which occur similarly in both men and women. Readiness for orgasm occurs when these two processes have reached adequate levels.

Orgasm, the third phase of sexual response, consists of a series of rhythmic muscular contractions of the orgasmic platform. Generally there is a series of 3 to 12 contractions, at intervals of slightly less than a second. The onset of the subjective experience of orgasm is an initial spasm of the orgasmic platform preceding the rhythmic contractions.

Orgasm: An intense sensation that occurs at the peak of sexual arousal and is followed by the release of sexual tensions.

The sensations of orgasm in the female have been described as follows:

In the female, orgasm starts with a feeling of momentary suspension followed by a peak of intense sensation in the clitoris, which then spreads through the pelvis. This stage varies in intensity and may also involve sensations of "falling," "opening up," or even emitting fluid. Some women compare this stage of orgasm to mild labor pains. It is followed by a suffusion of warmth

spreading from the pelvis through the rest of the body. The experience culmi-
nates in characteristic throbbing sensations in the pelvis. (Katchadourian and
Lunde, 1972, p. 58)

Contrary to popular belief, orgasm does not signal the end of sexual response. In the fourth phase, or *resolution phase*, of sexual response, the major
physiological changes are a release of muscular tensions throughout the body
and a release of blood from the engorged blood vessels. In the female, the
breasts, which were formerly enlarged with nipples erect, return to the unaroused
state. The clitoris returns to its normal, unretracted position and shrinks to normal size. The orgasmic platform relaxes, and the ballooned upper portion of the
vagina shrinks. The return of the female to the unstimulated state may require as
long as a half-hour following orgasm. If the woman reaches the plateau phase
without having an orgasm, the restoration process takes longer, often as much as
an hour. Indeed, prostitutes who habitually experience arousal without orgasm
may experience cumulative physiological effects, resulting in chronic engorgement of vaginal tissues (Masters and Johnson, 1966).

Criticisms of Masters and Johnson's work have been raised (e.g., Tiefer,
1991; Zilbergeld and Evans, 1980). One of the most important of these criticisms
is that Masters and Johnson's model focuses exclusively on physiological
processes and ignores cognition and affect—that is, what we are thinking and
feeling emotionally during sexual response.

An alternative model to address this criticism, the *triphasic model*, has been
proposed by the eminent sex therapist Helen Singer Kaplan (1979). According to
her, there are three components to sexual response: sexual desire, vasocongestion, and the muscle contractions of orgasm. The vasocongestion and orgasm
components are consistent with Masters and Johnson; the new component is sexual desire, which refers to an interest in or motivation to engage in sexual activity. Without this psychological component of desire, sexual activity is not apt to
take place, or if it does, it is less likely to be pleasurable. The desire component
is also important in understanding some sexual dysfunctions, to be discussed
later in this chapter.

Common Fallacies

Because sexuality has so often been the subject of superstition and so seldom the
subject of scientific research, even modern American culture is filled with distorted ideas about it. A discussion of several misconceptions about female sexuality and the results of relevant scientific research follow.

Clitoral and Vaginal Orgasm   Freud believed that women can experience two
different kinds of orgasm—clitoral and vaginal. According to his view, little
girls learn to achieve orgasm through stimulation of the clitoris during masturbation. However, in adulthood they have to learn to transfer the focus of their sex-

ual response from the clitoris to the vagina, and to orgasm from intercourse. Because some women fail to make this transfer, they can experience only clitoral orgasm, and are therefore "vaginally frigid." Freud thought that the only mature female orgasm was vaginal.

Masters and Johnson have dispelled this myth by showing convincingly that, physiologically, there is only one kind of orgasm. The major response is the contraction of the orgasmic platform. That is, physiologically an orgasm is the same whether it results from clitoral stimulation or from vaginal stimulation. Indeed, some women are even able to have orgasms through breast stimulation— and the physiological response is identical to that occurring from vaginal intercourse (Masters and Johnson, 1966). Moreover, even in vaginal intercourse, the clitoris is stimulated as described previously.

Although it is well established that orgasms resulting primarily from vaginal and clitoral stimulation are physiologically the same, psychologically they may be experienced differently. The sensations arising from heterosexual intercourse and clitoral masturbation, for example, may be quite different. Physiologically, the orgasm is the same, but the context (presence of the male and contact with his body) may lead to quite different perceptions of the sensation.

The Single, Satiating Orgasm   Traditionally it was thought that women, like men, experience only one orgasm, followed by a *refractory period* of minutes or even hours when they are not capable of arousal and orgasm. Research shows that this is not true and that in fact women can have multiple orgasms. Kinsey and his colleagues (1953) discovered this, reporting that 14 percent of the women he interviewed experienced multiple orgasms. The scientific establishment dismissed these reports as unreliable, however.

Observations from the Masters and Johnson laboratory provided convincing evidence that women do indeed experience multiple orgasms within a short time period. Moreover, these multiple orgasms do not differ from single ones in any significant way except that there are several. They are not minor experiences.

Physiologically, after an orgasm, the vaginal region loses its engorgement of blood. However, in the female, but not in the male, this process is immediately reversible. That is, under continued or renewed erotic stimulation the region again becomes engorged, the orgasmic platform appears, and another orgasm is initiated. This is the physiological mechanism that makes multiple orgasms possible in females. In some women, this process may continue to the point of exhaustion.

Most frequently, multiple orgasms are attained through masturbation rather than vaginal intercourse, because it is difficult for a male to postpone his orgasm for such long periods.

Sexuality and the Elderly   It is a popular belief that a woman's sexual responsiveness is virtually gone by the time she is 60 or so, and perhaps ceases at menopause. Some people believe that sexual activity is a drain on their health and physical resources, and they deliberately stop all sexual activity in middle age to prevent or postpone aging. Once again, Masters and Johnson have exploded these myths.

As they concluded, "There is no time limit drawn by the advancing years to female sexuality." For the male, also, under conditions of good health and emotional adjustment, there is "a capacity for sexual performance that frequently may extend beyond the eighty-year age level." In one sample of persons aged 70 and over who responded to a questionnaire in *Consumer Reports* magazine, 33 percent of the women and 43 percent of the men reported that they still masturbated; and 65 percent of the wives and 59 percent of the husbands still had intercourse with their spouse (Brecher, 1984).

It is true that certain physiological changes occur as women age that influence sexual activity. The ovaries sharply reduce their production of estrogen at menopause, causing the vagina to lose much of its resiliency, and the amount of lubrication is substantially reduced. However, it is common for women to be given hormone-replacement therapy after menopause, which minimizes these changes. Application of lubricants is also helpful. Sexual performance depends much more on the opportunity for regular, active sexual expression and physical and mental health than it does on hormone imbalance (Masters and Johnson, 1966).

The G-Spot

Gräfenberg spot (G-spot): A hypothesized small gland on the front wall of the vagina, emptying into the urethra, which may be responsible for female ejaculation.

There has been a great deal of publicity given to the discovery of the G-spot. The **G-spot** (short for **Gräfenberg spot**, named for a German obstetrician-gynecologist who discovered it originally in 1944, although his work was overlooked) is a small organ located on the top or front side of the vagina, about halfway between the pubic bone and the cervix (see Figure 11.1 on p. 293). It is thought to be an anatomical structure rather like the prostate in the male.

There are two reasons that the G-spot is thought to be important. First, the researchers who have been investigating it believe that it is the source of *female ejaculation* (Addiego et al., 1981; Belzer, 1981; Ladas et al., 1982; Perry and Whipple, 1981). Traditionally, it was thought that men ejaculate and women don't. However, sex researchers John Perry and Beverly Whipple (1981) reported that they discovered fluid spurting out of the urethra of some women during orgasm. According to one study, the fluid is chemically similar to the seminal fluid of men, but contains no sperm. Perry and Whipple estimate that 10 to 20 percent of women ejaculate during orgasm. This is an important discovery, because given the old wisdom that women don't ejaculate, many women who did ejaculate suffered extreme embarrassment and anxiety, thinking that they were urinating during sex.

There is a second reason that the G-spot might be important. Based on its discovery, Perry and Whipple theorized that there is a *uterine orgasm*. They believe that there are two kinds of orgasm: vulvar orgasm (the kind studied by Masters and Johnson, produced by clitoral stimulation, and named for the vulva, or external genitals, of the female) and uterine orgasm (felt more deeply and produced by stimulation of the G-spot). This sounds like the old argument about clitoral versus vaginal orgasm, and certainly we should withhold judgment on Perry and Whipple's work until there can be independent replication by other scientists.

In one study designed to test Perry and Whipple's hypotheses, two female gynecologists examined 11 women, 6 of whom claimed to be ejaculators. The gynecologists found an area like the G-spot in only 4 of the 11 women, but not in the rest, and the G-spot was not found more frequently among the ejaculators. Analysis of the ejaculate indicated that it was chemically like urine, not like semen (Goldberg, et al., 1983). Thus the G-spot research must be regarded as tentative and not definitive.

Psychological Aspects

Gender Differences in Sexuality   It is a traditional stereotype in our culture that female sexuality and male sexuality are quite different. Women were reputed to be uninterested in sex and slow to arouse. Men, in contrast, were supposed to be constantly aroused. What is the scientific evidence on gender differences in sexuality?

Mary Beth Oliver and I conducted a meta-analysis of studies reporting data on gender differences in sexuality (Oliver and Hyde, 1993). Two gender differences were particularly large: the incidence of masturbation and attitudes about casual sex. Women are less likely to have masturbated than men are ($d = .96$), and women are considerably less approving of sex in a casual or uncommitted relationship than men are ($d = .81$). Notice that the sizes of these gender differences, .96 and .81, are enormous compared with some of the other gender differences we have examined, such as gender differences in abilities (Chapter 6).

Let's first consider the gender difference in masturbation. Kinsey, based on his massive survey conducted in the 1940s, found that 92 percent of the men in his sample reported having masturbated to orgasm at least once in their lives, compared with 58 percent of the women (Kinsey et al., 1953). More recent surveys have found percentages very close to these. That is, this gender difference doesn't seem to have disappeared in recent years with the sexual revolution. In fact, every year I survey the students in my human sexuality course and find statistics on masturbation very close to Kinsey's.

One question we must ask, however, is whether this is a real gender difference or just an inaccuracy resulting from the use of self-reports. In our culture, particularly in previous decades, more restrictions have been placed on female sexuality than on male sexuality. It might be that these restrictions have discouraged females from ever masturbating. On the other hand, they might simply lead women not to report masturbating. That is, perhaps women do masturbate but are simply more reticent to report it on a sex survey than men are. I tend not to believe this argument. On today's sex surveys, women report on all kinds of intimate behaviors, such as fellatio and cunnilingus. More of them report having engaged in fellatio and cunnilingus than report having masturbated. It is hard to believe that these women honestly report about oral-genital sex and suddenly get bashful and lie about masturbation.

The other large gender difference was in attitudes about casual sex, such as sex in a "one-night stand." Men are more approving and women are more disapproving. Investigating this idea, Janell Carroll, Kari Volk, and I surveyed a random sample of students at Denison University (Carroll et al., 1985). The responses to the question "How would you feel about sex in a 'one-night stand'?" are shown in Table 11.1. Notice that virtually all the women said they would feel either guilty or anxious, whereas about half the men said they would feel comfortable, relaxed, or satisfied. This gender difference can be a source of great conflict between women and men.

Related to this finding is the stereotype that men and women differ in their motives for having sex. Men—at least according to the stereotype—are more interested in the physical aspects of sex and have a "love 'em and leave 'em" attitude. Women, on the other hand, are thought to be most interested in love and romance and to be concerned with the interpersonal more than the physical aspects of the relationship. We investigated this stereotype in the same survey of Denison students discussed earlier. The results generally tended to confirm the stereotype as being a real difference between women and men. In one open-ended question, we asked, "What would be your motives for having sexual intercourse?" These were some of the typical answers from women:

> emotional feelings that were shared, wonderful way to express LOVE!!

> my motives for sexual intercourse would all be due to the love and commitment I feel for my partner

> to show my love for my partner and to feel loved and needed

> wanting to share myself with someone I love, needing to be needed

> love, to feel loved, to express love to someone

These responses clearly indicate the importance most women attach to love and a close relationship as part of their sexual expression. Contrast those quotations with these typical responses from men:

> need it

> to gratify myself

> for the pleasure or the love

> to satisfy my needs

> when I'm tired of masturbation

TABLE 11.1
Percentages of Males and Females Giving Different Responses to the Question "How Would You Feel About Sex in a 'One-Night Stand'?"

	Guilty	Anxious	Comfortable/ Relaxed	Satisfied
Males	28	22	22	28
Females	68	23	6	3

Source: Carroll et al. (1985).

These responses reflect the greater importance men—at least in this college-aged group—attach to physical gratification from sex.

Of course, not every respondent gave typical responses. For example, a response to that same question from one woman was "to enjoy myself physically, for experimentation, exercise, fun, and to get to know someone better." And this atypical answer came from a male: "Intercourse makes me happy, and people enjoy doing things that make them happy. I express myself oftentimes better physically. I have lots of love to give, and it's one way that is a better avenue of expressing my feelings for others."

Another stereotype is that a gender difference exists in arousal to erotic materials, men being much more responsive to them than women are. Is there any scientific evidence that this is true?

The females in the Kinsey sample were considerably less likely to report responses to erotic materials than the males. For example, about half the males reported having been aroused at some time by erotic stories; although almost all the women had heard such stories, only 14 percent had been aroused by them. These data are often cited as evidence that women are not as easily aroused as men.[1]

Studies done in the past three decades, however, have provided little evidence that males and females differ in their arousal to erotic materials. For example, in one study the responses of 128 male and 128 female university students to erotic slides and movies were studied (Schmidt and Sigusch, 1970). The slides and movies showed petting and coitus. In several tests for gender differences, either there were no differences, or the differences were small, with about 40 percent of the females reporting a stronger arousal response than the average male. All the females and almost all the males reported genital responses to the slides and movies. And women, not men, showed an increase in petting and coitus in

---

[1]Actually, however, the Kinsey data were not that simple. Kinsey noted wide variability in women's responses and speculated that perhaps one-third of all women are as erotically responsive as the average male. Further, there were no gender differences in certain behaviors; for example, about the same number of females as males reported having been aroused by erotic literary materials.

the 24 hours after seeing the erotic stimuli. Therefore, there seems to be little basis for saying that women are not erotically responsive to such materials.

An interesting study by psychologist Julia Heiman (1975) provides a good deal of insight into the responses of males and females to erotic materials. Her participants were sexually experienced university students, and she studied their responses as they listened to tape recordings of erotic stories. Not only did Heiman obtain people's self-ratings of their arousal, as other investigators had done, but she also got objective measures of their physiological levels of arousal. To do this, she used two instruments: a penile strain gauge and a photoplethysmograph. The penile strain gauge is used to get a physiological measure of arousal in the male; it is a flexible loop that fits around the base of the penis. The photoplethysmograph measures physiological arousal in the female; it is an acrylic cylinder that is placed just inside the vagina. Both instruments measure vasocongestion in the genitals, which is the major physiological response during sexual arousal.

Participants heard one of four kinds of tapes. There is a stereotype that women are more turned on by romance, whereas men are more aroused by "raw sex," or the physical aspects of sex. The tapes varied according to which of these kinds of content they contained. The first group of tapes was *erotic*; they included excerpts from erotic material and popular novels giving explicit descriptions of heterosexual sex. The second group of tapes was *romantic*; a couple were heard expressing affection for each other, but they did not actually engage in sex. The third group of tapes was *erotic-romantic*; these tapes included erotic elements of explicit sex and also romantic elements. Finally, the fourth group of tapes served as a *control*; a couple were heard engaging in conversation but nothing else. The plots of the tapes also varied according to whether the male or the female initiated the activity and whether the description centered on the female's physical and psychological responses or on the male's. Thus the tapes were male-initiated or female-initiated and female-centered or male-centered. Three important results emerged from the study:

1. Explicit sex (the erotic and erotic-romantic tapes) was most arousing, both for women and for men. The great majority of both males and females responded most, both physiologically and in self-ratings, to the erotic and erotic-romantic tapes. Women, in fact, rated the erotic tapes as more arousing than men did. Neither men nor women responded—either physiologically or in self-reports—to the romantic tapes or to the control tapes.

2. Both males and females found the female-initiated, female-centered tape to be the most arousing.

3. Women were sometimes not aware of their own physiological arousal. Generally there was a high correlation between self-ratings of arousal and objective physiological measures of arousal, both for men and for women. When men were physically aroused, they never made an error in reporting this in their self-ratings—it's pretty hard to miss an erection. But when the women

were physically aroused, about half of them failed to report it in their self-ratings. (One might assume that women who were sophisticated enough to volunteer for an experiment of this sort and who were willing to insert a photoplethysmograph into their vagina would not suddenly become bashful about reporting their arousal; that is, it seems likely that these women honestly did not know when they were aroused.)

In sum, then, Heiman's study indicates that females and males are quite similar in their responses to erotic materials, but that women can sometimes be unaware of their own physical arousal. This study, however, dealt only with the preliminary stages of arousal; perhaps women vary in the point at which they recognize their arousal.

Development of Ideas About Sexuality   The earliest sexual experiences many people have are in masturbation. But as we have seen, the data indicate that substantial numbers of females never masturbate, and many of those who do, do so later in life than males do. This may have important consequences in other areas of sexuality as well.

Childhood and adolescent experiences with masturbation are important early sources of learning about sexuality. Through these experiences we learn how our bodies respond to sexual stimulation and what the most effective techniques for stimulating our own bodies are. This learning is important to our experience of adult, two-person sex. Perhaps the women who do not masturbate, and who are thus deprived of this early learning experience, are the same ones who do not have orgasms in sexual intercourse. This is exactly what Kinsey's data suggested—that women who masturbate to orgasm before marriage are more likely to have orgasms in intercourse with their husbands. For example, 31 percent of the women who had never masturbated to orgasm before marriage had not had an orgasm by the end of their first year of marriage, compared with only 13 to 16 percent of the women who had masturbated (Kinsey et al., 1953, p. 407). There seems to be a possibility, then, that women's lack of experience with masturbation in adolescence is related to their problems with having orgasms during intercourse.

It is interesting to note from the Kinsey data that boys and girls seem to learn about masturbation in different ways. Most males reported having heard about it before trying it themselves, and a substantial number had observed others doing it. Most females, on the other hand, learned to masturbate by accidental discovery of the possibility. Apparently communication about sexual behavior is not so free among girls as it is among boys, or perhaps girls are not so eager to pursue this information. At any rate, it appears that most males have learned to associate the genital organs with pleasure by the time of puberty, whereas many females have not.

Not only may women's relative inexperience with masturbation lead to a lack of sexual learning, but it may also create a kind of "erotic dependency" on men. Typically, boys' earliest sexual experiences are with masturbation. They learn that they can produce their own sexual pleasure. Girls typically have their earliest sexual experiences in heterosexual petting. They therefore learn about sex from boys, and they learn that their sexual pleasure is produced by the male. As sex researcher John Gagnon commented:

> Young women may know of masturbation, but not know *how* to masturbate— how to produce pleasure, or even what the pleasures of orgasm might be. . . . Some young women report that they learned how to masturbate after they had orgasm from intercourse and petting, and decided they could do it for themselves. (1977, p. 152)

An illustration of the way in which masturbation can expand female sexuality is given by what one young woman student wrote in an essay:

> At twelve years old, I discovered masturbation. . . . I was almost relieved to have, quite by accident, discovered this practice. This actually was one of the nicest discoveries that I've ever made. I feel totally comfortable with this and have actually discussed it with some of my friends. One of my favorite theories centers around this. When men have asked me to have intercourse with them and I felt that I was basically going to only serve the purpose of being an instrument to produce their orgasm, I usually tell them that I'm sure that they'd "have a better time by themselves." Masturbation does produce a better, more controlled, orgasm for me. I've read Shere Hite's study on male sexuality that the same is true for men. I'm not saying that it's better than sexual contact with a man for me but I do think it's more satisfying than waking up next to someone I don't care about and feel comfortable with. I'm surprised that according to Kinsey, only 58 percent of women masturbate at some time in their lives. I thought everyone did. It's very creative for me. I've tried several techniques and it certainly helps me in my sexual experiences. I know a great deal about my sexual responses and I think that in knowing about myself, some of it relates to men and their sexual responses.

Experiences with masturbation—or lack of such experiences—then, may be very important in shaping female sexuality and making it different from male sexuality.

Of course, socialization forces on the female's developing sexuality are also important. Our culture has traditionally placed tighter restrictions on women's sexuality than it has on men's, and vestiges of these restrictions linger today. It seems likely that these restrictions have acted as a damper on female sexuality, and thus they may help to explain why some women do not masturbate or do not have orgasms. In an essay one woman student recalled one of her childhood socialization experiences as follows:

> A big part of my childhood was Catholic grammar school. The principal and teachers were nuns of the old school. . . . I remember one day the principal called all of the girls (third grade to eighth) to the auditorium. "I can't blame the

boys for lifting your skirts to see your underwear," she scolded, "you girls wear your skirts so short it is temptation beyond their control." I had no idea what she was talking about, but throughout school the length of our skirts was of utmost importance. Nice girls did not show their legs.

Double standard: The evaluation of male behavior and female behavior according to different standards; used specifically to refer to holding more conservative, restrictive attitudes toward female sexuality.

One of the clearest examples of the differences in restrictions on female and male sexuality is the **double standard** (Sprecher et al., 1987). The double standard says, essentially, that the same sexual behavior is evaluated differently, depending on whether a male or a female engages in it. An example is premarital sex. Traditionally in our culture, premarital intercourse has been more acceptable for males than for females. Indeed, premarital sexual activity might be considered a status symbol for a male but a sign of cheapness for a female.

These different standards have been reflected in behavior. For example, the Kinsey data, collected in the 1940s, indicated that more than twice as many males (71 percent) as females (33 percent) had premarital sex. Apparently, society's message got through to young women of that era. Most of them managed to keep themselves chaste before marriage, whereas their male contemporaries tended to get the experience that was expected of them.

Generally, there seems to be less of a double standard today than there was in former times. For example, people now approve of premarital sex for females about as much as they do for males. In one sample, 82 percent of the men felt that premarital sex was acceptable for males when the couple is in love, and 77 percent felt that it was acceptable for females under the same circumstances (Hunt, 1974).

This change in attitude is reflected in behavior. A much higher percentage of women report having engaged in premarital intercourse now than in Kinsey's time. In one sample, 75 percent of college men and 60 percent of college women had engaged in premarital intercourse, as had 79 percent of noncollege men and 72 percent of noncollege women of the same age (DeLamater and MacCorquodale, 1979). Thus there is much less of a difference between females and males now than there was a generation ago.

On the other hand, there is still more disapproval of a woman who has many partners than of a man who does. In response to the statement, "A man who has had sexual intercourse with a great many women is immoral," 32 percent of men and 52 percent of women agree (Robinson, et al., 1991). But when the statement is about a woman, the percentages agreeing leap up to 51 and 64 for men and for women respondents, respectively.

As I noted in Chapter 6, *ambivalence* is an important theme in the psychology of women. In that chapter I discussed ambivalence about achievement and femininity. Sexuality is another area of ambivalence for women. Doubtless this ambivalence results from the kind of mixed message that females get from society. Beginning in adolescence, they are told that popularity is important for them, and being sexy increases one's popularity. But actually engaging in pre-marital intercourse, especially with many different partners, can lead to a loss of status. The ambivalence-producing message is "Be sexy but don't be sexual."

Ambivalence toward sexual relations is reflected in the large number of un-wanted pregnancies among unmarried women who were well informed about contraception (Luker, 1975). Among sexually active teenage girls, 29 percent use no method of contraception (Hofferth, 1990). Why? Taking a birth control pill every day indicates that the woman thinks intercourse is a real possibility. For unmarried women, particularly those not involved in a long-term relation-ship, this is a difficult admission to make. Constantly being ready for sexual rela-tions still suggests lack of morals. In fact, the antipathy toward taking a daily measure against conception is apparently so great that it outweighs the undesir-ability of pregnancy, as discussed in Chapter 10. The woman would much prefer to believe that she was "swept off her feet," rather than the implied alternative, that she was expecting to have sex.

Research on the development of sexuality suggests that discussing gender differences in sexuality is too simple an approach. It is the developmental process of sexuality that differs for males and females (Kaplan and Sager, 1971). In a sense, males and females appear to move through the stages of sexual devel-opment in adolescence and adulthood in opposite orders. For males, adolescent sexuality is genitally focused, with strong orgasmic needs—some report four to eight orgasms per day. But by the time a man reaches 50, emphasis has shifted away from genitally centered sensations to include more emphasis on the quality of the relationship with the partner, and two orgasms per week are considered satisfactory. For the female, adolescent sexuality is not genitally focused, with little emphasis on orgasm, but rather is relationship focused. Genital sexuality and orgasmic potential develop later, not reaching a peak until the thirties and forties. Orgasmic response in women is faster and more consistent in the forties than it is in the teens or twenties. It appears, then, that early male sexuality is genital and gradually evolves to add a relationship component, whereas female sexuality begins with a focus on the interpersonal, and only later develops the genital component.

Fantasies The psychoanalytic school traditionally considered fantasies during intercourse as a sign of pathology. Some women further resist fantasies because they seem to be a sign of disloyalty to their partners. These fantasies were con-sidered rare and received little attention in research until the 1970s.

A questionnaire study of 141 adult women volunteers indicated that 65 per-cent fantasized during intercourse with their husbands (Hariton, 1973). An addi-tional 28 percent reported occasional thoughts during intercourse that might be counted as fantasies, leaving only 7 percent of the sample indicating no fantasies at all. Statistically, then, it seems that it is the woman who does *not* fantasize who is unusual!

The following are the seven most common fantasies during masturbation, reported by women in another study (Hunt, 1974), listed in order of frequency:

1. Having intercourse with a loved one

2. Doing sexual things one would never do in reality

3. Having intercourse with a stranger

4. Being forced to have sex

5. Having sex with more than one person at the same time

6. Having sex with someone of the same gender

7. Forcing someone to have sex

Women who have fantasies are generally independent, impulsive, and non-conformist—all personality characteristics typical of creative people. Their fantasies do not appear to be signs of poor marital adjustment; on the contrary, they seemed to have better sexual relations than the nonfantasizers. This latter group, in contrast, were generally conciliatory, unassuming, nurturing, and affiliative (Hariton, 1973).

In previous sections, I have emphasized the need for interpersonal relationships as an important aspect of female sexuality. Here is the other side of the coin, the woman's experience of her own, individual, creative sexuality.

Sex and Androgyny Chapter 3 included a discussion of androgyny—integrating masculine and feminine traits into one's personality and behaviors—and some of the advantages it might have. Is androgyny advantageous to one's sexuality? Are androgynous people more sexually liberated? Are they more sexually satisfied? It might be expected that androgynous people would have the most flexible and satisfying sexuality, insofar as they can combine both masculine elements of sexuality (e.g., initiating sex, being easily aroused) and feminine elements of sexuality (integrating love and emotion with sex, communicating). What is the evidence?

In one study, androgynous females were more comfortable with sex than feminine females were, and androgynous males were more comfortable with sex than masculine males were (Walfish and Myerson, 1980). In another study, androgynous women reported having orgasms more frequently than feminine women did (Radlove, 1983). In a third study, college students viewed slides of couples having intercourse either in the traditional man-above position or in the woman-above position (Allgeier and Fogel, 1978). They then rated their attitudes toward the individuals in the slides. Females were more negative about the woman-above position than males were. The participants' gender-typing (androgynous versus stereotyped) was *unrelated* to their attitudes about the woman-above position. Thus, of these three studies, two indicate that androgynous people are more liberated and satisfied in their sexuality, whereas the third does not show that. Androgyny is probably related to some good things in sexuality, but we shouldn't expect it to be the surefire solution to everything.

As an interesting aside, another study found a relationship between sexual satisfaction and feminism among women who were married or cohabitating (Kirkpatrick, 1980). That is, the more feminist a woman was in her attitudes, the greater was her sexual satisfaction in her relationship.

Gender, Race, and Sexuality

The topic of the meeting of gender, race, and sexuality is a large and complex one that could easily fill several books. Many historical issues are involved. For example, during the period of slavery in the United States, white masters assumed that they had the right to sexual intercourse with African American slave women. On the other hand, the reverse—an African American slave man having sex with a white woman—was not only forbidden but grounds for death.

Here we will focus on contemporary data collected by social scientists that allow us to compare the sexual behavior of African American women and white women. Some of these data are summarized in Table 11.2. The data show evidence of both differences and similarities. For example, Black teenagers and white teenagers are about equally irresponsible with respect to using contraceptives. African American women, on average, have intercourse for the first time somewhat earlier than white women do, although the gap is not large. On the other hand, there is a fairly large difference in the sex ratio (number of males per 100 females); although the sex ratio is fairly even for whites, there are only about 86 Black men for every 100 Black women, a point that has important implications for patterns of marriage, as discussed in Chapter 8.

TABLE 11.2

A Comparison of the Sexual Behaviors of Black Women and White Women

	Whites	Blacks
Median age at first intercourse[a]	16.3 years	15.6 years
Percentage of unmarried women aged 17 who have ever had intercourse[b]	35%	57%
Percentage of sexually active teenage women who do not use contraceptives[b]	27%	35%
Sex ratio (number of males per 100 females), 30- to 34-year-olds[c]	101	85.3
Mean age of first masturbation, females[d]	14.3 years	12.6 years
Mean age of first masturbation, males[d]	13.1 years	13.3 years

[a]Zelnick and Kantner (1977).
[b]Hofferth (1990).
[c]U.S. Bureau of the Census (1990a).
[d]Belcastro (1985).

Earlier in the chapter I noted that females tend to begin masturbating at later ages than males do. When the data are broken down by ethnicity, however, it becomes clear that this statement is true for whites but not for African Americans. On average, Black women begin masturbating at an earlier age than Black men do and considerably earlier than white women do. This finding is a good reminder that we shouldn't look simply at gender differences, but should remember that gender often interacts with ethnicity.

Sexual Dysfunction and Therapy

Sexual dysfunction: A problem with sexual responding that causes a person mental distress; examples are erection problems in men and orgasm problems in women.

The term **sexual dysfunction** refers to various disturbances or impairments of sexual functioning, such as inability to have an orgasm (orgasmic dysfunction) or premature ejaculation. Masters and Johnson pioneered in therapy for these problems (Masters and Johnson, 1970; for a critique, see Zilbergeld and Evans, 1980).

The Masters and Johnson Approach Masters and Johnson rejected most of the traditional notions about the psychological sources of sex problems. They say,

FIGURE 11.4
One factor affecting African American women's sexual relationships is an imbalance in the gender ratio: There are more Black women than men.

Sociocultural deprivation and ignorance of sexual physiology, rather than psychiatric or medical illness, constitute the etiologic background for most sexual dysfunction. (1970, p. 21)

That is, sexual problems may not be symptoms of deep psychiatric disturbance, but may have simpler sources, such as educational deprivation. Their theoretical orientation, then, is learning theory rather than psychoanalytic theory. Therefore, Masters and Johnson adopted a rapid treatment program, two weeks in duration, which has attained remarkable success.

Their treatment program has a number of unusual features. One is that it requires that both partners participate in the therapy. Masters and Johnson maintain that there is no such thing as an uninvolved partner in cases of sexual dysfunction, even if only one person displays overt symptoms. For instance, a woman who does not experience orgasm is anxious and wonders whether there is anything wrong with her, or whether she is unattractive to her partner. The partner, on the other hand, may wonder why he is failing to stimulate her to orgasm. Both partners are deeply involved. Realizing the reciprocal nature of sexual gratification, Masters and Johnson employ the practice of having both partners participate.

The major objective in their therapy is abolishing goal-directed sexual performance. Most people think that certain things should be *achieved* during sexual activity—for example, that the woman should achieve or attain an orgasm. This emphasis on achieving leads to a fear of failure, which spells disaster for sexual enjoyment. Masters and Johnson therefore try to remove the individual from a spectator role in sex—observing her or his own actions, evaluating their success. Instead, the emphasis is on the enjoyment of all sensual pleasures. Clients use a series of "sensate focus" exercises, in which they learn to touch and to respond to touch. They are also taught to express sexual needs to their partners, which people generally are reluctant to do. For instance, the woman is taught to tell her partner in which regions of her body she enjoys being touched most and how firm or light the touch should be. Beyond this basic instruction, which includes lessons in sexual anatomy and physiology, Masters and Johnson simply allow natural sexual response to emerge. Sexual pleasure is natural; sexual response is natural. After removing artificial impediments to sexual response, they find that people quickly begin joyful, "successful" participation in sex.

Masters and Johnson evaluated the success of their therapy, both during the two-week therapy session and in follow-up studies five years after couples leave the clinic. Their research indicates that therapy is successful in approximately 75 percent of the cases (although their results have been disputed—see Zilbergeld and Evans, 1980).

Let us now look at some specific examples of sexual dysfunction in women.

Anorgasmia: The inability to have an orgasm; orgasmic dysfunction.

Orgasmic Dysfunction Orgasmic dysfunction (also termed **anorgasmia** or inhibited female orgasm) is the condition of being unable to have an orgasm. In *primary orgasmic dysfunction* the woman has had intercourse but has never experienced an orgasm (for a review, see Anderson, 1983). Sex therapists do not use the term *frigidity*, because it has a variety of imprecise, negative connotations.

In *situational orgasmic dysfunction*, the woman has orgasms in some situations, but not in others. Clearly in this case, there is no organic impairment of orgasm, because the woman is capable of experiencing it. The systematic nature of the situations in which the woman can and cannot experience orgasm often leads to an understanding of the psychological nature of the problem (Masters and Johnson, 1970). Sometimes a woman who has frequently experienced orgasm in intercourse with her husband is no longer capable of it. This may be related to a change in her identification with him. For instance, in one case a woman who strongly desired an increase in the family's social and economic status became sexually dysfunctional after her husband lost several jobs. Apparently she realized he would not accomplish what she wanted, and her disillusionment was channeled into her sexual response, or lack of it. Another example of situational orgasmic dysfunction is the case of women who are able to have orgasms through masturbation but not through sexual intercourse. This pattern is so common, however, that it probably shouldn't be classified as a dysfunction (Hyde, 1994).

Vaginismus | **Vaginismus** involves a tightening or spasm of the outer third of the vagina, possibly to such an extent that the opening of the vagina is closed and intercourse becomes impossible (Lieblum and Rosen, 1989). Factors in the woman's history that seem to cause this condition include family background in which sex was considered dirty and sinful, a previous sexual assault, and long experience of painful intercourse due to a physical problem (Masters and Johnson, 1970).

> **Vaginismus:** A strong, spastic contraction of the muscles around the vagina, perhaps closing off the vagina and making intercourse impossible.

In therapy, Masters and Johnson find it important to demonstrate to both partners the reality and nature of the vaginal spasm, of which the couple are frequently unaware. The treatment consists mainly of using vaginal dilators of progressive size to enlarge the opening. In cases where physical problems seem to be the source, treatment of these problems often seems to help the emotional problems.

Painful Intercourse | Painful intercourse, or **dyspareunia**, may be organic or psychogenic in origin. Too often, the woman's complaints of pain are dismissed, particularly if the physician cannot find an obvious physical problem. However, this is a serious condition and should be treated as such. When pain is felt in the vagina, it may be due to failure to lubricate, to infection, to special sensitivity of the vagina (such as to the contraceptives being used), or to changes in the vagina due to age. Pain may also be felt in the region of the vaginal outlet and clitoris, or deep in the pelvis. In this latter case, the causes may be infection or tearing of the ligaments supporting the uterus, particularly following childbirth.

> **Dyspareunia:** Painful intercourse.

Disorders of Sexual Desire In the 1980s, sex therapists began seeing a new kind of sexual dysfunction, and cases of it quickly became more common than cases of any of the preceding kinds. This new category was termed *disorders of sexual desire* (Kaplan, 1979; LoPiccolo, 1980). Contrary to stereotypes, this problem is found in both women and men.

Sexual desire, or libido, refers to a set of feelings that lead the individual to seek out sexual activity or to be pleasurably receptive to it. When sexual desire is inhibited, so that the individual is not interested in sexual activity, the dysfunction is termed *low sexual desire* or a disorder of sexual desire (Leiblum and Rosen, 1988). People with inhibited sexual desire often manage to avoid situations that will evoke sexual feelings. If, despite their best efforts, they find themselves in an arousing situation, they experience a rapid "turnoff" of their feelings. The turnoff may be so intense that some people report negative, unpleasant feelings; others simply report sexual anesthesia, that is, no sexual feeling at all, even though they may respond to the point of orgasm.

A survey of a "normal" (nonpatient) population indicated that 35 percent of the women and 16 percent of the men complained of disinterest in sex (Frank et al., 1978).

As with other dysfunctions, with disorders of sexual desire there are complex problems of definition. There are many circumstances when it is perfectly normal for a person's desire to be inhibited. For example, one cannot be expected to find every potential partner attractive. Sex therapist Helen Singer Kaplan (1979) recounts an example of a couple consisting of a shy, petite woman and an extremely obese (350 pounds, 5 feet 3 inches tall), unkempt man. He complained of her lack of desire, but one can understand her inhibition and would certainly hesitate to classify her as having a sexual dysfunction. One cannot expect to respond sexually at all times, in all places, and with all persons.

It is also true that an individual's absolute level of sexual desire is often not the problem—rather, the problem is a *discrepancy of sexual desire* between the partners (Zilbergeld and Ellison, 1980). That is, if one partner wants sex less frequently than the other partner wants it, there is a conflict.

Because recognition of this dysfunction is relatively recent, there is little agreement in the field about its definition or diagnosis. However, it seems unlikely that low sexual desire will turn out to be a single category (LoPiccolo, 1980). Rather, it probably represents a single symptom that can be caused by many factors. The following have been implicated as determinants of low sexual desire: hormones, psychological factors (particularly anxiety and/or depression), cognitive factors (not having learned to perceive one's arousal accurately or having limited expectations for one's own ability to be aroused), and sexual trauma such as sexual abuse in childhood (LoPiccolo, 1980; Rosen and Leiblum, 1987).

New Therapies for Women's Sexual Dysfunctions The incidence of women who have problems having orgasms, particularly in intercourse, is so high that it seems that this pattern is well within the range of normal female sexual response. It is questionable whether it should be called a dysfunction, except insofar as it causes unhappiness for the woman. With the growing awareness of the frequency of this problem have come a number of self-help sex therapy books for women, one of the best being Lonnie Garfield Barbach's *For Yourself: The Fulfillment of Female Sexuality* (1975; see also Heiman et al., 1976). Reading and working through the exercises in these self-help books actually has a fancy name—bibliotherapy—and it has been demonstrated to produce significant gains in women's frequency of orgasm during sexual intercourse (Dodge et al., 1982).

A common recommendation of Barbach and other therapists (e.g., Anderson, 1983; LoPiccolo and Stock, 1986) is that pre-orgasmic women practice masturbation to increase their capacity for orgasm. The idea is that women must first explore their own bodies and learn how to bring themselves to orgasm before they can expect to have orgasms in heterosexual intercourse. As noted earlier in this chapter, many women have not had this kind of practice, and sex therapists recommend that they get it.

Kegel exercises:
Exercises to strengthen the muscles surrounding the vagina; pubococcygeal muscle exercises.

Another exercise that is recommended is the **Kegel exercises** or *pubococcygeal muscle exercises* (Kegel, 1952). The pubococcygeal (PC) muscle runs along the sides of the entrance to the vagina. Exercising this muscle seems to increase women's sexual pleasure by increasing the sensitivity of the vaginal area. This exercise is particularly helpful to women who have had the PC muscle stretched in childbirth or who simply have poor tone in it. The woman is instructed first to find the PC muscle by sitting on a toilet with her legs spread apart, urinating, and stopping the flow of urine voluntarily. The muscle that stops the flow is the PC. After that, the woman is told to contract the muscle ten times during each of six sessions per day. Gradually she can work up to more.

Gender Similarities

In previous chapters I have stressed gender similarities in psychological processes. There are also great gender similarities in sexuality. A few decades ago, at the time of the Kinsey research, there were marked gender differences in several aspects of sexuality. However, more recent research shows that these differences are greatly decreased, or even absent now.

For example, according to Kinsey's data collected in the 1940s, 71 percent of males but only 33 percent of females had premarital intercourse by age 25 (Kinsey et al., 1953). There was, at that time, a marked gender difference in premarital sexual activity. In a more recent study, though, 75 percent of college men and 60 percent of college women had engaged in premarital intercourse (DeLamater and MacCorquodale, 1979), representing a clear trend toward gender similarities. In the meta-analysis discussed earlier in this chapter, a number of variables showed no gender difference, including sexual satisfaction and attitudes about masturbation (Oliver and Hyde, 1993). Although there are some large gender differences in sexuality (incidence of masturbation and attitudes about casual sex), there are many gender similarities.

EXPERIENCE THE RESEARCH

GENDER DIFFERENCES IN SEXUALITY

Administer the questionnaire below to ten students, five men and five women. Because the information you will collect is sensitive, be sure to explain to each participant that their answers will be anonymous. You must devise some method to insure anonymity, such as having respondents mail the questionnaire back to you, or having them place it into a large brown envelope that already contains others' questionnaires. Assure your respondent that the questionnaire will take less than five minutes to complete.

SEXUALITY QUESTIONNAIRE

1. Age: _____

2. Gender: ____ Female ____ Male

3. Ethnic heritage (check the one that applies):
   —— Black/African American
   —— Hispanic
   —— Asian American
   —— Native American
   —— White (not Hispanic)
   —— Biracial or multiracial

For each of the questions below, circle the letter that best reflects your response. Remember that your answers will be kept completely anonymous.

4. What is your attitude about a couple engaging in sexual intercourse when they are engaged?
   a. Strongly disapprove   d. Approve somewhat
   b. Disapprove somewhat   e. Strongly approve
   c. Neutral

5. What is your attitude about a couple engaging in sexual intercourse when they are only casually acquainted (i.e., a "one-night stand")?
   a. Strongly disapprove   d. Approve somewhat
   b. Disapprove somewhat   e. Strongly approve
   c. Neutral

6. Have you ever masturbated to orgasm?
   a. Yes (Go to question 7)
   b. No (Skip question 7 and go to question 8)

7. In the past month, how many times did you masturbate to orgasm?

   Number: _____

8. Have you ever engaged in sexual intercourse?
   a. Yes (continue on to question 9)
   b. No (Skip to the end)

9. With how many different partners have you engaged in sexual intercourse?

   Number: _____

Thank you for completing this questionnaire.

Suggestions for Further Reading

Barbach, Lonnie G. (1975). *For yourself: The fulfillment of female sexuality.* Garden City, NY: Anchor Press/Doubleday. This is the classic self-help book on female sexuality and, I think, still the best one around.

Hyde, Janet S. (1994). *Understanding human sexuality.* (5th ed.). New York: McGraw-Hill. Obviously, I have a prejudice in favor of this book, but I would like to recommend it if you want more information on sexuality than I could provide in one brief chapter here.

12

Lesbian and Bisexual Women

Between man and woman love is an act; each torn from self becomes other: what fills the woman in love with wonder is that the languorous passivity of her flesh should be reflected in the male's impetuosity; the narcissistic woman, however, recognizes her enticements but dimly in the man's erected flesh. Between women love is contemplative; caresses are intended less to gain possession of the other than gradually to re-create the self through her; separateness is abolished, there is no struggle, no victory, no defeat; in exact reciprocity each is at once subject and object; sovereign and slave; duality becomes mutuality.

SIMONE DE BEAUVOIR, THE SECOND SEX

With the sexual revolution and the feminist movement has also come the rise of gay liberation. The gay liberation movement can be counted as dating from June 1969, when, in response to police harassment, homosexuals rioted in Greenwich Village in New York. Lesbians have sometimes been united with the women's movement and sometimes in conflict with it. Radical lesbians argue that to be truly liberated, women must become separatists; that is, they must stay separate from men. Among other things, this would argue *against* heterosexuality and *for* lesbianism. More moderate lesbians join in working for the moderate goals of the women's movement, such as an end to job discrimination. A discussion of women today would be incomplete without a discussion of lesbian and bisexual women.

Bear in mind that there is no "typical lesbian" and no single lesbian experience. Lesbians vary tremendously from one to another, just as heterosexual women do. Some are professors and some work on assembly lines. Some are fat and some are thin. Some are white and some are African American.

Sexual orientation: A person's erotic and emotional orientation toward members of her or his own gender or members of the other gender.

Lesbian: A woman whose sexual orientation is toward other women.

Sexual orientation is defined as a person's erotic and emotional orientation toward members of her or his own gender or members of the other gender (Hyde, 1994). Sexual orientation is not just an issue of eroticism or sexuality, but also an issue of the direction of one's emotional attachments. It is not just a matter of whom one has sex with, but whom one loves. A **lesbian,** then, is a woman whose erotic and emotional orientation is toward other women. A *bisexual* is a person whose erotic and emotional orientations are toward both women and men.

Stereotypes and Discrimination

Some experts believe that many Americans' attitudes toward lesbians and gay men can best be described as homophobic (Fyfe, 1983; Hudson and Ricketts,

Homophobia: A strong, irrational fear of homosexuals.

Antigay prejudice: Negative attitudes and behaviors toward gay men and lesbians.

1980). **Homophobia** may be defined as a strong, irrational fear of homosexuals and, more generally, as fixed negative attitudes and reactions to homosexuals (Fyfe, 1983). Some scholars dislike the term *homophobia* because, although certainly some people have antigay feelings so strong that they could be called a phobia, what is more common is negative attitudes and prejudiced behaviors. Therefore, some prefer the term **antigay prejudice.**

Results of a well-sampled 1991 survey of Americans' attitudes are shown in Table 12.1. Notice that about three-quarters of Americans believe that sexual relations between adults of the same sex are always wrong. Notice also that these statistics have changed little in the approximately two decades from 1973 to 1991.

Many tangible instances of antigay prejudice exist. There are numerous documented cases of women being fired from their jobs or dishonorably discharged from the armed forces upon disclosure of their sexual orientation (Shilts, 1993), and in 1993 there was a great debate between President Bill Clinton and military leaders about whether the military should continue this practice of dishonorable discharge. The result was a "don't ask, don't tell" policy, in which it was all right to be gay or lesbian as long as one was secretive about it. Court cases have repeatedly upheld the right of employers to fire persons on the basis of sexual orientation.[1] Most states do not recognize lesbian partners in matters of health insurance or inheritance.

TABLE 12.1

Attitudes of Adult Americans Toward Homosexuality, 1973 and 1991

	Percentage of Sample	
Question and Responses	*1973*	*1991*
Are sexual relations between adults of the same sex:		
Always wrong	74	71
Almost always wrong	7	4
Wrong only sometimes	8	4
Not wrong at all	11	15

SOURCE: From Davis and Smith, *General Social Surveys, 1972–1991, Cumulative Codebook.* Copyright © 1991, National Opinion Research Center at the University of Chicago. Reprinted by permission.

---

[1] My own state, Wisconsin, as well as Hawaii and Massachusetts are the only states in the nation to have laws that ban discrimination on the basis of sexual orientation, in matters such as employment and housing.

Another form of discrimination is the prohibition against lesbians rearing children. In most states it is illegal for lesbians to adopt children, and lesbianism may be grounds for a father to regain custody from a lesbian mother of children they had when married. Yet many lesbians desire children, and these issues can be heartbreaking. There is currently a move in several states to modify some of this discrimination against lesbians.

The most extreme expressions of antigay prejudice occur in *hate crimes* against lesbians (Garnets et al., 1993). The following is one case:

> Late one night in July, Heidi Dorow was embracing another woman on the corner of Bleecker and Carmine Streets in the West Village [of New York], when a teenager began to taunt them. As they shoved past him, Ms. Dorow said, "He swung around and punched me in the head."
>
> The youth and 10 other teenagers then jumped on the women, felling them with their fists and kicking them as they lay on the pavement.
>
> Dazed and bleeding, Ms. Dorow and her friend staggered down the street in search of a cab, passing a man who shouted obscenities at them.
>
> At a nearby hospital, both women were treated for cuts and bruises, and Ms. Dorow's friend for a concussion, and released. Then the women, who are lesbians, went to the Sixth Precinct . . . to file a report. As they were leaving, someone on the street shouted more obscenities at them (Hays, 1990).

Other forms of discrimination are more subtle and psychological, involving the stereotyping of lesbians, who are expected to be unfeminine or even mannish, and certainly to be man-haters. In one study, participants were given written and tape-recorded descriptions of one of the following women: a feminine woman (described as feminine, emotional, warm toward others, and kind) or a masculine woman (described as masculine, competitive, active, feeling superior) with heterosexual or homosexual feelings (Storms et al., 1981). Then participants rated their perceptions of the woman described to them. The woman who was described as homosexual was rated as being more masculine than the heterosexual woman. The woman who was described as feminine and homosexual was perceived as having a confused, unstable sexual identity. This sort of stereotyping is another unpleasant fact of life for lesbians.

In considering this stereotype of the lesbian as masculine, it is important to make a distinction between gender identity and choice of sexual partner. Most lesbians have a female identification—that is, they are quite definitely women; they dress and behave like women; but they simply choose to direct emotional, sexual love toward other women. Indeed, a large proportion of them have had heterosexual relations, and many are or have been heterosexually married. According to a recent, well-sampled survey, 0.1 percent of the women reported that all of their sexual experiences had been with women; but 2.5 percent had had some experiences with men and some with women (Johnson et al., 1994, p. 187).

Finally, perhaps the most subtle and simultaneously most powerful belief is the assumption that heterosexuality is universal, or what Adrienne Rich (1980) has called *compulsory heterosexuality*. Perhaps you have seen the T-shirts that read "How Dare You Presume I'm Heterosexual?" But that is exactly the assumption that most people make in their day-to-day interactions. As a result, lesbians must tolerate co-workers asking if they have a boyfriend or mothers asking if a husband is on the horizon yet. Just as we have seen in previous chapters that the male is normative, so, too, heterosexuality is normative.

Lesbian Culture

Lesbian Community   Today there is a lesbian community or culture with its own norms and values. Even for lesbians who are in the closet, this culture has a profound impact on identity and behavior—such as the books they read, or the way they define sex. As one woman put it,

> I have seen lesbian communities all over the world (e.g., Zimbabwe) where the lesbians of that nation have more in common with me (i.e., they play the same lesbian records, have read the same books, wear the same lesbian jewelry) than the heterosexual women of that nation have in common with heterosexual women in the U.S. (Rothblum, 1993).

Participation in the lesbian community can then become a major force in the lives of lesbians who are out of the closet.

Lesbian Relationships   In studies of lesbians, close to 75 percent report being in a steady relationship (Peplau, 1993). Psychologist Anne Peplau and her colleagues (1978) have studied the nature of lesbian relationships based on lengthy questionnaires administered to 127 lesbians recruited through feminist and gay organizations in Los Angeles. They found a number of interesting results and concluded that two fundamental values were related to the nature of lesbian relationships: attachment to the partner and personal autonomy. That is, lesbians vary among one another in the extent to which they want a strong attachment to the partner, emphasizing emotional closeness, love, and security, and the extent to which they want personal independence. These two values are related to the kind of relationship that is formed. The feminist lesbians tended to emphasize the personal autonomy value.

The length of the longest lesbian relationship these women had had ranged from one month to 25 years, with a median of 2.5 years. In describing their current relationship, most of the women reported it as being close and loving. About 75 percent reported that they and their current partner were "in love." There was a high degree of satisfaction with the relationship (mean of 7.1 on a 9-point scale). There was also a great deal of satisfaction with the sexual aspects of the relationship. More than 70 percent of the women said that they almost always experienced orgasm when having sex with their partner. In regard to power in the relationship, the majority said that they and their partner shared equally in

FIGURE 12.1
Lesbian pop singer Melissa Ethridge. One important feature of lesbian culture is music.

power. Peplau and her colleagues concluded that lesbians can and do form committed, satisfying relationships.

One stereotype is that lesbians play "butch" and "femme" roles in their relationships, that is, that they mimic the male and female roles found in traditional marriages. Research shows this stereotype to be false (Peplau, 1982). Only a small minority of lesbian couples play such roles. In contrast, the majority of lesbian couples stress flexibility and taking turns—that is, equality—in their relationships. One woman said,

> I don't like role-playing because it copies the traditional male/female relationship. I'm proud I'm a woman. And I love women, not pseudo-men. (Jay and Young, 1979, p. 320)

Boston marriage: A romantic but asexual lesbian relationship.

Boston Marriages The term **Boston marriage** is used to refer to a romantic but asexual lesbian relationship. Historically, the term had a somewhat different meaning. Earlier in this century, the term was used to refer to two "spinsters" who set up housekeeping together, having failed to find husbands and given up the hope. We can't know whether these relationships were sexual or asexual. The term has been reappropriated today for lesbian relationships that are romantic but asexual.

Research on Boston marriages indicates that the partners typically had been sexual with each other for at least a short time in the past but are no longer (Rothblum and Brehony, 1993). Yet the women still felt sexually attracted to their partner. Their relationship was indistinguishable from other long-term lesbian relationships, with the exception of the lack of genital sex. Most of the couples were "out" in the lesbian community as well as in the workplace. Although some kept their asexuality secret in the lesbian community (it isn't very fashionable to be asexual these days), others were quite open about it.

Boston marriages are interesting in and of themselves, but they also raise some thought-provoking questions. How does one define a couple? For heterosexuals, legal marriage defines couple status, although certainly there are many heterosexual pairs who, though not married, would still be considered a couple. And there are some heterosexual married couples who are asexual. For gay male couples and lesbian couples, usually having a sexual relationship defines two people as being a couple. Where does that leave the Boston marriage, though? There is no marriage license and no sex, but the two women may have purchased a house together, lived together for 15 years, made out joint wills, perhaps raised children together. What defines two people as being a couple? That is a very complex question.

Coming Out

Coming out: The process of acknowledging to oneself, and then to others, that one is lesbian or gay.

The process of coming out of the closet, or **coming out,** involves acknowledging to oneself, and then to others, that one is gay or lesbian (Coleman, 1982).

Before coming out can occur, however, the person must have arrived at a lesbian identity. The process of identity development itself seems to proceed in six stages (Cass, 1979):

1. *Identity confusion.* The woman most likely began by assuming she was heterosexual because heterosexuality is so normative in our society. As same-gender attractions or behaviors occur, there is confusion. She wonders, "Who am I?"

2. *Identity comparison.* The woman now thinks, "I *may* be lesbian." There may be feelings of alienation because the comfortable heterosexual identity has been lost.

3. *Identity tolerance.* The woman now thinks, "I *probably* am lesbian." She seeks out other lesbians and makes contact with the lesbian community, hoping for affirmation. The quality of these initial contacts is critical.

4. *Identity acceptance.* The woman now thinks, "I am lesbian," and accepts rather than tolerates this identity.

5. *Identity pride.* The woman dichotomizes the world into lesbians and gays (who are good) and heterosexuals (who are not). There is strong identification with the lesbian group and increased coming out of the closet.

6. *Identity synthesis.* The person no longer holds an us-versus-them view of homosexuals and heterosexuals, and recognizes that there are some good and supportive heterosexuals. In this stage, the person is able to synthesize public and private identities.

The woman is very vulnerable in the process of coming out, whether in the lesbian community, to her old friends, or to her co-workers. Whether she experiences acceptance or rejection can be critical to self-esteem. The process of coming out can be highly stressful. There may also be fears of losing one's job or custody of one's children. Many lesbians make a decision to be selectively out— that is, to be out with people they know they can trust, and not with others.

Lesbians who are selectively out may face a distinct set of stresses. Consider a common situation in which a woman is not out at work, but is out in the lesbian community. At work, she must take care not to reveal her secret, be careful about the pronoun she uses when referring to her date, or worry that a worker will phone her at home and her partner will answer. On the other side, she may be pressured by the lesbian community to be completely out.

Some lesbians remember being lesbian ever since they became sexual, a pattern like that of almost all gay men. However, some lesbians come out in middle age, having been heterosexually married and had a heterosexual identity before that time (Burch, 1993).

Mental Health Issues

Lesbians' Adjustment   The majority of Americans disapprove of homosexuality and view it as abnormal. As noted earlier, in a well-sampled 1991 survey, 71 percent of the respondents said they believed that sexual relations between two adults of the same sex are always wrong; this statistic is essentially unchanged from 1973, when a similar survey was done (Davis and Smith, 1991). What scientific evidence is there regarding whether homosexuality is an abnormal form of adjustment?

To answer this question, I must first define what is meant by *abnormal.* A variety of definitions are possible (Hyde, 1994). The one that seems most appropriate here is that a sexual behavior is abnormal if it is associated with poor psychological adjustment and the person is unhappy about it.

Empirical research supports the view that lesbianism is not a deviant form of behavior (see the review by Rosen, 1974). First, much of the early research on lesbian adjustment studied lesbians who were in psychotherapy. The use of such respondents was not surprising, because these women were easy to recruit, and, with the assumption that lesbianism was an abnormal form of adjustment, the researcher could rationalize the sampling techniques by saying that the "typical" lesbian would be in therapy.

In view of the approach, it is not surprising that some of these early research efforts did find abnormal personality characteristics in lesbians. However, a major breakthrough occurred with the advent of research on *nonpatient* lesbians, recruited through homophile organizations or newspaper ads. Such studies have generally found that lesbian women do not differ psychologically from control groups of heterosexual women in any consistent ways, with the one exception of their choice of sex partner (Rosen, 1974). For example, in one large-scale study, lesbians and heterosexual women did not differ on most measures of adjustment (Bell and Weinberg, 1978). And in another study, lesbians had significantly higher self-esteem than college women (Spence and Helmreich, 1978; see also Green et al., 1986).

Thus the assumption that lesbianism is an inadequate form of adjustment is not supported by the available data, and, as Rosen concluded, "The only difference between the lesbian and other women is the choice of love object" (1974, p. 65). The comparative absence of psychological disturbance among lesbians is even more remarkable in view of the social pressures to which they are subject. The notion that lesbianism, and homosexuality more generally, is an adequate form of adjustment is reflected in the 1973 decision of the American Psychiatric Association to remove the term *homosexual* from its official list of diagnostic categories.

In one study the gender-role identities of lesbians were examined using the categories of androgynous, feminine, masculine, and undifferentiated discussed in Chapter 3 (Spence and Helmreich, 1978). The results, comparing lesbian women with college women, are shown in Table 12.2. It is true that a relatively

TABLE 12.2

Percentages of Lesbians and Unselected Female College Students in the Four Gender-Role Categories

	Gender-Role Category			
	Androgynous	*Feminine*	*Masculine*	*Undifferentiated*
Lesbians	33	13	22	32
College women	27	32	14	28

SOURCE: From *Masculinity and Femininity: Their Psychological Dimensions, Correlates, and Antecedents* by Janet T. Spence and Robert L. Helmreich, Copyright © 1978. By permission of the University of Texas Press.

low percentage of lesbians fall into the feminine category. We also find corresponding increases in the androgynous and masculine categories, and a slight increase in the undifferentiated category. The largest group of lesbians fall into the androgynous category. Given the earlier conclusions about androgyny being mentally healthy, this is a further indication that lesbianism is a healthy form of adjustment.

Rather than seeing lesbian identity as automatically causing adjustment problems or not causing problems, it is preferable to understand that being a lesbian may be a risk factor for some mental health problems and a protective factor from others. For example, the risk of alcohol use or abuse may be increased for those who socialize in bars, although a study using excellent sampling techniques found no differences between lesbian and heterosexual women in drinking patterns (Bloomfield, 1993). On the other hand, lesbians have fewer eating disorders and less preoccupation with weight than heterosexual women do (Brand, Rothblum, and Solomon, 1992).

Coping   There are stresses in lesbians' lives, some resulting from the kinds of discrimination discussed previously, some from the kinds of problems that everyone, heterosexual and homosexual alike, must deal with. How do lesbians cope? Far more research is needed in this area, but at least one study provides information (see also Brooks, 1981).

In this study, 79 lesbians, all working women, responded to a mailed questionnaire (Shachar and Gilbert, 1983). They were questioned about various conflicts they experienced and how they coped with them. Of the interrole conflicts—conflicts between two different roles that women must fulfill—the one most frequently mentioned was that between the lover and worker roles (mentioned by 41 percent of the women). As one woman commented,

> My lover wants the security of staying in one area and spending much time with me; I am very busy with my career . . . and I must move frequently to gain experience/opportunities. (Shachar and Gilbert, 1983, p. 249)

Other interrole conflicts mentioned with less frequency were conflicts between the roles of worker and political activist (13 percent), lover and daughter (7 percent), and lover and political activist (6 percent). Interestingly, certain other potential conflicts—for example, mother versus lover—were reported by no more than one respondent. On the other hand, those conflicts were rated as very stressful.

Intrarole conflicts are internal conflicts within a single role. As an area of intrarole conflict, work was mentioned most frequently (33 percent). One woman said,

> Expectations of co-workers and boss (all male) that I be heterosexual (dress, act, and have evidence of so being) when I really wish I could just be who I am

at work. I cannot, usually, because I am afraid of what'd result. (Shachar and Gilbert, 1983, p. 250)

On the other hand, the fact that one-third of the lesbian respondents reported intrarole conflicts at work implies that two-thirds do not experience such conflicts.

Coping mechanisms for dealing with role conflicts can be placed in three categories (Shachar and Gilbert, 1983):

1. Structural role redefinition—The individual deals directly with those people who communicate role demands and negotiates a change that is mutually acceptable.

2. Personal role redefinition—The individual changes her own perceptions of roles and role demands rather than changing the external environment.

3. Reactive behavior—The individual assumes that role demands are unchangeable and denies or tries to meet all role demands.

Generally, Type 1 or Type 2 coping is more successful, resulting in less stress and greater satisfaction with coping. In dealing with interrole conflicts, 82 percent of the lesbian respondents reported using Type 1 or Type 2 strategies. Further, those who used one of those two strategies had significantly higher self-esteem than those who used the Type 3 strategy. In general, then, the majority of lesbians use healthy strategies for coping with their stresses.

Children of Lesbian Mothers   As noted earlier, lesbian mothers often lose custody of children they had when heterosexually married, and being a lesbian may be grounds for being denied adoption (Falk, 1993). The underlying psychological assumption is that lesbians are bad mothers, in the sense that they will not do a good job rearing their children and the children will grow up poorly adjusted. There also is an assumption that these children will be stigmatized, teased by their peers, and so on. How well adjusted are the children of lesbian mothers?

Research has compared children of lesbian mothers with children of heterosexual parents on measures such as sexual identity, personal development, and social relationships. This research has found evidence that the children of lesbian mothers develop as well as children reared by heterosexual couples (Patterson, 1992).

Research has also shown that the child-rearing practices of lesbian mothers and heterosexual mothers are quite similar (Falk, 1993).

Regarding the issue of stigmatizing, one study found no differences between children from lesbian households and heterosexual households in peer group relationships, popularity, and social adjustment (Green et al., 1986).

In summary, although this research area is new and there are few studies, the evidence seems to indicate that there is no cause for concern about the adjustment of children growing up in a lesbian household.

Another concern is that lesbian parents might work to "convert" their chil-

FIGURE 12.2
An important political issue for lesbian couples is the right to have children. The child shown here was born to the woman holding her, as a result of artificial insemination.

dren to being lesbian or gay. In fact, the data indicate that children growing up with a gay or lesbian parent do not have an elevated incidence of being gay or lesbian (Green, 1978).

Theoretical Views

The Psychoanalytic View   Sigmund Freud was one of the first medical therapists to attempt the treatment of a lesbian, publishing his insights in a paper, "The Psychogenesis of a Case of Homosexuality in a Woman," in 1920.

Freud considered human beings to be bisexual in nature. In this assertion, he recognized that all humans are capable of homosexual behavior. According to Freud, the sources of sexual pleasure in the young are many and diffuse.

As noted in Chapter 2, at about age three the boy encounters the Oedipal complex. In the positive component of the complex, the mother is a love object for the boy and the father is the object of ambivalence. In resolving the Oedipal complex, the boy comes to identify with his father. A *negative Oedipal complex* occurs when the shift to identification with the father is not made, and the boy continues his initial identification with the mother, wanting (like her) to be loved by the father. According to Freud, people never really completely shed themselves of this negative component, but homosexual people remain fixated on it.

Freud initially viewed these psychological processes as highly similar for boys and for girls. It was some years before the gap between the logic of the theory and the realities of female development disposed Freud to a revised version of sexual development in women. He finally recognized that the boy's Oedipal development was far simpler than the girl's. The boy retains his original love object (mother), merely substituting another female for the original. For the girl, the mother is also the original love object, but the father must become the object. Thus presumably the negative Electra situation for the girl—in which she continues to love the same-gender parent, the mother—may well be more intense, last longer, and not be resolved. The lesbian alternative, according to Freud, occurs when the negative Electra component persists, so that mother and later other women are the object of love. The masculine component of the woman's personality is retained and the object choice is homosexual.

Freud speculated that the basis for homosexuality in men and in women may well be a matter of self-love, or *narcissism*. The outcome, then, is to love the self and to seek for a sex partner a same-gender person who resembles the self. From this perspective we may be seeing a positive aspect of lesbian development. A problem with "normal" female development is that many women end up with low self-confidence and low regard for other women. Lesbian development may be an alternative in which the self and the female can be loved and valued.

A Psychoanalytic Variant   In her book *Love Between Women* (1971), Charlotte Wolff provided a variant of the psychoanalytic model based on her research with nonpatient lesbians. Her theory of gender-role development in women emphasizes the normal, intense attachment of the young girl for her mother, wherein the mother is seen as all-powerful and godlike. It is not long before the developing girl realizes that the mother values males more highly than females in a man-valuing society, and that her chances of getting her mother's love are less than her father and brother have. This perception that the mother values her own gender less leads the developing girl to be insecure about her own value.

In a sense, then, the mother gives a second-rate status to the young girl. At this point the girl may choose to pursue one of two strategies for dealing with this situation: she may strive to be a very feminine female, ingratiating herself to the mother (the heterosexual course); or she may seek to become like the superior gender, becoming masculine and competitive (the lesbian course). More commonly, she chooses the first course of action, becoming like the mother and emulating those many aspects of femininity that the mother models.

According to Wolff's theory the homosexual woman has chosen a different strategy and therefore need not play such games. She fights for equality with men in order to be worthy of her mother's love. "Emotional incest with the mother is indeed the very essence of lesbianism" (p. 72). Further, there is a suggestion that males are basically alien to the lesbian. Wolff found that many of the lesbians she studied had a history of a father who was absent for a substantial period during their childhood—for example, during a war. Such girls grow up in a basically feminine world in which males are strange and alien. Thus, according to Wolff's view, lesbianism arises from the girl's taking a masculine, competitive strategy to deal with the insufficiency of her mother's love.

Wolff's theory rests on the questionable assumption that the mother is the girl's only real love object, that the girl continues to seek the mother's love throughout life, and that males are loved or manipulated only as a substitute. Further, Wolff commits an error similar to Freud's in confusing gender identity with choice of sexual partner—that is, she assumes that lesbian development leads to masculinity. Yet empirical research shows that lesbians generally have a feminine or androgynous identification, and that they may be aggressive and competitive, or passive and shy, just as heterosexual women may. Wolff assumes that all lesbians enter into direct competition with males, another questionable assumption. Nonetheless, her theory and research give some insights into the emotional and love aspects of lesbianism.

Learning Theory Learning theory (Bermant, 1972; Ford and Beach, 1951; McConaghy, 1987) emphasizes the point that all animals, including humans, display or are capable of homosexual activities. Thus, animals appear to be innately bisexual, and the environment may have a great influence on whether one or another choice of sex partner is made. In some primitive cultures, a male may be the appropriate sex partner for a young male, whereas in his adulthood the accepted partner may be a female (Herdt, 1984).

Therefore humans may have no inborn preference for the other gender as an appropriate sex partner, but the nature of conditioning and socialization channels this disposition. That is, cultural pressures channel a generalized drive in a culturally prescribed direction. Ford and Beach (1951), in their classic work on sexual behavior in humans and animals, gave detailed evidence of the bisexual inheritance of humans that tends to confirm the above notion. One might conclude that heterosexual behavior is an acquired, that is, a learned, state of being. Learning theory points out that heterosexual development is actually far more chancy than most people realize. We should ask not only, Why do lesbians develop? but also, Why do heterosexuals develop?

The learning theory view, then, is that humans have a general pool of sex drives that may, depending on experience and circumstance, be conditioned in one direction or another, into heterosexuality or into homosexuality. One problem with this view is that it assumes that gay male and lesbian development are similar. This would seem unlikely in view of the different experiences and status of men and women in our culture. On the other hand, the learning theory model readily accommodates lesbianism as a normal form of behavior, in contrast to the psychoanalytic theories, which treat it as deviant or compensatory.

The Feminist and Sociological Perspectives Feminists and modern sociologists have rather similar things to say about lesbianism, and so I have grouped them here. One of the main points of the feminist perspective is that, when trying to understand the behavior of a woman, the emphasis should be shifted away from *internal factors* (her personality, adjustment, early childhood) to *external factors* (institutions, laws, interactions with others). (See Chapter 2.) Sociological theories share this emphasis on external factors. They agree with the feminist perspective in criticizing previous theories for focusing too much on internal factors, such as disturbances in early childhood. They hold instead that researchers should focus on external forces acting on lesbians: institutions and laws discriminating against lesbians and stereotypes that produce unpleasant interactions with others.

Sociologists also focus on *norms,* rules for behavior that are understood by the people in a culture and that guide their behavior. Feminists point out that heterosexuality is a strong—indeed, a coercive—norm in our society. The term *compulsory heterosexuality* has been used to describe this norm (Rich, 1980). Thus lesbians can be understood as norm-violators, much as women who achieve are also norm-violators.

Both sociologists and feminists, then, view lesbians as a minority group (Brooks, 1981). As such, lesbians are denied civil rights, much as African Amer-

FIGURE 12.3
Lesbian social issues. In a march in New York, lesbians protest the fact they have been invisible in many ways, including in history. At the same time, they celebrate new archives to record their history.

icans have been denied those rights. They are also prevented from contributing to various social institutions that affect their lives—it is doubtful, for example, that an out-of-the-closet lesbian could be elected to most state legislatures. Lesbians, then, can be seen as occupying two minority statuses.

When lesbians have sought psychotherapy, traditional psychologists have assumed that the sexual orientation itself was the pathology. In contrast, feminists and sociologists see the problems of lesbians as resulting from the stress that falls on them because they are a minority group (Brooks, 1981). The emphasis in therapy, then, would be not on changing the woman's sexual orientation, but on helping her develop skills for coping with the stresses she experiences in a homophobic society. Research shows that three resources help lesbians cope with stress: positive identification as a lesbian, having higher socioeconomic status, and coming out of the closet or self-disclosing one's sexual orientation (Brooks, 1981).

Existentialism and Lesbianism   Existential philosophy maintains that anyone can change his or her self-view and view of the world at any time and can thus profoundly alter the course of his or her life—that humans are always free to reappraise their own condition and to take some action to alter it. People need not rely forever on the "crutches" of morals, social expectations, and past habits, but can in their own lives think for themselves and disavow all those things that they have been in the past. The only dictum is that humans should be authentic, and *authenticity* demands that one accept full responsibility for one's actions.

The existentialist who has commented most on lesbianism is the famous French philosopher Simone de Beauvoir (1952). Exemplifying the existentialist theme, she insists that "the truth is that homosexuality [lesbianism] is no more perversion deliberately indulged in than it is a curse of fate. It is an attitude *chosen in a certain situation*—that is at once motivated and freely adopted" (p. 398, italics de Beauvoir's). She views female homosexuality not as a compensatory condition of life, but as an instance of self-reappraisal and choice. Further, de Beauvoir agrees with the view that all women have a natural homosexual component. Thus, lesbianism from this viewpoint is merely the reflection of conscious choice and a willingness to accept the responsibilities for such a choice.

A woman who enters upon heterosexual relations enters upon a social contract society expects and reinforces. It appears to require much greater, not less, emotional strength and conviction (authenticity) for a woman to enter upon a homosexual relationship, risking social rejection. So, according to the existentialists, in some sense it requires a much more integrated woman to make the choice to be a lesbian.

Some Final Thoughts About the Theoretical Perspectives   Psychoanalysts, learning theorists, feminists, sociologists, and existentialists all have rather different things to say about lesbianism. Psychoanalysts and learning theorists focus on what causes lesbianism to develop. Feminists, sociologists, and existentialists reject the search for causes. Instead, they focus on understanding the lesbian's current experiences. Increasingly—though there are exceptions—that is the trend in research: to investigate the experiences of lesbians in trying to build strong romantic relationships, in dealing with co-workers, or in trying to balance love, work, and children.

Research on the Genesis of Lesbianism

Having tried to understand the nature of lesbian development through theoretical approaches, I must next bring these ideas to the test by comparing them with the available empirical data on the life histories and family backgrounds of lesbians, to see what factors appear to predispose a woman to choose another woman as her sexual and love partner.

There have been numerous speculations as to the factors causing lesbianism. As Rosen summarized them, they include

> fear of growing up and assuming adult responsibilities; fear of dominance and destruction; fear of rejection; fear of the opposite sex; fear of castration and of the penis; the desire to conquer and possess the mother; neurotic dependency; heterosexual trauma (including rape); seduction in adolescence by an older female; first sexual experience with someone of the same sex and finding it pleasurable; tomboy behavior in early childhood; prolonged absence of the mother; masturbation with a resulting clitoral fixation; social factors (such as heterosexual taboos and unisexual, all female, groups); and physical factors (genetic, constitutional, and endocrine abnormalities). (1974, p. 8)

What is striking in much of this research is that lesbians have not been studied; they have been invisible. For example, in a recent highly publicized study, neuroscientist Simon LeVay (1991) investigated differences in the hypothalamus between heterosexuals and homosexuals. There were three study groups: gay men, heterosexual men, and heterosexual women. There was no lesbian group.

A recent study raised the possibility that there is a genetic basis for sexual orientation (Bailey et al., 1993; for a critique, see Byne and Parsons, 1993). This study found a concordance rate for lesbian orientation of 48 percent for identical twins ("concordance" means that if one member of the twin pair is lesbian, so is the other). This was as compared with a concordance rate of 16 percent for nonidentical twins and 6 percent for adoptive sisters. The fact that identical twins have a much higher concordance rate than nonidentical twins is taken as evidence that there is a genetic basis. On the other hand, the 48 percent concordance rate means that 52 percent of the identical twin pairs are discordant—one is lesbian and the other heterosexual. If sexual orientation were completely genetically determined, there would be 100 percent concordance. Therefore, environmental factors must also be influential.

To be blunt, the state of the research is that no one really knows what causes lesbianism or heterosexuality to develop. In a major study of the development of sexual orientation, Kinsey Institute researchers Alan Bell, Martin Weinberg, and Sue Hammersmith (1981) reported on interviews with 979 homosexual and 477 heterosexual women and men living in the San Francisco area. The questions used in each interview covered a wide variety of topics, including early home life and previous sexual experiences, designed to test some of the theories proposed to account for the development of homosexuality. Their results showed *no* evidence for the following common explanations: (1) The psychoanalytic view is that homosexuality results from a disturbed early family experience, including dominant mothers or weak or detached fathers. There was little or no difference in family experiences between homosexuals and heterosexuals. (2) The learning theory view is that homosexuality results from conditioning, either in early unpleasant heterosexual experiences or in early pleasant homosexual experiences. Homosexuals were no more likely than heterosexuals to have had negative experiences such as rape or parental punishment for early heterosexual sex play with children of the opposite gender; nor were they more likely to have been seduced by an older person.

This same study has been widely cited in the press for its conclusion that homosexuality is biologically determined. However, if one reads the study critically, one notes that the researchers collected no biological data, such as measuring hormone levels. They speculated about biological causes only because all of the standard environment explanations failed the test of their data. The best conclusion, then, is that the cause of homosexuality remains unknown.

Perhaps the failure of research to uncover a consistent single "cause" of lesbianism is a result of the fact that there is no single cause, just as there is no single "lesbian personality." Variability among lesbians is great, and lesbians come in all sizes, shapes, and personality types, just as heterosexuals do. "Lesbian" is not a homogeneous category, although we have been misled into thinking it is because of the superficial similarity that all lesbians direct their erotic and emotional orientation toward other women. Because the category is non-homogeneous, a single cause would not be expected. In this chapter, I have referred to "lesbianism," using a single label with the understanding that it refers to a wide variety of behaviors, experiences, and developmental processes. Indeed, it has been recommended that we stop using the term *homosexuality* and substitute *homosexualities* (Bell, 1974) to recognize more adequately the diversity and heterogeneity of the category.

Differences Between Lesbians and Gay Men

Theorists frequently refer to homosexuality as if there were no difference between male and female homosexuality (or else as if male homosexuality were the only phenomenon of interest or concern). The interesting question arises as to whether these two phenomena are in fact different.

There do appear to be some differences between gay men and lesbians. First, lesbians appear to place more emphasis on the emotional intimacy of their relationship than gay men do (Peplau, 1982). Second, male homosexuals frequently have many different sex partners, whereas lesbians more often form long-term, exclusive relationships (Loney, 1972). In one study of female and male homosexuals, the males reported a median (average) of 75 different partners, contrasted with a median of 5 for the females; 56 percent of the men had had 50 or more partners, but only 5 percent of the women had had that number (Schafer, 1977). In a study of couples who had been together more than two years (often many more), 79 percent of the gay men had had sex with another partner in the previous year, compared with 19 percent for lesbians, and 11 percent for heterosexually married husbands and 9 percent for wives (Blumstein and Schwartz, 1983). Third, men with a male partner have sex (defined as genital sex) considerably more frequently than women with a female partner (Peplau, 1993). Gay men seem to be more interested in sexual activity, whereas lesbians emphasize companionship, affection, and emotional support (Bell and Weinberg, 1978). Fourth, the prevailing view, based on older research, was that bisexuality was more characteristic of lesbians and that exclusive homosexuality was less common than among gay men. According to the 1940s Kinsey data, 13 percent of adult women had had at least one same-gender sexual experience, but only about 1 percent were exclusively lesbian. However, a recent, well sampled survey showed somewhat different results (Laumann et al., 1994). Among people who reported having had at least one same-gender sexual partner, 38 percent of the women had had both male and female partners, compared with 28 percent of the men. That is, the incidence of bisexual behavior is somewhat higher in women than in men, but the difference is not large.

Psychologist Michael Storms (1981; see also Bermant, 1972) has constructed a theory of the development of erotic orientation that neatly explains some of these statistics, particularly that more men than women have had homosexual experiences. According to this theory, most people develop the sex drive in early adolescence, around the ages of 12 to 15. It is at that time that certain stimuli (e.g., a member of the same or the other gender) become conditioned to be arousing or erotic. If one examines the social patterns of preadolescents and adolescents, it is clear that homosocial patterns (same-gender friendships and groups) predominate in preadolescence, reaching a peak at around age 12. Heterosexual interactions begin to emerge after that time, and most people have engaged in heterosexual dating by age 15. According to Storms, homosexuality results when individuals have an early maturing sex drive, at about age 12, when they are still in homosocial groupings, so that erotic conditioning is more likely to focus on members of their own gender, because heterosexuality has not yet emerged as an alternative.

Supporting Storms's theory, data show that homosexual women are earlier sexual maturers than heterosexual women, as measured by age of beginning to masturbate, age of earliest feelings of sexual arousal, and age of first sexual fantasizing (Goode and Haber, 1977; Saghir and Robins, 1973). This theory therefore explains why there are more men than women who have experienced homosexual activity and who are exclusively homosexual: the sex drive in males emerges earlier, as evidenced by the more frequent and earlier appearance of masturbation, a point discussed in the previous chapter. Females are more likely to experience the emergence of their sex drive later, after heterosexuality has become the norm in their lives. In addition, it could be argued that the models girls are taught to emulate from their early years are more explicitly bound up with heterosexuality (wife, mother) than the models boys are taught to emulate (involving careers or sports) are. The theory is a recent one, and so it should not yet be accepted as definitive, but it does provide some intriguing ideas.

In sum, gay men and lesbians appear to be similar only in a superficial sense. The differences between the two are logical consequences of psychological differences between the genders and differences in their developmental experiences. Indeed, although it has been found that one's gender is a fairly good predictor of a number of psychological characteristics, one's homosexual status is not (Bell, 1974). Therefore, a lesbian is probably more like a heterosexual woman than she is like a gay man. Her identity is first as a woman and second as a lesbian.

Lesbians and Ethnicity

Lesbians who are women of color experience triple oppression: discrimination on the basis of gender, race, and sexual orientation. For the individual woman, there may be conflicts between lesbian identity and ethnic identity, because some ethnic groups in the United States have even more negative attitudes toward lesbians than Anglo society does.

As an example, we will consider Latina lesbians (Espin, 1987b, 1993). Although in Latin cultures emotional and physical closeness among women is considered acceptable and desirable, attitudes toward lesbianism are even more restrictive than in Euro-American culture. For instance, research indicates that most Puerto Ricans strongly reject lesbianism (Hidalgo and Hidalgo-Christenson, 1976). The special emphasis on family—defined as mother, father, children, and grandparents—in Latin cultures makes the lesbian even more of an outsider (Espin, 1987b). As a result, Latina lesbians often become part of a Euro-American lesbian community while remaining in the closet with their family and among Latinos, creating difficult choices among identities. As one Cuban woman responded to a questionnaire, "I identify myself as a lesbian more intensely than as Cuban/Latin. But it is a very painful question because I feel that I am both, and I don't want to have to choose" (Espin, 1987b, p. 47).

As a second example, we will consider Asian American lesbians (Chan, 1993). In one study, Asian American lesbians felt more strongly identified with their lesbian than with their Asian American identity (Chan, 1993). Some of the issues are the same as they are for Latina lesbians. In Asian cultures, being lesbian is typically viewed as a rejection of the most important roles for women, being a wife and mother. In addition, if a daughter is lesbian, there is an implication that the parents have failed in their role and that the child is rejecting the im-

FIGURE 12.4
Lesbians who are women of color may experience multiple forms of discrimination—on the basis of gender, sexual orientation, and ethnicity.

portance of family and Asian culture. Indeed, in Asian cultures it is often denied that Asian American lesbians and gay men exist—homosexuality is seen as a white, Western phenomenon (Chan, 1993; Ruan and Bullough, 1992). Asian American lesbians therefore face a conflict between ethnic identity and lesbian identity.

We have seen many times in this book that women have been rendered invisible in everything from history to science. Lesbians who are women of color are, in a sense, triply invisible—invisible because they are women, because they are people of color, and because they are lesbian. They deserve much more attention in psychological research in the future, for their complex identities have much to tell us about the interplay of gender, race, and sexuality.

Bisexual Women

Bisexuality: Being erotically and emotionally attracted to both females and males.

Bisexuality refers to being erotically and emotionally attracted to both males and females. As noted earlier, using this definition, bisexuality is actually more common than exclusive homosexuality is. For example, in a well sampled study, women were asked about their sexual partners in the past five years (Laumann et al., 1994);

FOCUS 12.1
JOAN, A BISEXUAL WOMAN

Joan, a professional woman in her middle thirties, considered herself exclusively heterosexual until about four years ago. Until that time she had never had homosexual fantasies or feelings, but she had been generally liberal about "sexual alternatives" and believed in equal rights for homosexuals. Four years ago, however, Joan became active in the women's liberation movement and developed closer friendships with some of the women with whom she worked. None of these relationships was sexualized, but her curiosity was aroused by sexual possibilities with women. Her approach to her own potential homosexual behavior was at this time still more intellectual than emotional and was not accompanied by graphic fantasies or feelings of attraction to other women whom she might meet or see in public.

During this period, Joan met another woman in her profession whom she found both intellectually and socially attractive. Vivian was also heterosexual, but she had had a few homosexual experiences. The relationship between the two women became closer, and during an exchange of confidences Joan learned that Vivian had had sexual experiences with women. At this point, Joan began to have sexual fantasies involving Vivian and began to be more overtly physical toward her, but she never crossed the bounds of female heterosexual friendship. The relationship intensified, and intimate discussions about sexuality turned to the possibility of sex between the two women. After about six months of such discussions, they slept together, first having overcome their initial worries concerning the effect that any guilt feelings about their "experimentation" might have on their friendship.

After the first successful sexual experience, Joan and Vivian repeated it approximately once every month for over a year. Vivian, however, continued to think of herself as a heterosexual, while Joan began to feel that she was in love with her friend and to want a more committed relationship. Joan stopped sleeping with Vivian when she realized that Vivian did not agree with her terms for the relationship. The two remained close friends, but Joan looked for someone else who might wish to share a committed relationship. She eventually fell in love with another woman, and an intense romantic and sexual relationship continued for two years. At the present, Joan is unsure of what sexual label to apply to herself, but she prefers "bisexual." At the time of her interview, she had both a male and a female lover.

SOURCE: Blumstein and Schwartz (1976), 156–157.

1.4 percent reported having both male and female partners, compared with only .8 percent reporting female partners only. That is, about twice as many were bisexual as were exclusively lesbian. The comparable statistics for men were 2.1 percent and 2.0 percent. Bisexuals are more than just a third category, although they are that. But they reveal the enormous variability and complexity of human sexual expression.

The case of Joan, a bisexual woman, is offered in Focus 12.1 to illustrate the life experience of a bisexual woman. One interesting fact that emerges from such cases is that women often become bisexual after a long history of exclusive heterosexuality or exclusive homosexuality, at relatively late ages (Blumstein and Schwartz, 1976).

Sociologists Philip Blumstein and Pepper Schwartz (1976, 1993) conducted interviews with bisexual women. On the basis of these interviews, they concluded that a number of factors contributed to a woman with a lesbian history moving toward bisexuality. Most lesbians—probably 50 to 80 percent (Hedblom, 1972; Saghir and Robins, 1973)—have had at least some heterosexual experience, including intercourse. When these are recalled as pleasurable it is reasonable to return to them later in life. Another factor is all the social rewards in our society that go with a heterosexual lifestyle, including having a husband and children. Bisexuality can be a way of avoiding the social ostracism that lesbians must often face, while still engaging in some lesbian activity. On the other hand, some forces discourage the movement from lesbianism to bisexuality. Many lesbians receive their major emotional support in a lesbian community, and they stand to lose this if they adopt bisexuality. Some lesbians view bisexual women with suspicion or downright hostility.

Blumstein and Schwartz feel that a number of factors contribute to heterosexual women moving in a bisexual direction. They believe that women learn, as part of learning how to compete with women in being attractive to men, what is attractive in other women. They thereby become aware of erotic qualities in other women. Furthermore, women are more permitted to be emotionally and physically expressive toward one another in our society, once again making a move toward bisexuality easier. As part of the more liberated sexual standards in recent years, some people experiment with having sex in groups of more than two persons at once, allowing an opportunity to experiment with lesbianism. Finally, the women's movement has created an environment that is relatively supportive of lesbianism, and some heterosexual women decide to experiment with lesbianism, and thereby become bisexuals, out of feminist convictions.

In Conclusion

This chapter has been based on the assumption—supported by the available data—that lesbianism is a normal form of behavior, and that lesbians and bisexual women are just as diverse in their physical attributes, personality characteristics, occupations, ethnicity, and family backgrounds as heterosexual women.

Lesbians frequently are stereotyped and may be the objects of various forms of discrimination, including hate crimes. A lesbian culture or community now exists in cities and towns around the world. The process of lesbian identification and coming out proceeds in several stages, beginning with identity confusion and eventually moving to identity synthesis. Theoretical views of the nature of lesbianism are varied. Psychoanalytic theory sees it as an outcome of a persisting negative Electra complex, so that the woman continues to love her mother, and later other women, throughout her life. Wolff's neoanalytic theory sees lesbianism as a continued competition with males for the mother's love, which the lesbian was deprived of as a child. Learning theory stresses that sex drive is a generalized drive that is channeled toward one or another object through conditioning; thus both heterosexuality and homosexuality are learned. Sociologists and feminists are more concerned with the impact on lesbians of institutions and norms. Existentialism does not concern itself with the developmental origins of lesbianism, but instead treats it simply as a free and legitimate choice. Research on the development of lesbianism suggests that there is probably no one single causal factor. Male and female homosexuality are different in nature as a consequence of psychological and developmental differences between females and males. Women of color who are lesbians experience triple oppression: on the basis of their gender, their race, and their sexual orientation.

Research on lesbianism is in its infancy, and the conclusions we draw must be tentative. Certainly the nature of research on lesbianism is changing as scientists shed the assumption that it is a form of pathology. We now no longer seek

EXPERIENCE THE RESEARCH

LESBIAN COMMUNITY

Does your campus have a gay/lesbian speakers' bureau? (If not, why do you think there is none?) Contact the speakers' bureau and arrange for three lesbians to attend your class to lead a panel discussion. When the speakers attend your class, have them introduce themselves first and then follow a question-and-answer format with the class. Be sure that the following questions are asked of the women:

1. What is your experience of the lesbian community? Explain, for a heterosexual audience, the features of the lesbian community.
2. Have you ever been the object of a hate crime because you are lesbian? What happened?
3. Describe the process of coming out as you experienced it.

to find what disturbances in development would create lesbianism; instead, we ask what developmental factors would lead a woman to develop heterosexuality or homosexuality or bisexuality. Indeed, some have argued that lesbianism is preferable to heterosexuality. As Szasz provocatively suggested:

> We might even advocate homosexuality over heterosexuality: this choice could be supported as a contraceptive technique, especially for women intellectually or artistically gifted, for whom the value of traditional feminine heterosexuality is a barrier to achievement. (1965, p. 137)

Suggestions for Further Reading

Boston Lesbian Psychologies Collective. (1987). *Lesbian psychologies.* Urbana, IL: University of Illinois Press. This book presents some of the most recent thinking by feminist psychologists about the lesbian experience.

Brown, Rita Mae. (1977). *Rubyfruit jungle.* New York: Bantam Books (paperback). This semiautobiographical novel gives a view of lesbianism that is both insightful and hilarious. It is delightful reading.

Herek, Gregory M., Kimmel, Douglas C., Amaro, Hortensia, & Melton, Gary B. (1991). Avoiding heterosexist bias in psychological research. *American Psychologist, 46,* 957–963. Just as in Chapter 1 we examined how psychological research has been based on male models and is sexist, so this article examines how research has been based on heterosexual models, and suggests ways to correct this problem.

Hutchins, Loraine, & Kaahumanu, Lani. (1991). *Bi any other name: Bisexual people speak out.* Boston: Alyson. This book explores the often misunderstood and neglected topic of bisexuality by sharing the personal stories of bisexuals.

Lorde, Audre. (1982). *Zami: A new spelling of my name.* Watertown, MA: Persephone Press. This well-known feminist writer explores what it means to be lesbian in the Black community.

Penelope, Julia, & Wolfe, Susan. (1989). *The original coming out stories.* Freedom, CA: Crossing Press. This book contains a collection of stories written about the personal experiences of women coming out and coming to terms with their identities as lesbians.

13

The Victimization of Women

> *Rape is a crime against the person, not against the hymen.*

DEENA METZGER, THE RAPE VICTIM

On December 6, 1989, a young man carrying a rifle invaded the engineering school at the University of Montreal. He rushed from room to room, shooting women. In some cases, women were told to line up against one wall and men against another; the women were then killed. By the time he was finished, 14 women were dead. He then killed himself (Associated Press, December 7, 1989).

This shocking incident drew strong emotional responses from women around the world. The symbolism of separating people by gender and then murdering those who were female seemed to embody the whole issue of systematic violence by men against women.

The women's movement, beginning in the early 1970s, brought the issue of the victimization of women into the public spotlight. Rape was the first topic to be addressed. Feminists assert that rape is one of the ways in which men exercise power and control over women (e.g., Brownmiller, 1975). More recently, attention has been drawn to the plight of battered women, to girls who are the victims of incest, and to the issue of sexual harassment. These topics have moved from being something a woman felt she should hide to being a subject of public debate.

This chapter is about the victimization of women as seen in rape, woman-beating, incest, and sexual harassment. A discussion of all aspects of these problems (e.g., legal, self-defense) is beyond the scope of this book. Here I will concentrate on the psychological aspects.

Rape

Rape: Nonconsenting oral, anal, or vaginal penetration obtained by force, by threat of bodily harm, or when the victim is incapable of giving consent.

Definition **Rape** is typically defined, following current laws in many states, as "nonconsensual oral, anal, or vaginal penetration, obtained by force, by threat of bodily harm, or when the victim is incapable of giving consent" (Koss, 1993, p. 1062; see also Searles and Berger, 1987). Notice that the definition includes not only forced vaginal intercourse, but forced oral sex and anal sex as well. The issue is that the activity is nonconsensual—that is, the victim did not consent to it. One type of nonconsent occurs when the victim is incapable of giving consent, perhaps because she is drunk, unconscious, or high on some type of drug.

Because this book is on the psychology of women, we will focus on rape of women by men, although certainly there are cases of men raping men and rare reports of women raping men.

Incidence Statistics In 1992 there were 102,500 cases of reported rape in the United States; that means there were 85 reported rapes for every 100,000 women (FBI, 1993). However, according to the FBI, forcible rape is one of the most

FIGURE 13.1
A key point of the feminist perspective is that gender roles have been and continue to be a powerful force casting women as victims. *(Source: Steiner/Cartoonists and Writers Syndicate)*

underreported crimes. One study found that only about one in five (21 percent) of stranger rapes had been reported, and only 2 percent of acquaintance rapes had been reported to the police (Koss et al., 1988). Based on interviews with a random sample of San Francisco women, researchers concluded—after adjusting for age—that there is a 26 percent chance that a woman will be the victim of a completed rape at some time in her life (Russell and Howell, 1983). A well-sampled national study of women college students found that 28 percent had experienced an act that met the legal definition of rape (Koss et al., 1987). Statistics vary somewhat from one study to another, but most find that the lifetime chance of a woman being raped is between 14 and 25 percent (Koss, 1993).

The Impact of Rape A large number of studies have investigated the psychological reactions of women following rape (e.g., Burgess and Holmstrom, 1974a, 1974b; Calhoun et al., 1982; Kilpatrick et al., 1981; Resick, 1983, 1987; see review by Koss, 1993). This research shows that rape is a time of crisis for a woman and that the effects on her adjustment may persist for a year or more. The term **rape trauma syndrome** has been used to refer to the emotional and physical effects a woman undergoes following a rape or an attempted rape (Burgess and Holmstrom, 1974a).

Rape trauma syndrome: The emotional and physical effects a woman undergoes following a rape or attempted rape.

Emotional reactions immediately after a rape (the acute phase) are generally severe. The high levels of distress generally reach a peak three weeks after the assault and then continue at a high level for the next month. A gradual improvement then begins two or three months after the assault (Koss, 1993; Rothbaum et al., 1992). Many differences between raped and nonvictimized women disappear after three months, except that raped women continue to report more fear, anxiety, self-esteem problems, and sexual dysfunctions. These effects may persist for 18 months or longer (Koss, 1993).

Some women experience self-blame. The woman may spend hours agonizing over what she did to bring on the rape or what she might have done to prevent it: "If I hadn't worn that tight sweater . . ."; "If I hadn't worn that short skirt . . ."; If I hadn't been dumb enough to walk on that dark street . . ."; "If I hadn't been stupid enough to trust that guy. . . . " This is an example of a tendency on the part of both the victim and others to *blame the victim.*

Researchers are finding increased evidence of the damage to women's *physical health* that results from violence such as rape and battering (Heise, 1993; Koss et al., 1991; Koss and Heslet, 1992). The woman may have physical injuries from the rape, such as cuts and bruises. Women who have been forced to have oral sex may suffer irritation or damage to the throat; rectal bleeding and pain are reported by women forced to have anal intercourse. The woman may contract a sexually transmitted disease, such as HIV/AIDS or herpes, from the rape. She may become pregnant; in about 5 percent of rape cases, pregnancy results (Koss et al., 1991). Women who have been sexually or physically assaulted at some time in their past visit their physician twice as often per year as nonvictimized women (Koss et al., 1991).

Recently it has been suggested that, rather than focusing on rape trauma syndrome, a "women's issue," we should instead recognize that rape victims are experiencing **post-traumatic stress disorder** (e.g., Koss, 1993). Post-traumatic stress disorder (PTSD) is an official diagnosis that was originally developed to describe the long-term psychological distress suffered by war veterans, most of whom are men. Symptoms can include anxiety, depression, nightmares, and a lack of feeling of safety. According to a cognitive-behavioral view of PTSD, people who have experienced a terrifying event form a memory schema that involves information about the situation and their responses to it (Foa et al., 1989). Because the schema is large, many cues can trigger it and therefore evoke the feelings of terror that occurred at the time; the schema is probably activated at some level all the time. Schemas also affect how we interpret new events, so that the consequences are far-reaching and long-lasting.

Post-traumatic stress disorder (PTSD): Long-term psychological distress suffered by someone who has experienced a terrifying, uncontrollable event.

Approximately half of college-age women who have been the victims of forced, nonconsensual sexual intercourse do not label the experience as rape, nor themselves as rape victims (Kahn et al., 1994). Why do some women fail to realize that they have been raped? We will call these women "unacknowledged victims," and those who realize that they were raped, "acknowledged victims." The difference lies in their rape scripts (Kahn et al., 1994). Unacknowledged victims are more likely to have a violent, stranger rape script for rape, whereas acknowledged victims are more likely to include acquaintance rape in their rape script. Unacknowledged victims often have experienced an acquaintance rape, which does not match their rape script, so they do not label the event as rape.

Rape affects many people besides the victim. Most women perform a number of behaviors that stem basically from rape fears. For example, a single woman is not supposed to list her full first name in the telephone book, because that is a giveaway that she is alone. Rather, she should list a first initial or a man's name. Many women, when getting into their car at night, almost reflexively check the backseat to make sure no one is hiding there. Most college

FIGURE 13.2
Female karate instructor and her student. Many experts feel that women should learn self-defense skills as a way of combating rape.

women avoid walking alone through dark parts of the campus at night. At least once in their lives, most women have been afraid of spending the night alone. If you are a woman, you can probably extend the list from your own experience. The point is that most women experience the fear of rape, if not rape itself (Burt and Estep, 1981; Warr, 1985). Furthermore, this fear restricts their activities.

Date Rape   In Mary Koss's national study of college women, among those who had experienced an act that met the legal definition of rape, 57 percent of the rapes involved a date (Koss et al., 1988; Koss and Cook, 1994). Date rape is one of the most common forms of rape, especially on college campuses.

In some cases, date rape seems to result from astounding male-female miscommunication. The traditional view in dating relationships has been that if the woman says no, she really means yes. Men need to learn that no means no. Consider this example of miscommunication and different perceptions in a case of date rape:

BOB: Patty and I were in the same statistics class together. She usually sat near me and was always very friendly. I liked her and thought maybe she liked me, too. Last Thursday I decided to find out. After class I suggested that she come to my place to study for midterms together. She agreed immediately, which was a good sign. That night everything seemed to go perfectly. We studied for a while and then took a break. I could tell that she liked me, and I was attracted to her. I was getting excited. I started kissing her. I could tell that she really liked it. We started touching each other and it felt really good. All of a sudden she pulled away and said "Stop." I figured she didn't want me to think that she was "easy" or "loose." A lot of girls think they have to say "no" at first. I knew once I showed her what a good time she could have, and that I would respect her in the morning, it would be OK. I just ignored her protests and eventually she stopped struggling. I think she liked it but afterwards she acted bummed out and cold. Who knows what her problem was?

PATTY: I knew Bob from my statistics class. He's cute and we are both good at statistics, so when a tough midterm was scheduled, I was glad that he suggested we study together. It never occurred to me that it was anything except a study date. That night everything went fine at first, we got a lot of studying done in a short amount of time, so when he suggested we take a break I thought we deserved it. Well, all of a sudden he started acting really romantic and started kissing me. I liked the kissing but then he started touching me below the waist. I pulled away and tried to stop him but he didn't listen. After a while I stopped struggling; he was hurting me and I was scared. He was so much bigger and stronger than me. I couldn't believe it was happening to me. I didn't know what to do. He actually forced me to have sex with him. I guess looking back on it I should have screamed or done something besides trying to reason with him but it was so unexpected. I couldn't believe it was happening. I still can't believe it did. (Hughes and Sandler, 1987, p. 1)

Kanin (1985) studied 71 unmarried college men who had disclosed they were date rapists, comparing them with a control group of unmarried college men. The date rapists tended to be sexually predatory. For example, when asked how frequently they attempt to seduce a new date, 62 percent of the rapists said "most of the time," compared with 19 percent of the men in the control group. The rapists were also much more likely to report using a variety of manipulative techniques with their dates, including getting them high on alcohol or marijuana, falsely professing love, and falsely promising "pinning," engagement, or marriage.

In summary, the consistent findings in studies of date rape are that such incidents are not rare, but rather are fairly common even in "normal" populations.

Marital Rape The possibility that a man could rape his wife was brought to public attention in 1978 when Greta Rideout sued her husband for marital rape. Defining marital rape is complicated by the fact that in many states, rape laws exclude the possibility of marital rape; the assumption has been that sex in marriage is always the husband's "right." This is a legacy of the Hale doctrine, formulated by Lord Matthew Hale in the seventeenth century, which states that "the husband cannot be guilty of a rape committed by himself upon his lawful wife, for by their mutual matrimonial consent and a contract the wife hath given up herself in this kind unto her husband which she cannot retract" (Whatley, 1993).

How common is marital rape? In a random sample of San Francisco women, 12 percent of the married women reported that they had experienced some form of forced sex in marriage (Russell, 1982). Other studies generally find that the prevalence of marital rape in the general population is between 7 and 14 percent (Whatley, 1993).

One phenomenon that emerges in research on marital rape is an association between it and marital violence—that is, the man who batters his wife is also likely to rape her. For example, in a study of 137 women who had reported being physically assaulted by their husbands, 34 percent reported being raped by their husbands (Frieze, 1983). The fact that some women are unwilling to define certain acts as marital rape is evident from the 43 percent of that sample (more than the number who reported being raped) who said that sex was unpleasant because it was forced upon them by their husbands. Asked why they had been raped, 78 percent said the cause was the husband's belief that the act would prove his manhood. An additional 14 percent attributed the rapes to the husband's drinking. The psychological consequences of marital rape were studied in this research, much as they have been in other rape research. The response of the majority of the women was anger toward the husband. However, women who had been frequently raped by their husbands began to experience self-blame. Marital rape also appeared to have consequences for the marriage: The raped women were more likely to say that their marriages had been getting worse over time.

Thus, research shows that marital rape is a real phenomenon, that it is associated with wife-battering, and that it has negative consequences, both for the woman and for the marriage.

Causes of Rape Four theoretical views of the causes of rape have been proposed (Albin, 1977; Baron and Straus, 1989):

FIGURE 13.3
There has been a tendency in cases of rape to blame the victim. This cartoon satirizes that point of view, showing how ridiculous it would be to take this stance in regard to another victim of crime, such as a man whose wallet was stolen. *(Source: Marian Henley. Reprinted by permission of the artist.)*

1. *Victim-precipitated.* This view holds that a rape is always caused by a woman "asking for it." Rape, then, is basically the woman's fault. This view represents the tendency to blame the victim.

2. *Psychopathology of rapists.* This theoretical view holds that rape is an act committed by a psychologically disturbed man. His deviance is responsible for the crime occurring.

3. *Feminist.* Feminist theorists view rapists as the product of gender-role socialization in our culture. They deemphasize the sexual aspects of rape and instead view rape as an expression of power and dominance by men over women. Gender inequality is both the cause and the result of rape.

4. *Social disorganization.* Sociologists believe that crime rates, including rape rates, increase when the social organization is disrupted and social disorganization results. Under such conditions the community cannot enforce its norms against crime. War is an extreme case of social disorganization.

What do the data say? Research indicates that a number of factors contribute to rape, ranging from forces at the cultural level to forces at the individual level. These factors include the following: cultural values, sexual scripts, early family influences, peer group influences, characteristics of the situation, characteristics of the victim, miscommunication, sex and power motives, and masculinity norms and men's attitudes. The data on each of these factors is considered below.

Cultural values can act in support of rape. Cross-culturally, rape is significantly more common in preliterate societies that are characterized by male dominance, a high degree of general violence, and an ideology of male toughness (Otterbein, 1979; Sanday, 1981). In the United States, research has documented widespread acceptance of rape myths and attitudes that foster rape among average citizens and police officers (Burt, 1980; Feild, 1978).

Sociologists Larry Baron and Murray Straus (1989), experts in violence research, did an extensive study to test the feminist theory and social disorganization theory described above. Both theories deal with rape as a product of cultural context or values. Baron and Straus collected extensive data on each of the 50 states in the United States, seeing them as representing variations in cultural context (think, for example, of the different cultures of Louisiana, New York, and North Dakota). They collected data on the extent of gender inequality in each state (for example, the gap between men's and women's wages). They also collected measures of social disorganization, such as the number of people moving into or out of the states, and the divorce rate. Their data gave strong support to three conclusions: (1) Gender inequality is related to rape (the states with the greatest gender inequality had the highest rape rates); (2) pornography provides cultural, ideological support for rape (the states with the highest circulation of pornographic magazines had the highest rape rates); and (3) social disorganization contributes to rape (those states with the greatest social disorganization tended to have the highest rape rates). This research shows that many complex factors in the culture may contribute to cultural values that encourage rape.

Sexual scripts play a role as well. Adolescents quickly learn society's expectations about dating and sex by culturally transmitted sexual scripts. These scripts support rape when they convey the message that the man is supposed to be the sexual "aggressor." By adolescence, both girls and boys endorse scripts that justify rape (Koss et al., 1994). A study of 1,700 middle school students revealed that approximately 25 percent of the boys said that it was acceptable for a man to force sex on a woman if he had spent money on her (cited in Koss et al., 1994). These findings have been replicated in a number of studies of high school and college students (e.g., Goodchilds and Zellman, 1984; Muehlenhard et al., 1985).

Early family influences may play a role in shaping a man into a sexual aggressor. Specifically, young men who are sexual aggressors are likely to have been sexually abused themselves in childhood (Friedrich et al., 1988; Koss et al., 1994).

The *peer group* can have a powerful influence encouraging men to rape. Anthropologist Peggy Sanday (1990) conducted a detailed ethnographic study of a case of fraternity gang rape at a particular university. According to her analysis, the initiation rituals of many fraternities follow a sequence of creating high levels of anxiety in the new members, followed by a male bonding ritual that makes them "brothers." Essentially the young man's identity as an individual is undermined while loyalty to the group is prized, in fact, enforced. Under these conditions, the peer group of the fraternity brothers becomes an extremely powerful force. In the particular case investigated by Sanday, the XYZ fraternity (she used this name to guard the anonymity of the population being studied, as required by the ethical standard for anthropologists) had a practice called the "XYZ express," referring to an express train. It involved what would be classified as a gang rape in which a woman, typically drunk or surreptitiously drugged so that she was barely conscious, is raped successively by a series of brothers who stand in line to take their turn, just as cars in a train are in a line.

When the case was brought to court, many of the brothers said that they had no idea that their activities were wrong or illegal. The culture of the fraternity—the peer group pressure and peer group norms—had dulled their capacity for rational judgment. And this was not a group of juvenile delinquents in a poor section of the city—it was a group of college students.

Characteristics of the situation play a role. Among these is social disorganization, as noted earlier. An extreme example is war, in which rape of women is common (Brownmiller, 1975). In the 1990s we saw graphic examples of this in the war in the former Yugoslavia. Bosnian women—Croats and Muslims—were frequently raped by the attacking Serbs. Secluded places foster rape, as do parties in which excessive alcohol use is involved (Koss et al., 1994).

Are some women especially likely to be rape victims? That is, are there *characteristics of the victim* that make her vulnerable to being raped? Although many studies have attempted to identify characteristics of women that make them vulnerable to rape—such as certain personality characteristics or appearance—these studies have uniformly failed to find differences between victims and nonvictims (Koss et al., 1994). That is, it doesn't seem to be something about the woman herself that is a key factor. On the other hand, studies have consistently shown that active resistance such as screaming, fleeing, or physically struggling are associated with higher rates of avoiding rape when a man is attempting rape (e.g., Bart, 1981). It pays to fight back.

Miscommunication between men and women is a factor. In the section on date rape, we saw a detailed example of a case in which the man and the woman had totally different understandings of what had occurred. Because many people in the United States are reluctant to discuss sex directly, they try to infer sexual interest from subtle nonverbal cues, a process that is highly prone to errors (Abbey, 1991). Specifically, men are apt to interpret a woman's friendly behavior as carrying a sexual message that she did not intend (Abbey, 1991).

Sex and power motives are involved in rape. Feminists have stressed that rape is an expression of power and dominance by men over women (Brownmiller, 1975). Current theorizing emphasizes that sexual motives and power motives are both involved and interact with each other. A number of processes may be involved (Barbaree and Marshall, 1991). For example, rapists may differ from nonrapists in their ability to suppress sexual arousal when it occurs under inappropriate circumstances. Rapists may be capable of experiencing sexual arousal and hostile aggression simultaneously, whereas other men find that hostile aggression inhibits sexual arousal.

Finally, *masculinity norms and men's attitudes* are another factor (Koss et al., 1994). Sexually aggressive men are more likely than nonaggressors to give themselves traditional masculine ratings. Sexually aggressive men are also more likely to endorse attitudes that are tolerant or supportive of rape, including rape myths. These attitudes allow them to believe that a victim wanted or deserved to be raped.

Battered Women[1]

One solution that some people propose to the rape problem is for women simply to stay home, off the streets. However, the data indicate that a woman may actually be less safe in her own home than on the street. Research indicates that women are more likely to be attacked, raped, injured, or killed by current or former male partners than by any other type of assailant (Koss et al., 1994). The following statistics give some indication of the extent of domestic violence (Browne, 1993; Diehm and Ross, 1988):

—Each year, an estimated 2 to 3 million women in the United States are beaten by their intimate partners (Straus and Gelles, 1990).
—Approximately 95 percent of the victims of domestic violence are women (U.S. Department of Justice, 1985, p. 21).
—Approximately 3 percent of women in any one year are *severely* beaten by their intimate partner (punched, kicked, choked, beaten, threatened with or had a gun or knife used on them) (Straus and Gelles, 1990).
—Battering results yearly in more injuries that require medical treatment than rape, auto accidents, and muggings combined (Stark and Flitcraft, 1987).

It was only in the late 1970s that the topic of battered wives was brought to the attention of the public, and thus it is a topic that has received less research than rape. In fact, wife-beating has a long history, and at many times has been considered a legitimate form of behavior, a logical extension of the roles of men and women. For example, in the sixteenth century in France, the Abbé de Brantôme, although reluctant to speak against the teachings of the Catholic Church, felt compelled to ask, "But however great the authority of the husband may be, what *sense* is there for him to be allowed to kill his wife?" (Davis, 1971, p. 261).

---

[1]Battering can occur in situations other than marriage—for example, when a man who is divorced or separated returns to beat the woman, or when battering occurs among couples who are simply living together. To simplify the terminology, I shall refer to battered wives in the discussion that follows. It is also true that in some cases it is the wife who beats the husband. However, when the violence is physical but not homicidal, the greater physical strength of the male means that far greater damage is done in wife-beating than in husband-beating (Steinmetz, 1977). The focus here will be on wife-beating rather than on husband-beating.

FIGURE 13.4
Battered women's shelters are a necessary part of aid to battered women. Here, battered women and caseworkers hold a discussion in the shelter's kitchen.

In Russia during the reign of Ivan the Terrible, the state church supported such practices by issuing a "Household Ordinance" that detailed how a man might most effectively beat his wife (Mandel, 1975, p. 12). Probably the first contemporary book exposing the topic was *Scream Quietly or the Neighbors Will Hear,* by Erin Pizzey (1974), who opened a shelter for battered women in England.

The 1994 case of the murder of Nicole Simpson, allegedly by her ex-husband, O. J. Simpson, highlighted to the public that batterers can kill. Battered women's shelters were flooded with women following the murder, apparently because many women realized that their situation was far more dangerous than they realized.

Although the family in America is romanticized as a haven of peace and safety, current estimates are that the incidence of family violence is high. In the largest and best study on the topic, sociologist Murray Straus (1980; see also Straus and Gelles, 1990) analyzed a probability sample of more than 2,000 families. The data indicated that 16 percent of the couples experienced some violence between themselves (ranging from slapping to actual beating) within the preceding year. Over the duration of a marriage, that would mean that about 28 percent of all couples would be involved in violence between spouses. Straus estimates that in about 5 percent of marriages the wife is actually beaten at some time during the marriage. The average frequency of beating is 2.4 times per year. These statistics doubtless represent an underestimate, because many people are unwilling to admit that beating occurs. In a sample of women at a battered women's shelter, 42 percent had been assaulted once a week or more (Gondolf et al., 1988).

The Batterer: Psychological Aspects   What kind of man beats his wife? As with the rapist, I can give no profile of the "typical" wife-beater. Such men are found in all social classes and in a wide variety of occupations.

Research does show, however, that characteristics of the batterer are much better predictors of violence than are characteristics of the woman (Hotaling and Sugarman, 1986). That is, it's something about the man, not something about the woman. The batterer has been found to be psychologically rigid and unstable, a person who is so self-absorbed that empathy and reciprocity are impossible for him (Hastings and Hamberger, 1988). Other studies have found other profiles, though, and the fact is that batterers are a diverse group (Dutton, 1988).

Violence in the man's family of origin also is a factor. Male batterers are more likely than a comparison sample of men to have been beaten as children or to have witnessed their father beat their mother (Caesar, 1988).

Batterers are likely to be heavy drinkers and to be drinking at the time of the battering incident (McHugh et al., 1993). However, some experts believe that batterers drink in order to excuse their own conduct.

Impact of Battering on the Woman   The physical consequences of being battered can be severe. In relationships with repeated violence, episodes often involve a combination of assault, verbal abuse, rape, and threats (Browne, 1993). Injuries range from bruises, cuts, black eyes, concussions, broken legs or back, and miscarriages to permanent injuries such as damage to joints, partial loss of hearing or vision, or even death.

Assault by a partner can be lethal. More than half (52 percent) of all women murdered in the United States are victims of murder by their partners (Browne, 1993).

The psychological impact can be devastating as well (Browne, 1993). Reactions of shock, denial, withdrawal, confusion, psychological numbing, and fear are common. Depression and suicide attempts are also common. Chronic fatigue and tension, startle reactions, disturbed sleeping and eating patterns, and nightmares are also often found among battered women. If battering continues over a long period of time, long-term responses include emotional numbing, extreme passivity, and helplessness.

Although the term *battered woman syndrome* was originally coined for these responses, psychologists now favor seeing them, like responses to rape, as instances of *post-traumatic stress disorder* (PTSD) (Browne 1993; Walker, 1991).

Why do battered women stay with the batterer? A number of reasons have been identified (Glazer, 1993; Roy, 1977b): (1) hope that the husband will

FOCUS 13.1
A LETTER FROM A BATTERED WIFE

I am in my thirties and so is my husband. I have a high school diploma and am presently attending a local college, trying to obtain the additional education I need. My husband is a college graduate and a professional in his field. We are both attractive and, for the most part, respected and well-liked. We have four children and live in a middle-class home with all the comforts we could possibly want.

I have everything, except life without fear.

For most of my married life I have been periodically beaten by my husband. What do I mean by "beaten"? I mean that parts of my body have been hit violently and repeatedly, and that painful bruises, swelling, bleeding wounds, unconsciousness, and combinations of these things have resulted. . . .

I have been kicked in the abdomen when I was visibly pregnant. I have been kicked off the bed and hit while lying on the floor—again, while I was pregnant. I have been whipped, kicked and thrown, picked up again and thrown down again. I have been punched and kicked in the head, chest, face, and abdomen more times than I can count.

I have been slapped for saying something about politics, for having a different view about religion, for swearing, for crying, for wanting to have intercourse.

I have been threatened when I wouldn't do something he told me to do. I have been threatened when he's had a bad day and when he's had a good day. . . .

Few people have ever seen my black and blue face or swollen lips because I have always stayed indoors afterwards, feeling ashamed. I was never able to drive following one of these beatings, so I could not get myself to a hospital for care. I could never have left my young children alone, even if I could have driven a car.

Hysteria inevitably sets in after a beating. This hysteria—the shaking and crying and mumbling—is not accepted by anyone, so there has never been anyone to call.

My husband on a few occasions did phone a day or so later so we could agree on the excuse I would use for returning to work, the grocery store, the dentist appointment, and so on. I used the excuses—a car accident, oral surgery, things like that.

Now, the first response to this story, which I myself think of, will be "Why didn't you seek help?"

I did. Early in our marriage I went to a clergyman who, after a few visits, told me that my husband meant no real harm, that he was just confused and felt insecure. I was encouraged to be more tolerant and understanding. Most important, I was told to forgive him the beatings just as Christ had forgiven me from the cross. I did that, too.

Next time I turned to a doctor. I was given little pills to relax me and told to take things a little easier. I was just too nervous.

I turned to a friend, and when her husband found out, he accused me of either making things up or exaggerating the situation. She was told to stay away from me. She didn't, but she could no longer really help me.

I turned to a professional family guidance agency. I was told there that my husband needed help and that I should find a way to control the incidents. I couldn't control the beatings—that was the whole point of my seeking help. At the agency I found I had to defend myself against the suspicion that I wanted to be hit, that I invited the beatings. Good God! Did the Jews invite themselves to be slaughtered in Germany? . . .

I called the police one time. They not only did not respond to the call, they called several hours later to ask if things had "settled down." I could have been dead by then!

I have nowhere to go if it happens again. No one wants to take in a woman with four children. Even if there were someone kind enough to care, no one wants to become involved in what is commonly referred to as a "domestic situation." . . .

No one has to "provoke" a wife-beater. He will strike out when he's ready and for whatever reason he has at the moment.

I may be his excuse, but I have never been the reason. . . .

I have suffered physical and emotional battering and spiritual rape because the social structure of my world says I cannot do anything about a man who wants to beat me. . . . But staying with my husband means that my children must be subjected to the emotional battering caused when they see their mother's face or hear her screams in the middle of the night.

I know that I have to get out. But when you have nowhere to go, you know that you must go on your own and expect no support. I have to be ready for that. I have to be ready to support myself and the children completely, and still provide a decent environment for them. I pray that I can do that before I am murdered in my own home. . . .

It must be pointed out that while a husband can beat, slap, or threaten his wife, there are "good days." These days tend to wear away the effects of the beating. They tend to cause the wife to put aside the traumas and look to the good—first, because there is nothing else to do; second, because there is nowhere and no one to turn to; and third, because the defeat is the beating and the hope is that it will not happen again. A loving woman like myself always hopes that it will not happen again. When it does, she simply hopes again, until it becomes obvious after a third beating that there is no hope. That is when she turns outward for help to find an answer. When that help is denied, she either resigns herself to the situation she is in or pulls herself together and starts making plans for a future life that includes only herself and her children.

For many the third beating may be too late. . . .

What determines who is lucky and who isn't? I could have been dead a long time ago had I been hit the wrong way. My baby could have been killed or deformed had I been kicked the wrong way. What saved me?

I don't know. I only know that it has happened and that each night I dread the final blow that will kill me and leave my children motherless. I hope I can hang on until I complete my education, get a good job, and become self-sufficient enough to care for my children on my own.

SOURCE: Excerpted from Martin (1976).

---

reform; (2) having no other place to go; (3) fear that there will be reprisals from the batterer and that he may even kill her; (4) concern about the children (they need a father, the woman cannot support them herself, and so on); and (5) economic dependence (the woman cannot support herself).

Impact on the Children   In addition to the impact on the woman herself, there is an impact on the children. The man who batters his wife is likely to abuse his children as well. According to the results of one study, in almost one-third of families in which there was spouse abuse, there was also child abuse (Straus, 1978, cited in Bowker et al., 1988). Children in homes in which the wife is battered are at a very high risk to be battered by their father (Bowker et al., 1988). And even witnessing their mother being beaten can be devastating to children.

Theories of the Causes of Woman-Battering   A number of theoretical perspectives are available for understanding why battering occurs (for reviews of these, see Straus, 1980; Walker, 1980). These perspectives in some ways parallel the different theoretical views of the nature of rape described earlier in this chapter.

Several different *psychological theories* are possible. One is that the man who batters his wife is simply a rare, psychologically disturbed individual, perhaps a psychopath. This view does not seem acceptable given the high incidence of wife-beating documented by research. A second psychological approach is to say that battering occurs because of the psychopathology of the wife. In this view, the woman is seen as a disturbed individual who brings on the attack and self-destructively stays with the man who batters her. The psychoanalyst might call her masochistic. Note that this view blames the victim.

A third psychological approach is a *learned helplessness theory* of battering proposed by Lenore Walker (1980), a psychologist who has done extensive research with battered women. This explanation rests on the same learned helplessness theory that is used in explaining depression in women in Chapter 14. It is based in learning theory. According to this view, the battered woman has a history of childhood gender-role socialization to passivity and helplessness. In adulthood, being battered increases her helplessness. This theory explains the depression experienced by battered women. It also explains why battered women stay with their husbands or return to them after having tried to escape. Their conditioning to helplessness is so complete that they cannot act to save themselves.

Sociological theory presents yet another view (Straus, 1980). It focuses on norms and attitudes in our society that condone violence within families, particularly violence by husbands to wives. Sociologists also call attention to the process of gender-role socialization in childhood, in which girls are expected to be passive and boys are expected to be aggressive.

The *feminist perspective* holds that wife-beating is both cause and effect of the inequality of power between men and women in our society (Walker, 1980). The inequality of power causes wife-beating because it serves as a rationale for a man to "discipline" his wife, much as a parent may discipline a child. But inequality of power is also affected by wife-beating, because battering serves to perpetuate the dominance of men over women. Feminists also note both the historical and contemporary approval of wife-beating.

What Can Be Done? The problems of battered women are complex, and no single measure is likely to solve them. If violence in American society could be reduced in general, that would help to a certain degree. Some of the problems of battered women, however, are special and require special solutions. One solution is providing refuge houses. These houses provide the woman with a safe place to go (one of her most immediate needs), with emotional support from those around her, and possibly with job counseling and legal advice. These shelters have sprung up like mushrooms in the past 15 years in the United States. Interestingly, these shelters and the paraprofessional and peer counseling they provide are the most successful treatment for battered women (Walker, 1980).

Community social services are also needed to deal with the problem of wife-beating. Crisis hot lines are important so that the woman can get immediate help. In addition, counseling services for the batterer, the victim, and the children are needed. Feminist therapy (see Chapter 14) should be particularly helpful to the battered woman.

Self-defense training for battered women has been recommended by some experts (e.g., Martin, 1976). The woman who is an expert in karate or some other system can offset the greater strength of her husband and assertively discourage his attacks.

Legal and police reform are also important (e.g., Martin, 1976; Roy, 1977a). One problem is that the American legal system has considered the family and home to be sacred and has been loath to interfere with them in any way. Somehow the police officer who intervened in a "family" fight was viewed as violating the sanctity of the family. Police officers were often unwilling to arrest a husband for assault unless the officer had actually witnessed the attack, which is rare since the police are usually called after the fact.

On a hopeful note, in 1984 Congress passed the Family Violence Prevention and Services Act, which allocated funds for victims of domestic violence. Domestic violence is now a crime in all 50 states (Diehm and Ross, 1988). Many communities have experimented with a "mandatory arrest" or "shock arrest policy" in which the man must be arrested and spend a minimum of one night in jail if the police are called in on a case of domestic violence. The idea is to convey clearly to the man that what he is doing is wrong and illegal. Research has shown mixed results as to how effective mandatory arrest is; it seems to work at least as well as anything else that has been tried (Berk, 1993). In an experiment with new technologies, an ankle bracelet for the batterer is being tried. It contains an electronic device that sounds an alarm if he gets within a block of the woman's house.

At least some of the blame must also rest with traditional gender roles and socialization. Wife-beating, after all, is a way of being dominant and thereby of fulfilling the male role. And staying with such a husband is consistent with the submissiveness for which women are socialized. Reforms in gender roles, socialization, and education, therefore, will be necessary to remedy the situation fully.

Sexual Harassment

The sexual victimization of women is not limited to cases of out-and-out rape. Most women have experienced incidents of varying degrees of sexual harassment, what one author called "the little rapes" (Offir, 1982).

Because incidents of sexual harassment differ in the degree of offensiveness and coercion, they are rather difficult to define, both in a legal or scholarly sense and in a personal sense. The official definition given by the U.S. government's Equal Employment Opportunity Commission (EEOC) is the following:

> Harassment on the basis of sex is a violation of Section 703 of Title VII (of the United States Civil Rights Act). Unwelcome sexual advances, requests for sexual favors, and other verbal or physical conduct of a sexual nature constitute sexual harassment when

1. submission to such conduct is made either explicitly or implicitly a term or condition of an individual's employment.

2. submission to or rejection of such conduct by an individual is used as the basis for employment decisions affecting such individual, or

3. such conduct has the purpose or effect of unreasonably interfering with an individual's work performance or creating an intimidating, hostile or offensive working environment.

The EEOC definition contains two parts. The first is often termed *quid pro quo harassment* and is captured in points 1 and 2. (*Quid pro quo* is a Latin phrase meaning "I'll give you something if you give me something in return," or "I'll scratch your back if you scratch mine.") Quid pro quo harassment refers to exchanges such as the following: "Have sex with me and I'll hire you," or "Have sex with me and I'll see to it that you get a big raise."

The second part of the definition refers to *hostile environment* and is captured in point 3. For this part of the definition, there does not have to be a requirement of sex in exchange for hiring, promotion, or pay. Rather, the issue is whether the behavior and environment in the workplace is so hostile to women that it interferes with their work performance. The classic example was the Jacksonville Shipyards Supreme Court case (*Robinson* v. *Jacksonville Shipyards,* 1991). In that case, Lois Robinson was employed at the shipyards and felt that her work was impaired by being surrounded by a hostile environment, including pornographic pictures prominently displayed (e.g., a pinup showing a meat spatula pressed against a woman's pubic area), crude and explicit graffiti on the walls, and a dart board covered with a picture of a woman's breast with the nipple as a bull's eye. The Supreme Court found in favor of Ms. Robinson and declared this kind of hostile environment to be illegal.

Sexual harassment can occur in a variety of settings—at work, in education, in psychotherapy (see Chapter 14), on the street.

Sexual Harassment at Work   Sexual harassment at work can take a number of different forms. A prospective employer may make it clear that sexual activity is a prerequisite to being hired. Stories of such incidents are rampant among actresses. On the job, sexual activity may be made a condition for continued employment, for a promotion, or for other benefits, such as a raise. Here is one case:

> June, a waitress in Arkansas, was serving a customer when he reached up her skirt. When she asked her manager for future protection against such incidents, she was harassed by him instead. "They put me on probation," she recalled, "as if I was the guilty one. Then things went from bad to worse. I got lousy tables and bad hours." (Phillips, 1977)

Such an incident is a clear case showing how the man uses his position of power to punish the woman for her noncompliance with sexual requests.

FIGURE 13.5
Sexual harassment at work may be blatant, such as making it clear that sexual activity is a prerequisite to being hired; or it may be more subtle, as is the case in this photograph. The woman cannot avoid physical contact. Yet, if the man is her boss, she may feel too intimidated to complain.

Research indicates that sexual harassment at work is far more common than many people realize. In one well-sampled study, 21 percent of women workers, compared with 9 percent of men workers, reported that they had been the object of incidents that an expert classified as definite sexual harassment (Gutek, 1985). The great majority of harassers—78 percent—are male (Tangri et al., 1982). In a massive study of federal government employees, 10 percent of the women had been directly pressured for sexual cooperation (U.S. Merit Systems Protection Board, 1981). And, in fact, the study estimated that 12,000 female federal workers were victims of rape or attempted rape by supervisors or co-workers in a two-year period.

In 1981, *Redbook* and the *Harvard Business Review* surveyed nearly 2,000 business executives about sexual harassment (Safran, 1981). They found that women in top-management positions had considerably different perceptions of this problem than men in similar positions did. Two-thirds of the men believed that the scope of the problem "is greatly exaggerated," whereas only one-third of the women agreed with that statement. Approximately three-quarters of both males and females, though, favored the issuing of a statement from management to all employees, expressing disapproval of sexual harassment.

Sexual harassment at work is more than just an annoyance. It can mean the difference between a career advancement or none. For the working-class woman who supports her family, being fired for sexual noncompliance is a catastrophe. The potential for coercing her is enormous. Women typically describe the experience as being degrading and humiliating, feeling a sense of helplessness similar to that reported by rape victims (Safran, 1976). There is evidence linking the experience of sexual harassment to depression and PTSD (Kilpatrick, 1992, cited in Fitzgerald, 1993a).

Sexual Harassment in Education The scene is also set for sexual harassment in an educational setting: the male teacher or professor wields power over the female student (Dziech and Weiner, 1983).

A survey of male professors at a prestigious research university indicated that fully 26 percent admitted to having had a sexual encounter or sexual relationship with a student (Fitzgerald et al., 1988). If anything, of course, that is probably an underestimate, because this is the kind of behavior that a respondent might hide in a survey.

The data indicate that about 50 percent of female students have been harassed in some ways by professors, ranging from insults and come-ons to sexual assault (Fitzgerald, 1993a).

> This professor made sexist and derogatory comments about the women in the class, women in public life, women in general:
>
> "You women are going to waste your education raising babies."
>
> "There is no future for women in political science. I don't believe in women in government at all."
>
> "Now if Justice Marshall had been a woman he would have sat down and cried, which is the reason—and a good one—we don't have a woman on the Supreme Court."
>
> "Any husband who is foolish enough to listen to what his wife says politically deserves anything he gets."
>
> I discussed with him the fact that his remarks were at first irritating and then progressively more offensive. I said that some of the women in the class felt intimidated and put down. The point is that if I, with all kinds of positive reinforcement from women professors and feminist friends, was brought down in spirit by this man, then surely so are other women students. (Williams, 1983, pp. 366–367)

The problem, once again, is unequal power. Women students in such a situation hardly have the power to protest, because the professor holds the power of having their grades in his hands. In the cases in graduate school, the professor controls critical evaluations and recommendations that affect the course of the woman's career. Women report dropping courses, changing majors, or dropping out of higher education as a result of sexual harassment (Fitzgerald, 1993a).

Feminist Analysis Feminists make several points about sexual harassment. First, traditional thinking often blames the victim, suggesting that the woman behaves provocatively or explicitly initiates sexual activity in the hope of getting a promotion, getting a good grade, and so on. In contrast, the feminist perspective is that such activity is usually initiated by the male in the powerful position. Second, feminist analysis emphasizes issues of power and control. It is precisely because men are so often in positions of greater power—whether at work or in education—that sexual harassment becomes a possibility. Sexual harassment functions as a form of social control; research indicates that women are most at risk in occupations traditionally reserved for men and that women who report harassment commonly experience retribution (Koss et al., 1994). Furthermore, the woman who is the victim of sexual harassment experiences a lack of control over her own life, perhaps much like that of a rape victim. More research on the psychological aspects of sexual harassment is sorely needed.

Incest

Incest is another topic that has come out of the closet in recent years. Two decades ago it was considered unmentionable and rare. Today one can flip on the television in the middle of the day and watch incest victims speak openly on talk shows.

Incest: Sexual activity between close relatives.

          Incest is typically defined as sexual relations between blood relatives, although the definition is often extended to include sex between non-blood relatives, for example, stepfather and stepdaughter (Maisch, 1972; Sagarin, 1977).

Incidence of Incest Traditionally, it was thought the incest was a rare and bizarre occurrence. Early research confirmed this notion, indicating that the incidence of incest prosecuted through the police and courts in the United States was only about one or two people per million per year (Weinberg, 1955). The catch, though, is that the overwhelming majority of cases go unreported and unprosecuted. To get a better idea of the true incidence of incest, it is necessary to survey the general population. In one such survey, 7 percent of the sample had had sexual intercourse with a relative (Hunt, 1974). In a general survey of undergraduates, 15 percent of the females and 10 percent of the males said they had had a sexual experience with a brother or sister (Finkelhor, 1980). In most cases, the activity was limited to fondling and exhibiting the genitals. Intercourse occurred in only 5 percent of the incidents where the respondent was under age 8 and 18 percent of the incidents where the respondent was over age 13. The point is that incest, particularly if it is defined to include sexual contact other than intercourse, is not at all rare.

    Of father-daughter incest and brother-sister, or sibling, incest, which is more common? In a study of *reported* incest (reported to the police or other authorities), father-daughter cases were by far the most common: father-daughter cases constituted 78 percent of the sample, 18 percent were brother-sister, 1 percent were mother-son, and the remaining 3 percent were multiple incestuous relationships (Weinberg, 1955). However, in surveys of the *general* population, brother-sister incest is far more common, outnumbering father-daughter incest by about five to one (Gebhard et al., 1965). Thus it appears that brother-sister incest is actually the most common form, but it is far less likely to be reported to the police than father-daughter incest is. However, most research has been done on reported cases, that is, on father-daughter incest, and it represents the clear case of a male victimizing a female.

Father-Daughter Incest What kind of man commits incest with his daughter? The stereotype is that such men are cases of extreme psychopathology. However, extensive reviews of the research literature on incest show that this stereotype is not true (Herman, 1981; Meiselman, 1978). Rather, the man who commits incest appears to be a classical patriarch within his family (Herman, 1981). He is a good provider, but he rules the family. The division of roles in the family in which father-daughter incest occurs is traditional, and the mother is typically a full-time housewife. She also seems somewhat isolated within the family, often because her health is poor. Given these family dynamics, the daughter-victim seems to take on the role of holding the family together and develops a "special" relationship with her father, within which the incest occurs.

The sexual activity with his daughter appears to fulfill several needs for the father (Herman, 1981). He often has feelings of dependency and a need for nurturance, which he receives in the relationship with his daughter (Justice and Justice, 1979). Doubtless he experiences a sense of power in the act, for he can control it exactly as he wishes and need not fear a rejection of his techniques, such as he might receive from a mature woman (Herman, 1981). The excitement coming from the secrecy may be pleasurable. Finally, it has been suggested that the daughter's unhappiness with the sexual activity may contribute to pleasure in the father, who is basically expressing hostility.

Psychological Impact on the Victim Many therapists who are experienced with cases of incest feel that the effects of father-daughter incest on the victim are serious and long-lasting, despite the fact that the incidents were not reported and seem to have been repressed (Herman, 1981). Consider the following case:

> A twenty-five-year-old office worker was seen in the emergency room with an acute anxiety attack. She was pacing, agitated, unable to eat or sleep, and had a feeling of impending doom. She related a vivid fantasy of being pursued by a man with a knife. The previous day she had been cornered in the office by her boss, who aggressively propositioned her. She needed the job badly and did not want to lose it, but she dreaded the thought of returning to work. It later emerged in psychotherapy that this episode of sexual harassment had reawakened previously repressed memories of sexual assaults by her father. From the age of six until midadolescence, her father had repeatedly exhibited himself to

her and insisted that she masturbate him. The experience of being trapped at
work had recalled her childhood feelings of helplessness and fear. (Herman,
1981, p. 8)

Research in this area has some inherent methodological difficulties. Most of
the research has been on reported or prosecuted cases, in which father-daughter
incest is overrepresented, and in which police and court proceedings may have
done as much damage to the victim as the incest itself did, a situation that is also
found with rape victims. Thus, most research gives little information on sibling
incest and its effects, or on the less traumatic cases that are not reported to the
police or do not result in the woman's seeking psychotherapy.

Two studies are worthy of attention. One of these is the general survey of
undergraduates, cited earlier, in which 15 percent of the females and 10 percent
of the males said they had had a sexual experience with a sibling (Finkelhor,
1980). Among those who had been involved in sibling incest, there was an almost even division between those who felt the experience had been positive for
them and those who felt it had been negative. There seemed to be some long-
term effects on sexuality. Women who had had sexual experiences with a sibling
had substantially higher levels of current (college-age) sexual activity than
women who had not experienced sibling incest. In addition, those who had had
experiences with a much older sibling before the age of nine suffered lowered
sexual self-esteem, but those who had had positive experiences after the age of
nine had heightened sexual self-esteem.

In a second, well-designed study, newspaper advertisements were used to recruit women falling into these three categories: women who were victims of
childhood molestation and were seeking therapy for the resulting problems
(called the clinical group); women who were victims of childhood molestation but
felt well adjusted and not in need of therapy (nonclinical group); and women who
were not victims of childhood molestation (control group) (Tsai et al., 1979). It
turned out that 73 percent of the clinical group and 63 percent of the nonclinical
group had been molested by their fathers, stepfathers, or grandfathers, and so the
study essentially became an investigation of father-daughter incest. The results
showed that the clinical and nonclinical groups differed in a number of ways (see
Table 13.1). The molestation went on for nearly five years, on average, for the
clinical group, whereas it lasted only about half that long for the nonclinical
group. Also, the molestation continued to older ages for the girls in the clinical
group. Attempted intercourse was more common in the clinical group. And finally, women in the clinical group were significantly less satisfied with their current, adult sexual relationships than women in the nonclinical group were, indicating the existence of long-term consequences of being a victim of incest during
one's childhood. This study is particularly interesting because it shows some of
the factors—long duration of molestation, attempted intercourse—that seem to be
related to long-term psychological damage in women who are incest victims.

Given the statistics cited previously showing a high frequency of sibling incest, it may seem peculiar that the study by Tsai and colleagues found father-

TABLE 13.1

Summary of Differences Between Two Groups of Molestation Victims

	Clinical* (n = 30)	Nonclinical[†] (n = 30)
Age at which last molestation occurred	12.4 years	9.2 years
Duration of molestation	4.7 years	2.5 years
Intercourse attempted	70%	40%
Intercourse completed	20%	17%
Feelings of satisfaction in current sexual relationships (7-point scale, 7 = very satisfied)	3.80	5.67

*"Clinical" indicates that the women felt that they were in need of therapy.
[†]"Nonclinical" indicates that the women felt well adjusted and not in need of therapy.

SOURCE: Tsai et al., (1979)

daughter and similar forms of incest to account for the great majority of cases. I think the answer lies in the fact that the newspaper ad recruiting participants in this study used the term *molestation*. An adult woman who was the victim of an incestuous relationship with her stepfather probably realizes that she was the victim of molestation. But sibling incest, particularly between a brother and sister close in age, may not seem to be "molestation," and therefore women who had experienced it might be relatively unlikely to respond to newspaper advertisements using that term.

In a major review of studies of children who were sexually abused (this included incestuous abuse by a family member and other forms of abuse such as by a preschool teacher), the researchers concluded that there is strong evidence of a number of negative effects on these children compared with control groups of nonabused children (Kendall-Tackett et al., 1993). Sexually abused children were significantly more likely to have symptoms of anxiety, post-traumatic stress disorder (PTSD), depression, poor self-esteem, health complaints, aggressive and antisocial behavior, inappropriate sexual behavior, school problems, and behavior problems such as hyperactivity. Victims had more severe symptoms when the perpetrator was a member of the family, when the sexual contact was frequent or over a long period of time, and when the sexual activity involved penetration (vaginal, oral, or anal). Gender did not seem to be a factor; that is, there were no differences in symptoms between boys and girls. However, the researchers noted that gender was not investigated in many studies, probably because so few boys appeared in most samples.

FOCUS 13.2

FALSE MEMORY SYNDROME? RECOVERED MEMORY?

One of the nastiest controversies in psychology today concerns the issue of what some call recovered memory and what others call false memory syndrome. The issue is sexual abuse or other severe trauma in childhood and whether the child victim can forget (repress) the memory of the event and later recover that memory.

FIGURE 13.6

The repressed memory/false memory debate. After Holly Ramona accused her father of child sexual abuse, he filed an $8 million lawsuit against her psychologist, her psychiatrist, and their medical center.

On one side of the argument, the *recovered memory* side, psychotherapists see adult clients who display serious symptoms of prior trauma, such as severe depression and anxiety. Sometimes these clients have clear memories of being sexually abused in childhood and have always known about the events, but never told anyone until they told the therapist. In other cases, the client doesn't remember that any abuse occurred but, during the process of therapy—or sometimes spontaneously before therapy—something triggers the memory and the client now recalls the sexual abuse. Psychotherapists are understandably outraged about the psychological trauma that results from childhood sexual abuse.

On the other side, some psychologists believe that these

memories for events that had been forgotten and then are remembered are actually *false memories.* They argue that un-
scrupulous therapists may induce these memories through hypnosis or strongly suggesting to clients that childhood abuse
occurred.

Why is this an issue in feminist psychology? The reason is
that a large proportion of cases of child sexual abuse involves a
female victim and a male perpetrator, such as a father or other
trusted adult such as an uncle or a priest. Feminists are concerned that, if the false memory syndrome side wins, women's
reports that they were sexually abused in childhood will not be
taken seriously.

What do the data say? First, there is evidence from laboratory
studies that information associated with unpleasant emotions is
more likely to be forgotten (e.g., Bootzin and Natsoulas, 1965).
Research directly on the issue of child sexual abuse also provides support for the existence of forgetting in some cases. In
one study, 100 women who were known to have been sexually
abused as children—they had been brought to a hospital for the
abuse and it had been medically verified—were subsequently interviewed; 38 percent could not remember their prior abuse
(Williams, 1992, 1994). In a study of adult women who reported
being victims of child sexual abuse, 30 percent reported that
they had completely blocked out any memory of the abuse for a
full year or more (Gold et al., 1994). In another, similar study, 19
percent of adult women reporting child sexual abuse said that
they forgot the abuse for a period of time (Loftus et al., 1994).
Therefore, the evidence seems to indicate that in some cases—
percentages range between 19 and 38 percent—memories of
childhood sexual abuse can be forgotten for a period of time and
then remembered again.

The other question is, Can memories of events that did not
occur be "implanted" in someone? In one study, the researcher
was able to create false memories of childhood events in 25 percent of the adults given the treatment (Loftus, 1993). Certain conditions seem to increase the chances of people thinking that they
remember things that did not occur, including suggestion by an
authority figure and suggestion under hypnosis.

What is the bottom line? There is evidence that some people
do forget memories of childhood sexual abuse and then later remember them. There is also evidence that some people can form
false memories based on suggestion by another person. It
seems to me likely that most of the cases of recovered memory

of child sexual abuse are true, but that a few are false and the product of suggestion. To put the matter in perspective, each year thousands of children are sexually abused; the vast majority of these cases go unreported and the perpetrators go unpunished. It is also probably true that false accusations of child abuse are made, often by a well-intentioned "victim" who is highly suggestible to press reports of other cases or who has been misled by an overly zealous therapist. As a result, an accused person who is actually innocent may be convicted and go to jail. There are errors of justice on both sides. Nonetheless, I believe that, statistically, there are many, many more cases of unreported and unpunished perpetrators than of falsely convicted persons.

SOURCES: Bootzin and Natsoulis (1965); Gold et al. (1994); Loftus (1993); Loftus et al. (1994); Williams (1992, 1994).

What, then, are the psychological consequences of incest or other childhood sexual abuse for the victim? Incest may not be damaging to the victim in some cases, particularly for brother-sister incest when the two are close in age. However, in most cases childhood sexual abuse is psychologically damaging and may lead to symptoms such as anxiety and PTSD. Several factors affect how severe the psychological consequences are; they seem to be more severe when the perpetrator is a close family member and when there is extensive sexual contact that involves penetration.

Feminist Analysis   Feminists make several points about incest. First, they warn against blaming the victim—that is, suggesting that a daughter initiates incest with her father by her seductive behavior and that he therefore cannot be held responsible. The evidence indicates that it is usually the father who is the initiator; even if the daughter were the initiator, the father, because of his age and position of responsibility in the family, must certainly refuse her. The most common pattern is for the incest to begin when the daughter is eight or nine years old (Herman, 1981), scarcely an age at which she can be held responsible. Second, feminists point out that this is another instance in which men exercise power and control over women—in this case a father uses his power in the family to coerce his daughter into sexual activity. Third, feminists want to alert the public to the frequency of incest and the psychological damage it can do to women. Feminist therapists report that women come to them with complaints apparently unrelated to sexual abuse, but that, in the course of therapy, a history of sexual abuse, which had been repressed, surfaces (Herman, 1981; Leidig, 1982).

There is a conflict of points of view here—feminists are alarmed by the psychological damage done by incest, whereas some sex researchers, looking at studies such as the one by Finkelhor (in 1980), conclude that incest is not always damaging, I feel a need to resolve this difference, particularly because I count myself a member of both those groups. I think the resolution lies in the fact that the two groups are looking at different kinds of incest. Sex researchers, alert to issues of sampling the general population, realize that sibling incest is the most common form and, studying it, find generally less serious consequences. Feminists focus on father-daughter incest because it represents a clear-cut case of male abuse of power, and find the consequences to be serious. Once again, the conclusion about the psychological impact of incest on the victim must be that it depends on many factors.

In Conclusion

In this chapter we have considered four situations in which women are victimized: rape, wife-battering, sexual harassment, and incest. All have in common

---

EXPERIENCE THE RESEARCH

A SCALE TO ASSESS VIEWS ON THE CAUSES OF RAPE

In this exercise, you are going to construct a scale to assess people's beliefs in the four theoretical views of the causes of rape (see page 350 in the text). Generate four statements for each theoretical view; the statements should be ones that can be rated on a scale from strongly disagree (1) to strongly agree (5). For example, for the victim-precipitated theory, one statement might be "Most rapes occur because the woman really wanted it." For the feminist theory, one statement might be "Men use rape to dominate women." Once you have the 16 statements, have another person in this class check them to see whether each really reflects one of the four theoretical views. Then administer your 16-item scale to five women and five men. Compute an average score for each theoretical view for each person; that is, each of your participants will have a score on victim-precipitated beliefs, psychopathology of rapist beliefs, feminist beliefs, and social disorganization beliefs.

Do you see patterns in your data? For example, do most people seem to hold most strongly to psychopathology of rapist beliefs? Are there differences between men's and women's responses? What is the pattern of those differences?

the reticence of the victims to report the occurrences and a corresponding diffi-culty in helping the unknown victims. In all four, the victim traditionally was blamed. Feminists emphasize the basic ways in which rape, wife-battering, sex-ual harassment, and incest represent male expressions of power and dominance over women.

We need to recognize the victimization of women. But we also need to move beyond that recognition. For example, contrast these two terms: *rape vic-tim* and *rape survivor.* The woman who has been raped yet manages to return to a productive life is a survivor, not a victim; she is strong, not weak. Even tragic situations in which women are made powerless can be a means for women to begin to discover and regain their strength and power, both at the individual level and at the level of the larger society.

Suggestions for Further Reading

Bates, Carolyn M., & Brodsky, Annette M. (1989). *Sex in the therapy hour.* New York: Guilford Press. Although sexual harassment in psychotherapy is discussed in Chapter 14, it also deserves mention here. In this book, the first author tells her story of being harassed in therapy. The second author, a feminist therapist, then analyzes the issues involved.

Brady, Katherine. (1979). *Father's days.* New York: Dell (paperback). This autobiogra-phy of an incest victim is both moving and insightful.

Gordon, Linda. (1988). *Heroes of their own lives.* New York: Viking. This noted feminist historian traces the lives of battered women in the early 1900s and concludes that they were remarkable survivors—heroes, indeed.

Koss, Mary P., Goodman, Lisa A., Browne, Angela, Fitzgerald, Louise, Keita, Gwen-dolyn P., & Russo, Nancy F. (1994). *No safe haven: Male violence against women at home, at work, and in the community.* Washington, DC: American Psy-chological Association. This is the most up-to-date, authoritative book on vio-lence against women.

Walker, Lenore E. (1989). *Terrifying love: Why battered women kill and how society re-sponds.* New York: Harper & Row. Walker, a psychologist who is an expert on battered women, has been an expert witness in the trials of more than 150 bat-tered women who eventually killed their batterers. This book gives voice to these women, telling their life stories and how they got to the point of murder.

14

Women and Mental Health Issues

I was eighteen when I started therapy for the second time. I went to a woman for two years, twice a week. She was constantly trying to get me to admit that what I really wanted was to get married and have babies and lead a "secure" life; she was very preoccupied with how I dressed, and just like my mother, would scold me if my clothes were not clean, or if I wore my hair down; told me that it would be a really good sign if I started to wear makeup and get my hair done in a beauty parlor (like her, dyed blond and sprayed); when I told her that I like to wear pants she told me that I had a confusion of sex roles. . . . I originally went to her when my friends started to experiment with sex, and I felt that I couldn't make it, and that my woman friends with whom I had been close had rejected me for a good lay. . . .

FROM PHYLLIS CHESLER, WOMEN AND MADNESS

Stories such as the one told by this woman are all too common among women who have been in psychotherapy. What is known about the experiences of such women? In this chapter we shall explore some of the adjustment problems women have, the evidence on whether there is sexism in traditional psychotherapy, and newly emerging therapies for women.

Gender Ratios and Mental Health

Studies consistently show that more women than men are patients in psychotherapy (Russo and Green, 1993). This is true whether one looks at psychotherapy done on an outpatient basis, or hospitalization for psychiatric problems. For example, there are 1.33 as many women as men in private psychiatric hospitals (Russo and Sobel, 1981).

How should this differential be interpreted? One possibility is that it simply means that more women than men have psychological disorders. Another possibility is that women in fact have no more adjustment problems than men do, but women are just more willing to admit their problems and seek psychotherapy. Both explanations have merit.

More important than overall gender ratios for psychological disorders is the finding that males and females receive different diagnoses. Gender differences are most pronounced for alcohol abuse, with a ratio of four or five men to every one woman, and for depression and anxiety (Myers et al., 1984; Robins et al., 1984; Russo and Green, 1993; Travis, 1988b). Approximately 20 to 26 percent of women will experience diagnosable depression at some time in their lives, compared with 8 to 12 percent of men (Wetzel, 1984).

Space does not permit a discussion of all possible problems of adjustment in women. Below we will consider three of special interest: depression, alcoholism and drug abuse, and the eating disorders (anorexia and bulimia). Depression and eating disorders are of interest because of the disproportionate number of women with these problems. Alcoholism and drug abuse are interesting because they are stereotyped as "masculine" problems, and therefore female abusers may be overlooked.

Depression

The symptoms of depression include (1) emotional aspects—a dejected mood, feelings of worthlessness; (2) cognitive aspects—low self-esteem and negative expectations about the future; (3) motivational aspects—motivation is low and there is an inability to mobilize oneself to action; and (4) behavioral aspects—appetite loss, sleep disturbance, loss of interest in sex, poor concentration, and tiredness (Beck and Greenberg, 1974).

Among persons given some treatment for depression, the ratio of women to men is 2:1 (Nolen-Hoeksema, 1987). Among persons with serious depression requiring hospitalization, the gender ratio is also 2:1 (Weissman and Klerman, 1979). Even in large-scale surveys of the general American population, women outnumber men in cases of diagnosable depression 2:1 (Weissman and Klerman, 1987). And the 2:1 ratio is found in studies of other nations (Weissman et al., 1993). It seems reasonable to conclude that there is more depression among women than among men. The evidence indicates that this gender difference emerges in adolescence and perhaps even earlier (Ruble et al., 1993).

Some have argued that these higher rates of depression in women are not cause for concern, because the gender difference in depression is an "artifact," not a true difference. That is, it is possible that in actuality, men and women suffer equally from depression, but women are overrepresented in the statistics, perhaps because they are more willing to admit mood symptoms or to seek help (therapy) for their problems. However, a detailed review of available research led to the conclusion that the gender difference in depression is a true difference, not an artifact (Weissman and Klerman, 1979). That is, the evidence is that women report more depression because they actually experience more depression.

Why do women have more problems with depression? There are a variety of factors associated with depression in women, including lack of reinforcements, social roles, helplessness and hopelessness, violence, and poverty. These factors are discussed below.

Learning Theory Learning theorists believe that depression occurs when the reinforcements a person is accustomed to—for example, a satisfying job or a congenial spouse—are suddenly withdrawn. The person responds by reducing activities. If there is not some reinforcement for the person's remaining efforts, he or she sinks further into depression. The pattern of inactivity itself may be rewarded if the person gets special attention for being "sick." Following these notions, a behaviorist might explain the greater occurrence of depression in women as being a result of women not receiving sufficient reinforcements for their actions (an assumption that is not too difficult to make); or as a result of women being especially likely to find themselves in situations in which their customary reinforcements are withdrawn (for example, having to leave one's friends and job and move to follow a husband's career, or having one's children leave home when they grow up) (Lewinsohn et al., 1979).

Two other factors are relevant in discussing the causes of depression in women: women's roles and learned helplessness or hopelessness.

Women's Roles The housewife role has been proposed as one source of women's depression (Travis, 1988b). Many of the tasks of a housewife are unchallenging, repetitive, and lacking in a sense of accomplishment, as, for example, making beds that will just be unmade that evening and made again the next day. Many housewife functions are performed in isolation, and so loneliness may be a factor. Childrearing, too, may contribute to depression; the mere presence of children in the home increases the risk of depression (Wetzel, 1984).

Gender roles are also involved in the ways in which females and males cope with depression. When depressed, men are more likely to engage in active behaviors that distract them; women, on the other hand, are more likely to be inactive and to ponder their depressed mood and its causes. This ruminating seems to increase depression rather than diminish it (Nolen-Hoeksema, 1987).

Learned helplessness theory: A theory that depression is caused by a person having learned that he or she is helpless or unable to control important outcomes in life.

Learned Helplessness and Hopelessness Psychologist Martin Seligman's (1975) **learned helplessness theory** as a cause of depression may be useful in explaining depression in women (Radloff, 1975, 1980; Radloff and Monroe, 1978). Seligman believes that depressives have a history of learning that they are incapable of successful mastery and control over their lives. In short, they have learned to regard themselves as helpless. When confronted with a difficult situation, such persons feel that they cannot deal with it successfully, and depression results. The sense of helplessness and lack of control Seligman talks about sound very much like the powerlessness that is characteristic of women. If women in our society do indeed lack power—in everything from interpersonal relationships to national politics—this may contribute to a sense of helplessness and thus to depression. Further, traits that women are socialized for, such as passivity, may contribute to helplessness. An observational study in nursery schools found that girls received fewer reactions from adults for all behaviors (Serbin et al., 1973). Perhaps even at an early age, girls learn that their behaviors do not produce results.

One large-scale study attempted to determine which of these factors—women's roles or women's powerlessness and learned helplessness—contributed more to psychological problems (Horwitz, 1982). The results provided some support for both factors, but indicated that powerlessness was particularly important in producing psychological distress.

Psychologist Lyn Abramson and her colleagues (1989) have proposed hopelessness theory as an improved version of helplessness theory. According to **hopelessness theory,** depression—or at least some types of depression—occurs as a result of the person having developed a sense of hopelessness. Hopelessness involves two components: (1) an expectation that good things will not happen to me and that bad things will; and (2) a belief that I am helpless to make the good things happen or to prevent the bad things from happening. Put these two components together, and you have a hopeless, depressed person. The second component, of course, is the same as helplessness theory. The first component, the negative expectations about future events, is the addition.

Hopelessness theory: A theory that one type of depression results from a pattern of cognition in which the person believes that good things will not happen to him or her and that he or she is helpless to control these outcomes.

Again, this theory may help explain why more women than men are depressed. A woman who is repeatedly battered by her husband is likely to have negative expectations about future events and to believe that she cannot control them; the same would be likely for a woman who is repeatedly sexually harassed on the job. And the evidence indicates that by adolescence, girls have lower expectations for future success than boys have (Ruble et al., 1993).

How can one deal with this situation? First, it is probably possible to apply some "preventive medicine" based on the learned helplessness and hopelessness theories. Childrearing practices and other factors should be examined to see whether they encourage helplessness in females, and if they do, they should be changed. As two authorities commented,

> . . . young women will do well to concentrate on preventing future depressions by cultivating habits of self-respect and self-reliance and by leading a balanced life, participating in a variety of activities rather than depending on family ties alone for emotional and intellectual sustenance. (Beck and Greenberg, 1974, p. 130)

But psychological changes in women alone will not be enough. As long as the society around them is unresponsive to their actions, problems will still result. As the same authors noted,

> A woman can learn to be aware of what she wants, to take direct action to get it, and to take credit for her successes. But to avoid helplessness, her environment must cooperate. (1974, p. 130)

Violence and Poverty Two additional factors contribute to depression in women and help to explain why more women than men are depressed: violence against women and poverty (Belle, 1990; Koss, 1990). Violence against women is discussed in detail in Chapter 13. Suffice it to say here that the experience of being battered, for example, can lead to depression. Regarding the second factor, poverty is becoming increasingly gender-related. An increasing proportion of those living below the poverty line are women or women and their children, a phenomenon known as the **feminization of poverty.** This in turn is related to factors such as the increased proportion of single-parent households headed by women, the inadequacy of child support payments following divorce, and the lack of decent, affordable childcare that would allow these women to work at jobs that could bring them to self-sufficiency (Belle, 1990). Abundant evidence shows a link between poverty and mental health problems (Belle, 1990). Therefore, the feminization of poverty has mental health implications for women. Research indicates that women who are financially stressed and have responsibility for young children experience more symptoms of depression than other women do (e.g., Pearlin and Johnson, 1977). One study found that nearly half the low-income mothers of young children in the sample had sufficient symptoms to be categorized as depressed (Hall et al., 1985). There is little doubt that the higher rates of poverty among women contribute to the higher incidence of depression in women.

Feminization of poverty: The increasing trend over time for women to be over-represented among the poor in the United States.

Alcoholism and Drug Abuse

Statistics on Gender and Alcohol Use   Just as depression has been viewed as a "feminine" problem, alcoholism has been seen as a "masculine" problem. In the Victorian era, drinking was viewed as a male-only activity, and the prohibition movement was led by women. Social norms have changed greatly and there is now tolerance of social drinking for women, although there is little tolerance for drunken women, and the drunk woman is viewed with more scorn and disgust than the drunk man (Gomberg, 1974).

The ratio of men problem drinkers to women problem drinkers is about 3:1 (McCrady, 1988). A convergence hypothesis has been proposed regarding statistics on gender and alcoholism. The hypothesis states that alcoholism rates for males and for females are getting closer to each other or are converging, in large part because gender roles are changing, making drinking more acceptable for women. There is actually little evidence that the convergence hypothesis is true; the male:female ratio has remained remarkably constant over many decades (Fillmore, 1984; Gomberg, 1993). However, one researcher found, among the youngest age group to be studied (those who were 21–29 in 1979), a much higher rate of heavy drinking for women than was found among women in that age range in previous generations (Fillmore, 1984). This is cause for some concern. The goal of women's liberation was not to liberate women to become heavy drinkers.

Predictors of Alcoholism in Women   Experts agree that there are multiple factors that predispose a woman to become an alcoholic or problem drinker. Factors that have been proposed include the following: a family history of alcoholism, disruption in early family life, childhood sexual abuse, a history of depression, and social roles (including gender roles and norms of one's ethnic group) (Gomberg and Lisansky, 1984; Gomberg, 1993).

A *family history of alcoholism* is one predisposing factor to alcoholism. Data from twin studies indicate that genetic factors play a large role in alcoholism in males; however, genetic factors appear to have little or no effect on alcoholism in females (McGue et al., 1992).

Disruptions in early family life, such as alcoholism in a parent, death of a parent, or divorce, are common among people who develop alcohol problems. Such traumatic events are all more likely among women alcoholics than among women in the general population (Gomberg, 1974, 1979; Travis, 1988b). Moreover, women alcoholics are more likely than men alcoholics to report such disruptions and to report feeling rejected and deprived in childhood (Gomberg and Lisansky, 1984). The data indicate that, for women, there is an association between *childhood sexual abuse* and problem drinking in adulthood (Gomberg, 1993).

Social roles, in particular, gender roles in one's ethnic group, play a role as well. Some ethnic groups tolerate or even encourage heavy drinking, whereas others discourage it, and still others encourage it for men and discourage it for women. This in turn is likely to affect patterns of alcoholism. For example, among Irish Americans alcoholism rates are high for both men and women, whereas among Hispanics the rates are high for men but very low for women (Gomberg and Lisansky, 1984). We will return to this point in the next section.

There appears to be a strong relationship between *depression* and drinking problems in women (Travis, 1988b). The evidence indicates that the depression occurs first, and heavy drinking becomes a way of coping with it (Gomberg, 1993). There is also a rather high rate of alcoholism among husbands of alcoholic women. The evidence suggests that alcoholism may begin with the husband and spread to the wife, although the reverse rarely occurs (Gomberg, 1974).

There are also important variations among alcoholic women. At least two basic types emerge (Gomberg, 1979). One group consists of women with an early onset of alcoholism in their teens or twenties; they are likely to have trouble with controlling their impulses and are very similar to delinquents. The other group consists of women with a later onset of alcoholism in their thirties or forties. Earlier in life they showed better coping skills, but they gradually began to use alcohol to cope with feelings of depression, and its use then accelerated.

Although men and women alcoholics have much in common, some gender differences are found (Gomberg, 1979). Women have their first drink and their first episode of intoxication at a later age than men do. In addition, women alcoholics are more likely to drink at home or alone, whereas men alcoholics are more likely to do their drinking in gregarious social settings.

Ethnicity, Gender, and Alcohol Abuse   As noted in Chapter 8, it is essential to consider interactions between gender and ethnicity, and alcohol abuse is a good case in point. Among teenage girls, heavy drinking has been found to be most common among American Indian girls (11 percent) and lowest among African

American girls (3 percent), with whites (6 percent), Hispanics (5 percent), and Asian Americans (4 percent) being intermediate (Travis, 1988b). For teenagers, the ratio of male:female heavy drinkers is 2:1 for American Indians, 2.5:1 for whites, 3:1 for African Americans, 3.6:1 for Hispanics, and 55:1 for Asian American (Travis, 1988b). Notice that the gender ratio is always greater than 1:1. That is, there are more male than female heavy drinkers in all these ethnic groups. Nonetheless, the gender imbalance is far greater for Asian Americans than it is for all other ethnic groups.

Other Drugs   About twice as many men as women use illegal drugs such as heroin, cocaine, and hallucinogens (Fidell, 1982). Data also show that large numbers of women are hooked on legal prescription drugs such as tranquilizers and diet pills. Physicians simply seem to be more willing to suggest drugs as cures for women's problems. For example, female depressives receive more drugs, and stronger ones, than males with the same symptoms (Stein et al., 1976). The ratio of women to men receiving prescriptions for tranquilizers is about 2:1. For example, in the United States, 16.9 percent of women and 8.5 percent of men have used tranquilizers in the past year (Ashton, 1991). This compares with figures of 15.3 percent for women and 6.7 percent for men in Britain, and 21.4 percent for women and 12.9 percent for men in Belgium. Thus dependence on or addiction to legal prescription drugs is a serious problem for some women and, once again, gender roles seem to play a part.

Eating Disorders

Have you ever heard the saying "A woman can never be too rich or too thin?" I'm not sure about the rich part, but I am sure about the thin part. A woman *can* be too thin. The condition is anorexia nervosa, and it can kill. It is fatal in about 5 percent of the cases (Hsu et al., 1993).

Anorexia nervosa: An eating disorder characterized by overcontrol of eating for purposes of weight reduction, sometimes to the point of starvation.

Anorexia Nervosa: Symptoms and Diagnosis   **Anorexia nervosa** is a disorder in which a person essentially starves herself. A typical definition is "overcontrol of eating for weight reduction" (Levenkron, 1982, p. 2). The pronoun *herself* is used intentionally here because the disorder is present disproportionately among females— 90 percent of anorexics are females, and the great majority are adolescents, the usual age of onset being between 13 and 25 (Levenkron, 1982; Russo and Green, 1993; Woodside and Garfinkel, 1992). Anorexia is estimated to afflict 1 in 250 adolescent girls (Levenkron, 1982). On the other hand, in one study, 20 percent of anorexics first showed symptoms when they were over 30 (Woodside and Garfinkel, 1992).

Although there is some disagreement among experts, the following are generally the criteria for diagnosis of anorexia (Garfinkel and Garner, 1982; Levenkron, 1982; Minuchin et al., 1978):

1. Loss of 20 percent or more of body weight—the person is emaciated.

2. Amenorrhea, or the absence of a menstrual period.

3. Thinning hair.

4. Dry, flaking skin.

5. Constipation.

6. Lanugo—a growth of downy hair on the body, probably part of the body's effort to keep warm when few calories are coming in.

7. Lowered body temperature—often 95–97° F. The anorexic may be found wearing four sweaters in the winter to keep herself warm.

The extreme weight loss results from the anorexic's compulsive dieting. Although she may begin with normal dieting, the dieting soon gets out of control. She limits herself to perhaps 600–800 calories per day (Garfinkel and Garner, 1982). Her thoughts become obsessively focused on food and eating, and rituals surrounding eating develop. She may limit herself to only a few low-calorie foods, perhaps existing solely on cottage cheese and apples. She eats in private

FIGURE 14.1
This artwork was done by an anorexic woman at the severest stage of her illness. It shows her feelings of isolation and distorted body image.

FOCUS 14.1

AN ANOREXIC TELLS HER STORY

At age 27 I am a recovered anorexic. I am 6 feet tall and weigh 140 pounds, which is just right for me. But things were not always that way.

At age 3 I was already fat. My mother loved to cook and I loved to eat. She was 5 feet 2 inches tall and weighed 180 pounds herself. When I got to school, I found that the other kids rejected me because I was fat. I quickly learned that the only way to get attention and have people like me was to cater to them, doing what they wanted, giving them things, never thinking of myself. When I was 14, my mother dieted down to 120 pounds. When my sister was 15 and I was 18, she became anorexic. I swore that would never happen to me.

At age 23 I weighed 187 pounds and had never had a date. One day a co-worker casually commented to me, "We both need to lose some weight." The comment instantly triggered something in me, and I started dieting. Within a few months, I was down to 140 pounds. I was asked on my first date. People said, "You look great, don't lose any more." I found that good things happen when you diet.

At that point, things were going so well that I decided, just to be on the safe side, that I should take off a few more pounds. I cut out sweets entirely. In the next three months, I went from 140 to 113 pounds. My menstrual period stopped.

When I reached 113 pounds, I decided to set 100 pounds as my goal. Dieting became an obsession. It was everything to me. I bought calorie counters, including seven copies of one of them. I cut almost all foods. Typically I consumed 500 calories per day maximum. Breakfast would be a slice of toast with a dab of peanut butter (I couldn't give up peanut butter). I skipped lunch. I ate dinner "out" so my family wouldn't know what I was doing. Usually it would be one bowl of chili, which has 280 calories. I drank lots of tea and chewed on ice so I could chew on something with no calories. Sometimes I also skipped breakfast, but got up early, before the rest of my family, and banged around the kitchen, pretending to fix breakfast but eating nothing. When I did eat, I always ate alone, never with others. I baked for my family, but then ate none of it. Everything was ritual and compulsion. I thought of nothing but food. Life with my family was a constant battle. The more they told me they wanted me to eat, the less I wanted to eat. When they asked me what I had for supper, I said, "I ordered a hamburger, french fries, and a milkshake." And I did. I ordered them at a fast food place, picked them up at the drive-through window, and then threw all of it in the trash can without eating any of it.

I never did make it to 100 pounds. The lowest I reached was 110. At that point, I missed work (I work as a dental assistant) and didn't care. I was perpetually cold and had my electric blanket on "high" in the middle of the summer. In the winter I would typically dress in panty hose, thermal underwear, two pairs of slacks, and several sweaters, and still be cold. Despite the small number of calories I consumed, my energy level was high. I sometimes woke up in the middle of the night and did sit-ups. I exercised while my co-workers were out at lunch.

Then I started having dizzy spells. That scared me. I got glasses, thinking my eyes were the problem and that glasses would help me. Needless to say, they didn't. Then I went to a physician. He told me to start eating. I didn't.

Soon after that I read a magazine article on anorexia. It triggered a rather dull click in my head. Some of the things that woman did sounded like me. The article contained the address of a national agency that made referrals for help.* I wrote to the address. They referred me to a nearby support group for anorexics. I went to it only twice. I didn't want to be with all of those thin people when I was so fat, as I saw myself.

The support group leader told me that I couldn't continue in the support group unless I also went for individual psychotherapy. Obedient person that I was, catering to her wishes as I always did to everyone's, I went to a therapist at a nearby community mental health clinic. I didn't want to go. At the first session I told him I didn't know why I was there. The first session converted me. Therapy was wonderful. Dr. G didn't tell me I had to eat or that I had to gain weight, as everyone else in my life was doing. He said, "We won't talk about weight. We'll talk about you." He helped me find out what my own wants were, a first for me because I had spent my life catering to others. After that first session, there was no doubt in my mind—I definitely wanted to continue therapy. In later sessions I learned to be assertive, doing something about my own wants. I learned how I had had no control of things in my life, and so chose to control one thing within my power—my weight. I came to realize that I had had chronically low self-esteem, and I learned that I was a worthy human being. Previously I had been afraid to be anything but an angel with other people. With Dr. G, I could be myself, and our relationship was still okay. I learned to take that out to the rest of the world. I made new friends and started dating. In sessions with Dr. G, I had his undivided attention.

In all, I was in intensive therapy for about seven months, once per week. I still go in for a session occasionally if I feel particularly stressed or feel like I need a "booster shot." After the first session, I decided that eating was safe. I ate, and it was the first thing I'd ever done for myself. I added one thing a day to my eating. After three months I was still eating only small amounts, but it was progress and I had gained 7 pounds. My eating habits were still rigid, though. Then I got up to 127 pounds and stayed there for a year. I was less of a loner and had more of a social life. After that I got up to 140 pounds, and I have been there ever since.

I'm confident that I will never be anorexic again. Occasionally, if I am under great stress, I stop eating. But I instantly recognize the signs, I remember how horrible it was to be anorexic, and I start eating again.

SOURCE: Based on an interview conducted by the author.
*One such organization is the National Anorexic Aid Society, 1925 East Dublin Granville Rd., Columbus, OH 43229. They make referrals to therapists, support groups, and hospitals, as well as offering many other services.

and generally becomes a loner. One anorexic described her ritualistic behavior to me: At work after her co-workers had eaten their lunches, she looked for opportunities when they were out of the office and then searched through the trash can for the waxed-paper wrappings from their lunches. She would finger the wrappings and sniff them for odors of food, then quickly return them to the trash can before she was discovered.

The compulsive dieting is a result of a phobia of gaining any weight and a corresponding drive toward thinness. But the anorexic's body image is often distorted, so that she believes herself to be fat even though she is emaciated, 20 percent or more under normal body weight. Despite the low intake of calories, the anorexic typically has abundant energy, to the point of being hyperactive. She often undertakes strenuous exercise programs to try to burn off further calories.

The title of one excellent novel about anorexia, which was made into a television special, is *The Best Little Girl in the World* (Levenkron, 1978). The title refers to the fact that most anorexics are good little girls, obedient and high-achieving at school. Despite this, they typically have feelings of inferiority about their intelligence and appearance. Depression and anxiety are also common, the anxiety being relieved only by weight loss and fasting. The anorexic is also typically uninterested in sexuality. Finally, the anorexic usually engages in denial:

she firmly maintains that she has no problem and that she is not underweight, and she resists undergoing psychotherapy.

Bulimia: An eating disorder in which the person binges on food and then purges the body of the calories by vomiting or using laxatives.

Bulimia **Bulimia** (also called bulimarexia) is a variation on anorexia in which the weight loss is achieved in another way (see the review by Striegel-Moore et al., 1986). It is sometimes called the bingeing-and-purging syndrome because the woman gorges herself by binge overeating, and then, before the calories enter her body, purges herself of the food either by forcing herself to vomit or by abusive use of laxatives. The bulimic may have an intake of 4,000 to 5,000 calories per day, yet continue to lose weight (Garfinkel and Garner, 1982). In one case, a bulimic spent six hours every evening eating, yet weighed 62 pounds (Levenkron, 1982).

Surveys of college populations indicate that as many as 13 to 20 percent of the women have engaged in bulimic behaviors, including binge eating followed by vomiting (Russo and Green, 1993). Thus this problem is not a rare one, and there is evidence that it is rapidly increasing. Like anorexia, it is primarily a female problem; 90 percent of bulimics are female (Striegel-Moore et al., 1986).

The prevalence of this disorder is disturbing, particularly because it has some serious health consequences. Some of those are the results of starvation and will be discussed in the next section. In addition, the bulimic may suffer serious damage to her teeth, due to the acidity of the repeated vomiting.

Theories and Therapies Many theories as to the causes of eating disorders have been proposed, leading to correspondingly different forms of therapy. All seem to agree, though, that therapy is slow and difficult—two to five years of therapy are common (Levenkron, 1982).

It has been proposed that anorexia is a result of *biological causes* (reviewed by Garfinkel and Garner, 1982). Anorexics do have many disturbances of their biological functioning. But the problem is that physicians never see these people until they are already anorexic. At that point, it is not clear whether the physiological problems are the cause of the anorexia or the result of starvation. Research indicates that most likely, the problematic conditions are the result of starvation because most of those conditions reverse themselves and return to normal as the person gains weight (Garfinkel and Garner, 1982). The functioning of the hypothalamus in the anorexic is disturbed. The hormones LH and FSH are at very low levels, comparable to those of a girl before puberty. Electrolytes are important for the proper functioning of the nervous system, and electrolyte levels (e.g., potassium) are disturbed in anorexics. Low potassium levels are a particular problem in bulimics, resulting from the vomiting and misuse of laxatives. Convulsions, low blood pressure, low heart rates, and irregular heartbeats are other results of the starvation. It seems, though, that all these biological abnormalities are results, rather than causes, of the anorexia.

Traditional psychoanalytic theory has viewed anorexia as resulting from a fear of oral impregnation (see the reviews by Minuchin et al., 1978; Garfinkel and Garner, 1982). That is, the anorexic sees food taken in through the mouth as causing pregnancy. Not eating prevents pregnancy. Simultaneously, the starvation produces amenorrhea, which further reduces fears about pregnancy. And the weight loss erases the curves of the adult female body, returning the anorexic to the straight body of a girl—a kind of regression. These problems are attributed to disturbed parent-child relationships. Disturbed family relationships are common among anorexics, but once again, it is not clear whether the disturbed family is cause or effect—that is, does the disturbed family cause the anorexia, or does having an anorexic in the family create disturbances?

A *behavior therapy* approach, based on learning theory, treats anorexia as an eating phobia (e.g., Brady and Rieger, 1975). The idea is that, for an anorexic, eating causes anxiety. Therefore, fasting causes anxiety reduction, which is a powerful reinforcer. An understanding of these principles can be useful in the hospital treatment of anorexics, the goal being to get them to eat. This may be an extremely important short-term goal because, as noted previously, there is some risk of death due to starvation or to complications resulting from it, such as organ failure or electrolyte imbalance. Behavior therapy can be used to reduce the anxiety that the patient associates with eating. Simultaneously, the patient may be taught to associate positive reinforcers with eating (reviewed by Garfinkel and Garner, 1982). Unfortunately, when patients treated this way return to their old home environment, they often revert to their previous anorexic behavior patterns.

Bulimia might seem difficult to explain using learning theory. Vomiting is so inherently aversive, why would anyone do it repeatedly? The answer, once again, lies in anxiety. The bulimic wants to lose weight; therefore an eating binge creates a high level of anxiety. Vomiting reduces the anxiety, and thus actually becomes a positive reinforcer.

Cognitive-behavioral therapy has now largely replaced the simpler behavioral therapies in many areas of psychotherapy, recognizing the importance of cognitions or thought processes in psychological disorders (e.g., Srebnik and Saltzberg, 1994). Cognitive-behavioral therapy helps people to change not only their behaviors, but also the way they think about themselves and the world around them. Research shows that people with eating disorders have a variety of dysfunctional thought processes (Butow et al., 1993). They have distorted perceptions of their own bodies, often believing themselves to be fat when they are emaciated. They believe that weight gain is a sign of indulgence or lack of control. They are almost morbidly fascinated with weight control, so that it enters their thoughts when food and eating are not an issue (such as while taking an exam). They base their own feelings of self-worth on how well they are controlling their eating and their weight. Typically they think of themselves as worthless and inadequate. And as if all this were not enough, they are extremely rigid in holding on to these ideas, making therapy difficult.

Pharmacotherapy or treatment with drugs is sometimes used with anorexics and bulimics (Mitchell et al., 1993). No drug has been developed specifically for the treatment of eating disorders. Rather, antidepressants are used, based on the belief that depression (as seen in the feelings of worthlessness and inadequacy) contributes to the eating disorder.

Research has been done on the effectiveness of cognitive-behavioral therapy and drug therapy in the treatment of eating disorders (Mitchell et al., 1993). Antidepressants seem to be somewhat successful in some, but certainly not all, cases. For example, the frequency of binge eating is typically reduced by about 70 percent, but only about 24 percent of bulimics abstain from binge eating by the end of treatment (Mitchell et al., 1993). Antidepressants may help some, but they aren't the "quick fix" for all, or even most, of those with eating disorders. Most experts agree that drugs by themselves are relatively ineffective and are best used together with a treatment such as cognitive-behavioral therapy (Herzog et al., 1992).

Cognitive-behavioral therapy seems to be somewhat more effective. It, too, is more effective in reducing the frequency of binge eating and less successful at bringing about complete abstinence from bingeing. Success rates vary widely, but typically 30 to 50 percent of clients are abstinent by the end of therapy (Mitchell et al., 1993). The eating disorders are difficult to treat, and no treatment to date has come close to a 100 percent success rate.

Systems theory and *family therapy* represent yet another approach to anorexia. Systems theory regards the anorexic not as an isolated, disturbed individual, but rather as a person embedded in a complex system that includes her family and society at large (Minuchin et al., 1978). Her parents may have done things in her early childhood to predispose the girl to anorexia. Family interaction and communication patterns trigger and then perpetuate the problem in adolescence. But the girl's problem behavior also has disastrous effects on the functioning of the family. Her pathology becomes the focus of the family, and if she were to get well, a whole new family organization would be required. The predominantly upper-middle-class families of anorexic girls tend to emphasize or place importance on beauty (and therefore thinness) and externally visible signs of success, such as good grades. The girl thus learns to subordinate herself. As one team of researchers commented,

> Her expectation from a goal-directed activity, such as studying or learning a skill, is therefore not competence, but approval. The reward is not knowledge, but love. (Minuchin et al., 1978, p. 59)

Dieting produces external, tangible signs of "success" and simultaneously allows the girl to gain a sense of control.

In following the systems theory approach, family therapy is necessary. Therapy for the girl alone will not work, because she remains embedded in the family that maintains her illness. Thus both the family and the anorexic must participate in therapy.

Feminist Perspectives   The *feminist perspective* emphasizes not the pathology of the individual, but rather the socialization practices and messages of our soci-

FIGURE 14.2
The media feature models who are un-realistically thin, which contributes to a culture that fosters eating disorders in women.

ety (e.g., Boskind-Lodahl, 1976). The anorexic shows an extreme reaction to the socialization messages that all women in American society hear while growing up. The emphasis is on thinness—as the saying quoted earlier put it, "A woman can never be too thin." High-fashion models, *Playboy* centerfolds, and Miss America contestants provide images of slimness that are difficult to live up to. Just as wealthy Chinese for centuries bound the feet of their daughters to achieve a culturally defined standard of beauty, so a particular standard of appearance of thinness is enforced in American society, not through physical methods but rather by socialization (Garfinkel and Garner, 1982).

Here are some of the data: Whereas a generation ago, female models weighed only about 8 percent less than the average American woman, today they weigh 23 percent less (Wolf, 1991). The average model, dancer, or actress today weighs less and looks thinner than 95 percent of the female population in the United States (Wolf, 1991). College women rate their ideal figure as consider-ably thinner than their actual figure (Lamb et al., 1993). In fact, dissatisfaction with weight is so common among adolescent girls and women that it has been termed a "normative discontent" (Rodin et al., 1985). In one study of sixth, seventh, and eighth grade girls, 72 percent dieted (Levine et al., 1994). These standards of attractiveness are attached to Euro-American culture. In one study, Ugandans rated somewhat overweight and fat figures as being significantly more attractive than British respondents did (Furnham and Baguma, 1994).

In another study, college students watched one of four videotapes of a woman eating a meal (Basow and Kobrynowicz, 1993). The woman and her behavior were the same on each videotape. The tapes differed only in the meal she ate. Videotape 1 showed her eating a small salad and a glass of seltzer. Videotape 2 showed a large Greek salad and a diet soda. Videotape 3 showed her eating a half-size meatball sandwich, six mozzarella sticks, and a large Coke. Videotape 4 showed her eating a full-size meatball sandwich (approximately 1 foot in length), six mozzarella sticks, large fries, a piece of cake, and a large Coke. The woman in Videotape 1 was rated as having significantly better eating habits and as having significantly more social appeal than the same woman in the other videotapes. We have developed not only powerful cultural norms about the proper, thin body for women, but also norms about what women should eat.

Feminist therapists also note that anorexia is often precipitated by breaking up with a boyfriend or some other perceived rejection by a male (Boskind-Lodahl, 1976). The problem here is that the anorexic has given males the power to define her life and control her self-esteem.

Where does this vast array of possible explanations leave us? Garfinkel and Garner (1982) have proposed what I think is a useful way of organizing and understanding why anorexia develops, incorporating most of the foregoing ideas (see Figure 14.3). First, there are a number of *predisposing factors* to anorexia: a disturbed family, cultural pressures for thinness, disturbed cognitions such as a distorted body image, and so on. Compulsive dieting may be started when someone who is characterized by many of the predisposing factors is then exposed to a *precipitating factor,* such as the loss of a boyfriend or a demand from a boyfriend for the beginning of sexual activity. Once excessive dieting begins, several *sustaining factors* keep it going—starving and vomiting reduce anxiety, and there may be secondary gains when the anorexia attracts attention. Thus many factors play their parts, and all must be understood and addressed if therapy is to be successful.

Sexism and Psychotherapy

With the rise of the women's movement in the late 1960s, psychotherapists and the institution of psychotherapy became the object of sharp attacks for sexism (e.g., Chesler, 1972). What evidence is there that sexism in psychotherapy is a problem?

The Broverman Study By far the most frequently cited study used as evidence of sexism in psychotherapy is one done by psychologist Inge Broverman and her

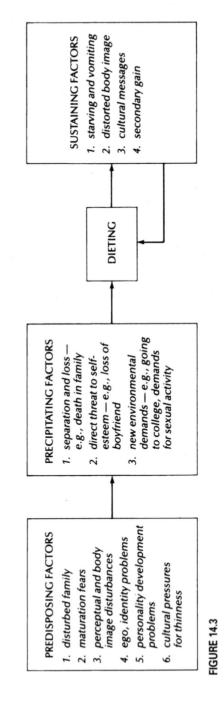

FIGURE 14.3

A model proposed for understanding the causes of anorexia. (*Source: After Garfinkel and Garner, 1982.*)

colleagues (1970). They investigated the judgments of clinicians (psychiatrists, clinical psychologists, and social workers) on criteria of mental health for males and females. The clinicians in the sample were given a personality questionnaire with a series of bipolar rating scales of gender-typed personality characteristics, for example:

very aggressive   *not at all aggressive*

One-third of the clinicians were instructed to indicate on each item the pole to which a mature, healthy, socially competent *male* would be closer. Another third were told to do this for a *female,* and the remaining third were told to do so for an *adult.* Three interesting results emerged. First, although no significant differences were seen between the standards for males and for adults, there were differences between the standards for females and for adults. This is a good example of the male-as-normative principle in psychology. The standards for human mental health are for males, and females are a deviation from them— or, as one feminist put it, the Broverman results show that "a normal, average, healthy woman is a crazy human being." A second result was that socially desirable personality characteristics tended to be assigned to males, undesirable ones to females. For example, a mature, healthy, socially competent woman is supposed to be more submissive, more excitable in minor crises, have her feelings more easily hurt, and be more conceited about her appearance than a mature, healthy, socially competent man. A third result was that there was no difference in the results depending on whether the clinician-rater was a man or a woman (more than one-third of the clinicians were females). Apparently female clinicians are no more exempt than males from these views of "healthy" womanhood.

On the basis of this study, it appears that the same double-bind situations that bring women to therapy may be present in the therapy situation. Basically the woman has two alternatives: she can adjust to female norms, in which case she will have a number of undesirable personality characteristics (e.g., being excitable in minor crises); or she can develop certain desirable human traits such as independence and assertiveness, in which case she may be accused of rejecting her femininity, and therefore of being abnormal. Of course, not every clinician is guilty of creating such situations, but the general trends discovered in this study are disturbing.

As evidence of sexism in psychotherapy, there are some problems with the Broverman study. The basic problem is that it does not provide a direct measure of what we are concerned with: whether therapists, in their treatment of clients, act in a sexist manner. This study does not measure what therapists actually do in therapy, but rather what their attitudes are, based on their responses to a paper-and-pencil questionnaire. What we need are data on therapists' actual treatment of clients (Stricker, 1977), but such information is in short supply. (I shall review those data that are available in a later section.) The Broverman study has also been criticized for being methodologically flawed (Widiger and Settle, 1987). Another problem with the Broverman study is that it is now some 25 years old. It is possible that therapists have changed their attitudes substantially in the past 25 years, in response to changing attitudes about gender roles in our culture. In sum, the Broverman study does not provide good evidence of sexism in psychotherapy today.

From the perspective of the 1990s, three areas are causes for concern about sex bias in therapy: gender bias in diagnosis, bias in treatment, and sexual misconduct by therapists with their clients. Each of these is discussed below.

Gender Bias in Diagnosis   Gender stereotypes may influence clinicians' diagnoses of women who come to them for help. For example, in one study clinicians labeled a stereotyped description of a single, middle-class white woman as an hysterical personality (Landrine, 1987). But clinicians given the same description for a *married,* middle-class woman labeled her depressed. As another example, a female client might be labeled histrionic, but a male client with the same characteristics might be labeled as antisocial (Ford and Widiger, 1989).

Focus 14.2 provides an illustration of the ways in which the very diagnostic labels that are available in the American Psychiatric Association's official ***Diagnostic and Statistical Manual*** (**DSM**) are influenced by gender and political considerations.

Diagnostic and Statistical Manual (DSM): The American Psychiatric Association's official manual of psychiatric diagnosis.

In short, the diagnosis of a mental disorder is not an objective, value-free process. The therapist's values and gender stereotypes enter the process. On an institutional level, gender considerations affect the very diagnostic categories that are officially available.

Gender Bias in Treatment   The American Psychological Association (1975b) identified a number of ways in which gender bias may occur in psychotherapy:

1. Fostering of traditional gender roles.

   Example:
   The therapist assumes that the woman's problems will be solved by marriage or by being a better wife.

   > My therapist suggested that my identity problems would be solved by my marrying and having children; I was 19 at the time and in no way ready for marriage.

2. Bias in expectations and devaluation of women.

   Example:
   The therapist denies self-actualization or assertiveness for female clients and instead fosters concepts of women as passive and dependent.

Whenever a female becomes active, assertive, and aggressive in group [therapy] situations the label "castrating bitch" is applied to her.

3. Sexist use of psychonanalytic concepts.

   Examples:
   a. The therapist maintains that vaginal orgasm is a prerequisite for emotional maturity and thus a goal of therapy.
   b. The therapist labels assertiveness and ambition with the Freudian concept of "penis envy."

4. Responding to women as sex objects, including the seduction of female clients.

Sexual Misconduct by Therapists   One of the most serious problems for women in therapy today is the possibility of a male therapist initiating sex with a female client.

The 1978 revision of the APA's ethical code states: "Sexual intimacies between therapist and client are unethical." This means that under no circumstances is a therapist to have a sexual relationship with a client. A survey investigated the sexual activities of a sample of licensed Ph.D. psychologists with their clients (Holroyd and Brodsky, 1977); 5.5 percent of the male and 0.6 percent of the female psychologists returning the questionnaire admitted having engaged in sexual intercourse with a client during the time the patient was in therapy, and an additional 2.6 percent of male and 0.3 percent of female therapists had intercourse with clients within three months of termination of therapy. These are probably best regarded as minimum figures, because they are based on the self-reports of the therapists and some might not be willing to admit such activity, even though the questionnaire was anonymous. Of those therapists who had intercourse with clients, 80 percent repeated the activity with other clients.

Experts regard this situation as having the potential for serious emotional damage to the client (Williams, 1992). Like other cases of sexual coercion, it is a situation of unequal power, in which the more powerful person, the therapist, imposes sexual activity on the less powerful person, the client. The situation is regarded as particularly serious, because patients in psychotherapy have opened themselves up emotionally to the therapist and therefore are extremely vulnerable emotionally.

How Traditional Therapies Apply to Women

One of the most important factors influencing a woman's experience in therapy is the theoretical orientation of the therapist and the corresponding type of therapy she or he uses. Below we shall consider two kinds of therapy to see how they relate to women and whether they are likely to be biased.

FOCUS 14.2
GENDER AND THE POLITICS OF PSYCHIATRIC DIAGNOSIS

The American Psychiatric Association publishes a thick book called the *Diagnostic and Statistical Manual* (DSM). The latest edition, DSM-IV, came out in 1994. Why is this book important? It contains the listing of all the official labels or diagnoses that psychiatrists and psychologists can give to people's mental disorders, together with a list of the criteria or symptoms that a patient must show in order to be given a particular diagnosis. Money is involved because, in order for your health insurance to pay for psychotherapy, the therapist must give you an official diagnosis from this book, which then becomes part of your record.

The DSM-IV contains a new diagnosis, not present in previous editions: Premenstrual Dysphoric Disorder (PMDD). ("Dysphoria" is the opposite of "euphoria"; "dysphoria" means unhappiness or depressed mood.) To be diagnosed with PMDD, a woman (and obviously only women can get this diagnosis) must display

> symptoms such as markedly depressed mood, marked anxiety, marked affective lability, and decreased interest in activities. These symptoms have regularly occurred during the last week of the luteal phase in most menstrual cycles during the past year. The symptoms begin to remit within a few days of the onset of menses . . . and are always absent in the week following menses. . . . This pattern of symptoms must have occurred most months for the previous 12 months. (American Psychiatric Association, 1994, p. 715)

Clearly this is the American Psychiatric Association's attempt to incorporate PMS into its diagnoses. Although this might sound like an innocent enough idea, gender politics are involved.

The PMDD diagnosis may do harm to women in several

Psychoanalysis: A system of therapy based on Freud's psychoanalytic theory in which the analyst attempts to bring repressed, unconscious material into consciousness.

Psychoanalysis **Psychoanalysis** is a system of therapy based on Freud's theory (see Chapter 2). Both Freudian theory and psychoanalysis have received sharp criticism from feminists. Some feminists feel that psychoanalysis is inherently, or at least very likely to be, sex biased (e.g., American Psychological Association, 1975b). Others, however, feel that it can be applied in an unbiased way, and even speak of feminist psychoanalysis (e.g., Eichenbaum and Orbach, 1983; Shainess, 1977).

The problem was psychoanalysis is that some of its central concepts *are* sex biased. For example, women's achievement strivings

ways. For example, if a woman is diagnosed with PMDD, an ex-husband might use this to argue that he should get custody of their children because she has psychiatric problems. As another example, physicians may fail to properly diagnose and treat serious pelvic problems—such as pain resulting from an untreated sexually transmitted disease—because their focus is shifted to "treating" psychological issues because of the PMDD diagnosis. One should generally be suspicious of a psychiatric diagnosis that can be applied to one gender only.

Another cause for suspicion about PMDD is that it has little or no scientific evidence backing it. The DSM is supposed to contain only diagnoses that have been validated scientifically. However, in an important study, a group of women reporting severe premenstrual symptoms was compared with a group of women with no symptoms (Gallant et al., 1992). The women responded to a checklist that contained the symptoms listed in the criteria for PMDD. There were no differences between the two groups! That is, the PMDD criteria fail to differentiate between a group of women who believe they have PMS and a group of women who do not. To establish the validity of PMDD, differences existing between the two groups would be essential. Therefore, there is serious question about the scientific validity of PMDD.

What about women who do feel depressed just before their period? Don't we need a diagnosis for them? There already is one—depression. They can be treated for it, with no need for complex and potentially harmful labels of premenstrual dysphoria.

Even a process as seemingly innocent as psychiatric diagnosis may involve gender stereotypes and practices that can be harmful to women.

SOURCE: Caplan (1995).

may be interpreted as penis envy. Women who enjoy orgasm from masturbation may be regarded as immature and thus be urged to strive for the more mature, vaginal orgasm. The evidence indicates that women in psychoanalysis have sometimes been convinced that they are inferior, masochistic, and so on (American Psychological Association, 1975b). Therefore, although feminist or nonsexist psychoanalysis may be a possibility, clients should be sensitized to the potential sexism of psychoanalysis.

Behavior therapy: A system of treatment based on the principles of learning theory.

Behavior Therapy **Behavior therapy** (behavior modification or behavior mod) is a set of therapies based on principles of classical conditioning (usually associated with Pavlov) and operant conditioning (usually associated with Skinner). In contrast to psychoanalysis, behavior therapy attempts no in-depth analysis of the patient's personality or unconscious motives. Instead, the focus is on problematic behavior and how it can be modified by learning principles such as rewarding desired behaviors or punishing undesired ones (for a detailed discussion of behavior therapy and its implications for women, see Bleckman, 1980).

A number of specific therapy techniques may be used. One is **systematic desensitization,** which is used in the treatment of phobias. The client and therapist make a list of events that arouse the patient's anxiety, and these are listed in a "hierarchy" from least anxiety-provoking to most anxiety-provoking (Table 14.1) The client is then trained in deep muscle relaxation. Next, the client relaxes and, while relaxed, is asked to imagine the least anxiety-provoking item on the hierarchy; if there is any tension, the patient goes back to concentrating on relaxation. Once the client is relaxed while imagining that situation, the therapist moves on to the next situation on the hierarchy, and so on, until the client is relaxed while imaging the most anxiety-provoking situation. Once clients feel relaxed imagining these events, they are often able to feel relaxed and confident when actually confronting them.

Systematic desensitization: A method used by behavior therapists in the treatment of phobias; it involves associating a relaxed, pleasant state with gradually increasing anxiety-provoking stimuli.

TABLE 14.1
A Client's Hierarchy for Systematic Desensitization

Most anxiety-arousing	
	1. An argument she raises in a discussion is ignored by the group.
	2. She is not recognized by a person she has briefly met three times.
	3. Her mother says she is selfish because she is not helping in the house (studying instead).
	4. She is not recognized by a person she has briefly met twice.
	5. Her mother calls her lazy.
Least anxiety-arousing	6. She is not recognized by a person she has briefly met once.

SOURCE: Adapted from Joseph Wolpe and A. A. Lazarus, *Behavior Therapy Techniques: A Guide for the Treatment of Neuroses,* 1966, Pergamon Press. Used by permission.

Another therapy technique that is practiced is *positive reinforcement,* in which desired behaviors are rewarded. *Observation* and *imitation* can also be used, such as assertiveness training for women, which we will discuss later in this chapter. Finally, *aversive learning procedures*—in which some unpleasant stimulus functions to eliminate an undesired behavior—may be another technique applied. For example, the drug antabuse may be given to alcoholics; if they drink, the drug causes unpleasant body reactions such as nausea and vomiting. Such therapy is called *aversive counterconditioning.*

There is no inherent sexism in the concepts of behavior therapy (Lazarus, 1974). It does not assume that there should be gender differences, or that only women should engage in certain behaviors. Of course, behavior therapy does contain value judgments, but these should be applied equally to females and males. For example, assertiveness is valued by behavior therapists, but it should be valued both for males and for females. Of course, an individual behavior therapist may be sex biased, but there is nothing in the theoretical system itself that is biased.

As an example of the treatment of a particularly common problem for women, the behavior therapist would attack depression by trying to increase the level of positive reinforcement the woman receives in her environment (Beck and Greenberg, 1974). For instance, it might be that her husband is unresponsive, or even that he responds negatively, to her attempts at conversation or her work around the house, or to discussion of her job. Her husband might be trained to be more responsive to her, thus providing more positive reinforcement. Or she may receive little positive reinforcement in her job, in which case she might be encouraged to alter her work or find a different job that would provide more positive reinforcement.

Cognitive-behavioral therapy: A system of psychotherapy that combines behavior therapy and restructuring of dysfunctional thought patterns.

As noted earlier in this chapter, **cognitive-behavioral therapy** has now largely replaced behavior therapy (e.g., Srebnik and Saltzberg, 1994). In cognitive-behavioral therapy, the therapist and client identify not only dysfunctional behaviors, but also dysfunctional thought patterns. As an example of a problem behavior, a woman might have become so concerned that her hips are fatter than those of the models she sees on TV and in magazines that she refuses to go to the swimming pool because she will have to be seen in a swimming suit, despite the fact that she loves to swim and it's a hot summer. The therapist can help the woman confront such *avoidant behaviors* and substitute adaptive behaviors. In the cognitive realm, the therapist can help the client discover *negative beliefs* (my hips are fat and therefore no one can love me). The client can then discover how irrational those beliefs are and engage in *cognitive restructuring,* in which she substitutes positive beliefs (my hips are just fine, they're just fatter than those of skinny models, and I have lots of lovable qualities that people will notice, rather than staring at my hips).

Again, there is nothing inherently sex-biased about cognitive-behavioral therapy, although certainly an individual therapist could use it in a biased manner. Some feminist therapists are developing feminist cognitive-behavioral therapy (e.g., Srebnik and Saltzberg, 1994).

New Therapies for Women

With the critiques of traditional therapies, particularly psychoanalysis, has come the suggestion that there is a need for feminist therapy or nonsexist therapy, or therapies especially tailored to the needs of women. In this section we shall discuss some of these alternatives.

Feminist Therapy and Nonsexist Therapy Feminist and nonsexist therapies may be characterized as allowing

> clients to determine their own destinies without the construction of culturally prescribed sex-role stereotypes based upon assumed biological differences. Both approaches attempt to facilitate equality (in personal power) between females and males. (Rawlings and Carter, 1977, p. 50)

Feminist therapy: A system of therapy informed by feminist theory.

Clinical psychologists Edna Rawlings and Dianne Carter (1977) distinguish between nonsexist therapy and feminist therapy. **Feminist therapy,** in particular, includes an advocacy of positions of the women's movement. They state that *nonsexist therapy* has the following particular values and assumptions:

1. The therapist should be aware of her or his own values.

2. There are no prescribed gender-role behaviors.

3. Gender-role reversals (e.g., female breadwinner, male at home) are not labeled pathological.

4. Marriage is not regarded as any better an outcome of therapy for a female than for a male.

5. Females are expected to be as autonomous and assertive as males; males are expected to be as expressive and tender as females.

6. Theories of behavior based on anatomical differences (e.g., Freud, Erikson) are rejected.

The assumptions of *feminist therapy* are as follows (Gilbert, 1980; Rawlings and Carter, 1977; Worell and Remer, 1992):

1. The inferior status of women is due to their having less political and economic power than men. Power analysis is central to feminist thought (see, for example, Chapter 2) and to feminist therapy.

2. The primary source of women's pathology is social, not personal; external, not internal.

3. The focus on environmental stress as a major source of pathology is not used as an avenue of escape from individual responsibility.

4. Feminist therapy is opposed to personal adjustment to social conditions; the goal is social and political change.

5. The therapist-client relationship is viewed as egalitarian.

6. Clients are encouraged to express anger and then deal with it.

7. Women must be economically and psychologically autonomous.

8. Relationships of friendship, love, and marriage should be equal in personal power.

9. Major differences between "appropriate" gender-role behaviors must disappear.

10. Racial, economic, handicapped, heterosexist, and ageist oppression are also important sources of social pathology. Social change needs to include all oppressions.

Terminology in this area is not standardized, however, and so some therapists might refer to themselves as feminist therapists when in fact their assumptions correspond to what I have here called nonsexist therapy.

Perhaps the two points that are most central to feminist therapy, and that most distinguish it from traditional psychotherapy, are points 2 and 4. Regarding point 2, traditional therapies have viewed people's problems as being internal (within the individual) and have correspondingly prescribed personal changes to achieve better adjustment. Feminist therapists, in contrast, view women's problems as being external in origin, caused by oppression in the society around them. From this follows point 4: if the problems are external in origin, then the goal should be to change society, not oneself.

Empowerment is a key feature of feminist therapy (Worell and Remer, 1992). This process begins by declaring that the therapist and client are equal in the therapy process—equal in the sense that both are persons of equal worth. Therapy cannot empower women if it begins by making them less powerful than the therapist. The client is then encouraged to develop two sets of skills, one dealing with the internal and the other with the external. She is empowered in dealing with her personal situation by developing flexibility in problem solving and by developing a wide range of interpersonal and life skills. In addition, focusing on external issues, the woman is empowered by encouraging her to identify and challenge external conditions in her life that devalue her as a woman and perhaps as a member of an ethnic minority group or sexual minority as well. Rather than "fixing" the client's problems, the feminist therapist encourages the client to discover her strengths and develop new strengths that empower her to deal with situations that have previously caused her distress.

Assertiveness Training   Assertiveness training—a technique of behavior therapy—has become popular among women, and it can take place as a part of formal psychotherapy, in informal self-help groups, or in classes. (For more detailed discussions, see Jakubowski-Spector, 1973; Jakubowski, 1977.) First, some terms need to be defined.

Assertion, or **assertiveness,** involves standing up for one's basic interpersonal rights in such a way that the rights of another person are not violated. Assertion should be a direct, honest, and appropriate expression of one's feelings. *Aggression,* in this context, involves standing up for one's rights in such a way that the rights of the other person are violated. It involves dominating, humiliating, or putting down the other person. *Nonassertion* is failing to stand up for one's rights and, consequently, permitting one's rights to be violated by others (Jakubowski-Spector, 1973).

Assertiveness: Standing up for one's basic interpersonal rights in such a way that the rights of another person are not violated.

Women tend to have more problems with being assertive than men do. In part that is because assertiveness is confused with aggressiveness, and aggressiveness is definitely not part of the feminine role—but then neither is assertiveness. Passivity and many of the other traits females are socialized for are contrary to assertiveness. Women are often concerned with maintaining harmonious relationships with others, and they may fear that being assertive will cause friction. The problem is that there is a cost in always swallowing one's feelings—a sense of frustration, ineffectiveness, or hurt. Some therapists believe that depression can result from lack of assertion (Jakubowski, 1977). Because assertiveness is a valuable human quality, many women are taking courses in assertiveness training.

Assertiveness training often consists of role playing in which students respond to people who are being aggressive or infringing on their rights, the idea being that assertiveness is learned through practice and through seeing models of assertive behavior. The following is an example of how high-quality assertion can be used to resolve a conflict.

A graduate professor often continued evening class ten minutes or more beyond the normal class period. Although many students were irked by this behavior, one student was assertive and approached the professor after class one evening.

STUDENT: I recognize that sometimes we get so involved in the discussion that you may not realize that the class is running overtime. I'd appreciate your ending the class on time because I have several commitments which I need to keep immediately after this class.

PROFESSOR: I don't really think that I've been late so often.

STUDENT: I guess that you haven't noticed but the last three classes have been ten or fifteen minutes late. Is there any way I could help you end it on time?

PROFESSOR: As a matter of fact there is. I'm often so interested in the class that I don't look at my watch. It'd help me if you'd raise your hand five minutes before the end of the class period. If I don't stop in five minutes, signal me again.

STUDENT: I'd be happy to do that. (Jakubowski, 1977, pp. 157–158)

Notice that the student was assertive, expressing her feelings directly, but in a way that showed regard for the professor. She did not show aggression (e.g., "You're so damned inconsiderate of us, making us stay late all the time"). Neither was the nonassertive (in this case, doing nothing and continuing to suffer). The situation proceeded to a satisfactory resolution.

New Directions

As we look to the future of women's mental health, we should bear in mind a central tenet of feminist theory: The primary source of women's pathology is societal, not individual. If we could stop men from battering, there would be no need for therapy for battered women. Therefore, we must continue to press for social change. In regard to the future of therapy for women, two issues seem particularly important: dependency and anger (Travis, 1988b). From the point of view of feminist analysis, both issues must be examined within the context of unequal power relations between women and men. As noted in Chapter 2, a basic tenet of feminist theories is that the personal is political, and nowhere is this more true than in the area of women's mental health. The "self" and problems of the self must be understood within their social context. Another major issue involves addressing the mental health needs of women of color and poor women.

Dependency   *Dependency* is part of the traditional female role. Dependency includes dependent acts, such as expressions of helplessness or frailty, and psychological dependency, in which the person is so emotionally dependent on another that an independent identity is lacking and the person may feel helpless without the other (Travis, 1988b). Dependency is simply not a functional way to live in the United States in the 1990s, if it ever was. Therefore one of the most important future directions in the area of women's mental health involves women's need to overcome dependency, always bearing in mind that dependency is a personal problem that is often created or exaggerated by unequal power relations between men and women. Dependency, of course, should not be confused with mature interdependency between two people, which can be a major strength for many women.

Anger   A second issue is *anger.* Traditional gender roles make it more acceptable for men to express anger than for women to do so. Nonetheless, both genders have difficulty with anger, although in different ways. For example, women tend to say they are hurt when what they really feel is anger, and men tend to say they are angry when what they really feel is hurt (Lerner, 1980; Miller, 1983).
    Part of the problem women have with anger concerns the fact that it is not particularly socially acceptable for women to express anger; a woman who expresses anger honestly may be greeted with negative feedback (punishments, in the terms of learning theory), such as being called a "man-hater" or a "pushy, ag-

gressive broad." Women's desire to preserve harmonious relations in a group may also inhibit the expression of anger. It is always difficult—if not downright dangerous—for members of a subordinate group to express anger toward members of a dominant group. Inability to express anger may be particularly harmful to mental health if the suppressed anger turns itself into depression.

Whether in a self-help program or as part of therapy, many women will benefit from working on issues of dependency and anger. But a feminist analysis of the issue suggests that it will be difficult to resolve these issues completely so long as there is an unequal balance of power between males and females. One goal of many feminist processes—ranging from feminist therapy to women's studies courses—is the *empowerment* of women. As women are empowered, many other problems may solve themselves. The empowerment of women, in everything from personal relationships to national politics, is therefore one of the most important directions we can take to improve women's mental health in the future.

Addressing the Mental Health Needs of Women of Color and Poor Women
Mental health services have been most available to middle- and upper-middle-class whites, and the services have been designed to meet their needs. Women of color and poor women have had less access to these services. Furthermore, the services to which they have had access have not been sensitive to their needs (Comas-Diaz and Greene, 1994).

In therapy with women of color, therapists need to assess the woman's degree of identification with her ethnic group and her degree of acculturation (Worell and Remer, 1992). A Mexican American woman, for example, might speak Spanish almost exclusively and live in a Mexican American community in California. On the other hand, another Mexican American woman's family might have been in the United States for four generations, and she might live in a suburb of Minneapolis and speak little Spanish. Such factors affect the cultural values the woman brings to therapy and therefore affect the goals that she and the therapist set for her. In general, feminist therapists need to make themselves familiar with the cultures from which women of color come.

In therapy with women of color, therapists must assess women's experiences not only of sex discrimination, but of race discrimination as well (Worell and Remer, 1992). These experiences can have a profound negative effect on psychological well-being.

In general, there are few psychotherapists who are women of color. Clients who are women of color may prefer to have a therapist of their own ethnic group, with whom they will feel comfortable and who will understand their cultural background better. One of the important things that psychology as an institution must do is support more women of color in becoming psychotherapists. In the meantime, in many instances white women therapists will work with clients who are women of color. These therapists need to make extra efforts to provide ethnic-sensitive therapy.

As an example, we will consider the particular needs of Asian American women (Bradshaw, 1994; Chin et al., 1993; True, 1990). A number of potential

FIGURE 14.4
Therapy for women of color needs to be
culturally sensitive.

sources of stress exist in their lives. Some stresses arise from traditional Asian cultures, which are patriarchal and expect women to be passive and obedient. Younger, educated Asian American women may embrace modern egalitarian values in the United States and thus may come in conflict with older family members. Interracial dating and marriage can be another source of stress. Although such relationships are common statistically for Asian American women, they are strongly discouraged by Asian families (True, 1990), again producing conflict and stress. There are, of course, stresses such as work-family conflicts that are experienced by white women as well, but Asian American women are likely to experience these stresses more keenly.

Culturally sensitive or culturally adapted therapy for Asian American women involves several features (True, 1990):

1. Use of bilingual therapists for non-English-speaking clients.

2. Use of family-focused rather than individual-focused approaches, with a respect for the woman's family ties.

3. Respect for Asian American women who are not verbally or emotionally expressive.

4. Attention to the woman's physical (somatic) complaints as possible reflections of psychological distress, knowing that in Asian culture it is more acceptable to have physical health problems than it is to have mental health problems.

5. Recognition that there may be strong sentiment against feminism within the Asian American community.

Just as we have discussed the importance of woman-valuing in a feminist approach to therapy, so an ethnic validity model has been proposed in working with people of color (Chin et al., 1993; Tyler et al., 1985). In this model, the values and lifestyle of people of color must be valued. In addition, the deficit hypothesis, which views ethnic cultures other than Euro-American culture to be deficient, must be abandoned and replaced by a difference hypothesis, which

EXPERIENCE THE RESEARCH

GENDER STEREOTYPES AND PSYCHOTROPIC DRUGS

In your school's library, locate the medical journals, particularly those in the area of family medicine and psychiatry (e.g., *Archives of General Psychiatry, American Journal of Psychiatry*). If your school's library does not carry these specialty journals, it probably will at least carry *New England Journal of Medicine* and *Journal of the American Medical Association,* and you can use those for this exercise, too. Inspect three issues. Locate all the ads for drugs for treating psychological disorders. These ads will mostly be for antianxiety drugs (tranquilizers) and antidepressants. For each ad, record the following: the gender of the physician in the ad, the gender of the patient, and the emotion expressed by the patient's facial expression. How does the ad signal which person is the physician and which is the patient? Also analyze the text of the ad. Does it carry a message about the expected gender of patients receiving this drug? How does it describe these patients and their problem?

Are the ads gender stereotyped? That is, do they portray physicians as men and people suffering from depression or anxiety as women? Or do the ads try to break down stereotypes, for example, by showing a woman physician? What kinds of effects do you think these ads might have?

acknowledges differences between cultures while at the same time valuing them equally.

These are important new directions for feminist therapy in the next decade.

Suggestions for Further Reading

Chernin, Kim. (1981). The *obsession: Reflections on the tyranny of slenderness.* New York: Harper (Colophone paperback). This moving book documents our society's demand that women be thin, and what the consequences of that demand can be.

Lerner, Harriet G. (1985). *The dance of anger: A woman's guide to changing the patterns of intimate relationships.* New York: Harper & Row. Lerner, a psychotherapist, writes wonderful books for the lay public. This one deals with anger. Another good one is *The dance of intimacy* (1989).

15

Psychology of Men

> *The divergence in men's and women's attitudes passed several benchmarks in [the] 1980s. . . . The American Male Opinion Index found that the proportion of men who fell into the group opposing changes in sex roles and other feminist objectives had risen from 48 percent in 1988 to 60 percent in 1990—and the group willing to adapt to these changes had shrunk from 52 percent to 40 percent. . . . While pollsters can try to gauge the level of male resistance, they can't explain it. And unfortunately our social investigators have not tackled "the man question" with one-tenth the enterprise that they have always applied to "the woman problem."*

SUSAN FALUDI, BACKLASH

Perhaps it seems odd to you to have a chapter on the psychology of men in a book on the psychology of women, particularly when I argued earlier that much of traditional psychology has been a psychology of men, one that has, for example, ignored women's issues (menstruation, woman-battering) and done research with male participants only. But even though that is true, traditional psychology was not purposeful in or conscious of being a psychology of men. Emerging from the feminist movement and feminist scholarship of the 1970s has been a self-aware psychology of men. It is rooted in feminism and aware of the power of gender roles, and particularly of how the male role influences the lives of men. It is this emerging feminist psychology of men that we will consider in this chapter.

A milestone in this new field was the publication of psychologist Joseph Pleck's *The Myth of Masculinity* (1981). It provides a summary and critique of both traditional and emerging research on the psychology of men. It will form the basis for many of the concepts of this chapter.

Male Roles

Just as there are gender-role stereotypes about women, there are such stereotypes about men (Chapter 3). Socially desirable masculine characteristics include aggressiveness, independence, being unemotional, and self-confidence (Rosenkrantz et al., 1968; Ruble, 1983).

Several methods have been suggested for organizing the long list of masculine traits. For example, research suggests that there are four major factors in stereotypes about males (Brannon and David, 1976; Kilmartin, 1994):

1. No sissy stuff—Masculinity involves the avoidance of anything feminine (such as eating quiche). Note that in this aspect of masculine stereotypes, masculinity is defined negatively; it means avoiding femininity.

2. The big wheel—The masculine person is a "big wheel." He is successful, is looked up to, and makes a lot of money, thereby being a good breadwinner.

3. The sturdy oak—Masculinity involves exuding confidence, strength, and self-reliance.

4. Give 'em hell—The masculine person is aggressive (perhaps to the point of violence) and daring.

Research also shows that there are four stereotyped types of men in American culture (Edwards, 1992):

1. The businessman—A professional man, dressed in a suit, who is educated, money-oriented, and success-oriented.

2. The athlete—A muscular jock who is a football player or weightlifter; he is physically fit, coordinated, competitive, and determined, and he talks sports.

3. The family man—He is the father and the breadwinner, working full-time to support his family; he is married, responsible, and devoted to his family.

4. The loser—A jerk or a wimp, he has a bad attitude, has low self-confidence, and is a quitter.

Recent History: Changes in the Male Role Today there are ambiguities and strains in the male role. For example, men are supposed to be aggressive, yet it is increasingly unacceptable for them to rape or beat their wives. They are expected to be aggressive lions at work in the corporation or on the athletic field, yet they are expected magically to transform themselves into tender, loving pussycats as they walk through the door to their own homes. Men are supposed to possess great physical strength and be active, yet what is adaptive in today's society is to be able to interact intelligently with a computer while sitting quietly at the keyboard.

Pleck (1981) argues that the sources of these ambiguities and strains become clear if we look at the recent history of changes in the male role. Whenever roles change, ambiguities are created because of contradictions between the old role and the new one. The individual feels a personal sense of strain in the tension between these roles, perhaps having been raised by the standards of the old role and then needing to function as an adult in the new role, and perhaps not even being aware that there is an old role and a new role.

In the late 1800s, the Victorian era in the United States and England, differences between men and women were controlled externally, and very strictly, by institutions (Pleck, 1981). Men went to all-male colleges, lived in fraternities, and drank at the all-male saloon. Later they functioned in the corporate boardroom, where no woman ever entered. Indeed, in those days my own alma mater, Oberlin College, although amazingly progressive in being coeducational, required men to walk on the sidewalk on one side of the street and women to walk on the sidewalk on the opposite side. In those days it was clear—though oppressive to those involved—what a man should do, and no one questioned the meaning of masculinity.

But somehow, in less than a century, we jolted from men and women walking on separate sidewalks to men actually becoming women through transsexual surgery. All-male colleges became coeducational, all-male saloons became singles' bars, and some women even entered the corporate boardroom. In short, external, institutional definition and control of masculinity declined.

Pleck argues that as society loses one kind of control over people's lives, it increases control over other aspects of their lives. Thus, as external, institutional control of masculinity declined, emphasis shifted to internal, psychological masculinity and gender identity. And at that point the psychologists stepped in. Pleck believes it was no accident that the first major work on psychological masculinity-femininity, Terman and Miles's *Sex and Personality* (1936), was published at the height of the Great Depression, just when traditional definitions of masculinity—having a job and being a breadwinner—were threatened most seriously. Thus the shift was from externally defined masculinity to internally defined masculinity—or from what side of the street you were supposed to walk on, to what end of a masculinity-femininity scale you score on and what your gender identity is. As Pleck put it, "If holding a job to support a family could no longer be counted on to define manhood, a masculinity-femininity test could" (1981, p. 159).

Paralleling these historical changes from external to internal definitions of masculinity was a shift in the traits and behaviors expected of men. That is, there was a shift from the traditional male role to the modern male role.

The *traditional male role* has been found in all social classes in the United States during the nineteenth century, in most nonindustrial societies studied by anthropologists, and in working-class communities today. In the traditional male role, physical strength and aggression are of primary importance. Tender emotions are not to be expressed, although anger is permitted. The traditional male likes to spend his time with other men and defines his masculinity in the male group. Although he is married, he regards himself as superior to women, and does not value an egalitarian, emotionally close relationship with women.

By contrast, in the *modern male role,* primary importance is given to success on the job and earning a lot of money. Thus, working well in the corporation (which requires interpersonal skills and intelligence) and gaining power over others are far more important than physical strength. The modern male prefers the company of women and validates his masculinity through them. A high-quality intimate relationship with one woman, rather than numerous anonymous conquests, is his goal. Emotional sensitivity may—indeed, should—be expressed with women, but self-control is still the name of the game on the job.

Some men, of course, find even the modern male role to be oppressive and seek new options and liberation from it. Many others are caught in historical change, in the conflicts and strains between the traditional male role and the modern male role.

FIGURE 15.1
Are modern men caught in the shift from traditional roles to modern roles?
(Source: © 1983 King Features Syndicate, Inc.)

Traditional Psychology's View of Men and Masculinity

Traditional psychology has been greatly concerned with gender-role identity in males. As noted above, beginning in the 1930s the notions of masculinity and masculine identity were considered critical, and a large body of research, continuing to the present, was spawned. Pleck (1981) sees this body of research as based on the belief in the critical importance of masculine identity, or as based on the **male sex-role identity (MSRI) paradigm.** He has analyzed the set of assumptions involved in this traditional view, as well as whether or not the data support these assumptions. Some of the most critical assumptions are reviewed below.

Male sex-role identity (MSRI) paradigm: Traditional psychology's approach to the psychology of men, based on the assumption that a masculine identity is essential for good adjustment.

One critical assumption of the MSRI paradigm is that *gender-role identity results from identification/modeling and, to a lesser extent, reinforcement and cognitive learning, and that cognitive learning is more important in males than in females.*[1] This assumption appears to be quite reasonable and certainly is consistent with traditional psychological theories (see Chapter 2). On reviewing the evidence, however, Pleck (1981) concluded that research does not support any of the several parts of this assumption. Let us consider why in a bit more detail.

Both psychoanalytic theory and social learning theory view identification/modeling as the cause of gender-role identity in children. The idea is that children identify with and model the same-gender parent (see Chapter 2). But psychoanalytic theory and social learning theory contradict each other as to which traits of the father encourage identification. Psychoanalytic theory says the boy identifies with his father out of fear of the father's wrath. Therefore, a punishing

---

[1]*Gender-role identity* is defined as the hypothetical psychological structure representing the individual's identification with his or her own gender group; it demonstrates itself in the individual's gender-appropriate behavior, attitudes, and feelings.

father should encourage identification. Social learning theory says it is the warm, nurturant, reinforcing father who encourages identification. Research does not support the punishing father idea from psychoanalytic theory. There is some support for the notion that warm fathers foster masculine identification in their sons, but the evidence is mixed and, at best, correlational (see, for example, Mussen, 1961; Sears et al., 1965). The identification/modeling assumption also predicts that sons should be more like their fathers than they are like their mothers, because boys should identify with and model their fathers. For example, if a boy has a talkative, outgoing father and a quiet, shy mother, the theories say that the boy should be talkative and outgoing because he identifies with his father and tries to be like him. But the data don't support this idea either—boys are not very similar to either parent on gender-typed traits (Maccoby and Jacklin, 1974).

The other part of this first assumption is that cognitive learning of gender roles should be more important for boys than it is for girls. The reasoning is something like this. In their formative, preschool years, boys spend most of their time with their mothers and little time with their fathers, because mothers are at home and fathers are off at work. This makes it rather difficult to identify with the father, because he is not there. Thus identification with the father does not work well as a source of masculine identity. The boy must then resort to other means for gaining a masculine identity, specifically, cognitive learning of masculinity (cognitive-developmental theory—see Chapter 2) from general cultural sources such as TV and books. Although there is one pair of studies supporting this whole idea (McArthur and Eisen, 1976a, 1976b), far more research on the issue is needed.

In short, we do not really know how males develop a masculine identity. The research is often contradictory or inadequate, much of it having been based on unidimensional measures of masculinity-femininity (see Chapter 3), which do not recognize the possibility of androgyny.

A second assumption of the MSRI paradigm is that *the development of gender identity is risky and prone to errors, particularly in males.* The belief that errors are more likely in the development of a masculine identity is based in part on the point noted above, namely, that fathers are not around often enough for boys to identify with them. Data on transsexuals are also often presented as evidence. Transsexuals are persons who feel they are trapped in the body of the wrong gender; they are the people who seek sex-change operations. The person who has a male body but believes he is truly a woman is called a male-female transsexual. Data indicate that, among those people seeking sex-change operations, male-female transsexuals outnumber female-male transsexuals by a ratio of 3:1 (Abramowitz, 1986). That is, it is more common to have a person with a male body who has failed to form a (correct) masculine identity and instead has a feminine identity. This would be evidence that masculine identity development is more prone to error. The problem is that these data are only for reported cases and may ignore many female-male transsexuals who never seek a sex-change operation, in part because the operation in that direction is far more difficult. There is other evidence on the second assumption, but it, too, turns out to be weak. Overall, then, the evidence is poor that males are more vulnerable than females are to problems in the development of their gender identities (Pleck, 1981).

A third assumption of the MSRI paradigm is that *men's negative attitudes and behaviors toward women are a result of problems of gender-role identity that are caused by mothers.* Three possible ideas have been proposed about exactly what feature of the mother-son relationship causes problems; all three include an assumption that fathers do not participate much in rearing their sons. One possibility is that the little boy experiences the power his mother has over him as overwhelming and threatening. In adulthood, then, men try to control and subordinate women in order to defend against their fear of women's (mother's) control of them (this is the idea of Karen Horney, whose theories were discussed in Chapter 2). A second possibility is that the issue is not power, but rather identification. The idea is that the little boy mistakenly identifies with his mother because his father is not around, but he later realizes that he must get rid of this identification and become masculine. Thus men fear the feminine part of their identity and react to this fear by dominating and controlling those who are feminine—namely, women (this is the idea of Nancy Chodorow, whose theory was also discussed in Chapter 2). A third possibility considers mothers as agents of socialization. Socialization of boys frequently consists of punishing feminine behaviors, and mothers, who do most of the socialization, therefore punish boys for femininity. As a result, boys come to dislike their mothers and to generalize this dislike to all women. Actually, the second and third possibilities contradict each other—in the second the problem is that mothers make boys feminine, whereas in the third the problem is that mothers make boys masculine.

Any or all of these possibilities, then, could be used to explain why men have negative attitudes toward women. In extreme cases, they might be used as explanations of rape or woman-battering. What the feminist would note, though, is that in all cases the mother is being blamed.

There really is not enough definitive research on this third assumption to decide whether it is accurate or not. But perhaps the more important point is that there are two much simpler explanations about why men hold negative attitudes toward women: (1) men do so because it is to their advantage (negative attitudes about women justify and perpetuate men's privileged position in society), and (2) such attitudes are widespread in our culture and it is not surprising that each new generation of little boys picks them up.

A fourth assumption of the MSRI paradigm is the school feminization hypothesis: *boys have academic and adjustment problems in school because schools are feminine* (most teachers are female, teachers encourage femininity, and schools have a feminine "image") *and that only makes boys' identity problems worse.* Once again, the data do not support this assumption (Pleck, 1981). For example, research on academic performance shows that there is no differ-

FIGURE 15.2
Some have argued that boys have more problems in school than girls do because most teachers are women, with whom boys have trouble identifying. The research, however, does not support this claim; there are no differences between boys with male teachers and boys with female teachers.

ence between boys who have female teachers and those who have male teachers (Gold and Reis, 1982).

In summary, none of the assumptions of the MSRI paradigm, which has been psychology's traditional view of men, has much evidence backing it.

Perhaps you are wondering why I have told you all these things and then told you each of them is wrong. There are two reasons. First, it is important to understand the assumptions underlying traditional psychology's view of men and to understand that those assumptions are questionable at best. Second, a significant conclusion comes out of this discussion, namely, that psychology's obsessive concern with masculine identity is simply not useful and not validated by data. If we let go of the concept of masculine identity—as a crucial thing and a goal of development—we are in turn freed from some worries, for example, about boys in father-absent families and whether they will "turn out all right" (which often is defined as developing a masculine identity).

Although the conclusion here is that the male sex-role identity paradigm is not a very good one, there is an alternative approach for the future, the sex-role strain paradigm, which is discussed in the next section.

A New View: Sex-Role Strain

Current feminist research on both the female role and the male role is often based on a new set of assumptions, called collectively the **sex-role strain (SRS) paradigm** (Pleck, 1981). Here are some of the assumptions of the SRS paradigm.

The first assumption is that *gender roles are contradictory and inconsistent.* There are multiple aspects of these inconsistencies in gender roles. For example, research indicates that today's college men are caught in the tension between the traditional norm that men should be intellectually superior to women and the modern norm that men and women should be intellectual equals (Komarovsky, 1973). As noted earlier in this chapter, some of these inconsistencies are created because gender roles have changed over time. The more general point is that these contradictions in gender-role norms are sources of stress to men, because men may be uncertain as to which role they are to follow, or because in following one they violate another—for example, by establishing an intellectually egalitarian relationship with a woman, a man fails the male superiority test. Note that the SRS paradigm focuses on gender roles as a source of strain to individuals, compared with the MSRI paradigm, which views gender roles and masculine identity as positive goals to be achieved.

A second assumption of the SRS paradigm is that *a large proportion of individuals violate gender roles.* The idea here is that gender roles often become so idealized, so difficult, and so unrealistic that most people cannot live up to them, at least not on all occasions. Therefore, only a few people are actually perfect examples of their gender role, and the rest bumble along in various degrees of failure to live up to it. That gap between what men think they actually are and what they think is expected of them causes strain.

A third assumption of the SRS paradigm is that *violating gender roles has worse consequences for males than it does for females.* The evidence on this point is actually rather mixed. Pleck reviewed some of those studies, and they show that although male-role violators are sometimes viewed negatively, in other cases they are accepted.

A fourth assumption of the SRS paradigm is that *some characteristics that are prescribed by gender roles are actually maladaptive.* That is, some gender-role characteristics do not help a person function well psychologically. The aggressive component of the male role is a prime instance (Pleck, 1981). For example, men's liberationist Marc Fasteau (1974) analyzed the Pentagon Papers and showed how expansion of the Vietnam War was linked to concerns about power, strength, and dominance in the writings of influential male leaders. If socialization of males for aggressiveness plays a role in creating wars, it seems reasonable to call it maladaptive. It also leads to a whole series of interesting questions about what things would be like if socialization practices were different. If men were not socialized for aggressiveness, would there still be wars?

In this section we have considered the SRS paradigm. It shifts emphasis away from traditional psychology's concern with masculine identity. Instead, it views gender roles as sources of strain for people: gender roles are contradictory, many individuals violate them, some aspects of gender roles are maladaptive, and males pay a particularly high price for violation of their role. Because this model is relatively new, there are fewer data to test it critically, as has been done with the MSRI paradigm. Until more evidence accumulates, the SRS paradigm will provide new perspectives on gender roles, and particularly on the male role.

Lifespan Development

In this section we will adopt the developmental perspective, tracing issues for males as they arise from infancy to adulthood.

Infancy Most of the evidence indicates that *gender similarities* are the rule in infancy (see Chapter 5). Yet there is evidence that boy babies have a higher activity level than girls (Block, 1976; Eaton and Enns, 1986). The question is, What does that mean in terms of later behavior? Does it predict the higher rate of hyperactivity in boys in the elementary school years? Does it create the higher level of aggressiveness in boys? And what causes the higher activity level in boys? Unfortunately, we do not yet know the answers to these questions.

One experience of male infants that is worth noting and investigating more is circumcision. Circumcision (surgical removal of the foreskin of the penis, usually done within a few days of birth) is routinely done to 59 percent of male infants born in hospitals in the United States, although the procedure has been questioned (Lindsey, 1988). There are several reasons for circumcision. One is religious—it is part of Jewish religious practice, symbolizing the covenant between God and His people. There are also health reasons. Removal of the foreskin permits better cleaning of the penis. And there is some new evidence that uncircumcised babies are more vulnerable to urinary tract infections and that uncircumcised men have a greater risk of infection with the AIDS virus (Moses et al., 1990; Touchette, 1991; Wiswell et al., 1987).

The more interesting question for us, though, is what the psychological effects of this early trauma might be on the male infant. Research actually indicates there is no effect (Brackbill and Schroder, 1980). That is, there appear to be no differences in behavior between circumcised and uncircumcised boy babies.

Childhood As a boy moves from infancy to childhood, the peer group becomes increasingly important as an influence. School-age children spend considerably more time with their peers than with their parents (Bronfenbrenner, 1970). Furthermore, children care a great deal about the approval of their peers, so that the peer group is a powerful shaper of behavior through modeling, positive reinforcers, or punishments (Carter, 1987).

Children tend to be gender segregated in their play—that is, boys play with boys, and girls play with girls. In an interesting study, naturalistic observations were made of preschoolers' play (Fagot and Patterson, 1969). When teachers suggested that boys switch to some "feminine" activities, the boys resisted. The teachers' views appeared to mean little to them; what they wanted was the company and approval of the other boys.

Gender-segregated play and the gender typing of toys and activities seem to have mutually facilitating effects. That is, the more a boy plays in the all-male group, the more he plays with trucks, and the more he plays with trucks, the more playing house seems alien; thus he avoids playing with girls and shows an even stronger preference for the company of boys, which means more play with trucks, which means more play with boys, and so the pattern spirals.

Boys have more problems in school—in the sense that they are more frequently put in remedial classes and more frequently referred to psychologists than girls are (see Chapter 5). One possible explanation comes from the well-established finding that the incidence of *hyperactivity* is far higher in boys than in girls. The most common estimate is that among hyperactive children the ratio of males to females is about 4:1, or about 80 percent of hyperactive children are male and only 20 percent are female (Holborow and Berry, 1986). Hyperactive children are characterized by an extremely high activity level in situations—such as the school classroom—where it is clearly inappropriate. Hyperactive children characteristically also have problems of attention; that is, their attention span tends to be short. The greater incidence of hyperactivity in boys may help to explain their school difficulties. The attentional problems are likely to create learning problems and referral to remedial classes. The hyperactivity itself is irritating to teachers and probably leads them to refer children to psychologists. This line of reasoning raises two further questions. First, how would schools change if there were more male elementary school teachers who themselves had been hyperactive as children—would they be more sympathetic, as well as more skillful as teachers of hyperactive boys? Second, why are there so many more hyperactive boys than girls? No one really has an answer to this second question. One speculation is that hyperactivity is a result of a developmental or maturational lag; that is, children gain more control of their activity level with age, and the hyperactive child may simply be a very slow maturer (Wright et al., 1979). If boys generally are slower to mature than girls are, perhaps boys' greater rate of hyperactivity is a result of their slower maturation.

Adolescence   An increase in the intensity of peer demands for conformity to gender roles occurs in adolescence (see Chapter 5). Here we will concentrate on one aspect of the male role that is highly demanding in adolescence: athleticism (Messner, 1990). As the popular song put it, "You've got to be a football hero to get the love of a beautiful girl." Athletic participation is the single most important factor in high school boys' social status (Kilmartin, 1994).

Consider the athlete role from the perspective of the SRS paradigm. In one study, 24 men in their twenties were interviewed. Half of them had been varsity athletes, and the others had not been involved in athletics (Stein and Hoffman,

FIGURE 15.3
Success in the athlete role is critical for
males—but is this little guy ready for it?

1978). The study was aimed at identifying sources of male-role strain, based on
the SRS paradigm. The sources of strain, of course, varied between the athletes
and the nonathletes. The athletes reported a strain resulting from ambiguity as to
whether it was most important to succeed as an individual or as a team. A second
source of strain resulted from a changing value attached to athletics at different
times in the lifespan. In high school, athletics is a supreme, unquestioned value.
In college, it continues to be important for some but is less important for most.
At age 30, no one cares a bit about one's high school varsity letter in football,
nor about the thousand hours that went into earning it. Another source of strain
for the athletes was the obsession with winning, expressed so eloquently by
Vince Lombardi: "Winning isn't everything. It's the only thing." The problem is
that in a contest between two teams, only one can win, and that means that half
the players go home losers. Sports, of course, do not have to be structured com-
petitively. Feminists have emphasized "new games" and noncompetitive sports.
But the dominant reality in American athletics has been competition, and that
produces losers. In focusing on the psychological strains created by the athlete
role, we should not forget that actual physical damage is also part of the reality

(Sabo, 1992). For example, I knew one boy who continued to play as a quarterback on the high school football team despite the fact that he had broken several ribs in a previous game. Each year, between 13 and 40 high school boys in the United States die playing football (Kilmartin, 1994).

The athlete role also creates strain for the male nonathlete (Stein and Hoffman, 1978). The boy who is a nonathlete is essentially flunking part of the masculinity test. Remember how children choose others one by one when forming teams? The uncoordinated or unskilled boy is chosen last. The message can be devastating: "Not only are you a poor athlete, but your peers don't want you on their team." A friend of mine, who spent his high school years being an intellectual, recounted a story about himself that is a perfect illustration of the way the male nonathlete is treated. He was in a football scrimmage in a gym class. The teacher was giving instructions to members of the team as to what to do in the next play. After all the others had been given specific things to do, the teacher looked at the last poor fellow and said, "When the ball is snapped, you fall down and we'll hope that someone on the other team trips over you." The message to the nonathlete is clear: "You're a failure."

In sum, the competitive, success-oriented emphasis on athletics, particularly in high school, seems to create problems for both the athlete and nonathlete. We need a new, noncompetitive, health-oriented vision of athletics. You may get shin problems from jogging or sore muscles from aerobics, but you won't get a bruised ego.

Adulthood   In this section on the period of adulthood for men, we will first consider two traditional roles for men: that of provider and that of soldier. Next, we will discuss a role of emerging interest, fatherhood. Finally, we will consider whether there is a male midlife crisis that is perhaps analogous to the menopause experience for women.

The provider role: The male role in preindustrial societies, which required the man to provide food and shelter for his family.

The provider role: Several centuries ago, before the industrial revolution, men and women shared **the provider role** (for a review of these concepts, see Doyle, 1989). Men were responsible for providing food, either by hunting or by farming, and shelter, perhaps by building it themselves. But women, too, were expected to be providers. They provided food, in such activities as growing a garden, milling flour, and cooking. They were responsible for other kinds of providing as well, such as producing clothing by spinning, weaving, and sewing it. In short, men and women shared the provider role. In an agricultural society, they shared time and space as well, for men were not off in factories while women remained at home.

Then came the industrial revolution. Men went out to work in factories, and women stayed home. Thus their roles became far more divided. The work men did became less intrinsically satisfying—for example, forging a particular part for a particular machine is likely to be less satisfying than growing and harvesting one's own grain to become food on the table. Often the only good thing about the work was the money that was earned. Simultaneously, there was a shift

The good provider role: The male role in industrialized societies, in which the man is expected to earn money and provide well for his family.

for men from the provider role to **the good provider role.** That is, with the shift to an emphasis on earning money, the man was expected to be a good provider for his family—to earn a lot of money. The more money he earned, the more successful and manly he was.

It is an understatement to say that the good provider role is a high-pressure one. Once again, the SRS paradigm is applicable: the good provider role for men is a source of strain. There is the pressure of being the sole provider, with a great deal of money needed to support the modern family, particularly if the wife does not earn anything. Furthermore, the good provider role is a highly competitive role; a man is in competition with other men to provide for his family better than the way those other men provide for theirs. Finally, it is a role that is destroyed by unemployment, which may occur through no fault of one's own but rather as a result of economic conditions. It is no wonder that the Great Depression shook the foundations of manhood. Nor is it a wonder that one of the slogans of the men's liberation movement is "We're not just success objects."

Current conditions may ease some of the strains of the good provider role for men. Most notably, the majority of wives now hold paying jobs, and the two-paycheck marriage has become the norm. This reduces the pressure on the man of being the sole provider. But other trends may be working in the opposite direction. In contrast to the social activism of the 1960s and 1970s, the decades of the 1980s and 1990s showed every sign of a return to concern over success on the job and making money. With that, the pressure of the good provider role increases. Best-selling self-help books offered ample testimony to the trend, with titles such as *Winning Through Intimidation* and *Looking Out for Number One.* Rather than offering alternatives to the good provider role, these books show men how to go about it more intensely.

The military: The military experience has been a standard one for American men. All have in common having experienced the rite of passage known as basic training. Most go through the experience when they are between the ages of 17 and 20, a critical junction between adolescence and adulthood and an important time in identity development.

What is the result of the military experience for the individual male? It makes a man out of him, of course. Slogans such as "The Army will make a man out of you" and "The Marines take only a few good men" provide ample testimony to the cultural notion that the military experience turns boys into men. Appeals to masculinity are used as recruiting and training tools (Doyle, 1989).

To gain a better view of what actually transpires as men go through the military experience, consider one man's recollections of his training:

> I went into the Army like a lot of people do—a young scared kid of 17 told he should join the Army to get off probation for minor crimes. At the time the Army sounded real fine: three meals, rent-free home, adventure and *you would come out a man.* (It's amazing how many parents put this trip on their kids.)
>
> In basic training I met the dregs of the Army. (Who else would be given

such an unimportant job as training "dumb shit kids"?) These instructors were constantly making jokes such as "don't bend over in the shower" and encouraging the supermasculine image of "so horny he'll fuck anything." People talked about fucking sheep and cows and women with about the same respect for them all.

Not many 17-year-olds could conform to such hard core experience. You're told the cooks were gay (pieces of ass for your benefit). The "hard core" sergeants with all these young "feminine" bodies (everyone appears very meek, i.e., feminine, when constantly humiliated, by having his head shaved and being harassed with no legitimate way of fighting back) were always dunghole talking ("your ass is grass and Jim's the lawnmower").

These "leaders" are the *men;* that pretty much makes you the "pussy's"— at the very most "boys." You have to conform to a hard core, tough image or you're a punk. And I began to believe it because of my insecure state of mind, which was so encouraged in training. I was real insecure, so I wanted to be a superman and went Airborne, which, unlike most of the Army, is more intense and worse than basic training. The pressures of assuming manhood are very heavy.

Not only are you hard, you're Airborne hard—sharp, mean, ruthless. You have to be having an impressive sexual life or a quick tongue to talk one up. You've got to be ready to fight a lot because you're tough and don't take shit from anyone. All these fronts were very hard for me to keep up because they contradicted everything I felt. I didn't feel tougher than anyone. I was very insecure about my dick size and ability to satisfy women.

All I had was my male birthright ego. I stayed drunk to be able to struggle through the barroom tests of strength and the bedroom obstacle courses. The pressures became heavier and stronger, requiring more of a facade to cover up the greater insecurity. To prove I was tougher I went looking for fights and people to fuck over. To prove I was "cock strong" I fucked over more women and talked more about it. I began to do all the things I was most insecure about doing, hoping that doing them would make me that "real man."

Having survived the initial shock of such a culture I became very capable in such required role-playing as toughest, meanest, and most virile—the last meaning a cold unreproachable lover (irresistible to women and unapproachable by other men). (Anonymous, "Life in the Military," 1974, pp. 127–128)

The military's operational definition of manhood is clear: The real man is hyperaggressive, has no emotions, and treats women as objects. Some scholars have referred to this process, particularly combat training, as "military socialization" (Arkin and Dobrofsky, 1978), a socialization into the male role (at least as defined by the military) at the beginning of adulthood.

In 1973 there was a shift to an all-volunteer army, but in 1980 the draft was reinstituted. Therefore, at this time men in the United States can be drafted and women can volunteer, and the 1981 Supreme Court decision in *Rotsker* v. *Goldberg* says that this is not discriminatory. With the shift to a more modern army, advertising promotions for recruits have a different pitch. Instead of selling the macho marine image, the emphasis is now on presenting military enlistment as a chance to acquire job skills. It has been argued, though, that the male socialization is still powerfully present. The content is no longer toughness, but rather being successful as a breadwinner, and here the good provider role surfaces once more.

The entry of women into the military is a scene set for conflict. As the above excerpt testifies, basic training is not designed to have women be a part of it. Which side of the conflict will emerge triumphant? Will women change the military, making it more humane and androgynous? Or will the military change women recruits, producing platoons of macho women? Only time and research will tell.

Fatherhood: The father role is one of the major adult roles for men. In considering this role, there are two interesting topics for the psychologist to investigate. One is to examine the effects of the father on his children, technically called *paternal influence* (e.g., Phares and Compas, 1992). The other is to consider the father role and its meaning for the man himself—what are the satisfactions of being a father, what are the frustrations, and so on (Cohen, 1993). Because there is so much more research on the first topic, it will be discussed first.

What kinds of effects do fathers have on their children? Or do they have much influence at all, given the limited number of hours of father-child contact? Studies indicate that fathers can be as competent in caring for infants and as responsive to them as mothers are (Parke, 1979). It is also clear that, from the earliest interactions, mothers and fathers give different kinds of attention to their children. Specifically, mothers are more likely to engage in caregiving activities, whereas fathers engage in play, particularly rough, stimulating play (Parke and O'Leary, 1976). In short, mothers exchange dirty diapers for clean ones, and fathers give horseback rides. Research also shows that once children pass their first birthday, fathers begin directing more attention to their sons and less to their daughters (Lamb, 1979). Thus children's interest is drawn to the same-gender parent, and children develop a preference for the same-gender parent. This, of course, may be the heart of the whole gender-typing process.

Much of the evidence on the effects of fathers on their children has been based on studies of *father absence.* The logic is that if we compare children in intact (both parents present) families with those in father-absent (usually through divorce) families, any differences between children in the two situations must be indicative of the effects of fathers on children. A major meta-analysis of 67 studies of the effects of father absence found little or no evidence of harmful effects (Stevenson and Black, 1988). There was a decided lack of effect for girls. There were some small effects for boys: preschool father-absent boys were less stereotyped in their choice of toys and activities, in comparison with father-present boys. But there was a slight tendency for older father-absent boys to be more stereotyped than father-present boys.

Notice that the motivation for this line of research is rooted in the MSRI paradigm discussed earlier in this chapter. It is based on the notion that gender identity is essential for development and that males get their gender identity from their fathers. Thus father absence is expected to be dangerous, particularly to sons. However, as Pleck (1981) concluded, the MSRI paradigm is not a particularly good one and is not supported by research evidence. Specifically, researchers fail to find much of a correlation between fathers and sons in masculinity.

In any case, there do not seem to be any substantial effects of father absence to be concerned about. What would be more useful is to conceptualize fathers' influence as part of a more complex system of influence on children. For example, sons are probably more likely to identify with and to be like their fathers if father and son have a warm, nurturant relationship (Lamb, 1979). Thus only some fathers and sons would be expected to be similar—namely, those with warm, nurturant relationships. Further, the father's influence doubtless depends not only on the father-son relationship but also on other relationships, such as the father-mother relationship and the mother-son relationship.

When fathers are present, how much time do they spend with their children? In one widely cited study, Rebelsky and Hanks (1971) attached tape-recorder microphones to newborn infants. They found that fathers spent an average of only 38 seconds per day talking with their infants. This low level of paternal involvement seemed scandalous. However, there is reason to think that the results of the study may have been idiosyncratic—for example, only ten fathers were sampled. More recent, better-sampled research indicates that fathers spend more than 38 seconds per day on their children. One way to approach questions of how time is spent is the *time budget* or *time diary method,* in which individuals keep a careful record of all their activities for a 24-hour day, usually on a detailed diary form. The results of one such study are shown in Table 15.1 (Pleck, 1983). As you can see in the table, fathers spend only about a quarter of an hour per day, on average, on childcare. But childcare was defined very nar-

TABLE 15.1

Time Use for Housework and Childcare (in hours/day) of Employed Husbands and of Wives

	Housework		Childcare	
	Husband	*Wife*	*Husband*	*Wife*
Wife employed	1.63	3.37	0.24	0.64
Wife not employed	1.59	5.60	0.25	1.16

SOURCE: In H. Lopata & J. Pleck, eds., *Research in the Interweave of Social Roles,* Vol. 3: *Families and Jobs.* Greenwich, CT: J.A.I. Press, 1983. Used by permission.

TABLE 15.2

Hours per Week Spent on Household Labor by Men and Women as a Function of Ethnic Group

	Whites	Blacks	Hispanics
Men	19.6	25.0	23.2
Women	37.3	38.0	41.8

SOURCE: Shelton and John, "Ethnicity, Race, and Difference" in J. C. Hood (ed.), *Men, Work, and Family*, pp. 131–150. Copyright © 1993, reprinted by permission of Sage Publications, Inc.

rowly in this study, including only direct interaction with children; thus a father who sits and reads the newspaper but is available to his children while his wife is off shopping would not count the time as childcare. Another important result can also be seen in the table—husbands of employed wives spend no more time on housework or childcare than husbands of nonemployed wives do. This points up the important problem that men's behavior has not changed in ways necessary to complement the changes in women's roles as women have increasingly entered the labor force.

In another study, a well-sampled national survey, husbands and wives were asked to estimate their time spent on household tasks per week (Shelton and John, 1993). The results are shown in Table 15.2. Note that the pattern of contributions varies as a function of ethnicity. For both white and Hispanic families, wives spend about twice as many hours per week doing household work, whereas there is a little more equality for African Americans. Given stereotypes about macho Hispanic men, it is interesting to note that they actually spend somewhat more time than white men do on household work.

The other side of the father role is the way the father perceives and responds to that role. Is it a source of satisfaction, or of inadequacy and frustration? Research indicates that men shift in their sources of satisfaction at different times in the life cycle. Specifically, when a man is a father of young or school-age children, he tends to define his happiness in terms of family life (Harry, 1976). At earlier times and later times, his happiness is found outside the family, in activities such as sports or hobbies. Thus fatherhood does seem to have a major impact, becoming a focus of attention and a source of happiness. There is a stereotype that men get most of their satisfaction from work, whereas women get most of their satisfaction from their families. However, well-sampled studies find that both men and women rate marriage and the family as more satisfying than work (Campbell et al., 1975).

Male midlife crisis? One author summed up the midlife period (I will define this roughly as the decade between the ages of 40 and 50) as follows:

The hormone production levels are dropping, the head is balding, the sexual vigor is diminishing, the stress is unending, the children are leaving, the parents dying, the job horizons are narrowing, the friends are having their first heart attacks; the past floats by in a fog of hopes not realized, opportunities not grasped, women not bedded *[sic]*, potentials not fulfilled, and the future is a confrontation with one's own mortality. (Lear, 1973)

This points to the complex forces, biological, personal, and social, that converge on the middle-aged man.

Traditional psychology, as well as the general public, has viewed personality as changing and developing only in childhood and adolescence, and then remaining stable and unchanging throughout adulthood. Perhaps this represents a need many of us have to see adults as stable and predictable. For example, it may be difficult for many college students to comprehend that their parents are currently going through as much development and change as a college student is. Nonetheless, there is considerable evidence that substantial personality changes occur throughout adulthood (Brim, 1976).

Let us consider in more detail the nature of the changes that were summarized in the above quotation. First, testosterone levels begin to decline around age 40. One consequence is that erections may occur more slowly. If a man understands this as a normal developmental change, it will not be traumatic, but if there is a lack of such understanding, the changes may become traumatic and be interpreted as a sign of a loss of ability to function sexually.

Several extensive research programs have investigated various psychological and social factors that are important to the midlife male (Levinson, 1978; Lowenthal et al., 1975; see also the review by Brim, 1976). These factors are discussed below.

Most human beings have a desire to feel good about themselves based on their achievements. For men, this positive sense of self comes mainly from the job or career. Around age 40 many men recognize that there is an *aspiration-achievement gap,* that is, that their actual achievements have not matched the high aspirations they had in their twenties. The question is, How does a man resolve this aspiration-achievement gap for himself? For many men, perhaps the majority, there is a gradual reconciliation, with a downward shift in aspirations until they are at a realistic level, and the man emerges feeling good about himself. For others, the reconciliation is not easy, and there is a crisis and depression.

Erik Erikson (1950) considered one of the major tasks of adult development to be a resolution of the issue of *stagnation versus generativity.* Most people seem to have a deep-seated desire to feel a sense of growth, or generativity, in their lives. At age 40, with a receding hairline, one finds it difficult to see oneself as continually growing, and a sense of stagnation may set in. It is possible to resolve this issue in adulthood by finding a sense of growth in other sources, such as the growth of one's children or grandchildren, and that represents a positive resolution of this issue. The question arises as to how men with no children can gain a continual sense of generativity. There are, however, many other ways to maintain that sense, such as taking an interest in fostering the careers of one's younger co-workers.

Confrontation with death is another theme of the midlife period. Signs of aging are apparent on the man's own body, and it is likely that one of his close friends will die of a heart attack or other causes. Once again, this experience may lead to negative outcomes such as depression. Or it may lead to a positive outcome in which the man comes to terms with the idea of his own death; reorders the priorities of his life, perhaps in some wonderful ways; and recognizes that happiness is not always to be found in the future, but must be sought in the present.

Relationships within the family also shift (Brim, 1976). The children grow up and leave home, leaving the husband and wife alone together. Although it is a popular stereotype that this is a difficult time in marriage, producing many divorces, in fact the data indicate that married couples on average rate the postparental period as one of the happiest in their lives (Brim, 1976). The man's own parents may become increasingly dependent on him, requiring a transformation of that relationship. And the man's wife, freed from childcare responsibilities, may seek more education, a new career, or a more active involvement in a career she already has, requiring a renegotiation of the marital relationship.

Systematic, well-sampled research indicates that men in their forties, compared with men aged 25 to 39 and 50 to 69, do show significantly higher depression scores and more alcohol and drug use; on the other hand, their levels of anxiety are no higher, nor do they report any less life satisfaction or happiness (Tamir, 1982). Thus it seems that men in their forties have some problems, but the problems are probably not much worse than those men face at other ages.

This section began with a question, Is there a male midlife crisis? The answer must be that things are a bit too complicated to give a yes-or-no answer. First, it is important to question the notion that there are fixed stages of adult development, meaning there is a "crisis stage" at age 40 or some other age. Popularized books such as Gail Sheehy's *Passages* have given the public the impression that there are specific crises that predictably happen to people at certain ages. The actual research does not support that idea at all (Brim, 1976). In part, things are not so predictable because different things happen to different people at different times. For instance, if in the 12 months after his fiftieth birthday a man fails to get a promotion, has his best friend die of a heart attack, has to move his parents to a nursing home, and has frequent episodes of erection problems, he probably will have a crisis. But another man may not experience these things, or they may happen in a different order, or they may be spread out over a period of five or ten years. The changes for such a person will be much more gradual, never reaching a crisis. Rather than talking about "stages" and "crises," it is preferable to talk about "transitions" (Brim, 1976). This last term expresses the notion that there are changes in adult personality, but that they do not occur at fixed times; they do not have to be of crisis proportions; and they often lead to positive, growth-promoting outcomes.

Men of Color

Men of color in the United States share some experiences in common. Among these are high unemployment rates and low wages compared with those of white men (although not necessarily compared with those of white women). Data on this point are shown in Table 15.3. Economic adversity due to low wages or unemployment, as well as experiences of race discrimination, are common for men of color. Beyond that, we must look at specific ethnic groups, each with its own history and set of cultural values that shape men's roles.

African American Men   Both theories and research in the social sciences have traditionally viewed the African American man as being downtrodden, having a poor self-concept, and being psychologically castrated. There are several reasons that this view is neither very realistic nor very useful. First, the traditional view is based on historical tracing of the African American male role back to the days of slavery. This historical analysis has ignored the strong contributions of Black men to their families, even within the confines of slavery (Staples, 1978). For example, Alex Haley's *Roots* portrayed many male characters who were responsible and strong and who had a good sense of themselves.

TABLE 15.3
Unemployment Rates and Earnings as a Function of Ethnicity and Gender

Unemployment rates of adults, 1994

	Women	Men
African Americans	12.1%	14.2%
American Indians	11.9%	14.5%
Hispanics	11.0%	11.1%
Whites	5.6%	6.8%

Median earnings for year-round, full-time workers, 1991

	Women	Men
African Americans	$18,720	$22,075
Hispanics	$16,244	$19,771
Whites	$20,794	$30,266

SOURCES: U.S. Department of Labor (1993, 1994); LaFromboise et al., (1990). Data for American Indians are from 1987 (LaFromboise et al., 1990), because the Department of Labor reports only on whites, Blacks, and Hispanics.

FIGURE 15.4
There are many African American culture heroes with whom African American youths can identify. (Left) Political activist Jesse Jackson. (Right) Basketball star Shaquille O'Neal.

A second problem with the notion of the castrated Black male is that it rests on the concept of Black matriarchy. Black matriarchy is an interpretation of the fact that the percentage of female-headed households is larger among Blacks than it is among whites (see Chapter 8). But this ignores the fact that the *majority* of Black households are headed by men. Once again, the Black man's contributions have not been sufficiently recognized. From a feminist point of view, it is interesting that the relatively egalitarian African American family, when viewed by white male social scientists, has appeared matriarchal (Staples, 1978).

The view of African American men as having a poor self-concept ignores the various ways in which people learn to cope with their situations in life. The results of oppression may seem less severe, depending on the context in which one is making judgments. For example, unemployment is often a terribly depressing experience for white men. The Black man may be better able to cope with unemployment if many of his friends are also unemployed, although that scarcely makes unemployment pleasant. Yet African American men have a reference group within their own culture by which they judge themselves, and against which they may come out quite well (Staples, 1978). Attribution theory (see Chapter 6) points out that it is important what attributions people make for their successes and failures. The civil rights movement has made African Americans aware of discrimination as a force in their lives. Thus a Black man who fails to get a promotion on the job may make the external attribution that the failure was due to discrimination, rather than the internal attribution that the failure was due to his own lack of ability. The former attribution helps to keep one's self-concept intact.

Development Issues   In a 1968 best-seller, *Black Rage,* psychiatrists William Grier and Price Cobbs said, "Whereas the white man regards his manhood as an ordained right, the black man is engaged in a never-ending struggle for its possession." There has been concern within traditional psychology about the development of adequate male identity in African Americans, particularly among youths, given the high percentage of female-headed Black households (e.g., Pettigrew, 1964). Such a view ignores the time fathers may spend with their sons, even though they are not part of the same household, and the contributions of older brothers, uncles, and grandfathers. Furthermore, there are many African American culture heroes with whom the Black youth can identify. Depending on his concerns at the time, the young Black male identifies with different heroes from his culture (Taylor, 1976)—for instance, if his passion is sports, his idol may be Shaquille O'Neal, or if his interest is in politics and civil rights, it may be Martin Luther King, Jr. Thus there are many sources of identification for an African American youth besides his own father.

Earlier in this chapter the MSRI paradigm was discussed. The concern over African American male identity is clearly part of this paradigm. Having concluded that the MSRI paradigm is not a very good one and that concerns over gender identity are overblown, we must conclude that there has been too much emphasis on Black male identity. If we shift to the SRS paradigm, we see gender roles as sources of psychological strain for Black men, which is probably a more productive approach.

Roles: Breadwinner, Husband, Father   There is a high unemployment rate among Black men. For example, as the data in Table 15.3 indicate, in 1994 the unemployment rate was 6.8 percent for white males over age 16; for Black males, it was 14.2 percent (U.S. Department of Labor, 1994), more than double the rate for whites. The high unemployment rate creates a gender-role problem because the role of breadwinner or good provider is an important part of the male role in the United States. Thus Black men, and particularly Black male teenagers (for whom the unemployment rate is 34 percent), may feel that they are not fulfilling this part of their role. From the perspective of the SRS paradigm, we again see gender roles as a source of strain.

Not being able to fulfill this part of the male role may express itself in a number of ways. It may turn into antisocial behavior, violence, and crime, accounting for the high crime rate among male African American teenagers. It has also been suggested that volunteering for the army becomes an alternative means of fulfilling the male role—one-third of army recruits are African American men (Staples, 1978).

The role of husband is closely tied to the breadwinner role. African American men are understandably reluctant to take on the responsibility of marriage when unemployment is such a justified fear, and the rules of the welfare system essentially force low-income men to be absent. On the other hand, middle-class African Americans place an especially strong emphasis on the provider role (Cazenave and Leon, 1987).

The father role, too, is closely tied to the breadwinner role, and the responsibility of supporting children is a source of stress to the unemployed African American man. On the other hand, fathering children can be a means of fulfilling the male role for the lower-class Black man who is denied much success in the breadwinner role. Interestingly, middle-class Black men father fewer children than any other group in our society and, in particular, father fewer children than lower-class Black men do (McKay, 1978). Research shows that middle-class Black men are very child-oriented and participate more in childrearing than white men do (Daneal, 1975).

In sum, the SRS paradigm seems to be most useful in understanding the experience of the Black male. We can examine, for instance, how the breadwinner role is a source of strain to a group that has such a high unemployment rate. Data are scarce, but the SRS paradigm suggests many interesting and productive approaches for future research—for example, what is the impact of the "no sissy stuff" part of the male role on Black men? Does it contribute to their devaluing of women, or does it help them find satisfaction in their role, or is it not relevant in African American culture?

Asian American Men   Asian American men share some things in common with African American men—the experience of racial discrimination and being "the other" in a white-dominated society. Still, there are some substantial differences. Asian Americans do not have the heritage of slavery. And there is great diversity among Asian American groups, from recent refugees who escaped from Vietnam or Cambodia under dangerous and traumatic conditions, to those Japanese Americans or Chinese Americans who are fifth generation in the United States.

U.S. immigration policies and the manner in which some Asian Americans (e.g., Chinese men brought to build the transcontinental railway in the 1860s) came to the United States created a great imbalance in the gender ratio, with far more Asian American men than Asian American women. For example, in the year in which Carlos Bulosan arrived in Seattle from the Philippines, the ratio of Filipino men to Filipino women in the state of Washington was 33:1 (Bulosan, 1960). In the context of laws and norms prohibiting interracial marriage, this meant a permanently enforced bachelorhood for a great many Asian American men. The problem is confounded by the fact that in many Asian societies, one is a full-fledged adult only when one is married and becomes a parent. Therefore, in the context of their own cultural values, many Asian American men were condemned to a life of perpetual boyhood (Kim, 1990).

Just as the sexuality of African Americans has been stereotyped, so, too, has the sexuality of Asian Americans. The Asian American man has been stereotyped as asexual (lacking in sexuality), whereas the Asian American woman has been stereotyped as exotic and entirely sexual (Kim, 1990).

Asian American men, of course, share many of the same difficulties faced by Asian American women (see Chapter 8), including bilingualism and conflicts between Asian cultural values and the dominant cultural values of America.

Hispanic Men   Hispanic culture is typically viewed as highly patriarchal, with men expected to live up to the ideal of machismo. However, Chicanos in the United States are different from Mexicans in Mexico, and it seems that Chicano family structure in the United States is less patriarchal, although the strong emphasis on the importance of *la familia,* the family, remains (Vasquez and Baron, 1988). Recent psychological research refutes the notion of extreme male dominance in Hispanic families (Vasquez-Nuttall et al., 1987). For example, studies of marital decision making by Hispanic couples gives little support to the notion of male dominance (Cromwell and Ruiz, 1979).

American Indian Men   At least some Indian tribes, including the Cherokee, Navajo, Iroquois, Hopi, and Zuni, traditionally had relatively egalitarian gender roles (LaFromboise et al., 1990). Women had important economic, political, and spiritual roles, and there was even a matrilineal pattern of inheritance. Men tended to have more authority in the public sphere, but women's power in the private sphere of the family was great.

The overwhelming result of acculturation resulting from contact with the dominant white culture in the United States has been an increase in male dominance among Indians (LaFromboise et al., 1990). It remains to be seen whether this is beneficial to Indian men. The realities of high unemployment rates probably have a greater impact.

Health Issues

A baby boy born in the United States today can expect to live 72 years if he is white and 65 years if he is Black; a baby girl can expect to live 79 years if she is white and 73 years if she is Black (Kilmartin, 1994). In short, men live about 7 fewer years than women do. The argument rages as to whether the difference in life expectancy is due to biological factors or environmental factors. That is, are men more biologically vulnerable, more susceptible to disease, genetic defects, and so on; or are men the victims of their environment, specifically of the male role—the "lethal aspects of the male role," as one psychologist put it? In this section we will examine the evidence on both sides of the issue (for more extended discussions, see Harrison, 1978; Turner, 1982).

On the biological side of the argument, it has been found that males have a higher death rate than females, even prenatally. At conception, the ratio of males to females is probably about 110:100.[2] At birth the male to female ratio is down to about 105:100 (Harrison, 1978). That is, even before birth, males have a higher death rate (Kilmartin, 1994). One can scarcely attribute this to socialization into the male role. The higher prenatal mortality rate for males is probably due to sex-linked recessive genetic defects or diseases, such as hemophilia (see Chapter 9). It has also been found that females have more resistance to infectious diseases than males do, because there are genes on the X chromosome that increase one's immune resistance (Goble and Konopka, 1973).

X-linked diseases probably cause a relatively small proportion of the excess male deaths, though. Of the biological factors, sex hormones are far more important (Kilmartin, 1994). Specifically, heart disease is a leading cause of death for both men and women, but heart disease tends to strike men at much younger ages than women. This contributes to men's shorter life expectancy. Estrogen appears to be a protective factor against heart disease, and so women are more protected. Estrogen seems to have this protective effect because of its action against LDL, the "bad cholesterol" that increases the risk of heart disease.

A classic study by Madigan (1957) is often cited as evidence for the biological determination of higher mortality rates in males. This study was designed to test the hypothesis that higher male mortality rates are due to the greater stresses of the male role—the competitiveness of male jobs, the pressure for success and high earnings—compared with the "easy life" of the housewife/mother. Cleverly, Madigan thought of one population in which the roles and stresses on males and females would be identical, or nearly so—nuns and monks. The results were that the nuns lived longer than the monks, and both had life expectancies essentially the same as that in the general population. Because environment was equalized for the two groups, the conclusion must be that biological factors determined the shorter lives of the monks. There have been serious criticisms of the Madigan study, however. Specifically, the monks smoked more than the nuns did, and, as we shall see, smoking is a critical factor. Thus the nuns and monks did not have truly equal experiences.

There is evidence on the environmental side of the argument. A thorough analysis of the causes of deaths in males and females indicates that about one-third of the male-female difference is due to smoking (Waldron, 1976; Waldron and Johnston, 1976). Of the leading causes of death in which males outnumber females, two are lung cancer and heart attacks, and cigarette smoking is implicated in both. Another leading cause of death in which males outnumber females is cirrhosis of the liver, and that is related to excessive drinking, a behavior pat-

---

[2]You may be wondering why males and females are not conceived in equal numbers. The answer seems to be that sperm that bear the Y chromosome (Y-bearing sperm), and therefore produce a male at conception, are lighter than X-bearing sperm. This in turn is because the Y chromosome is smaller than the X chromosome. This allows the Y-bearing sperm to swim faster and makes them more likely to reach the egg.

tern that is considered more appropriate for males than females. Accidents—specifically, car and truck accidents and shooting accidents during hunting—are another cause of death in which males outnumber females; these kinds of deaths too can clearly be linked to patterns of socializing males for such traits as aggressiveness and risk taking. Thus some specific behaviors associated with the male role—smoking, drinking, aggression, and risk taking—can be linked to higher death rates in males. It doesn't stretch the data to call these "lethal aspects of the male role."

There has been a great deal of publicity about the Type A, or coronary-prone, behavior pattern (Friedman and Rosenman, 1974; Matthews, 1982). Type A behaviors include extremes of aggressiveness and hostility, competitiveness, difficulty in relaxing, impatience, and a chronic sense of urgency about time, or "hurry sickness." Type A behaviors have been linked significantly to coronary heart disease (Matthews, 1982), and, as mentioned earlier, that is a leading cause of the greater number of male deaths. It is hard to avoid noticing that the list of Type A traits reads like a litany of the male role. Thus, insofar as males are socialized into such traits, it seems likely that they will become Type A individuals and will have a greater risk of developing heart disease. In fact, research indicates that extreme masculinity is related to severity of heart attacks and to Type A behaviors (Helgeson, 1990). From a feminist point of view, most of the research on Type A has been conducted with men only, and it is important that such research be extended to women.

An important related question is, What will happen to women as they become increasingly liberated and able to do things formerly reserved for males? If the liberation of women means liberating them to smoke, drink, and be aggressive, competitive, and hurried, will the ultimate reward be an earlier death? The available data indicate that this is not likely. For example, from 1940 to 1977 women's participation in paid jobs and careers increased substantially, yet deaths from coronary heart disease among women fell rapidly during this period (Siegel, 1978)—indeed, the rates for women declined faster than the rates for men did, both declines being due to greatly improved medical techniques. There is also evidence that Type A women who have been in the work force for more than half of their lives are no more likely to have heart disease than Type A homemakers (Haynes et al., 1978). Thus it may be that women can take on some aspects of the male role without too much risk. Nonetheless, I would not want to be part of the group of women who tests whether the female body can survive three packs of cigarettes and four martinis a day.

In conclusion, it seems that neither biological factors nor environmental factors alone can explain the higher mortality rates of males. Male deaths from heart disease and cirrhosis of the liver seem linked to environmental factors, specifically, the male role and smoking and drinking behaviors. But these can scarcely explain the higher rate of male deaths prenatally. Thus the higher male mortality rate is most likely due to a combination of biological factors (sex-linked genetic defects, immune factors) and environmental factors (the male role, which encourages smoking, drinking, and Type A behaviors).

Male Sexuality

The research of Masters and Johnson (1966) indicates that men go through the same biological stages in sexual arousal as women do: excitement, plateau, orgasm, and resolution (see Chapter 11). A major process during both male and female arousal is vasocongestion, or increased blood flow into the genitals. In men, the vasocongestion produces erection of the penis. In males past puberty, orgasm is accompanied by ejaculation, the penis emitting a milky fluid containing sperm. One difference between males and females is that males have a refractory period following orgasm. A refractory period is a period of time during which one cannot be restimulated to orgasm. Women have no such refractory period, and thus can have multiple orgasms, whereas men are generally limited to single ones. The length of the refractory period in men varies, depending on a number of factors, including age. In young men, the refractory period may be as short as a few minutes, whereas in men over the age of 65, it might be 24 hours.

What is more intriguing than biology is the psychology of male sexuality. An important first point is that, according to traditional definitions, sexuality—specifically, heterosexuality—is a central aspect of male identity (Gross, 1978). Males are supposed to be very interested in sex and good at it. The increasing recognition of women's interest in sex does not diminish its centrality for men—in fact, it may heighten it.

Psychologist and sex therapist Bernie Zilbergeld has provided a superb analysis of male sexuality—and how to cope with it—in his book *The New Male Sexuality* (1992). His central thesis is that men in our culture are taught a "fantasy model of sex," an unrealistic, idealistic set of expectations that put intense performance pressures on them. He captures the message of the fantasy model of sex in the title of one of his chapters: "It's Two Feet Long, Hard as Steel, Always Ready, and Will Knock Your Socks Off," referring to the fantasy model of the enormous, ever-erect, aroused penis. He details the various aspects of the fantasy model in a list of cultural myths about male sexuality, discussed below.

Myth 1 A real man isn't into sissy stuff like feelings and communicating. A central part of the male role is being unemotional. That means that feelings of love, tenderness, and perhaps even vulnerability are inappropriate and unmasculine. Unfortunately, those are precisely the emotions that are essential in developing intimate relationships. They are the emotions that enrich the sexual experience. Is it any wonder that males—particularly adolescent males for whom masculine identity is a key concern—focus mainly on the physical aspects of sexuality and neglect the emotional aspects? It is as though the culture had handicapped them from birth, crippling their tenderness, intimacy, and sensuality. Zilbergeld urges women to understand this problem as a handicap and, rather than resenting men's lack of emotional expressiveness, to help them overcome their handicap and discover their tender, intimate selves.

Zilbergeld argues that it is this myth which leads men to mislabel their feelings and to think that what they are feeling is a sexual need for intercourse, when in fact what they are experiencing is love, or tenderness, or just a need for a good cuddle. Growing up thinking that they experience only lust, men mislabel their feelings. They think they want intercourse when what they are really experiencing is a need for a hug or for someone to say "I love you."

Myth 2 A real man performs in sex. A man must perform because sex is seen as an achievement situation. Our culture is highly achievement-oriented, and we tend to turn sex into just one more achievement situation (Albee, 1977; Slater, 1973). We express this in language such as *achieving* orgasm, and in setting up achievement goals in sex, such as simultaneous orgasms for the man and woman. In addition, achievement is a key feature of the male role.

Myth 3 A man should be able to make the earth move for his partner, or at the very least knock her socks off. Put this myth together with the preceding one, and you have a situation in which sex becomes, for the man, an achievement situation in which he is expected to perform skillful tricks. However, the work of Masters and Johnson (1970) and others indicates that achievement-orientation and performance-orientation contribute importantly to sexual dysfunctions such as erection problems. When one sets up an achievement goal, one is also setting up the possibility of failure. Fear of failure creates anxiety, and anxiety quickly ruins the pleasure of sexual expression and produces sexual dysfunction.

The extent of performance pressures on men is strikingly illustrated in this account by two sex therapists:

> We'll never forget the man who called himself a premature ejaculator even though fairly regularly he lasted for forty-five minutes of vigorous thrusting. We know he lasted this long because his partner confirmed it. Actually, she had never been orgasmic in intercourse and had no desire to become so. She much preferred shorter intercourse because she sometimes became so sore through almost an hour of thrusting that she could barely sit down the next day. That had little influence on the thinking of our client, who was convinced that she would have orgasms if only he could last an hour. (Zilbergeld, 1978, p. 257)

Myth 4 A man is always interested in and always ready for sex. Men are portrayed as always interested in sex and easily arousable. But that is not always true. Men need to learn to acknowledge that sometimes, in certain situations, or when they are tired, or with a certain partner, they are just not in the mood. Men need to learn to say no, something women received more than adequate training for, but men learned was not part of their script.

Myth 5 All touching is sexual.

Myth 6 Sex equals intercourse.

Myth 7 Sex is centered on a hard penis. These three myths go together. In our culture we have learned a script for sexual interactions. The script specifies what should occur and in what order. Touching, kissing, and hugging progress to heavy petting, which progresses to intercourse, at least if everything goes well. As a result, we do not know how to relax and enjoy sex that consists only of kissing and touching. I once gave a talk on sex to a group of adolescent girls whom a social worker considered predelinquents. I was supposed to convey some information or inspiration that would keep them from getting pregnant. I suggested oral-genital sex as a way of having enjoyable sex with no risk of pregnancy. One girl raised her hand and said, with a penetrating honesty of the adolescent, "But that isn't *real* sex." She expressed perfectly the sentiment in our culture. Anything other than intercourse is not "real" sex, or is merely a ritualistic prelude to the real thing. The problem with all of this, from the male point of view, is that an erection is absolutely essential if intercourse is to take place. Erections are nice if they happen on their own; when they are an entrance requirement, things are not such fun. Once again, the stage is set for anxiety, fear of failure, and failure. Part of the remedy is to learn that there are many enjoyable aspects of sex that require no erection—in fact, the only thing that requires an erection is intercourse.

Myth 8 Good sex is spontaneous with no planning and no talking. Of course, spontaneous sex can be nice, but not all good sex has to be that way. The problem with the emphasis on spontaneity is that it discourages some important things from happening. For example, some people fail to plan for and talk about birth control because they say it interferes with the spontaneity of sex. That logic has a high chance of producing an unwanted pregnancy. In the AIDS era, it is crucial to talk about safer sex. The spontaneity/naturalness myth is also responsible for many men neglecting to educate themselves about sex. It is better to recognize that good sex sometimes does take planning, learning, and talking, which is in contradiction to beliefs that sex is just natural and that men are born sex experts.

Zilbergeld recommends that men try to shed the sexual scripts that they have learned and to spend some time discovering what is truly pleasing to them sexually, expressing those ideas, and then trying to have sex that way, rather than the way society dictates.

Recent sex research has turned up many unexpected findings about male sexuality. For example, men sometimes fake orgasm. They want more emotional involvement in sex. And they feel under great performance pressure (e.g., Shanor, 1978). What is happening is that we are beginning to appreciate the complexity of male sexuality, in part by adopting the feminist perspective of examining the influence of gender roles on male sexuality, and then considering ways in which men can be liberated from some of the restrictions and demands of those roles.

In Conclusion

An important point in this chapter was the distinction between the male sex-role identity paradigm and the sex-role strain paradigm. The MSRI paradigm was part of traditional psychology and was based on the assumption that a man must have a masculine identity in order to be psychologically healthy. As we saw, the MSRI paradigm is just not borne out by the evidence—boys' masculinity is not

EXPERIENCE THE RESEARCH

CHILDHOOD EXPERIENCES OF THE MOTHER AND MEN'S DESIRE TO CONTROL WOMEN

One assumption of the male sex-role identity (MSRI) paradigm is that men's negative attitudes toward women are a result of problems of gender-role identity caused by mothers. One hypothesis is that little boys experience the mother as overwhelming and therefore try to control and dominate women in adulthood. If this is the case, there should be a correlation between men's ratings of their childhood experiences of their mother and their attitudes, as adults, toward women. Men who experienced their mothers as overwhelming should want to control women, and men who did not experience their mothers as overwhelming should be less interested in controlling women. You will collect data to see whether this is true.

Use the following items to assess men's experience of their mothers in childhood:

1. When I was a child, my mother seemed overwhelming to me.
2. When I was a child, my mother tried to control me all the time.

Use the following items to assess men's attitudes toward women:

1. The husband should have the final say in family decisions.
2. In the traditional marriage vows, the wife promises to obey the husband, and there is great wisdom in that.

Participants should rate each item on a scale from (1) strongly disagree to (5) strongly agree, with (3) meaning neither agree nor disagree. To make the purpose of these items less obvious, construct at least ten items assessing attitudes on some other topics and intersperse the four critical items among them.

Administer your 14-item scale to five men who are *not* in your class (men who take a psychology of women course are not a random sample of the male population). If possible, include in your sample several men who are older than traditional college age.

Take the average of the two items on experience of the mother as the man's score on Experience of Mother. Take the average of the two control of women items as the man's score on Control Women. For your five respondents, does there appear to be a correlation between Experience of Mother scores and Control Women scores? That is, do men who have high scores on one tend to have high scores on the other? If you have taken a statistics course, compute the actual correlation between the two scales. You may also put your data together with that of other students in your class to obtain a larger sample and then compute the correlation.

Do the results support or go against the hypothesis?

correlated with their fathers' masculinity, father absence does not necessarily produce inadequate masculinity, and so on. The alternative model is the SRS paradigm, which views gender roles as sources of strain in our culture. Although this paradigm is too new to have much evidence backing or contradicting it, it is useful in understanding some of the topics covered later in the chapter. For instance, it is useful in understanding the problems created by the emphasis on athletic prowess for males, an emphasis that produces strains for both the athlete and the nonathlete; and it is useful in understanding the problem of unemployment for the Black male in a culture that stresses the breadwinner or good provider role as a definition of manhood.

Suggestions for Further Reading

Doyle, James A. (1989) *The male experience.* 2d ed. Dubuque, IA: Wm. C. Brown. This is a nicely written, modern account of the psychology of men.

Kilmartin, Christopher T. (1994). *The masculine self.* New York: Macmillan. Another good psychology of men textbook.

Kimmel, Michael S. & Messner, Michael A. (1992). *Men's lives.* 2d ed. New York: Macmillan. An excellent collection of readings about men on topics including work, health, sexuality, and families.

Rotundo, E. Anthony. (1993). *American manhood: Transformations in masculinity from the Revolution to the modern era.* New York: Basic Books. This is an excellent tracing of historical changes in the male role in the United States.

Zilbergeld, Bernie. (1992). *The new male sexuality.* New York: Bantam Books. Zilbergeld's writing is delightful and insightful. This is must reading on the topic of male sexuality.

16

Retrospect and Prospect

Future Research

Feminism Revisited

Future Roles for Women

> *Standing on the ground of common sense and the*
> *constitution of the human mind, I deny that anyone knows,*
> *or can know, the nature of the two sexes, so long as they*
> *have only been seen in their present relation to one*
> *another. . . . What is now called the nature of woman is an*
> *eminently artificial thing—the result of forced repression in*
> *some directions, unnatural stimulation in others.*
>
> JOHN STUART MILL, THE SUBJECTION OF WOMEN

The great philosopher and feminist John Stuart Mill, quoted at the opening of the chapter, lived in an era in which there was no science of psychology. He believed that no one could understand the true nature of women and men. More than 100 years—and a great deal of psychological research—later, how can one respond to Mill?

Certainly scientists would not claim to know the "true nature" of woman any more than Mill did. But I would argue that that is not the right question. Rather than trying to establish the "true nature" of woman, we would do better to try to understand how women function psychologically now in our culture, how they function in some other cultures and other times, and what their potential for the future is.

This book has focused particularly on trying to understand how women function psychologically in our contemporary culture. To do this, I have reviewed the existing scientific theories and research. They provide some reasonable ideas that further research will continue to refine.

Several important themes have cropped up repeatedly in this book. One is gender similarities, the notion that women and men are more similar to each other than they are different. Another theme has been ambivalence, as seen in the conflict between motherhood and career, and in ambivalence about sexuality. Finally, it is important to consider both gender and ethnicity as definers of people's identity and roles.

Future Research

In 1974, in writing the first edition of this book, I commented that research on the psychology of women was in its infancy. However, coming away from the most recent (1994) convention of the American Psychological Association, I felt that real progress had been made and that research and theory were becoming increasingly sophisticated. We understand the ways in which gender bias can enter psychological research, and we have some ways to correct it. There are some fairly well documented differences in the verbal and nonverbal communication styles of females and males, and research is proceeding to determine exactly what these differences mean. Feminist therapy is more than a twinkle in some feminist's eye and is now widely practiced. And so the list goes.

Of course, this does not mean that we know everything there is to know about women. Far from it. There is much information that we do not yet have. The reader may want to spend some time thinking about what the most important questions for future research are. I will suggest a few that I think are important.

A great deal of research on the psychology of women has focused on high-achieving women, looking at their personality characteristics, common biographical themes, and so on. Such an approach has merit if one's goal is to improve women's achievements; studying high-achieving women may give suggestions as to how one "creates" a high-achieving female through childrearing practices or other factors. The problem is that we concentrate 90 percent of the research on 1 percent of the population, and compound the problem by calling it the psychology of women, implying all women. Although we need research on high-achieving women, we also need to redirect our efforts toward understanding the psychology of housewives, the psychology of secretaries, the psychology of mentally retarded women, the psychology of handicapped women, and many others. I am not suggesting that all studies must involve random sampling, but that groups other than high achievers, who are also of importance or interest, be defined. Of course, the study of all these groups of women is as important a task for psychology in general as it is for the psychology of women.

Following from this point is perhaps the most important need: to study women of color. The psychology of women has been too much the psychology of white middle-class women. We need to know far more about African American, Asian American, Latina, and American Indian women, of all social classes. We need to know about those who have become enormously successful despite the odds, and about those who are on welfare. We need to know far more about

FIGURE 16.1
Three generations of women. Far more research on women of color is needed in psychology.

how different ethnic groups in the United States define gender roles and regulate women's sexuality. In doing this, we will always have to keep a balanced perspective between ethnic similarities and ethnic differences.

We need more research on adjustment problems in women, particularly on depression, anxiety, alcoholism, and eating disorders, because they are all so frequent. We need to know what causes depression and what can be done to prevent it (e.g., changing childrearing practices, school policy, violence against women, or family roles). Along with this, we need more work on psychotherapy for women's problems and research on the effectiveness of these therapies. Related research should be directed toward the psychological aspects of women's health issues such as wanted and unwanted pregnancy, HIV/AIDS, and breast cancer.

We need to know more scientifically about feminism. What leads women to become feminists? What happens to women psychologically when they become feminists? How do other people react to women who are feminists? What impact does feminism have on men?

In one relevant study, Adena Bargad and I evaluated the impact of women's studies courses on the students who take them (Bargad and Hyde, 1991). We looked particularly at the development of feminist identity in women taking the courses compared with a group of women not taking women's studies. According to one theory, feminist identity develops in five stages:

Stage 1, Passive Acceptance   In this stage, women passively accept traditional gender roles and discrimination and do not question either.

Stage 2, Revelation   In this stage, catalyzed perhaps by a crisis or by taking a women's studies course, the woman questions gender roles and sexism. She often experiences great anger and holds a negative view of men.

Stage 3, Embeddedness   The woman develops a sense of connectedness with other women and receives affirmation and strength from them.

Stage 4, Synthesis   The woman develops a positive feminist identity and transcends gender roles. She no longer blames men as a group, but evaluates men on an individual basis.

Stage 5, Active Commitment   Feminist identity is consolidated and the woman becomes committed to working actively to promote a nonsexist world.

We developed a scale, the Feminist Identity Development Scale (FIDS), to measure women's scores on each of the stages and administered the scale at the beginning and end of the semester. Our research indicated that women taking women's studies courses, compared with the control group, showed significant declines in their degree of passive acceptance. That is, those in women's studies decreased significantly in Passive Acceptance from the beginning to the end of the semester. At the same time, they increased significantly in their scores on

Revelation, Embeddedness, and Active Commitment. Women's studies courses do seem to have an impact on women who take them.

In another study, the researcher found that in a women's studies course, the attitudes of both men and women changed, although the women's attitudes changed more than the men's did (Steiger, 1981). The author concluded that it was the consciousness-raising component of the course that changed people's attitudes. Furthermore, he speculated that the consciousness-raising component of the women's movement is having a significant impact on people.

We need to know what impact recent advances in sex-related technology will have on women's lives. Some have argued that the greatest single stimulus to the current liberation of women was the development of the birth control pill. If a single technological advance of that sort can have such far-reaching consequences, what will be the impact of other technologies? What will be the effect of test-tube babies, surrogate mothering, sex-choice technologies? Regarding the last issue, it may be possible within the next decade to choose the gender of one's offspring. In a sense, that is possible now; a woman could have amniocentesis, find out the gender of her child, and have an abortion if it were the "wrong" one. Personally, I would hate to see women abort fetuses on the basis of gender, and I think very few women would do so. But more sophisticated methods of gender choice will be available soon. One study investigated the impact of gender-choice technology by surveying 710 undergraduates (Fidell et al., 1979). As previous surveys had shown, people have an overwhelming preference for a boy as the first child; 85 percent express that preference. Having the second child be a girl was preferred by 73 percent. Given the preference people express as to the size of families, more boys (55 percent) would be born than girls. And given previous findings on differences between first-borns and second-borns, psychological gender differences would probably be magnified. Much more research of this sort is needed.

As I have discussed in earlier chapters, feminist scholars stress the importance of power relations between women and men. More psychological research is needed in this area. We need to know how men express power over women and how women might more effectively begin to express power themselves. Psychologists Wendy McKenna and Florence Denmark (1978) did an interesting study that shows some of the possibilities for future research in this area. They attempted to find out whether women really could improve their perceived status by adopting some of the nonverbal communication patterns typical of males and high-status individuals. To do this, they made videotapes of a short skit involving two people who were described as working for the same company. One person asked for a favor, and the other at first refused but then complied. In all possible combinations of men and women in the two roles, the researchers had one person exhibit high-status nonverbal behaviors (e.g., smiling infrequently, touching the person she or he is dealing with) and the other, low-status nonverbal behaviors. College students rated the job level of each of the videotaped men and women. Overall, the subjects thought that the person who showed high-status behaviors held the high-level job, regardless of the person's gender. Therefore, it seems that if women convey their competence nonverbally, they will be recog-

FOCUS 16.1

PARADIGMS, SCIENCE, AND FEMINISM

Thomas Kuhn's *The Structure of Scientific Revolutions* (1970) has become a modern classic in the philosophy of science. A consideration of Kuhn's analysis will help us to understand science, and specifically how feminism fits into science.

The general public tends to view science as advancing continually in small steps by accumulating facts. One of Kuhn's fundamental points is that if we look at the history of science, that is not at all the way it works. His analysis indicates that science instead proceeds in occasional revolutionary leaps that disrupt calm periods of data collection. Essential to his conceptualization is the term *paradigm*. As he defines it, a paradigm refers to the set of beliefs, underlying assumptions, values, and techniques shared by a particular community of scientists. In a sense a paradigm is a "worldview," or at least a view of the piece of the world that is the focus of the particular scientific specialty. A new paradigm is usually drastically different from the paradigm that preceded it in its field, but it gains followers because it solves some problems that the old paradigm could not handle; a radical revolution occurs as the science shifts from the old paradigm to the new. A paradigm is also sufficiently open-ended that it creates within it a whole new set of questions that scientists can busy themselves with answering.

A specific example that may clarify these concepts is Copernicus and the Copernican revolution in astronomy. In Europe at the beginning of the fifteenth century, everyone, scientists included, believed that the earth was the center of the universe and that the sun revolved around the earth, a view known as the geocentric (earth-centered) or Ptolemaic view. Copernicus (1473–1543) proposed a new view, or paradigm—namely, that the sun was the center (heliocentric view) around which the earth rotated yearly, while the earth spun on its own axis daily. The Copernican view solved some problems that existed with the old, geocentric view. One of these was that in order for geocentrism to be correct, the other planets must be traveling at irregular speeds around the earth, darting ahead and then slowing down. Using the Copernican view, the planets could be seen as moving at constant speed, while the earth (with the astronomer on it) moved simultaneously. Copernicus's ideas were opposed by the Catholic Church as erroneous and possibly heretical, which is often the case with new scientific paradigms. But eventually his ideas were widely accepted by astronomers, who then used them as the basis for their research. Kuhn's point is clear: science proceeds in occasional revolutionary leaps as new paradigms, representing radically different ideas, arise.

The general public, as well as many scientists, tends to view science as fundamentally objective. Kuhn also disputes this notion. He believes that there is no such thing as a pure fact in science; rather, there are only facts that exist within the context of a particular paradigm. Once a new paradigm has taken over, the old "facts" will seem wrong or downright stupid. For example, if we had lived before the time of Copernicus, we would naturally have observed the "fact" that the sun rises in the East every morning and sets in the West every evening. We would further have taken this as ample evidence of the "fact" that the sun is revolving around the earth. From our modern, post-Copernican perspective, these do not seem to be facts at all. This illustrates Kuhn's argument that there are no objective facts in science; facts exist only from the point of view of a particular paradigm.

How does all this relate to psychology? Psychology has had several paradigms, the actual number depending on how broad or narrow one wants to be in identifying paradigms. Certainly *learning theory* has been a dominant paradigm in psychology. Rosnow (1981) has traced the history of *experimentalism* as a dominant paradigm in social psychology. The belief in social psychology has been that the tightly controlled laboratory experiment is the best, perhaps the only, way to get good "facts" on people's social behavior. Rosnow also documents a crisis that experimentalism faces. Experimenter effects and observer effects (discussed in Chapter 1) mean that scientists may get poor data from their experiments, or only data that conform to their own biases.

Feminists point out that the paradigms of psychology have been *androcentric,* that is, focusing on males and coming from a male perspective.

In the context of Kuhn's arguments, feminism can be seen as an emerging new paradigm in the science of psychology. Feminism fits the definition of a paradigm in that it comprises a set of beliefs, values, and techniques (explained in other chapters of this book) that are shared by a community of scientists, namely, feminist psychologists. Feminism provides a new worldview. Traditional psychology could be viewed as seeing the world revolving around men (androcentrism), just as the pre-Copernicans saw the sun revolving around the earth. Feminists do not want to shift to viewing the world as revolving around women. Rather, the feminist desire is to view the world revolving around men and women jointly.

Another characteristic of a paradigm, according to Kuhn, is that it provides answers to a set of problems that could not be solved by the old paradigm and were creating a crisis. There are a number of such problems that have not been solved by traditional psychology. One of these is the nature of masculinity and femininity (Pleck, 1981). Traditional psychology has viewed masculinity-femininity as an essential personality dimension (see Chapter 3). Furthermore, gender typing was supposed to be essential to mental health. That is, the highly masculine male and the highly feminine female were supposed to be the most well adjusted, according to that paradigm. Actual research, however, shows that this is not true. For example, highly masculine males are actually less well adjusted than less masculine males are (e.g., Mussen, 1961, 1962). Traditional psychology's paradigm cannot handle that result. Feminism provides a framework that answers that difficulty. It suggests the possibility that people can be androgynous and that the androgynous person would be most healthy psychologically.

Paradigms, according to Kuhn, also create a whole new set of research questions because they present a different way of looking at the world. And so the feminist paradigm has created a new set of research topics that had not come to light in traditional psychology: rape, wife-battering, sexual harassment of women at work, how different ethnic groups define gender roles, and sexism in psychotherapy, to name a few.

Feminist psychology, then, fits Kuhn's definition of a paradigm nicely. One final comment is in order, however. It is sometimes argued that feminism has no place in scientific psychology because feminism consists merely of a set of political biases and these biases do not permit objective research. Concerning this point, it is well to remember Kuhn's argument that science is not truly objective and that facts are facts only in the context of a particular paradigm. Thus feminist psychology is neither more nor less objective than other paradigms in psychology. What it does is provide a set of "facts" that make sense in the feminist context.

SOURCES: Kuhn (1970), Rosnow (1981), Pleck (1981).

nized as being competent and of high status. That is an encouraging finding. Unfortunately, there was also a suggestion that a man who showed low-status behaviors in the presence of a woman showing high-status behaviors was judged as having a lower-level job than when his partner was a man showing high-status behaviors. Therefore, men may lose prestige by working for high-status women, and male resentment may ensue. It is exactly this kind of information—about the positive and negative consequences of new patterns of behavior—that we need.

Feminism Revisited

In Chapter 1 a short definition of feminism was given: "a feminist is a person who favors political, economic, and social equality of women and men, and therefore favors the legal and social changes that will be necessary to achieve

ENGLEMAN

" I'LL PLAY 'DOCTOR' ONLY IF I'M THE DOCTOR. "

FIGURE 16.2
Has society changed so that girls understand the complexities of power, gender, roles, and occupations? *(Source: Engleman/Rothco.)*

that equality." Your understanding of feminism is now much more complex than that. I hope that your view of feminism has been transformed in reading this book. Feminists are not a bunch of ugly women burning their bras; nor are they a group of screaming picketers protesting discrimination. Feminism, or the feminist perspective, or the feminist paradigm, whichever term you prefer, offers a substantially different view of the world, and specifically of psychology, than traditional science has offered (see Focus 16.1, "Paradigms, Science, and Feminism"). The feminist paradigm says that the focus of psychology should be on women as much as on men. Issues of concern to women—rape, battering, menstruation—should be given research attention. Scientists must be careful in interpreting outcomes: for example, when they investigate rape, they must not automatically blame it on the victim, the woman. People need to be aware of the power of gender roles in their lives. And so the list continues. The point is that feminism provides a new view in psychology, a new set of questions, a fresh set of hypotheses. I find that exciting, and I hope you do, also.

Future Roles for Women

How will the female role emerge in the United States from the present upheaval in gender roles? In many ways, ours may be an optimal time for gender-role change for women. The de-emphasis on fertility and childrearing may be critical. The nature of the female role is intimately tied to whether or not a society wants to reproduce at a high rate. With a strong emphasis on reproduction, maternal aspects of the female role are stressed. With the current de-emphasis on fertility, careers for women are much more viable alternatives than they formerly were. Indeed, childlessness is becoming an option for women, freeing them for substantially different roles than housewife/mother (Hoffman, 1974).

On the other hand, we must recognize the emergence of a political movement known as the New Right (for a feminist analysis of the New Right, see Eisenstein, 1982). The New Right abhors recent social change. It claims that its stance is "profamily," but it narrowly defines the family as a married heterosexual couple with children, with the husband working in the labor force and the wife staying home full-time. The New Right rues the demise of patriarchy and the loss of the father's authority within the family. To say the least, the forces of the New Right act in opposition to the forces of feminism. Focus 16.2, Backlash!, details some of these anti-women forces. It remains to be seen which will win out. Interestingly, the New Right has lost some key legislative battles; in 1983 it lost a critical Senate vote attempting to put into law a constitutional amendment that would have prohibited abortion. (On the other hand, the Equal Rights Amendment also went down to defeat.) And the New Right lost in its efforts to keep George Bush in the White House when Bill Clinton won the 1992 presidential election.

One problem to be faced is that we really have no adequate measure of social change. There has been a tendency to equate work outside the home with progress for women. Yet working outside the home is the opposite of progress if

FOCUS 16.2

BACKLASH!

Pulitzer Prize–winning author Susan Faludi's 1991 book *Backlash* has helped to energize a new surge of feminist activism. The feminist movement that began in the 1960s is now referred to as the "second wave" (the first wave being the suffragettes who won the right to vote for women in the early 1900s), and a new, third wave of feminism is vigorous in the 1990s. Susan Faludi's book is passed around as eagerly today as Betty Friedan's *The Feminine Mystique* was in the 1960s.

FIGURE 16.3

The backlash has many manifestations. In December 1994, two abortion clinic employees were slain in Brookline, Massachusetts, allegedly by a known anti-abortion protester. Here flowers and candles on the steps of the Planned Parenthood clinic memorialize those who died.

Faludi's basic argument is that women have made some progress—legal, economic, political—in the United States in the last two decades and that a counterassault of antifeminism has been launched to attack this progress. This is the backlash against women and feminism.

The basic argument of the backlash forces is that women have made progress yet they are still unhappy, so their unhappiness must be the fault of the feminist movement. The alternative explanation—that women's unhappiness may be related to continued sexism in every place from the bedroom to the board room—is ignored.

What evidence does Faludi present for the existence of this backlash movement? Much of it comes from analyses of the popular media's reporting of stories that gnaw away at the psyche of liberated women. For example, there was much publicity in 1986 of a study that found that a single, college-educated woman over the age of 30 had only a 20 percent chance of ever marrying, and a single, college-educated woman of 40 had only a 1.3 percent chance. The clear messages were, "If you're a single woman with some education, you're going to end up a miserable old spinster" and "There's a terrible man shortage. Better treat men as precious resources." It turns out that the story originated when a newspaper reporter at the Stamford (Connecticut) *Advocate* wanted to do a Valentine's Day article and phoned the sociology department at Yale. She reached a faculty member, Neil Bennett, who gave her the statistics noted above, which had come from data analyses just completed, and the study was not yet published. These results, which had not even been published in a scientific journal, spread like wildfire. Associated Press picked up the story, and the results were discussed in magazines ranging from *Mademoiselle* to *Cosmo,* on television shows such as "Designing Women" and "Kate and Allie," and in movies such as *When Harry Met Sally.* As it turned out, the Bennett statistics were flawed (Faludi recounts the flaws in gripping detail, for which there isn't space here). A better study by Jeanne Moorman of the U.S. Census Bureau indicated that at 30, a never-married college-educated woman had a 58 to 66 percent chance of marriage, and at 40, she had a 17 to 23 percent chance. Moorman's findings received only muted publicity, were in fact attacked in op-ed articles in places such as the *New York Times,* and were suppressed by her superiors at the Census Bureau under the Reagan administration.

As another example, in the 1980s there was much publicity over child sexual abuse in daycare centers—toxic daycare, as some said. Working women couldn't help but feel guilty over leaving their children in such dangerous situations. In fact, though, child sexual abuse was verified in relatively few daycare centers. More importantly, statistics indicate that most child sexual abuse occurs in the home, not in daycare centers.

As a third example, in 1982 the *New England Journal of Medicine* published an article on the "infertility epidemic"—women between the ages of 31 and 35 stood a nearly 40 percent chance of being infertile, according to the research. There was a fatherly editorial admonishing women to reevaluate their goals and have their babies before their careers. The findings were on the front page of the *New York Times* the next day and were widely publicized throughout the country. Again, the study was seriously flawed. The participants were French women being treated at artificial insemination centers—that is, their husbands were completely sterile and they were trying artificial insemination, which is far less effective in producing pregnancies than good old-fashioned sexual intercourse. Moreover, the declines in fertility were attributed to women building careers and postponing childbearing. In fact, any increases in women's infertility are far more likely to be a result of the epidemic of sexually transmitted diseases such as chlamydia, which, if not treated, can cause blockage of the fallopian tubes.

The message to women in the publicity in all three examples was "Don't worry about developing a career. Marry early, have babies early, or you'll be sorry. And once the babies are born, don't get a job and leave them in daycare, or you'll be even sorrier."

Faludi's evidence includes far more than overpublicized, flawed research. She analyzes images of women on TV and in high fashion, the New Right, Robert Bly's men's movement, and many other influences. In all cases, the effort is to reverse the trends set in motion by the women's movement, and the messages are often quite frightening.

The critical question is, Are we now in a decade of a resurgence of feminism—a third wave—energized by college-age women and young working women, who can fight the backlash and continue to press for women's rights?

SOURCE: Faludi (1991).

it must be done in addition to all the housewife and mother tasks. The work of women, whether inside the home or outside the home, must be evaluated in terms of its contributions to society in general and to the growth of the individual. A much more complex and adequate measure of social change would result.

We need, then, to expand our notion of the meaning of equality—it means more than just women holding jobs outside the home, for example. Part of the expansion must include changes in the male role. Equality requires modification of the male role, not only to make true equality possible, but because the male role itself is in need of revision.

But I must add one note of caution, and this is in regard to the values attached to gender roles. Cross-culturally (at least currently) it is a universal phenomenon that the male role is more powerful and the female role is valued less. This devaluing of the female role surely has many consequences, among them psychological ones such as the higher frequency of psychiatric problems found in women. In my opinion it is imperative that whatever the reallocation or modification of gender roles, the result be that the male role and the female role be valued equally.

Although I am emphasizing the need for a higher valuing of the female role, this higher valuing must come not only from without, but also from within. That is, institutional change aimed at raising the value of the female role—for example, treating childrearing as a profession—and changing male attitudes are not enough. Women must also value themselves. This is an important goal of self-help groups formed by women across the country.

Whatever the reallocation of gender roles in the future, equal respect and value must be attached to both roles. In part, I am suggesting that gender roles in some form will probably continue, and that rather than trying to eliminate them, we might more profitably concentrate on improving the valuation attached to the female role. Much as Blacks shifted from an emphasis on integration and assimilation into white culture to a proclamation that Black is beautiful, so I hope women will increasingly believe that female is good. As Christabel Pankhurst, a turn-of-the-century British suffragette, said,

> Remember the dignity
> of your womanhood.
> Do not appeal,
> do not beg,
> do not grovel.
> Take courage,
> join hands,
> stand beside us.

EXPERIENCE THE RESEARCH

FEMINIST IDENTITY

Think about the stages of feminist identity development described in the Bargad and Hyde (1991) study (see page 442). They go from Stage 1, Passive Acceptance, to Stage 5, Active Commitment. You have just taken a psychology of women course. Do you think that you passed through one or several of those stages as the term progressed? What stage would you say you are in now?

Appendix
Psychology of Women
Resource Directory

Below are listed various organizations that may provide services useful to you. All have focuses on issues related to the psychology of women.

I.   **General**
     American Men's Studies Association
     22 East Street
     Northampton, MA 01060

The American Men's Studies Association (AMSA) is an organization of men and women dedicated to teaching, research, and clinical practice in the field of men's studies. We conceive "men's studies" to be concerned with the analyses of male experience as social-historical-cultural constructions.

American Psychological Association
750 First St., N.E.
Washington, DC 20002-4242
(202) 336-5500

This is the major organization of psychologists in the United States. Division 35 of the APA is Psychology of Women. APA has a Women's Program Officer. Numerous useful publications can be obtained from APA, such as *Graduate Faculty Interested in the Psychology of Women* and *Understanding the Manuscript Review Process: Increasing the Participation of Women.*

Association for Women in Psychology
Joan Chrisler
Psychology Department
Connecticut College
New London, CT 06320
(203) 439-2336

This is a political action group of women psychologists. It sponsors an annual feminist psychology conference.

Center for Women Policy Studies
2000 P Street, N.W., Suite 508
Washington, DC 20036
(202) 872-1770

The Center publishes reports on a range of women's issues, including violence against women, girls and violence, women's health, and women and AIDS.

The Feminist Press
P.O. Box 334
Old Westbury, NY 11568
(212) 360-5790

This organization publishes books with a feminist perspective in a wide variety of disciplines.

National Anorexic Aid Society
Harding Hospital
1925 East Dublin Granville Rd.
Columbus, OH 43229
(614) 436-1112

Provides information and referrals on eating disorders.

National Council for Research on Women
530 Broadway at Spring St., 10th floor
New York, NY 10012-3921
(212) 274-0730

This is an organization of more than 60 women's research centers committed to research on women from disciplines in the humanities, social sciences, and natural/health sciences.

National Organization for Women
1000 16th St. N.W., Suite 700
Washington, DC 20036
(202) 331-0066

NOW seeks to take action to bring women into full participation in the mainstream of American society now, so that they will exercise all the privileges and responsibilities thereof in truly equal partnership with men.

National Women's Studies Association
University of Maryland
7100 Baltimore Ave., Suite 301
College Park, MD 20740
(301) 403-0525

This organization is devoted to women's studies in all disciplines, including psychology. It sponsors a yearly women's studies conference that includes many excellent activities.

Women's Bureau
U.S. Department of Labor
200 Constitution Ave. N.W.
Washington, DC 20210
(202) 219-6611

The Women's Bureau alerts women about their rights in the workplace; proposes policies and legislation that benefit working women; researches and analyzes information about women and work; reports findings to the president, Congress, and the public; and makes sure that the voices of America's working women count.

II.   **Health Issues: Contraception, Abortion, Sexuality**
CDC National AIDS Clearinghouse
P.O. Box 6003
Rockville, MD 20849-6003
1-800-458-5231

Operated by the U.S. Public Health Service, this clearinghouse provides information and referrals on HIV/AIDS.

National Abortion and Reproductive Rights Action League
1156 15th St., N.W
Washington, DC 20005
(202) 973-3000

NARAL is a political action organization working at both state and national levels and is dedicated to preserving a woman's right to legal abortion and to teaching its members effective use of the political process to ensure abortion and reproductive rights.

National Gay and Lesbian Task Force
2320 17th St., N.W.
Washington, DC 20009-3409
(202) 332-6483

NGLTF is a lesbian and gay civil rights and lobbying organization dedicated to building a movement to promote freedom and full equality for all lesbians and gay men.

National Women's Health Network
10th St., N.W., Suite 400
Washington, DC 20004
(202) 347-1140

This feminist group is concerned with women's health issues; it provides a newsletter, news alert, information clearinghouse, health resource guides, speakers bureau, and educational conferences.

Planned Parenthood of America, Inc.
810 Seventh Avenue
New York, NY 10019
(212) 541-7800

PPFA is the nation's largest family planning agency. Through local clinics (check your telephone directory) it offers birth control instruction and prescriptions; pregnancy testing; infertility care; voluntary sterilization for men and women; prenatal care; early abortions; testing for sexually transmitted diseases; screening for sickle cell anemia, cancer, DES exposure, and diabetes; blood and urine tests; and pelvic and breast exams.

III. Victimization Issues: Rape, Battering, Harassment
Violence and Traumatic Stress Research Branch
National Institute of Mental Health
5600 Fishers Lane, Room 10C-26
Rockville, MD 20857
(301) 443-3728

This is the focal point in the National Institute of Mental Health for research on violent behavior, including sexual abuse and sexual assault.

National Center for Women and Family Law
Room 402, 799 Broadway
New York, NY 10003
(212) 674-8200

This is a legal services backup center, providing assistance on legal issues affecting women and families, such as battering, rape, marital rape, divorce, and child snatching.

Glossary

Acculturation The process by which one takes on the beliefs and customs of a new culture as one's own.

Achievement motivation The desire to accomplish something of value or importance through one's efforts; the desire to meet standards of excellence.

Adrenogenital syndrome *See* Congenital adrenal hyperplasia.

African Americans Americans of African descent.

Aggression Behavior intended to harm another person.

Androcentric Male centered; the belief that the male is the norm.

Androgens A group of sex hormones, including testosterone, produced more abundantly in males than females.

Androgyny The combination of masculine and feminine psychological characteristics in an individual.

Anorexia nervosa An eating disorder characterized by overcontrol of eating for purposes of weight reduction, sometimes to the point of starvation.

Anorgasmia The inability to have an orgasm; orgasmic dysfunction.

Antigay prejudice Negative attitudes and behaviors toward gay men and lesbians.

Asian Americans Americans of Asian descent.

Assertiveness Standing up for one's basic interpersonal rights in such a way that the rights of another person are not violated.

Attribution The process by which people make judgments about the causes of behavior.

Behavior therapy A system of treatment based on the principles of learning theory.

Berdache *See* Two-Spirit.

Bilingualism Knowing two languages.

Bisexuality Being erotically and emotionally attracted to both females and males.

Boston marriage A romantic but asexual relationship between two women.

Bulimia An eating disorder in which the person binges on food and then purges the body of the calories by vomiting or use of laxatives.

Care perspective According to Gilligan, an approach to moral reasoning that emphasizes relationships between people and caring for others and the self.

Chicana A female American of Mexican descent.

Chicano Americans of Mexican descent; may also refer specifically to male Mexican Americans.

Cognitive-behavioral therapy A system of psychotherapy that combines behavior therapy and restructuring of dysfunctional thought patterns.

Coming out The process of acknowledging to oneself, and then to others, that one is lesbian or gay.

Comparable worth The principle that people should be paid equally for work that is comparable in responsibility, educational requirements, and so forth.

Congenital adrenal hyperplasia (CAH) A rare genetic condition that causes the fetus's adrenal glands to produce abnormally large amounts of androgens. In genetic females, the result may be a girl born with masculinized genitals. Also called adrenogenital syndrome.

Conventional morality In Kohlberg's theory, an intermediate level of moral reasoning, in which children and adults understand rules and obey them rigidly.

Couvade A custom in which the man is assumed to be the major contributor to childbirth, and therefore suffers the symptoms such as fatigue.

Deindividuation A state in which a person

has become anonymous and has therefore lost his or her individual identity.

Double standard Tolerance of male promiscuity and disapproval of female promiscuity.

Double standard of aging Cultural norms by which men's status increases with age but women's decreases.

Diagnostic and Statistical Manual (DSM) The American Psychiatric Association's official manual of psychiatric diagnoses.

DSM *See Diagnostic and Statistical Manual*

Dysmenorrhea Painful menstruation; cramps

Dyspareunia Painful intercourse.

Dysphoria Unhappiness or sad mood.

Electra Complex In psychoanalytic theory, a girl's sexual attraction to and intense love for her father.

Empowerment Helping people to find their own strength.

Empty next syndrome Depression that middle-aged people supposedly feel when their children are grown and have left home, leaving an empty nest.

Enhancement hypothesis In research on women and multiple roles, the hypothesis that multiple roles are good for mental health, because they provide more opportunities for stimulation, self-esteem, and so on.

Entitlement The individual's sense of what he or she is entitled to or deserves.

Erogenous zones Areas of the body that are particularly sensitive to sexual stimulation.

Estrogen A "female" sex hormone produced by the ovaries; also produced in smaller quantities in males.

Estrogen-deficiency theory The hypothesis that the symptoms of menopause are due to low levels of estrogen.

Estrogen-replacement therapy (ERT) Replacement doses of estrogen given to some women to treat menopausal symptoms.

Ethnic group A group of people who share a common culture and language.

Ethnocentrism The tendency to regard one's own ethnic group as superior to others and to believe that its customs and way of life are the standards by which other cultures should be judged.

Euro-Americans White Americans of European descent. An alternative to the term *whites.*

Eurocentrism The tendency to view the world from a Euro-American point of view and to evaluate other ethnic groups in reference to Euro-Americans.

Experimenter effects Some characteristics of the experimenter affect the way participants behave and therefore affect the research outcome.

Female-as-the-exception phenomenon If a category is considered normatively male and there is a female example of the category, gender is noted because the female is the exception. The men's basketball team is called simply the basketball team, whereas the women's basketball team is called the women's basketball team. A byproduct of androcentrism.

Female deficit model A theory or interpretation of research in which women's behavior is seen as deficient.

Feminine evil The belief that women are the source of evil or immorality in the world, as in the Adam and Eve story.

Femininity-achievement incompatibility The cultural belief that, beginning in adolescence, achievement is not appropriately feminine for girls.

Feminist A person who favors political, economic, and social equality of women and men, and therefore favors the legal and social changes necessary to achieve that equality.

Feminist research Research growing out of feminist theory, which seeks radical reform of traditional research methods.

Feminist therapy A system of psychotherapy informed by feminist theory.

Feminization of poverty The increasing trend over time for women to be overrepresented among the poor in the United States.

Field independence Witkin's term for the ability to make perceptual judgments and not be influenced by misleading surroundings.

Fitness In evolutionary theory, an animal's relative contribution of genes to the next generation.

Follicle The capsule of cells surrounding an egg in the ovary.

Follicle-stimulating hormone (FSH) A hormone secreted by the pituitary; in females it stimulates follicle and egg development.

Follicular phase The first phase of the menstrual cycle, beginning just after menstruation.

Gender The state of being male or female.

Gender constancy In cognitive-developmental theory, a child's understanding that gender is a permanent, unchanging characteristic of oneself.

Gender-fair research Research that is free of gender bias.

Gender identity In cognitive-developmental theory, the individual's concept or knowledge that she or he is a female or male.

Gender-role stereotype A set of shared cultural beliefs about males' and females' behavior, personality traits, and other attributes.

Gender schema A person's general knowledge framework about gender; it processes and organizes information on the basis of gender-linked associations.

Gender similarities Ways in which males and females are similar rather than different.

Glass ceiling "Invisible" barriers to the promotion of women and ethnic minorities into upper management and executive levels.

Gonadotropin-releasing hormone (GnRH) A hormone secreted by the hypothalamus that regulates the pituitary's secretion of hormones.

Good provider role The male role in industrialized societies, in which the man is expected to earn money and provide well for his family.

Gräfenberg spot (G-spot) A hypothesized small gland on the front wall of the vagina, emptying into the urethra, which may be responsible for female ejaculation.

Hispanics People of Spanish descent, whether from Mexico, Puerto Rico, or elsewhere.

Homophobia A strong, irrational fear of homosexuals.

Hopelessness theory A theory that one type of depression results from a pattern of cognition in which the person believes that good things will not happen to him or her, and that he or she is helpless to control these outcomes.

Hypothalamus A part of the brain that is important in regulating certain body functions including sex hormone production.

Hysterectomy Surgical removal of the uterus.

Imitation When people do what they see others doing.

Incest Sexual activity between close relatives.

Infantilizing Treating people, for example, women, as if they were children or babies.

Justice perspective According to Gilligan, an approach to moral reasoning that emphasizes fairness and the rights of the individual.

Kegel exercises Exercises to strengthen the muscles surrounding the vagina; pubococcygeal muscle exercises.

Lateralization The extent to which one hemisphere of the brain organizes a particular mental process or behavior.

Latina A female Latin American.

Latinos People of Latin American descent.

Learned helplessness theory A theory that depression is caused by a person having learned that he or she is helpless or unable to control important outcomes in life.

Lesbian A woman whose sexual orientation is toward other women.

Lumpectomy A surgical treatment for breast cancer in which only the lump and a small bit of surrounding tissue are removed.

Luteal phase The third phase of the menstrual cycle, after ovulation.

Luteinizing hormone (LH) A hormone secreted by the pituitary; in females it triggers ovulation.

Machismo The ideal of manliness in Hispanic cultures.

Male as normative A model in which the male is seen as the norm for the species, and the female is seen as a deviation from the norm.

Male sex-role identity (MSRI) paradigm Traditional psychology's approach to the psychology of men, based on the assumption that a masculine identity is essential for good adjustment.

Marianismo The ideal of womanliness in Hispanic cultures.

Masochism The desire to experience pain.

Maternity leave *See* Parental leave

Measurement *See* Psychological measurement.

Menstruation A bloody discharge of the lining of the uterus; the fourth phase of the menstrual cycle.

Meta-analysis A statistical technique that allows a researcher to combine the results of many separate research studies.

Motherhood mandate the cultural belief that all women should have children, that is, be mothers.

Motive to avoid success A hypothesized fear of success that leads people to avoid being successful.

Myotonia Muscle contraction.

Natural selection According to Darwin, the process by which the fittest animals survive, reproduce, and pass their genes on to the next generation, whereas animals that are less fit do not reproduce and therefore do not pass on their genes.

Observational learning When a person observes someone doing something, and then does it at a later time.

Observer effects When the researcher's expectations affect his or her observations and recording of the data.

Oedipal complex In psychoanalytic theory, a boy's sexual attraction to and intense love for his mother, and his desire to do away with his father.

Orgasm An intense sensation that occurs at the peak of sexual arousal and is followed by the release of sexual tensions.

Overgeneralization A research error in which the results are said to apply to a broader group than the one sampled; for example, saying that results from an all-male sample are true for all people.

Ovulation Release of an egg from an ovary.

Ovum An egg.

Paradigm The set of beliefs, underlying assumptions, values, and techniques shared by a particular community of scientists.

Paradigm shift A radical revolution in science, in which scientists change from one paradigm to another.

Parental investment In sociobiology, behaviors or other investments in the offspring by the parent that increase the offspring's chance of survival.

Parental leave A leave from work for purposes of recovering from childbirth and/or caring for the child, at the time of birth or adoption.

PC exercises *See* Kegel exercises.

Pejoration The process by which a term takes on negative connotations.

Phallic stage The third stage of development in psychoanalytic theory, around 3 to 6 years of age, during which the pleasure zone is the genitals and sexual feelings arise toward the parent of the other gender.

Phallocentric Male centered, or, specifically, penis centered.

Postconventional morality In Kohlberg's theory, the most mature level of moral reasoning, in which the person understands that rules are not absolute, but rather are part of a social contract; the person behaves from internalized ethical principles.

Post-traumatic stress disorder (PTSD) Long-term psychological distress suffered by someone who has experienced a terrifying, uncontrollable event.

Preconventional morality In Kohlberg's theory, the earliest stage of moral reasoning, in which children do the right thing simply to gain rewards or avoid punishments.

Premenstrual dysphoric disorder (PMDD) The American Psychiatric Association's controversial new diagnostic category for PMS.

Premenstrual syndrome (PMS) A combination of several physical and psychological symptoms (such as depression) occurring in some women for a few days before menstruation.

Prenatal Before birth.

Progesterone A "female" sex hormone produced by the ovaries; also produced in smaller quantities in males.

Projective test A method of psychological measurement that uses ambiguous stimuli; the person's responses are thought to reflect his or her personality, based on the assumption that one's personality is projected onto the ambiguous stimulus.

Prostaglandins Hormone-like biochemicals that stimulate the muscles of the uterus to contract.

Provider role The male role in preindustrial societies, which required the men to provide food and shelter for his family; *See also* Good provider role.

Pseudohermaphrodite An individual who has a mixture of male and female reproductive structures, so that it is not clear whether the individual is a male or female.

Psychoanalysis A system of therapy based on Freud's psychoanalytic theory, in which the analyst attempts to bring repressed, unconscious material into consciousness.

Psychoanalytic theory A psychological theory originated by Freud; its basic assumption is that part of the human psyche is unconscious.

Psychological measurement The process of assigning numbers to people's characteristics, such as aggressiveness or intelligence.

Pubococcygeal muscle exercises (PC exercises) *0* Kegel exercises.

Quasi-experimental design A research design that uses two or more groups, but participants are not randomly assigned to groups so it is not a true experiment. An example is two-group designs comparing males and females.

Race A biological concept referring to a group of people with a common set of physical features who have mated only within their race.

Radical mastectomy A surgical treatment for breast cancer in which the entire breast, as well as underlying muscle and lymph nodes, are removed.

Rape Nonconsenting oral, anal, or vaginal penetration obtained by force, by threat of bodily harm, or when the victim is incapable of giving consent.

Rape trauma syndrome The emotional and physical effects a woman undergoes following a rape or attempted rape.

Reinforcement In operant conditioning, something that occurs after a behavior and makes the behavior more likely to occur in the future.

Replicate To repeat a research study and obtain the same basic results.

Scarcity hypothesis In research on women and multiple roles, the hypothesis that adding a role (e.g., worker) creates stress, which has negative consequences for physical health and mental health.

Schema In cognitive psychology, a general knowledge framework that a person has about a particular topic; the schema then processes and organizes new information on that topic.

Sex-linked trait A trait controlled by a gene on the X chromosome (or occasionally on the Y chromosome).

Sex-role strain (SRS) paradigm Feminist psychology's approach to the male role, based on the assumption that gender roles for men are contradictory and stressful.

Sexism Discrimination or bias against people based on their gender. Sex bias.

Sexual dysfunction A problem with sexual responding that causes a person mental distress; examples are erection problems in men and orgasm problems in women.

Sexual orientation A person's erotic and emotional orientation toward members of her or his own gender or members of the other gender.

Sexual selection According to Darwin, the processes by which members of one gender (usually males) compete with each other for mating privileges with members of the other gender (usually females), and members of the other gender (females) choose to mate only with certain preferred members of the first gender (males).

Social constructionism A theoretical viewpoint that humans do not discover reality directly; rather, they construct meanings for events in the environment based on their own prior experiences and beliefs.

Socialization The process by which society conveys to the individual its expectations for his or her behavior, values, and beliefs.

Sociobiology The application of evolutionary theory to explaining the social behavior of animals, including people.

Superego Freud's term for the part of the personality that contains the person's ideals and conscience.

Systematic desensitization A method used by behavior therapists in the treatment of phobias; it involves associating a relaxed, pleasant state with gradually increasing anxiety-provoking stimuli.

Testosterone A sex hormone; one of the androgens.

Trait An enduring characteristic of a person, such as extraversion.

Two-Spirit Among Native Americans, a third gender category.

Vacuum curettage A method of abortion that is performed in the first trimester.

Vaginismus A strong, spastic contraction of the muscles around the vagina, perhaps closing off the vagina and making intercourse impossible.

Vasocongestion An accumulation of blood in the blood vessels of a region of the body, especially the genitals; a swelling or erection results.

Whorfian hypothesis The theory that the language we learn influences how we think.

Womb envy In Horney's analytic theory, the male's envy of woman's uterus and reproductive capacity.

Women's resistance Occurs when women do not passively accept discriminatory treatment, but instead take active steps to resist it.

Bibliography

In the bibliography I have followed the style of spelling out first names of authors. I do this to help readers become aware of the scientific contributions made by women.

AAUW. (1991). *Shortchanging girls, shortchanging America.* Washington, DC: American Association of University Women.

Abbey, Antonia. (1982). Sex differences in attributions for friendly behavior: Do males misperceive females' friendliness. *Journal of Personality and Social Psychology, 42,* 830–838.

Abbey, Antonia. (1991). Misperception as an antecedent of acquaintance rape: A consequence of ambiguity in communication between men and women. In A. Parrott & L. Bechhofer (Eds.), *Acquaintance rape: The hidden crime.* New York: Wiley.

Abramowitz, Stephen I. (1986). Psychosocial outcomes of sex reassignment surgery. *Journal of Consulting and Clinical Psychology, 54,* 183–189.

Abramowitz, Stephen I., et al. (1976). Sex bias in psychotherapy: A failure to confirm. *American Journal of Psychiatry, 133,* 706–709.

Abramowitz, Stephen I., Abramowitz, C. V., & Gomes, Beverly. (1973). The politics of clinical judgment: What nonliberal examiners infer about women who do not stifle themselves. *Journal of Consulting and Clinical Psychology, 41,* 385–391.

Abramson, Lyn Y., Metalsky, Gerald I., & Alloy, Lauren B. (1989). Hopelessness depression: A theory-based subtype of depression. *Psychological Review, 96,* 358–372.

Abramson, P. R., et al. (1977). The talking platypus phenomenon as a function of sex and professional status. *Psychology of Women Quarterly, 2,* 114–117.

Adams, Kathryn A., & Landers, Audrey D. (1978). Sex difference in dominance behavior. *Sex Roles, 4,* 215–224.

Adamsky, Catherine. (1981). Changes in pronomial usage in a classroom situation. *Psychology of Women Quarterly, 5,* 773–779.

Addiego, F., et al. (1981). Female ejaculation: A case study. *Journal of Sex Research, 17,* 13–21.

Adelman, Clifford. (1991). *Women at thirtysomething: Paradoxes of attainment.* Washington, DC: U.S. Department of Education.

Adler, Nancy E., David, Henry P., Major, Brenda N., Roth, Susan H., Russo, Nancy F., & Wyatt, Gail E. (1990). Psychological responses after abortion. *Science, 248,* 41–44.

Adler, Nancy E., David, Henry P., Major, Brenda N., Roth, Susan H., Russo, Nancy F., & Wyatt, Gail E. (1992). Psychological factors in abortion. *American Psychologist, 47,* 1194–1204.

Alba, Joseph W., & Hasher, Lynn. (1983). Is memory schematic? *Psychological Bulletin, 93,* 203–231.

Albee, George W. (1977). The Protestant ethic, sex, and psychotherapy. *American Psychologist, 32,* 150–161.

Albin, Rochelle S. (1977). Psychological studies of rape. *Signs, 3,* 423–435.

Allen, Paula Gunn. (1986). Who is your mother? Red roots of white feminism. In P. G. Allen, *The sacred hoop: Recovering the feminine in American Indian traditions.* Boston: Beacon Press.

Allgeier, Elizabeth R., & Fogel, A. (1978). Coital position and sex roles: Responses to cross-sex behavior in bed. *Journal of Consulting and Clinical Psychology, 46,* 588–589.

Allport, G. (1954). *The nature of prejudice.* Reading, MA: Addison-Wesley.

Almquist, Elizabeth. (1977). Women in the labor force. *Signs, 2,* 843–853.

Almquist, E. M., & Angrist, S. (1970). Career salience and atypicality of occupational choice among college women. *Journal of Marriage and the Family, 32,* 242–249.

Amaro, Hortensia. (1988). Considerations for prevention of HIV infection among Hispanic women. *Psychology of Women Quarterly, 12,* 429–444.

Amaro, Hortensia, & Russo, Nancy F. (1987). Hispanic women and mental health: An overview of contemporary issues in research and practice. *Psychology of Women Quarterly,* 393–408.

Amaro, Hortensia, Russo, Nancy F., & Johnson, Julie. (1987). Family and work predictors of psychological well-being among Hispanic women professionals. *Psychology of Women Quarterly, 11,* 505–522.

American Cancer Society. (1987). *Cancer facts and figures—1987.* New York: Author.

American Cancer Society. (1991). *Facts on breast cancer.* New York: Author.

American Psychiatric Association. (1994). *Diagnostic and statistical manual,* 4th ed. New York: Author.

American Psychological Association. (1975a). Task force on issues of sexual bias in graduate education. Guidelines for nonsexist use of language. *American Psychologist, 30,* 682–684.

American Psychological Association. (1975b). Report of the task force on sex bias and sex-role stereotyping in psychotherapeutic practice. *American Psychologist, 30,* 1169–1175.

American Psychological Association. (1994). *Publication manual* (4th ed.). Washington, DC: Author.

Anastasi, Anne. (1958). *Differential psychology* (3rd ed.). New York: Macmillan.

Anderson, Barbara L. (1983). Primary orgasmic dysfunction: Diagnostic considerations and review of treatment. *Psychological Bulletin, 93,* 105–136.

Aneshensel, Carol S. (1986). Marital and employment role strain, social support, and depression among adult women. In S. E. Hobfall (Ed.), *Stress, social support, and women* (pp. 99–114). New York: Hemisphere.

Angrist, Shirley S. (1969). The study of sex roles. *Journal of Social Issues, 25,* 215–232.

Ankney, C. Davison. (1992). Sex differences in relative brain size: The mismeasure of woman, too? *Intelligence, 16,* 329–336.

Anonymous. (1974). Life in the military. In J. Pleck & R. Sawyer (Eds.), *Men and masculinity.* Englewood Cliffs, NJ: Prentice-Hall.

Arendell, Terry. (1987). Women and the economics of divorce in contemporary America. *Signs, 13,* 5.

Argyle, Michael, et al. (1968). The effects of visibility on interaction in a dyad. *Human Relations, 21,* 3–17.

Arkin, W., & Dobrofsky, Lynne R. (1978). Military socialization and masculinity. *Journal of Social Issues, 34*(1), 151–168.

Asch, Seymour E. (1956). Studies of independence and conformity: I. A minority of one against an unanimous majority. *Psychological Monographs, 70*(9, Whole No. 416).

Asher, S. R., & Gottman, I. M. (1973). Sex of teacher and student reading achievement. *Journal of Educational Psychology, 65,* 168–171.

Ashton, Heather. (1991). Psychotropic drug prescribing for women. *British Journal of Psychiatry, 158* (Suppl. 10), 30–35.

Associated Press. (1989, December 7). 14 women slain in rampage. *Wisconsin State Journal,* A1.

Astin, Helen S., & Leland, C. (1991). *Women of influence, women of vision: A cross-generational study of leaders and social change.* San Francisco: Jossey-Bass.

Atkin, David. (1991). The evolution of television series addressing single women, 1966–1990. *Journal of Broadcasting & Electronic Media, 35,* 517–523.

Baber, Kristine M., & Monaghan, Patricia. (1988). College women's career and motherhood expectations: New options, old dilemmas. *Sex Roles, 19,* 189–204.

Baenninger, Maryann, & Newcombe, Nora. (1989). The role of experience in spatial test performance: A meta-analysis. *Sex Roles, 20,* 327–344.

Bailey, J. M., Pillard, R. C., Neale, M. C., & Agyei, Y. (1993). Heritable factors influence sexual orientation in women. *Archives of General Psychiatry, 50,* 217–223.

Bancroft, John. (1987). A physiological approach. In J. H. Geer and W. T. O'Donohue (Eds.), *Theories of human sexuality* (pp. 411–421). New York: Plenum.

Bandura, Albert. (1965). Influence of model's reinforcement contingencies on the acquisition of imitative responses. *Journal of Personality and Social Psychology, 1,* 589–595.

Bandura, A., & Walters, R. H. (1963). *Social learning and personality development.* New York: Holt, Rinehart & Winston.

Barash, David P. (1982). *Sociobiology and behavior* (2nd ed.). New York: Elsevier.

Barbach, Lonnie G. (1975). *For yourself: The fulfillment of female sexuality.* Garden City, NY: Anchor Press/Doubleday.

Barbaree, H. E., & Marshall, W. L. (1991). The role of male sexual arousal in rape: Six models. *Journal of Consulting and Clinical Psychology, 59,* 621–630.

Bardwick, Judith M. (1971). *Psychology of women: A study of biocultural conflicts.* New York: Harper & Row.

Bargad, Adena, & Hyde, Janet S. (1991). Women's studies: A study of feminist identity development in women. *Psychology of Women Quarterly, 15,* 181–201.

Baron, Larry, & Straus, Murray A. (1989). *Four theories of rape in American society.* New Haven: Yale University Press.

Barraclough, C. A., & Gorski, R. A. (1961). Evidence that the hypothalamus is responsible for androgen-induced sterility in the female rat. *Endocrinology, 68,* 68–79.

Barry, H., Bacon, Margaret K., & Child, I. L. (1957). A cross-cultural survey of some sex differences in socialization. *Journal of Abnormal and Social Psychology, 55,* 327–332.

Bart, Pauline B. (1971). Depression in middle-aged women. In V. G. Gornick & B. K. Moran (Eds.), *Women in sexist society.* New York: Basic Books.

Bart, Pauline B. (1981). A study of women who both were raped and avoided rape. *Journal of Social Issues, 37,* 123–136.

Barth, Robert J., & Kinder, Bill N. (1988). A theoretical analysis of sex differences in same-sex friendships. *Sex Roles, 19,* 349–364.

Baruch, Grace K. (1975). Sex-role stereotyping, the motive to avoid success, and parental identification. *Sex Roles, 1,* 303–309.

Baruch, Grace et al. (1983). *Lifeprints: New patterns of love and work for today's women.* New York: McGraw-Hill.

Baruch, Grace K., Biener, Lois, & Barnett, Rosalind C. (1987). Women and gender in research on stress. *American Psychologist, 42,* 130–136.

Basow, Susan A., & Kobrynowicz, Diane. (1993). What is she eating? The effects of meal size on impressions of a female eater. *Sex Roles, 28,* 335–344.

Bates, Carolyn M., & Brodsky, Annette M. (1989). *Sex in the therapy hour.* New York: Guilford Press.

Baxter, I. C. (1970). Interpersonal spacing in natural settings. *Sociometry, 33,* 444–456.

Beach, Frank A. (1947). Evolutionary changes in the physiological control of mating behavior in mammals. *Psychological Review, 54,* 5.

Beall, Anne E. (1993). A social constructionist view of gender. In A. E. Beall & R. J. Sternberg (Eds.), *The psychology of gender* (pp. 127–147). New York: Guilford.

Beauvoir, Simone de. (1952). *The second sex.* New York: Knopf.

Beck, A. T., & Greenberg, Ruth L. (1974). Cognitive therapy with depressed women. In V. Franks & V. Burtle (Eds.), *Women in therapy.* New York: Brunner/Mazel.

Belcastro, P. A. (1985). Sexual behavior differences between black and white students. *Journal of Sex Research, 21,* 56–67.

Bell, Alan P. (1974). Homosexualities: Their range and character. In *Nebraska symposium on motivation 1973.* Lincoln: University of Nebraska Press.

Bell, Alan P., & Weinberg, Martin S. (1978). *Homosexualities.* New York: Simon & Schuster.

Bell, Alan P., Weinberg, Martin S., & Hammersmith, Sue K. (1981). *Sexual preference: Its development in men and women.* Bloomington: Indiana University Press.

Bell, R. Q. (1960). Relations between behavior manifestations in the human neonate. *Child Development, 31,* 463–477.

Belle, Deborah. (1990). Poverty and women's mental health. *American Psychologist, 45,* 385–389.

Belzer, E. G. (1981). Orgasmic expulsions of women: A review and heuristic inquiry. *Journal of Sex Research, 17,* 1–12.

Bem, Sandra L. (1974). The measurement of psychological androgyny. *Journal of Consulting and Clinical Psychology, 42,* 155–162.

Bem, Sandra L. (1975). Sex-role adaptability: One consequence of psychological androgyny. *Journal of Personality and Social Psychology, 31,* 634–643.

Bem, Sandra L. (1977). On the utility of alternative procedures for assessing psychological androgyny. *Journal of Consulting and Clinical Psychology, 45,* 196–205.

Bem, Sandra L. (1981). Gender schema theory: A cognitive account of sex-typing. *Psychological Review, 88,* 354–364.

Bem, Sandra L. (1983). Gender schema theory and its implications for child development: Raising gender-aschematic children in a gender-schematic society. *Signs, 8,* 598–616.

Bem, Sandra L. (1993). *The lenses of gender.* New Haven, CT: Yale University Press.

Bem, Sandra L., & Bem, Daryl J. (1970). Case study of nonconscious ideology: Training the woman to know her place. In D. J. Bem (Ed.), *Beliefs, attitudes, and human affairs.* Belmont, CA: Brooks/Cole.

Bem, Sandra, L., & Lenney, Ellen. (1976). Sex-typing and the avoidance of cross-sex behavior. *Journal of Personality and Social Psychology, 33,* 48–54.

Bem, Sandra L., Martyna, W., & Watson, C. (1976). Sex typing and androgyny: Further explorations of the expressive domain. *Journal of Personality and Social Psychology, 34,* 1016–1023.

Bengtson, Vern L. (1985). Diversity and symbolism in grandparental roles. In V. L. Bengtson & J. F. Robertson (Eds.), *Grandparenthood.* Beverly Hills: Sage.

Bepko, Claudia. (Ed.). (1991). *Feminism and addiction.* New York: Haworth.

Berenbaum, Sheri A., & Hines, Melissa. (1992). Early androgens are related to childhood sex-typed toy preferences. *Psychological Science, 3,* 203–206.

Berg, Phyllis, & Hyde, Janet S. (1976, September). *Gender and race differences in causal attributions.* Paper presented at American Psychological Association Meetings.

Bergen, D. J., & Williams, J. E. (1991). Sex stereotypes in the United States revisited: 1972–1988. *Sex Roles, 24,* 413–423.

Berk, Richard A. (1993). What the scientific evidence shows: On the average, we can do no better than arrest. In R. J. Gelles & D. R. Loseke (Eds.), *Current controversies on family violence.* Newbury Park, CA: Sage.

Berman, Phyllis W., O'Nan, Barbara A., & Floyd, W. (1981). The double standard of aging and the social situation. *Sex Roles, 7,* 87–96.

Bermant, G. (1972). Behavior therapy approaches to modification of sexual preferences: Biological perspective and critique. Paper presented at the California State Psychological Association. Reprinted in J. Bardwick (Ed.), *Readings on the psychology of women.* New York: Harper & Row.

Bernstein, A. (1988, February 29). So you think you've come a long way, baby? *Business Week.*

Berscheid, Ellen, et al. (1971). Physical attractiveness and dating choice: A test of the matching hypothesis. *Journal of Experimental Social Psychology, 7,* 173–189.

Betancourt, Hector, & Lopez, Steven R. (1993). The study of culture, ethnicity, and race in American psychology. *American Psychologist, 48,* 629–637.

Bettelheim, Bruno. (1962). *Symbolic wounds.* New York: Collier Books.

Betz, Nancy. (1993). Women's career development. In F. L. Denmark & M. A. Paludi (Eds.), *Psychology of women: Handbook of issues and theories* (pp. 627–684). Westport, CT: Greenwood.

Bingham, Shereen G., & Scherer, Lisa L. (1993). Factors associated with responses to sexual harassment and satisfaction with outcome. *Sex Roles, 29,* 239–269.

Bird, Chloe E., & Ross, Catherine E. (1993). Houseworkers and paid workers: Qualities of the work and effects on personal control. *Journal of Marriage and the Family, 55,* 913–925.

Blackwood, E. (1984). Sexuality and gender in certain Native American tribes: The case of the cross-gender females. *Signs: Journal of Women in Culture and Society, 10,* 27–42.

Blank, Rebecca M. (1988). Women's paid work, household income, and household well being. In S. Rix (Ed.), *The American woman 1988–89.* New York: Norton.

Blau, Francine B., & Ferber, Marianne A. (1985). Women in the labor market: The last twenty years. In L. Larwood, A. H. Stromberg, & B. A. Gutek (Eds.), *Women and work* (Vol. 1). Beverly Hills: Sage.

Blaubergs, Maija S. (1978). Changing the sexist language: The theory behind the practice. *Psychology of Women Quarterly, 2,* 244–261.

Bleckman, Elaine A. (1980). Behavior therapies. In A. M. Brodsky & R. Hare-Mustin (Eds.), *Women and psychotherapy.* New York: Guilford.

Block, Jeanne H. (1973). Conceptions of sex role: Some cross-cultural and longitudinal perspectives. *American Psychologist, 28,* 512–526.

Block, Jeanne H. (1976). Issues, problems and pitfalls in assessing sex differences. *Merrill-Palmer Quarterly, 22,* 283–308.

Block, Jeanne H. (1978). Another look at sex differentiation in the socialization behaviors of mothers and fathers. In J. Sherman & F. Denmark (Eds.), *Psychology of women: Future directions of research.* New York: Psychological Dimensions.

Bloomfield, Kim. (1993). A comparison of alcohol consumption between lesbians and heterosexual women in an urban population. *Drug and Alcohol Dependence, 33,* 257–269.

Blumstein, Philip W., & Schwartz, Pepper. (1976). Bisexual women. In J. P. Wiseman (Ed.), *The social psychology of sex.* New York: Harper & Row.

Blumstein, Philip W., & Schwartz, Pepper. (1983). *American couples.* New York: William Morrow.

Blumstein, Philip W., & Schwartz, Pepper. (1993). Bisexuality: Some social psychological issues. In L. D. Garnets & D. C. Kimmel (Eds.), *Psychological perspectives on lesbian and gay male experiences* (pp. 168–184). New York: Columbia University Press.

Bock, E. W., & Webber, I. (1972). Suicide among the elderly: Isolating widowhood and mitigating alternatives. *Journal of Marriage and the Family, 34,* 24–31.

Bock, R. D., & Kolakowski, D. (1973). Further evidence of sex-linked major-gene influence on human spatial visualizing ability. *American Journal of Human Genetics, 25,* 1–14.

Bodine, Ann. (1975a). Sex differentiation in language. In B. Thorne & N. Henley (Eds.), *Language and sex: Difference and dominance.* Rowley, MA: Newbury House.

Bodine, Ann. (1975b). Androcentrism in prescriptive grammar: Singular 'they,' sex indefinite 'he,' and 'he or she.' *Language in Society, 4,* 129–146.

Bohman, M., Sigrardsson, S., & Cloniger, C. R. (1981). Maternal inheritance of alcohol abuse: Cross-fostering analysis of adopted women. *Archives of General Psychiatry, 38,* 965–969.

Bonaparte, Marie. (1953). *Female sexuality.* New York: International Universities Press. (Reprinted 1965. New York: Grove Press.)

Bootzin, R. R., & Natsoulas, T. (1965). Evidence for perceptual defense uncontaminated by response bias. *Journal of Personality and Social Psychology, 1,* 461–468.

Boskind-Lodahl, Marlene. (1976). Cinderella's stepsisters: A feminist perspective on anorexia nervosa and bulimia. *Signs, 2,* 120–146.

Boskind-Lodahl, Marlene, & Sirlin, Joyce. (1977, March). The gorging-purging syndrome. *Psychology Today,* p. 50.

Bosselman, Beulah C. (1960). Castration anxiety and phallus envy: A reformulation. *Psychiatric Quarterly, 34,* 252–259.

Boston Lesbian Psychologies Collective. (1987). *Lesbian psychologies.* Urbana: University of Illinois Press.

Boston Women's Health Book Collective. (1976). *Our bodies, ourselves.* New York: Simon & Schuster.

Boston Women's Health Book Collective. (1984). *The new our bodies, ourselves.* New York: Simon & Schuster.

Bouchard, Thomas I., & McGee, Mark G. (1977). Sex differences in human spatial ability: Not an X-linked recessive gene effect. *Social Biology, 24,* 332–335.

Bowker, Lee H., Arbitell, Michelle, & McFerron, J. Richard. (1988). On the relationship between wife beating and child abuse. In K. Yllo & M. Bogard (Eds.), *Feminist perspective on wife abuse.* Newbury Park, CA: Sage.

Boyd, Carol J. (1989). Mothers and daughters: A discussion of theory and research. *Journal of Marriage and the Family, 51,* 291–301.

Brabant, Sarah, & Mooney, Linda. (1986). Sex role stereotyping in the Sunday comics: Ten years later. *Sex Roles, 14,* 141–148.

Brackbill, Yvonne, & Schroeder, Kerri. (1980). Circumcision, gender differences and neonatal behavior: An update. *Developmental Psychobiology, 13,* 607–614.

Bradshaw, Carla K. (1994). Asian and Asian-American women: Historical and political considerations in psychotherapy. In L. Comas-Diaz & B. Greene (Eds.), *Women of color.* New York: Guilford.

Brady, I. P., & Rieger, W. (1975). Behavioral treatment in anorexia nervosa. In T. Thompson & W. Dockens (Eds.), *Applications of behavior modification.* New York: Academic Press.

Brady, Katherine. (1979). *Father's days.* New York: Dell paperback.

Brand, Pamela A., Rothblum, Esther D., & Solomon, Laura J. (1992). A comparison of lesbians, gay men, and heterosexuals on weight and restrained eating. *International Journal of Eating Disorders, 11,* 253–259.

Brannon, R., & David, D. S. (1976). The male sex role: Our culture's blueprint of manhood, and what it's done for us lately. In D. S. David & R. Brannon (Eds.), *The forty-nine percent majority.* Reading, MA: Addison-Wesley.

Brecher, Edward M. (1984). *Love, sex, and aging.* Mt. Vernon, NY: Consumers Union.

Brend, Ruth M. (1971). Male-female intonation patterns in American English. *Proceedings of the 7th International Congress of Phonetic Sciences,* 866–869. The Hague: Mouton. (Reprinted in B. Thorne & N. Henley (Eds.), *Language and sex: Difference and dominance.* Rowley, MA: Newbury House, 1975.)

Bretl, Daniel J., & Cantor, Joanne. (1988). The portrayal of men and women in U.S. television commercials: A recent content analysis and trends over 15 years. *Sex Roles, 18,* 595–610.

Brim, Orville I. (1976). Theories of the male mid-life crisis. *Counseling Psychologist, 6*(1), 2–9.

Brinson, Susan L. (1992). The use and opposition of rape myths in prime-time television dramas. *Sex Roles, 27,* 359–376.

Brody, Leslie R., Hay, Deborah H., & Vandewater, Elizabeth. (1990). Gender, gender role identity, and children's reported feelings toward the same and opposite sex. *Sex Roles, 23,* 363–387.

Brodsky, Annette. (1977). Therapeutic aspects of consciousness-raising groups. In E. I. Rawlings & D. K. Carter (Eds.), *Psychotherapy for women.* Springfield, IL: Charles C Thomas.

Bronfenbrenner, Urie. (1970). *Two worlds of childhood.* New York: Sage.

Brooks, Linda, & Perot, Annette R. (1991). Reporting sexual harassment: Exploring a predictive model. *Psychology of Women Quarterly, 15,* 31–48.

Brooks, Virginia R. (1981). *Minority stress and lesbian women.* Lexington, MA: Lexington Books.

Broverman, Inge K., Broverman, D. M., Clarkson, F. E., Rosenkrantz, P. S., & Vogel, S. R. (1970). Sex role stereotypes and clinical judgments of mental health. *Journal of Consulting and Clinical Psychology, 34,* 1–7.

Broverman, Inge K., Vogel, Susan R., Broverman, D. M., Clarkson, F. E., & Rosenkrantz, P. S. (1972). Sex role stereotypes: A current appraisal. *Journal of Social Issues, 28,* 59–78.

Brown, Laura, & Root, Maria. (Eds.). (1990). *Diversity and complexity in feminist therapy.* New York: Harrington Park Press.

Browne, Angela. (1993). Violence against women by male partners. *American Psychologist, 48,* 1077–1087.

Brownell, K. D., & Foreyt, J. P. (Eds.). (1986). *Physiology, psychology, and treatment of eating disorders.* New York: Basic Books.

Brownmiller, Susan. (1975). *Against our will: Men, women, and rape.* New York: Simon & Schuster.

Buchanan, K. M. (1986). *Apache women warriors.* El Paso, TX: Texas Western Press.

Buczek, Teresa A. (1981). Sex biases in counseling: Counselor retention of the concerns of a female and male client. *Journal of Counseling Psychology, 28,* 13–21.

Budoff, Penny W. (1981). *No more menstrual cramps and other good news.* New York: Penguin Books.

Buffery, A. W. H., & Gray, I. A. (1972). Sex differences in the development of spatial and linguistic skills. In C. Ounsted & D. C. Taylor (Eds.), *Gender differences: Their ontogeny and significance.* Baltimore, MD: Williams & Wilkins.

Bugental, Daphne E., Love, Leonore R., Gianetto, Robert M. (1971). Perfidious feminine faces. *Journal of Personality and Social Psychology, 17,* 314–318.

Bulosan, Carlos. (1960). *Sound of falling light: Letters in exile.* Quezon City: University of the Philippines.

Burch, Beverly. (1993). *On intimate terms: The psychology of difference in lesbian relationships.* Urbana: University of Illinois Press.

Burgess, Ann W., & Holmstrom, Lynda L. (1974a). Rape trauma syndrome. *American Journal of Psychiatry, 131,* 981–986.

Burgess, Ann W., & Holmstrom, Lynda L. (1974b). *Rape: Victims of crisis.* Bowie, MD: Robert J. Brady Company.

Burnell, G. M., & Norfleet, M. A. (1987). Women's self-reported responses to abortion. *The Journal of Psychology, 121,* 71–76.

Burt, Martha. (1980). Cultural myths and support for rape. *Journal of Personality and Social Psychology, 38,* 217–230.

Burt, Martha R., & Estep, Rhoda E. (1981). Apprehension and fear: Learning a sense of sexual vulnerability. *Sex Roles, 7,* 511–522.

Burton, Linda M. (1992). Black grandparents rearing children of drug-addicted parents: Stressors, outcomes, and social service needs. *Gerontologist, 32,* 744–751.

Buss, David. (1991). Evolutionary personality psychology. *Annual Review of Psychology, 42,* 459–491.

Butow, Phyllis, Beumont, Pierre, & Touyz, Stephen. (1993). Cognitive processes in dieting disorders. *International Journal of Eating Disorders, 14,* 319–329.

Bylsma, Wayne H., & Major, Brenda. (1992). Two routes to eliminating gender differences in personal entitlement. *Psychology of Women Quarterly, 16,* 193–200.

Byne, William, & Parsons, B. (1993). Human sexual orientation: The biologic theories reappraised. *Archives of General Psychiatry, 50,* 228–239.

Caesar, P. L. (1988). Exposure to violence in the families of origin among wife abusers and maritally nonviolent men. *Violence and Victims, 3,* 49–64.

Caldwell, Mayta A., & Peplau, Letitia Anne. (1982). Sex differences in same-sex friendship. *Sex Roles, 8,* 721–732.

Calhoun, Karen S., Atkeson, B. M., & Resick, P. A. (1982). A longitudinal examination of fear reactions in rape victims. *Journal of Counseling Psychology, 29,* 655–661.

Campbell, A., Converse, P. E., & Rodgers, W. L. (1975). *The quality of American life.* Ann Arbor, MI: ISR Social Science Archive.

Campbell, Susan B., & Cohn, Jeffrey F. (1991). Prevalence and correlates of postpartum depression in first-time mothers. *Journal of Abnormal Psychology, 100,* 594–599.

Candy, Sandra G., Troll, Lillian E., & Levy, S. G. (1981). A developmental exploration of friendship functions in women. *Psychology of Women Quarterly, 5,* 456–472.

Caplan, Paula. (1995). *How do they decide who is normal?* Reading, MA: Addison-Wesley.

Caplan, Paula J., & Caplan, Jeremy B. (1994). *Thinking critically about research on sex and gender.* New York: Harper Collins.

Carani, Cesare et al. (1990). Effects of androgen treatment in impotent men with normal and low levels of free testosterone. *Archives of Sexual Behavior, 19,* 223–234.

Carli, Linda L. (1990). Gender, language, and influence. *Journal of Personality and Social Psychology, 59,* 941–951.

Carlson, Rae. (1971). Where is the person in personality research? *Psychological Bulletin, 75,* 203–219.

Carlson, Rae. (1972). Understanding women: Implications for personality theory and research. *Journal of Social Issues, 28*(2), 17–32.

Carroll, Janell, Volk, Kari, & Hyde, Janet S. (1985). Differences between males and females in motives for engaging in sexual intercourse. *Archives of Sexual Behavior, 14,* 131–139.

Carter, D. B. (1987). The roles of peers in sex role socialization. In D. B. Carter (Ed.), *Current conceptions of sex roles and stereotyping* (pp. 101–121). New York: Praeger.

Cass, Vivienne C. (1979). Homosexual identity formation: A theoretical model. *Journal of Homosexuality, 4,* 219–235.

Castle, C. S. (1913). A statistical study of eminent women. *Archives of Psychology, 27.*

Cazenave, Noel, & Leon, George. (1987). Men's work and family roles and characteristics: Race, gender, and class perceptions of college students. In M. Kimmel (Ed.), *Changing man* (pp. 244–262). Newbury Park, CA: Sage.

Chan, Connie S. (1993). Issues of identity development among Asian-American lesbians and gay men. In L. D. Garnets & D. C. Kimmel (Eds.), *Psychological perspectives on lesbian and gay male experience* (pp. 376–387). New York: Columbia University Press.

Cherlin, Andrew J. (1992). *Marriage, divorce, remarriage* (rev. ed.). Cambridge, MA: Harvard University Press.

Cherlin, Andrew, & Furstenberg, Frank F. (1985). Styles and strategies of grandparenting. In V. L. Bengtson & J. F. Robertson (Eds.), *Grandparenthood.* Beverly Hills: Sage.

Cherry, Frances, & Deaux, Kay. (1978). Fear of success versus fear of gender-inappropriate behavior. *Sex Roles, 4,* 97–102.

Chesler, Phyllis. (1972). *Women and madness.* Garden City, NY: Doubleday.

Chin, Jean L., De La Cancela, Victor, & Jenkins, Yvonne M. (1993). *Diversity in psychotherapy: The politics of race, ethnicity, and gender.* Westport, CT: Praeger.

Chodorow, Nancy. (1978). *The reproduction of mothering.* Berkeley: University of California Press.

Clark, Kenneth B., & Clark, Mamie P. (1947). Racial identification and preferences in Negro children. In T. M. Newcomb & E. L. Hartley (Eds.), *Readings in social psychology.* New York: Holt, Rinehart & Winston.

Cobb, Nancy J., et al. (1982). The influence of televised models on toy preference in children. *Sex Roles, 8,* 1075–1080.

Cohan, Catherine L., Dunkel-Schetter, Christine, & Lydon, John. (1993). Pregnancy decision-making: Predictors of early stress and adjustment.

Psychology of Women Quarterly, 17, 223–240.

Cohen, Jacob. (1969). *Statistical power analysis for the behavioral sciences.* New York: Academic Press.

Cohen, T. F. (1993). What do fathers provide? In J. C. Hood (Ed.), *Men, work, and family.* Newbury Park, CA: Sage.

Colby, Ann, Kohlberg, L., et al. (1983). A longitudinal study of moral development. *Monographs of the Society for Research in Child Development, 48*(200).

Coleman, Eli. (1982). Developmental stages of the coming out process. In W. Paul et al. (Eds.), *Homosexuality: Social, psychological, and biological issues.* Beverly Hills: Sage.

Coleman, Lerita M., Antonucci, Toni C., Adelmann, Pamela K., & Crohan, Susan E.. (1987). Social roles in the lives of middle-aged and older Black women. *Journal of Marriage and the Family, 49,* 761–771.

Collins, Karen S., Rowland, Diane, Salganicoff, Alina, & Chait, Elizabeth. (1994). Assessing and improving women's health. In C. Costello & A. J. Stone (Eds.), *The American woman 1994–95.* New York: Norton.

Collins, Nancy L., Dunkel-Schetter, Christine, Lobel, Marci, & Scrimshaw, Susan C. M. (1993). Social support in pregnancy: Psychosocial correlates of birth outcomes and postpartum depression. *Journal of Personality and Social Psychology, 65,* 1243–1258.

Collins, Patricia H. (1989). The social construction of Black feminist thought. *Signs: Journal of Women in Culture and Society, 14,* 745–773.

Collins, B. (1985). Psychological implications of sex differences in attitudes toward computers: Results of a survey. *International Journal of Women's Studies, 8,* 207–213.

Comas-Diaz, Lillian. (1987). Feminist therapy with mainland Puerto Rican women. *Psychology of Women Quarterly, 11,* 461–474.

Comas-Diaz, Lillian. (1991). Feminism and diversity in psychology: The case of women of color. *Psychology of Women Quarterly, 15,* 597–610.

Comas-Diaz, Lillian, & Greene, Beverly. (1994). *Women of color: Integrating ethnic and gender identities in psychotherapy.* New York: Guilford.

Condry, J. C., & Condry, S. (1976). Sex differences: A study of the eye of the beholder. *Child Development, 47,* 812–819.

Connors, Mary E., & Morse, Wayne. (1993). Sexual abuse and eating disorders: A review. *International Journal of Eating Disorders, 13,* 1–11.

Constantinople, Anne. (1973). Masculinity-femininity: An exception to a famous dictum. *Psychological Bulletin, 80,* 389–407.

Cooper, Joel, Hall, Joan, & Huff, Charles. (1990). Situational stress as a consequence of sex-stereotyped software. *Personality and Social Psychology Bulletin, 16,* 419–429.

Cordaro, L., & Ison, I. R. (1963). Psychology of the scientist: X. Observer bias in classical conditioning of the planarian. *Psychological Reports, 13,* 787–789.

Costello, Cynthia, & Stone, Anne J. (Eds.). (1994). *The American Woman 1994–95.* New York: Norton.

Cozzarelli, Catherine. (1993). Personality and self-efficacy as predictors of coping with abortion. *Journal of Personality and Social Psychology, 65,* 1224–1236.

Crabb, Peter B., & Bielawski, Dawn. (1994). The social representation of material culture and gender in children's books. *Sex Roles, 30,* 69–80.

Craig, Steve. (Ed.). (1992). *Men, masculinity, and the media.* Newbury Park, CA: Sage.

Crandall, Virginia C. (1969). Sex differences in expectancy of intellectual and academic reinforcement. In C. P. Smith (Ed.), *Achievement-related motives in children.* New York: Russell Sage Foundation.

Crandall, Virginia C. (1978, August). *Expecting sex differences and sex differences in expectancies: A developmental analysis.* Paper presented at American Psychological Association Meetings, Toronto, August.

Crawford, Mary, & English L. (1984). Generic versus specific inclusion of women in language: Effects on recall. *Journal of Psycholinguistic Research, 13,* 373–381.

Crawford, Mary, & Marecek, Jeanne. (1989). Feminist theory, feminist psychology: A bibliography of epistemology, critical analysis, and applications. *Psychology of Women Quarterly, 13,* 479–494.

Crohan, Susan, et al. (1989). Job characteristics and well-being at midlife: Ethnic and gender comparisons. *Psychology of Women Quarterly, 13,* 223–236.

Cromwell, R. E., & Ruiz, R. A. (1979). The myth of macho dominance in decision making within Mexican and Chicano families. *Hispanic Journal of Behavioral Sciences, 1,* 355–373.

Crosby, Faye. (1991). *Juggling: The unexpected advantages of balancing career and home for women and their families.* New York: Free Press.

Cross, Susan F., & Markus, Hazel R. (1993). Gender in thought, belief, and action: A cognitive approach. In A. E. Beall & R. J. Sternberg (Eds.), *The psychology of gender* (pp. 55–98). New York: Guilford.

Dalton, Katharina. (1964). *The premenstrual syndrome.* Springfield, IL: Charles C Thomas.

Dalton, Katharina. (1966). The influence of mother's menstruation on her child. *Proceedings of the Royal Society for Medicine, 59,* 1014.

Daneal, J. (1975). *A definition of fatherhood as expressed by black fathers.*

Unpublished doctoral dissertation, University of Pittsburgh.

David, Henry P. (1992). Born unwanted: Long-term developmental effects of denied abortion. *Journal of Social Issues, 48*(3), 163–181.

David, Henry P., Dytrych, Zdenek, Matejcek, Zdenek, & Schuller, Vratislav. (Eds.). (1988). *Born unwanted: Developmental effects of denied abortion.* New York: Springer.

David, Henry P., & Matejcek, Z. (1981). Children born to women denied abortion: An update. *Family Planning Perspectives, 13,* 32–34.

Davidson, Lynne R., & Duberman, Lucile. (1982). Friendship: Communication and interactional patterns in same-sex dyads. *Sex Roles, 8,* 809–822.

Davidson, S., & Packard, T. (1981). The therapeutic value of friendship between women. *Psychology of Women Quarterly, 5,* 495–510.

Davis, Angela. (1981). *Women, race and class.* New York: Random House.

Davis, Donald M. (1990). Portrayals of women in prime-time network television: Some demographic characteristics. *Sex Roles, 23,* 325–332.

Davis, Elizabeth Gould. (1971). *The first sex.* New York: G. P. Putnam's Sons.

Davis, J. A., & Smith, T. (1991). *General social surveys, 1972–1991: Cumulative data.* Storrs: University of Connecticut, Roper Center for Public Opinion Research.

Deaux, Kay, & Emswiller, T. (1974). Explanations of successful performance on sex-linked tasks: What is skill for the male is luck for the female. *Journal of Personality and Social Psychology, 29,* 80–85.

Deaux, Kay, & Kite, Mary. (1993). Gender stereotypes. In F. L. Denmark & M. A. Paludi (Eds.), *Psychology of women: Handbook of issues and theories.* Westport, CT: Greenwood.

Deaux, Kay, & Lewis, Laurie L. (1983). Components of gender stereotypes.

Psychological Documents, 13, 25. (Ms. No. 2583).

Deaux, Kay, & Lewis, Laurie L. (1984). Structure of gender stereotypes: Interrelationships among components and gender label. *Journal of Personality and Social Psychology, 46,* 991–1004.

Deckard, Barbara S. (1983). *The women's movement* (3rd ed.). New York: Harper & Row.

DeFries, John C., et al. (1976). Parent-offspring resemblance for specific cognitive abilities in two ethnic groups. *Nature, 261,* 131–133.

DeLamater, John D., & MacCorquodale, Patricia. (1979). *Premarital sexuality: Attitudes, relationships, behavior.* Madison: University of Wisconsin Press.

Delaney, Janice, Lupton, Mary Jane, & Toth, Emily. (1976). *The curse: A cultural history of menstruation.* New York: Dutton.

Dellas, M., & Gaier, E. L. (1975). The self and adolescent identity in women: Options and implications. *Adolescence, 10,* 399–407.

Denmark, Florence L. (1993). Women, leadership, and empowerment. *Psychology of Women Quarterly, 17,* 343–356.

Denmark, Florence L., & Goodfield, Helen M. (1978). A second look at adolescence theories. *Sex Roles, 4,* 375–380.

Denmark, Florence, Russo, Nancy F., Frieze, Irene H., & Sechzer, Jeri A. (1988). Guidelines for avoiding sexism in psychological research. *American Psychologist, 43,* 582–585.

Deutsch, A. (1944). The first U. S. census of the insane (1840) and its use as pro-slavery propaganda. *Bulletin of the History of Medicine, 15,* 469–482.

Deutsch, Francine M., LeBaron, Dorothy, & Fryer, Maury M. (1987). What is in a smile? *Psychology of Women Quarterly, 11,* 341–352.

Deutsch, Helene. (1924). The psychology of women in relation to the functions of reproduction. *International Journal of Psychoanalysis, 6.*

Deutsch, Helene. (1944). *The psychology of women.* New York: Grune & Stratton.

Diamond, Milton. (1965). A critical evaluation of the ontogeny of human sexual behavior. *Quarterly Review of Biology, 40,* 147–175.

Diamond, Milton. (1979). Sexual identity and sex roles. In V. Bullough (Ed.), *The frontiers of sex research.* Buffalo, NY: Prometheus Books.

Diamond, Milton. (1982). Sexual identity, monozygotic twins reared in discordant sex roles, and a BBC followup. *Archives of Sexual Behavior, 11,* 181–186.

Dickson, Lynda. (1993). The future of marriage and the family in Black America. *Journal of Black Studies, 23,* 472–491.

Diehm, Cynthia, & Ross, Margo. (1988). Battered women. In S. Rix (Ed.), *The American woman 1988–89.* New York: Norton.

Dion, Kenneth L., & Cota, Albert A. (1991). The Ms. stereotype. *Psychology of Women Quarterly, 15,* 403–410.

Dobert, Margarete. (1975). Tradition, modernity and woman power in Africa. In M. S. Mednick, L. W. Hoffman, & S. S. Tangri (Eds.), *Women and achievement: Social and motivational analyses.* Washington, DC: Hemisphere.

Dodge, Laura J. T., et al. (1982). Bibliotherapy in the treatment of female orgasmic dysfunction. *Journal of Consulting and Clinical Psychology, 50,* 442–443.

Donelson, Elaine. (1977). Becoming a single woman. In E. Donelson & J. Gullahorn (Eds.), *Women: A psychological perspective.* New York: Wiley.

Donenberg, Geri R., & Hoffman, Lois W. (1988). Gender differences in moral development. *Sex Roles, 18,* 701–718.

Douvan, Elizabeth. (1970). New sources of conflicts in females at adolescence and early adulthood. In J. Bardwick, E. Douvan, M. Horner, & D. Gutman (Eds.), *Feminine personality and conflict.* Belmont, CA: Brooks/Cole.

Douvan, Elizabeth, & Adelson, J. (1966). *The adolescent experience.* New York: Wiley.

Dovidio, J. F., Ellyson, S. L., Keating, C. F., Heltman, K., & Brown, C. E. (1988). The relationship of social power to visual displays of dominance between men and women. *Journal of Personality and Social Psychology, 54,* 233–242.

Doyle, James A. (1989). *The male experience* (2nd ed.). Dubuque, IA: William C. Brown.

Dugger, Karen. (1988). Social location and gender-role attitudes: A comparison of Black and White women. *Gender & Society, 2, 425–448.*

Duncan, Greg J., & Hoffman, Saul D. (1985). A reconsideration of the economic consequences of marital dissolution. *Demography, 22,* 485.

Duncan, Greg J., & Hoffman, Saul D. (1988). What are the economic consequences of divorce? *Demography, 25,* 641.

Dutton, D. G. (1988). Profiling of wife assaulters: Preliminary evidence for a tri-modal analysis. *Violence and Victims, 3,* 5–30.

Dweck, Carol, Goetz, Therese E., & Strauss, Nan L. (1980). Sex differences in learned helplessness: IV. An experimental and naturalistic study of failure generalization and its mediators. *Journal of Personality and Social Psychology, 38,* 441–452.

Dziech, Billie W., & Weiner, Linda. (1983). *The lecherous professor: Sexual harassment.* Boston: Beacon.

Eagly, Alice H. (1978). Sex differences in influenceability. *Psychological Bulletin, 85,* 86–116.

Eagly, Alice H. (1987). *Sex differences in social behavior: A social role interpretation.* Hillsdale, NJ: Erlbaum.

Eagly, Alice H., & Carli, Linda L. (1981). Sex of researchers and sex-typed communications as determinants of sex differences in influenceability: A meta-analysis of social influence studies. *Psychological Bulletin, 90,* 1–20.

Eagly, Alice H., & Crowley, Maureen. (1986). Gender and helping behavior: A meta-analytic review of the social psychological literature. *Psychological Bulletin, 100,* 283–308.

Eagly, Alice H., & Johnson, B. T. (1990). Gender and leadership style. *Psychological Bulletin, 108,* 233–256.

Eagly, Alice H., Makhijani, M. G., & Klonsky, B. G. (1992). Gender and the evaluation of leaders: A meta-analysis. *Psychological Bulletin, 111,* 3–22.

Eagly, Alice H., Mladinic, A., & Otto, S. (1991). Are women evaluated more favorably than men? An analysis of attitudes, beliefs, and emotions. *Psychology of Women Quarterly, 15,* 103–216.

Eagly, Alice H., & Steffen, Valerie J. (1986). Gender and aggressive behavior: A meta-analytic review of the social psychological literature. *Psychological Bulletin, 100,* 309–330.

Earle, John R., & Harris, Catherine T. (1985). Modern women and the dynamics of social psychological ambivalence. *Psychology of Women Quarterly, 9,* 65–80.

Eaton, Warren O., & Enns, Lesley R. (1986). Sex differences in human motor activity level. *Psychological Bulletin, 100,* 19–28.

Eccles, Jacquelynne S. (1987). Gender roles and women's achievement-related decisions. *Psychology of Women Quarterly, 11,* 135–172.

Edwards, D. A. (1969). Early androgen stimulation and aggressive behavior in male and female mice. *Physiology and Behavior, 4,* 333–338.

Edwards, Gwenyth H. (1992). The structure and content of the male gender role stereotype: An exploration of subtypes. *Sex Roles, 27,* 533–552.

Ehrhardt, Anke A., & Meyer-Bahlburg, Heino. (1981). Effects of prenatal sex hormones on gender-related behavior. *Science, 211,* 1312–1318.

Eichenbaum, Luise, & Orbach, Susie. (1983). *Understanding women: A feminist psychoanalytic approach.* New York: Basic Books.

Eicher, Margrit. (1988). *Nonsexist research methods: A practical guide.* Boston: Allen & Unwin.

Eichler, Anita, & Parron, D. L. (1987). *Women's mental health: Agenda for research.* Rockville, MD: National Institute of Mental Health.

Eisenberg, Nancy, & Lennon, Randy. (1983). Sex differences in empathy and related capacities. *Psychological Bulletin, 94,* 100–131.

Eisenstein, Zilla R. (1982). The sexual politics of the New Right: Understanding the "Crisis of Liberalism" for the 1980s. In N. O. Keohane et al. (Eds.), *Feminist theory.* Chicago: University of Chicago Press.

Erickson, Erik H. (1950). *Childhood and Society.* New York: Norton.

Eron, Leonard, et al. (1974). The convergence of laboratory and field studies of the development of aggression. In J. de Wit & W. W. Hartup (Eds.), *Determinants and origins of aggressive behavior.* The Hague: Mouton.

Espin, Oliva. (1987a). Psychological impact of migration on Latinas: Implications for psychotherapeutic practice. *Psychology of Women Quarterly, 11,* 489–504.

Espin, Oliva M. (1987b). Issues of identity in the psychology of Latina lesbians. In Boston Lesbian Psychologies Collective, *Lesbian psychologies.* Urbana: University of Illinois Press.

Espin, Oliva M. (1993). Issues of identity in the psychology of Latina lesbians. In L. D. Garnets & D. C. Kimmel (Eds.), *Psychological perspectives on lesbian and gay male experiences* (pp. 348–363). New York: Columbia University Press.

Etaugh, Claire. (1993). Women in the middle and later years. In F. L. Denmark & M. A. Paludi (Eds.), *Psychology of women: Handbook of issues and theories.* Westport, CT: Greenwood.

Everitt, Barry J., & Bancroft, John. (1991). Of rats and men: The comparative approach to male sexuality. *Annual Review of Sex Research, 2,* 77–118.

Fagot, Beverly, & Patterson, Gerald. (1969). An in vivo analysis of reinforcing contingencies for sex-role behaviors in the preschool child. *Developmental Psychology, 1,* 563–568.

Fairchild, Halford H. (1988). Curriculum design for Black (African American) psychology. In P. Bronstein & K. Quina (Eds.), *Teaching a psychology of people.* Washington, DC: American Psychological Association.

Falk, Patricia J. (1993). Lesbian mothers: Psychosocial assumptions in family law. In L. D. Garnets & D. C. Kimmel (Eds.), *Psychological perspectives on lesbian and gay male experience* (pp. 420–436). New York: Columbia University Press.

Faludi, Susan. (1991). *Backlash: The undeclared war against American women.* New York: Anchor Books/ Doubleday.

Fasteau, M. F. (1974). *The male machine.* New York: McGraw-Hill.

Fausto-Sterling, Anne. (1992). *Myths of gender* (2nd ed.). New York: Basic Books.

Fausto-Sterling, Anne. (1993, October). Sex, race, brains, and calipers. *Discover, 14*(10), 32–37.

FBI. (1988). *Uniform crime reports 1987.* Washington, DC: U.S. Department of Justice.

FBI. (1993). *Uniform crime reports.* Washington, DC: U.S. Government Printing Office.

Feild, Hubert S. (1978). Attitudes toward rape: A comparative analysis of police, rapists, crisis counselors, and citizens. *Journal of Personality and Social Psychology, 36,* 156–179.

Feingold, Alan. (1988). Cognitive gender differences are disappearing. *American Psychologist, 43,* 95–103.

Feingold, Alan. (1995). Gender differences in personality: A meta-analysis. *Psychological Bulletin, 116,* 429–456.

Fidell, Laura S. (1982). Gender and drug use and abuse. In I. All-Issa (Ed.), *Gender and psychopathology* (pp. 221–236). New York: Academic Press.

Fidell, Linda, Hoffman, Donnie, & Keith-Spiegel, Patti. (1979). Some social implications of sex-choice technology. *Psychology of Women Quarterly, 4,* 32–42.

Fillmore, Kaye M. (1984). "When angels fall": Women's drinking as cultural preoccupation and as reality. In S. Wilsnack and L. Beckman (Eds.), *Alcohol problems in women.* New York: Guilford.

Fine, Michelle. (1992). *Disruptive voices: The possibilities of feminist research.* Ann Arbor: University of Michigan Press.

Fine, Reuben. (1990). Anna Freud (1895–1982). In A. N. O'Connell & N. F. Russo (Eds.), *Women in psychology: A bio-bibliographical sourcebook* (pp. 96–103). Westport, CT: Greenwood Press.

Finkelhor, David. (1980). Sex among siblings: A survey on prevalence, variety and effects. *Archives of Sexual Behavior, 9,* 171–194.

Finkelhor, David, Hotaling, G., Lewis, I., & Smith, C. (1989). Sexual abuse and its relationship to later sexual satisfaction, marital status, religion, and attitudes. *Journal of Interpersonal Violence, 4,* 379–399.

Firestone, Shulamith. (1970). *The dialectic of sex.* New York: Bantam.

Fisher, Seymour. (1973). *Understanding the female orgasm.* New York: Basic Books.

Fishman, Pamela M. (1978). Interaction: The work women do. *Social Problems, 25,* 397–405.

Fiske, Susan T. (1993). Controlling other people: The impact of power on stereotyping. *American Psychologist, 48,* 621–628.

Fitzgerald, Louise F. (1993a). Sexual harassment. *American Psychologist, 48,* 1070–1076.

Fitzgerald, Louise F. (1993b). *The last great open secret: The sexual harassment of women in the work place and academia.* Washington, DC: Federation of Behavioral, Psychological, and Cognitive Sciences.

Fitzgerald, Louise A., & Ormerod, Alayne J. (1993). Breaking silence: The sexual harassment of women in academia and the work place. In F. L. Denmark & M. A. Paludi (Eds.), *Psychology of women: Handbook of issues and theories.* Westport, CT: Greenwood.

Fitzgerald, Louise F., et al. (1988). Academic harassment: Sex and denial in scholarly garb. *Psychology of Women Quarterly, 12,* 329–340.

Fivush, Robin. (1989). Exploring sex differences in the emotional content of mother-child conversations about the past. *Sex Roles, 20,* 675–691.

Foa, E. B., Steketee, G., & Olasov, B. (1989). Behavioral/cognitive conceptualization of post-traumatic stress disorder. *Behavior Therapy, 20,* 155–176.

Ford, Clellan S., & Beach, Frank A. (1951). *Patterns of sexual behavior.* New York: Harper & Row.

Ford, M., & Widiger, T. (1989). Sex bias in the diagnosis of histrionic and antisocial personality disorders. *Journal of*

Consulting and Clinical Psychology, 57, 301–305.

Forrest, Jacqueline D., & Singh, Susheela. (1990). The sexual and reproductive behavior of American women, 1982–1988. *Family Planning Perspectives, 22,* 206–215.

Frank, E., et al. (1978). Frequency of sexual dysfunction in "normal" couples. *New England Journal of Medicine, 299*(3), 111–115.

Frank, R. T. (1931). The hormonal causes of premenstrual tension. *Archives of Neurological Psychiatry, 26,* 1053.

Freud, Sigmund. (1933). *New introductory lectures in psychoanalysis.* New York: Norton.

Freud, Sigmund. (1948). Some psychical consequences of the anatomical distinction between the sexes. In I. Riviere (Trans.), *Collected papers* (Vol. V, pp. 186–197). London: Hogarth Press.

Freud, Sigmund. (1955). *The interpretation of dreams.* (J. Strachey, trans.). New York: Basic Books.

Friedman, M., & Rosenman, R. H. (1974). *Type A behavior and your heart.* New York: Fawcett Books.

Friedman, William J., Robinson, Amy B., & Friedman, Britt L. (1987). Sex differences in moral judgments? A test of Gilligan's theory. *Psychology of Women Quarterly, 11,* 37–46.

Friedrich, W. N., Beilke, R. L., & Urquiza, A. J. (1988). Behavior problems in young sexually abused boys. *Journal of Interpersonal Violence, 3,* 1–12.

Frieze, Irene H. (1983). Causes and consequences of marital rape. *Signs, 8,* 532–553.

Frieze, Irene H., et al. (1982). Assessing the theoretical models for sex differences in causal attributions for success and failure. *Sex Roles, 8,* 333–334.

Frodi, Ann, Macauley, Jacqueline, & Thome, Pauline R. (1977). Are women always less aggressive than men? A re-view of the experimental literature. *Psychological Bulletin, 84,* 634–660.

Fudge, Judy, & McDermott, Patricia. (1991). *Just wages: A feminist assessment of pay equity.* Toronto: University of Toronto Press.

Fullilove, Mindy Thompson, et al. (1990). Black women and AIDS prevention: Understanding the gender rules. *Journal of Sex Research, 27,* 47–64.

Furnham, Adrian, & Baguma, Peter. (1994). Cross-cultural differences in the evaluation of male and female body shapes. *International Journal of Eating Disorders, 15,* 81–89.

Fyfe, B. (1983). "Homophobia" or homosexual bias reconsidered. *Archives of Sexual Behavior, 12,* 549–554.

Gagnon, John H. (1977). *Human sexualities.* Glenview, IL: Scott, Foresman.

Gallant, Sheryle J., Popiel, Debra A., Hoffman, Denise M., Chakraborty, Prabir, K., & Hamilton, Jean. (1992). Using daily ratings to confirm premenstrual syndrome/Late Luteal Dysphoric Disorder, Part II, What makes a "real" difference? *Psychosomatic Medicine, 54,* 167–181.

Gannon, Linda, et al. (1992). Sex bias in psychological research: Progress or complacency? *American Psychologist, 4,* 389–396.

Gannon, Linda, & Ekstrom, Bonnie. (1993). Attitudes toward menopause: The influence of sociocultural paradigms. *Psychology of Women Quarterly, 17,* 275–288.

Garcia, Alma M. (1989). The development of Chicana feminist discourse, 1970–1980. *Gender & Society, 3,* 217–238.

Garfinkel, Paul E., & Garner, D. M. (1982). *Anorexia nervosa: A multidimensional perspective.* New York: Brunner/Mazel.

Garnets, Linda, Herek, Gregory M., & Levy, Barrie. (1993). Violence and victimization of lesbians and gay men: Mental health consequences. In L. D.

Garnets & D. C. Kimmel (Eds.), *Psychological perspectives on lesbian and gay male experience* (pp. 579–598). New York: Columbia University Press.

Garnets, Linda D., & Kimmel, Douglas C. (Eds.). (1993). *Psychological perspectives on lesbian and gay male experiences.* New York: Columbia University Press.

Gartrell, Nanette K., Loriaux, D. L., & Chase, T. N. (1977). Plasma testosterone in homosexual and heterosexual women. *American Journal of Psychiatry, 134,* 1117–1119.

Gebhard, Paul H., Gagnon, J. H., Pomeroy, W. B., & Christenson, Cornelia V. (1965). *Sex offenders: An analysis of types.* New York: Harper & Row.

Gentry, Jacquelyn H. (1993). Women and AIDS. In *Psychology & AIDS exchange.* Washington, DC: American Psychological Association.

George, Linda K., Fillenbaum, G. G., Palmore, E. (1984). Sex differences in the antecedents and consequences of retirement. *Journal of Gerontology, 39,* 364–371.

Gerdes, Eugenia P., Miner, Rebecca S., Norchi, M., Ranallo, M., & Joshi, R. (1992). White males' bias against black female job applicants. In J. C. Chrisler & D. Howard (Eds.), *New directions in feminist psychology* (pp. 179–187). New York: Springer.

Gerson, Mary-Joan. (1980). The lure of motherhood. *Psychology of Women Quarterly, 5,* 207–218.

Gibbons, Ann. (1991). The brain as "sexual organ." *Science, 253,* 957–959.

Giddings, Paula. (1984). *When and where I enter: The impact of black women on race and sex in America.* New York: Bantam Books.

Gidycz, Christine A., Coble, C. N., Latham, L., & Layman, M. J. (1993). Sexual assault experience in adulthood and prior victimization experi-

ences: A prospective analysis. *Psychology of Women Quarterly, 17,* 151–168.

Gigy, Lynn L. (1980). Self-concept of single women. *Psychology of Women Quarterly, 5,* 321–340.

Gilbert, Lucia A. (1980). Feminist therapy. In A. Brodsky & R. Hare-Mustin (Eds.), *Women and psychotherapy.* New York: Guilford.

Gilbert, Lucia A. (1985). *Men in dual-earner families: Current realities and future prospects.* Hillsdale, NJ: Erlbaum.

Gilbert, Lucia A. (1989). *Sharing it all: The rewards and struggles of two-career families.* New York: Plenum.

Gilbert, Lucia A. (1993). *Two careers/one family.* Newbury Park, CA: Sage.

Gilbert, Lucia A., & Dancer, L. S. (1992). Dual-earner families in the United States and adolescent development. In S. Lewis, D. N. Izraeli, & H. Hootsmans (Eds.), *Dual-earner families: International perspectives* (pp. 151–171). Newbury Park, CA: Sage.

Gilley, H. M., & Collier, S. S. (1970). Sex differences in the use of hostile verbs. *Journal of Psychology, 76,* 33–37.

Gilligan, Carol. (1982). *In a different voice: Psychological theory and women's development.* Cambridge, MA: Harvard University Press.

Gilpatrick, Naomi. (1972). The secret life of Beatrix Potter. *Natural History, 81* (8).

Glazer, Sarah. (1993, February). Violence against women. *CQ Researcher,* 171–192.

Glenn, Evelyn Nakano. (1985). Racial ethnic women's labor: The intersection of race, gender and class oppression. *Review of Radical Economics, 17*(3), 86–108.

Glenn, Evelyn Nakano. (1992). From servitude to service work: Historical continuities in the racial division of paid reproductive labor. *Signs, 18*(1), 1–43.

Goble, F. C., & Konopka, E. A. (1973). Sex as a factor in infectious disease. *Transactions of the New York Academy of Science, 35,* 325.

Gold, Delores, & Reis, Myrna. (1982). Male teacher effects on young children: A theoretical and empirical consideration. *Sex Roles, 8,* 493–514.

Gold, Steven N., Hughes, Dawn, & Hohnecker, Laura. (1994). Degrees of repression of sexual abuse memories. *American Psychologist, 49,* 441–442.

Goldberg, Daniel C., et al. (1983). The Gräfenberg spot and female ejaculation: A review of initial hypotheses. *Journal of Sex and Marital Therapy, 9,* 27–37.

Goldberg, Philip. (1968, April). Are some women prejudiced against women? *Transaction, 5,* 28–30.

Golombok, Susan, & Fivush, Robyn. (1994). *Gender development.* New York: Cambridge University Press.

Golub, Sharon. (1976). The effect of premenstrual anxiety and depression on cognitive function. *Journal of Personality and Social Psychology, 34,* 99–104.

Golub, Sharon. (1992). *Periods: From menarche to menopause.* Newbury Park, CA: Sage.

Gomberg, Edith S. (1974). Women and alcoholism. In V. Franks & V. Burtle (Eds.), *Women in therapy.* New York: Brunner/Mazel.

Gomberg, Edith S. (1979). Problems with alcohol and other drugs. In E. S. Gomberg & V. Franks (Eds.), *Gender and disordered behavior.* New York: Brunner/ Mazel.

Gomberg, Edith S. L. (1986). Women: Alcohol and other drugs. *Drugs and Society, 1,* 75–109.

Gomberg, Edith S. (1993). Gender issues. In M. Galanter (Ed.), *Recent developments in alcoholism, Volume 11: Ten years of progress.* New York: Plenum.

Gomberg, Edith S. L., & Lisansky, Judith M. (1984). Antecedents of alcohol problems in women. In S. Wilsnack and L. Beckman (Eds.), *Alcohol problems in women.* New York: Guilford.

Gondolf, E. W., Fisher, E., & McFerron, J. R. (1988). Racial differences among shelter residents: A comparison of Anglo, Black, and Hispanic battered women. *Journal of Family Violence, 3,* 39–51.

Gonsiorek, John C. (1993). Mental health issues of gay and lesbian adolescents. In L. D. Garnets & D. C. Kimmel (Eds.), *Psychological perspectives on lesbian and gay male experience* (pp. 469–485). New York: Columbia University Press.

Gonzalez-Calvo, Judith T. (1993). *Gender: Multicultural perspectives.* Dubuque, IA: Kendall/Hunt.

Goodchilds, Jacqueline, & Zellman, Gail. (1984). Sexual signaling and sexual aggression in adolescent relationships. In N. Malamuth & E. Donnerstein (Eds.), *Pornography and sexual aggression.* New York: Academic Press.

Goode, E., & Haber, L. (1977). Sexual correlates of homosexual experience: An exploratory study of college women. *Journal of Sex Research, 13,* 12–21.

Gordon, Linda. (1988). *Heroes of their own lives.* New York: Viking.

Gordon, R. E., Kapostins, E. E., & Gordon, Katherine K. (1965). Factors in postpartum emotional adjustment. *Obstetrics and Gynecology, 25,* 158–166.

Gough, Harrison G. (1957). *Manual for the California Psychological Inventory.* Palo Alto, CA: Consulting Psychologists Press. (Rev. ed., 1964.)

Gould, Stephen J. (1987). *An urchin in the storm.* New York: Norton.

Gove, William R., & Tudor, Jeannette F. (1973). Adult sex roles and mental illness. *American Journal of Sociology, 78,* 812–835.

Grady, Kathleen. (1979). Androgyny reconsidered. In J. H. Williams (Ed.), *Psychology of women: Selected read-*

ings (pp. 172–177). New York: Norton.

Grady, Kathleen E. (1981). Sex bias in research design. *Psychology of Women Quarterly, 5,* 628–636.

Grant, Linda. (1984). Black females' "place" in desegregated classrooms. *Sociology of Education, 57,* 98–111.

Green, Beth L., & Russo, Nancy F. (1993). Work and family roles: Selected issues. In F. L. Denmark & M. A. Paludi (Eds.), *Psychology of women: Handbook of issues and theories.* Westport, CT: Greenwood.

Green, Richard. (1978). Sexual identity of 37 children raised by homosexual or transsexual parents. *American Journal of Psychiatry, 135,* 692–697.

Green, Richard, Mandel, J. B., Hotvedt, M. E., Gray, J., & Smith, L. (1986). Lesbian mothers and their children. *Archives of Sexual Behavior, 15,* 167–184.

Greenglass, Esther R., & Devins, Reva. (1982). Factors related to marriage and career plans in unmarried women. *Sex Roles, 8,* 57–72.

Greenhaus, Jeffrey H., & Parasuraman, Saroj. (1993). Job performance attributions and career advancement prospects: An examination of gender and race effects. *Organizational Behavior and Human Decision Processes, 55,* 273–297.

Grier, William H., & Cobbs, Price M. (1968). *Black rage.* New York: Basic Books.

Grinde, Donald A. (1977). *The Iroquois and the founding of the American nation.* San Francisco: American Historian Press.

Gross, Alan E. (1978). The male role and heterosexual behavior. *Journal of Social Issues, 34*(1), 87–107.

Gruber, James E. (1992). A typology of personal and environmental sexual harassment: Research and policy implications for the 1990s. *Sex Roles, 26,* 447–464.

Guinan, Mary E., & Hardy, Ann. (1987). Epidemiology of AIDS in women in the United States, 1981 through 1986. *Journal of the American Medical Association, 257,* 2039–2042.

Gullone, Eleonora, & King, Neville J. (1992). Psychometric evaluation of a Revised Fear Survey Schedule for children and adolescents. *Journal of Child Psychology and Psychiatry, 33,* 987–998.

Gutek, Barbara A. (1985). *Sex and the workplace.* San Francisco: Jossey-Bass.

Guthrie, R. V. (1976). *Even the rat was white: A historical view of psychology.* New York: Harper.

Guttentag, Marcia, & Secord, P. (1983). *Too many women?* Beverly Hills, CA: Sage.

Haan, Norma. (1975). Hypothetical and actual moral reasoning in a situation of civil disobedience. *Journal of Personality and Social Psychology, 32,* 255–270.

Haas, Adelaide. (1979). Male and female spoken language differences: Stereotypes and evidence. *Psychological Bulletin, 86,* 616–626.

Halberstadt, Amy G., & Saitta, M. B. (1987). Gender, nonverbal behavior, and perceived dominance: A test of the theory. *Journal of Personality and Social Psychology, 53,* 257–272.

Hall, Judith A. (1984). *Nonverbal sex differences.* Baltimore: Johns Hopkins University Press.

Hall, L. A., Williams, C. A., & Greenberg, R. S. (1985). Supports, stressors, and depressive symptoms in low-income mothers of young children. *American Journal of Public Health, 75,* 518–522.

Hall, N., & Dawson, W. R. (1989). *Broodmales.* Dallas, TX: Spring.

Halpern, Diane F. (1992). *Sex differences in cognitive abilities* (2nd ed.). Hillsdale, NJ: Erlbaum.

Hamilton, Mykol C. (1991). Masculine bias in the attribution of personhood:

People = male, male = people. *Psychology of Women Quarterly, 15,* 393–402.

Hansen, Christine H., & Hansen, Ronald D. (1988). How rock music videos can change what is seen when boy meets girl: Priming stereotypic appraisal of social interactions. *Sex Roles, 19,* 287–316.

Hare-Mustin, Rachel T., & Marecek, Jeanne. (1988). The meaning of difference: Gender theory, postmodernism and psychology. *American Psychologist, 43,* 455–464.

Hariton, E. Barbara. (1973, March). The sexual fantasies of women. *Psychology Today, 6,* 39–44.

Harrigan, Jinni A., & Lucic, Karen S. (1988). Attitudes about gender bias in language: A reevaluation. *Sex Roles, 19,* 129–140.

Harris, Gloria G., & Osborn, Susan M. (1974). *Assertiveness training for women.* Springfield, IL: Charles C Thomas.

Harris, G. W., & Levine, S. (1965). Sexual differentiation of the brain and its experimental control. *Journal of Physiology, 181,* 379–400.

Harris, S. (1971). Influence of subject and experimenter sex in psychological research. *Journal of Consulting and Clinical Psychology, 37,* 291–294.

Harris, Shanette M. (1993). The influence of personal and family factors on achievement needs and concerns of African-American and Euro-American college women. *Sex Roles, 29,* 671–690.

Harrison, J. (1978). Warning: The male sex role may be dangerous to your health. *Journal of Social Issues, 34*(1), 65–86.

Harry, J. (1976). Evolving sources of happiness for men over the life cycle: A structural analysis. *Journal of Marriage and the Family, 38,* 289–296.

Hartlage, L. (1970). Sex-linked inheri-

tance of spatial ability. *Perceptual and Motor Skills, 31,* 610.

Hartley, Ruth E. (1959). Sex role pressures and socialization of the male child. *Psychological Reports, 5,* 457–468.

Hartley, Ruth E. (1960). Some implications of current changes in sex role patterns. *Merrill-Palmer Quarterly, 3,* 153–164.

Hastings, J. E., & Hamberger, L. K. (1988). Personality characteristics of spouse abusers: A controlled comparison. *Violence and Victims, 3,* 31–48.

Havens, Elizabeth. (1973). Women, work and wedlock: A note on female marital patterns in the United States. *American Journal of Sociology, 78,* 975–981.

Hawkins, Joellen, & Aber, Cynthia S. (1983). Women in advertisements in medical journals. *Sex Roles, 28,* 233–242.

Haynes, S. G., et al. (1978). The relationship of psychosocial factors to coronary heart disease in the Framingham Study. II. Prevalence of coronary heart disease. *American Journal of Epidemiology, 107,* 384–402.

Hays, Constance R. (1990, Sept. 30). Reports of assaults on homosexuals increase. *New York Times.*

Hays, H. R. (1964). *The dangerous sex: The myth of feminine evil.* New York: G. P. Putnam's Sons.

Heatherington, Laurie, et al. (1993). Two investigations of "female modesty" in achievement situations. *Sex Roles, 29,* 739–754.

Hedblom, J. H. (1972). The female homosexual: Social and attitudinal dimensions. In J. A. McCaffrey (Ed.), *The homosexual dialectic.* Englewood Cliffs, NJ: Prentice-Hall.

Heiman, Julia R. (1975). The physiology of erotica: Women's sexual arousal. *Psychology Today, 8*(11), 90–94.

Heiman, Julia, LoPiccolo, Leslie, & LoPiccolo, Joseph. (1976). *Becoming or-*

gasmic: A sexual growth program for women. Englewood Cliffs, NJ: Prentice Hall.

Heise, Lori. (1993). Violence against women: The hidden health burden. *World Health Statistics Quarterly, 46,* 78–85.

Helgeson, Vicki S. (1990). The role of masculinity in a prognostic predictor of heart attack severity. *Sex Roles, 22,* 755–790.

Hemmer, Joan D., & Kleiber, D. A. (1981). Tomboys and sissies: Androgynous children? *Sex Roles, 1,* 1205–1212.

Henahan, John. (1984). Honing the treatment of early breast cancer. *Journal of the American Medical Association, 251,* 309–310.

Henley, Nancy. (1973). Status and sex: Some touching observations. *Bulletin of the Psychonomic Society, 2,* 92–93.

Henley, Nancy M. (1989). Molehill or mountain? What we do know and don't know about sex bias in language. In M. Crawford & M. Gentry (Eds.), *Gender and thought* (pp. 59–78). New York: Springer-Verlag.

Henshaw, Stanley K. (1990, April). Induced abortion: A world review, 1990. *Family Planning Perspectives, 22,* 76–89.

Herdt, Gilbert H. (Ed.). (1984). *Ritualized homosexuality in Melanesia.* Berkeley: University of California Press.

Herek, Gregory M. (1993). The context of antigay violence: Notes on cultural and psychological heterosexism. In L. D. Garnets & D. C. Kimmel (Eds.), *Psychological perspectives on lesbian and gay male experience* (pp. 89–108). New York: Columbia University Press.

Herek, Gregory M., & Berrill, K. T. (1992). *Hate crimes: Confronting violence against lesbians and gay men.* Newbury Park, CA: Sage.

Herek, Gregory M., Kimmel, Douglas C., Amaro, Hortensia, & Melton, Gary B.

(1991). Avoiding heterosexist bias in psychological research. *American Psychologist, 46,* 957–963.

Herman, Judith L. (1981). *Father-daughter incest.* Cambridge, MA: Harvard University Press.

Hernandez, Ines. (1990, April). *American Indian women writers.* Colloquium presented at the University of Wisconsin-Madison.

Hersey, R. B. (1931). Emotional cycles in man. *Journal of Mental Science, 77,* 151–169.

Herzog, David B., et al. (1992). The current status of treatment for anorexia nervosa and bulimia nervosa. *International Journal of Eating Disorders, 12,* 215–220.

Hidalgo, Hilda, & Hidalgo-Christenson, Elia. (1976). The Puerto Rican lesbian and the Puerto Rican community. *Journal of Homosexuality, 2,* 109–121.

Hines, Melissa. (1982). Prenatal gonadal hormones and sex differences in human behavior. *Psychological Bulletin, 92,* 56–80.

Hines, Melissa, & Collaer, Marcia L. (1993). Gonadal hormones and sexual differentiation of human behavior. *Annual Review of Sex Research, 4,* 1–48.

Hines, Melissa, & Kaufman, F. R. (1994). Androgen and the development of human sex typical behavior: Rough-and-tumble play and sex of preferred playmates in children with congenital adrenal hyperplasia (CAH). *Child Development, 65,* 1042–1053.

Ho, Christine K. (1990). An analysis of domestic violence in Asian American communities: A multi-cultural approach to counseling. *Women & Therapy, 12,* 129–150.

Hochschild, Arlie. (1989). *The second shift: Working parents and the revolution at home.* New York: Viking.

Hodgson, J. W., & Fischer, Judith L. (1981). Pathways of identity development in college women. *Sex Roles, 7,* 681–690.

Hofferth, Sandra L. (1990). Trends in adolescent sexual activity, contraception, and pregnancy in the United States. In J. Bancroft & J. M. Reinisch (Eds.), *Adolescence and puberty.* New York: Oxford.

Hoffman, Lois W. (1972). Early childhood experiences and women's achievement motives. *Journal of Social Issues, 28*(2), 129–155.

Hoffman, Lois W. (1974). The employment of women, education and fertility. *Merrill-Palmer Quarterly, 20,* 99–119.

Hoffman, M. L. (1977). Sex differences in empathy and related behaviors. *Psychological Bulletin, 84,* 712–722.

Holborow, P. L., & Berry, P. S. (1986). Hyperactivity and learning difficulties. *Journal of Learning Disabilities, 11,* 426–431.

Holden, Constance. (1989). Koop finds abortion evidence "inconclusive." *Science, 243,* 730–731.

Holland, Dorothy C., & Eisenhart, Margaret A. (1990). *Educated in romance: Women, achievement, and college culture.* Chicago: University of Chicago Press.

Holroyd, Jean C., & Brodsky, Annette M. (1977). Psychologists' attitudes and practices regarding erotic and nonerotic physical contact with patients. *American Psychologist, 34,* 843–849.

Holstein, Constance. (1976). Development of moral judgment: A longitudinal study of males and females. *Child Development, 47,* 51–61.

Hood, Jane C. (Ed.). (1993). *Men, work, and family.* Newbury Park, CA: Sage.

Hopkins, Joyce, Marcues, M., & Campbell, S. B. (1984). Postpartum depression: A critical review. *Psychological Bulletin, 95,* 498–515.

Horner, Matina S. (1969). Fail: Bright women. *Psychology Today, 3*(6), 36.

Horner, Matina S. (1970a). Femininity and achievement: A basic inconsistency. In J. Bardwick, E. Douvan, M. Horner, & D. Gutman (Eds.), *Feminine personality and conflict.* Belmont, CA: Brooks/Cole.

Horner, Matina S. (1972). Toward an understanding of achievement-related conflicts in women. *Journal of Social Issues, 28*(2), 157–175.

Horney, Karen. (1924). On the genesis of the castration complex in women. *International Journal of Psychoanalysis, 5,* 50–65.

Horney, Karen. (1926). The flight from womanhood. *International Journal of Psychoanalysis, 7,* 324–339.

Horwitz, A. V. (1982). Sex-role expectations, power, and psychological distress. *Sex Roles, 8,* 607–624.

Hotaling, G. T., & Sugarman, D. B. (1986). An analysis of risk markers in husband to wife violence: The current state of knowledge. *Violence and Victims, 1,* 101–124.

House, W. C. (1974). Actual and perceived differences in male and female expectancies and minimal goal levels as a function of competition. *Journal of Personality, 42,* 493–509.

Houseknecht, Sharon K. (1979). Timing of the decision to remain voluntarily childless: Evidence for continuous socialization. *Psychology of Women Quarterly, 4,* 81–96.

Hrdy, Sarah B. (1981). *The woman that never evolved.* Cambridge: Harvard University Press.

Hsu, L. K. George, Kaye, Walter, & Weltzin, Theodore. (1993). Are the eating disorders related to obsessive compulsive disorder? *International Journal of Eating Disorders, 14,* 305–318.

Hudson, Walter W., & Ricketts, Wendell A. (1980). A strategy for the measurement of homophobia. *Journal of Homosexuality, 5,* 357–372.

Huff, Charles, & Cooper, Joel. (1987). Sex bias in educational software: The effect of designers' stereotypes on the software they design. *Journal of Applied Social Psychology, 17,* 519–532.

Hughes, Jean O., & Sandler, Bernice R. (1987). *"Friends" raping friends: Could it happen to you?* Washington, DC: Association of American Colleges.

Hunt, Morton. (1974). *Sexual behavior in the 1970s.* Chicago: Playboy Press.

Hutchins, Loraine, & Kaahumanu, Lani. (1991). *Bi any other name: Bisexual people speak out.* Boston: Alyson.

Hyde, Janet S. (1979). *Understanding human sexuality.* New York: McGraw-Hill.

Hyde, Janet S. (1981). How large are cognitive gender differences? A meta-analysis using ω^2 and *d. American Psychologist, 36,* 892–901.

Hyde, Janet S. (1984a). Children's understanding of sexist language. *Developmental Psychology, 20,* 697–706.

Hyde, Janet S. (1984b). How large are gender differences in aggression? A developmental meta-analysis. *Developmental Psychology, 20,* 722–736.

Hyde, Janet S. (1990). *Understanding human sexuality,* 4th ed. New York: McGraw-Hill.

Hyde, Janet S. (1994). *Understanding human sexuality,* 5th ed. New York: McGraw-Hill.

Hyde, Janet S., & Essex, Marilyn J. (Eds.). (1991). *Parental leave and child care: Setting a research and policy agenda.* Philadelphia: Temple University Press.

Hyde, J. S., Essex, M. J., & Horton, F. (1993). Fathers and parental leave. *Journal of Family Issues, 14,* 616–641.

Hyde, Janet S., Fennema, Elizabeth, & Lamon, Susan J. (1990). Gender differences in mathematics performance: A meta-analysis. *Psychological Bulletin, 107,* 139–155.

Hyde, Janet S., Geiringer, Eva R., & Yen, Wendy M. (1975). On the empirical relation between spatial ability and sex differences in other aspects of cognitive performance. *Multivariate Behavioral Research, 10,* 289–310.

Hyde, Janet S., Klein, M., Essex, M. J., & Clark, R. (1995). Maternity leave and women's mental health. *Psychology of Women Quarterly.*

Hyde, Janet S., Krajnik, Michelle, & Skuldt-Niederberger, Kristin. (1991). Androgyny across the life span: A replication and longitudinal follow-up. *Developmental Psychology, 27,* 516–519.

Hyde, Janet S., & Linn, Marcia C. (Eds.). (1986). *The psychology of gender: Advances through meta-analysis.* Baltimore: Johns Hopkins University Press.

Hyde, Janet S., & Linn, Marcia C. (1988). Gender differences in verbal ability: A meta-analysis. *Psychological Bulletin, 104,* 53–69.

Hyde, Janet S., & Phillis, Diane E. (1979). Androgyny across the lifespan. *Developmental Psychology, 15,* 334–336.

Hyde, Janet S., & Rosenberg, B. G. (1976). *Half the human experience: The psychology of women* (1st ed.). Lexington, MA: D. C. Heath.

Hyde, Janet S., Rosenberg, B. G., & Behrman, JoAnn. (1977). Tomboyism. *Psychology of Women Quarterly, 2,* 73–75.

Hyde, Janet S., & Schuck, J. R. (1977). *The development of sex differences in aggression.* Paper presented at American Psychological Association Meetings, San Francisco.

Imperato-McGinley, Julianne, et al. (1974). Steroid 5-Alpha-Reductase deficiency in man: An inherited form of male pseudohermaphroditism. *Science, 186,* 1213–1215.

Instone, Debra, Major, Brenda, & Bunker, Barbara B. (1983). Gender, self-confidence, and social influence strategies: An organizational simulation. *Journal of Personality and Social Psychology, 44,* 322–333.

Irvine, Jacqueline J. (1985). Teacher communication patterns as related to the race and sex of the student. *Journal of Educational Research, 78,* 338–345.

Irvine, Jacqueline J. (1986). Teacher-student interactions: Effects of student race, sex, and grade level. *Journal of Educational Psychology, 78,* 14–21.

Ivey, M. E., & Bardwick, Judith M. (1968). Patterns of affective fluctuation in the menstrual cycle. *Psychosomatic Medicine, 30,* 336–345.

Jackson, Linda A. (1992). *Physical appearance and gender: Sociobiological and sociocultural perspectives.* Albany: State University of New York Press.

Jadack, Rosemary, Hyde, Janet S., & Moore, Colleen F. (1995). Gender differences in moral reasoning about sexually transmitted diseases. *Child Development,*

Jaffe, Peter G., Wolfe, David A., & Wilson, Susan K. (1990). *Children of battered women.* Newbury Park, CA: Sage.

Jaggar, Alison M. (1977). Political philosophies of women's liberation. In M. Vetterling-Braggin et al. (Eds.), *Feminism and philosophy.* Totowa, NJ: Littlefield, Adams.

Jaggar, Alison M., & Struhl, Paula R. (1978). *Feminist frameworks.* New York: McGraw-Hill.

Jakubowski, Patricia A. (1977). Assertive behavior and clinical problems of women. In E. I. Rawlings & D. K. Carter (Eds.), *Psychotherapy for women.* Springfield, IL: Charles C Thomas.

Jakubowski-Spector, Patricia. (1973). Facilitating the growth of women through assertiveness training. *The Counseling Psychologist, 4,* 75.

James, Stanlie M., & Busia, Abena. (Eds.). (1993). *Theorizing Black feminisms: The visionary pragmatism of Black women.* New York: Routledge.

Jamison, Kay R., Wellisch, D. K., & Pasnau, R. O. (1978). Psychosocial aspects of mastectomy: I. The woman's perspective. *American Journal of Psychiatry, 135,* 432–436.

Janson-Smith, Deirdre. (1980). Sociobiology: So what? In Brighton Women & Science Group, *Alice through the microscope.* London: Virago.

Jay, Karla, & Young, Allen. (1979). *The gay report.* New York: Summit Books.

Jeanquart-Barone, Sandy. (1993). Trust differences between supervisors and subordinates: Examining the role of race and gender. *Sex Roles, 29,* 1–12.

Jick, H., Walker, A. M., & Rothman, K. J. (1980). The epidemic of endometrial cancer: A commentary. *American Journal of Public Health, 70,* 264–267.

Johnson, Anne M., Wadsworth, Jane, Wellings, Kaye, & Field, Julia. (1994). *Sexual attitudes and lifestyles.* London: Blackwell.

Johnson, Catherine D., Stockdale, Margaret S., & Saal, Frank E. (1991). Persistence of men's misperceptions of friendly cues across a variety of interpersonal encounters. *Psychology of Women Quarterly, 15,* 463–475.

Jones, James M. (1991). Psychological models of race: What have they been and what should they be? In J. D. Goodchilds (Ed.), *Psychological perspectives on human diversity in America.* Washington, DC: American Psychological Association.

Josephs, Robert A., Markus, Hazel R., & Tafarodi, R. W. (1992). Gender and self-esteem. *Journal of Personality and Social Psychology, 63,* 391–402.

Jourard, Sydney M. (1974). *Healthy personality: An approach from the viewpoint of humanistic psychology.* New York: Macmillan.

Justice, Blair, & Justice, Rita. (1979). *The broken taboo: Sex in the family.* New York: Human Sciences Press.

Kahn, Arnold. (1981). Reactions of profeminist and antifeminist men to an expert woman. *Sex Roles, 7,* 857–866.

Kahn, Arnold S., Mathie, V. A., & Torgler, C. (1994). Rape scripts and rape acknowledgement. *Psychology of Women Quarterly, 18,* 53–66.

Kalisch, Philip A., & Kalisch, Beatrice J. (1984). Sex-role stereotyping of nurses and physicians on prime-time television. *Sex Roles, 10,* 533–554.

Kane, F. J., Lipton, M. A., & Ewing, J. A. (1969). Hormonal influences in female sexual response. *Archives of General Psychiatry, 20,* 202–209.

Kanin, Eugene J. (1985). Date rapists: Differential sexual socialization and relative deprivation. *Archives of Sexual Behavior, 14,* 219–232.

Kanter, Rosabeth Moss. (1977). Women in organizations: Sex roles, group dynamics, and change strategies. In A. Sargent (Ed.), *Beyond sex roles.* St. Paul, MN: West.

Kaplan, Helen Singer. (1979). *Disorders of sexual desire.* New York: Simon & Schuster.

Kaplan, Helen S., & Sager, Clifford J. (1971, June). Sexual patterns at different ages. *Medical Aspects of Human Sexuality,* 10–23.

Kart, C. S., Metress, E. K., & Metress, S. P. (1988). *Aging, health, and society.* Boston: Jones & Bartlett.

Katchadourian, H. A., & Lunde, D. D. (1972). *Fundamentals of human sexuality.* New York: Holt, Rinehart & Winston.

Katz, Joseph. (1983). White faculty struggling with the effects of racism. In J. H. Cones, J. F. Noonan, & D. Janha (Eds.), *Teaching minority students.* San Francisco: Jossey-Bass.

Kegel, A. H. (1952). Sexual functions of the pubococcygeus muscle. *Western Journal of Surgery, 60,* 521–524.

Kendall-Tackett, Kathleen, Williams, L., & Finkelhor, D. (1993). Impact of sexual abuse on children: A review and synthesis of recent empirical studies. *Psychological Bulletin, 113,* 164–180.

Kessler, S. J., & McKenna, Wendy. (1985). *Gender: An ethnomethodological approach.* Chicago: University of Chicago Press.

Key, Mary Ritchie. (1975). *Male/female language.* Metuchen, NJ: Scarecrow Press.

Kibria, Nazli. (1990). Power, patriarchy, and gender conflict in the Vietnamese immigrant community. *Gender & Society, 4,* 9–24.

Kidwell, C. S. (1976, December). The status of American Indian women in higher education. In National Institute of Education, *Conference on the Educational and Occupational Needs of American Indian women* (pp. 83–123). Washington, DC: U.S. Department of Education.

Kilmartin, Christopher T. (1994). *The masculine self.* New York: Macmillan.

Kilpatrick, D. G., Resick, P. A., & Veronen, L. J. (1981). Effects of a rape experience. *Journal of Social Issues, 37*(4), 105–122.

Kim, Elaine H. (1990, Winter). "Such opposite creatures": Men and women in Asian American literature. *Michigan Quarterly Review, 29,* 68–93.

Kimball, Meredith M. (1989). A new perspective on women's math achievement. *Psychological Bulletin, 105,* 198–214.

Kimmel, Michael S., & Messner, Michael A. (Eds.). (1989). *Men's lives.* New York: Macmillan.

Kimura, Doreen, & Hampson, E. (1994). Cognitive pattern in men and women is influenced by fluctuations in sex hormones. *Current Directions, 3,* 57–60.

Kinsey, Alfred C., Pomeroy, Wardell B., & Martin, Clyde E. (1948). *Sexual behavior in the human male.* Philadelphia: Saunders.

Kinsey, Alfred C., Pomeroy, Wardell B., Martin, Clyde E., & Gebhard, Paul H. (1953). *Sexual behavior in the human female.* Philadelphia: Saunders.

Kirkpatrick, Carole S. (1980). Sex roles and sexual satisfaction in women. *Psychology of Women Quarterly, 4,* 444–459.

Kivnick, Helen Q. (1983). Dimensions of grandparenthood meaning: Deductive conceptualization and empirical derivation. *Journal of Personality and Social Psychology, 44,* 1056–1068.

Klebanov, Pamela K., & Jemmott, John B. (1992). Effects of expectations and bodily sensations on self-reports of premenstrual symptoms. *Psychology of Women Quarterly, 16,* 289–310.

Knop, C. A. (1946). The dynamics of newly born babies. *Journal of Pediatrics, 29,* 721–728.

Kohlberg, Lawrence. (1966). A cognitive-developmental analysis of children's sex-role concepts and attitudes. In E. E. Maccoby (Ed.), *The development of sex differences.* Stanford: Stanford University Press.

Kohlberg, Lawrence. (1969). Stage and sequence: The cognitive-developmental approach to socialization. In D. A. Goslin (Ed.), *Handbook of socialization theory and research.* Chicago: Rand McNally.

Kollock, P., Blumstein, P., & Schwartz, P. (1985). Sex and power in interaction: Conversational privileges and duties. *American Sociological Review, 50,* 34–46.

Komarovsky, Mirra. (1973). Cultural contradictions and sex roles: The masculine case. *American Journal of Sociology, 78,* 873–884.

Konopka, Gisela. (1975). *Young girls: A portrait of adolescence.* Englewood Cliffs, NJ: Spectrum Books.

Koonin, L. M., et al. (1991, July). Abortion surveillance, United States, 1988. *Morbidity and Mortality Weekly Report, 40,* No. SS-1, 15–42.

Kortenhaus, Carole M., & Demarest, Jack. (1993). Gender role stereotyping in children's literature: An update. *Sex Roles, 28,* 219–232.

Koss, Mary P. (1990). The Women's Mental Health Research Agenda: Violence against women. *American Psychologist, 45,* 374–380.

Koss, Mary P. (1993). Rape: Scope, impact, interventions, and public policy responses. *American Psychologist, 48,* 1062–1069.

Koss, Mary P., et al. (1987). The scope of rape: Incidence and prevalence in a national sample of higher education students. *Journal of Consulting and Clinical Psychology, 55,* 162–170.

Koss, Mary P., et al. (1988). Stranger and acquaintance rape: Are there differences in the victim's experience? *Psychology of Women Quarterly, 12,* 1–24.

Koss, Mary P., & Cook, Sarah L. (1994). Facing the facts: Date and acquaintance rape are widespread forms of violence. In M. Koss et al. (Eds.), *No safe haven.* Washington, DC: American Psychological Association.

Koss, Mary P., Goodman, Lisa A., Browne, Angela, Fitzgerald, Louise F., Russo, Nancy F., & Keita, Gwendolyn P. (1994). *No safe haven: Male violence against women at home, at work, and in the community.* Washington, DC: American Psychological Association.

Koss, Mary P., & Heslet, Lynette. (1992). Somatic consequences of violence against women. *Archives of Family Medicine, 1,* 53–59.

Koss, Mary P., Koss, Paul G., & Woodruff, W. Joy. (1991). Deleterious effects of criminal victimization on women's health and medical utilization. *Archives of Internal Medicine, 151,* 342–347.

Koss, Mary P., & Mukai, Takayo. (1993). Recovering ourselves: The frequency, effects, and resolution of rape. In F. L. Denmark & M. A. Paludi (Eds.), *Psy-*

chology of women: Handbook of issues and theories. Westport, CT: Greenwood.

Kramer, Cheris. (1974a, June). Folk-linguistics: Wishy-washy mommy talk. *Psychology Today,* 82–89.

Kramer, Cheris. (1974b). Women's speech: Separate but unequal. *Quarterly Journal of Speech,* February, 14–24.

Kramer, Cheris. (1976). Stereotypes of women's speech: The word from cartoons. *Journal of Popular Culture.*

Kramer, Cheris, Thorne, Barrie, & Henley, Nancy. (1978). Perspectives on language and communication. *Signs, 3,* 638–651.

Kravetz, Diane. (1980). Consciousness-raising and self-help. In A. Brodsky & R. Hare-Mustin (Eds.), *Women and psychotherapy.* New York: Guilford.

Kuhn, D. (1976). Short-term longitudinal evidence for the sequentiality of Kohlberg's early stage of moral development. *Developmental Psychology, 12,* 162–166.

Kuhn, Thomas S. (1970). *The structure of scientific revolutions.* Chicago: University of Chicago Press.

Ladas, Alice K., Whipple, Beverly, & Perry, J. D. (1982). *The G-spot.* New York: Holt, Rinehart & Winston.

Ladner, Joyce A. (1971). *Tomorrow's tomorrow: The black woman.* Garden City, NY: Doubleday.

LaFrance, Marianne. (1981). Gender gestures: sex, sex-role, and nonverbal communication. In C. Mayo & N. Henley (Eds.), *Gender and nonverbal behavior.* New York: Springer-Verlag.

LaFrance, Marianne. (1992). Gender and interruptions: Individual infraction or violation of the social order? *Psychology of Women Quarterly, 16,* 497–512.

LaFromboise, Teresa, Coleman, H., & Gerton, J. (1993). Psychological impact of biculturalism: Evidence and theory. *Psychological Bulletin, 114,* 395–412.

LaFromboise, Teresa D., Heyle, Anneliese M., & Ozer, Emily J. (1990). Changing and diverse roles of women in American Indian culture. *Sex Roles, 22,* 455–476.

Lakoff, Robin. (1973). Language and woman's place. *Language and Society, 2,* 45–79. (Reprinted 1975 in paperback. New York: Harper & Row.)

Lamb, C. Sue, Jackson, Lee A., Cassiday, Patricia B., & Priest, Doris J. (1993). Body figure preferences of men and women: A comparison of two generations. *Sex Roles, 28,* 345–358.

Lamb, Michael E. (1979). Paternal influences and the father's role. *American Psychologist, 34,* 938–943.

Landrine, Hope. (1985). Race × class stereotypes of women. *Sex Roles, 13,* 65–75.

Landrine, Hope. (1987). On the politics of madness: A preliminary analysis of the relationship between social roles and psychopathology. *Psychological Monographs, 113*(3), 341–406.

Landrine, Hope. (1988a). Depression and stereotypes of women: Preliminary empirical analyses of the gender-role hypothesis. *Sex Roles, 19,* 527–541.

Landrine, Hope. (1988b). Revising the framework of abnormal psychology. In P. Bronstein & K. Quina (Eds.), *Teaching a psychology of people.* Washington, DC: American Psychological Association.

Landrine, Hope. (1989). The politics of personality disorder. *Psychology of Women Quarterly, 13,* 325–339.

Landrine, Hope, Klonoff, Elizabeth A., & Brown-Collins, Alice. (1992). Cultural diversity and methodology in feminist psychology. *Psychology of Women Quarterly, 16,* 145–163.

Larwood, Laurie, Szwajkowski, Eugene, & Rose, Suzanna. (1988). When discrimination makes "sense": The rational bias theory. In B. Gutek et al. (Eds.), *Women and work: An annual review* (Vol. 3). Beverly Hills: Sage.

Laumann, Edward O., Gagnon, John H., Michael, Robert T., & Michaels, Stuart. (1994). *The social organization of sexuality: Sexual practices in the United States.* Chicago: University of Chicago Press.

Lazarus, Arnold A. (1974). Women in behavior therapy. In V. Franks & V. Burtle (Eds.), *Women in therapy.* New York: Brunner/Mazel.

Lazarus, A. (1985). Psychiatric sequelae of legalized elective first trimester abortion. *Journal of Psychosomatic Obstetrics and Gynecology, 4,* 141.

Lear, M. W. (1973, January 28). Is there a male menopause? *New York Times Magazine,* January 28.

Leiblum, Sandra R., & Rosen, Raymond C. (Eds.). (1988). *Sexual desire disorders.* New York: Guilford.

Leiblum, Sandra R., & Rosen, Raymond C. (1989). *Principles and practice of sex therapy* (2nd ed.). New York: Guilford.

Leidig, Marjorie W. (1982, April). Incest. Colloquium presented at Denison University.

Leifer, Myra. (1980). *Psychological effects of motherhood: A study of first pregnancy.* New York: Praeger.

Lenney, Ellen. (1977). Women's self-confidence in achievement settings. *Psychological Bulletin, 84,* 1–13.

Lenney, Ellen. (1981). What's fine for the gander isn't always good for the goose: Sex differences in self-confidence as a function of ability area and comparison with others. *Sex Roles, 7,* 905–924.

Leppard, Wanda, Ogletree, Shirley M., & Wallen, Emily. (1993). Gender stereotyping in medical advertising: Much ado about something? *Sex Roles, 29,* 829–838.

Lerman, Hannah. (1986). From Freud to feminist personality theory. *Psychology of Women Quarterly, 10,* 1–18.

Lerner, Harriet E. (1980). Internal prohibitions against female anger. *American Journal of Psychoanalysis, 40*(2), 137–148.

Lerner, Harriet G. (1985). *The dance of anger: A woman's guide to changing the patterns of intimate relationships.* New York: Harper & Row.

LeVay, Simon. (1991). A difference in hypothalamic structure between heterosexual and homosexual men. *Science, 253,* 1034–1037.

Levenkron, Steven. (1978). *The best little girl in the world.* Chicago: Contemporary Books.

Levenkron, Steven. (1982). *Treating and overcoming anorexia nervosa.* New York: Charles Scribner's.

Levine, Michael P., Smolak, Linda, Moodey, Anne F., Shuman, Melissa D., & Hessen, Laura D. (1994). Normative developmental challenges and dieting and eating disturbances in middle school girls. *International Journal of Eating Disorders, 15,* 11–20.

Levinson, Daniel J. (1978). *The seasons of a man's life.* New York: Ballantine.

Levy, Gary D. (1994). High and low gender schematic children's release from proactive interference. *Sex Roles, 30,* 93–108.

Levy, Jere. (1976). Cerebral lateralization and spatial ability. *Behavior Genetics, 6,* 171–188.

Levy-Agresti, Jere, & Sperry, Roger W. (1968). Differential perceptual capacities in major and minor hemispheres. *Proceedings of the National Academy of Science, 61,* 1151.

Lewin, Miriam, & Wild, Cheryl L. (1991). The impact of the feminist critique on tests, assessments, and methodology. *Psychology of Women Quarterly, 15,* 581–596.

Lewinsohn, P. M., Youngren, M. A., & Grosscup, S. J. (1979). Reinforcement and depression. In R. A. Depue (Ed.), *The psychobiology of depressive disorders: Implications for the effects of stress.* New York: Academic Press.

Lewis, Michael. (1972). State as an infant-environment interaction: Analysis of mother-infant interaction as a function of sex. *Merrill-Palmer Quarterly, 18,* 95–121.

Lewis, Michael, Meyers, W., Kagan, J., & Grossberg, R. (1963). *Attention to visual patterns in infants.* Paper presented at the Symposium on Studies of Attention in Infants, American Psychological Association, Philadelphia.

Lightdale, Jenifer R., & Prentice, Deborah A. (1994). Rethinking sex differences in aggression: Aggressive behavior in the absence of social roles. *Personality and Social Psychology Bulletin, 20,* 34–44.

Lindsey, Robert. (1988, February 1). Circumcision under criticism as unnecessary to newborn. *New York Times,* A1.

Linn, Marcia C., & Hyde, Janet S. (1990). Gender, mathematics, and science. *Educational Researcher, 18*(8), 17–19, 22–27.

Linn, Marcia C., & Petersen, Anne C. (1985). Emergence and characterization of sex differences in spatial ability: A meta-analysis. *Child Development, 56,* 1479–1498.

Lipman-Blumen, Jean. (1972). How ideology shapes women's lives. *Scientific American, 226*(1), 34–42.

Lips, Hilary M. (1989). Gender-role socialization: Lessons in femininity. In Jo Freeman (Ed.), *Women: A feminist perspective* (4th ed.). Mountain View, CA: Mayfield Publishing.

Lockhart, Lettie, & White, Barbara. (1989). Understanding marital violence in the Black community. *Journal of Interpersonal Violence, 4,* 421–436.

Loewenstein, Sophie F., et al. (1981). A study of satisfactions and stresses of single women in midlife. *Sex Roles, 7,* 1127–1141.

Loftus, Elizabeth F. (1993). The reality of repressed memories. *American Psychologist, 48,* 518–537.

Loftus, Elizabeth F., Polonsky, Sara, & Fullilove, Mindy T. (1994). Memories of childhood sexual abuse: Remembering and repressing. *Psychology of Women Quarterly, 18,* 67–84.

Loney, J. (1972). Background factors, sexual experiences and attitudes toward treatment in two "normal" homosexual samples. *Journal of Consulting and Clinical Psychology, 38,* 57–65.

Lopata, Helen Z. (1979). *Women as widows.* New York: Elsevier.

LoPiccolo, Joseph, & Lobitz, C. (1972). The role of masturbation in the treatment of sexual dysfunction. *Archives of Sexual Behavior, 2,* 163–171.

LoPiccolo, Joseph, & Stock, Wendy E. (1986). Treatment of sexual dysfunction. *Journal of Consulting and Clinical Psychology, 54,* 158–167.

LoPiccolo, Leslie. (1980). Low sexual desire. In S. R. Leiblum & L. A. Pervin (Eds.), *Principles and practice of sex therapy.* New York: Guilford Press.

Lorber, Judith, et al. (1981). On *The Reproduction of Mothering:* A methodological debate. *Signs, 6*(3), 482–513.

Lorber, Judith, & Farrell, Susan A. (Eds.). (1991). *The social construction of gender.* Newbury Park, CA: Sage.

Lorde, Audre. (1982). *Zami, a new spelling of my name.* Watertown, MA: Persephone Press.

Lott, Bernice. (1981). A feminist critique of androgyny: Toward the elimination of gender attributions for learned behavior. In C. Mayo & N. Henley (Eds.), *Gender and nonverbal behavior.* New York: Springer-Verlag.

Lott, Bernice, & Maluso, D. (1993). The social learning of gender. In A. E. Beall & R. J. Sternberg (Eds.), *The psychology of gender* (pp. 99–126). New York: Guilford.

Lott, Juanita Tamayo. (1990). A portrait of Asian and Pacific American women. In S. Rix (Ed.), *The American woman 1990–91.* New York: Norton.

Lovdal, Lynn T. (1989). Sex role messages in television commercials: An update. *Sex Roles, 21,* 715–724.

Lowenthal, M. F., et al. (1975). *Four stages of life: A comparative study of women and men facing transitions.* San Francisco: Jossey-Bass.

Loyd, B. H., Loyd, D. E., & Gressard, C. P. (1987). Gender and computer experience as factors in the computer attitudes of middle school students. *Journal of Early Adolescence, 7,* 13–19.

Luker, Kristin. (1975). *Taking chances: Abortion and the decision not to contracept.* Berkeley: University of California Press.

Luria, Zella. (1974). Recent women college graduates: A study of rising expectations. *American Journal of Orthopsychiatry, 44,* 312–326.

Lynn, David B. (1974). *The father: His role in child development.* Monterey, CA: Brooks/Cole.

Lytton, Hugh, & Romney, David M. (1991). Parents' differential socialization of boys and girls: A meta-analysis. *Psychological Bulletin, 109,* 267–296.

Maccoby, Eleanor E. (1966). Sex differences in intellectual functioning. In E. E. Maccoby (Ed.), *The development of sex differences.* Stanford: Stanford University Press.

Maccoby, Eleanor E. (1972). The meaning of being female. *Contemporary Psychology, 17,* 369–372.

Maccoby, Eleanor E., & Feldman, S. Shirley. (1972). Mother-attachment and stranger reactions in the third year of life. *Monographs of the Society for Research in Child Development, 37*(1), 1–86.

Maccoby, Eleanor E., & Jacklin, Carol N. (1973). Stress, activity and proximity seeking: Sex differences in the year-old child. *Child Development, 44,* 34–42.

Maccoby, Eleanor E., & Jacklin, Carol N. (1974). *The psychology of sex differences.* Stanford: Stanford University Press.

Macdonald, Nancy E., & Hyde, Janet S. (1980). Fear of success, need achievement, and fear of failure: A factor-analytic study. *Sex Roles, 6,* 695–712.

Machung, Anne. (1986). *Talking career, thinking job: Gender differences in career and family expectations of Berkeley seniors.* Final report, Center for the Study, Education and Advancement of Women, University of California, Berkeley.

Mack, Thomas M., et al. (1976). Estrogens and endometrial cancer in a retirement community. *New England Journal of Medicine, 294,* 1262–1267.

MacKinnon, Catharine A. (1979). *Sexual harassment of working women.* New Haven: Yale University Press.

MacKinnon, Catharine A. (1982). Feminism, Marxism, method, and the state: An agenda for theory. In N. O. Keohane et al. (Eds.), *Feminist theory.* Chicago: University of Chicago Press.

MacLusky, Neil I., & Naftolin, F. (1981). Sexual differentiation of the central nervous system. *Science, 211,* 1294–1303.

Madigan, F. C. (1957). Are sex mortality differentials biologically caused? *Milbank Memorial Fund Quarterly, 35,* 203–223.

Maisch, H. (1972). *Incest.* New York: Stein and Day.

Major, Brenda. (1989). Gender differences in comparisons and entitlement: Implications for comparable worth. *Journal of Social Issues, 45*(4), 99–115.

Major, Brenda. (1993). Gender, entitlement, and the distribution of family labor. *Journal of Social Issues, 49,* 141–159.

Major, Brenda. (1994). From social inequality to personal entitlement: The role of social comparisons, legitimacy appraisals, and group membership. In M. P. Zanna (Ed.), *Advances in Exper-*

imental Social Psychology (Vol. 26, pp. 293–355). New York: Academic Press.

Malone, T. W., & Lepper, M. R. (1986). Making learning fun: A taxonomy of intrinsic motivation for learning. In R. Snow & M. Farr (Eds.), *Aptitude, learning, and instruction* (Vol. 3). Hillsdale, NJ: Erlbaum.

Mandel, William. (1975). *Soviet women.* Garden City, NY: Anchor.

Marchetti, Gina. (1993). *Romance and the "yellow peril": Race, sex, and discursive strategies in Hollywood fiction.* Berkeley: University of California Press.

Marcus, Dale E., & Overton, W. F. (1978). The development of cognitive gender constancy and sex preferences. *Child Development, 49,* 434–444.

Marks, Michelle A., & Nelson, Eileen S. (1993). Sexual harassment on campus: Effects of professor gender on perception of sexually harassing behaviors. *Sex Roles, 28,* 207–218.

Markus, Hazel, et al. (1982). Self-schemas and gender. *Journal of Personality and Social Psychology, 42,* 38–50.

Martin, Carol L., & Halverson, C. F. (1983). The effects of sex-typing schemas on young children's memory. *Child Development, 54,* 563–574.

Martin, Carol L., & Little, J. K. (1990). The relation of gender understanding to children's sex-typed preferences and gender stereotypes. *Child Development, 61,* 1427–1439.

Martin, Del. (1976). *Battered wives.* San Francisco: Glide Publications.

Martin, Del, & Lyon, Phyllis. (1972). *Lesbian/Woman.* San Francisco: Glide Publications.

Martin, M. K., & Voorhies, B. (1975). *Female of the species.* New York: Columbia University Press.

Martyna, Wendy. (1980). Beyond the he/man approach: The case for nonsexist language. *Signs, 5,* 482–493.

Marx, Jean L. (1976). Estrogen drugs: Do they increase the risk of cancer? *Science, 191,* 838.

Masters, William H., & Johnson, Virginia E. (1966). *Human sexual response.* Boston: Little Brown.

Masters, William H., & Johnson, Virginia E. (1970). *Human sexual inadequacy.* Boston: Little Brown.

Matthews, Karen A. (1982). Psychological perspectives on the Type A behavior pattern. *Psychological Bulletin, 91,* 293–323.

Mayo, Clara, & Henley, Nancy M. (Eds.) (1981). *Gender and nonverbal behavior.* New York: Springer-Verlag.

Mays, Vickie M., & Cochran, Susan D. (1987). Acquired immunodeficiency syndrome and Black Americans: Social psychological issues. *Public Health Reports, 102,* 224–231.

McArthur, Leslie, & Eisen, S. (1976a). Achievement of male and female storybook characters as determinants of achievement behavior by boys and girls. *Journal of Personality and Social Psychology, 33,* 467–473.

McArthur, Leslie, & Eisen, S. (1976b). Television and sex-role stereotyping. *Journal of Applied Social Psychology, 6,* 329–351.

McClelland, David C., Atkinson, J. W., Clark, R. A., & Lowell, F. L. (1953). *The achievement motive.* New York: Appleton-Century-Crofts.

McClintock, Martha K. (1971). Menstrual synchrony and suppression. *Nature, 229,* 244–245.

McConaghy, Nathaniel. (1987). A learning approach. In J. H. Geer & W. T. O'Donohue (Eds.), *Theories of human sexuality* (pp. 287–334). New York: Plenum.

McConnell-Ginet, Sally. (1978). Intonation in a woman's world. *Signs, 3,* 541–559.

McCormick, Naomi, & McCormick, John. (1991). Not for men only: Why so few women major in computer science. *College Student Journal, 85,* 345–350.

McCrady, Barbara S. (1988). Alcoholism. In E. A. Blechman & K. D. Brownell (Eds.), *Handbook of behavioral medicine for women.* New York: Pergamon.

McFarlane, Jessica M., & Williams, Tannis M. (1994). Placing premenstrual syndrome in perspective. *Psychology of Women Quarterly, 18,* 339–374.

McFarlane, Jessica, Martin, Carol L., & Williams, Tannis M. (1988). Mood fluctuations: Women versus men and menstrual versus other cycles. *Psychology of Women Quarterly, 12,* 201–224.

McGinnis, M. (1974). *Single: The woman's view.* Old Tappan, NJ: Fleming H. Revell.

McGrath, Ellen, · Keita, Gwendolyn P., Strickland, Bonnie R., & Russo, Nancy F. (1990). *Women and depression: Risk factors and treatment issues.* Washington, DC: American Psychological Association.

McGraw-Hill Book Company. (1974). *Guidelines for equal treatment of the sexes in McGraw-Hill Book Company publications.* New York: McGraw-Hill.

McGue, Matt, Pickens, Roy, & Svikis, Dace. (1992). Sex and age effects on the inheritance of alcohol problems: A twin study. *Journal of Abnormal Psychology, 101,* 3–17.

McHugh, Maureen C., Frieze, Irene H., & Browne, Angela. (1993). Research on battered women and their assailants. In F. L. Denmark & M. A. Paludi (Eds.), *Psychology of women: Handbook of issues and theories.* Westport, CT: Greenwood.

McHugh, Maureen C., Frieze, Irene H., & Hanusa, Barbara H. (1982). Attributions and sex differences in achievement: Problems and new perspectives. *Sex Roles, 8,* 467–479.

McHugh, Maureen C., Koeske, Randi D., & Frieze, Irene H. (1986). Issues to consider in conducting nonsexist psychological research: A guide for researchers. *American Psychologist, 41,* 879–890.

McKay, R. (1978). One child families and atypical sex ratios in an elite black community. In R. Staples (Ed.), *The black family.* Belmont, CA: Wadsworth.

McKenna, Wendy, & Denmark, Florence L. (1978, March). *Gender and nonverbal behavior as cues to status and power.* Paper presented at the New York Academy of Sciences.

McKenna, Wendy, & Kessler, Suzanne J. (1977). Experimental design as a source of sex bias in social psychology. *Sex Roles, 3,* 117–128.

McKinlay, Sonja M., & Jeffreys, Margot. (1974). The menopausal syndrome. *British Journal of Preventive and Social Medicine, 28*(2), 108.

McKinley, John B., McKinley, Sonja M., & Brambilla, Donald J. (1987). Health status and utilization behavior associated with menopause. *American Journal of Epidemiology, 125,* 110–121.

McLanahan, Sara, & Adams, Julia. (1987). Parenthood and psychological well-being. *Annual Review of Sociology, 5,* 237–257.

McMahan, Ian D. (1971, April). *Sex differences in causal attributions following success and failure.* Paper presented at Eastern Psychological Association Meetings.

McMahan, Ian D. (1972, April). *Sex differences in expectancy of success as a function of task.* Paper presented at Eastern Psychological Association Meetings.

McMillan, Julie R., et al. (1977). Women's language: Uncertainty or interpersonal sensitivity and emotionality? *Sex Roles, 3,* 545–560.

Mead, Margaret. (1935). *Sex and temperament in three primitive societies.* New York: William Morrow.

Mead, Margaret. (1949). *Male and female.* New York: William Morrow.

Mead, Margaret, & Kaplan, Frances B. (Eds.) (1965). *American women: The report of the President's Commission on the Status of Women.* New York: Charles Scribner's.

Medicine, B. (1982). Native American women look at mental health. *Plainswoman, 6,* 7.

Mednick, Martha T. (1989). On the politics of psychological constructs: Stop the bandwagon, I want to get off. *American Psychologist, 44,* 1118–1123.

Mednick, Martha T., & Thomas, Veronica G. (1993). Women and the psychology of achievement: A view from the eighties. In F. L. Denmark & M. A. Paludi (Eds.), *Psychology of women: A handbook of issues and theories.* Westport, CT: Greenwood.

Meece, Judith L., Eccles-Parsons, Jacquelynne, et al. (1982). Sex differences in math achievement: Toward a model of academic choice. *Psychological Bulletin, 91,* 324–448.

Meeker, B. F., & Weitzel-O'Neill, P. A. (1977). Sex roles and interpersonal behavior in task-oriented groups. *American Sociological Review, 42,* 91–104.

Meiselman, Karin. (1978). *Incest.* San Francisco: Jossey-Bass.

Messner, Michael. (1990). Boyhood, organized sports, and the construction of masculinities. *Journal of Contemporary Ethnography, 18,* 416–444.

Meyerowitz, Beth E. (1980). Psychosocial correlates of breast cancer and its treatments. *Psychological Bulletin, 87,* 108–131.

Milburn, Norweeta, & D'Ercole, Ann. (1991). Homeless women: Moving toward a comprehensive model. *American Psychologist, 46,* 1161–1169.

Milgram, Stanley. (1965). Some conditions of obedience and disobedience to authority. *Human Relations, 18,* 57–76.

Milgram, Stanley. (1974). *Obedience to authority.* New York: Harper & Row.

Mill, John Stuart. (1869). The subjection of women. (Reprinted in *Three essays by J. S. Mill.* London: Oxford University Press, 1966.)

Miller, Casey, & Swift, Kate. (1991). *Words and women* (2nd ed.). New York: Harper Collins.

Miller, Jean B. (1983). The construction of anger in women and men. *Work in progress,* No. 83-01. Wellesley, MA: Stone Center.

Millett, Kate. (1969). *Sexual politics.* Garden City, NY: Doubleday.

Minuchin, Salvador, Rosman, Bernice L., & Baker, L. (1978). *Psychosomatic families: Anorexia nervosa in context.* Cambridge, MA: Harvard University Press.

Mischel, Walter. (1966). A social-learning view of sex differences in behavior. In E. E. Maccoby (Ed.), *The development of sex differences.* Stanford: Stanford University Press.

Mitchell, James E. Raymond, Nancy, & Specker, Sheila. (1993). A review of the controlled trials of pharmacotherapy and psychotherapy in the treatment of bulimia nervosa. *International Journal of Eating Disorders, 14,* 229–247.

Mitchell, Valory, & Helson, Ravenna. (1990). Women's prime of life: Is it the 50s? *Psychology of Women Quarterly, 14,* 451–470.

Monahan, Lynn, Kuhn, Deanna, & Shaver, Philip. (1974). Intrapsychic versus cultural explanations of the "fear of success" motive. *Journal of Personality and Social Psychology, 29,* 60–64.

Money, John, & Ehrhardt, Anke. (1972). *Man & woman, boy & girl.* Baltimore: Johns Hopkins University Press.

Montagu, Ashley. (1964). *The natural superiority of women.* New York: P. F. Collier. (First published, 1952.)

Moore, Kristin A., Simms, M. C., & Betsey, C. L. (1986). *Choice and circumstance: Racial differences in adoles-*

cent fertility. New Brunswick, NJ: Transaction Books.

Moos, R. (1968). Psychological aspects of oral contraceptives. *Archives of General Psychiatry, 30,* 853–867.

Morrison, Ann M., et al. (1992). *Breaking the glass ceiling: Can women reach the top of America's largest corporations?* (Updated ed.). Reading, MA: Addison-Wesley.

Moses, Stephen, et al. (1990). Geographical patterns of male circumcision practices in Africa: Association with HIV seroprevalence. *International Journal of Epidemiology, 19,* 693–697.

Moses, Yolanda T. (1989). *Black women in academe.* Washington, DC: Association of American Colleges.

Moss, H. A. (1967). Sex, age and state as determinants of mother-infant interaction. *Merrill-Palmer Quarterly, 13,* 19–36.

Moulton, Janice R., Robinson, G. M., & Elias, Cherin. (1978). Psychology in action: Sex bias in language use: "Neutral" pronouns that aren't. *American Psychologist, 33,* 1032–1036.

Moulton, R. (1970). A survey and re-evaluation of the concept of penis envy. *Contemporary Psychoanalysis, 7,* 84–104.

Mowbray, Carol T., & Herman, Sandra E. (1992). Gender and serious mental illness: A feminist perspective. *Psychology of Women Quarterly, 16,* 107–126.

Muehlenhard, Charlene, Friedman, D. E., & Thomas, C. M. (1985). Is date rape justifiable? The effects of dating activity, who paid, and men's attitudes toward women. *Psychology of Women Quarterly, 9,* 297–310.

Muehlenhard, Charlene L., & McCoy, Marcia L. (1991). Double standard/double bind: The sexual double standard and women's communication about sex. *Psychology of Women Quarterly, 15,* 447–462.

Murrell, Audrey J., Frieze, Irene H., & Frost, Jacquelyn L. (1991). Aspiring to careers in male- and female-dominated professions. *Psychology of Women Quarterly, 15,* 103–126.

Mussen, Paul H. (1961). Some antecedents and consequents of masculine sex-typing in adolescent boys. *Psychological Monographs, 75*(2), 1–24.

Mussen, Paul H. (1962). Long-term consequents of masculinity of interests in adolescence. *Journal of Consulting Psychology, 26,* 435–444.

Myers, J. K., et al. (1984). Six-month prevalence of psychiatric disorders in three communities. *Archives of General Psychiatry, 41,* 959–967.

Naples, Nancy A. (1992). Activist mothering: Cross-generational continuity in the community work of women from low-income urban neighborhoods. *Gender & Society, 6,* 441–463.

Nardi, Peter M. (Ed.). (1992). *Men's friendships.* Newbury Park, CA: Sage.

National Committee on Pay Equity. (1989). *Briefing paper #1: The wage gap.* Washington, DC: National Committee on Pay Equity.

Neugarten, Bernice L., & Kraines, Ruth J. (1965). Menopausal symptoms in women of various ages. *Psychosomatic Medicine, 27,* 266.

Niemann, Yolanda F., Jennings, Leilani, Rozelle, Richard M., Baxter, James C., & Sullivan, Elroy. (1994). Use of free responses and cluster analysis to determine stereotypes of eight groups. *Personality and Social Psychology Bulletin, 20,* 379–390.

Nieva, Veronica F., & Gutek, Barbara A. (1981). *Women and work: A psychological perspective.* New York: Praeger.

No sexism please, we're Webster's. (1991, June 24). *Newsweek,* p. 59.

Nolen-Hoeksema, Susan. (1987). Sex differences in unipolar depression: Evidence and theory. *Psychological Bulletin, 101,* 259–282.

Nolen-Hoeksema, Susan. (1991). *Sex differences in depression.* Stanford, CA: Stanford University Press.

Nolen-Hoeksema, Susan, & Girgus, Joan S. (1994). The emergence of gender differences in depression during adolescence. *Psychological Bulletin, 115,* 424–443.

Norton, Arthur J., & Moorman, Jeanne E. (1987). Current trends in marriage and divorce among American women. *Journal of Marriage and the Family, 49,* 3–14.

Oakley, Anne. (1974). *The sociology of housework.* Bath, England: Pitman.

O'Connell, Agnes N. (1990). Karen Horney (1885–1952). In A. N. O'Connell & N. F. Russo (Eds.), *Women in psychology: A biobibliographical sourcebook.* Westport, CT: Greenwood Press.

Offir, Carole W. (1982). *Human sexuality.* New York: Harcourt, Brace, Jovanovich.

O'Hara, Michael W. (1986). Social support, life events, and depression during pregnancy and the puerperium. *Archives of General Psychiatry, 43,* 569–573.

O'Hara, Michael W., Zekoski, Ellen M., Philipps, Laurie H., & Wright, Ellen J. (1990). Controlled prospective study of postpartum mood disorders: Comparison of childbearing and nonchildbearing women. *Journal of Abnormal Psychology, 99,* 3–15.

O'Keefe, Eileen S. C., & Hyde, Janet S. (1983). The development of occupational sex-role stereotypes: The effects of gender stability and age. *Sex Roles, 9,* 481–492.

Oliver, Mary Beth, & Hyde, Janet S. (1993). Gender differences in sexuality: A meta-analysis. *Psychological Bulletin, 114,* 29–51.

O'Neill, June. (1985). Role differentiation and the gender gap in wage rates. In L. Larwood, A. Stromberg, & B. Gutek (Eds.), *Women and work: An annual review* (Vol. 1, pp. 50–75). Beverly Hills: Sage.

Orloff, Kossia. (1978). The trap of androgyny. *Regionalism and the Female Imagination, 4*(ii), 1–3.

Otterbein, K. F. (1979). A cross-cultural study of rape. *Aggressive Behavior, 5,* 425–435.

Paige, Karen E. (1971). Effects of oral contraceptives on affective fluctuations associated with the menstrual cycle. *Psychosomatic Medicine, 33,* 515–537.

Paige, Karen E. (1973, September). Women learn to sing the menstrual blues. *Psychology Today, 7*(4), 41.

Paludi, Michelle. (Ed.). (1990). *Ivory power: Sexual harassment on campus.* Albany: State University of New York Press.

Papanek, Hanna. (1973). Men, women and work: Reflections on the two-person career. *American Journal of Sociology, 78,* 852–872.

Parke, Ross D. (1979). Perspectives in father-infant interaction. In J. D. Osofsky (Ed.), *Handbook of infant development.* New York: Wiley.

Parke, Ross D., & O'Leary, S. E. (1976). Father-mother-infant interaction in the newborn period. In K. Riegel & J. Meacham (Eds.), *The developing individual in a changing world* (Vol. 2). The Hague: Mouton.

Parlee, Mary B. (1973). The premenstrual syndrome. *Psychological Bulletin, 80,* 454–465.

Parlee, Mary B. (1978). The rhythms in men's lives. *Psychology Today,* 82–91.

Parlee, Mary B. (1981). Appropriate control groups in feminist research. *Psychology of Women Quarterly, 5,* 637–644.

Parlee, Mary B. (1983). Menstrual rhythms in sensory processes: A review of fluctuations in vision, olfaction, audition, taste, and touch. *Psychological Bulletin, 93,* 539–548.

Parlee, Mary B. (1993). Psychology of menstruation and premenstrual syndrome. In F. L. Denmark & M. A. Paludi (Eds.), *Psychology of women: Handbook of issues and theories.* Westport, CT: Greenwood.

Patterson, Charlotte. (1992). Children of lesbian and gay parents. *Child Development, 63,* 1025–1042.

Pearlin, Leonard, & Johnson, J. S. (1977). Marital status, life-strains and depression. *American Sociological Review, 42,* 704–715.

Pearson, Jane L., Hunter, Andrea G., Ensminger, Margaret F., & Kellam, Sheppard G. (1990). Black grandmothers in multigenerational households. *Child Development, 61,* 434–442.

Peplau, L. Anne. (1993). Lesbian and gay relationships. In L. D. Garnets & D. C. Kimmel (Eds.), *Psychological perspectives on lesbian and gay male experience* (pp. 395–419). New York: Columbia University Press.

Peplau, Letitia Anne. (1982). Research on homosexual couples: An overview. *Journal of Homosexuality, 8*(2), 3–8.

Peplau, Letitia Anne, Cochran, Susan, Rook, Karen, & Padesky, Christine. (1978). Loving women: Attachment and autonomy in lesbian relationships. *Journal of Social Issues, 34*(3), 7–27.

Peplau, L. Anne, et al. (1982). Being old and living alone. In L. A. Peplau & D. Perlman (Eds.), *Loneliness.* New York: Wiley.

Peplau, L. Anne, & Conrad, Eva. (1989). Beyond nonsexist research: The perils of feminist methods in psychology. *Psychology of Women Quarterly, 13,* 381–402.

Perlman, D., et al. (1978). Loneliness among senior citizens: An empirical report. *Essence, 2*(4), 239–248.

Perry, J. D., & Whipple, Beverly. (1981). Pelvic muscle strength of female ejaculators: Evidence in support of a new theory of orgasm. *Journal of Sex Research, 17,* 22–39.

Peterson, John, & Bakeman, Roger. (1988). The epidemiology of adult minority AIDS. *Multicultural Inquiry and Research on AIDS, 2*(1), 1–2.

Peterson, Rolf A. (1983). Attitudes toward the childless spouse. *Sex Roles, 9,* 321–332.

Pettigrew, Thomas. (1964). *A profile of the Negro American.* Princeton, NJ: Van Nostrand.

Phares, Vicky, & Compas, Bruce E. (1992). The role of fathers in child and adolescent psychopathology: Make room for daddy. *Psychological Bulletin, 111,* 387–412.

Pharr, Suzanne. (1988). *Homophobia, a weapon of sexism.* Iverness, CA: Chardon Press.

Pheterson, G. I., Kiesler, S. B., & Goldberg, P. A. (1971). Evaluation of the performance of women as a function of their sex, achievement, and personal history. *Journal of Personality and Social Psychology, 19,* 114–118.

Phillips, Leslie. (1977, September 9). For women, sexual harassment is an occupational hazard. *Boston Globe.*

Phinney, Jean S., & Rotheram, Mary Jane. (Eds.). (1987). *Children's ethnic socialization.* Newbury Park, CA: Sage.

Phoenix, C. H., Goy, R. W., Gerall, A. A., & Young, W. C. (1959). Organizing action of prenatally administered testosterone propionate on the tissues mediating mating behavior in the female guinea pig. *Endocrinology, 65,* 369–382.

Piaget, J. (1954). *The construction of reality in the child.* New York: Basic Books.

Pizzey, Erin. (1974). *Scream quietly or the neighbors will hear.* London: If Books.

Pleck, Joseph H. (1975). Masculinity-femininity: Current and alternate paradigms. *Sex Roles, 1,* 161–178.

Pleck, Joseph H. (1981). *The myth of masculinity.* Cambridge, MA: MIT Press.

Pleck, Joseph H. (1983). Husbands' paid work and family roles: Current research issues. In H. Lopata & J. Pleck (Eds.), *Research in the interweave of social roles, Vol. 3: Families and Jobs.* Greenwich, CT: JAI Press.

Pleck, Joseph H. (1992). Families and work: Small changes with big implications. *Qualitative Sociology, 15,* 427–432.

Pope, Kenneth S., Levenson, H., & Schover, L. R. (1979). Sexual intimacy in psychology training: Results and implications of a national survey. *American Psychologist, 34,* 682–689.

Porter, Natalie P., Geis, Florence L., & Walstedt, Joyce J. (1978). *Are women invisible as leaders? Paper presented at American Psychological Association Meetings, Toronto, August.*

Powell, Barbara. (1977). The empty nest, employment, and psychiatric symptoms in college-educated women. *Psychology of Women Quarterly, 2,* 35–43.

Prange, A. J., & Vitols, M. M. (1962). Cultural aspects of the relatively low incidence of depression in southern Negroes. *International Journal of Social Psychiatry, 8,* 104–112.

Profet, Margie. (1993). Menstruation as a defense against pathogens transported by sperm. *Quarterly Review of Biology, 68,* 335–381.

Psathas, G. (1968). Toward a theory of occupational choice for women. *Sociology and Social Research, 52,* 253–265.

Pugliesi, Karen. (1992). *The social construction of premenstrual syndrome: Explaining problematic emotion.* Paper presented at the American Sociological Association meetings, Pittsburgh.

Rabinowitz, Vita C., & Sechzer, Jeri A. (1993). Feminist perspectives on research methods. In F. L. Denmark & M. A. Paludi (Eds.), *Psychology of women: Handbook of issues and theories.* Westport, CT: Greenwood.

Radloff, Lenore. (1975). Sex differences in depression: The effects of occupation and marital status. *Sex Roles, 1,* 249–265.

Radloff, Lenore G., & Monroe, Megan K. (1978). Sex differences in helplessness—with implication for depression. In L. H. Hansen & R. S. Rapoza (Eds.), *Career development and counseling of women.* Springfield, IL: Charles C Thomas.

Radlove, Shirley. (1983). Sexual response and gender roles. In E. R. Allgeier & N. B. McCormick (Eds.), *Changing boundaries: Gender roles and sexual behavior.* Palto Alto, CA: Mayfield.

Ragan, Janet H. (1982). Gender displays in photographs. *Sex Roles, 8,* 33–44.

Ramey, Estelle. (1972). Men's cycles. *Ms.,* Spring, 8–14.

Rawlings, Edna I., & Carter, Dianne K. (1977). Feminist and nonsexist psychotherapy. In E. I. Rawlings & D. Carter (Eds.), *Psychotherapy for women.* Springfield, IL: Charles C Thomas

Rebecca, Meda, Hefner, Robert, & Oleshansky, Barbara. (1976). A model of sex-role transcendance. *Journal of Social Issues, 32*(3), 197–206.

Rebelsky, Freda, & Hanks, C. (1971). Fathers' verbal interaction with infants in the first three months of life. *Child Development, 42,* 63–68.

Reid, Pamela T. (1993). Poor women in psychological research: Shut up and shut out. *Psychology of Women Quarterly, 17,* 133–150.

Reid, Pamela T., & Paludi, Michele A. (1993). Developmental psychology of women: Conception to adolescence. In F. L. Denmark & M. A. Paludi (Eds.), *Psychology of women: Handbook of issues and theories.* Westport, CT: Greenwood.

Reid, Pamela T., & Trotter, Katherine H. (1993). Children's self-presentations with infants: Gender and ethnic comparisons. *Sex Roles, 29,* 171–182.

Reinharz, Shulamit. (1992). *Feminist methods in social research*. New York: Oxford University Press.

Reinisch, June M. (1974). Fetal hormones, the brain, and human sex differences: A heuristic, integrative review of the literature. *Archives of Sexual Behavior, 3,* 51–90.

Reinisch, June M. (1981). Prenatal exposure to synthetic progestins increases potential for aggression in humans. *Science, 211,* 1171–1173.

Repetti, Rena L., Matthews, Karen A., & Waldron, Ingrid. (1989). Employment and women's health. *American Psychologist, 44,* 1394–1401.

Resnick, Patricia, et al. (1981). Social adjustment of victims of sexual assault. *Journal of Consulting and Clinical Psychology, 49,* 705–712.

Resick, Patricia. (1983). The rape reaction: Research findings and implications for intervention. *The Behavior Therapist, 6,* 129–132.

Resick, Patricia A. (1987). Psychological effects of victimization: Implications for the criminal justice system. *Crime and Delinquency, 33,* 468–478.

Reskin, Barbara F. (1988). Occupational resegregation. In S. Rix (Ed.), *The American woman 1988–89.* New York: Norton.

Reskin, Barbara F., & Hartmann, Heidi I. (Eds.). (1986). *Women's work, men's work: Sex segregation on the job.* Washington, DC: National Academy Press.

Resnick, S. M., Berenbaum, Sheri A., Gottesman, Irving I., & Bouchard, Thomas J. (1986). Early hormonal influences on cognitive functioning in congenital adrenal hyperplasia. *Developmental Psychology, 22,* 191–198.

Rich, Adrienne. (1980). Compulsory heterosexuality and lesbian existence. *Signs, 5,* 631–660.

Rix, Sara E. (Ed.). (1988). *The American woman 1988–89.* New York: Norton.

Rix, Sara E. (Ed.). (1990). *The American woman, 1990–91.* New York: Norton.

Roberts, Shauna S. (1990, Jan.–Feb.). Koop's aborted report. *The Journal of NIH Research. 2,* 28.

Robins, Lee N., et al. (1984). Lifetime prevalence of specific psychiatric disorders in three sites. *Archives of General Psychiatry, 41,* 949–958.

Robinson, Ira, Ziss, Ken, Ganza, Bill, Katz, Stuart, & Robinson, Edward. (1991). Twenty years of the Sexual Revolution, 1965–1985. *Journal of Marriage and the Family, 53,* 216–220.

Robinson-Staveley, Kris, & Cooper, Joel. (1990). Mere presence, gender, and reactions to computers: Studying human-computer interaction in the social context. *Journal of Experimental Social Psychology, 26,* 168–183.

Rodin, Judith, Silberstein, L. R., & Striegel-Moore, R. H. (1985). Women and weight: A normative discontent. In T. B. Sonderegger (Ed.), *Psychology and gender: Nebraska Symposium on Motivation* (pp. 267–307). Lincoln: University of Nebraska Press.

Rodin, Mari. (1992). The social construction of premenstrual syndrome. *Social Science and Medicine, 35,* 49–56.

Rogers, Lesley, & Walsh, Joan. (1982). Shortcomings of the psychomedical research of John Money and co-workers into sex differences in behavior. *Sex Roles, 8,* 269–282.

Root, Maria P. P. (1990). Disordered eating in women of color. *Sex Roles, 22,* 525–536.

Rosaldo, Michelle Z. (1974). Women, culture, and society: A theoretical overview. In M. Z. Rosaldo & L. Lamphere (Eds.), *Woman, culture, and society.* Stanford: Stanford University Press.

Rosen, D. H. (1974). *Lesbianism: A study of female homosexuality.* Springfield, IL: Charles C Thomas.

Rosen, Raymond C., & Leiblum, Sandra R. (1987). Current approaches to the evaluation of sexual desire disorders. *Journal of Sex Research, 23,* 141–162.

Rosenberg, Florence R., & Simmons, Roberta G. (1975). Sex differences in the self-concept in adolescence. *Sex Roles, 1,* 147–159.

Rosenberg, Morris. (1965). *Society and the adolescent self-image.* Princeton, NJ: Princeton University Press.

Rosenkrantz, P. S., et al. (1968). Sex-role stereotypes and self-concepts in college students. *Journal of Consulting and Clinical Psychology, 32,* 287–295.

Rosenthal, Robert. (1966). *Experimenter effects in behavioral research.* New York: Appleton-Century-Crofts.

Rosnow, Ralph L. (1981). *Paradigms in transition: The methodology of social inquiry.* New York: Oxford University Press.

Ross, C. W., & Mirowsky, J. (1988). Child care and emotional adjustment to wives' employment. *Journal of Health and Social Behavior, 29,* 127–138.

Rothbaum, B. O., Foa, E. D., Riggs, D. S., Murdock, T., & Walsh, W. (1992). A prospective examination of post-traumatic stress disorder in rape victims. *Journal of Traumatic Stress, 5,* 455–475.

Rothblum, Esther D. (1993). Personal communication.

Rothblum, Esther D., & Brehony, Kathleen A. (1993). *Boston marriages.* Amherest: University of Massachusetts Press.

Rothenberg, Paula S. (1992). *Race, class, and gender in the United States.* New York: St. Martin's Press.

Rotundo, E. Anthony. (1993). *American manhood: Transformations in masculinity from the Revolution to the modern era.* New York: Basic Books.

Roy, Maria. (Ed.). (1977a). *Battered women.* New York: Van Nostrand.

Roy, Maria (1977b). A current survey of 150 cases. In M. Roy (Ed.), *Battered women.* New York: Van Nostrand.

Rozée, Patricia D. (1993). Forbidden or forgiven? Rape in cross-cultural perspective. *Psychology of Women Quarterly, 17,* 499–514.

Ruan, Fang Fu, & Bullough, Vern L. (1992). Lesbianism in China. *Archives of Sexual Behavior, 21,* 217–226.

Rubin, Lillian. (1979). *Women of a certain age.* New York: Harper & Row.

Rubin, Robert T., Reinisch, June M., & Haskett, R. F. (1981). Postnatal gonadal steroid effects on human behavior. *Science, 211,* 1318–1324.

Ruble, Diane N. (1977). Premenstrual symptoms: A reinterpretation. *Science, 197,* 291–292.

Ruble, Diane N., Greulich, F., Pomerantz, E. M., & Gochberg, B. (1993). The role of gender-related process in the development of gender differences in self-evaluation and depression. *Journal of Affective Disorders, 29,* 97–128.

Ruble, Thomas L. (1983). Sex stereotypes: Issues of change in the 1970s. *Sex Roles, 9,* 397–402.

Rumenick, Donna K., Capasso, Deborah R., & Hendrick, C. (1977). Experimenter sex effects in behavioral research. *Psychological Bulletin, 84,* 852–887.

Rushton, J. Philippe. (1992). Cranial capacity related to sex, rank, and race in a stratified random sample of 6,325 U.S. military personnel. *Intelligence, 16,* 401–413.

Russell, Diana. (1975). *The politics of rape: The victim's perspective.* New York: Stein and Day.

Russell, Diana. (1982). *Rape in marriage.* New York: Macmillan.

Russell, Diana E. H., & Howell, Nancy. (1983). The prevalence of rape in the United States revisited. *Signs, 8,* 688–695.

Russo, Nancy F. (1979). Overview: Sex roles, fertility, and the motherhood mandate. *Psychology of Women Quarterly, 4,* 7–15.

Russo, Nancy F. (1990). Overview: Forging research priorities for women's mental health. *American Psychologist, 45,* 368–373.

Russo, Nancy F., Amaro, Hortensia, & Winter, M. (1987). The use of inpatient mental health services by Hispanic women. *Psychology of Women Quarterly, 11,* 427–442.

Russo, Nancy F., & Green, Beth L. (1993). Women and mental health. In F. L. Denmark & M. A. Paludi (Eds.), *Psychology of women: Handbook of issues and theories.* Westport, CT; Greenwood.

Russo, Nancy F., Horn, Jody D., & Schwartz, Robert. (1992). U.S. abortion in context: Selected characteristics and motivations of women seeking abortions. *Journal of Social Issues, 48*(3), 183–202.

Russo, Nancy Felipe, & O'Connell, Agnes N. (1980). Models from our past: Psychology's foremothers. *Psychology of Women Quarterly, 5,* 11–54.

Russo, Nancy F., & Sobel, S. B. (1981). Sex differences in the utilization of mental health facilities. *Professional Psychology, 12,* 7–19.

Ruth, Sheila. (Ed.). (1990). *Issues in feminism: An introduction to women's studies* (2nd ed.). Mountain View, CA: Mayfield.

Sabo, Don. (1992). Pigskin, patriarchy, and pain. In M. S. Kimmel & M. A. Messner (Eds.), *Men's lives.* New York: Macmillan.

Sadker, Myra, & Sadker, David. (1985, March). Sexism in the schoolroom of the '80s. *Psychology Today, 19,* 54–57.

Saenz, Rogelio, Goudy, W. J., & Lorenz, F. O. (1989). The effects of employment and marital relations on depression among Mexican American women. *Journal of Marriage and the Family, 51,* 239–251.

Safran, C. (1976, November). What men do to women on the job: A shocking look at sexual harassment. *Redbook,* p. 148.

Safran, C. (1981, March). Sexual harassment: The view from the top. *Redbook.*

Sagarin, E. (1977). Incest: Problems of definition and frequency. *Journal of Sex Research, 13,* 126–135.

Saghir, M., & Robins, E. (1973). *Male and female homosexuality.* Baltimore: Williams & Wilkins.

St. Lawrence, Janet S., & Joyner, Doris J. (1991). The effects of sexually violent rock music on males' acceptance of violence against women. *Psychology of Women Quarterly, 15,* 49–63.

Salgado de Snyder, V. Nelly, Cervantes, Richard C., & Padilla, Amado M. (1990). Gender and ethnic differences in psychosocial stress and generalized distress among Hispanics. *Sex Roles, 22,* 441–454.

Salhanick, H. A., & Margulis, R. H. (1968). Hormonal physiology of the ovary. In J. J. Gold (Ed.), *Textbook of gynecologic endocrinology.* New York: Harper & Row.

Sanday, Peggy R. (1981). The socio-cultural context of rape: A cross-cultural study. *Journal of Social Issues, 37,* 5–27.

Sanday, Peggy R. (1988). The reproduction of patriarchy in feminist anthropology. In M. M. Gergen (Ed.), *Feminist thought and the structure of knowledge.* New York: New York University Press.

Sanday, Peggy R. (1990). *Fraternity gang rape.* New York: New York University Press.

Sanders, Cheryl J. (1988). Ethics and the educational achievements of Black women. *Religion and Intellectual Life, 5*(4), 7–16.

Sayers, Dorothy. (1946). *Unpopular opinions.* London: Victor Gollancz.

Sayers, Janet. (1991). *Mothers of psychoanalysis.* New York: Norton.

Sayre, Anne. (1978). *Rosalind Franklin and DNA.* New York: Norton.

Schafer, Siegrid. (1977). Sociosexual behavior in male and female homosexuals: A study in sex differences. *Archives of Sexual Behavior, 6,* 355–364.

Schmidt, Gunter, & Sigusch, V. (1970). Sex differences in responses to psychosexual stimulation by films and slides. *Journal of Sex Research, 6,* 268–283.

Schulz, Muriel R. (1975). The semantic derogation of woman. In B. Thorne & N. Henley (Eds.), *Language and sex: Difference and dominance.* Rowley, MA: Newbury-House.

Searles, P., & Berger, R. J. (1987). The current status of rape reform legislation: An examination of state statutes. *Women's Rights Law Reporter, 10,* 25–43.

Sears, Robert R., Maccoby, Eleanor E., & Levin, H. (1965). *Patterns of child rearing.* New York: Harper & Row.

Seavy, Carol A., Katz, Phyllis A. & Zalk, Sue R. (1975). Baby X: The effects of gender labels on adult responses to infants. *Sex Roles, 1,* 103–110.

Seegmiller, Bonnie. (1993). Pregnancy. In F. L. Denmark & M. A. Paludi (Eds.), *Psychology of women: Handbook of issues and theories.* Westport, CT: Greenwood.

Segura, Denise A., & Pierce, Jennifer L. (1993). Chicana/o family structure and gender personality: Chodorow, familism, and psychoanalytic sociology revisited. *Signs, 19,* 62–91.

Seligman, Martin E. P. (1975). *Helplessness: On depression, development and death.* San Francisco: Freeman.

Serbin, Lisa A., et al. (1973). A comparison of teacher response to the preacademic and problem behavior of boys and girls. *Child Development, 44,* 796–804.

Serbin, Lisa A., Connor, Jane M., & Iler, Iris. (1979). Sex-stereotyped and nonstereotyped introductions of new toys in the preschool classroom: An observational study of teacher behavior and its effects. *Psychology of Women Quarterly, 4,* 261–265.

Shachar, Sandra A., & Gilbert, Lucia A. (1983). Working lesbians: Role conflicts and coping strategies. *Psychology of Women Quarterly, 7,* 244–256.

Shainess, Natalie. (1977). The equitable therapy of women in psychoanalysis. In E. I. Rawlings & D. K. Carter (Eds.), *Psychotherapy for women.* Springfield, IL: Charles C Thomas.

Shanor, Karen. (1978). *The sexual sensitivity of the American male.* New York: Ballantine.

Shaver, Phillip. (1976). Questions concerning fear of success and its conceptual relatives. *Sex Roles, 2,* 305–320.

Shaw, L. B. (1984). Retirement plans of middle-aged married women. *Gerontologist, 24,* 154–159.

Shelton, Beth A., & John, Daphne. (1993). Ethnicity, race, and difference: A comparison of white, Black, and Hispanic men's household labor time. In J. C. Hood (Ed.), *Men, work, and family* (pp. 131–150). Newbury Park, CA: Sage.

Sherfey, Mary Jane. (1966). The evolution and nature of female sexuality in relation to psychoanalytic theory. *Journal of the American Psychoanalytic Association, 14,* 28–128.

Sherman, Julia A. (1971). *On the psychology of women: A survey of empirical studies.* Springfield, IL: Charles C Thomas.

Sherman, Julia A. (1978). *Sex-related cognitive differences.* Springfield, IL: Charles C Thomas.

Sherman, Julia A. (1982). Mathematics, the critical filter: A look at some residues. *Psychology of Women Quarterly, 6,* 428–444.

Sherwin, Barbara B. (1991). The psychoendocrinology of aging and female sexuality. *Annual Review of Sex Research, 2,* 181–198.

Shields, Stephanie A. (1975). Functionalism, Darwinism, and the psychology of women: A study in social myth. *American Psychologist, 30,* 739–754.

Shields, Stephanie A., & Cooper, Pamela E. (1983). Stereotypes of traditional and nontraditional childbearing roles. *Sex Roles, 9,* 363–376.

Shilts, Randy. (1993). *Conduct unbecoming: Lesbians and gays in the U.S. military, Vietnam to the Persian Gulf.* New York: St. Martin's Press.

Shusterman, Lisa R. (1979). Predicting the psychological consequences of abortion. *Social Science and Medicine, 13,* 683–689.

Shuy, Roger W. (1969). Sex as a factor in sociolinguistic research. Paper presented at the Anthropological Society of Washington. (Available from Educational Resources Information Clearinghouse, no. ED027522.)

Siegel, A., Stolz, L., Hitchock, E., & Adamson, J. (1963). Dependence and independence in children. In F. Nye & L. Hoffman (Eds.), *The employed mother in America.* Chicago: Rand McNally.

Siegel, J. S. (1978). *Prospective trends in the size and structure of the elderly population, impact of mortality trends, and some implications.* U.S. Bureau of the Census, Current Population Reports (Special Studies Series P-23, no. 59, 2nd printing, rev.). Washington: U.S. Government Printing Office.

Simon, J. G., & Feather, N. T. (1973). Causal attributions for success and failure at university examinations. *Journal of Educational Psychology, 64,* 45–56.

Simon, R., & Fleiss, J. (1973). Depression and schizophrenia in hospitalized patients. *Archives of General Psychiatry, 28,* 509–512.

Simonds, Wendy. (1992). *Women and self-help culture.* New Brunswick, NJ: Rutgers University Press.

Slater, Philip E. (1973, December). Sexual adequacy in America. *Intellectual Digest,* 132–135.

Smith, Howard L., & Grenier, Mary. (1982). Sources of organizational power for women: Overcoming structural obstacles. *Sex Roles, 8,* 733–746.

Smith-Lovin, L., & Brody, C. (1989). Interruptions in group discussions: The effects of gender and group composition. *American Sociological Review, 54,* 424–435.

Snodgrass, Sara E. (1992). Further effects of role versus gender on interpersonal sensitivity. *Journal of Personality and Social Psychology, 62,* 154–158.

Sohn, David. (1982). Sex differences in achievement self-attributions: An effect-size analysis. *Sex Roles, 8,* 345–357.

Sommer, Barbara. (1973). The effect of menstruation on cognitive and perceptual motor behavior: A review. *Psychosomatic Medicine, 35,* 515–535.

Sontag, Susan. (1979). The double standard of aging. In J. H. Williams (Ed.), *Psychology of women: Selected readings.* New York: Norton.

Sorenson, Susan, & Telles, Cynthia. (1991). Self-reports of spousal violence in a Mexican American and non-Hispanic white population. *Violence & Victims, 6*(1), 3–15.

Spelman, Elizabeth V. (1988). *Inessential woman: Problems of exclusion in feminist thought.* Boston: Beacon Press.

Spence, Janet T., & Helmreich, Robert L. (1978). *Masculinity and femininity.* Austin: University of Texas Press.

Spence, Janet T., & Helmreich, Robert L. (1980). Masculine instrumentality and feminine expressiveness: Their relationships with sex-role attitudes and behaviors. *Psychology of Women Quarterly, 5,* 147–163.

Spence, Janet T., & Helmreich, Robert L. (1981). Androgyny versus gender schema: A comment on Bem's gender schema theory. *Psychological Review, 88,* 365–368.

Spence, Janet T., Helmreich, Robert L., & Stapp, Joy. (1975). Ratings of self and peers on sex-role attributes and their relation to self-esteem and conceptions of masculinity and femininity. *Journal of Personality and Social Psychology, 32,* 29–39.

Spivack, G., & Spotts, J. (1965). The Devereux Child Behavior Scale: Symptoms behaviors in latency age children. *American Journal of Mental Retardation, 67,* 839–853.

Sprecher, Susan, McKinney, Kathleen, & Orbuch, Terri L. (1987). Has the double standard disappeared? An experimental test. *Social Psychology Quarterly, 50,* 24–31.

Spreitzer, Elmer, & Riley, Lawrence. (1974). Factors associated with singlehood. *Journal of Marriage and the Family, 36,* 533–542.

Spreitzer, Elmer, Snyder, Eldon E., & Larson, D. (1975). Age, marital status, and labor force participation as related to life satisfaction. *Sex Roles, 1,* 235–247.

Srebnik, Debra S., & Saltzberg, Elayne A. (1994). Feminist cognitive-behavioral therapy for negative body image. *Women & Therapy, 15,* 117–133.

Stafford, R. (1961). Sex differences in spatial visualization as evidence of sex-linked inheritance. *Perceptual and Motor Skills, 13,* 428.

Staples, Robert. (1978). Masculinity and race: The dual dilemma of black men. *Journal of Social Issues, 34*(1), 169–183.

Stark, Evan, & Flitcraft, Ann. (1987). Violence among intimates: An epidemiological review. In V. N. Haslett et al. (Eds.), *Handbook of family violence.* New York: Plenum.

Steiger, John C. (1981). The influence of the feminist subculture in changing sex-role attitudes. *Sex Roles, 7,* 627–634.

Stein, Aletha H., & Bailey, Margaret M. (1973). The socialization of achievement orientation in females. *Psychological Bulletin, 80,* 345–366.

Stein, L. S., et al. (1976). A comparison of female and male neurotic depressives. *Journal of Clinical Psychology, 32,* 19–21.

Stein, P. J., & Hoffman, Steven. (1978). Sports and male role strain. *Journal of Social Issues, 34*(1), 136–150.

Steinmetz, Suzanne K. (1977). Wifebeating, husband beating—A comparison of the use of physical violence between spouses to resolve marital rights. In M. Roy (Ed.), *Battered women.* New York: Van Nostrand.

Stephens, W. N. (1961). A cross-cultural study of menstrual taboos. *Genetic Psychology Monographs, 64,* 385–416.

Stern, Marilyn, & Karraker, Katherine H. (1989). Sex stereotyping of infants: A review of gender labeling studies. *Sex Roles, 20,* 501–522.

Stevenson, Michael R., & Black, Kathryn N. (1988). Paternal absence and sex-role development: A meta-analysis. *Child Development, 59,* 793–814.

Stewart, Abigail J., & Chester, N. L. (1982). The exploration of sex differences in human social motives: Achievement, affiliation, and power. In A. J. Stewart (Ed.), *Motivation and society* (pp. 172–218). San Francisco: Jossey-Bass.

Storms, Michael D. (1981). A theory of erotic orientation development. *Psychological Review, 88,* 340–353.

Storms, Michael D., et al. (1981). Sexual scripts for women. *Sex Roles, 7,* 699–708.

Straus, Murray A. (1978). Wife beating: How common and why? *Victimology, 2,* 443–458.

Straus, Murray A. (1980). Wife beating: How common and why? In M. A. Straus and G. T. Hotaling (Eds.), *The social causes of husband-wife vio-*

lence. Minneapolis: University of Minnesota Press.

Straus, Murray A., & Gelles, Richard J. (1990). *Physical violence in American families.* New Brunswick NJ: Transaction.

Straus, Murray A., Gelles, R. J., & Steinmetz, S. K. (1980). *Behind closed doors: Violence in the American family.* Garden City, NY: Anchor/Doubleday.

Stricker, G. (1977). Implications of research for psychotherapeutic treatment of women. *American Psychologist, 32,* 14–22.

Strickland, Bonnie R. (1988). Sex-related differences in health and illness. *Psychology of Women Quarterly, 12,* 381–399.

Striegel-Moore, Ruth H., Silberstein, Lisa R., & Rodin, Judith. (1986). Toward an understanding of risk factors in bulimia. *American Psychologist, 41,* 246–263.

Strodtbeck, F. L., James, Rita M., & Hawkins, C. (1957). Social status in jury deliberations. *American Sociological Review, 22,* 713–719.

Stroebe, Margaret S., & Stroebe, W. (1983). Who suffers more? Sex differences in health risks of the widowed. *Psychological Bulletin, 93,* 279–301.

Struckman-Johnson, Cindy, & Struckman-Johnson, David. (1993). College men's and women's reactions to hypothetical sexual touch varied by initiator gender and coercion level. *Sex Roles, 29,* 371–385.

Sue, Stanley. (1977). Community mental health services to minority groups: Some optimism, some pessimism. *American Psychologist, 32,* 616–624.

Sue, Stanley, & Morishima, J. (1982). *The mental health of Asian Americans: Contemporary issues in identifying and treating mental problems.* San Francisco: Jossey-Bass.

Summers, Russel J. (1991). Determinants of judgments of and responses to a complaint of sexual harassment. *Sex Roles, 25,* 379–392.

Sutherland, H., & Stewart, I. (1965). A critical analysis of the premenstrual syndrome. *Lancet, 1,* 1180–1183.

Sutton-Smith, B., & Rosenberg, B. G. (1970). *The sibling.* New York: Holt, Rinehart & Winston.

Svarstad, Bonnie L., et al. (1987). Gender differences in the acquisition of prescribed drugs: An epidemiological study. *Medical Care, 25,* 1089–1098.

Swacker, Marjorie. (1975). The sex of the speaker as a sociolinguistic variable. In B. Thorne & N. Henley (Eds.), *Language and sex: Difference and dominance.* Rowley, MA: Newbury House.

Swim, Janet K. (1994). Perceived versus meta-analytic effect sizes: An assessment of the accuracy of gender stereotypes. *Journal of Personality and Social Psychology, 66,* 21–36.

Swim, Janet, Borgida, E., Maruyama, G., & Myers, D. G. (1989). Joan McKay versus John McKay: Do gender stereotypes bias evaluations? *Psychological Bulletin, 105,* 409–429.

Szasz, Thomas S. (1965). Legal and moral aspects of homosexuality. In J. Marmor (Ed.), *Sexual inversion: The multiple roots of homosexuality.* New York: Basic Books.

Taleisnik, S., Caligaris, L., & Astrada, I. I. (1971). Sex differences in hypothalamo-hypophysial functions. In C. H. Sawyer & R. A. Gorski (Eds.), *Steroid hormones and brain function.* Berkeley: University of California Press.

Tamir, Lois M. (1982). *Men in their forties: The transition to middle age.* New York: Springer.

Tangri, Sandra, Burt, M. R., & Johnson, L. B. (1982). Sexual harassment at work: Three explanatory models. *Journal of Social Issues, 38*(4), 33–54.

Tannen, Deborah. (1991). *You just don't understand: Women and men in conversation.* New York: Ballantine.

Tannen, Deborah. (1994). *Talking from 9 to 5: How women's and men's conversational styles affect who gets ahead, who gets credit, and what gets done at work.* New York: Morrow.

Task Force on the Glass Ceiling Initiative. (1993). *Report of the Governor's Task Force on the Glass Ceiling Initiative.* Madison, WI: State of Wisconsin.

Tavris, Carol. (1992). *The mismeasure of woman.* New York: Simon & Schuster.

Taylor, Jerome, & Jackson, Beryl B. (1991). Evaluation of a holistic model of mental health symptoms in African American women. *The Journal of Black Psychology, 18,* 19–45.

Taylor, Marylee C., & Hall, Judith A. (1982). Psychological androgyny: Theories, methods, and conclusions. *Psychological Bulletin, 92,* 347–366.

Taylor, R. (1976). Psychosocial development of black youth. *Journal of Black Studies, 6,* 353–372.

Terman, Lewis M., & Oden, Melita H. (1947). *The gifted child grows up.* Stanford, CA: Stanford University Press.

Terman, Lewis, & Miles, C. (1936). *Sex and personality.* New York: McGraw-Hill.

Thomas, A., & Sillen, S. (1972). *Racism and Psychiatry.* Secaucus, NJ: Citadel.

Thomas, Jerry K., & French, Karen E. (1985). Gender differences across age in motor performance: A meta-analysis. *Psychological Bulletin, 98,* 260–282.

Thompson, Janice L. (1991). Exploring gender and culture with Khmer refugee women: Reflections on participatory feminist research. *Advances in Nursing Science, 13,* 30–48.

Thorne, Barrie, & Henley, Nancy. (1975). Difference and dominance: An overview of language, gender, and society. In B. Thorne & N. Henley (Eds.), *Language and sex: Difference and dominance.* Rowley, MA: Newbury House.

Tiefer, Lenore. (1991). Historical, scientific, clinical, and feminist criticisms of "The Human Sexual Response Cycle" model. *Annual Review of Sex Research, 2,* 1–24.

Tong, Rosemarie. (1989). *Feminist thought: A comprehensive introduction.* Boulder, CO: Westview.

Torres, Sara. (1991). A comparison of wife abuse between two cultures: Perceptions, attitudes, nature, and extent. *Issues in Mental Health Nursing, 12,* 113–131.

Touchette, Nancy. (1991, July). HIV-1 link prompts circumspection on circumcision. *Journal of NIH Research, 3,* 44–46.

Travis, Cheryl B. (1988a). *Women and health psychology: Biomedical issues.* Hillsdale, NJ: Lawrence Erlbaum.

Travis, Cheryl B. (1988b). *Women and health psychology: Mental health issues.* Hillsdale, NJ: Lawrence Erlbaum.

Travis, Cheryl B. (1993). Women and health. In F. L. Denmark & M. A. Paludi (Eds.), *Psychology of women: Handbook of issues and theories.* Westport, CT: Greenwood.

Tresemer, David. (1974). Fear of success: Popular, but unproven. *Psychology Today, 7*(10), 82.

Trivers, R. L. (1972). Parental investment and sexual selection. In B. Campbell (Ed.), *Sexual selection and the descent of man.* Chicago: Aldine.

True, Reiko Homma. (1990). Psychotherapeutic issues with Asian American women. *Sex Roles, 22,* 477–486.

Tsai, Mavis, Feldman-Summers, S., & Edgar, M. (1979). Childhood molestation: Variables related to differential impacts on psychological functioning in adult women. *Journal of Abnormal Psychology, 88,* 407–417.

Tsai, Mavis, & Uemura, Anne. (1988). Asian Americans: The struggles, the conflicts, and the successes. In P. Bronstein & K. Quina (Eds.), *Teaching a psychology of people* (pp. 125–133).

Washington, DC: American Psychological Association.

Tsai, Mavis, & Wagner, N. (1978). Therapy groups for women sexually molested as children. *Archives of Sexual Behavior, 7,* 417–428.

Turner, Barbara F. (1982). Sex-related differences in aging. In B. B. Wolman (Ed.), *Handbook of developmental psychology.* Englewood Cliffs, NJ: Prentice-Hall.

Tyler, B. B. (1958). Expectancy for eventual success as a factor in problem-solving behavior. *Journal of Educational Psychology, 49,* 166–172.

Tyler, F. B., Sussewell, D. R., & Williams-McCoy, J. (1985). Ethnic validity in psychotherapy. *Psychotherapy, 22,* 311–320.

Tyler, Leona E. (1965). *The psychology of human differences.* New York: Appleton-Century-Crofts.

Udry, J. Richard, & Eckland, Bruce K. (1984). Benefits of being attractive: Differential payoffs for men and women. *Psychological Reports, 54,* 47–56.

Ullian, Dorothy Z. (1976). The development of conceptions of masculinity and femininity. In B. Lloyd & J. Archer (Eds.), *Exploring sex differences.* New York: Academic Press.

Ullrich, H. E. (1992). Menstrual taboos among Havik Brahmin women: A study of ritual change. *Sex Roles, 26,* 19–40.

Unger, Rhoda. (1979). Toward a redefinition of sex and gender. *American Psychologist, 34,* 1085–1094.

U.S. Bureau of the Census. (1990a). Marital status and living arrangements: March 1990. *Current Population Reports,* Series P-20, No. 450.

U.S. Bureau of the Census. (1990b). *Statistical abstract of the United States: 1990* (110th ed.). Washington, DC: U.S. Government Printing Office.

U.S. Bureau of the Census. (1993). *Statistical abstract of the United States* (113th ed.). Washington, DC: U.S. Government Printing Office.

U.S. Bureau of Labor Statistics. (1976, January). *Employment and earnings* (Table 2). Washington, DC: U.S. Government Printing Office.

U.S. Bureau of Labor Statistics. (1990, January). *Employment and earnings* (Table 22). Washington, DC: U.S. Government Printing Office.

U.S. Bureau of Labor Statistics. (1993, January). *Employment and earnings* (Table 22). Washington, DC: U.S. Government Printing Office.

U.S. Department of Justice. (1985). *Report to the nation on crime and justice: The data.* Washington, DC: Author.

U.S. Department of Labor. (1992). *Pipelines of progress: A status report on the glass ceiling.* Washington, DC: U.S. Government Printing Office.

U.S. Department of Labor. (1994, April). *Employment and earnings.* Washington, DC: U.S. Government Printing Office.

U.S. Department of Labor, Women's Bureau. (1988). *20 facts on women workers.* Washington, DC: Author.

U.S. Department of Labor, Women's Bureau. (1993). *Facts on working women.* Washington, DC: Author.

U.S. Merit Systems Protection Board. (1981). *Sexual harassment of federal workers: Is it a problem?* Washington, DC: U.S. Government Printing Office.

U.S. National Center for Health Statistics. (1987). *Vital and health statistics,* series 10.

U.S. Public Health Service, Center for Disease Control. (1976). Comparative risks of three methods of midtrimester abortion. *Morbidity and Mortality Weekly Report,* November 26, 370.

Van den Bergh, Nan. (Ed.). (1991). *Feminist perspectives on addictions.* New York: Springer.

Vasquez, Melba J. T., & Baron, Augustine. (1988). The psychology of the Chicano experience: A sample course structure. In P. Bronstein & K. Quina

(Eds.), *Teaching a psychology of people*. Washington, DC: American Psychological Association.

Vazquez-Nuttall, Ena, Romero-Garcia, I., & DeLeon, B. (1987). Sex roles and perceptions of femininity and masculinity of Hispanic women: A review of the literature. *Psychology of Women Quarterly, 11,* 409–426.

Veronesi, Umberto, et al. (1981). Comparing radical mastectomy with quadrantectomy, axillary dissection, and radiotherapy in patients with small cancers of the breast. *New England Journal of Medicine, 305,* 6–11.

Voydanoff, Patricia, & Donnelly, Brenda W. (1989). Work and family roles and psychological distress. *Journal of Marriage and the Family, 51,* 923–932.

Waldron, J. (1976). Why do women live longer than men? *Social Science and Medicine, 10,* 349–362.

Waldron, J., & Johnston, S. (1976). Why do women live longer than men? *Journal of Human Stress, 2,* 19–29.

Walfish, S., & Myerson, Marilyn. (1980). Sex role identity and attitudes toward sexuality. *Archives of Sexual Behavior, 9,* 199–204.

Walker, Lawrence J. (1984). Sex differences in the development of moral reasoning: A critical review. *Child Development, 55,* 677–691.

Walker, Lenore E. (1980). Battered women. In A. Brodsky & R. Hare-Mustin (Eds.), *Women and psychotherapy*. New York: Guilford.

Walker, Lenore E. (1989). *Terrifying love: Why battered women kill and how society responds*. New York: Harper & Row.

Walker, Lenore E. (1991). Post-traumatic stress disorder in women: Diagnosis and treatment of battered women syndrome. *Psychotherapy, 28,* 1–9.

Wallston, Barbara S. (1981). What are the questions in psychology of women? A feminist approach to research. *Psychology of Women Quarterly, 5,* 597–617.

Walsh, Mary R. (1977). *Doctors wanted: No women need apply*. New Haven: Yale University Press.

Walters, Cathryn, Shurley, J. T., & Parsons, O. A. (1962). Differences in male and female responses to underwater sensory deprivation: An exploratory study. *Journal of Nervous and Mental Diseases, 135,* 302–310.

Warr, M. (1985). Fear of rape among urban women. *Social Problems, 32,* 239–250.

Watzlawick, P. (Ed.). (1984). *The invented reality: Contributions to constructivism*. New York: Norton.

Weinberg, S. K. (1955). *Incest behavior*. New York: Citadel Press.

Weiss, Noel S., et al. (1976). Increasing incidence of endometrial cancer in the United States. *New England Journal of Medicine, 294,* 1259–1261.

Weissman, Myrna M., Bland, Roger, Joyce, Peter R., Newman, Stephen, Wells, J. Elisabeth, & Wittchen, Hans-Ulrich. (1993). Sex differences in rates of depression: Cross-national perspectives. *Journal of Affective Disorders, 29,* 77–84.

Weissman, Myrna M., & Klerman, G. L. (1979). Sex differences and the epidemiology of depression. In E. S. Gomberg & V. Franks (Eds.), *Gender and disordered behavior*. New York: Brunner/Mazel. (Originally in *Archives of General Psychiatry, 1977, 34,* 98–111.)

Weissman, Myrna M., & Klerman, G. L. (1987). Gender and depression. In R. Formanek & A. Gurian (Eds.), *Women and depression: A lifespan perspective* (pp. 3–18). New York: Springer.

Weisstein, Naomi. (1971). Psychology constructs the male, or the fantasy life of the male psychologist. In M. H. Garskof (Ed.), *Roles women play: Readings toward women's liberation*. Belmont, CA: Brooks/Cole.

Weisstein, Naomi. (1982, November). Tired of arguing about biological inferiority? *Ms.,* 41–46.

Weitzman, Lenore J. (1986). *The divorce revolution.* New York: Free Press.

West, Candace, & Zimmerman, D. H. (1983). Small insults: A study of interruptions in cross-sex conversations between unacquainted persons. In B. Thorne, C. Kramarae, & N. Henley (Eds.), *Language, gender, and society* (pp. 102–117). Rowley, MA: Newbury House.

Wetzel, J. W. (1984). *Clinical handbook of depression.* New York: Gardner Press.

Whatley, Mark A. (1993). For better or worse: The case of marital rape. *Violence and Victims, 8,* 29–39.

White, Evelyn C. (Ed.). (1994). *The Black women's health book.* Seattle: Seal Press.

Whitley, Bernard E., McHugh, Maureen C., & Frieze, Irene H. (1986). Assessing the theoretical models for sex differences in causal attributions of success and failure. In J. S. Hyde & M. C. Linn (Ed.), *The psychology of gender: Advances through meta-analysis.* Baltimore: Johns Hopkins University Press.

Whorf, B. L. (1956). *Language, thought, and reality.* Cambridge, MA: MIT Press.

Widiger, T. A., & Settle, S. A. (1987). Broverman et al. revisited: An artifactual sex bias. *Journal of Personality and Social Psychology, 53,* 463–469.

Wilder, Gita, Mackie, Diane, & Cooper, Joel. (1985). Gender and computers: Two surveys of computer-related attitudes. *Sex Roles, 13,* 215–228.

Williams, John E., & Best, Deborah L. (1990). *Measuring sex stereotypes: A multination study* (rev. ed.). Newbury Park, CA: Sage.

Williams, Juanita H. (1983). *Psychology of women* (2nd ed.). New York: Norton.

Williams, Linda M. (1992). Adult memories of childhood abuse: Preliminary findings from a longitudinal study. *The APSAC Advisor, 5,* 19–20.

Williams, Linda M. (1994). Recall of childhood trauma: A prospective study of women's memories of child sexual abuse. *Journal of Consulting and Clinical Psychology, 62,* 1167–1176.

Williams, Martin H. (1992). Exploitation and inference: Mapping the damage from therapist-patient sexual involvement. *American Psychologist, 47,* 412–421.

Williams, Norma. (1988). Role making among married Mexican American women: Issues of class and ethnicity. *Journal of Applied Behavioral Science, 24,* 203–217.

Wilson, Edward O. (1975). *Sociobiology: The new synthesis.* Cambridge, MA: Harvard University Press.

Wilson, Edward O. (1978). *On human nature.* Cambridge, MA: Harvard University Press.

Wilson, J. D., et al. (1984). Recent studies on the endocrine control of male phenotypic development. In M. Serio et al. (Eds.), *Sexual differentiation: Basic and clinical aspects.* New York: Raven.

Wiswell, Thomas, et al. (1987). Declining frequency of circumcision: Implications for changes in the absolute incidence and male to female sex ratio of urinary tract infections in early infancy. *Pediatrics, 79,* 338–342.

Witkin, Herman A. (1964). Origins of cognitive style. In C. Sheerer (Ed.), *Cognition: Theory, research, promise.* New York: Harper & Row.

Witkin, Herman A., Lewis, H. B., Hertzman, M., Machover K., Meissner, P. B., & Wapner, S. (1954). *Personality through perception.* New York: Harper & Row.

Wittig, Michele A. (1979). Genetic influences on sex-related differences in intellectual performance: Theoretical and methodological issues. In M. A.

Wittig & A. C. Peterson (Eds.), *Sex-related differences in cognitive functioning: Developmental issues.* New York: Academic Press.

Wittig, Michele A. (1985). Metatheoretical dilemmas in the psychology of gender. *American Psychologist, 40,* 800–811.

Wittig, Michele A., & Skolnick, Paul. (1978). Status versus warmth as determinants of sex differences in personal space. *Sex Roles, 4,* 493–503.

Wolf, Naomi. (1991). *The beauty myth.* New York: William Morrow.

Wolff, Charlotte. (1971). *Love between women.* New York: Harper & Row.

Wolpe, Joseph, & Lazarus, A. A. (1966). *Behavior therapy techniques: A guide to the treatment of neuroses.* New York: Pergamon Press.

Wood, Julia T. (1994). *Gendered lives: Communication, gender, and culture.* Belmont, CA: Wadsworth.

Woodside, D. Blake, & Garfinkel, Paul E. (1992). Age of onset of eating disorders. *International Journal of Eating Disorders, 12,* 33–36.

Worell, Judith, & Remer, Pam. (1992). *Feminist perspectives in therapy: An empowerment model for women.* New York: Wiley.

Wright, Logan, Schaefer, Arlene B., & Solomons, G. (1979). *Encyclopedia of pediatric psychology.* Baltimore: University Park Press.

Wright, Paul H. (1982). Men's friendships, women's friendships, and the alleged inferiority of the latter. *Sex Roles, 8,* 1–20.

Yen, Wendy M. (1975). Sex-linked major-gene influences on selected types of spatial performance. *Behavior Genetics, 5,* 281–298.

Yllo, Kersti A. (1993). Through a feminist lens: Gender, power, and violence. In R. J. Gelles & D. R. Loseke (Eds.), *Current controversies on family violence* (pp. 47–62). Newbury Park, CA: Sage.

Yoder, Janice D., & Kahn, Arnold S. (1992). Toward a feminist understanding of women and power. *Psychology of Women Quarterly, 16,* 381–388.

Yoder, Janice D., & Kahn, Arnold S. (1993). Working toward an inclusive psychology of women. *American Psychologist, 48,* 846–850.

Young, W. C., Goy, R., & Phoenix, C. (1964). Hormones and sexual behavior. *Science, 143,* 212–218.

Zabin, Laurie S., Hirsch, Marilyn B., & Emerson, Mark R. (1989). When urban adolescents choose abortion: Effects on education, psychological status, and subsequent pregnancy. *Family Planning Perspectives, 21*(6), 248–255.

Zambrana, Ruth. (1988). A research agenda on issues affecting poor and minority women: A model for understanding their health needs. *Women & Health, 12,* 137–160.

Zelnick, Melvin, & Kantner, J. F. (1977). Sexual and contraceptive experiences of young unmarried women in the United States, 1976 and 1971. *Family Planning Perspectives, 9*(2), 55–71.

Zigler, Edward F., & Frank, Meryl. (Eds.). (1988). *The parental leave crisis.* New Haven: Yale University Press.

Zilbergeld, Bernie. (1978). *Male sexuality.* Boston: Little, Brown.

Zilbergeld, Bernie. (1992). *The new male sexuality.* New York: Bantam Books.

Zilbergeld, Bernie, & Ellison, Carol R. (1980). Desire discrepancies and arousal problems in sex therapy. In S. R. Leiblum & L. A. Pervin (Eds.), *Principles and practice of sex therapy.* New York: Guilford Press.

Zilbergeld, Bernie, & Evans, M. (1980, August). The inadequacy of Masters and Johnson. *Psychology Today, 14* (3), 28–43.

Zimmerman, Don H., & West, Candace. (1975). Sex roles, interruptions and silences in conversation. In B. Thorne & N. Henley (Eds.), *Language and sex:*

Difference and dominance. Rowley, MA: Newbury House.

Zimmerman, E., & Parlee, Mary B. (1973). Behavioral changes associated with the menstrual cycle: An experimental investigation. *Journal of*

Applied Social Psychology, 3, 335–344.

Zuckerman, M., & Wheeler, L. (1975). To dispel fantasies about the fantasy-based measure of fear of success. *Psychological Bulletin, 82,* 932–946.

Acknowledgments

pp. 21–22, Nancy Felipe Russo and Agnes N. O'Connell, "Models from Our Past: Psychology's Foremothers," *Psychology of Women Quarterly,* 1980, *5,* 11–54.

pp. 28–29, Abridged from R. Moulton, "A Survey and Re-evaluation of the Concept of Penis Envy," *Contemporary Psychoanalysis, 7* (1970), pp. 84–104. Used with permission.

p. 89, Swim (1994). Copyright © 1994, the American Psychological Association.

p. 172, From Naomi Gilpatrick, "The Secret Life of Beatrix Potter." Used with permission from *Natural History,* Vol. 81, No. 8. Copyright © 1972, the American Museum of Natural History.

p. 184, Excerpted from the poem "The Token Woman" by Marge Piercy. Copyright © 1974, 1976 by Marge Piercy and Middlemarsh, Inc. Reprinted by permission of the Wallace Literary Agency, Inc.

p. 260, Reprinted by permission of The Putnam Publishing Group from *No More Menstrual Cramps and Other Good News* by Penny Wise Budoff, Ph.D. Copyright © 1980 by Penny Wise Budoff, Ph.D.

p. 338, Philip W. Blumstein and Pepper Schwartz, "Bisexual Women." In J. P. Wiseman, ed., *The Social Psychology of Sex* (New York: Harper & Row, 1976), pp. 156–57.

p. 356, Excerpted from *Battered Wives.* Copyright © 1976, 1981 by Del Martin. All rights reserved. Published by Volcano Press, Inc., P.O. Box 270, Volcano, CA 95689 ($11.95). Used with permission

Photo Credits

CHAPTER 9

p. 245, *Man & Woman, Boy & Girl* by John Money & Anke A. Ehrhardt, Johns Hopkins University Press; p. 248, A Delta Book Published by Dell Publishing, a division of Bantam Doubleday Dell Publishing Group, Inc.

CHAPTER 10

p. 277, Courtesy, Planned Parenthood/Association of Utah; p. 282, Courtesy, American Cancer Society

CHAPTER 11

p. 309, Robert Brenner/PhotoEdit

CHAPTER 12

p. 322, Steve Allen/Gamma Liaison; p. 328, Photo Researchers; p. 331, Kevin Larkin/Sygma; p. 337, Mark Richards/PhotoEdit

CHAPTER 13

p. 347, © Deborah Dapolito; p. 354, © Mark Antman/Stock, Boston; p. 362, Frank Siteman/Picture Cube; p. 368, Holly Ramona/Sygma

CHAPTER 14

p. 381, Susan Rosenberg/Photo Researchers; p. 388, Bill Bachmann/PhotoEdit; p. 403, Michael Newman/PhotoEdit

CHAPTER 15

p. 414, Michael Newman/PhotoEdit; p. 418, Michael Newman/PhotoEdit; p. 428 (left), AP/World Wide Photos; p. 428 (right), Reuters/Bettmann

CHAPTER 16

p. 441 (left), Robert Brenner/PhotoEdit; p. 441 (right), Tony Freeman/PhotoEdit; p. 449, Mark Richards/Sygma

Index